Practical Woody Plant Propagation for Nursery Growers

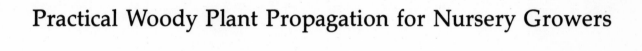

PRACTICAL WOODY
Plant Propagation
FOR NURSERY GROWERS

Bruce Macdonald

Bruce Macdonald.

VOLUME I

Hartness Library
Vermont Technical College
One Main St.
Randolph Center, VT 05061

TIMBER PRESS
Portland, Oregon

To my wife, Liz,
for her patience, support and encouragement in writing this book
and to all friends who enjoy and appreciate the art and science of plant propagation.

DISCLAIMER CLAUSE

The author and publisher are in no way responsible for
the application or use of the chemicals mentioned or
described herein. They make no warranties, expressed or
implied, as to the accuracy or adequacy of any of the
information presented in this book, nor do they guarantee the current status of registered uses of any of
the chemicals with the U.S. Environmental Protection
Agency. Also, by the omission, either unintentionally or
from lack of space, of certain trade names and of some of
the formulated products available to the public, the
author is not endorsing those companies whose brand
names or products are listed.

© Timber Press 1986

All rights reserved.
Printed in Hong Kong

ISBN 0-88192-062-2

TIMBER PRESS
9999 SW Wilshire
Portland, Oregon 97225 USA

CONTENTS

References and Suggested Sources for Further Reading are located at the end of each chapter.

FOREWORD

All readers of this book will recognise the importance of woody plants in beautifying our landscape and providing economic resources throughout the world. The huge areas of land devoted to urban development have put increasing demands on the need for plants with predictable characteristics to be grown to a specific shape and size. The economic pressures on plantation and forestry crops of woody species are such that there is a constant need for cultivars which give higher yields. Such plants need to be available in very significant numbers. As a result, there is an ever increasing need for plants to be propagated by vegetative means. At the same time, the more traditional method of propagation by seed is still of vital importance to the nursery stock and forestry industries.

The amount of effort put into woody plant propagation throughout the world has never been documented but the statistics must be staggering. For example, it has recently been estimated that in Great Britain alone at least one hundred million leafy cuttings of woody plants are prepared and inserted each year. The number of seedlings raised in nurseries is certain to be more than the number of plants raised by cuttings. Add to this the highly significant techniques of plant propagation by budding, grafting and micropropagation and it becomes obvious that the whole amount of effort put into the production of woody plants is very considerable indeed. Furthermore, the woody plant propagator could claim that the diversity of plant species, forms and clones under his sphere of infuence surpasses any other sector of agriculture or horticulture.

Today, the propagator of woody plants occupies a very important position within the international nursery stock and forestry industries. He has to master a diverse range of techniques from manual craft skills to the management of labour and materials. The art and science of plant propagation has been refined and developed over many generations and continues to forge ahead. It is important that such development is periodically reviewed, recorded and documented so that those involved can embrace the existing information, appraise their needs from within it and proceed along their chosen path with a foundation of sound knowledge and good technique. Newcomers to the subject must be able to refer to the current information related to their chosen profession as quickly and easily as possible.

This book sets out to accomplish such a review and documentation. In it, the author, who has experience of all facets of plant propagation from research work to the practical needs of industry, provides an invaluable guide to the person who has to carry out the work. However, the beginner and student will find the information is presented in such a way that there is no diffculty in drawing any required information from it. This information never strays from a practical base but draws from a combination of research and experimental work blended with good practice. The hard work and dedication of the author has resulted in a work of such excellence and comprehensiveness that it is certain to stand for many years as an important landmark in the literature of woody plant propagation.

BRIAN HUMPHREY
Hillier Nurseries (Winchester) Ltd.
Ampfield House
Ampfield, Romsey
Hants SO5 9PA, England
June 1985

PREFACE

The extensive number of plant species provides the plant propagator with a continual challenge to both exercise and extend his or her skills. Propagators centuries ago used their ingenuity with but very basic facilities. Today's technology has made it possible to use very highly specialized methods, permitting the successful propagation of plants which were formerly difficult, if not virtually impossible, to regenerate.

This book is directed to those entering the nursery trade as a career and to students of practical nursery production, as well as to the nursery owner and employee who wish to revise their present practices by learning of other procedures or to add other methods of regenerating plants to their propagation program. For example, an established open-ground seedling nursery whose production schedule makes it necessary to initiate a bench grafting program will find this book quite useful. (The proposed Volume 2 will be essentially a concise documentation of the specific propagation methods used for many different genera, species and cultivars.)

In writing this book, I have tried to combine both fundamental principles of plant growth and detailed descriptions of the methods used in the context of commercial nursery production procedures. It is important that the reader has a good understanding of nursery work. With this in mind, I have purposely included numerous photographs that have been kindly given to me or that I have photographed in various European and North American nurseries. The book grows out of over 18 years of personal propagation experience, as well as extensive travel to many of the leading nurseries in North America, the United Kingdom and Europe.

The nomenclature for the plants follows that used in the following references: *Hortus Third* (L. H. Bailey Hortorium Staff, 1976); *An Annotated Checklist of Woody Ornamental Plants of California, Oregon, and Washington* (M .E. McClintock & A. T. Leiser, 1979); *Trees and Shrubs Hardy in the British Isles* (W. J. Bean, 1970–80, 8th rev. ed., 4 volumes); *Vascular Plants of British Columbia: A Descriptive Resource Inventory* (R. L. Taylor & B. MacBryde, 1977); *Hillier's Manual of Trees and Shrubs* (Hillier Nurseries [Winchester] Ltd., 1974, 4th ed.); and *Naamlijst van houtige gewassen* (H. J. van de Laar, 1985).

The twenty chapters in the book cover the spectrum of practices successfully used for commercial propagation, ranging from traditional layering methods to the recent developments of direct sticking and micropropagation. Some chapters provide more detail than others—for example, I felt it was important to cover protected propagation facilities, clonal selection programs and bench grafting in greater depth, as they have not necessarily been covered adequately in texts to date. It is important the reader appreciates that "something new" is not necessarily better—many of the principles passed down through generations provide the sound basis to successful propagation today. With this in mind, I have made a point of describing a number of traditional practices.

The reader must also appreciate that propagation should not be considered an isolated activity in nursery production. Many plants are easy to propagate so that a quality product depends largely on the knowledge and skills employed during the growing-on period up to the point-of-sale.

My interest in propagation was stimulated by my grandfather, father and the late Fred Ward of Wards Nurseries (Sarratt) Ltd., Rickmansworth, England. This interest developed further when I was a student at Hertfordshire College of Agriculture and Horticulture, St. Albans, and at Wye College (University of London). My major influence was derived from the "seek and share" motto of the International Plant Propagators' Society, of which I have had the privilege of being a member. The IPPS philosophy of sharing knowledge, 10 rewarding years teaching at Hadlow College of Agriculture and Horticulture, and 6 years at the University of British Columbia Botanical Garden have all made very significant contributions. I particularly wish to acknowledge the assistance of the three practical instructors while I was at Hadlow College—Brian Elliot, David Ridgeway and Chris Lane—as well as Percy Read, formerly open-ground production foreman at Hadlow College.

This book could not have been written without the encouragement from my wife, Liz, friends, colleagues and past students. I am immensely grateful to all the people who have reviewed individual chapters.

I wish to record a sincere thank you to Brian Humphrey, formerly Production Director of Hillier Nurseries (Winchester) Ltd., England, who has been my "mentor" throughout the writing of this book. His advice and helpful comments on each chapter were gratefully received. I am grateful to him also for writing the foreword.

In conclusion, I hope that the reader will appreciate that one cannot be dogmatic about woody plant propagation. Different propagators achieve the same outcome using different methods. Further, differing weather conditions from one year to the next can lead to varying results. I hope this book will encourage the reader to be observant, to "seek and share" knowledge, and to understand that it is vital to learn from both the successes and failures in propagation. The reward is that plant propagation provides a continuing satisfaction to those who have an enquiring mind and are prepared to learn and develop their practical skills.

ACKNOWLEDGMENTS

I wish to acknowledge the help and advice from colleagues at the University of British Columbia Botanical Garden: Roy L. Taylor, past Director of the Garden (currently President and Chief Executive Officer, Chicago Horticultural Society, and Director of the Chicago Botanic Garden), for his encouragement and for allowing time for me to research material for the text; Sylvia Taylor for the unenviable task of editing my initial manuscript and systematically checking nomenclature; Gwynneth Quirk and Pam Robin for their patience in typing the manuscripts; and Charles Tubesing for freely sharing his propagation experience and information, and for reviewing specific chapters.

I am very grateful to Ann Thorsteinsson, a former student in Art Education at the University of British Columbia, for the many illustrations she prepared, mainly from live material as well as color transparencies.

I sincerely thank those individuals, in addition to Brian Humphrey, who gave up their time to review chapters on subjects in which they have specific expertise and experience. The text would not have been as substantial and accurate without their help and amendments. Bruce Briggs (Briggs Nursery, Inc., Olympia, WA, U.S.A.) spent many hours with me explaining his experiences with micropropagation and allowed me to visit his laboratory on numerous occasions. Chris Bunt (formerly of the Glasshouse Crops Research Institute, Rustington, U.K.) for his help with the chapter on rooting media. Henri Calle (Henri Calle Nurseries, Wetteren, Belgium) for help with the chapter on layering and for adding some traditional layering procedures used in Belgium. Brian Christie (Christie Nursery Ltd., Pitt Meadows, B.C., Canada) for the chapter on direct sticking. Nat Clayton (formerly at E. R. Johnson Nursery Ltd., Whixley, York, U.K.) for the section dealing with open-ground deciduous hardwood cutting propagation. Les Clay, Jr. (Les Clay & Son Ltd., Langley, B.C., Canada) for the chapter on micropropagation. Nick Dunn (Frank P. Matthews Ltd., Tenbury Wells, U.K.) for the chapter on layering and the section dealing with rooting deciduous hardwood cuttings in heated bins. Robert Garner (formerly with the East Malling Research Station, Maidstone, U.K.) for the chapters on the principles of grafting, open-ground grafting, layering, and tools and materials, together with "snippets" of information contained in his many letters. Lauchlan Glenn and colleagues (Reid Collins Nurseries Ltd., Aldergrove, B.C., Canada) for explaining the procedures and reviewing the chapter on greenhouse seedling production. David Hutchinson (Ministry of Agriculture, Fisheries and Food, Winchester, U.K.) for the chapter on plant propagation facilities. Stephen Haines (James Coles & Sons [Thurnby] Ltd., Leicester, U.K.) for the chapter on open-ground budding and grafting. Brian Howard (East Malling Research Station, Maidstone, U.K.) for the chapters on factors affecting the rooting of cuttings, softwood, semi-ripe wood and evergreen hardwood cuttings, deciduous hardwood cuttings and open-ground budding—his expertise on the fundamental principles and research work was particularly valuable. Neil Hall (Wells Nurseries, Inc., Mount Vernon, WA, U.S.A.) for the chapter on bench grafting. Jean Iseli (Iseli Nursery, Inc., Boring, OR, U.S.A.) for the chapter on bench grafting. Brian Morgan (Ministry of Agriculture, Fisheries and Food, Coley Park, Reading, U.K.) for the sections dealing with the handling of cuttings in the chapters on softwood, semi-ripe wood, evergreen and deciduous hardwood cuttings. Keith Loach (Glasshouse Crops Research Institute, Rustington, U.K.) for the chapters on rooting media, softwood, semi-ripe wood and evergreen hardwood cuttings, and protected plant propagation facilities—his research relating to softwood cutting propagation was particularly helpful. Bruce Morton (Hybrid Nurseries Ltd., Pitt Meadows,

B.C., Canada) for the chapter on direct sticking and sections of the rooting media chapter. John Mathies (Cannor Nurseries Ltd., Chilliwack, B.C., Canada) for the chapter on open-ground budding. Philip McMillan Browse (Saratoga Horticultural Foundation, San Martin, CA, U.S.A.) for the chapter on open-ground seedling production and factors affecting the rooting of cuttings—including personal communications related to other sections of the text. Bruce McTavish (Reid Collins Nurseries Ltd., Aldergrove, B.C., Canada) for sections dealing with seedling production of British Columbia native plants. Steven McCulloch (Briggs Nursery, Inc., Olympia, WA, U.S.A.) for the chapter on micropropagation and his patience in answering numerous questions on the topic. Dan Milbocker (Virginia Truck and Ornamentals Research Station, Virginia Beach, VA, U.S.A.) for the section dealing with fogging in the protected propagation facilities chapter. Margaret Scott (Ministry of Agriculture, Fisheries and Food, Lymington, U.K.) for the chapter on rooting hormones and for updating me on various aspects of her research work on energy saving. George Sheard (formerly Deputy Director of the Glasshouse Crops Research Institute, Rustington, U.K.) for the chapter on protected propagation facilities, and particularly for his help on greenhouse construction and heating. Ralph Shugert (Zelenka Evergreen Nursery, Inc., Grand Haven, MI, U.S.A.) for the chapter on open-ground seedling production, where he was particularly helpful in amending the text to include some North American practices. Pauline Smith (formerly with the Glasshouse Crops Research Institute, Rustington, U.K.) for the chapter on disease prevention and control. Rick Sorenson (Homestead Nurseries Ltd., Clayburn, B.C., Canada) for many specific sections. John Stanley (Nursery Business Consultants, Rode, Avon, U.K.) for the chapter on unit containers. Gayle Suttle (Microplant Nurseries, Inc., Gervaise, OR, U.S.A.) for the chapter on micropropagation. Robert L. Ticknor (North Willamette Experimental Station, University of Oregon, OR, U.S.A.) for the chapter on rooting hormones. B. van Elk (Proefstation voor de Boomkwekerij, Boskoop, Holland) for his assistance with the formulation of the appendices on scion/rootstock combinations for the chapters on budding and bench grafting. Tom Wood and Dennis Fordham (Oakover Nurseries Ltd., Ashford, Kent, U.K.) for the chapter on open-ground seed production. Besides extra information on this chapter, Tom Wood provided considerable encouragement in the writing of this book.

I am also grateful to Tom Campbell and the Agricultural Training Board (Beckenham, Kent, U.K.) for permission to use some of the diagrams from their Trainee Guides and their outline format in describing some specific techniques.

Numerous individuals were particularly helpful with personal communications to provide additional information and/or photographs. These include: Douglas Anderson and John Watts (Darby Nursery Stock Ltd., Methwold Hythe, Norfolk, U.K.); Poul E. Brander (State Research Centre for Horticulture, Hornum, Denmark); John Byland (Byland Nursery, Kelowna, B.C. Canada); Dennis Connor and Rick Wells (Monrovia Nursery Co., Inc., Azusa, CA, U.S.A.); Jim L. W. Deen (Horticulture Weekly, Twickenham, Middlesex, U.K.); Donald R. Egolf and Sylvester G. March (U.S. National Arboretum, Washington, D.C., U.S.A.); Raymond J. Evison (Treasures of Tenbury Ltd., Tenbury Wells, Worcestershire, U.K.); S. R. Freeman (Nobel Engineering Ltd., Goring-by-Sea, Sussex, U.K.); Don Gilbert (M.A.F.F., Agricultural Development Advisory Service, Cambridge, U.K.); Francis Hancock (Woodland Nurseries, Mississauga, ON, Canada); Verl Holden (Holden Wholesale Growers Inc., Silverton, OR, U.S.A.); Gary Kenwood (Reid Collins Nurseries Ltd., Aldergrove, B.C., Canada); Paul Labous (Merrist Wood Agricultural College, Worplesdon, Surrey, U.K.); Roy Lancaster (Horticultural Consultant & Plantsman, Chandlers Ford, Hampshire, U.K.); Ernest G. Parsons (Plumtree Nursery Equipment Ltd., Mapperley, Nottinghamshire, U.K.); David Redekop (Aldergrove Nurseries, Aldergrove, B.C., Canada); Richard Revel (Clovis Lande Associates, Hildenborough, Kent, U.K.); Paul Reimer (Reiner Nurseries Ltd., Yarrow, B.C., Canada); Wilbert Ronald (Jefferies Nursery, Portage la Prairie, MB, Canada); Geoffrey Schwyn (Westham Island Nursery, Delta, B.C., Canada); Norman Stewart (Camland Products Ltd., Cambridge, U.K.); Arie van Vliet (Klijn & Co., Boskoop, Holland); David Whalley (Glasshouse Crops Research Institute, Rustington, Sussex, U.K.); and Terry Wiggin (Wells Nursery, Inc., Mount Vernon, WA, U.S.A.).

Finally, I would like to acknowledge the many nurseries where I have been allowed to photograph their operations or who have provided me with photographs. It is impossible to name them all, but I particularly wish to thank the following: Briggs Nursery, Inc.; East Malling Research Station; Efford Experimental Horticulture Station; Hadlow College of Agriculture and Horticulture; Hillier Nurseries (Winchester) Ltd.; Oakover Nurseries Ltd.; Microplant Nurseries, Inc.; Reid Collins Nurseries Ltd.; J. Frank Schmidt & Sons Co.; and Wells Nurseries, Inc.

Bruce Macdonald
June 1986

SECTION A

SECTION A

Chapter 1

PROPAGATION FROM SEED
Principles and Open-Ground Production

Propagation by seed is an important technique for raising horticultural crops worldwide. This method is of extreme importance to the propagation of woody plants, whether for forestry or ornamental use. These chapters will explain both the reasons and the methods used to propagate woody ornamentals from seed commercially. It describes the practices used to germinate seed, both in open ground and for the intensive greenhouse methods used in a regulated environment, from selecting the seed source to successful germination of the crop.

Nursery operators have been raising woody plants from seed for many decades to produce both a few specialized items of specific interest and numerous quantities of plants for hedging and rootstocks. Modern techniques in forestry and vegetable production have helped to provide general background knowledge from which the nursery industry can adapt specific ideas or understand the reason why viable seed may fail to germinate.

The reasons why seed propagation has become increasingly important for the nursery industry include:—

(i) Market—This was well illustrated in Britain during the mid-1970s when sterling was weak in relation to some European currencies and made it attractively viable to produce British-grown rootstocks. At this time, a considerable quantity of seedling stock for rootstocks and hedging was imported—much of it being of variable quality and often with unreliable delivery dates. This situation laid the foundation for a number of nurseries to orientate their operations to seedling production, providing a quality product for the home market. Two examples were the formation of Bristocks, Wisbech, Cambridgeshire, specializing in the production of seedling Laxa rose rootstocks for open-ground budding, and Oakover Nurseries, Ashford, Kent, now a leading supplier of seedlings used for rootstocks, hedging materials, amenity plantings and ornamental specimens. Subsequent experience has shown that there is a continuing demand for a high-quality product even during times of over-production.

(ii) Mechanization—The development of specialized machinery—e.g., for sowing large numbers of seeds, seed bed formation, soil fumigation, spraying, undercutting and lifting—and of cold storage facilities has led to more efficient production. The Danish company Egedal, at Horsens, has been a world-wide leader in providing custom-built machinery for various jobs from precision seed sowing to spreading sand for covering seed to lifting the marketable crop. Their catalogue provides a useful, up-to-date reference on appropriate machinery. Other manufacturers include Baertschi Ltd., Heuswil, Switzerland, who have recently made a significant impact in Michigan, U.S.A., with their "multi-row" lifter/shaker harvesting equipment and their vertical root pruning tool.

(iii) Seed Sources—Greater encouragement and knowledge of self-collection of seed and the increasing range of plant materials being offered by seed sources has had a favorable impact on the quantities and range of species available.

(iv) Crop Husbandry—Improved materials and equipment for crop irrigation, shading, and protection from vermin have become available over the last decade. This has led to a less variable and more consistent product.

Figure 1-1.
A tractor-powered Egedal lifting machine fitted with a double shaking system is an example of the specialized equipment developed for open-ground nursery seedling production.

The term "Accelerated Growth" (A/G) has been used in recent years—it refers to the production of seedlings in a growth cabinet or greenhouse under a controlled environment. "Accelerated Growth" production is used for intensive systems to raise seedlings for forestry, shipping them in their media plugs. It has been successfully adapted for raising ornamental seedling stock—particularly for native plants, rootstocks, and choice and slightly tender species.

REASONS AND MERITS FOR SEED PROPAGATION

The major reasons and advantages of seed propagation are outlined below.

1. It is a primary method for raising large numbers of plants, particularly where small differences in genetical variation are not important. In addition to forestry applications, seed is used for:—

Hedging Plants	— *Berberis thunbergii* (Japanese Barberry) *Carpinus betulus* (European Hornbeam) *Fagus sylvatica* (European Beech)
Amenity and Mass Highway Plantings	— *Acer ginnala* (Amur Maple) *Betula pendula* (European White Birch) *Cornus sanguinea* (Blood-twig Dogwood)
Rootstocks	— *Acer platanoides* (Norway Maple) *Picea abies* (Norway Spruce) *Sorbus aucuparia* (European Mountain Ash)
Street Trees	— *Corylus colurna* (Turkish Filbert) *Gleditsia triacanthos* var. *inermis* (Thornless Honey Locust) *Liquidambar styraciflua* (American Sweet Gum) *Liriodendron tulipifera* (Tulip Tree) *Quercus palustris* (Pin Oak) *Tilia cordata* (Little-leaf Linden) *Zelkova serrata* (Japanese Zelkova)
Ground Covers	— *Gaultheria procumbens* (Creeping Wintergreen) *Hypericum calycinum* (Aaron's-beard)
Native Plants for Mine Reclamation	— *Elaeagnus commutata* (Silverberry, Wolfwillow) *Rosa acicularis* (Prickly Rose) *Rosa woodsii* (Woods' Rose)

Shepherdia canadensis (Soopolallie, Soapberry or Russet Buffalo-berry)

Climbing Plants — *Campsis radicans* (Common Trumpet Creeper)
Clematis tangutica (Golden Clematis)
Mutisia oligodon

Specimen Plants — *Arbutus menziesii* (Pacific Madrone)
Cedrus deodara (Himalayan Cedar)
Cornus nuttallii (Western Flowering Dogwood)
Eucalyptus gunnii (Cider Gum)
Nyssa sylvatica (Black Gum or Tupelo)

Figure 1-2. The production of seedling Rose rootstocks is a major crop in Europe. A (above). Open-ground seed beds in West Germany. B (right). A bundle of ungraded seedlings lifted after one season's growth, and ready for dispatch to the grading shed (Denmark). C (below). The graded product trimmed and bundled for shipping to the customer.

Figure 1-3. *Acer pensylvanicum* (Pennsylvania Maple), an ornamental tree noted for the striated markings on the bark, is readily propagated from seed.

2. It has been a means of introducing new cultivars to the nursery trade when both controlled and uncontrolled hybridization has taken place. This has been particularly important with *Rosa, Rhododendron, Camellia* and *Clematis*. Important inter-generic and inter-specific hybrids have been produced by plant breeding programs.

James Hanover at Michigan State University produced an inter-specific hybrid, the Spartan Spruce, by crossing *Picea abies* (Norway Spruce) with *P. pungens* 'Glauca' (Colorado Blue Spruce). The second generation of progeny has resulted in little need for roguing. This consistency, the good branching habit and the fact that cones are produced in five years are reasons for some growers to feel that the Spartan Spruce could revolutionize the Michigan Christmas tree market.

3. Seed is generally a low cost method of production, when compared to the number of plants produced vegetatively from a known mother plant. In addition, vegetative propagation methods are more likely to require sophisticated propagation facilities.

4. The use of native plants for screening and re-colonizing areas designated for land reclamation is increasing with more public awareness of the environment and more encouragement by governments. The majority of these plants are raised from seed. In British Columbia and Alberta, popular seed-raised subjects for the appropriate reclamation sites are *Alnus viridis* ssp. *fruticosa* (syn. *A. crispa*) (American Green Alder), *Gaultheria shallon* (Salal), *Prunus virginiana* (Choke Cherry), *Rosa acicularis* (Prickly Rose), *Rubus parviflorus* (Thimbleberry) and *Shepherdia canadensis* (Soopolallie or Russet Buffalo-berry).

5. A major problem associated with vegetative propagation is the transmission of virus diseases. In many species, there is far less risk of virus transmission from one generation to the next with seed propagation. Some exceptions occur in the Rosaceae where *Prunus avium* (Mazzard) is known to transmit up to six viruses by seed, e.g., Plum Ring Spot and Cherry Mosaic Viruses.

6. Rate of growth, and ability to establish following transplanting, is very often faster with a seed-raised crop as compared to plants of the same species raised from cuttings. Nursery operators sometimes refer to this as "seedling vigor." Good examples are exhibited with some Pines, Maples and *Amelanchier* (Serviceberry).

7. The import and export of seeds is much less restricted by phytosanitary regulations than is the movement of vegetative material. In addition, there is very often less bulk, thus lowering the shipping costs. [The Province of British Columbia, Canada, for example, completely bans the entry of any species of *Corylus* (Filbert) as seedlings, cuttings, layers or grafts, but the importation of seed is allowed. Similarly, the importation of living material of *Prunus* is prohibited unless it has been registered as virus-tested by the appropriate authority in its country of origin. Seed importation of *Prunus* is also prohibited as it is known that this seed can transmit viruses. Legislation also exists for the importation of seed in relation to its source (see p. 7).]

LIMITATIONS OF SEED PROPAGATION

There are limitations to propagation by seed, as indicated below.

1. Genetical variation can be so marked that subsequent progeny can yield a high percentage of low quality stock at the time of sale, e.g., bent stems, lack of dominant leader or undesirable leaf color. An example of the latter is seen with *Fagus sylvatica* 'Atropunicea' (Purple or Bronze Beech) where seed selected from this purple-leaved tree will produce forms with leaves ranging in color from purple to green. The green and intermediate colored forms have to be rogued out when the first and second true leaves have formed, so that the cultivar can be sold as a purple-leaved seedling form and a premium price obtained. Genetical variation can be minimized by using correct provenances, growing trees for seed sources in isolation, and by selection after germination.

2. There can be difficulties in germination due to lack of viability (see p. 30), and seed dormancy problems (see p. 32) may make it necessary to carry out pre-germination treatments to remove or damage hard or waxy seed coats so that seed can germinate successfully. This should be taken into account when comparing seed propagation with vegetative techniques. For example, softwood cuttings of *Potentilla fruticosa* cvs. (Shrubby Cinquefoil) are easy to root, but some woody plants are traditionally difficult to root from cuttings, making it necessary to be precise with timing and rooting hormone concentrations, e.g., *Kalmia latifolia* (Mountain Laurel). Conversely, *Betula pendula* (European White Birch) presents few problems from seed, but seeds of plants such as *Davidia involucrata* (Dove or Handkerchief Tree) can be unreliable in germination.

3. Seed crops can be unreliable, whether the seed is purchased or self-collected. This important aspect is discussed on p. 11.

Figure 1-4.
A reliable seed source of *Fagus sylvatica* 'Atropunicea' (Bronze or Purple Beech) will minimize the need to rogue out green and intermediate colored seedlings. Note that the unwanted seedlings are cut off at ground level to avoid disturbance of the adjacent seedlings and are discarded into the pathways.

4. The sex of the progeny may not necessarily be known. This is important for some dioecious street trees where the fruits from female trees may cause problems, either because of their smell or unsightliness after falling onto the pavement or sidewalk. *Ginkgo biloba* (Maidenhair Tree) is a good example. The squashed fruits from the female plant have an unpleasant odor, hence the reason for planting vegetatively propagated clonal selections of male forms in urban areas.

5. The root systems are often considerably more dominant in seed propagated crops than in those from cuttings or layers. This may be advantageous for anchorage, and, it is sometimes claimed, longevity (life of the plant). However, a dominant root system can mean firstly, that a plant is less prone to develop a fibrous root system which is important when balling and burlapping open-ground stock, and secondly, that it is more prone to root curl (see p. 91) of container-grown stock. These conditions can be avoided by transplanting, root pruning and growing in specialized containers during the production cycle.

SOURCES OF SEED AND PROVENANCE

During the last decade, considerable emphasis has been placed on the importance of seed sources, resulting from the exchange of knowledge between nursery operators, advice from specialist extension officers, and published literature. It is fair to say that many nurseries have been haphazard in the past in adequately assessing their seed sources, in the storage and treatment of seed prior to sowing, and in recording the performance of the subsequent progeny, thus leading to variable and unpredictable seedling crops. Also, seed collectors and seed houses have sometimes used unreliable storage procedures before the seed is shipped.

Both seed quality and known seed sources are vital to the success of the enterprise. Nursery operators should find the best commercial seed source or select the best stands of plants when collecting locally. Botanical gardens, in particular, will wish to obtain wild collected seed from different known geographical locations when developing their collections. The following comments will be useful in formulating guidelines for obtaining seed from different sources.

Provenance

Provenance may be defined as either the geographical origin of seed or the source of the seed in relation to its geographical location. Provenance is extremely important in forestry for successful forest management and to obtain quality timber. The principles of provenance can also be successfully utilized by nursery operators for the improvement and production of woody ornamentals.

There is legislation in the European Economic Community (EEC) governing the use of 14 major species in forestry. Provenances are registered and must be declared by seed houses, nurseries and plantation owners. The controlling agency in each country (this is the Forestry Commission in the United Kingdom) conducts inspections at the nursery stage. All consignments of plants for forest use must be accompanied by a certificate of origin stating the provenance. Seed orchards and registered stands approved for collection are also inspected.

The provenance of the seed can directly affect a number of characteristics of plant growth. These include drought and cold resistance, flushing of growth, bud setting, onset of dormancy, root system development, habit, viability of seed, shape and color of leaves, and pest and disease susceptibility. Growth problems may occur with seed collected in a cold temperate climate but sown in a warm temperate region—irregular growth patterns can occur because the progeny is not exposed to sufficiently cold temperatures during the winter to break dormancy of the buds.

An incident that brought home the importance of provenance to me was at an English nursery growing *Tsuga canadensis* (Canadian Hemlock) obtained from two different origins. The seed bed was in a site where late spring frosts could be a problem, thus affecting the new growth. The buds on the plants from the more southerly provenance flushed about four weeks earlier than on those from the more northerly region. The former showed considerable frost damage when a late spring frost arrived, while the latter were virtually unaffected.

Many plant species are widely dispersed geographically, e.g., *Acer rubrum* (Red Maple) occurs from Newfoundland to Florida, so it is inadvisable to buy seed collected from the south for sowing in more northerly latitudes. *Acer rubrum* (Red Maple) plants grown from seed collected in Florida and sown in northern latitudes will rarely, if ever, assume fall color. The seedlings will also be subject to winter injury.

Another vivid recollection is of a nursery in Denmark, where the owner had collected *Pinus mugo* var. *mugo* (Mugo Pine) and *Pinus mugo* var. *pumilio* (Shrubby Mugo Pine) at different altitudes to establish and make selections for landscape plantings. The habit, particularly with relation to height and degree of compactness, varied considerably in different collections made in the wild at a range of altitudes. The mother plants selected from these collections provided progeny that was virtually true-to-type so that his customers could select according to their landscape requirements.

A good example of provenance is seen in British Columbia with the native *Pinus contorta* (Shore or Lodgepole Pine). This conifer is widely distributed over Western North America and shows considerable differences in morphology (habit and appearance) over its range. The coastal form is sufficiently distinct from the form found in the interior of British Columbia to be separated as a different variety. The coastal form is called *Pinus contorta* var. *contorta* (Shore Pine) and is found growing in coastal bogs, sand dunes and rocky outcrops. It has dark green needles and twisted, contorted branches on inferior quality trees. The interior form, *Pinus contorta* var. *latifolia* (Lodgepole Pine), grows on dry gravelly and sandy soils. Its habit is very different—the trunks are straight with a symmetrical branching framework and the needles are yellow-green in color. This habit makes it valuable as a timber tree for use in the construction of houses, and for railway ties, poles and mine timbers.

Finally, an outline of the work carried out to improve forest tree management and timber quality by selection and breeding to provide registered and tested certified seed may be useful to nursery operators. These programs are not used for woody ornamentals but the fundamental principles could be used, in part at least, to improve these plants. The same principle has been used to establish seed orchards of broad-leaved trees.

To obtain Registered Conifer Seed, superior plantations are identified and undesirable trees removed. The seed collected from the remaining trees is then grown to supply registered seed from the offspring. To obtain Tested Certified Seed, outstanding trees are selected, sometimes being referred to as "plus trees". These trees are vegetatively propagated, normally by grafting, to produce clonal material which is then planted up in tree banks. The trees in these banks are either wind or artificially pollinated. The subsequent progeny are tested on different sites and their performance documented. The very best plants are then selected on the basis of these progeny trials to form what is referred to as an Improved Seed Orchard. The seed from these plants is sold as Tested Certified Seed.

Seed Sources

Essentially there are four main categories into which seed sources can be classified.

(1) Wild Collected Seed for Botanical Gardens, Arboreta and Professional Collectors

A considerable amount of commercial seed is collected in the wild, e.g., *Cedrus deodara* (Himalayan Cedar). Seed of known wild provenance is available from seed houses for some species, particularly species that are important in forestry and Christmas tree production, e.g., *Picea*

Figure 1-5. Container-grown "plus trees" of *Picea sitchensis* (Sitka Spruce), selected for such qualities as vigor, form, timber quality, stability, hardiness and disease resistance, form an integral part of the tree improvement program of Elite Trees Ltd., North Kessock, Scotland. These "plus trees" are further monitored for superior genetic quality, with the best ones being selected as "elite tree". (Reproduced by courtesy of W. Crowder & Sons, Ltd., Horncastle, Lincolnshire, U.K.)

abies (Norway Spruce), *Pinus sylvestris* (Scots Pine) and *Pseudotsuga menziesii* (Douglas Fir).

Wild collected seed is a very important source of seeds for botanical gardens when building up plant collections in different components of the garden. It is also important for the nursery operator interested in collecting specific species or populations of plants so that seed collected at different geographical locations can be compared. Wild collected seed is particularly useful for a propagator or researcher interested in breeding new plants. For example, winter hardiness may be an objective in the breeding program so that seed collected from a species at a high elevation or northerly latitude would be a major criterion for one of the parents. Further, collecting in the wild has become increasingly important for large-scale native and environmental plantings.

The merits of wild collected seed are:—

(i) It is obtained from a known and recorded provenance.

(ii) There is often less chance of cross pollination of the species to give variability, compared with seed collected from cultivated plants.

The problems of physically reaching and reliably collecting the seed set limits on wild collecting. For example, the plant seen in the wild may be in flower with ripened seed not ready until early fall. Local botanists must be found to collect the seed at the required time. Obviously, they must be given explicit directions and maps to locate the plant(s) from which seed is to be collected.

The collection of small quantities of seed in the wild is often carried out by plant collecting expeditions under the auspices of botanical gardens and societies, or occasionally by a keen amateur or professional horticulturist. The first step in obtaining wild collected seed is to write or make personal contact with plantsmen, specialist societies or botanical gardens in the area, stating your requirements. This request is likely to require some funding, which may take the form of buying one or more shares in the plant collecting expedition or of making a donation to the collector. The seed is normally labelled at the time of collection with the plant collector's number and a code giving details of plant identification, date and exact site of collection, with more detailed records being kept either on cards or in the collector's field note-book.

(2) Seed Exchanges

Many botanical gardens and arboreta have seed exchange programs that play an important role in the international exchange of seed. It is sometimes possible for an individual to become a member of a botanical garden and thus receive copies of the seed exchange list (or Index Seminum).

Seed is also available to members of plant and horticultural societies—for example,

Figure 1-6. Botanical garden seed exchange lists (index semina) can provide a very useful source for small quantities of seeds of rare, unusual and native plants.

specialist hardy plant societies. The Royal Horticultural Society Garden at Wisley, Surrey, England, produces an annual seed list from which members of the Society can obtain seed.

There is a risk that seed of some species received from botanical gardens, arboreta and societies, may be hybrid seed because of the possibility of cross pollination occurring in cultivated plant collections.

Seed exchanges offer:—

(i) A wide range of seed, much of which may be rare or obtainable only in certain years.

(ii) A useful way to obtain seed of plants native to the particular geographical area of the botanical garden or society.

(iii) Reliable information on provenance and date of collection is often available.

However, seed exchanges usually offer only small quantities of seed unless a request is made in advance, usually accompanied by pre-payment.

To summarize, the role of seed exchanges by botanical gardens, arboreta, societies and foundations in supplying seed is limited for the average nursery operator due mainly to the small quantity of seed available. However, they fulfill an important role for the small specialist producer.

(3) Local Collections (Commercial Collections)

This is a primary source of seed for the nursery operator, particularly for the large-scale production of hedging and rootstock material.

Local collection has the advantages of offering:—

(i) The nursery virtually complete control of the collection, storage and treatment of seed prior to sowing.

(ii) Seed which is generally cheaper. Costs are obviously dependent on distance, transport availability, quantity of seed for collection, access to the collecting area, and problems of seed extraction.

(iii) The opportunity to obtain, and thus personally build up, local knowledge of available seed (e.g., the reliability of correct identification). This knowledge can be gained by visiting the sites at different times of the year to obtain a broader picture of the seed source.

(iv) Better assurance of the progeny's performance in the nursery seed bed and suitability in its final planting position in a given locality.

The limitations of local collecting are:—

(i) Unknown factors about the seed source until growing records have been built up over a number of years.

(ii) Inadequate seed quantities to meet the requirements of the nursery. Some trees may set little viable seed in a particular location. For example, *Liriodendron tulipifera* (Tulip Tree) is hard to come by in southern England. Also, some trees may not set sufficient viable seed every year, for example, *Pistacia chinensis* (Chinese Pistachio), *Fraxinus excelsior* (European Ash) and the native California evergreen tree *Lyonothamnus floribundus* ssp. *asplenifolius* (Island Ironwood) may set viable seed only every 2 years while *Fagus sylvatica* (European Beech) may set seed only every 3–5 years.

I strongly recommend that record cards be carefully formulated and maintained for each plant or population from which seed is collected. The record card should contain the following information:—

(a) Actual location of local seed source
(b) Ease of collecting
(c) Specific equipment required for collection
(d) Viability of seed at the time of collection
(e) Date of collection
(f) Brief report(s) on visit(s) to source earlier in season to assess potential crop, indicating possible reasons for crop failure.

This resource information should be supplemented with information on the germinated seedlings:—

(a) Method and period of storage
(b) Pre-sowing treatment to overcome dormancy and improve germination
(c) Viability at sowing
(d) Date of sowing
(e) Rate of sowing
(f) Percentage germination
(g) Grade out after lifting for selling or transplanting
(h) Summary of habit, specifically indicating any desirable or undesirable qualities.

This record will provide a virtually complete picture of the performance of the collected seed. A medium to large nursery will find that a desk computer is an ideal way to record the information for subsequent evaluation.

TABLE 1-1. An Example of a Nursery Crop Record Sheet

CROP RECORD SHEET

NAME:	CAT. NO.
ORIGIN: (1) Own Collection (2) Commercial Source	
DATE: RECEIVED:	YEAR OF CROP:
QUANTITY	QUANTITY SOWN
WEIGHT	WEIGHT
PRICE: EXTRAS:	COST:

CONDITION ON RECEIPT:

SAMPLE: NO: SAMPLE: WT:

VIABILITY: Suppliers information: Estimated field factor:

Own estimates:

SEED TREATMENT:

SOWING DATE: AREA SOWN:

GERMINATION: Sample count:
Date:

NUMBER SEEDLINGS LIFTED:

Source: Oakover Nurseries Ltd., Potters Corner, Ashford, Kent, U.K.

TABLE 1-2. Nursery Record Sheet for Native Plant Propagation

NATIVE PLANT PROPAGATION

SEED
Date collected _____ Time spent _____
Collector's name _____
Place of collection _____
Elevation _____ Soil type _____ Associated spp _____
Remarks _____
_____ Pre-extraction wt. _____
Date extracted _____ By _____ Time spent _____
Method _____
_____
_____ Post-extraction wt. _____

CUTTINGS
Date collected _____ Time spent _____ Type of cutting _____
Collector's name _____
Place of collection _____
Elevation _____ Soil type _____ Associated spp _____
Remarks _____
Date propagated _____ By _____ Time spent _____
Mix _____ Hormone _____ Wound _____ Total quantity _____
Remarks _____

TRIAL No.	1	2	3	4
Pregermination treatment				
Date sown				
Date germinated				
Germination %				
Mix				

Source: Reid Collins Nurseries, Aldergrove, B.C., Canada

The above information illustrates the importance of adapting the underlying principles of provenance used in forestry for the improvement of nursery stock.

Some years ago I recall these principles being used by an English nursery that was sowing a large number of *Quercus robur* (English Oak) seeds annually. The owner toured his local area identifying the superior native trees, mapped them and then recorded the performance of the progeny. The variation from each source was considerable—some were notably more susceptible to Downy Mildew, which was sufficiently severe to kill the growing point in some cases. One source contained a high percentage of stems that were bent near ground level, while another showed a lack of apical growth so that the laterals resulted in twin leaders, thus making it necessary to prune the crop during the production cycle.

Figure 1-7. The degree of Downy Mildew infection on *Quercus robur* (English Oak) is sometimes attributable to a specific seed source.

Local collection of seed is encouraged by the Landscape Alberta Nursery Trades Association in Canada. Nursery operators from different locations bring locally collected seed to the annual convention and have it available for purchase by other operators. This not only gives an opportunity to compare different provenances, but also helps to finance the Nurserymen's Research Fund.

Reid Collins Nurseries in Aldergrove, B.C., is one of several companies in Western Canada specializing in the nursery production of native British Columbian and Albertan plants for mine reclamation schemes. As is the case with most of these nurseries, they designate one of their management team to be responsible for determining local seed sources within a 19 km (12 mi) radius around the site to be reclaimed, organizing seed collecting contracts and shipping the seed back to the nursery. Collecting is done on contract by agents who may, in turn, contract with local Indian bands to do the actual collecting. University or college faculty, who take students into the bush as part of a course, may also be requested to collect seed of specific species. Most of the collected seed is packed into used, washed milk cartons and sent by bus to Aldergrove for subsequent processing.

Local collections must be well supervised, particularly when the actual collecting is contracted out. The criteria required include correct identification of the species and an early reconnaissance to evaluate the potential seed crop.

It is important that the nursery operator knows the native plants in the locality. A keen eye is necessary to observe changes in growth and seed development. This knowledge should be passed on to one's staff, and time spent walking through the local habitat with them should not be considered as time wasted.

Finally, local collections are to be strongly encouraged, as well as the maintenance of accurate records. The information obtained from these records should be acted upon so that long-term financial benefits can be obtained.

(4) Commercial Seed Houses

As with local collections, commercial seed houses play a major role in providing both small and large quantities of seed annually to the nursery operator. The principal seed companies are located in North America, West Germany, France, Austria, Holland, Denmark, Britain, Australia and Japan.

Figure 1-8. Commercial seed houses principally offer large quantities of seed, but many companies will readily supply small amounts to nurseries.

Commercial seed houses offer the advantages of:—

(i) Convenience of the collection and supply of the seed being implemented by someone else.

(ii) A far wider range of species is available than the nursery operator can possibly collect locally.

(iii) The correct provenance of the seed should be available. If not, the same species may be ordered from several seed houses for comparison.

(iv) A source of seed when local sources do not set regular or sufficient viable seed.

The disadvantages of commercial seed houses are:—

(i) It is more expensive—both for cost of the seed and shipping. Large seeds of *Castanea* (Chestnut) and *Quercus* (Oak) are bulky and heavy and are therefore expensive to ship.

(ii) A considerable number of factors about the seed, such as its age, method of storage and percentage viability, are not known. Legislation in some countries makes it mandatory to provide this information for certain species. Many seed houses sometimes purchase seed from other seed houses, or even go to an agent in a particular country to arrange collection in that area. This can mean that there is little control of the actual method and time of collection. Errors are compounded in trading. There have been many failures in the system. There have been instances of failure to supply seed true-to-name (which can occur in some cases when local contract labor collects the wrong seed), deliberate confusion of documentation to hide malpractice, and mixing poor and low viability seed lots with high viability ones. Conventional dry storage may also kill certain seeds so that the nursery receives dead seed (always check the viability of seed as soon as it arrives). However, good communication and the use of reputable agents and seed houses will minimize these problems.

(iii) Problems resulting from unreliable delivery can occur. Delivery is a problem when seed arrives either too late to carry out a specific pre-sowing treatment to overcome dormancy, or means sowing so late as to create the obvious cultural problems.
    A further problem is that the buyer may not be informed under separate cover that a certain species is not included in the order. If the omission is not noted until the order is opened, there may not be sufficient time to order from elsewhere. Having said this, I must point out that many seed houses have provided an excellent service to nurseries for many years. However, it is important to be aware of some of the problems experienced by nurseries who have not been sufficiently careful in their choice of seed house(s).

The following advice may prove helpful when ordering from seed houses.
    1. Ask other nursery operators about their experiences with different suppliers, particularly with respect to reliability of seed quality and delivery date.
    2. Before ordering large quantities of seed, initially order small amounts from several suppliers so that their reliability can be evaluated. The seed from each supplier should be inspected on arrival and records kept on subsequent performance.
    3. Order only sufficient seed for a specified seed bed area. This means that the annual requirements should be roughly calculated in advance. There are exceptions to this rule, however—when seed is rare and suddenly becomes available or where it is projected that there will be shortages in the following year.
    4. Place the order early and ask for confirmation of quantities available and prices (including shipping costs) at the shipper's earliest convenience.
    5. Check statutory requirements governing the importation of seed from a seed house in another country.
    6. Encourage the seed house to provide details on provenance, origin and viability, even though an extra charge may be made. [Seed should be sold as the number of viable seeds per unit of weight, with the price based on the number of seeds rather than on the weight.]
    7. It is helpful to have a record of the number of live seeds in a given weight—e.g., per gram, ounce, kilogram or pound. Seed houses may be able to provide the information or it can later be based on accumulated experience.
    8. Develop a relationship with your seed supplier so that you are notified well in advance of possible shortfalls.

(5) Government Agencies

The Departments of Forestry in many countries supply seed to nurseries producing forest trees. Most of the seed so offered is for coniferous timber trees, but other species may well be available. For example, the New Zealand Forest Service and British Forestry Commission catalogues list a number of deciduous trees and shrubs suitable for hedging or amenity landscape planting. Seed may also be offered as "Arboretum Collections", which could include a number of more ornamental and less known species, e.g., *Acer* spp. (Maple).

COLLECTION OF SEED

The following information is provided for the propagator or nursery operator planning to collect seed locally.

The first step is to map the location of the local seed sources and to set up record cards. The next stage is to "get out and know your trees". As previously indicated, this entails visiting the trees at various times throughout the growing season every year to assess the potential seed crop. The gradual accumulation of this information will indicate any irregular seed-bearing features of a particular location. The success of a source providing a good quantity of viable seed will be very dependent on the weather during both pollination and the developing and ripening process. A wet summer and fall can mean that the seed does not ripen sufficiently.

Equipment

The basic equipment needed for collecting includes reliable transport, maps, labels, tarpaulins and burlap (hessian) sheets, canvas hoppers, burlap (hessian) sacks, polyethylene bags, rigid wooden and plastic containers, and hooks or poles to draw branches down to the picker. Extension ladders or a power-operated gantry platform may be necessary if the seed is high up in the trees. Appropriate climbing and safety equipment must be available if trees are to be climbed.

Time of Ripening

The correct time of year for gathering the seed is very largely related to the type of tree and to its geographical location. Seed of *Populus* (Poplar) may be available for collection in June while *Quercus* (Oak) will not be available until October. Factors that can make the time of collection more critical are:—

(i) Climatic variations such as periods of prolonged wet or drought. This variation may be up to 6 or 8 weeks either side of the norm, depending on the prevailing weather in the summer from flowering (pollination) to development and final ripening of the seed.

(ii) Consumption of the fruits by birds, voles, mice, squirrels, etc. I have gone out to collect seed of *Sorbus aucuparia* (European Mountain Ash) only to find that birds had already devoured most of the fruits. Crows and jays are fond of acorns, while I have seen fallen fruits of *Acer platanoides* (Norway Maple) destroyed by mice eating out the seed contents. *Daphne mezereum* (February Daphne) fruits are particularly prone to being removed by birds, even before they turn red. In Michigan, it is not unusual to have seed of *Amelanchier alnifolia* (Common or Western Saskatoon) completely eaten by birds within 24 hours of ripening.

Figure 1-9.
The ripened fruits of
Sorbus intermedia
(Swedish White Beam)
are readily consumed by
birds.

A technique that is sometimes successfully used with fleshy fruits if there is a problem with birds eating them, is to collect the fruits before ripening. They are then mixed with moist peat and stored to allow the ripening process to continue.

(iii) Seed may only remain on the tree for a short period and then be quickly dispersed by wind—for example, *Populus* (Poplar) and *Salix* (Willow). However, some seed may remain on the tree for a considerable period, e.g., *Fraxinus excelsior* (European Ash).

(iv) The seed may be rapidly ejected when the fruit is ripe—for example, legumes such as *Laburnum, Cytisus* (Broom) and *Cercis* (Redbud) whose seeds are ejected as the pod splits. Seed of *Hamamelis virginiana* (Common Witch Hazel) are rapidly ejected as the ripened capsule splits.

The table shows the optimum period for collecting seed in southeast England, and can be used as a guide for northern temperate climates.

TABLE 1-3. Seed Collection Dates for Deciduous Woody Plants

The dates in this table are *approximate* dates based on average years in southern England and the stage of ripening reached when collection is considered to be both optimal and economical. This means that some seeds are taken early before birds can reduce the crop to an uneconomical level for collecting and are then allowed to complete their development to maturity in artificial storage conditions, e.g., *Sorbus aucuparia* (European Mountain Ash or Rowan) is taken by birds in July if the weather is dry but the berries can be kept in moist peat while the seeds complete their development. Although this information has been collated from a known geographical source, it does provide a useful guide for all north temperate climates and demonstrates that seed collection periods can vary considerably from one species to another. There will be considerable variation from year to year depending on the season and weather conditions.

SPECIES	COLLECTION DATES
Acer campestre (Hedge Maple)	November
A. capillipes	September/October
A. cappadocicum (Coliseum Maple)	October
A. davidii (David Maple)	September/October
A. grosseri var. *hersii* (Hers' Maple)	September/October
A. negundo (Box Elder)	October/November
A. palmatum plus forms (Japanese Maple)	September/October
A. pensylvanicum (Pennsylvania Maple)	October
A. platanoides (Norway Maple)	October/November
A. pseudoplatanus (Sycamore Maple)	October
A. rufinerve (Red-vein Maple)	October
A. saccharinum (Silver Maple)	Imported from U.S.A. in June as fresh (new season's crop), germinates immediately.
Aesculus hippocastanum (Common Horse-chestnut)	October/November
Alnus cordata (Italian Alder)	November/January
A. glutinosa (Black or Common Alder)	November/December
Amelanchier canadensis (Shadblow Serviceberry)	June/July
Arbutus unedo (Strawberry Tree)	November/December
Azalea ponticum see *Rhododendron luteum*	
Berberis darwinii (Darwin Barberry)	July
Betula pendula (European White Birch)	September
Carpinus betulus (European Hornbeam)	October/November
Castanea sativa (Spanish Chestnut)	October/November
Cornus alba (Red-bark Dogwood)	September/October

SPECIES	COLLECTION DATES
C. sanguinea (Blood-twig Dogwood)	September/October
Corylus spp. (Filbert)	September
Cotoneaster bullatus (Hollyberry Cotoneaster)	August
C. horizontalis (Rock Cotoneaster)	October/November
C. simonsii (Simon's Cotoneaster)	October
Crataegus monogyna (Single-seed or Common Hawthorn)	September/November
Cytisus scoparius (Scotch Broom)	August/September
Daphne mezereum (February Daphne)	June/July
Fagus sylvatica (European Beech)	September/October
Fraxinus excelsior (European Ash)	August (direct sowing) October/November (preferable) (store & stratify over year)
F. ornus (Flowering or Manna Ash)	October/November
Hamamelis virginiana (Common Witch Hazel)	October/November
Juglans regia (English or Persian Walnut)	October
Kalmia latifolia (Mountain Laurel)	January/February
Laburnum anagyroides (Golden-chain Tree)	September/November
Ligustrum vulgare (English Privet)	September/October
Magnolia spp. (Magnolia)	October/November
Mahonia aquifolium (Tall Oregon-grape)	July
Prunus avium (Mazzard)	July (picking) September (sweeping)
P. lusitanica (Portugal Laurel)	August/September
P. spinosa (Blackthorn, Sloe)	September
Quercus cerris (Turkey Oak)	October/November
Q. robur (English Oak)	October/November
Rhododendron luteum (Pontic Azalea) + Exbury and Knaphill Hybrids	October/December
R. ponticum (Pontic Rhododendron)	November/December
Rosa canina (Dog Rose)	September/November
R. rugosa (Rugosa Rose)	September/November
Sorbus aria (White Beam)	September/November
S. aucuparia (European Mountain Ash, Rowan)	July/September
S. intermedia (Swedish White Beam)	September/October
S. torminalis (Wild Service Tree)	October/November
Tilia cordata (Little-leaf Linden)	October
T. platyphyllos (Large-leaved Linden)	October
Ulex europaeus (Gorse)	July/September
Viburnum lantana (Wayfaring Tree)	September/October
V. opulus (European Cranberry Bush)	October/November

Source: Oakover Nurseries Ltd., Potters Corner, Ashford, Kent, U.K.

Methods of Collecting Seed

The first task before collecting any seed is to correctly identify the plant. It is very important to carry out an assessment during the flowering period to determine the seed crop potential. Notes should be made on possible frost damage to flowers and on failure to set and/or develop. Weather conditions should be noted, with particular reference to drought which can cause "hollow seeds", resulting in non-viable seed. Sufficient sunshine and temperature for full embryo and endosperm development is necessary nearer to the normal time of ripening. Provenance and latitude should also be recorded to determine the constancy of production of viable crops of seeds. For example, *Castanea sativa* (Spanish Chestnut) is a native of the Mediterranean region and cultivated specimens will only set seed in more northerly latitudes (e.g., northern England) during an exceptional summer.

At collection time, ensure that the seed is viable before collecting (see p. 30). It is important to take a thorough, random sampling of both single plants and of populations. The viability of species with larger seeds (e.g., *Fagus*, Beech, or *Castanea*, Chestnut) can be checked simply by easing the outer coat of the seed apart with the thumb nails to visually assess whether or not there is a living embryo. Hard-coated seeds may require mechanical opening—but care is necessary when using a knife or hand pruners to undertake this, as the blade may easily slip on the hard coat. Viability tests (described on p. 31) are recommended if the seed is too small for either of these techniques. Viability tests can be carried out before the actual time of collecting. The seed must also be checked for pest damage, e.g., weevil attack on *Quercus* (Oak) seed.

The following methods are used to collect seed of woody ornamentals.

(1) Handpicking

Handpicking the fruits from trees and shrubs is generally the most widely used method. It is particularly convenient for *Acer* (Maple), *Crataegus* (Hawthorn), *Fraxinus* (Ash), *Alnus* (Alder), *Betula* (Birch), *Sorbus* (Mountain Ash) and *Viburnum*, as well as numerous other genera.

A hopper or bag made of sacking and tied to the picker's waist is a very convenient method of holding the collected seed. A plastic sack (e.g., a fertilizer bag cut in half) should be used for fleshy (pulpy) fruit, otherwise there can be embarrassment for the picker. Tying the bag to the waist frees both hands, thus speeding up the rate of picking. Other useful containers include rigid plastic or burlap-lined boxes. Polyethylene bags can be used, but the seed should be transferred to a container that allows air circulation immediately on return to the nursery, otherwise the seed will begin to sweat and deteriorate.

Only seeds (or fruits) should be picked, leaving as many stalks, twigs and leaves behind as possible to reduce the work required to clean the seed later. A useful tool is a pole with a hook at one end that can be used to pull the branches down to the picker. This avoids breaking branches to obtain seed that would otherwise be out of reach. Ladders similar to those used for fruit picking are also helpful.

A scaffold tower is useful when collecting seeds from trees in parkland and on highways.

Figure 1-10. An open burlap (hessian) sack attached to a support around the neck of the picker leaves both hands free to collect the seed. (Tom Wood, Oakover Nurseries, Ashford, Kent, U.K.)

The base of the scaffold is roped to the trunk of the tree. The height should be adjustable to suit the size of the tree and to the height of wide spreading and overhanging branches. The platform must be large enough to allow two people to work with considerable freedom of movement and be equipped with a strong guard-rail for safety. Hard hats and eye protection are recommended safety precautions when using a scaffold tower.

(2) Collecting from the Ground

This method is particularly useful for larger, heavier seeds that are not dispersed by wind as they fall—for example, *Aesculus* (Horse-chestnut) *Quercus* (Oak), *Castanea* (Chestnut), *Fagus* (Beech) and *Juglans* (Walnut). The timing of collection must be well organized so that the seed is collected when the maximum amount has fallen but before it is attacked by birds and rodents. The first seed that falls should be carefully checked as they tend not to be viable.

Two methods are generally used to collect seed from the ground:—

(i) Rake away the ground litter around the tree to prevent it being mixed with the seed, and then collect the seed by hand after it has fallen.

(ii) Lay a continuous strip of woven polypropylene netting (heavy grade shade cloth) or burlap (hessian) sacking around the base of the tree, and peg down to prevent it being lifted by wind. There must be sufficient material to cover the ground beneath the area of the tree canopy. The sheets are carefully removed when sufficient seed has fallen. The seed is then carried back to the nursery in containers. Tarpaulin sheets should be avoided when collecting seed because rain water will collect on the surface, thus inducing the seed to rot. Polyethylene sheets should also be avoided, not only for the same reason, but because they have the additional disadvantage of making the seed sweat.

One method used in the United States to collect *Berberis* (Barberry) seed is to flail the plants with either bamboo poles or short lengths of rubber hose. The seed then falls onto netting or tarpaulin sheets.

(3) Cutting Branches

Collecting seeds of *Populus* (Poplar) and *Salix* (Willow) can be a problem because they are quickly dispersed by wind. Branches may be cut just before seed dispersal, placed in water and kept in a greenhouse or shed for easier collection of seed.

(4) Mechanical Aids for Picking

Mechanical pickers of he following types are sometimes used.

(a) Vacuum Pumps—These have been successfully used in North America and can be mounted on the operator's back as a "back-pack". The flexible suction extension pipe is passed over the plants to remove the fruits. It is useful for some lower-growing shrubs and vines such as *Clematis* where seed is within reach from the ground. Problems include collecting over-ripe fleshy fruits and a lot of unwanted litter, thus making cleaning of the seed a problem.

(b) Tree Shakers—Hydraulically-operated shakers are used in some fruit industries, e.g., for *Olea europaea* (Olive), and have been used successfully for other, relatively small trees. The trunk is held firmly while the tree is shaken, and the seed falls to the ground for easy collection.

(c) Mounted Platform Gantries—These are power driven from a tractor and allow the picker to get up into the higher parts of trees. It is important to wear hard hats and to have a strong guard rail surrounding the platform.

Figure 1-11.
A front-mounted gantry for collecting seed. Note the safety guard rail around the picking platform.

(d) Rifles—These have been used occasionally to obtain small amounts of seed, particularly in cones, that are otherwise inaccessible by conventional methods.

(e) Climbing Equipment—Extension ladders and specialized climbing equipment can be used to obtain seed high up in trees. Full safety procedures must be carried out and the climber trained in the use of such equipment. It is also important that another person be at hand to assist as necessary.

(f) Helicopters—These have been used to collect cones from the tops of tall coniferous trees. The collector is suspended from the helicopter on a safety harness.

(5) Conifers

Conifer cones are usually collected before they are fully mature. They are allowed to complete development and to dry slowly before being put in a kiln to extract the seed. Cones of *Abies* (Fir) are particularly prone to shattering following collection. Consequently, seed collectors will harvest the cones while they are still immature so that the seed is retained.

Cones can be collected by cutting lower branches, by using special poles with a curved blade for severing cones from the trees, and by climbing the trees. Collection from the ground must be done quickly to prevent seed being destroyed by mammals. Fleshy cones can be hand-picked off the trees.

EXTRACTION AND CLEANING OF SEED (PROCESSING SEED)

The collected seed must be prepared so that it can be successfully stored without deteriorating. It is no use just leaving the seed in a shed without any attention, hoping all will be well when it is time for the appropriate pre-sowing treatments and seed sowing. The majority of seeds will still have a relatively high moisture content and be actively respiring when collected, therefore any delays in appropriate handling will lead to deterioration.

Always remove fresh seed from air-tight containers on return to the nursery. It is best to place the seed in sacks or open boxes in a cool ventilated shed where there is little variation in temperature. This allows a number of seeds, e.g., *Betula* (Birch) and *Alnus* (Alder), to remain in a satisfactory condition for a number of weeks before cleaning. Refrigerated cold storage is ideal for most species, both prior to and after cleaning.

A number of the methods used in preparing seed of particular species or types for storage are outlined. Further details on the procedures can be found in the *Seed Manual for Ornamental Trees and Shrubs* by A. G. Gordon and D. C. F. Rowe (Forestry Commission U.K., Bulletin No. 59), *Seeds of Woody Plants in the United States* (USDA, Agriculture Handbook No. 450) and other texts in the reference list.

METHODS OF PREPARING SEED FOR STORAGE

Pod

e.g., *Laburnum, Robinia* (Locust), *Cytisus* (Broom), *Cercis* (Redbud)

These, and other legumes, present few problems. Moist or almost ripe pods are spread out on flats in a greenhouse or warm shed. Newspaper is placed over the pods to prevent the seed from being ejected away from the flats. Small quantities of seed pods can be put in a paper bag laid on a flat. Ripe pods can be held dry in sacks.

The seeds are extracted by breaking the pods by hand or machine (threshing). The seeds and debris are separated by sieving or by using a directed flow of air from a fan (it is advisable to wear eye protection).

Samara

e.g., *Acer* (Maple), *Fraxinus* (Ash), *Liriodendron* (Tulip Tree)

The wings are not removed if the seed is to be sown broadcast, so it is normally not handled further unless debris must be removed or large clumps have been picked and must be separated. For machine sowing, it is desirable to physically remove the winged appendages by rubbing between the hands or against a screen. A de-winging machine may be used for large quantities. The debris can be removed by sieving or a fan.

Figure 1-12. Seed-containing pods of *Cercis siliquastrum* (Judas Tree). If necessary, the pods are dried before extracting the seed.

Figure 1-13. *Acer davidii* (David Maple) produces numerous clusters of samaras which readily lend themselves to hand-picking.

Figure 1-14. *Carpinus betulus* (European Hornbeam) seed being fed into a machine to remove the winged appendages in order to facilitate mechanical sowing.

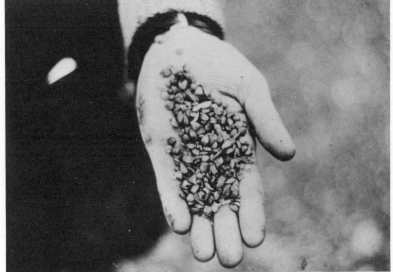

Figure 1-15. "De-winged" *Carpinus betulus* (European Hornbeam) seed ready for sowing.

Nutlet

e.g., *Carpinus* (Hornbeam)

Some nutlets have a winged appendage, as in *Carpinus*. They should be surface dried and then treated as for samaras.

Nut

e.g., *Fagus* (Beech), *Castanea* (Chestnut), *Corylus* (Filbert), *Quercus* (Oak)

Nuts are partially enclosed in a surrounding appendage called the husk or cup. Nuts are usually free of the husk when collected, or it can be removed at that time. A convenient method to remove non-viable seed, husks or cups and other debris is to float the seed in water (flotation). The viable seed will sink while the empty nuts and debris will float to the surface. The seed should be surface dried after flotation. Some viable seed often remains in suspension with the non-viable seed, so it may be necessary to carry out 2 or 3 flotations, surface drying the seed between each one. Small lots of seed can be processed by hand without floating in water.

Winged Nut

e.g., *Betula* (Birch), *Alnus* (Alder)

Birch catkins are collected prior to disintegration, usually when they are still green. The catkins (strobiles) are laid on flats lined with paper, placed in a warm shed or greenhouse and turned 2 or 3 times a week. This will encourage them to disintegrate. *Alnus* seeds do not easily come away from the catkin and may require longer drying and storage to simplify the task. *Alnus rubra* (Red Alder) can be extracted by kiln drying the catkins at 32°C (90°F) for 24 hours within 4–6 weeks of collecting. The seed is then stripped by hand from the dried catkins.

Capsule

e.g., *Hamamelis* (Witch Hazel)

The capsules must be collected before they are fully ripe and still soft as the seed is rapidly ejected on ripening. The procedure is similar to that described for legumes. The capsules must be covered with paper or placed in a paper bag to prevent loss of seed from the flats.

Follicle

e.g., *Magnolia*

The fruits are fleshy, oily follicles and are best collected as they begin to open up, being laid on flats in a greenhouse to dry. The seeds can be shaken out when the fruits are sufficiently dry. However, some fleshy tissue will remain around the seed and must be removed prior to storage. Removal of this fleshy tissue can be speeded up by using hot water instead of cold water for macerating the seed.

Fleshy Fruit

Fleshy fruits should be surface dry at the time of collection, although this is not necessary if the fruit is to be macerated or pulped. Stalks should be left on to allow aeration of drupes, as the resulting air spaces between the drupes will delay deterioration of the flesh during shipping.

There are two ways to handle fleshy fruits. Firstly, to remove the flesh or pulp from the seed and, secondly, to dehydrate the pulp on the seed. If storage is necessary, burlap (hessian) sacks containing the fruits should be stored in a cool shed or, alternatively, the fruits can be spread out on the floor of a well-aerated building.

Figure 1-16.
Black fleshy fruits
(drupes) of *Cornus mas*
(Cornelian Cherry) ready
for collection.

1. Removal of Pulp

The fruits should be allowed to partially ferment as this will help the seed extraction process. Placing the fruits in a water tank for 2 or 3 days encourages fermentation. Note that there is a risk that fermentation will damage the seed embryo unless it is carefully controlled. There are then several different methods used to remove the pulp from the seeds.

Figure 1-17.
Fleshy fruits (berries) of
Sorbus intermedia
(Swedish White Beam)
ready for seed extraction
by flotation.

(a) Flotation—This is probably the most widely used method for cleaning seed and is suitable for both small and medium quantities, e.g., *Aronia* (Chokeberry), *Berberis* (Barberry), *Parthenocissus* (Woodbine), *Sorbus* (Mountian Ash) and *Vitis* (Grape). The first stage is to partially separate the seed from the flesh by maceration. Pome fruits of *Malus* (Apple) and *Pyrus* (Pear) should be cut into pieces first to make the maceration easier. Bruising the fruit to encourage limited fermentation will make seed extraction easier.

One method to improve flotation is to encourage fermentation of the fruits, particularly those with thicker skins and/or harder flesh. This is done by macerating the fruits and then placing them in some warm water in a rigid plastic container. The mixture is thoroughly stirred and the container placed in a warm room for 2–4 days. The addition of 15% sodium carbonate (washing soda) to the mixture assists separation. This process liquifies the fruits, thus making the subsequent flotation easier. Fermentation must not be allowed to proceed for too long as anerobic respiration (respiration in the absence of air) will build to a level that will damage the seed embryo. One beneficial side effect for some of the thicker coated seeds, for example, some *Rosa* ssp. (Rose), is that fermentation may partially break down the seed coat (pericarp).

An effective method used by one nursery for the thin-skinned fruits of *Viburnum opulus* (European Cranberry Bush) was to simply place the fruits in a plastic bin with a small amount of water. The lid of the bin was partially closed and left in full sun for one day. Sufficient fermentation occurred to turn the contents into a virtually fully liquified state, so that flotation was hardly necessary. Similarly, *Mahonia aquifolium* (Tall Oregon-grape) seed can be extracted by making an acidic slurry of the fruits by fermenting the fruits at room temperature.

Figure 1-18.
Fruits of *Viburnum opulus*
(European Cranberry
Bush) undergoing
fermentation in a plastic
bucket. Considerable care
must be taken during
fermentation to avoid
damage to the seed
embryo.

As all fermentation techniques could damage the embryo, the general recommendation is that it is preferable to physically remove the pulp to produce a clean seed sample.

Patience and a certain amount of skill is required to carry out flotation correctly—both should develop as the propagator becomes more experienced. A procedure that I was taught and subsequently found effective is:—

1. Pour the macerated fruits into a deep container, such as a bucket or plastic garbage can.
2. Allow a continuous flow of water from a tap or hose to slowly enter the bucket.
3. Stir the contents at frequent intervals. It is important to keep the contents moving.
4. Tilt the container so that the water slowly runs over the edge, taking with it the flesh, debris and non-viable seeds.
5. Repeat until clean seed is left at the bottom of the bucket.
6. Surface dry the seed.

Figure 1-19.
The final stages of flotation lead to a small amount of floating debris with the clean viable seed remaining at the bottom of the bucket.

The novice will find that the knack is to control the flow of water into the container to provide a steady over-flow of water and debris. It is also important to tilt the container at the correct angle so that the viable seed remains on the bottom and is not lost with the overflowing water. Rubber gloves should be worn—some people have experienced allergic reactions to fruit pulp.

Small pieces of flesh may still remain on the seed, and the addition of a 10–15% sodium carbonate (washing soda) solution may prove helpful. Stir the mixture and leave for 18–24 hours.

(b) "Popping" the Seed—This is convenient for fruits that have both a relatively large seed and relatively hard flesh. It is useful in obtaining small quantities of seed from fruits of *Crataegus* (Hawthorn) and *Rosa* (Rose) before the flesh has fully ripened. The thumb or a rolling pin is used to create pressure on the fruit that will squeeze out the seed.

(c) Maceration (Pulping)—Maceration is done either with a rolling pin or a fruit press. Pulling a garden roller over the fruits laid on a concrete floor is effective for large quantities.

After maceration, the fruits are mixed with a moist stratification medium for chilling (see p. 37). This procedure eliminates further handling as the seed and medium are sown together. This method has been used successfully for *Sorbus aucuparia* (European Mountain Ash). Captan is sometimes added to the medium if there is a risk that fungal molds will develop.

Best results are obtained if the seed is sieved, cleaned and air dried before it is stratified (p. 37). It is then possible to make an estimate of the amount of clean seed before it is mixed with the stratification medium. It is not possible to do this when the pulp and seed are mixed together. Pulp in the stratification medium can continue to ferment and thus cause rotting and deterioration of the seed during the stratification process. The pulp of some seeds also contains chemical inhibitors to germination, making it important to have a clean seed sample.

Macerating machines (e.g., Dybvig) have been successfully used for larger quantities of fruits. Hillier Nurseries (Winchester) Ltd., Ampfield, Romsey, U.K., use the German-manufactured

Allesmusser for all but the most delicate pulp fruits (e.g., *Viburnum opulus,* European Cranberry Bush) to macerate the fruit. Water is poured through during maceration and the resulting slurry is poured into a bucket. The pulp floats but is still usually "teased" by hand. The seed drops to the bottom of the bucket, together with fruit not yet macerated or "de-seeded". The un-macerated fruit is then poured into the macerator machine again, with the process being repeated until all the pulped fruit and dead seed is poured off. Clean seed is surface dried only when it is to be stored before subsequent treatment or sowing.

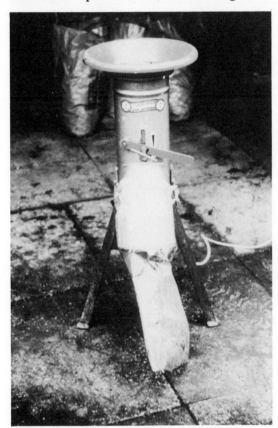

Figure 1-20. An electrically-powered machine for macerating fleshy fruits.

Figure 1-21. The slurry produced by the macerating machine shown in Figure 1-20 is released from the polyethylene retaining bag into a bucket.

Soft delicate fruit like *Viburnum opulus* (European Cranberry Bush) is best macerated by squeezing out the contents between the fingers and then using flotation to obtain the seed.

2. Dehydration

Fruits can be dried if the flesh does not contain chemical inhibitors that will affect subsequent germination. For example, fruits of *Mahonia* (Oregon-grape) and *Berberis* (Barberry) are surfaced washed and then laid on trays placed in full sun or in a greenhouse, turning the fruits as necessary. The debris is separated from the dried fruits when the moisture content is down to about 10–12%. The seed is then stored dry in muslin bags or burlap (hessian) sacks kept in a refrigerator or cool shed. *Arctostaphylos uva-ursi* (Kinnikinnick) and *Shepherdia canadensis* (Soopolallie, Soapberry or Russet Buffalo-berry) are examples of fruits that have been successfully dried and sown in British Columbia.

The disadvantages of dehydration are that it firstly, encourages the presence of chemical inhibitors on or around the actual seed, and secondly, there is a tendency for the seed to be sown in "bunches" (uneven seed sowing).

EXTRACTION AND HANDLING OF CONIFER SEED

The procedures used in the extraction and handling of coniferous seed by the forestry industry provides a "model" which may be adapted by a nursery wishing to obtain small quantities of seed.

Forestry Procedures

Seed extraction usually is carried out in a custom-designed building using specialized equipment, some of which is traditional in design but; nevertheless, has been very satisfactory for many years. The custom-designed building is referred to as a "seed extractory".

The following procedure is based upon the seed extraction system used at Reid Collins Nurseries, Aldergrove, British Columbia.

1. The cones are removed from the collection bags on arrival and re-bagged. This allows the cones to expand as they are usually tightly packed in the collection sacks. During this process, the cones are checked for moisture content, mold and insects.

The re-bagged cones are placed on slatted racks in a building that has a roof but open sides to allow plenty of air movement. This building is an extension of the seed extractory.

Sample sacks are opened every 7–10 days and checked for fungal molds. Good aeration is essential to prevent sweating and heat build-up of the cones. Cones of *Pseudotsuga menziesii* (Douglas Fir) have a moisture content of 65–80% on arrival, but this is reduced during the initial storage period (cones of most coastal species have a high moisture content). Cones of *Pinus contorta* var. *latifolia* (Lodgepole Pine) have a considerably lower moisture content of around 20%. *Abies* (Fir) cones stored for 6–8 weeks have a moisture content in the region of 40%. The moisture content is determined by either a moisture-detecting probe which is placed among the cones or by oven drying.

2. The sacks are removed from the racks and the cones emptied onto a conveyor that carries them into the extractory.

3. The cones are placed on large trays with wire-mesh bases and the trays moved on trolleys into a kiln for further drying to encourage the cone scales to open and release the seed. This procedure is usually referred to as "kilning". The period of kilning is based on the species and on the provenance of the seed. Depending on the species, the kilns normally work on a 24-hour cycle during which time the temperature rises to 41°C (105°F). The moisture content of the air in the kilns is kept high to assist the cone opening process and then reduced. Air is continually circulated over the cones.

Two terms used during kilning of the cones are:—

(a) *Serotinous Cone*—Refers to a cone with a high resinous content which acts as a bond to prevent the cones from opening up, e.g., *Pinus contorta* var. *latifolia* (Lodgepine Pine). Temperatures up to 77°C (170°F) are needed to break the resin bond of these cones.

(b) *Case Hardening*—Refers to cones in which the outside surface does not allow moisture to pass through it so that they will not open up during kilning. Case hardening can occur when the initial air temperatures are too high or when the cones have been exposed to irregular periods of drying. Case-hardened cones should be discarded.

4. The cones are removed from the kilns and placed in a tumbler to extract the seeds. This tumbler is a long, square, wire-mesh basket which shakes the cones as it rotates and thus separates the seed from the cones. The seeds then fall through the wire mesh into a hopper.

5. Cleaning of the seed begins with "scalping". This rough cleaning removes any large debris that could damage the seed during the de-winging process.

6. Next is de-winging—the physical removal of the wings from the seeds. It is not possible to remove the wings from seed of *Thuja* (Arborvitae), *Chamaecyparis* (False Cypress) and *Cupressus* (Cypress) species. De-winging is claimed to reduce the viability of seed in *Libocedrus* (Incense Cedar).

One of three mechanical methods may be used to de-wing the seed. First, a mechanism called a brush de-winger that physically strips off the wings. This method is suitable for hard-coated seeds, such as *Picea sitchensis* (Sitka Spruce). Second, an auger de-winger that rubs the seeds against each other, and is suitable for softer-coated seeds such as *Pseudotsuga menziesii* (Douglas Fir). Third, a conventional cement mixer is suitable for both hard- and softer-coated seeds. Water is added to the seeds as they rotate within the drum of the mixer. The resulting friction rubs the wings off the seeds.

7. By this time, a considerable amount of debris—dust, cone fractions, etc.—has accumulated and must be separated from the seed. Separation, sometimes referred to as fanning and winnowing, is accomplished with air blowers lifting the debris and allowing the seed to fall under gravity through a series of sieves.

8. The final cleaning process is to transfer the seed to a vibrating "gravity table". This separates the viable and non-viable seed.

9. The clean seed is placed in polyethylene bags, which are labelled and packed into double-walled, waxed cardboard boxes ready for shipment. These boxes are generally better than rigid boxes for shipment, as they take impact with less likelihood of damage to the seed. The boxes are stored at −6°C (21°F) until shipped.

A detailed account of the seed extraction process can be found on pages 110–113 in *Seeds of Woody Plants in the United States* (USDA, Handbook No. 450).

Small Conifer Seed Lots

Some useful information is contained in the excellent publication, *Propagation Manual of Selected Gymnosperms,* produced by the Arnold Arboretum (Arnoldia 37(1), Jan.–Feb. 1977), and largely based on the experience of Alfred J. Fordham, former Head Propagator at the Arnold Arboretum, Jamaica Plain, Mass., whom I first met in 1973 at the Great Britain and Ireland Regional I.P.P.S. Conference and Tour. He recommends that the seed of most species can be best recovered by simply putting the cones in a paper bag, which is then placed on top of a radiator until the scales come apart sufficiently to shake out the seed. If the seed is not released, the cones are placed in an oven heated to about 54°C (130°F). A laboratory oven fitted with a fan, if available, is useful as it allows ventilation. Cones of *Cedrus* (Cedar) and *Abies* (Fir) may be soaked in water to encourage them to disintegrate. If this is not sufficient, freeze the moist cones as ice crystals will force the scales to open up.

It is important to avoid any more drying than is absolutely necessary, because the seeds may dry too much and be killed if the cones open—especially *Abies* (Fir), *Cedrus* (Cedar) and *Picea* (Spruce).

The seeds can be separated from the debris by fanning or winnowing with a small electric fan, or simply use a hand sieve with a mesh slightly larger than the seed. Such a sieve will allow the seeds to fall through, while retaining the larger scales and other debris. The scales and seeds of some species are almost the same size, and A. J. Fordham recommends that these be dropped from one hand into the other while gently blowing. The seed is lighter and the air current caused by blowing encourages it to fall on the bench below, leaving most of the debris in the hand.

De-winging is done by simply rubbing the seeds in a dry cloth. Resin from the resin pockets in the wings can sometimes make the procedure difficult if bare hands are used.

A method successfully used for obtaining seed from closed *Cupressus* (Cypress) cones is to place the cones in boiling water for 30–60 seconds and then allow them to dry. This procedure encourages the cones to open more rapidly than if they are just dried.

The seed of fleshy cones such as *Juniperus* (Juniper) and *Taxus* (Yew) can be extracted by maceration and flotation as described for extracting seed from fleshy fruits of broad-leaved trees and shrubs (p. 22).

STORAGE OF SEEDS

Over the years nursery operators have benefited enormously from the knowledge and technology available in the forestry and vegetable seed industry relative to the storage of seed. Storage of seed is the period of time between collection or purchase of the seed and sowing. Seed storage is not as straightforward as it might appear, as the seed may have to be treated to overcome germination problems after removal from storage and before sowing. Seed storage has often been haphazard on nurseries, leading to rapid deterioration of what was formerly viable seed. The *Seed Manual for Ornamental Trees and Shrubs* (U.K. Forestry Commission Bulletin No. 59) is a very welcome addition to present-day knowledge, and further details may be obtained from this publication.

The primary aim of successful storage is to retain the seed at maximum viability and in prime condition for as long a period as possible. Longevity is a term often used to describe the length of time that a seed may be successfully stored and still germinate satisfactorily.

It must be appreciated that one is dealing with live tissue, so it is not just a case of collecting or receiving seed, placing it on a shelf in a shed, office or, even worse, a greenhouse, forgetting about it until sowing time, and then hoping it will germinate satisfactorily.

A number of species, e.g., *Aesculus* (Horse-chestnut), *Juglans* (Walnut) and *Cedrus* (Cedar), store all or part of their food reserves as fats, oils and waxes, plus some as protein. If these seeds are dried below a critical level, they will not imbibe (take up water) in a way that will allow the food reserve to be used by the embryo. This may result in the percentage viability declining very rapidly. (Excessive drying out results in loss of water from the seed and the "waterproofing" of food reserves then prevents the take up of water.)

There are two general "rules-of-thumb" that are sometimes used for annual and herbaceous plants. First, longevity is doubled with every 1% reduction of the moisture content within the seed. Second, that longevity is doubled with each 5°C (9°F) reduction in storage temperature. In practice, however, other factors must be taken into account for successful seed storage.

(i) The Plant Species—Species with very thin seed coats tend to lose their viability quickly. For example, *Salix* (Willow) and *Populus* (Poplar) can be stored successfully for only a few days, *Acer saccharinum* (Silver Maple) can normally be stored for only 3–4 weeks, while hard-coated seed such as *Rhus typhina* (Staghorn Sumac) can be stored for many years.

(ii) Collection and Extraction—The time of seed collection and the procedures used in extracting and cleaning the seed, as previously indicated, have a direct effect on longevity. Problems will result when it is not handled correctly, particularly if the seed is not fully developed.

(iii) Moisture Content of the Seed—The moisture content for storage normally falls in the range of 5–14%, with the optimum around 8–10%. A general guideline for the storage of nutty seeds is to store at the moisture content present at collection, unless there is evidence to indicate otherwise. Nutty seeds such as *Fagus* (Beech) are often stored at 5°C (41°F) with a moisture content of 20–25%, while *Quercus robur* (English Oak) should not fall below 40%. There can be a loss of at least 50% viability after one year in storage. [Nutty seeds refers to seeds which store the food mainly as fats, oils, waxes and even proteins.]

(iv) Temperature—Lowering the temperature is essential for successful storage. The optimum temperature range is −1 to + 5°C (30–41°F), with 3°C (37°F) being a good compromise. Many seeds can be stored below these temperatures, but there will be increased refrigeration costs. Below freezing temperatures coupled with high relative humidity can cause ice crystals to form. This will destroy seed tissues, so the seed is best stored in sealed containers under these conditions. Storing seeds below freezing is not fully effective unless the moisture content is reduced. This may be achieved by placing a small amount of desiccant (e.g., calcium chloride or silica gel) in the container for about 4 weeks. Nutty seeds should not be stored below freezing.

(v) Relative Humidity—The relative humidity of the air must remain low during storage. The air absorbs water as the temperature increases, and increased humidity levels encourage the seeds to absorb moisture. However, the relative humidity around nutty seeds is sometimes raised to prevent water loss. Some of the largest nuts with a very high moisture content are best stored in a jacketed (indirect) cold store in which both the relative humidity and the temperature are kept constant.

Sealed containers should be used for seed that is to be stored for more than one year, e.g., *Fagus* (Beech), *Corylus* (Filbert) and *Nothofagus* (Southern Beech), to ensure that low humidity levels are maintained in the immediate environment of the seed.

(vi) Atmospheric Fluctuations—Temperature, moisture levels of the seed and relative humidity should all remain constant during storage. Fluctuating moisture and temperature regimes will encourage disease infection. Lowering the temperature to 1–5°C (34–41°F) reduces the risk of infection.

(vii) Aeration—Good ventilation is required during storage, especially for nutty seeds. This can be achieved by storing the seed in a ventilated building, turning the seed regularly, and using well-ventilated storage containers, e.g., burlap (hessian) sacks. It is better to direct sow nutty seeds in the fall following collection whenever possible.

(viii) Damaged Seed—It is essential that damaged seed is not stored. Damaged seed will infect the other seed with disease, so decreasing its longevity. Seed of *Fagus sylvatica* (European Beech) is particularly prone to damage during collection and handling, and therefore must be carefully examined before storage.

(ix) Pest and Disease Infection—Seeds infected by pests should be eliminated during the processing stages before storage, e.g., weevil attack on *Quercus* (Oak) seed. Vermin such as mice and rats can play havoc with nutty seed if it is not protected.

Treating the seed with fungicides such as thiram prior to storage is beneficial.

Receipt of Purchased Seed

As previously indicated (p. 14), the propagator is sometimes confronted by the unknown treatment of seed prior to its arrival at the nursery. The seed should be carefully examined on arrival for damage and, where practical, a viability test performed if this information is not provided. Any deficiencies should be reported immediately to the supplier. Suppliers should be encouraged to send small quantities of seed in Ziploc® packs.

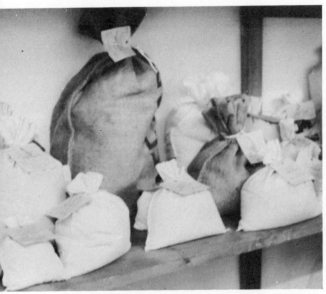

Figure 1-22. Well-labelled seed lots received from a commercial seed house can be stored temporarily in a refrigerator prior to any necessary pre-sowing treatments.

Figure 1-23. Boxes lined with burlap (hessian) in a well-ventilated cool shed are ideal for storing *Acer* (Maple), *Carpinus* (Hornbeam) and *Fraxinus* (Ash) seed.

Storage Techniques

Seeds with hard seed coats, such as *Cytisus* (Broom), *Koelreuteria* (Golden Rain Tree), *Rhus* (Sumac), *Pinus* (Pine) and *Robinia* (Locust), are surface dried and placed in metal or rigid plastic containers which are then sealed and placed in a refrigerator at 0–5°C (32–41°F). Seed stored in this way will be viable for a number of years. In practice, these hard-coated seeds are often stored in cloth bags but a sealed container is preferable.

Betula (Birch) and *Alnus* (Alder) seeds should be stored dry in sealed containers at 0–5°C (32–41°F). Normal refrigerated (direct) cold storage in cloth bags, particularly with *Betula* seed, leads to dehydration of the seed, thus decreasing its storage life. I have successfully stored small amounts of *Cedrus deodara* (Himalayan Cedar) by mixing the seed with a small amount of sawdust and placing the mixture in a sealed container. This ensures that the seed will remain plump and does not shrivel in the short term.

The winged seeds of *Acer* (Maple), *Fraxinus* (Ash) and *Carpinus* (Hornbeam) are placed in burlap (hessian) sacks that will allow air movement. The seed is stored dry either by hanging the sacks from the roof of a well-ventilated, cool shed or by placing in large boxes, lined with burlap (hessian) sacking if necessary. The boxes are placed on supports to allow air movement from underneath. The bags should be shaken regularly and the seed in the boxes turned over. Some *Acer* (Maple), seeds, e.g., *A. palmatum* (Japanese Maple), will fail to germinate in the first year after sowing if they have been allowed to dry excessively during storage.

Nutty seeds, such as *Aesculus* (Horse-chestnut), *Castanea* (Chestnut), *Quercus* (Oak) and *Fagus* (Beech), will not germinate well if they are not handled properly after collection. Essentially the problems are three-fold:—

(i) They are prone to rapid moisture loss after collection. The outer tissues become wrinkled if the loss is severe. It is sometimes necessary to dampen the seed before it is turned, using a fine spray of water.

(ii) Heaps of newly-collected seed are prone to heat build-up and sweating unless regularly turned.

(iii) They are prone to attack by mice.

Potential storage problems can be overcome by fall sowing—the merits and limitations of this are discussed on p. 60.

The trick is to reduce the moisture content of the seed that has to be stored without lowering it enough to be detrimental. Two methods successfully used on nurseries to reduce the moisture content of nutty seeds that must be stored until the following spring are:—

(i) Mix the seed with dry peat moss or wood shavings and place in a rodent-free frame adjacent to the north side of a building to reduce temperature fluctuation. The frame should be sited under an over-hanging roof (or have other means of protection) to ensure that rain does not reach the seed and thus increase the moisture content. The dry peat moss or wood shavings reduce air movement around the seed and help to prevent it from drying out.

(ii) Mix the seed with charcoal and place in 50 kg (100 lb) polyethylene sacks. The sacks are not tied but left open at the neck. They are then placed in a cold store at a temperature of 0–2°C (32–36°F) and left until sowing time. Commercial experience has demonstrated that this is a very good method of storing nutty seeds.

Storage of *Fagus sylvatica* (European Beech) seed has given nurseries some trouble, but it has been stored successfully at 3–5°C (37–41°F) with a 20–25% moisture content. This kept the seed in viable condition until sowing in the spring following collection.

Further details on the storage of nutty seeds can be found in the *Seed Manual for Ornamental Trees and Shrubs* (Chapter 5) by A. G. Gordon and D. C. F. Rowe (U.K. Forestry Commission, Bulletin No. 59).

SEED VIABILITY

Viability is a term used to denote the proportion of seed that is live when a sample is assessed, and therefore the potential number of seeds capable of germination. Today there are a number of techniques used to determine the percentage viability of certain plants in order to comply with the standards required by international agreement. It is important to document the percentage viability of seed every year.

There are essentially four periods when viability of woody ornamentals can be assessed by the nursery operator:—

(i) Before or at the time of collection of local seed. This period is useful for larger seed, e.g., *Acer palmatum* (Japanese Maple). However, this assessment should be treated only as an early indication of viability. It will be necessary to re-assess the viability following pre-sowing treatments to remove dormancy.

(ii) On receipt of purchased seed, even if the information has been supplied by the commercial seed house. This is particularly important when seed is suspect in quality and/or there has been a chance of damage during transit. Note that seed houses should provide information on viability, such as viability at time of collection, when the seed is consigned to their customers.

(iii) After the seed has been extracted, cleaned and stored for a short while. This is also a useful time to re-check viability if the seed has been placed under stress during preparation and storage. It is also useful to re-check the viability if the seed has been kept for more than one season prior to sowing.

(iv) Just prior to sowing to help to determine the rate of sowing. Testing at this time is important for accurate broadcasting and precision drilling by machines.

Methods of Assessing Seed Viability

1. Cutting Through the Seed

This method gives only a rough estimate of viability, but is invaluable prior to collecting seed and during subsequent processing. A good experienced eye, backed up by a hand lens, can provide a reasonable assessment of the situation. The method used is described on p. 18 under local collections.

Some propagators use the cutting test procedure to get a rough estimate of sowing density. One hundred seeds are selected at random and the percentage of live embryos recorded. This then governs the decision on whether to sow either "heavy" or "light".

2. Test Sowing

A small quantity of seed can be sown in a flat in the greenhouse about 4–6 weeks before outdoor sowing, providing seed dormancy requirements have been met.

One procedure that has been found satisfactory is as follows:—

(i) Weigh and count the seed before sowing. A convenient number for each sample is 100.

(ii) Count the number of radicles that have emerged after a given or optimum period.

(iii) Calculate this number as a percentage of both weight and number in the sample to provide both the viability information and sowing density.

Figure 1-24.
Laboratory viability testing techniques used for forest tree seed can also be used by a nursery to give an accurate assessment of germination capability.

3. Tetrazolium Test (Biochemical Staining)

This relatively straightforward technique is used internationally to assess the viability of seeds and can be adapted for the nursery situation. It provides a more accurate assessment than cutting through the seed. The tetrazolium test requires both experience and skill to make the correct judgments.

The chemical used is 2,3,5-Triphenyltetrazolium Chloride, which readily dissolves in water to form a colorless solution. An optimum strength of 1% with a pH of 6.5–7.0 is normally recommended. The tetrazolium salt reacts with tissues that are able to respire, breaking down to form insoluble triphenylformazan. This stains the live tissues reddish-pink, while dead tissues remain unstained as triphenylformazan is not formed.

International standards of viability require that four replicates of each seed lot be tested, with each replicate containing one hundred seeds. The results are combined and averaged to provide a viability figure. Four replicates of 25 seeds each should be sufficient for nursery testing.

The seed can be prepared in one of three ways for testing, depending on the shape and structure—cut longitudinally on long thin seeds (e.g., *Fraxinus,* Ash), cut transversely on more rounded seeds (e.g., *Sorbus,* Mountain Ash), while the removal of a hard seed coat (e.g., *Pinus,* Pine) is advisable before treatment. The process can be made easier by soaking the seed in water for 24 hours prior to preparation. The seeds must be covered by the tetrazolium solution—a small beaker or petri dish is sufficient unless the seed is unusually large. Small seeds are best soaked for 24 hours on moist filter paper, with the paper being folded over the seed just before the addition of the tetrazolium salt. This will prevent the seeds from dispersing in the liquid. The treated seeds are placed in a dark cupboard or drawer for 24 hours at a temperature of 21–30°C (70–86°F)—the higher temperature may reduce the time period necessary for the reaction to occur.

Examination of the seeds will show that live tissue has stained reddish-pink while dead tissue remains colorless. The advantage of this method is that it gives a relatively fast result combined with a visual determination of live and dead tissue. A simple hand lens or a binocular microscope may be needed for very small seeds.

4. Indigo Carmine Test

This is a lesser known technique. It stains in the opposite way to the tetrazolium test—the dead tissue is stained blue while the live tissue is untouched. I have no personal experience of this test.

5. Excised Embryo Test

This technique provides a very accurate assessment but should be carried out in a specialized facility. International specifications state that a set number of embryos should be carefully removed (excised) from the seed and allowed to develop independently under controlled light and temperature conditions.

The usual method is to culture the excised embryos on moist filter paper in covered dishes under light for 10–14 days at 18–20°C (64–68°F). A percentage figure is derived to compare the number of embryos that develop or at least remain firm and white compared with those which deteriorate (become dark or covered with mold).

6. X-ray Test

This is also a specialized technique giving a fast and accurate determination of live, dead and damaged seed. Specialized apparatus is needed. The seeds are soaked in solutions of heavy-metal salts and then photographed.

This summary of the methods by which viability can be determined will provide the reader with some initial background. It should be noted that only the tetrazolium and excised embryo tests are officially accepted by regulatory agencies at the present time.

In conclusion, it is suggested that the propagator should:—

(i) Use the seed cutting technique, backed up where necessary with the tetrazolium test, to determine seed viability. Records should be kept every year of both locally collected and purchased seed.

(ii) Learn of testing services which will perform specialized viability tests for a fee. For example, the Forestry Commission in Britain (Alice Holt Lodge, Wrecclesham, Farnham, Surrey) provides a service to foresters and others requiring a proper seed test certificate.

(iii) Obtain further details of the tetrazolium test and other specialized techniques by referring to the appropriate sections in *Seeds of Woody Plants in the United States* (USDA, Agriculture Handbook No. 450), *Seed Manual for Ornamental Trees and Shrubs* by A. G. Gordon and D. C. F. Rowe (U.K. Forestry Commission, Bulletin No. 59), the chapter "Tetrazolium Staining for Assessing Seed Quality" by R. P. Moore in the book *Seed Ecology* (University of Nottingham Nineteenth Easter School in Agricultural Science 1972, edited by W. Heydecker), *Plant Propagation: Principles and Practices* (4th edition) by H. T. Hartmann and D. E. Kester, and *Hardy Woody Plants from Seed* by P. D. A. McMillan Browse. These publications all provide invaluable information on the techniques.

SEED DORMANCY

Seed dormancy is the term used for viable seed which does not germinate when placed in conditions suitable for germination. In nature, it represents a vital form of protection ensuring the survival of plants—either external or internal conditions prevent the seed germinating at the wrong time of year. This factor is particularly important in climates with extremes of cold or heat, where germination at the wrong period would result in instant death of the seedling. A live seed is considered to be dormant if it is incapable of imbibing (taking up water), developing growth of the embryo, or of activating biochemical reactions. Some seeds exhibit only one of these factors but two may be involved—this latter case is referred to as "double dormancy". The propagator essentially overcomes dormancy with treatments that imitate conditions in nature. Remember, however, that results may not be consistent from one year to the next, and that the time period of treatment may vary for seed batches of the same species collected at different geographical locations.

Dormancy usually results from processes that occur during the seed's development after fertilization (usually after completion of development of the embryo and food stores). There are, however, two other periods when seed dormancy can develop. This is generally referred to as "secondary dormancy".

(i) During the processing and storage of seed—for example, excessive drying-out of the seed.

(ii) After sowing of the seed. Unfavorable conditions, such as high temperature build-up when seed is sown under glass or polyethylene, can re-induce dormancy.

Research programs throughout the world have played a vital role in coming to grips with the practical problems of overcoming dormancy. An excellent example occurred in Britain when there were strong pressures to create a home-based Rose rootstock industry. The outcome of J. B. Blundells' work was a procedure which combined temperature and acid treatment to dramatically increase the potential germination of seeds of Laxa rose rootstocks compared to the lower germination percentages obtained by the traditional method of stratification pits.

The aim of this section is to outline the causes of seed dormancy, and to explain the methods that can be used on the nursery to overcome it. Seed dormancy has often been misunderstood and, until recently, many treatments were haphazard for particular species, resulting in unreliable results. For simplicity, the causes of seed dormancy can be attributed to either physical or physiological reasons. In reality, however, it should be appreciated that a number of species exhibit dormancy as a result of combinations of these two categories.

Information on the detailed classification of seed dormancy may be obtained by referring to several of the texts in the reference list.

The aim of treatments to overcome dormancy is to bring the highest proportion or percentage of viable seed to the point of germination. This then helps to ensure even germination and a well-graded crop, compared to irregular germination with the resultant poorer quality end-product.

TYPES OF SEED DORMANCY AND PRE-SOWING TECHNIQUES TO OVERCOME DORMANCY

A. Physical Dormancy

a. Hard Seed Coats

Hard seed coats make it difficult for the seed to take up water, thus causing slow and irregular germination. Many of these plants are in the Fabaceae (Leguminosae) family, (which grow well in warm climates), such as *Acacia, Cercis* (Redbud), *Gleditsia* (Honey Locust) and *Robinia* (Locust). Other genera, including species of *Pinus* (Pine), *Tilia* (Linden), *Rhus* (Sumac) and *Eucalyptus,* also develop hard seed coats. The degree of hardness of the seed coat depends on the species, and also on the geographical location where the seed was collected as weather conditions during the seed ripening process can influence hardness.

Techniques to Overcome Hard Seed Coat Dormancy

Various methods are used to overcome hard seed coat dormancy.

1. Mechanical Scarification

The aim is to puncture, crack or reduce the thickness of the dry seed coat to make it more permeable to water and air. Filing, cracking or chipping the seed coat with small hand tools is successful for small quantities of large seeds. The thickness of the seed coat can be reduced by rubbing individual seeds on a wooden block covered with sand paper. An electrically-powered rotating drum lined with sand paper on the inside may be used for large quantities of seed. The rotation of the drum gradually reduces the thickness of the seed coat. An ordinary cement mixer can be used if a special sanding drum is not available. The seed is mixed with coarse sharp sand and tumbled in the mixer. This 'method does take quite a long time to scarify each seed batch sufficiently. *Prunus* (Cherry) seeds have been satisfactorily scarified by this method.

Whichever technique is used, it is important to regularly check the degree of seed coat reduction to ensure that the internal tissues of the seed are not damaged.

Burning the seed has been used occasionally to improve germination. Seed of *Arctostaphylos* spp. (Manzanita), *Eucalyptus* spp. and *Dendromecon rigida* (Tree or Bush Poppy) can be sown in flats and covered with 6 mm (¼") of soil. A 7.5–10 cm (3–4") layer of straw is then placed over the soil cover and ignited. This method is not, however, always reliable.

2. Hot Water Soak

Soaking in hot water for a set period of time will soften the seed coat and thus allow the seed to imbibe water. The seeds swell, become paler in color and may have a gelatinous feel when handled. This technique is particularly useful for many of the Fabaceae (Leguminosae). I have had excellent results with *Acacia, Gleditsia* (Honey Locust), *Robinia* (Locust) and *Cercis occidentalis* (Western Redbud). Cold water is normally adequate for *Robinia,* and should be tried first. *Tilia* (Linden) seed has been successfully imbibed by leaving in hot water while it cools. The imbibed seed falls to the bottom, and seeds that are still floating are removed and re-treated.

Procedure:

1. Heat sufficient water to between 77–100°C (170–212°F) for *Gleditsia* (Honey Locust). The volume of water should be equal to approximately 4–6 times the volume of seed. Too little water results in a rapid temperature drop which is less effective. [Test a small handful of seed first to check that the water temperature is not too high, otherwise the seed will turn to "mush".] Some species are liable to embryo damage when very hot water is used, and some propagators prefer to heat the water only to 65–70°C (149–158°F) to reduce this risk when dealing with these species.

2. Place the seeds in a heat-resistant container, labelling as necessary.

3. Pour the water over the seeds, ensuring that they are well covered.

4. Leave the seed to soak in the cooling water for 18–24 hours, agitating at regular intervals with a glass or metal rod.

5. Remove the seed after the specified soaking period, mix with moist peat and leave for a further 24 hours.

6. Sow the seed within 4 days of the initial treatment. Do not roll the seed bed after sowing because the seeds are very soft and easily damaged.

Some propagators try cold water before resorting to the hot water soak. Cold water is adequate for seeds with thinner coats. The effect and necessary soaking time should be tested on a small sample before treating large lots of seed.

Finally, two important items for consideration:—

1. Do not leave the seeds in solution too long as they will deteriorate.

2. Ensure that the seeds do not dry out between removal from the water and sowing or between sowing and germination. I recall a seed bed of *Robinia pseudoacacia* (Black Locust) that had been successfully soaked in hot water only to germinate erratically because the necessary irrigation had not been given after sowing. In other words, sow as soon as possible after treatment and provide good aftercare following sowing.

One difficulty that can arise with seeds soaked in water is that they swell and stick to each other, and therefore make it difficult to calibrate a mechanical seed sower. Oakover Nurseries, Ashford, Kent, England, have successfully used the following method to overcome this problem. The seed is removed from the cooled water after 18–24 hours, drained briefly and placed in moist peat for 4–7 days. This allows the seed to continue the imbibing process under aerobic conditions. The seed and medium are sown together after the seed has chitted (p. 62). There is thus little chance of the seeds drying out or of sticking together. The beds are irrigated as soon as sowing is completed.

3. Acid Scarification (Acid Digestion)

Concentrated sulfuric acid (commercial grade, specific gravity 1.84) is an efficient technique for reducing the thickness of hard seed coats. It is sometimes referred to as acid digestion because the action "eats away" at the seed coat. This action can be seen by the rapid discoloration of the acid around, say, a *Gleditsia* seed. This shows how strong and corrosive the acid is, and the primary recommendation before attempting this technique is *safety*. The following precautions need to be taken:—

    1. Proper instruction and training should be given to the person carrying out the treatment.

    2. Full protective clothing (acid-resistant rubber gloves, eye goggles, and rubber boots and leggings) should be worn to protect eyes and skin.

    3. Acid-resistant utensils (glass or glazed earthenware) must be used for handling and treating the seed.

    4. Water should *not* be added to the acid or it will boil and splash back on to the operator.

    5. The acid should be carefully and slowly poured into large volumes of water to reduce the concentration or for disposal. Do *not* simply pour it down a sink or drain.

Figure 1-25.
Even germination of
Gleditsia triacanthos
(Honey Locust) following
a 90-minute acid
digestion treatment with
concentrated sulfuric
acid.

The majority of seeds are placed in the concentrated acid for 15–90 minutes of treatment—e.g., *Gleditsia triacanthos* (Honey Locust)—90 minutes, *Robinia pseudoacacia* (Black Locust)—20 minutes, and *Cercis chinensis* (Chinese Redbud)—20 minutes. Some seeds may require 2–3 hours (*Gymnocladus dioica*, Kentucky Coffee Tree) and others up to 5–6 hours (*Rhus typhina*, Staghorn Sumac). Note that the time period of acid treatment can vary from year to year. For example, J. B. Blundells in England has shown that the seed coat of the Laxa rose rootstock varies in thickness in different seed lots, making it necessary to treat with acid for periods ranging from a few minutes to 90 minutes. A preliminary test should be carried out to determine the length of the acid scarification period before treating the entire batch of seeds. Two methods of testing that are used are as follows:—

    (i) The USDA Agriculture Handbook No. 450 suggests that a sample be taken from the seed lot, divided into several small groups and each of these be treated for one of a range of time periods suitable for that particular species. The seeds are soaked in water for 1–5 days after the acid treatment and then examined. The seed batch with the highest proportion of undamaged swollen seeds indicates the optimum time period for acid scarification.

    (ii) Treat the whole sample with acid, removing some seeds at regular timed intervals and cut them to assess the amount of reduction of the seed coat. This technique has worked well with seed of the Laxa rose rootstock.

A guideline sometimes used for shiny seeds is that the seed coat should take on a dull and slightly pitted appearance after treatment. The seed coat will still be glossy if the treatment is too short, while there will be excessive pitting if it has been too long. A more accurate assessment is obtained by examining the seed through a low power microscope—the testa should be burnt almost all the way through.

One method of acid scarification is outlined below. Note that the seed should not be taken straight from cold storage and treated—moisture may have formed which will cause a dangerous reaction with the acid.

1. Place clean, dry seed in an acid-resistant container such as glass or glazed earthenware. (The seed must be clean in order to avoid the risk of heat build-up.)

2. Carefully add twice the volume of acid to one volume of seed and stir the contents with a glass rod. The container and contents are left at room temperature. (Some propagators stand the container in a tub of cold water to reduce heat build-up.)

3. Stir the contents at regular intervals both to prevent temperature and charcoal build-up and also to prevent the seeds from sticking to each other.

4. Prepare a container with a large volume of a 5% solution of sodium carbonate in water as a neutralizing agent.

5. Carefully pour off the acid and transfer the seeds to the sodium carbonate solution until effervescing ceases. Stir to start the process of acid neutralization and removal of acid from the seed coat.

6. Thoroughly wash the seeds in running water to remove all traces of the acid.

7. Depending on the species, the seed is dried ready for immediate sowing, a pre-germination treatment, or short-term storage.

Some seed, e.g., Laxa rose rootstock, may still contain a layer of "charcoal" which is removed by rubbing the dry seed on sandpaper or a fine sieve. An excessive build-up of this layer of "charcoal" during the treatment reduces the effect of the acid.

4. Warm Moist Stratification

This important technique for breaking physiological dormancy is described on p. 41, but is also useful for seeds with hard coats because:—

(i) It encourages a more "natural" way of degrading the seed coat. The seed is mixed with moist screened leaf mold or peat moss and then placed in a polyethylene bag at a temperature of 21–24°C (70–75°F).

(ii) It can be used as a follow-up procedure to acid scarification to continue the breakdown of the seed coat at a much slower rate.

[*Calcium Hypochlorite Soak*—Soaking seed in a solution of calcium hypochlorite until the seed coat begins to crack has been used successfully in Australia for overcoming dormancy of some native plants with hard seed coats. Species of *Eucalyptus* were particularly responsive, while *Acacia, Albizia* (Albizzia) and *Pavonia* showed less response. An optimum strength of 10 g calcium hypochlorite in 140 ml water (0.75 oz in 10 fl. oz.) was used.]

b. Waxy Seed Coats

Some species, e.g., *Sapium* (Tallow Tree) and *Myrica pensylvanica* (Bayberry), retain wax within or on the seed coat, thus making it impermeable to water. This impermeability protects the seed by preventing loss of water. The seed can be soaked in hot water to cause the wax to melt out and float, but a faster method is to soak the seed in an organic solvent such as acetone. This last method also means that there is no imbibition of water.

B. Physiological Dormancy

For the purpose of this text, physiological dormancy means the biochemical processes in seeds and/or seed coat that induce dormancy. The causes of physiological dormancy can be divided into two main categories:—

1. Those caused by insufficient development of the embryo, sometimes referred to as rudimentary embryo—for example, seeds of *Fraxinus excelsior* (European Ash) and *Ilex* (Holly).

2. Biochemical factors caused by chemical inhibitors or the failure of chemical reactions that should make the food reserves available for the developing embryo, e.g., *Mahonia* (Oregongrape), *Sorbus* (Mountain Ash) and *Betula* (Birch). Studies have shown that physiological dormancy in some plants, for example, *Rosa* spp., is extremely dependent on the ratio between the chemical growth inhibitor abscisic acid (ABA) and the growth promoter gibberellic acid (GA). Essentially, the seed remains dormant if the level of ABA is higher than that of GA, while germination results if the level of GA is higher than that of ABA.

In a number of rosaceous plants, it is known that the chemical inhibitor is contained in the ripened flesh of the fruit. The chemical inhibitor is able to build up within the seed coat if this fleshy tissue remains on the seeds, either due to over-ripening before collection or because it is not removed before the seeds are stored.

The level of physiological dormancy varies for different species. Some authorities further subdivide the biochemical causes into shallow, intermediate and deep dormancy based on the complexity of the physiological mechanisms involved and the length of time under low temperatures and moisture that is necessary for germination to occur.

Physiological dormancy is sometimes further complicated in species possessing two dormancy factors causing non-germination, e.g., *Tilia* (Linden) and *Crataegus* (Hawthorn)—referred to as double dormancy (see p. 33 and p. 42). Seed of double dormancy species (often due to one physical and one physiological dormancy factor) must be given two treatments before germination will occur.

Epicotyl Dormancy—One specialized form of physiological dormancy is referred to as epicotyl dormancy. This is exhibited in the magnificent specimen tree *Davidia involucrata* (Dove or Handkerchief Tree), *Paeonia suffruticosa* (Tree Peony), *Chionanthus retusus* (Chinese Fringe Tree) and *Aesculus parviflora* (Dwarf Horse-chestnut). The radicle (rudimentary root) emerges during the first year after sowing but a cold temperature period is required before the shoot will emerge. Cold temperatures during the next winter overcome this second stage of dormancy and the shoot then grows in the second season following sowing.

As can be seen, the reasons for physiological dormancy are complex, and the degree in which it occurs varies considerably from species to species. It is not the intent of this book to discuss further the reasons for physiological seed dormancy, but rather to address the practical techniques available to overcome the problems.

Techniques to Overcome Physiological Dormancy

1. Cold Moist Stratification (Chilling)

This is the most widely used technique and is sometimes referred to as cold temperature period. Because the seed is placed in cold and moist conditions for a period ranging from a few days to several months, depending on the species, I prefer the term "cold moist stratification" rather than cold temperature period because it emphasizes that both of these requirements are essential. The five criteria which will determine the success of the treatment are:—

(i) Temperature Level—The critical temperature at which cold moist stratification occurs is usually related to the provenance of the species. Warm temperature species may respond to 20°C (50°F) temperatures, while cold temperature species may only respond below 5°C (41°F) or even lower. Freezing essentially dries the seed and stops the stratification process. The optimum temperature range for most temperate woody plants is 0–5°C (32–41°F).

(ii) Stratification Medium—The following comments apply to both cold and warm moist stratification (see p. 41). The stratification medium must retain *moisture* around the seed, be clean, and, where appropriate, not hinder the sowing of the seed. I have seen the following media successfully used for stratifying seed:—

(a) Sphagnum peat moss—Medium coarse peat moss will require shredding if it is to be used alone. Dry *Acer platanoides* (Norway Maple) seed is mixed with moist peat moss for four weeks before sowing.

(b) Sand—This is a convenient material that facilitates the sowing of smaller seed, but does have the problems of weight and tendency to dry out quickly.

Figure 1-26.
A moist sand stratification medium is sometimes used for small seeds to facilitate sowing.

(c) **Vermiculite**—A light material that retains water well.

(d) **Natural leaf mold**—Shredded, well-rotted leaf mold creates a more natural medium for biological degradation. The effect is enhanced in warm moist stratification. Note that natural leaf mold may contain pests.

(e) **Mixtures**—It is more likely that a mixture of two of these components will be used in commercial practice. These range from a 1:1 to a 4:1 mixture of sphagnum peat moss with either sand, vermiculite or perlite. A good medium to start with is 4 parts sphagnum peat moss and 1 part sand.

Traditionally, the seed and stratification medium were placed in alternating layers. However, it is preferable to mix the seed with the stratification medium to allow regular inspection and turning.

Water-retaining gels could have a use as a medium for stratification as they provide a reliable water supply and good aeration.

(iii) **Moisture**—The stratification medium must be damp but not too wet. Major causes of failure result from a medium being too dry initially and/or allowing the medium to dry out during the stratification process. *The seed must be able to imbibe* (take up water). Many propagators soak their seed in water prior to stratification. This helps to ensure that the seed will take up water.

(iv) **Time Period**—This will largely depend on the plant species, but normally falls within a 4–20 week period. It is essential that stratification is begun well in advance of the intended sowing date. This time period must be accurate for each plant species.

(v) **Aeration**—The medium must allow the movement of air so it must be turned over during the period of stratification. Aeration prevents both temperature and carbon dioxide build-up.

There are several different ways to carry out cold moist stratification, including both traditional and modern methods.

(a) Traditional Techniques

Many of the traditional techniques have been superseded by more modern methods, although they still have uses in the industry.

(i) **Stratification Pits**—This method has been used for many decades and is still practised in a number of European countries. I have seen it being used successfully in West Germany, using a series of concrete pits sunk into the soil. Ideally, the site should be north-facing to reduce temperature variation and must be protected from vermin. Shading is necessary in direct sunlight. The seed is mixed with the medium, placed into the pit, labelled, and regularly turned and inspected for moisture content. Shading will be necessary in direct sunlight. A map giving details of which seed lot is in each pit should be made in case labels are mislaid.

(ii) **Plunging Containers**—This is essentially a traditional modification of the stratification pit that is used for small quantities of seed. As for pits, the site should be away from direct sun and should be rodent-proof with galvanized wire netting, both above and below where the containers are to be plunged. Woven polypropylene fabric (shade cloth) could be used although there is a risk that mice would be able to eat through it.

Holes are made in the base of either tin cans or rigid plastic containers (e.g., used ice cream or freezer containers), the seed layered or mixed with the stratification medium in the container, labelled and plunged. A map indicating the site of each species is necessary in case the labels are removed.

(iii) **Stratification Mounds or Clamps**—I have seen this traditional method used in France for stratifying *Sorbus* (Mountain Ash) and *Rosa* spp. (Rose). The principle is the same in that the seed is mixed with a stratification medium of peat moss and sand and placed in a rodent-proof site on a base of chopped straw and sieved soil. It is then covered over with a further layer of chopped straw, moss and soil, followed by a layer of moist straw held down with galvanized wire netting. Aeration is improved by leaving a central vent hole from the top of the mound down to the stratification medium. The vent is filled with loose straw.

(iv) **Bins**—The mixed seed and stratification medium can be placed into large plastic bins. The bins should be kept on the north side of a building. The medium should be turned regularly and checked for moisture.

Figure 1-27. Traditional outdoor stratification pits in the Pinneberg area, West Germany. Note the use of individual pits for different seed lots and the wire mesh enclosure to exclude vermin.

Figure 1-28. Rows of traditional stratification mounds or clamps being used for individual seed lots of rosaceous species in Angers, France.

Figure 1-29. Cold frames being utilized for stratifying *Rosa canina* (Dog Rose) seed in the Pinneberg area, West Germany. Note the use of bamboo cane rolls for covering the frames to reduce drying out of the stratification medium.

Figure 1-30. A mixture of macerated fruits and seeds ready to be thoroughly mixed with a moist stratification medium.

(v) Frames—A similar set-up to that described for storing nutty seeds (p. 30) can be used for stratifying seed. Rodent-proofing, shading, turning and checking moisture content are of paramount importance.

(vi) Fall Sowing—The seed is sown in outdoor seed beds soon after collection, extraction and cleaning. In some cases, it is broadcast as a macerated mixture of flesh and seed. Seeds that have been successfully treated this way include species of *Berberis* (Barberry), *Mahonia* (Oregon-grape) and *Sorbus* (Mountain Ash).

The advantage of this technique is that it eliminates any further handling of the seed. The disadvantage is that the seed beds are open to winter damage and that, like the previous methods described, there is little control over the degree of cold temperature. A mild winter can cause erratic germination in the following spring.

(b) Modern Techniques—Refrigeration

The most common method of cold stratifying seed today is in a refrigerator or cold store. Refrigeration is the best method for the propagator to use because there is greater control of the level and duration of the cold temperature period. A domestic refrigerator that can be adjusted down to 3°C (38°F) is ideal for small seed lots, while a nursery cold store facility is required for larger quantities. The advantage of this method is that cold treatments can be given at any time of the year if necessary. Propagators using a cold storage facility set the temperature within the range 0–5°C (32–41°F), although just below 3°C (38°F) can be considered as the optimum level. Some nurseries have experienced better results when the temperature is reduced to 1–2°C (34–35.6°F). The lower temperature range means that there is less risk of the seeds beginning to germinate during the chilling period.

There are two main ways of providing cold treatment under refrigeration, one with stratification medium and one without.

(i) **Mixed with Stratification Medium**—This is the most widely used method of cold stratifying seed. A recommended procedure to use is outlined below:—

1. Thoroughly mix the seed with the moist stratification medium.
2. Soak the seed in water for 10–12 hours before mixing if previous experience has shown that it does not imbibe moisture readily. Imbibing the seed in a 5% thiram solution will help to reduce the incidence of damping-off diseases.
3. Place the seed and medium in a polyethylene bag. Captan is sometimes incorporated with the medium if there is a tendency for fungal molds to develop, e.g., *Amelanchier alnifolia* (Common or Western Saskatoon).
4. Place a label in the bag to indicate the species and starting date of stratification.
5. Tie the neck of the bag. Some propagators tie the neck tightly to retain humidity and prevent drying out of the seed when using thin polyethylene bags (2–3 mil) as these allow atmospheric diffusion through the polyethylene. The neck should be loosely tied when using bags made of a thicker gauge polyethylene.
6. Tie a duplicate label to the outside of the bag.
7. (a) Leave the bag and contents at room temperature until the seed is fully imbibed. The cold temperature period will not be effective unless the seed has reached this stage as imbibition is slower under cold temperatures.
   (b) Place bag and contents in a refrigerator set at 3°C (38°F)—this being the optimum temperature for most species.
8. Gently turn the contents of the bag routinely twice a week, more often if necessary. Check and adjust the moisture levels as necessary. It is very important to check the seeds daily towards the end of the stratification period for premature emergence of the radicle— *Acer* (Maple) and *Sorbus* (Mountain Ash) are very prone to this. If this happens, the seed must either be removed and sown immediately, or the temperature reduced to −3 to −4°C (24–26°F) if sowing conditions are unsuitable.
9. Keep records of the species, method of treatment, and the dates of starting and ending the treatment.

(ii) **Naked Stratification**—Some propagators prefer the technique of "naked stratification" in which the imbibed seed is not mixed or covered with a stratification medium. This technique essentially requires thoroughly soaking the seed for 12–24 hours (depending on the species), draining off the excess water, and surface drying. The seed is then placed in polyethylene bags, glass containers with a cotton plug over the top or in dishes or flats lined with polyethylene. The imbibed condition of the seed must be carefully maintained during the stratification period.

The technique can be illustrated by describing a method devised by the Canada Department of Agriculture Research Station at Harrow in Ontario, and now adapted by Byland Nurseries, Kelowna, B.C., for raising *Prunus persica* 'Nemaguard' (a strain of seedling Peach resistant to nematodes). This method not only stratifies the seed, but also takes the process one stage further by allowing the tip of the radicle to emerge through the softened seed coats. This is referred to as pre-chitting. The principles behind pre-chitting are described on p. 62 under seed sowing. The process is as follows:—

1. Remove the seeds from the "pits" by cracking them in a vise, followed by a thorough rinsing in water.
2. Soak the seed overnight in a solution of the fungicide ferbam (Fermate®)—1 heaped tablespoon of 76% wettable powder is thoroughly mixed in one quart of water.

3. Place the seed in sterilized flats lined with polyethylene, ensuring that the depth of the seed is not more than 2.5 cm (1″).
4. Place the flats in a cool, dark building or cold store at 2–3°C (36–38°F).
5. Inspect and turn over the seed every day. Remove seeds that develop a fungal mold. Use a water mister to distribute a fine spray of either rain or distilled water over the seeds. Small holes can be made in the polyethylene to drain water if it collects on the bottom of the flat.
6. The radicle should begin to break through the seed coat after about 60–90 days.
7. Direct sow the seed on previously prepared open-ground seed beds or in individual containers in a greenhouse.

An alternative method of naked stratification found to be successful elsewhere is outlined below.

1. Imbibe the seed in water in a polyethylene bag.
2. Stir the contents so that seed which is beginning to dry out on the surface of the water is replaced with moist seed from below.
3. *Very carefully* re-wet the seed with a hand-operated mister as the water in the bag evaporates.
4. Treat as in the previous method once the radicle breaks through the seed coat.

If only small quantities of chitted seed are required, the seed can be placed in glass bottles with cotton stoppers after the initial treatment. Any excess water resulting from the daily misting is simply drained off.

Naked stratification at 0–1°C (32–34°F) is also used for some trees requiring stratification for 4–6 weeks, such as *Alnus* (Alder), *Betula* (Birch) and conifers (see p. 90).

It is possible that water-soluble gels could be a useful alternative to water for naked stratification, but more research is needed.

2. Warm Moist Stratification

The principles are similar to cold moist stratification in that the seed is mixed with a previously moistened medium, but the temperature at which it is kept is increased to 21–24°C (70–75°F). In practice, the temperature may vary from 18–29°C (65–85°F). Seed is normally held in warm moist stratification for between 4–12 weeks, depending on the species. The purpose of warm moist stratification is two-fold:—

(i) To aid the development of an under-developed embryo. In nature, the seed obtains this warm period during the summer of the year following fertilization, with the cold period being provided the following winter. This means that the seed can successfully germinate the next spring (i.e., 18 months after fertilization).

Warm moist stratification is an artificial means of providing the summer warmth. Without it, a few seedlings would germinate the spring after sowing but the remainder would not germinate until 12 months later. This not only ties up the seed bed for an extra year, but results in unevenly graded seedlings at harvesting.

(ii) To soften and break down the seed coat.

The cleaned seed is thoroughly mixed with the stratification medium, placed in polyethylene bags and labelled—using the same procedures as described for cold moist stratification. It is important that the seed coat is imbibed with water before placing in the medium. Pre-soaking in water for up to 24 hours may be necessary for some seed. Three ways of subsequently handling the seed at the required temperature range are:—

(a) Hang the filled polyethylene bags from the roof structure inside a warm greenhouse. Results are not always consistent with this method.

(b) Place the filled polyethylene bags on the heated bench or floor in a mist propagation unit.

(c) Oakover Nurseries, Ashford, Kent, England, have found that a second-hand cold meat storage trailer is a very satisfactory unit for warm moist stratification. Insulation is improved by fixing additional polystyrene (Styrofoam®) sheets on the inside to form an insulated box equipped with shelves. Three radiant heat lamps raise the temperature of this box to 24–27°C (75–80°F). This has proved to be more convenient and more economical than using space in a greenhouse.

Figure 1-31. Seeds of *Fraxinus excelsior* (European Ash) mixed with the stratification medium were kept in plastic bags in a storage trailer equipped with radiant heat lamps to provide an 8-week period of warm moist stratification at 21°C (70°F). This was then followed by a 12-week period of cold moist stratification (chilling) at 1–3°C (34–38°F).

In all three cases, the seed and medium is inspected at least twice a week to ensure that the moisture content is maintained at the correct level. The medium should be re-moistened as necessary.

Warm moist stratification is normally followed by a cold moist stratification period as many seeds requiring a warm temperature period also require a period of cold temperatures, i.e., they show double dormancy. *Fraxinus excelsior* (European Ash) is a good example. I have had good results with this species by collecting the seed when yellow in color, giving a warm moist stratification at 21°C (70°F) for 8 weeks followed by cold moist stratification at 1–3°C (34–37°F) for 12 weeks.

3. Early Local Collection of Seed

Early collection of seed is sometimes used to avoid the hard seed coat condition. For example, the fruits of *Carpinus betulus* (European Hornbeam), *Acer campestre* (Hedge Maple), *Fraxinus excelsior* (European Ash), *Daphne mezereum* (February Daphne) and *Hamamelis virginiana* (Common Witch Hazel) are collected while still green in the late summer/early fall. They are sown in the same fall and should germinate in the following spring. The fruits have not been allowed to become brown in color or to form thick seed coats so dormancy has not fully developed. Germination of *Acer circinatum* (Vine Maple) should be more consistent if the seed is collected when the "wings" are green rather than allowing them to dry. Conclusions reached by David Vanstone (formerly at Agriculture Canada, Morden, Manitoba) suggest that *Tilia americana* (American Linden or Basswood) is best collected when the outside (pericarp) of the fruit is a green to grayish-brown color and should then be sown immediately.

A number of fruits are known to build up a level of chemical inhibitors (see p. 36) as they ripen. These inhibitors pass from the fruit into the seed itself. Early collection of the seed interferes with this natural process of events.

Rosaceous trees, e.g., *Crataegus* (Hawthorn) and *Rosa* (Rose), are best collected when the fruits are orange-red in color and still firm in texture, and the seeds immediately extracted. Fruits collected when fully ripe are very likely to have high levels of chemical inhibitors in the seed (see p. 36). However, the native Rose species of western Canada are generally collected when the fruit *is* fully ripe to ensure that the seed is fully developed at the time of collection.

Some propagators have found that collecting seeds of *Cornus mas* (Cornelian Cherry), *Viburnum lantana* (Wayfaring Tree) and *Viburnum dentatum* (Arrowwood) 2–3 weeks before they are fully ripe and immediately sowing while there is still sufficient warmth in the seed bed has given better results than sowing in the spring.

The timing of collection is critical to ensure first year germination. Early collection and sowing does ensure the maximum possible germination over a two-year period, but is likely to result in an uneven stand of seedlings in the seed bed. Naked stratification (see p. 40) of early collected seeds will given an indication as to whether first or second year germination can be expected.

Commercially, more consistent results have generally been obtained by moving away from the early collection of fruits. Instead, the fruits are collected when fully ripe and the seeds then treated, stratified and imbibed as necessary to induce germination, This normally gives a consistently more even stand of seedlings and greater production efficiency than early collection and sowing. The early collection and sowing method is helpful following a year of crop failures as it helps to maintain continuity of production.

4. Chemical Soak

There has been research on the effects of soaking seeds of various species in a chemical solution to stimulate germination, with the aim of completely or partially overcoming the need to use the conventional treatments previously described. These experiments have used various solutions of thiourea, ethylene, cytokinins, hydrogen peroxide and sodium hypochlorite. Further information can be obtained from *Plant Propagation: Principles and Practices* (4th edition) by H. T. Hartmann and D. E. Kester.

More recently, there has been a renewed interest in soaking seeds in gibberellic acid (GA) to partially or fully replace the necessary cold requirements. The list of crops showing a positive response to such treatment is presently limited. Research by A. G. Gordon and D. C. F. Rowe in England using gibberellic acid to obviate the need for cold moist stratification on *Nothofagus obliqua* (Roblé Beech) has shown good results when the seed was soaked for 24 hours in a 50 ppm mixture of GA_4 and GA_7 formulations of gibberellic acid. This replaced a cold moist stratification period of up to six weeks.

Research elsewhere has demonstrated that the best response to GA is obtained with the concentration varying from 10–100 ppm. Gibberellic acid seed soaks for 12–24 hours are said to partially replace the stratification period for peaches and *Myrica pensylvanica* (Bayberry). A 100 ppm GA soak combined with a seven-day cold stratification has produced positive results in promoting germination of *Liquidambar styraciflua* (American Sweet Gum). Encouraging results in improving germination have been claimed with *Betula pendula* (European White Birch), *Corylus avellana* (European Filbert) and *Fagus sylvatica* (European Beech).

TABLE 1-4. Pre-Sowing Germination Treatments to Overcome Seed Dormancy of Selected Species

NOTE: **(i)** This tabulated information should be treated as an initial guideline only as time periods will vary from year to year due to the state of ripeness of the seed caused by weather conditions, and in different climates. **(ii)** The cold stratification temperature used is 0.5–1°C (33–34°F). Many nurseries stratify at 3–4°C (38–40°F) and some species will behave differently at these higher temperatures.

SPECIES	WARM STRATIFICATION 18–21°C (65–70°F)	COLD STRATIFICATION 0.5–1°C (33–34°F)	OTHER
A. DECIDUOUS			
Acer capillipes	—	4–8 weeks	
A. cappadocicum (Coliseum Maple)	—	4–8 weeks	
A. davidii (David Maple)	—	4–8 weeks	
A. grosseri var. *hersii* (Hers' Maple)	—	4–8 weeks	
A. negundo (Box Elder)	—	3–6 weeks	
A. palmatum (Japanese Maple)	8–12 weeks +	8–12 weeks	Fall collected and spring sown

SPECIES	WARM STRATIFICATION 18–21°C (65–70°F)	COLD STRATIFICATION 0.5–1°C (33–34°F)	OTHER
A. pensylvanicum (Pennsylvania Maple)	—	4–8 weeks	
A. platanoides (Norway Maple)	—	4–8 weeks	
A. pseudoplatanus (Sycamore Maple)	—	4–8 weeks	
A. rubrum (Red Maple)	—	—	Sown fresh
A. rufinerve (Red-vein Maple)	—	4–8 weeks	
A. saccharinum (Silver Maple)	—	—	Sown fresh
Aesculus hippocastanum (Common Horse-chestnut)	—	—	Fall sown, little dormancy shown
Ailanthus altissima (Tree-of-Heaven)	—	3 weeks	
Alnus cordata (Italian Alder)	—	3–5 weeks	
A. glutinosa (Black or Common Alder)	—	3–5 weeks	
A. incana (White Alder)	—	3–5 weeks	
A. rubra (Red Alder)	—	3–5 weeks	
Amelanchier canadensis (Shadblow Serviceberry)	—	8–10 weeks	
Arbutus menziesii (Pacific Madrone)	—	4–6 weeks	
A. unedo (Strawberry Tree)	—	4–6 weeks	
Azalea pontica see *Rhododendron luteum*			
Berberis darwinii (Darwin Barberry)	—	6–12 weeks	
B. julianae (Wintergreen Barberry)	—	6–12 weeks	If seed is over-dried, the more dormant it will be
B. thunbergii (Japanese Barberry)	—	6–12 weeks	
B. thunbergii 'Atropurpurea' (Red Barberry)	—	6–12 weeks	
B. wilsoniae (Wilson Barberry)	—	6–12 weeks	
Betula pendula (European White Birch)	—	3–4 weeks	
Caragana arborescens (Siberian Pea Shrub)	—	—	48 hrs cold water
Carpinus betulus (European Hornbeam)	8 weeks +	8–12 weeks	Collected in fall, extracted, treated. Spring sown
Castanea sativa (Spanish Chestnut)	—	—	Fall sown due to storage problems
Catalpa bignonioides (Indian Bean)	—	3 weeks	
Cercis siliquastrum (Judas Tree)	—	—	24 hr hot water followed by 24 hr cold water OR gibberellic acid (GA) at 500 ppm for 24 hrs
Cornus alba (Red-bark Dogwood)	—	8–12 weeks	
Cotoneaster franchetii (Franchet Cotoneaster)	6 weeks +	8–10 weeks	Collected fresh. Spring sown
Crataegus monogyna (Single-seed or Common Hawthorn)	In summer after collection	After warm stratification and prior to spring sowing	Fall collected. Sown second spring after collecting

SPECIES	WARM STRATIFICATION 18–21°C (65–70°F)	COLD STRATIFICATION 0.5–1°C (33–34°F)	OTHER
Daphne mezereum (February Daphne)	—	—	Collected as fruit ripens. Sown immediately
Fraxinus americana (White Ash)	—	8–14 weeks	
F. angustifolia (Narrow-leaved Ash)	—	6–14 weeks	
F. excelsior (European Ash)	12 weeks +	8 weeks	OR collect and hold until June, damp down, give 8 weeks cold. Fall sow
F. ornus (Flowering or Manna Ash)	12 weeks	8 weeks	Spring sown
Gleditsia triacanthos (Honey Locust)	—	—	Hot water or acid treatment
Hamamelis virginiana (Common Witch Hazel)	8 weeks +	24 weeks	
Hibiscus syriacus (Rose-of-Sharon)	—	—	48 hr water soak
Hippophae rhamnoides (Common Sea Buckthorn)	—	8–12 weeks	
Juglans nigra (Black Walnut)	—	—	Kept moist after collection. Spring sown
J. regia (English or Persian Walnut)	—	—	
Kalmia latifolia (Mountain Laurel)	—	—	Sown fresh
Laburnum anagyroides (Golden-chain Tree)	—	—	Cold or hot water treatment depending on hardness of seed coat.
Ligustrum vulgare (English Privet)	—	8–12 weeks	
Liquidambar styraciflua (American Sweet Gum)	—	4–6 weeks	
Liridendron tulipifera (Tulip Tree)	—	10–16 weeks	
Magnolia wilsonii (Wilson Magnolia)	8 weeks +	8–12 weeks	
Malus sylvestris (Crab Apple)	—	8–12 weeks	
M. 'Bittenfelder'	—	8–12 weeks	
Nothofagus obliqua (Roblé Beech)	—	—	50 ppm GA₃ soak for 24 hrs. GA₄ & GA₇ seem to work better than GA₃. Seed must not be allowed to dry out during germination.
N. procera (Rauli)	—	—	
Prunus cerasifera (Myrobalan Plum)	—	8 weeks (fall) 8–12 weeks (late winter)	
P. lusitanica (Portugal Laurel)	—	—	Cold treatment only with fresh seed.
P. spinosa (Blackthorn, Sloe)	*4 weeks +	4–8 weeks	*Warm stratification only given to dry seed arriving in the fall. Not required for fresh collected seed.

SPECIES	WARM STRATIFICATION 18–21°C (65–70°F)	COLD STRATIFICATION 0.5–1°C (33–34°F)	OTHER
Pyrus communis (Common Pear)	—	8–12 weeks	
Quercus cerris (Turkey Oak)	—	—	Fall sown due to storage problems.
Q. robur (English Oak)	—	—	Fall sown as above.
Q. rubra (Red Oak)	—	—	Fall sown as above.
Rhododendron luteum (Pontic Azalea)	—	—	48 hr water soak, mixed with dry sand when sowing.
Robinia pseudoacacia (Black Locust)	—	—	Hot or cold water treatment depending on hardness of seed coat
Rosa rugosa (Rugosa Rose)	—	8–12 weeks	
Salix caprea (Goat Willow)	—	—	Spring collected. Sown fresh
Sambucus nigra (European Elder)	8 weeks +	8–12 weeks	
Sorbia aria (White Beam)	—	10–12 weeks	
S. aucuparia (European Mountain Ash or Rowan)	—	12–16 weeks	
S. intermedia (Swedish White Beam)	—	10–12 weeks	
S. torminalis (Wild Service Tree)	—	8–10 weeks	
Syringa vulgaris (Common or French Lilac)	—	6–10 weeks	
Ulex europaeus (Gorse)	—	—	48 hr water soak
Viburnum opulus (European Cranberry Bush)	—	—	Stored dry. Sown early summer to germinate following spring
Wisteria sinensis (Chinese Wisteria)	—	—	Warm water

B. CONIFERS

SPECIES	WARM STRATIFICATION 18–21°C (65–70°F)	COLD STRATIFICATION 0.5–1°C (33–34°F)	OTHER
Abies concolor (White Fir)	—	4–5 weeks	
A. procera (Grand Fir)	—	3 weeks	
Cedrus deodara (Himalayan Cedar)	—	1–2 weeks	
Chamaecyparis lawsoniana (Lawson Cypress)	—	3 weeks	
Larix decidua (European Larch)	—	3 weeks	Necessary only if seed is dormant
L. × eurolepis (Dunkeld Larch)	—	3 weeks	
L. kaempferi (Japanese Larch)	—	3 weeks	
Picea abies (Norway Spruce)	—	3 weeks	
P. engelmanii (Engelmann Spruce)	—	3 weeks	
P. omorika (Serbian Spruce)	—	3 weeks	
P. sitchensis (Sitka Spruce)	—	3 weeks	
Pinus aristata (Bristlecone Pine)	—	3 weeks	
P. mugo var. *pumilio* (Shrubby Mugo Pine)	—	3 weeks	
P. nigra subsp. *nigra* (Austrian Pine)	—	3 weeks	
P. nigra var. *maritima* (Corsican Pine)	—	3 weeks	

SPECIES	WARM STRATIFICATION 18–21°C (65–70°F)	COLD STRATIFICATION 0.5–1°C (33–34°F)	OTHER
P. radiata (Monterey Pine)	—	3 weeks	
P. strobus (Eastern White Pine)	—	3 weeks	
P. sylvestris (Scots Pine)	—	3 weeks	
Pseudotsuga menziesii (Douglas Fir)	—	3 weeks	
Taxodium distichum (Bald Cypress)	—	3–4 weeks	
Thuja plicata (Western Red Cedar)	—	3 weeks	
Tsuga canadensis (Canadian Hemlock)	—	3 weeks	
T. heterophylla (Western Hemlock)	—	3 weeks	

Source: Oakover Nurseries Ltd., Potters Corner, Ashford, Kent, U.K.

APPENDIX 1-1

Pollination, Fertilization, Seed and Fruit Development, and Periodicity

Pollen from the anther (male reproductive organ) must be transferred to the stigma (female reproductive part) of the flower before seed can be produced. This process is referred to as pollination.

Self-pollination is the term given when pollen is transferred from the anther to the stigma of the same flower or of another flower on the same plant.

Cross-pollination is the transference of pollen from the anther of one flower on one plant to the stigma of a flower on another plant.

It is important to understand this process so that mother seed plants of species notorious for hybrid variation may be isolated to prevent cross-pollination from the wrong source, for example, *Berberis* (Barberry). An example is *Berberis thunbergii* 'Atropurpurea' (Red Barberry) where one wants the highest possible percentage of seedlings to have purple leaves. The presence of forms with inferior colored leaves and of other species in the area will defeat this aim. *Berberis polyantha* (Chrome-flower Barberry) and *B. wilsoniae* (Wilson Barberry) are two species that are particularly likely to have a high proportion of undesirable intermediate forms if cross-pollination occurs.

There are two major ways in which cross-pollination can occur—by wind and by insects. The flowers of wind-pollinated plants tend to be numerous, inconspicuous and lacking scent—e.g., *Salix* (Willow), *Betula* (Birch), *Quercus* (Oak), *Populus* (Poplar), *Corylus avellana* (European Filbert) and the strobili of conifers. The abundant pollen is dry and can be carried a considerable distance, although a lot is wasted because of this.

Insect-pollinated flowers, on the other hand, normally are more conspicuous and scented in order to attract their pollinating agent. The flower structure often requires that a specific species or group of insects be necessary for successful pollination—for example, *Robinia pseudoacacia* (Black Locust) and *Pyrus communis* (Common Pear).

The majority of species have perfect flowers, i.e., they have functional male and female parts in the same flower. They are sometimes referred to as hermaphrodite plants. Exceptions to this usual characteristic are:—

(i) **Monoecious Plants**—These species have separate male and female flowers on the same plant, e.g., *Alnus* (Alder), *Betula* (Birch), and *Quercus* (Oak).

(ii) **Dioecious Plants**—These species have separate male and female flowers on different plants, e.g., *Skimmia japonica* (Japanese Skimmia) and *Ilex aquifolium* (English Holly).

The final stage of pollination occurs when a pollen grain develops a pollen tube that travels down through the stigma and style to the ovary and enters the ovule to effect fertilization of the egg.

Fertilization

Fertilization occurs when the nuclei of the specialized male and female cells (derived from the pollen grain and the ovule) fuse to form an embryo that will, in turn, give rise to the seed. Successful fertilization is followed by the development of the seed and the fruit. The latter protects the embryo until conditions, both inside and outside, are suitable for germination.

Each seed contains one embryo and stored food material, while a fruit may contain one, several, or many seeds. Two terms are sometimes used when true fertilization does not occur:—

(i) Parthenocarpic Fruit—The fruits develop without actual fertilization taking place, e.g., *Diospyros kaki* (Japanese Persimmon). The seeds are non-viable (dead).

(ii) Apomictic Seed—Viable (live) seed develops without fertilization of the ovule, although cross-pollination will occur in other flowers on the same plant as apomixis is rarely 100%. The off-type seedlings that result from fertilization have to be rogued out, if they can be distinguished from the apomictic ones.

Apomixis produces progeny identical to the parent. An example can be found in the seedling selections of *Rosa canina* (Dog Rose), e.g., *R. canina* 'Pfänder', where the mother seed-bearing plants produce apomictic seeds that germinate to form plants identical to the parent bush. Specialist catalogues sometimes list suckering and non-suckering forms of *Sorbus reducta*, which can be grown true-to-type even if the mother plants grow near each other. This is probably due to the formation of apomictic seed. Trees showing apomixis include *Malus toringoides* (Cut-leaf Crab Apple), *Sorbus hupehensis* (Hupeh Mountain Ash), and *S. vilmorinii* (Vilmorin Mountain Ash).

Periodicity

This term refers to the quantity of viable seed reliably produced each year once a tree has passed through its non-flowering (juvenile) to its flowering and fruiting (mature) phase. Some species are far more reliable in producing a good quantity of seeds each year, e.g., *Alnus rubra* (Red Alder) (also known as *A. oregana*), while others may produce a "bumper crop" only once every 5–7 years, e.g., *Fraxinus sylvatica* (European Beech). Periodicity poses a problem to the seed propagator because it is necessary to plan well ahead by forward ordering seed from a seed house or by developing efficient long-term storage techniques for those species characterized by marked periodicity.

The reasons for periodicity are not fully understood. Internal reasons, such as the carbohydrate levels in the tree, have been suggested, but it is also known that outside agencies such as late spring frosts can directly affect the efficiency of the pollination process.

OPEN-GROUND PRODUCTION FROM SEED

In most countries, the largest proportion of woody plant seed is used for open-ground production.

SITE

I would strongly recommend that the past history of a new site be obtained, no matter whether you are purchasing, renting or utilizing a new area on or near the nursery. Items to check in particular are:—previous crops grown; weather patterns; frost incidence in relation to topography; drainage; availability of water; and, history of past herbicide applications (testing for herbicide build-up in the soil may be necessary to determine whether there has been any carry-over). Good homework at this early stage will minimize production problems in years to come and govern the species suitable for production. The information can be obtained by contacting local growers and farmers, extension officers and meterological offices, as well as the previous user of the site.

The following items should be considered carefully when determining the suitability of a site intended for open-ground sowing of seed.

1. Aspect

Ideally, the site should be flat or slightly sloping, and with a southern or south-western exposure. The soil temperature on such sites raises the seed bed temperature earlier in the year, which assists germination and gives a longer growing period. Eastern exposures are particularly likely to experience cold winds, which retard seedling growth and desiccate plants during subsequent transplanting. The aspect in relation to soil erosion and the ability to use mechanization effectively are also major considerations.

Frost pockets should be avoided, particularly those susceptible to late spring radiation frosts, which can critically injure the growing shoots of such trees as *Fraxinus* (Ash) and *Tsuga* (Hemlock).

2. Soil Type

The soil should ideally meet the following requirements:—

(a) Should warm up quickly in spring to ensure even germination.

(b) Should be easily worked for bed preparation, sowing, cultivation, undercutting and lifting under reasonable weather conditions.

(c) Should encourage fibrous root systems to form on the seedlings.

(d) Should retain nutrients and water, but allow free drainage.

(e) Should be free from pests, diseases and perennial weeds.

Having stated the ideal, it is not always possible to obtain them all in practice, therefore, modifications to the site will be necessary. The ideal soil to select is a deep sandy loam with a high organic matter content and an irrigation facility. The subsoil must allow free drainage. High levels of organic matter will be difficult to maintain on sandy soils. The optimum pH range for most broad-leaved trees and shrubs is 5.5–6.5, while it is 4.5–5.5 for ericaceous plants and conifers. (A fairly coarse and sandy soil should produce the best fibrous root systems and will be naturally free draining to facilitate winter preparation of the site and subsequent lifting of the crop.)

[During the 1930s, Alfred Dunemann, a German, devised a well-drained seed frame bed comprised of a mixture of *Picea abies* (Norway Spruce) and *P. sitchensis* (Sitka Spruce) "leaf litter" collected from local forests. A layer of sifted *Fagus sylvatica* (European Beech) leaf litter was placed over the coniferous mix and the seed sown on to this. Nurseries later adapted the original mix to approximately equal quantities of coniferous and deciduous broad-leaf tree "leaf litter". High-quality seedlings with well-developed root systems were harvested with the Dunemann seed bed system, but it is little used today, mainly due to costs.

One significant reason for the good root system development of many species grown under the Dunemann system was undoubtedly due to mycorrhizal associations (p. 364) existing within the seed beds. Plant species vary considerably in their dependence on mycorrhiza (e.g., leguminous species do not generally make mycorrhizal associations, while many coniferous species depend on them). The resurgence of interest in using mycorrhiza to inoculate media for rooting cuttings means that it is possible that the inoculation of nursery seed beds with mycorrhiza may become accepted practice for some species in the future.]

3. Soil Analysis

A complete soil analysis should be obtained for any new site before carrying out any preparations. The analysis should show:—

(a) pH level.

(b) Nutritional content—necessary modifications can be made with base dressings and subsequent top dressings.

(c) Pest and disease incidence to meet national and local statutory requirements. For example, it is necessary to have a P.C.E.-nematode (Potato Cyst Eelworm) count when marketing nursery stock from Britain to other member countries within the European Economic Community (EEC).

4. Drainage

Good drainage is essential for virtually all horticultural crops, and must be especially

Figure 1-32. Uneven germination of *Fagus sylvatica* (European Beech) seed beds due to impeded drainage caused by a hardpan in the subsoil.

Figure 1-33. A centrally-located, well-designed building to accommodate office space, open-ground machinery, seed extraction and grading equipment, cold storage and shipping facilities is very advantageous for a modern seedling nursery operation. (Oakover Nurseries, Ashford, Kent, U.K.)

efficient for seedling crops—particularly in high rainfall areas. Bad drainage means poor aeration, which will hinder germination, subsequent growth of both shoots and roots, general mechanization, and the ability to finally undercut and lift the crop. This point was brought home to me in northern Europe where a large area had been sown with *Fagus sylvatica* (European Beech). The crop was growing satisfactorily only near the headlands area. The rest of the crop was stunted because a hardpan below the soil surface hindered the downward flow of water. If such problems exist, attention to sub-soiling and the provision of a well-designed drainage system are essential. Good advice can be obtained from specialist officers in the regional agricultural and horticultural extension services.

5. Basic Services and Facilities

(i) **Covered building(s)**—to house offices, seed extraction, cold storage, field equipment, and facilities for grading, storage and shipping of the seedlings.

(ii) **Electrical power.**

(iii) **Roadways**—to provide access to and from the seed beds. This is particularly important during the winter when shipping, and to avoid compaction of the seed beds.

(iv) **Water.**

A clean and reliable water supply is essential for open-ground seedling production. The aim must be to hold the soil as near to field capacity as possible. This will ensure even germination and regular growth of the shoot and root systems during the summer. Stresses caused by lack of water during the growth flushes reduce the overall quality of the crop. However, this latter statement is not always true. Some stress to an established crop in late summer can be beneficial—it can help to produce a better balanced plant as more roots develop to exploit all the available water when somewhat dry. Too much irrigation on soils with a high water table will cause imbalance to crop growth.

Economical and clean sources of water need to be thoroughly evaluated. Main water supply is often expensive or restricted for nursery use, so the use of bore holes (wells), streams and rivers are preferable for larger areas. A reservoir and pumps are likely to be necessary to provide a sufficient quantity and pressure of water. Damming a creek or stream may be feasible if local regulations permit. It is important to contact the local water authority and the extension advisor specializing in irrigation before undertaking any plans for developing sources of water. They will be able to explain local restrictions and suggest the most economical source for the particular situation. Water samples should be taken annually for analysis to monitor the pH and any possible build-up of soluble salts (particularly sodium and chloride compounds).

A thorough study of the equipment available for irrigation is necessary so that the correct type can be obtained at the best price. The size of water droplets and spray pattern are

Figure 1-34. An ample, reliable, clean water supply is essential for reliable germination and subsequent development of a quality product. This reservoir was created by damming a local stream. (Oakover Nurseries, Ashford, Kent, U.K.)

Figure 1-35. Many *Alnus* spp. (Alder) make excellent permeable windbreaks for open-ground seedling production. (Oakover Nurseries, Ashford, Kent, U.K.)

of foremost importance. The two main alternatives for irrigation equipment are rotating sprinklers and spray lines. Oscillating spray lines with nozzles to give more even water application serve well on relatively sheltered areas. The oscillation may be controlled to give an arc of up to 100° by having a water tank (spring-loaded for return) at the front end of the spray line. The tank slowly fills with water until the water supply is cut off as the arc of the spray line reaches its lowest point. The return arc is made by the water slowly trickling away from the tank. This system is particularly useful under low water pressure conditions. Multi-jet spray lines are static and do not oscillate, but do have up to six times as many nozzles as the oscillating types.

6. Shelter from Wind

Crop shelter in exposed areas is a fundamental essential for open-ground seedling production to prevent uneven growth, stunted seedlings, damage to stem and leaf tissue, irrigation problems, and soil erosion. Natural shelter from the prevailing wind, if present, forms a good basis for site protection, but on larger fields it is necessary to further slow the wind with a windbreak (a hedge, trees or manufactured fabric, or a combination) to give the protection required.

The objective of a windbreak is to slow the wind without creating a turbulent flow as would a solid barrier. Therefore, the windbreak should provide an optimum of 50% permeability to the prevailing wind. A general guideline given is that the shelter should give maximum protection on its leeward side to about ten times the height of the windbreak. For example, a windbreak of 3 m (10′) in height will protect plants for a distance of up to 30 m (100′). Under very exposed conditions, the maximum protection distance is reduced by half or to 15 m (50′) in the example.

(a) Hedges and Trees

Plantings provide a long-term crop shelter. The choice of the actual plants is largely dependent on the geographical location and the soil type. *Populus* (Poplar) should be avoided, except in some areas of extreme cold, because the vigorous suckering root system competes with the crop, in addition to trees harboring pests and diseases. In many areas of Europe, some *Alnus* spp. (Alder) meet the requirements for effectiveness and relative ease of maintenance, e.g., *A. cordata* (Italian Alder) which holds its leaves well into late fall and early winter but is late to break in spring. *Alnus rubra* (Red Alder), a native of the west coast of North America, is beginning to gain popularity in Europe. *Salix alba* cvs. (White Willow) make successful windbreaks, and have the advantage that they are less likely to self-sow than some alders.

Conifers are successful windbreaks in many climates because they provide maximum shelter for the entire year. Trees such as × *Cupressocyparis leylandii* (Leyland Cypress), *Thuja plicata* (Western Red Cedar), *Pinus nigra* ssp. *nigra* (Austrian Pine) and *Picea sitchensis* (Sitka Spruce) have achieved the desired effect on the correct site. Some conifers are poorly anchored and must be staked in the early years. They will also need maintenance later to retain their habit. For example, × *Cupressocyparis leylandii* (Leyland Cypress) is often poorly anchored in the early years, the tops blow out in high winds, and the tree becomes excessively dense in later years so that wind permeability is severely reduced. A significant reduction in permeability creates a turbulent air flow similar to an impermeable barrier, leading to crop damage. These problems have led to the removal of some hedges, and their replacement with alternative species. However, × *Cupressocyparis leylandii*, once established, is a reliable windbreak in some northern temperate climates, providing it is regularly pruned by cutting out sufficient major branches to achieve 50% permeability. Pruning not only improves wind filtering but also reduces wind rock.

Another alternative is to combine some conifer species with alders, for example, with *Alnus cordata* (Italian Alder). I saw an effective combination on an exposed seed site in Denmark alternating *Picea sitchensis* (Sitka Spruce) and *Alnus incana* (White Alder). The eventual aim is to fell the *A. incana* when the slower-growing *P. sitchensis* have developed sufficiently to provide adequate protection. This arrangement provides both a relatively short-term and a long-term solution. An accepted practice in Michigan is to have a windbreak consisting of 3 rows of trees. The outer row is *Picea abies* (Norway Spruce) and the 2 inner rows are a canker-resistant hybrid Poplar such as *Populus canescens* 'Imperialis' (Gray Poplar cv.). The rows are planted 3 m (10') apart, with the plants 2.5 m (8') apart within the row.

(b) Manufactured (Artificial) Windbreaks

These are generally more expensive, but do have the great advantage of providing immediate protection. Firstly, they are very adaptable when coupled with a well-designed support system so that they can be moved to and from different areas in the nursery as and when immediate seed bed protection is required. Secondly, some types of manufactured fabric materials or rigid plastic mesh materials (e.g., Tensar®) can be used also to cover the seed bed to provide shade for such crops as *Fagus sylvatica* (European Beech), *Hamamelis virginiana* (Common Witch Hazel) and *Tsuga* (Hemlock). The heavier grade woven plastic fabrics are ideal for shelter providing they contain an ultra-violet light inhibitor (U.V.I.) to minimize degradation in sunlight.

Further information on appropriate plants and types of manfactured windbreaks should be obtained from regional publications. These include in England, for example, *Windbreaks* (Maidstone Division of the Ministry of Agriculture, Fisheries and Food) and *Shelter Hedges and Trees* (Rosewarne Experimental Horticulture Station, Camborne, Cornwall). In Western Canada, the Agriculture Canada publications *Hedges for the Prairies* (No. 1153) and *Shelterbelts for the Peace River Region* (No. 1384) provide useful reference material. In the United States, the local Soil Conservation Service (S.C.S.) office should be contacted for a list of species recommended for planting to provide crop shelter in a particular locality.

7. Vermin Control

It is easy to under-estimate the damage that rabbits, hares and deer can do to seed beds and seedlings. Perimeter fencing custom-designed for vermin control is expensive but an invaluable investment in the long-term. The gate into a protected seed bed area must be kept locked at all times. Leaving the gate open, whether by casual visitors or careless staff, can allow the animals entrance into the area where they could then be trapped. This can result in a potential enclosed breeding site. Unlocked gates are often more of a problem than holes in the perimeter fencing. Some nursery operators have been known to organize rabbit society shoots over their land to reduce the numbers, but the aim should be to keep them *out* initially. Netting the seed beds against birds and trapping mice are normally necessary after sowing.

8. Equipment

Basic hand tools such as spades, shovels, forks, rakes, hoses, etc., are required. Ploughs and cultivating equipment, as well as tractors, are necessary for the initial preparation of the seed bed area. Some specialized equipment is needed by the medium- to large-sized operation. Specialized catalogues, such as those produced by Egedal Masinfabrik (Egebjerr, D. K. 8700 Horsens, Denmark), M. J. F. Ltd. (Godalming, Surrey, England), and Baertschi Co. Ltd. (6152 Hueswil, Switzerland), provide a good source of reference for equipment currently available. Equipment for the propagation stage of production include soil fumigant applicators, bed former to "throw-up" the seed beds, precision seed drill, bed roller, and a sand box (sand spreader).

Figure 1-36. × *Cupressocyparis leylandii* (Leyland Cypress) windbreaks require pruning to retain good anchorage and sufficient permeability. (Oakover Nurseries, Ashford, Kent. U.K.)

Figure 1-37. A combination of *Picea sitchensis* (Sitka Spruce) and *Alnus incana* (White Alder) has been used successfully as a windbreak in exposed locations. (Rodekro, Denmark)

Figure 1-38. A well-designed windbreak constructed of a manufactured fabric with a reliable support system has the advantage of providing immediate protection to the crop. (This photograph shows a suitable fabric in use as a windbreak for a strawberry plantation in Holland.)

Figure 1-39. A well-designed perimeter fence to prevent the entry of rabbits and other animals is essential in many locations. Note the newly-established *Alnus cordata* (Italian Alder) windbreak adjacent to the fencing.

LAND HUSBANDRY

Good soil husbandry is of fundamental importance for successful seed bed culture. Nowhere has this been more carefully thought out, based on past experience, or more successfully implemented than at Oakover Nurseries, Ashford, Kent, U.K. Essentially, their system is based on a three-year production cycle. The first year is used to prepare the soil, while the second and third years are devoted to sowing and development of the seedling crop.

The first year involves the improvement of drainage by subsoiling, improvement of the organic matter content and soil structure, amendment of the pH and nutritional status, and removal of perennial weeds. These aims are assisted by either leaving the soil fallow with light cultivation and/or application of paraquat (a contact herbicide) to control the annual weeds or by sowing a crop of Weldera, a selected fast-growing, perennial rye grass which is cut 4–5 times during the season.

Glyphosate (Roundup®) is effective when both perennial and annual weeds are present, while trichloroacetic acid (TCA) is effective for perennial grasses.

Subsoiling to reduce compaction is carried out in mid-summer when the soil is dryer so that the subsoil cracks and shatters more effectively.

Well-decomposed farmyard (steer) manure is applied during the first summer at the rate of 148–198 metric tons per hectare (60–80 tons/acre) (1 metric ton = 1000 kg) and then ploughed in later in the summer. The manure is applied before subsoiling as the wheel pressure from the tractor used for the manuring destroys the effect of subsoiling. Waterlogging can be induced during the winter months if heavy rates of organic matter and their immediate ploughing-in is done during the fall. Steer manure does introduce weed seeds into the soil, and the soil fumigant dazomet (Basamid®) does not necessarily kill all weed seeds in the manure.

There are two alternative methods that have been used successfully to supply organic matter to the soil:—

(i) Spread peat moss over the soil surface before incorporating the grass ley.

(ii) Apply Basamid® to the prepared beds and then incorporate peat moss into the soil before sowing the seed.

Fall sowing of the beds requires that the soil be cultivated by disking and tilling to a sufficient tilth ready for seed bed formation in the late summer, with checks being made on the nutrient status and pH level. For spring sowing, the ploughed land is left to weather over the winter, with cultivation beginning the following spring. Power harrows are particularly useful in seed bed preparation as they reduce the number of times that equipment passes over the field, and do not have the harmful effect of rotavation which breaks down the soil structure and encourages the development of soil pans.

Forrest Keeling Nursery, Elsberry, Missouri, successfully use a green manuring program of Sudan Grass and chicken manure to improve soil fertility and structure of prepared seed beds. This vigorous growing grass is allowed to reach a height of 2 m (6½') and then it is cut with a rotary mower, with up to five mowings per season required. Buckwheat offers an alternative to Sudan Grass for green manuring.

DESIGN OF SEED BEDS

Seed beds are constructed after the initial land husbandry has been carried out. Seed beds are essentially categorized into two types.

1. Frameyards

These are seed beds contained within a wooden framework made of railway ties (sleepers) or lengths of wood 1.3 cm (½") thick and about 15–20 cm (6–8") deep. This system is particularly useful for a small permanent area. Frameyards are a great asset to nurseries when sited immediately adjacent to the greenhouse propagation unit. This type of seed bed is quite useful for raising rootstocks for bench grafting as well as a wide range of smaller quantities of seedlings.

Frameyards are not suitable for medium- to large-scale open-ground production because the initial set-up expense is high, subsequent cultivation can be very difficult to mechanize, and there may be less flexibility in rotating the seed beds.

2. Raised Seed Beds

Raised seed beds have no retaining walls. They are formed by merely raising the soil level between pathways. This system provides far more flexibility, initial set-up costs are lower, and the beds lend themselves to mechanization. They are suitable for all sizes of nursery operation. The reasons for raising seed beds are:—

(i) To asssist drainage.

(ii) To reduce erosion.

(iii) To encourage root development.

(iv) To more easily mechanize undercutting in heavier soils.

Figure 1-40.
Undercutting of *Picea* sp. (Spruce) seedlings after the first season's growth. This operation is made easier by using raised seed beds.

The main disadvantage of raised seed beds is that there is a tendency for the beds to dry out faster, particularly at the edges adjacent to the pathways.

The height of the raised seed bed varies. For example, it is about 15 cm (6″) for fall sowing of *Quercus* (Oak) and *Aesculus* (Horse-chestnut), but about 7.5–10 cm (3–4″) for spring sowing of *Acer* (Maple) and *Fraxinus* (Ash). However, it is quite feasible and less work to simply mark out the beds with the compression made by tractor wheels for smaller seeded species such as *Alnus* (Alder), *Betula* (Birch) and *Sorbus* (Mountain Ash) sown on light sandy soils. These beds will be raised just a few centimeters after covering over the seed.

Bed Width

An optimum bed width is 1.0 m (3½′), with 0.45 m (1½′) pathways. A bed width of 1.2 m (4′) with 0.6 m (2′) pathways is more common in the United States. The final bed width should be determined by:—

(a) The width of the machinery used for seed sowing, seed covering, cultivation, undercutting and lifting.

(b) The efficient use of land.
   (i) Wider seed beds of between 1.2–1.5 m (4–5′) utilize land more effectively but could hinder some cultural operations.
   (ii) Narrow seed beds of between 0.6–0.9 m (2–3′) utilize land less effectively, but operations such as hand weeding are easier.

FORMATION OF SEED BEDS

The following factors should be considered when designing the layout of the beds:—

(i) The aspect of the site.

(ii) The headland space. There must be a minimum of 4.5 m (15′) headland space to allow turning of tractor-drawn equipment.

(iii) The orientation of the seed beds. Try to orientate the seed beds so that they run north/south. East/west orientation provides a "sunny side/shaded side" situation, resulting in uneven crop growth.

(iv) The length of the seed beds. A bed pattern consisting of blocks of seed beds 65–90 m (210–300′) long has been successfully used. This optimum length conveniently allows the seed to be covered with one pass of a standard-size sanding (sandbox) machine.

(v) The type of irrigation equipment.

"Throwing-up" of Seed Beds

Seed beds are made in one of three ways.

(1) Spades

The bed is marked out with handlines, then spades are used to move tilled soil from the pathways to the bed, thus raising it. The soil from the pathways must be well-cultivated and not compacted, otherwise the structure of the bed is affected, giving rise to both germination and root development problems.

This system is suitable for small areas or when fall sowing large-seeded species, e.g., *Quercus* (Oak), on heavier soils. Seed of *Quercus* is covered to a depth of 2.5–4.0 cm (1–1½″), using cultivated soil from the pathways to create the raised bed effect.

(2) Ridging Plough

A simple piece of tractor-drawn equipment can be made with two potato-ridger ploughs, spaced 1.5 m (5′) apart, center to center. A metal bar, firmly attached between the two ploughs, will ensure that the bed is levelled off at the desired height in a single operation. The unit is then fixed to the 3-point linkage of the tractor.

The tractor operator must ensure that enough soil reaches the middle of the bed from the edges, otherwise the center will be loose after firming with a roller.

(3) Tractor Wheels

This is a straightforward technique for light sandy soils. The tractor wheels are set so that the unconsolidated area left between them is the desired width of the seed bed. For example, the tractor wheels are set at 1.55 m (62″) center to center to obtain a seed bed width of 1.0 m (3½′). It is normally necessary to travel up and down 3 or 4 times to mark out the pathways and seed bed. A bed cultivator is used at the same time to break up the soil surface.

This is the preferred technique for bed layout and may be linked to the soil fumigation program, with the runs of polyethylene used to seal in the fumigant determining the seed bed width. The marking out is effectively done by the wheels of the tractor and of the polyethylene-laying machine and the marks then remain for the life of the crop.

SOIL FUMIGATION (PARTIAL SOIL STERILIZATION)

The soil fumigation of seed beds to improve the quality of seedling crops has been a major development during the last decade. The aim of fumigation is to encourage plant growth by controlling soil-borne diseases, insects and weeds, and to increase crop growth. It is fair to say that the main objective on some nurseries is to control weeds, thus preventing competition to the crop during the early weeks of seedling growth. Soil fumigation may well reduce the effectiveness of soil mycorrhizae, so that growth may be less in the early part of the season until natural re-inoculation occurs.

Six criteria to consider prior to using chemical soil fumigants are:—

1. The safety of the chemical. Regulations must be checked before applying potentially hazardous compounds such as chloropicrin and methyl bromide. Statutory regulations may require hiring a licensed contractor. Appropriate safety clothing and equipment must be used, no matter who applies the chemical. Rates of application must be according to the manufacturers' instructions.

2. The size of the area to be treated.

3. The effectiveness of the chemical under local conditions for killing pests, diseases and weeds.

4. The cost of the chemical and the equipment to apply it.

5. The soil type in relation to time of application, temperature of the soil and the effective penetration of the chemical.

6. The time period from application to sowing of the crop. Considerable damage can be done if residues remain in the soil when the crop is sown.

Chemical soil fumigants are applied before the seed beds have been finally constructed, bearing in mind the weather conditions, soil moisture, soil temperature and the planned time of sowing the crop. As a general rule, manufacturers usually recommend that fumigation for fall-sown crops should be carried out in late summer to early fall before the winter rains occur and soil temperatures drop. For spring-sown crops, they recommend fumigating after the soil temperature has risen sufficiently and the soil moisture content has fallen. It is vital to carry out a cress or similar test before seed sowing to determine whether fumigant residues remain in the soil.

In commercial practice, some nurseries have found that fumigation in the fall is preferable for both fall and spring sowings. For example, Oakover Nurseries, Ashford, Kent, England, schedule application of the fumigant Basamid® and the time of sowing as follows. Basamid® is applied during August, which allows a 6-week fumigation and aeration period before fall sowing in October/November. Seed beds to be sown with large seeds such as *Aesculus* (Horse-chestnut) and *Quercus* (Oak) are not fumigated. For all other sowings, the polyethylene cover is left on until mid-winter when it has begun to deteriorate and blow around in the wind. The beds are cleared of polyethylene and allowed to aerate and weather naturally, producing an excellent tilth for sowing from March to May. This long-term system is convenient for the overall schedule of this nursery and ensures that no chemical residues are present to damage the germinating crop.

The following procedures have been successfully used to fumigate seed beds with the major chemicals.

1. Basamid® (Dazomet)

This chemical is now widely used in Britain for open-ground seed beds. It is relatively safe and is available in convenient prill form. These small standardized granules ensure more accurate application and create less problems under windy conditions. The prills vaporize to yield the active ingredient methyl isothiocyanate. It is particularly effective for nematodes and weed seeds, but merely retards the development of deep-rooted perennials if not incorporated to a sufficient depth. Basamid® does not control leguminous weed seeds, e.g., clovers and vetches. There are also doubts as to its effectiveness in controlling some soil diseases.

Basamid® should not be used if the soil temperature at 15 cm (6″) deep is less than 7°C (45°F). The condition of the soil in the seed bed prior to application is important—it should be moist and cultivated so that the prills can be incorporated down to a depth of approximately 20–23 cm (8–9″).

The optimum rate of application ranges from 381 kg/ha (340 lbs per acre) for light, sandy soils to 627 kg/ha (560 lbs per acre) for heavier, loamy clay soils. The physical condition and constitution of the soil are important in determining the optimum rate of application.

Basamid® can be applied to small areas using a hand box on wheels (similar to a home lawn fertilizer applicator). Accurate application on larger areas is achieved with a tractor-mounted "microband" applicator—e.g., the Sisis Lospread® manufactured in Britain and designed as a seeder and fertilizer spreader for sports grounds. This is a very accurate machine with 96 settings ranging from 5.6 kg/ha (5 lb per acre) to 1344 kg/ha (1200 lb per acre) to compensate for minor variation in rates. The prills are then incorporated into the soil with a cultivator. A tractor-mounted Vicon® fertilizer spreader is relatively cheap and reasonably accurate.

It is very important to keep a record of the depth to which the prills have been incorporated, so that unsterilized soil is not brought up by the cultivator tines when carrying out the post-application treatment to release the gases. I have seen this happen, and it makes the application of the Basamid® virtually worthless.

Once the prills have been incorporated into the soil, it is necessary to seal in the gas. This can be carried out in one of two ways:—

a) Sealing the soil surface with a light flat roller. The soil must be moist to make this seal effective. Experience has shown that this is not as satisfactory in sealing seed beds as covering with polyethylene film. There has also been poor growth of the seedlings in the beds due to the compression of the moist cultivated soil.

b) The beds are covered over with 1.5 mil (150 gauge) polyethylene film. This is done on a small scale by placing the polyethylene over the treated area and either burying the edges or holding them down with heavy objects such as metal bars and chains. It may be necessary to place heavy objects at intervals across the polyethylene to prevent the sheets lifting on exposed sites. This is the better system to use.

Laying down of polyethylene is mechanized for larger areas with machines that automatically roll out the polyethylene film. These machines can be fitted to the 3-point linkage unit of the tractor. A pair of reverse shares can be fitted so that the machine will also turn back the soil over the edges of the polyetheylene, thus holding it firmly in place over the seed bed. This turned-back soil is unsterilized, so care must be taken when the plastic is removed that it is returned to the pathways and not placed on to the seed bed. Machines are also available that "glue" the polyethylene on one edge, thus reducing the amount of unsterilized soil.

Figure 1-41. Fumigation of a seed bed by incorporating Basamid® into the soil and then sealing it in with polyethylene film (far left). (Reproduced by courtesy of Oakover Nurseries, Ashford, Kent, U.K.)

The treated area is opened up after 2–4 weeks to release traces of gas. This is done by taking a cultivator over the area, ensuring that the tines do not go below the treated depth. This operation should be repeated at 7-day intervals until all traces of gas have been removed.

A cress test (crop safety test) should be carried out before sowing the crop. This is done by taking a minimum of 6 random samples of soil, and placing each sample in individual glass jars so that they are half-filled. Another glass jar is half-filled with untreated soil as a control. Cress seed is scattered over the moist surface, the jars sealed and placed in a warm room for 48 hours. The samples are compared to the control to estimate potential damage to the germinating seedlings. Yellowing of the cotyledons or other damage indicates that traces of the gas still exist in the treated area. Further information on this procedure and the use of Basamid® can be obtained from the manufacturer's literature.

2. Methyl Bromide

Methyl bromide is widely-used for the fumigation of open-ground seed beds, particularly in North America. It is an odorless, colorless gas that penetrates the soil to effectively kill most weed seeds, pests and diseases. It is not fully effective on leguminous weed seeds. It is particularly effective against nematodes, but there is some doubt about its effectiveness against *Verticillium* sp. (Verticillium Wilt). It is considerably more expensive than Basamid® (the cost of methyl bromide application by a contractor in the United States was quoted at $900–1200 per acre in 1985).

Methyl bromide has the advantage over Basamid® of a quicker "turn-around" between application and sowing, and it is also probably more effective in controlling pests, diseases and weeds.

Methyl bromide must be handled with extreme care, and some countries require that it be applied by a licensed contractor. For safety reasons, approximately 2% chloropicrin is added to the methyl bromide so that the gas can be detected by the operator. It is also available in the United States as a "jelled-fumigant"—a mixture of 70% methyl bromide and 28.75% ethylene dibromide (plus inert materials)—that is applied below soil level by machine.

Methyl bromide is conveniently supplied in pressurized canisters that can be used for smaller areas—it is released under a sheet of polyethylene that seals in the gas. For larger areas, the gas can be released from a large vaporizing unit and then distributed through flat polyethylene tubing laid under a large sheet of polyethylene. Alternatively, a specialized application unit is mounted on the 3-point linkage unit of a tractor. This unit applies the methyl bromide through plastic tubes fitted to the rear of the chisel tines. Machines are available that will both apply the chemical and lay down the polyethylene over the seed beds in one operation.

Depending to some extent on soil temperature, the polyethylene covers are removed after 5 days and sowing can begin 3–5 days after that.

3. Chloropicrin

Chloropicrin is supplied in sealed containers as a liquid that volatizes into the pungent-smelling gas trichloronitromethane. This chemical must be handled with great care as it is very corrosive and very harmful to humans unless full safety precautions are taken. The rate of application depends very much on the soil type, e.g., an optimum rate for sandy loams has been quoted as 280 litres per hectare (25 Imp. gal/acre).

Chloropicrin is particularly effective against fungal pathogens, such as *Phytophthora* spp. (Root and Collar Rots), *Verticillium* spp. (Verticillium Wilt) and *Thielaviopsis basicola*, the Specific Cherry Replant Disease problem of *Prunus* (Cherry). Chloropicrin will reduce the numbers of nematodes, but is considered to be only moderately effective against weed seeds. It is more widely used on soil that is to be planted with young nursery stock rather than for seed sowing.

The chemical is applied either during the early fall or in spring when the soil temperature allows good volatilization of the liquid. It can be hand-injected into small areas, or by machine on larger seed bed sites. The treated area is then covered by polyethylene. Alternatively, the treated area can be sealed with a heavy roller.

The polyethylene is removed and the soil opened up after a minimum period of 21 days, with sowing possible some three weeks later. The cress test must be used to check the treated area for traces of residue prior to sowing. A mixture of methyl bromide and chloropicrin is sometimes used to make the treatment more effective.

4. Vapam® (Metam)

Vapam® [metham sodium (dihydrate)] is a well-tested material for soil fumigation and volatizes into sodium N-methyldithiocarbamate dihydrate, which has an unpleasant odor. It is applied in a fashion similar to chloropicrin, by hand injection or machine. It is less toxic than chloropicrin but should still be handled with care. This fumigant is effective against nematodes, weed seeds and most fungi. It disappears from the soil in about two weeks.

5. Formaldehyde

Formaldehyde (Formalin®) is more specific in its action than other soil fumigants because it is good against fungal pathogens but is of limited value against nematodes and weed seeds. [Research at East Malling Research Station, England, has shown formaldehyde to be particularly effective against Specific Apple Replant Disease (Chapter 15).]

Full safety precautions must be taken, including wearing protective clothing, when handling formaldehyde—particularly in enclosed areas.

6. Allyl Alcohol

Allyl alcohol was used in North America during the 1950s for fumigating seed beds, and occasionally used on some European nurseries. It has now lost favor and has been replaced by other chemicals.

Its action is chiefly herbicidal in that it prevents weed seeds germinating in the top 5 cm (2″) of soil. There is also some beneficial effect against damping-off diseases, but it is ineffective against nematodes. It is considerably cheaper than many other materials.

It is a toxic and inflammable chemical that must be used with the utmost caution. Full safety precautions *must* be taken. Some countries require a special licence for its application.

In Europe, allyl alcohol was applied as a drench or through the tubes of a slitter or "'nicker" bar unit laid about 5 cm (2″) below the surface. In the United States, allyl alcohol was applied through irrigation lines during the early morning when the air was still and the air temperature cool. Extreme care was necessary with respect to wind movement as allyl alcohol can cause eye damage when drift occurs. The treated area was rolled after fumigation. Sowing of the seed could begin some 7–10 days later.

Conclusions

In conclusion, the two compounds most widely used for soil fumigation of seed beds are Basamid® and methyl bromide. The others are utilized for more specific circumstances, while allyl alcohol is now little used.

Before using soil fumigants, advice should be sought from extension officers as to the type to use; local health and safety departments contacted for information on the appropriate safety procedures to be used; and careful reference made to the manufacturer's literature and labels for the method and rates of application. An even better method is to contact either a nursery operator or contractor who has actually fumigated soil. This will probably result in a number of practical hints that will not be found either in the manufacturer's or government publications. Do ensure that these hints do not reduce the effectiveness of the fumigant, endanger the employees or damage the future crop.

"STALE SEED BED"

Some nurseries find that the "stale seed bed" practice meets their requirements for weed control.

In this system, the seed beds are prepared for sowing but the crop is not immediately sown. Weed seeds are allowed to germinate and are then sprayed with a contact herbicide, e.g., paraquat (Gramoxone®). The crop seeds are then sown with minimum disturbance of the seed bed.

The practice of using a "stale seed bed" curtails weed competition during the critical early stages of crop development.

SEED SOWING

Seed sowing can begin after the seed has been purchased or collected, provided that it has been treated to aid germination when necessary and that the seed beds have been finally prepared.

It is important to realize that sowing is not just a matter of hurriedly broadcasting seed and then leaving nature to look after the crop. Seed sowing and the immediate aftercare must be planned methodically in order to obtain an economic and well-graded crop. Seedling growth during the early stages is fast, and failure to observe the fundamental principles of good husbandry can adversely affect the crop during the year and is often impossible to rectify. These basic principles are incorporated in the following sequence of events during and after seed sowing.

Time of Year

The date of sowing depends on the geographical location of the area. As a guideline, the dates mentioned in the text refer to an optimum period for a northern temperate climate, and are based on experiences in southern England and southwestern (coastal) British Columbia, Canada.

(a) Fall Sowing

Fall sowing in mid-October through to early November is used essentially for the following reasons.

(i) It is the traditional time in some European countries to sow many of the larger nutty seeds that have a tendency to deteriorate after collection if correct storage procedures are not followed, e.g., *Aesculus* (Horse-chestnut), *Castanea* (Chestnut), *Corylus* (Filbert) and *Quercus* (Oak). More even stands of *Quercus* and *Aesculus* are obtained by grading the seed to size before sowing.
[It is perhaps interesting to note that seed of the White Oak group (e.g., *Quercus prinus*, Chestnut Oak) produce the radicle in the fall before winter sets in, while the Black Oaks (e.g., *Q. palustris*, Pin Oak) produce their radicle in the following spring.]
It is also the traditional time for species with large-winged seeds (samaras), e.g., *Acer pseudoplatanus* (Sycamore). *Acer macrophyllum* (Big-leaf Maple) should be sown as soon as possible after collection.
Species that are fall sown in Michigan (midwestern United States) include *Acer ginnala* (Amur Maple), *Berberis* (Barberry), *Chaenomeles* (Flowering Quince), *Cornus florida* (Eastern Flowering Dogwood), *C. kousa* (Kousa Dogwood), *Cotinus* (Smoke Tree), *Crataegus* (Hawthorn), *Fraxinus* (Ash), *Malus* (Apple), *Sorbus* (Mountain Ash), *Syringa* (Lilac) and *Yucca*.

Figure 1-42.
Raised beds of fall-sown *Quercus robur* (English Oak). The seed is covered with soil taken from the pathways. (Oakover Nurseries, Ashford, Kent, U.K.)

(ii) To prevent seed from developing a hard seed coat by sowing while it is still "green" and keeping it moist (see p. 42), e.g., *Fraxinus excelsior* (European Ash) and *Carpinus betulus* (European Hornbeam).

(iii) To allow the natural winter temperature to provide the necessary cold period to overcome dormancy in seeds of trees and shrubs such as *Berberis* spp. (Barberry), *Mahonia* spp. (Oregon-grape) and *Sorbus* spp. (Mountain Ash).

(iv) To handle seed that was received from the seed house too late in the spring to stratify adequately for good germination. The seed can be kept for fall sowing, thus allowing a 12–16 week stratification period. However, most long-period dormant species can be kept for a full year and sown in the following spring. There is a risk of frost damage should seed germinate in early spring.

The advantages of fall sowing include taking some of the pressure off spring sowing and reducing the space needed to store seeds over the winter. The disadvantages are that the sown seed is at risk from vermin attack, particularly the nutty and winged seeds; a mild winter may not meet the cold temperature requirements of some species, resulting in irregular germination; and early germination in the spring will increase the risk of frost damage. Seeds of conifers should not be sown too early in cold areas because of the risk of damage should the seed germinate before the onset of winter.

(b) Spring Sowing

The main period for sowing the majority of seed is March to early May. Sowing in the later weeks reduces the risk arising from late spring frosts. Earlier sowing can cause problems as there is a risk of uneven germination caused by lower seed bed temperatures, excessive moisture, and insufficient time to prepare the actual seed bed properly. Later sowing reduces the length of the growing season, and there is a greater risk of the germinating crop being subject to stress from dry conditions if irrigation requirements are not met. A useful guide to the sowing of frost-tender species is to determine the time required to prepare the seed and for imbibition and germination to occur and then to calculate back from the latest expected date of frost.

The fact that both soil and average air temperatures are rising all the time means that later sowings will germinate and develop faster, therefore little time is actually lost. Also, the field factor (p. 66) may be reduced by late sowings. Commercially, many sowings are delayed to reduce the size of the seedlings so that they will fit transplanting machines, for example, *Alnus* (Alder) and *Betula* (Birch). Also, many legumes develop into superior plants if grown rapidly after the soil has warmed up. This applies particularly to *Gleditsia triacanthos* (Honey Locust) and *Robinia pseudoacacia* (Black Locust).

Annual weeds may have germinated since the formation of the seed bed and it may be necessary to apply paraquat as a contact herbicide before sowing.

(c) Summer Sowing

Summer sowing is rarely used, except when collecting or receiving seed that is viable for only a few days or weeks.

There are four situations in which summer sowing has been found to be successful in Europe.

(i) *Acer rubrum* (Red Maple) and *A. saccharinum* (Silver Maple)—Fresh seed usually arrives from the United States around mid-June. The moisture status of the seed is determined and it is then imbibed and chitted in moist peat at around 21°C (70°F) for 5–7 days (up to 10 days if the seed is very dry). It is then sown in the normal way, ensuring that the seed bed is covered by a shade cloth for protection.

(ii) *Populus* (Poplar) and *Salix* (Willow)—Seed is collected around mid-May, extracted and germinated immediately. It is important to frequently damp the seed bed with fine water droplets to ensure germination. It is necessary to provide heavy shading by using two layers of shade cloth set 15 cm (6″) apart (p. 74).

(iii) *Ulmus* (Elm)—*Ulmus* species such as *U. procera* (English Elm) are collected in June, chitted in moist peat and then sown. Again it is important to provide a cover of a shade cloth.

(iv) Seed collected early to avoid hard seed coat problems, e.g., *Daphne mezereum* (February Daphne) collected and sown in mid-June to early July.

In the United States, seed of most *Viburnum* species can be collected "slightly ripe" and sown throughout the summer. This accepted practice is used to avoid double dormancy (p. 33).

Nutrition

The nutritional requirements of the crop depend on the species being grown and on the soil. The fertilizer program should be based on the data obtained from analyses of samples of the soil. There are two times when fertilizers are applied—as a base dressing (fertilizer application prior to crop sowing) or as a top dressing (fertilizer application following germination of the crop).

The general rule for the base dressing is to place the emphasis on phosphate, with lower potash and little or no nitrogen levels. An application of 14 g superphosphate per m² (½ oz./sq. yd.) provides a useful base dressing for the average seed bed. This should be raked or lightly cultivated into the top few centimeters (inches) of the seed bed. Some soils have a naturally high phosphate content and may require only a "topping-up" every four years.

Any major nutritional deficiency should be corrected with a base dressing plus subsequent top dressing. A magnesium deficiency on acid soil can be corrected during the initial preparation of the land by applying ground magnesium limestone (Dolomite). This is best applied during the fallow year or on the previous crop as it is only slowly released. *Prunus avium* (Mazzard) is particularly prone to magnesium deficiency.

Chitting of Seed

Chitting of the seed (see also p. 40) is a process by which the radicle is allowed to just break through the seed coat prior to sowing. Seeds that fail to chit successfully are discarded. The purpose of this pre-sowing treatment is two-fold. Firstly, to obtain more even germination of the crop, thus improving the grade-out of the crop. Secondly, it reduces the field factor (p. 66) by shortening the period from sowing to germination when the seed is at greatest risk from vermin, birds, etc., thus improving evenness of stand and accuracy of bed density.

Timing of sowing is critical as the radicle is very likely to damage if allowed to become too long. I realized the importance of this point some years ago after seeing an entire bin of *Castanea* (Chestnut) and *Fagus* (Beech) that had to be discarded because the seed had been excessively chitted in a cold store. Poor germination would have resulted if the seed had been sown and the resulting seedlings would have developed crooked stems that would either break on lifting or have to be graded into waste. Species that have been successfully pre-chitted prior to sowing are *Fagus* (Beech), *Castanea* (Chestnut), *Quercus* (Oak), *Rosa* spp. (Rose) and *Camellia*.

Chitted seed can be held back by keeping them in a cold store at a temperature of −2 to −3°C (26.5–28°F). This useful procedure is likely to require an additional cold storage facility. I recall seeing some fine even-graded seed beds of *Fagus sylvatica* (European Beech) that had been chitted by mixing the seed with moist peat and left in a cold store before sowing in late April.

Seed Dressings

The seed coat is sometimes covered with a compound before sowing for the following reasons.

(i) To give the sower a visual assessment of the dispersal of the seed on the seed bed. This is particularly useful for machine broadcasting dark seeds on dark-colored soil.

One material used for this is lithofar red in the proportion of 19 parts talc to 1 part dye. This gives the seed coat a bright orange-red color. A small quantity of linseed oil is mixed with the seed to act as a "sticker" for the dye before addition of the lithofar red. The treated seed can be stored before sowing. Further details and a useful table on the amount of linseed oil and the weight of lithofar red to use per kg (lb) of seed is given in *Nursery Practice* by J. R. Aldhous (U.K. Forestry Commission No. 43). In some countries, lithofar red plus lead arsenate is used on conifer seeds to protect against finches and other small birds.

(ii) To dress the seed with a coating of fungicide—for example, thiram. The aim is to control disease, particularly the various damping-off diseases. Benomyl (Benlate®) has been used but has been observed to retard germination in *Acer platanoides* (Norway Maple). However, thiram has been shown to significantly improve germination and growth in the seed bed of this same species.

(iii) To act as a bird repellent. The traditional method used was a red-lead dressing, which also reduced damage by mice. Thiram has been successful in repelling birds when used at heavier rates of application than in the previous section. There is presently interest in the use of commercial alum (aluminum sulfate) to protect larger seeds from birds. The material is manufactured as a sticky compound for use as a bird repellent so that it will adhere to the surface of the seeds.

(iv) To act as a mouse repellent. Diesel oil has been added to seed for this purpose.

Density of Sowing

Determining the correct density of sowing is critical for the profit margin of the open-ground seedling operation. The density of sowing is largely determined by the required seedling size. A sowing rate that is too low gives a reduced number of seedlings and results in the bulk of the crop being above the final size requirement. A low density can also lead to the production of "feathered" or bushy seedlings that will either be unsaleable as rootstocks or mean more work for the customer trying to bud them in the following year. Sowing density is critical for crops such as *Rosa* (Rose) rootstocks, where the optimum sowing rate is the one that will produce the 5–8 mm grade (diameter of hypocotyl)—too few seedlings result in a greater proportion of 8–10 mm grade, which may be unmarketable.

However, there are instances when the sowing density is sometimes reduced—for example, *Berberis darwinii* (Darwin Barberry)—in order to maximize the use of seed, produce a better quality plant and minimize the grade-out of the finished crop. Oakover Nurseries, Ashford, Kent, England, have demonstrated that if 350 seeds per m² are sown instead of 500 (290 versus 420 per sq. yd.), the result is that virtually every seedling produces a bushy plant by harvesting time. These plants establish well to give two-year potted liners that will produce high-quality container plants after a further year of growing-on. The crop resulting from a 500-seed sowing density per square metre has a high proportion of single-stemmed, "leggy" seedlings, thus necessitating extra trimming and possibly an extra year to produce quality finished plants.

Conversely, too high a sowing rate will create more competition for light, water and nutrients, leading to lower grade material. This will mean increased grading work after lifting, discarded seedlings, lower prices, and, sometimes, a need to transplant the seedlings so that they can be grown on for a further year. Too high a density of sowing can usually be rectified by the costly operation of manually thinning the seedlings.

There are instances when the sowing rate is increased. For example, if a species grows very rapidly (e.g., *Robinia pseudoacacia*, Black Locust, and *Acer platanoides*, Norway Maple), the sowing may be delayed to enable the seed sowing density to be increased. The size of seedling is reduced at harvesting, so giving the maximum number of optimum-sized seedlings per square metre (sq. yd.) of seed bed area for selling as rootstocks.

Table 1-5 lists a selection of species and their optimum sowing rates for use as a guideline.

TABLE 1-5. Seed Density Sowing for Open-Ground Seed Beds

The densities for sowing are based on leaf size and intended use of the plant. All densities are rates per m^2 (square meter).

SPECIES	LINING-OUT STOCK (seeds per m^2)	FOR ROOTSTOCKS (seeds per m^2)
A. DECIDUOUS		
Acer palmatum (Japanese Maple)	200/300 (for potting-up as liners)	150/200
A. platanoides (Norway Maple)	200/250	100/150
A. rubrum (Red Maple)	200/250	150
A. saccharinum (Silver Maple)	100/150	100
Aesculus hippocastanum (Common Horse-chestnut)	80/120	80
Alnus cordata (Italian Alder)	350	—
A. rubra (Red Alder)	400	—
Berberis darwinii (Darwin Barberry)	350/500 (for potting-up as liners)	—
B. thunbergii (Japanese Barberry)	350/400	—
B. wilsoniae (Wilson Barberry)	350/400	—
Carpinus betulus (European Hornbeam)	250 (bushy)	150/250
Castanea sativa (Spanish Chestnut)	60/80	—
Catalpa bignonioides (Indian Bean)	150	200
Cornus alba (Red-bark Dogwood)	300/400	200
Corylus avellana (European Filbert)	150/200	150
Cotoneaster bullatus (Hollyberry Cotoneaster)	300	200
C. horizontalis (Rock Cotoneaster)	250	—
Crataegus monogyna (Single-seed or Common Hawthorn)	200/250	150
C. × *prunifolia* (Plum-leaf Hawthorn)	250	150
Fagus sylvatica (European Beech)	150/200	—
Fraxinus americana (White Ash)	120/150	100
F. excelsior (European Ash)	120/150	100
Gleditsia triacanthos (Honey Locust)	120/200	100/150
G. triancanthos var. *inermis* (Thornless Honey Locust)	120/200	100/150
Hamamelis virginiana (Common Witch Hazel)	120	100 (for potting-up as liners)
Juglans nigra (Black Walnut)	80/100	120
J. regia (English or Persian Walnut)	60/80	100
Laburnum anagyroides (Golden-chain Tree)	150/200	100/150
Mahonia aquifolium (Tall Oregon-grape)	200/250	—
Malus sylvestris (Crab Apple)	150/200	120/150
Nothofagus obliqua (Roblé Beech)	150/200	—
N. procera (Rauli)	150	—

SPECIES	LINING-OUT STOCK (seeds per m²)	FOR ROOTSTOCKS (seeds per m²)
Parthenocissus quinquefolia (Virginia Creeper)	200	120
Prunus avium (Mazzard)	150	80
P. cerasifera (Myrobalan Plum)	150/200	100
P. padus (European Bird Cherry)	150/200	80/100
P. spinosa (Blackthorn, Sloe)	150/200	—
Pyrus communis (Common Pear)	150/200	100/120
Quercus robur (English Oak)	120/150	—
Q. rubra (Red Oak)	80/100	—
Rhododendron ponticum (Pontic Rhododendron)	800/1000	600 (for potting-up as liners)
Robinia pseudoacacia (Black Locust)	100/150	80/100
Rosa canina (Dog Rose)	300	150
R. rubrifolia (Red-leaf Rose)	200	—
R. rugosa (Rugosa Rose)	250	—
Sorbus aria (White Beam)	200/250	—
S. aucuparia (European Mountain Ash or Rowan)	300/350	150/200
S. intermedia (Swedish White Beam)	150/200	100/150
Syringa vulgaris (Common or French Lilac)	250/300	150/200
Tilia cordata (Little-leaf Linden)	150/200	100/150
T. platyphyllos (Large-leaved Linden)	120/150	100
Viburnum lantana (Wayfaring Tree)	250	150/200
V. opulus (European Cranberry Bush)	200/300	150/200
Wisteria sinensis (Chinese Wisteria)	150/200	100/150

B. CONIFERS

SPECIES	LINING-OUT STOCK (seeds per m²)	FOR ROOTSTOCKS (seeds per m²)
Abies concolor (White Fir)	250	—
A. grandis (Grand Fir)	250	—
A. procera (Noble Fir)	250	—
Cedrus deodara (Himalayan Cedar)	200/250	200 (for potting-up)
Chamaecyparis lawsoniana (Lawson Cypress)	400/500	250/300
Ginkgo biloba (Maidenhair Tree)	150/200	—
Juniperus virginiana (Eastern Red Cedar)	400	400
Larix spp. (Larch)	250/300	—
Picea spp. (Spruce)	500/600	—
Pinus mugo (Mugo Pine)	300/400	—
P. nigra (Austrian Pine)	200/300	—
P. strobus (Eastern White Pine)	300/400	—
P. sylvestris (Scots Pine)	400/500	—
Sequoiadendron giganteum (Giant Sequoia)	100/150	
Taxus baccata (English Yew)	250/300	—
Thuja plicata (Western Red Cedar)	300/400	—
Tsuga heterophylla (Western Hemlock)	300/400	—

Source: Oakover Nurseries Ltd., Potters Corner, Ashford, Kent, U.K.

NOTE: Many of the plants that are used as rootstocks for bench grafting are selected for potting-up from the lining-out stock grade, rather than being sown at special densities.

Some propagators refer to text books for sowing rates (e.g., *Seeds of Woody Plants of the United States,* USDA, Agriculture Handbook No. 450). The recommendations in many books are a useful guideline but do not necessarily take into account important criteria such as variations in seed viability and the field factor. The "cutting test" for seed viability is sometimes used to give a rough estimate to determine whether to sow "heavy" or "light" (see p. 31). A much more accurate method is to use a well-tried formula to determine the sowing rate.

Evaluation of the correct sowing rate has been calculated in both the vegetable and forestry industries, using well-tried formulae. A formula may be used to calculate the rate of broadcasting seed per square metre (sq. ft.) of seed bed. See Table 1-6 for a working nursery example of the formula which will be helpful to the inexperienced propagator. However, experience developed over the years means that the calculation becomes a matter of mental arithmetic based on known germination factors.

The terms used in calculating the sowing density are:—

Required Plant Population—The number of established seedlings (density) needed per square meter (or sq. yd.) of seed bed in order to give the desired grade at the time of lifting.

Viability of Seed—The percentage of live seeds at the time of sowing.

Field Factor—The field factor represents an assessment of the likely survival rate of viable seeds to establishment as seedlings. It is written as a percentage (%). [The field factor brings together all the various factors that will determine the initial growth of the crop, such as soil type, sowing date and losses from pests and diseases. It is difficult to give a single figure precisely because it is based on many unknowns. In fact, it is really based on the nursery operator's own experiences and observations, and is another reason why record keeping is important.]

Seed Count—The number of seeds per gram (or pound).

Firming (Consolidating)

The seed bed must be relatively firm to ensure that the individual seeds are in direct contact with the soil so that they can obtain the water and nutrients necessary for even germination. A procedure sometimes used as a rough guide is to see if a slight depression can be made into the bed with the back of a tightly-closed fist.

An over-firm bed will slow down water movement through the soil, encourage water run-off, and hinder root development. A loose bed will allow both the bed and the imbibed seed to rapidly dry out. The secret to obtaining a level and evenly firmed seed bed is in the initial bed formation by ensuring that the middle of the bed has the same degree of firmness as the outside edges.

Firming of the seed beds is carried out at the following stages:—

(i) Before sowing. Very firm seed beds have been particularly recommended by the Forestry Commission in the United Kingdom for conifers that are slow to develop as seedlings and where there is no irrigation facility available. A more open, aerated seed bed is preferred for broad-leaved trees and shrubs, but there must be irrigation available for use when necessary. Excellent results are now achieved with no firming before sowing by using the stale seed bed system (p. 60) when preparing the seed beds, followed by consolidation after raking down.

(ii) Immediately after sowing when the seed bed is just lightly rolled. This is necessary because it ensures that the seed is in contact with the soil and cover. It also utilizes less seed covering material—particularly for larger seeds. In practice, this post-sowing firming is all that is necessary if the seed beds have been allowed to settle for a period prior to sowing.

The equipment used for firming seed beds is:—

(i) **Hand roller**—Some hand rollers are designed so that the weight can be increased by filling the center of the roller bar with water.

(ii) **Tamper**—This consists of a flat square piece of wood attached to a large handle. The flat base is pressed down on the seed beds. These are suitable for very small areas, but are somewhat clumsy to use as compared to a hand roller. It also takes experience to obtain an even firmness across the bed.

TABLE 1-6. Calculation of Seed Sowing Rate

The following calculations show one method to determine the sowing rate needed to produce the required number of plants.

$$\text{Plant Population Required} = 200/m^2$$

Given: Viability of Seed $= 50\%$

Seed Count from sample of 1 gm $= 200$ seeds/gm

A. Field Factor (based on experience) $= 40\%$

$$\text{Seed Sowing Rate} = \frac{\text{Plant Population Required}}{\text{Viability} \times \text{Field Factor} \times \text{Seed Count}}$$

$$= 200 \times \frac{100}{50} \times \frac{100}{40} \times \frac{1}{200}$$

$$= \cancel{200} \times 2 \times \frac{10}{4} \times \frac{1}{\cancel{200}}$$

$$= \frac{20}{4}$$

$$\text{Sowing Rate} = 5 \text{ gm/m}^2$$

B. Field Factor $= 80\%$

$$= 200 \times \frac{100}{50} \times \frac{100}{80} \times \frac{1}{200}$$

$$= \cancel{200} \times 2 \times \frac{10}{8} \times \frac{1}{\cancel{200}}$$

$$= \frac{20}{8}$$

$$\text{Sowing Rate} = 2.5 \text{ gm/m}^2$$

Using Example A, 5 gm seed are required per square meter

$$\text{Bed size} = 50 \text{ m}^2 = 5 \times 50 = 250$$

$\therefore$ 250 gm seed will be required to produce 200 plants per square meter.

NOTE: It is preferable to use the actual germination count from a sample test rather than the viability figure provided by the supplier. The viable seed count and actual germination rate are often very different. Germinable seed is a more accurate figure.

Reference: McMillan Browse, P.D.A. 1979. Hardy, Woody Plants from Seed. Grower Books, London.

(iii) Tractor-drawn Roller—These larger flat rollers are suitable for larger seed beds.

Methods of Sowing Seed

Procedures will vary slightly from nursery to nursery, but some guidelines can be obtained from the following comments. Seeds are sown either by:—

(i) Broadcasting—The seed is either hand sown or applied through a seed box pulled by a tractor so that it is distributed evenly across and along the length of the seed bed. A 60 cm (24") wide lawn seeder can be used on a small area.

(ii) Space Sown—The seed is sown at set distances apart. This method is sometimes used for large seeds such as *Aesculus* (Horse-chestnut), *Juglans* (Walnut) and *Araucaria araucana* (Monkey-puzzle Tree). Depending on the species, the seed bed is marked into squares, e.g., 5 × 5 cm (2 × 2"), using either a pre-made marker or a rake with pegs 5 cm (2") apart and pulled in two directions to form the squares.
[Experiments have demonstrated that the polarity (orientation) of the seed at sowing can influence seedling size and quality for some species with very large seeds, e.g., *Aesculus* (Horse-chestnut). Maximum vertical growth of *Aesculus* is encouraged if the seed is sown with the seed scar (hilum) downward. Conversely, seed sown at other orientations (with the seed scar upwards or sideways) encourages seedlings with angled or bent stems, or even with shoot/root "crossover". Space sowing by hand enables the propagator to ensure correct polarity in these circumstances.]

(iii) Drilling—Shallow drills are made with a hand rake or a hand-pushed or tractor-drawn seed drill so that the seed is directed evenly into and down the drills. An optimum row spacing across the bed is normally 4–6 rows.

The choice of whether to broadcast or drill the seed depends on the size of the nursery, personal preferences and mechanization. The choice is also sometimes dictated by soil type.

Drilling is not possible if the soil texture has a tendency to "crust", and this necessitates broadcasting. Drilling generally produces a greater variation in seedling size while broadcasting results in more uniform seedlings. Drilling the seed makes it easier to carry out some subsequent mechanical operations (for example, if weeding should become necessary or if contact herbicides can be applied with a nozzle covered by a spray guard).

The sowing method will also determine the type of lifting equipment that can be used. Broadcast beds restrict mechanical lifting to the use of an under-cutting blade (and its adaptations) that cuts under and across the bed. Drilled beds allow the additional option of "row-lifters" that undercut, lift and sometimes bundle a row in one operation. Examples of this type of machine are the "Plantlift" manufactured in Holland, the Famo machine from Belgium and the Fobro machine from Switzerland.

Hand broadcasting of stratified and imbibed seed is the safest way to prevent germination failures.

Hand Broadcasting

A well-tried procedure for hand broadcasting seed is outlined below.

1. Rake the surface of the seed bed with a wooden rake or light mechanical cultivator. A wooden rake is used for the final raking down of the beds to break up the soil surface and to remove any exposed lumps or stones, thus helping to prevent the seed from bouncing as it falls onto the surface.

2. Weigh out sufficient seed for each metre (yard) length of the bed, using the calculation for determining seed density. Place the weighed seed into separate containers.

3. Mark out the seed bed into metre (yard) lengths by placing 1 m (3') long bamboo canes along the surface.

4. Take the correct amount of seed in the hand and use relatively quick, short, sideways movements just above the bed so that the seed falls between the fingers and over the sides of the hand. The seed should not be sown right up to the edge of the bed as these seedlings could later be dislodged in heavy rains, as well as being prone to drying out.

The seed may be divided into two lots for each bed length to allow the sower to go up one side of the bed and down the other. Evenness of sowing throughout the seed bed is helped by making two or more passes.

As the sowers become experienced, it may be more efficient to divide the seed into 4–6 lots for a 23 m (75') long seed bed instead of dividing the bed into 1 m (3') lengths. Sowing of smaller seed, e.g., *Betula* (Birch), *Alnus* (Alder), *Cornus sanguinea* (Blood-twig Dogwood) and *Viburnum opulus* (European Cranberry Bush), is made easier by bulking-up the seed with fine peat moss or fine sand to a known volume.

5. Lightly firm the seed bed to ensure that the seed is in good contact with the soil surface.

Considerable skill is involved in the efficient hand broadcasting of seed. There is no point in using an untrained employee for hand sowing. The following comments should be helpful:—

(i) Ensure that the sower has had instruction from a skilled person and has had the opportunity to practice, using old seed in an unused area. Practice is also useful for experienced personnel when sowing different sizes and/or shapes of seed.

(ii) Retain the stratification medium (bulking-up where necessary) and sow it with the seed, or mix the seed with fine peat moss or sand. This increased bulk can help to obtain more even seed dispersal, especially for smaller seeds.

(iii) Ensure that the sower, and the supervisor, regularly checks over the seed bed areas to ensure that an even distribution of the seed is being maintained.

Drilling Seed

Three methods may be used for drilling seed.

1. Hand Sowing—This is suitable for small areas where rows across the bed can be marked out at the required distance, using either a heavy rake with appropriate V-shaped pegs or a wood plank laid across the bed. Drills can be made down the bed by using a hand roller shaped to make compressions in the surface. The seed is then just simply hand sown into the pre-made drills.

Figure 1-43.
Hand sowing of *Acer platanoides* (Norway Maple) in pre-formed drills in a 9-row seed bed. Any hand sowing method requires considerable skill in order to obtain an even seed sowing density. (Reproduced by courtesy of J. Frank Schmidt & Co., Boring, OR, U.S.A.)

2. Hand Push Drills—Simple hand push drills (e.g., the Jubilee Drill) have been used for many years on small, intensive vegetable nurseries and can also be used on larger nurseries. A single row of seeds is sown and covered at a time down the bed.

3. Tractor-Drawn Precision Drills—These are designed to straddle the width of the bed so that multiple rows can be sown down the length. Drills used in the vegetable industry have been adapted for nurseries, but there are often limitations in the seed size that can be sown. One machine specifically designed for woody seed is the Egedal Sowing Machine (Model 76), which has numerous calibration settings so that it is possible to uniformly sow a wide range of seed sizes. The seed is placed into a large seed box that has a dial at the base to allow various settings for different seed sizes. The seed is distributed from this box to individual sowing units that are adjustable for row width and, if necessary, height. The Plantox® seed drill made by Zilstra and Bolhuis is also claimed to be very efficient. Some types of precision seed drilling machines for vegetables have been adapted for use on forestry nurseries.

The Planet Junior Drill is widely used in the United States for seed sowing. This equipment has seed buckets fixed to a draw bar, generally spaced for 15 cm (6″) rows in the bed. A series of plates can accommodate most seed sizes. The plates are removed entirely for larger seed such as *Corylus* (Filbert) and *Quercus* (Oak) to enable the tractor speed and gear range to control seed density in the row.

Figure 1 - 45. A tractor-drawn sowing machine for direct drilling of seed on to a prepared seed bed. Note that the seed beds have been marked out by the compressions of tractor wheels instead of with a ridging plough. (Pinneberg area, West Germany)

Figure 1 - 44. Tractor-drawn sowing machines have been designed for broadcasting seed on to the seed bed. The seed beds are lightly harrowed to remove surface capping (right). The evenness of seed distribution is checked after a trial run with the sowing machine (center). The seed is covered with coarse sand after sowing (left). (Surrey, U.K.)

Figure 1 - 47. A tractor-drawn Egedal mechanical seed sower in which adjustments can be made for many varying seed sizes. Note the roller attachment for lightly firming the seed bed after drilling. (Reproduced by courtesy of Plumtree Nursery Equipment, Mapperley, Nottingham, U.K.)

Figure 1 - 46. Germination of *Prunus cerasifera* (Myrobalan Plum) in drilled seed beds. (Pinneberg area, West Germany.)

Pelleted Seed

Pelleting is the covering of seed with an artificial layer of an inert material. This inert material can be talc, gypsum, lime or clay held together by a compound such as gum arabic. Pelleted seed has been used successfully for many years in the vegetable and greenhouse industries. Its main advantage is that irregularly shaped seeds become circular, thus allowing precision sowing. If desired, the inert cover can be impregnated with nutrients, insecticides, fungicides or even bird repellents. The inert coating disintegrates when the soil moisture level has risen sufficiently to allow germination to occur. Thus, a further advantage of pelleted seed is that germination does not occur if the soil conditions are too dry. One drawback of pelleted seed is the increased cost.

There is some question as to the application of pelleted seed for woody plants as many of these are sown in the imbibed state which will break down the pelleting material. It could be used on dried woody plant seed, remembering that sowing dried seed will give mixed results and it is therefore a matter of chance as to whether the maximum potential crop is obtained. It is a procedure that perhaps should be investigated further for small, irregular seed of selected ornamentals having little or no dormancy problems.

Seed Priming

Seed researchers have recently been spending considerable time on developing methods of, and uses for, priming seed. Seed priming is essentially "conditioning" the seed in a way that will both hasten and encourage more uniform germination. The methods investigated have included the use of organic solvents for diffusing fungicides, insecticides or growth regulators into the seed. However, one method that has now become firmly established in the horticultural industry is fluid drilling.

Fluid drilling is a technique that was developed during the 1970s by the National Vegetable Research Station, Wellesbourne, England. The concept is to directly sow pre-germinated seed dispersed in a fluid gel. This technique has given vegetable growers better control over the germination and early establishment of crops, particularly celery and parsley. The benefits include faster germination in the open ground, higher germination percentages, the ability to discard non-germinated seeds before sowing, and more even spacing of seedlings within the row. The capital investment for large-scale production is relatively high as the procedure requires germination and separation cabinets, a fluid carrier, a fluid carrier mixer, and either a hand or tractor-mounted drill to disperse the gel-like fluid containing the pre-germinated seed.

The technique has been very much simplified for use by the home gardener in small outdoor areas or greenhouses. The seed is pre-germinated on layers of moisture-absorbent paper and then mixed carefully with a prepared gel. This gel can be dispersed in lines in the open ground or prepared flats by either placing the mixture in a polyethylene bag with one corner cut off so that the contents can be pushed out by hand pressure or by using a cake-icing dispenser with a wide nozzle. As a guide, the optimum rate of application is 130 ml of gel and seeds per 10 m row (4 fl. oz./30′).

To the best of my knowledge, fluid drilling has been little utilized for woody seeds. However, it may play a role in the future in both large- and small-scale seed sowing for the nursery operator—especially for small seeds and for sowing seeds in flats.

Further information of fluid drilling can be obtained by writing to the Scientific Liaison Officer, National Vegetable Research Station, Wellesbourne, Warwick, CV35 9EF, England.

Covering the Seed

After sowing, the seed is lightly rolled, and the next stage is to ensure that the seed is efficiently and evenly covered with an appropriate material. As a guideline, the recommended depth for covering is to the depth of the longest axis of the seed. In practice, it is often a good deal deeper than this. There are three principal types of material used for covering the seeds.

1. Soil from Pathways—This is useful for large seeds such as *Aesculus* (Horse-chestnut) and *Quercus* (Oak). Soil from the pathways is shovelled by hand onto the beds until the required depth is reached. This is particularly useful in the fall when the soil is likely to be in a more friable condition than in the spring after the winter rains.

The usual practice in the fall is to cover the seed to a depth of 3.5–5.0 cm (1½–2″) and leave in a "rough" condition. The soil cover will then be broken down by winter frosts. Compaction of this soil cover in the fall, or the use of a fine tilth, will lead to surface capping in the spring which will make it difficult for seeds to emerge.

One means of deterring mice and birds from the seed bed is to cover the seed with a 6 mm (¼″) deep layer of sawdust before covering with soil.

2. Coarse Sand—Lime- and silt-free coarse sand with a particle size of 3–5 mm (1/8–1/5″) is widely used, particularly in Europe. Dark-colored coarse sand should be avoided as it absorbs the heat. Light-colored sand will reflect the light, thus reducing the soil temperature around the seed during long periods of sunshine. Germination will be affected if the sand contains silt which solidifies around the seed.

The advantages of using a coarse sand for covering the seeds are:—

(i) It is easily handled by machinery.

(ii) It improves aeration around the seed.

(iii) It reduces capping of the seed bed surface.

(iv) It encourages even percolation of water into the seed bed.

(v) It encourages easier removal of small weeds by hand.

(vi) It deters slugs and the development of moss and algae.

Small areas can be covered by simply placing the sand in a sieve, holding it over the seed bed and shaking to ensure an even distribution over the seed. Another method to use for smaller areas is to have a quantity of sand on a spade, and then make sideways movements with the wrists so that the sand falls off the sides of the spade. The sand can be evenly distributed with some practice. A tractor-drawn sand spreader that straddles the seed bed is an efficient means of covering long beds. Some sanders have a moving floor (conveyor) that carries the sand to the outlet. The large box is filled with sand from a front-end loader, and the material falls onto the seeds by gravity. The amount of sand falling onto the seed bed surface can be adjusted by calibrating the box openings. Change of tractor speed makes little difference to the depth of cover as this is essentially controlled by aperture size and by the moisture status of the sand. Dry sand will have to be re-moistened. A sanding machine manufactured by Egedal, Denmark, has a power-driven spinning roller to provide an even spread.

Examples of covering depths are 3 mm (⅛″) used for *Betula* (Birch) and 5 cm (2″) for *Fagus sylvatica* (European Beech).

The sand is sometimes lightly rolled after application.

If the seed is sown in drills, it may be convenient to cover only the seed and not the whole bed. For example, I have seen *Rosa* (Rose) rootstock seed growing on stony or heavy soils with only the drills covered with sand rather than the entire seed bed. This ensures that the hypocotyls will grow straight.

3. Plant-Derived Products—The choice of plant-derived products will depend on an economical local source. These products range from peat moss, sawdust, spent rice hulls and chopped straw to crushed peanut husks. A mixture of sawdust and bark has provided a satisfactory combination. Many of these materials are used successfully in North America. Manure spreaders have been adapted to apply sawdust. Two problems that may be encountered are poor aeration of the seed and poor drainage as the water is slow to move away from the surface, leading to a subsequent nitrogen deficiency. However, these materials do reduce weed growth and help maintain water in seed beds on dryer sites, thus allowing less frequent irrigation. A mixture that provides a more open structure is equal parts of peat moss, perlite and sand.

In some areas of the United States, spent rice hulls (a by-product of the apple processing industry where they are used to filter the juice) are utilized to cover seed. The rice hulls are applied by a manure spreader and the depth of the cover varies according to species (seed size) and time of year.

Plant-derived products such as spent rice hulls must be held in place by erosion matting or burlap (hessian) when used to cover seed in the fall. The matting or burlap is removed at the time of germination in the spring.

Immediate Aftercare

The seed sowing operation is not over when the seed is covered. Attention to the following details is critical during the four weeks following sowing to ensure successful germination.

Figure 1-48. An ample supply of clean, lime-free, 3–5 mm (1/8–1/5″) coarse sand (grit) is popular in Europe for covering seed. (Oakover Nurseries, Ashford, Kent, U.K.)

Figure 1-49. A tractor-drawn Egedal sand spreader (sand box) straddles the seed bed and gives an even coverage of sand after sowing. (Denmark)

Figure 1-50. Long runs of seed beds sown with *Abies* sp. (Fir) and then covered with coarse sand (grit). Note the wind protection on each side of the seed beds to provide shelter.

Figure 1-51. Pumice is an alternative to coarse sand for covering conifer seed beds. Note the use of wooden slats to provide shading and some initial frost protection. (Oregon, U.S.A.)

1. Irrigation

The importance of watering the germinating seed has already been stressed. Spraylines or sprinklers to ensure an even water pattern should be set up immediately after sowing. The soil should be maintained at field capacity and may well require in excess of 1.3 cm (½″) of water per week during dry summers. It is best to water "little and often" rather than to allow the water requirements to build up until a prolonged period of irrigation is necessary. It may be necessary to give 3–4 applications of water each day during dry weather after sowing imbibed seed until the radicle has developed sufficiently to function and maintain moisture status. This is also critical during the first few days for small seeds such as *Alnus* (Alder) and *Betula* (Birch).

Irrigation also increases the efficiency of post-sowing applications of herbicide. Care is needed regarding the timing of application of herbicides—for example, chlorthal (Dacthal®, DCPA®) should not be applied until the first true pair of leaves have appeared.

2. Frost Protection With Overhead Irrigation

A technique that I have seen used successfully on *Abies* (Fir) seed beds in Denmark to protect the young seedling crop from late spring radiation frosts is to apply a continuous overhead application of water from sprinkler nozzles. Irrigation is synchronized to come on at the temperature at which the crop will be at risk of damage.

It is based on the principle that protection is given by the transference of heat from the water. The mixture of ice and water keeps the temperature around the plant tissue at 0°C (32°F). Damage to the plant tissues will occur if there is a break in irrigation so that there is no water but only ice. This technique has been widely used in fruit orchards to protect the blossoms from frost damage. However, obvious problems will occur if there are drainage difficulties in the seed beds.

3. Vermin Protection

The need for vermin protection has already been stressed. Traps and bait for mice can be placed in a series of old drainage tiles down the seed beds and protect the crop by reducing the population. Chicken netting should be placed around each drain tile to reduce the risk of birds eating the poisoned bait. Birds can be a real problem by having "dust baths", eating the seeds, and pulling, dislodging and eating the cotyledons of young seedlings. Rooks, crows and pigeons are particularly fond of *Fagus* (Beech) and *Quercus* (Oak), and some finches like *Pinus* (Pine) seeds. Galvanized wire hoops can be placed at 1 m (3′) intervals down the beds and covered with a thin plastic netting in areas where birds are a major problem. Netlon® plastic netting is favored in England. Oakover Nurseries, Ashford, Kent, have used lightweight black Netlon®, 1.9 cm (¾″) square mesh, in 1.8 m (6′) wide strips for 7 seasons without marked deterioration. This width allows for the curvature of the hoops.

4. Shading

Depending on the location, shading may be necessary to prevent leaf scorch of some seedlings, for example, *Abies* (Fir), *Tsuga* (Hemlock), *Fagus* (Beech) and *Hamamelis* (Witch Hazel). It can also provide frost protection to *Acer campestre* (Hedge Maple) and *Fraxinus excelsior* (European Ash), and allows a more even moisture status of the seed bed. In nature, this protection would be provided by the surrounding canopy of trees. A material that will provide about 35–40% shade should be placed over the bed after sowing. This will also provide protection against vermin.

Rolls of wooden slats attached to a length of wire at either end have been used but are clumsy to handle and the wood is liable to break. Polypropylene woven shade cloths provide a much more efficient alternative, and can be used successfully for several years. A woven polypropylene fabric with a 40% shade factor will keep out approximately 1°C (2°F) of frost. A double layer of shade cloth separated by a 15 cm (6″) gap is said to increase this effectiveness by a further 2°C (4°F). This gap can be created by using hoops in two sizes with one layer laid over the lower hoop and the other over the higher. It is necessary to continue frost protection through to late May in some climates.

The remaining operations after seedling germination are not strictly propagation and thus are not included in this book. Details of roguing, top dressing, post-germination pest, disease and weed control, undercutting, lifting, grading and shipping can be obtained from other books. Two publications that provide very useful information are *Hardy Woody Plants from Seed* by P. D. A. McMillan Browse and *Nursery Practice* by J. R. Aldhous (Forestry Commission Bulletin No. 43).

Figure 1-52. A sturdy label, clearly showing the species and seed source, should be placed in the seed bed after sowing and covering the seed. The date of sowing can also be added to the label.

Figure 1-53. Attention to detail during the aftercare following sowing is essential. Note the multi-jet spray line for irrigation, the supported plastic net for protection against birds, and (far left) shade fabric for initial frost protection and shading. (Oakover Nurseries, Ashford, Kent, U.K.)

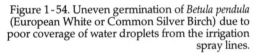

Figure 1-54. Uneven germination of *Betula pendula* (European White or Common Silver Birch) due to poor coverage of water droplets from the irrigation spray lines.

Figure 1-55. Close-up of plastic net material supported on sturdy wire hoops used to cover conifer seed beds. (W. Crowder & Sons, Horncastle, Lincolnshire, U.K.)

Figure 1-56. Quality beds of seedlings resulting from good seed sources, correct land preparation and pre-sowing treatments, even seed sowing densities, and good aftercare. (Oakover Nurseries, Ashford, Kent, U.K.)

APPENDIX 1-2

A Selected List of Commercial Seed Sources of Woody Plants for Nurseries

NORTH AMERICA

CANADA

Reid Collins Nurseries Ltd., Box 430, 2396-272nd St., Aldergrove, B.C. V0X 1A0
Rocky Mountain Seed Service, Box 215, Golden, B.C. V0A 1H0

UNITED STATES

Brown Seed Co, P.O. Box B, Jaroso, CO 81138
Byers Nursery Inc., 6001 Moores Hill Rd., Huntsville, AL 35811
Callahan Seeds, 6045 Foley Lane, Central Point, OR 97502
Carters Seeds, P.O. Box 4006, Sylmar, CA 91342
Cascade Forestry Service Inc., R.R. #1, Cascade, IA 52033
Environmental Seed Producers Inc., P.O. Box 5904, El Monte, CA 91734
R. Herbst Wholesale Seed Inc., 108 Candlewood Isle, New Fairfield, CT 06812
Herbst Brothers Seedsmen Inc., 1000 N. Main St., Brewster, NY 10509
Lawyers Nurseries, Plains, MT 59859
Maplewood Seed Co., 6219 S.W. Dawn St., Lake Oswego, OR 97034
Mellingers Inc., 2310 W. South Range Rd., North Lima, OH 44452
Mistletoe Sales, 910 Alphonse, Santa Barbara, CA 93103
Mortensen Landscaping, West 2407 Olympic, Spokane, WA 99208
Native Plants, 9180 South Wasatch Blvd., Sandy, UT 84092
Northplan Seed Producers Inc., P.O. Box 9107, Moscow, ID 83843
Ojai Seeds, P.O. Box 543, Ojai, CA 93023
Palouse Seed Co., P.O. Box 866, Tekoa, WA 99033
Quality Tree Seed, Inc., Prospect Hill Rd., Brewster, NY 10509
Rob Lovelace Seeds, Brown Mill Rd., Elsberry, MO 63343
Seedco, Box H, Vista, CA 92083
F. W. Schumacher Co. Inc., 36 Spring Hill Rd., Sandwich, MA 02563-1023
Sheffields Seed Co., P.O. Box 624, Ithaca, NY 14950
Silvaseed, P.O. Box 118, Roy, WA 98580
George W. Park Seed Co. Inc., Box 31, Greenwood, SC 29647
Vans Pines Inc., West Olive, MI 49460
V.B.M. Seeds, 4607 Wendover Blvd., Alexandria, LA 71301

AUSTRALASIA

AUSTRALIA

Australian Seed Co., P.O. Box 67, Hazelbrook, Blue Mountains, N.S.W. 2779
Ellison Horticultural Pty. Ltd., P.O. Box 365, Nowra, N.S.W.
Flamingo Enterprises Pty. Ltd., P.O. Box 1037, East Nowra, N.S.W. 2541
T. Holl, Lot 6 Badgerup Rd., Wanneroo, W.A. 6065
H. G. Kershaw, P.O. Box 84, Terry Hills, N.S.W. 2084
         or P.O. Box 88, Mona Vale, N.S.W. 2103
Kimberley Seeds Pty. Ltd., 51 King Edward Rd., Osborne Park, W.A. 6017
Vaughan's Wildflower Seeds, P.O. Box 1037, East Nowra, N.S.W. 2541

NEW ZEALAND

Peter B. Dow & Co., Ltd., P.O. Box 696, Gisborne
New Zealand Forest Services, Private Bag, Wellington

ASIA

INDIA

Chandra, Upper Cart Rd, P.O. Kalimpong 734301, West Bengal
P. Kohli & Co., Park Rd., Srinagar, Kashmir
Udai C. Pradhan, Himalayan Flower Seeds, Atish Villa, Atisha Rd., Kalimpong 734301, Darjeeling

JAPAN

Fujita Seed Co. Ltd., P.O. Box 211, Osaka Central, Osaka

AFRICA

SOUTH AFRICA

Honingklip Nurseries, W. J. & Mrs. E. R. Middelmann & Son, 13 Lady Anne Ave., Newlands, Cape Province 7700

Parsley's Cape Seeds, 1 Woodlands Rd., Somerset West, Cape Province 7130

EUROPE

AUSTRIA

Franz Kluger, A-1222 Wien, Schrickgasse 9

BELGIUM

Paul Raeymaekers, Turnhoutsebaan 143, Mol B-2400

DENMARK

A. J. Frost, 7080-Borkop

Soren Levinsen, Kollerød Byugade 25, 3450-Allerød

FRANCE

Les Établissements Versepuy, Le Puy—4300, Haute Loire

Vilmorin—Andrieux S.A., Service Graines d'Arbres, La Ménitré—49250, Beaufort-en-Vallée, Maine et Loire

ITALY

Barilli & Blagi, Casella Postale 1645-AD, 1-40 100 Bologna

Florsilva Ansaloni, Casella Postale 2100-EL, 1-40 Bologna

NETHERLANDS

H. den Ouden & Zoon B.V., The Old Farm Nurseries, Boskoop

Van Dijk & Co. B. V., Postbus 20, Enkhuizen

WEST GERMANY

Mosbacher Geholz und Waldsamen, Conrad Appel KG, Postfach 1123, D-6124 Beerfelden-Gammelsbach

Renz Nachf, Gmbh & Co. KG, D-7270 Nagold-Emmingen

G. J. Steingaesser & Co. Gmbh., Postfach 1756, 8760-Miltenburg

UNITED KINGDOM

E. F. G. Nurseries Ltd., Maelor Nursery, Bronington, Whitchurch, Salop SY13 3EZ

Forestry Commission, Seed Section, Alice Holt Lodge, Wrecclesham, Farnham, Surrey GU10 4LH

Asmer Seeds Ltd., Asmer House, Ash St., Leicester

Greenfinger Tree Sales, Inigo Rd., Stoneycroft, Liverpool

NOTE: A number of specialist nurseries and organizations offer small quantities of seed—for example, Thuya Alpine Nursery, Glebelands, Hartpury, Glos GL19 3BW; The Royal Horticultural Society, R.H.S. Garden, Wisley, Surrey GU23 6QB (for members only); and Chiltern Seeds, Bortree Stile, Ulverston, Cumbria LA12 7PB.

REFERENCES AND SUGGESTED SOURCES FOR FURTHER READING

Aldhous, J. R. 1972. Nursery Practice. *Bulletin No. 43*, Forestry Commission, London.

Allen, G. S. 1967. Stratification of tree seed. *Comb. Proc. Inter. Pl. Prop. Soc.* **17**: 99–106.

Barton, L. V. 1956. Gathering, stratification, and sowing seeds. *Proc. Pl. Prop. Soc.* **6**: 95–107.

Boyd, H. 1960. The treatment of seed. *Austral. Pl.* **1**(2): 5–6.

Carville, L. 1978. Seed bed production in Rhode Island. *Comb. Proc. Inter. Pl. Prop. Soc.* **28**: 114–117.

Collins, E. P. 1981. Seed coatings. *Garden* (N.Y. Botanical Garden) 5(2): 14, 16, 17, 29.

Dummer, P. 1969. Problems in raising ornamental stock from seed. *Comb. Proc. Inter. Pl. Prop. Soc.* **19**: 213–215.

Emery, D. E. 1969. The propagation of some native California plants. *Comb. Proc. Inter. Pl. Prop. Soc.* **19**: 145–148.

Fordham, A. J. 1960. Germination of double-dormant seeds. *Comb. Proc. Pl. Prop. Soc.* **10**: 206–210.

———. 1973. Dormancy in seeds of Temperate Zone woody plants. *Comb. Proc. Inter. Pl. Prop. Soc.* **23**: 262–266.

——— & L. J. Spraker. 1977. Propagation manual of selected gymnosperms. *Arnoldia* **37**(1): 1–88.

Fordham, D. 1976. Production of plants from seed. *Comb. Proc. Inter. Pl. Prop. Soc.* **26**: 139–145.

Forestry Commission of New South Wales. no date. *Raising Trees and Shrubs from Seed.* Forestry Commission, New South Wales, Australia.

Gage, B. 1969. Seed propagation at the Saratoga Horticultural Foundation. *Comb. Proc. Inter. Pl. Prop. Soc.* **19**: 138–141.

Galle, F. C. 1953. The propagation of Magnolias by seed. *Proc. Pl. Prop. Soc.* **3**: 105–108.

Gordon, A. G. 1977. Speeding dormancy break in hardwoods. *GC & HTJ* **181**(3): 30–31 (Jan. 21, 1977).

———. 1977. Tree seed sources. *GC & HTJ* **182**(17): 20–21 (Oct. 21, 1977)

——— & D. C. F. Rowe. 1982. *Seed Manual for Ornamental Trees and Shrubs.* Bulletin No. 59, Forestry Commission, London.

Hartmann, H. T. & D. E. Kester. 1983. 4th ed. *Plant Propagation: Principles and Practices.* Prentice-Hall, Inc., Englewood Cliffs, N.J.

Heydecker, W., Ed. 1973. *Seed Ecology.* Butterworths & Co. (Publishers) Ltd., London.

Humphrey, B. E. 1970. The large scale raising of nursery plants by seed in England. *Comb. Proc. Inter. Pl. Prop. Soc.* **20**: 188–192.

Hutchinson, P. A. 1971. Propagation of Acers from seed. *Comb. Proc. Inter. Pl. Prop. Soc.* **21**: 233–235.

King, P. J. 1980. Reviewing Seed Pretreatments Required for Germination of Candidate Native Tree and Shrub Species in the Eastern Slopes of the Rocky Mountains and Foothills of Alberta. *ENR Report No. 154*, Alberta Energy and Natural Resources.

———, G. Grainger & A. Straka. (?date?) Testing of Seed Pre-germination Treatments for Selected Native Shrub Species. *ENR Report No. T/43*, Alberta Energy and Natural Resources.

Marchant, C. & J. Sherlock. 1984. A Guide to Selection and Propagation of Some Native Woody Species for Land Rehabilitation in British Columbia. *Research Report RR84007-HQ.* B.C. Ministry of Forests, Victoria, B.C.

McMillan Browse, P. D. A. 1979. *Hardy Woody Plants from Seed.* Grower Books, London.

———. 1982. Propagation of the hardy horse chestnuts and buckeyes. *The Plantsman* **4**: 150–164.

McTavish, B. 1983. Propagation and use of native woody plants in northern latitudes. Unpubl. report presented at the 7th Ann. B.C. Mine Reclamation Symp., 1983.

Ministry of Agriculture, Fisheries & Food, U.K. 1978. *Windbreaks.* Agriculture Development Advisory Service, Ministry of Agriculture, Fisheries and Food, Maidstone, Kent, U.K.

Moore, R. P. 1973. Tetrazolium staining for assessing seed quality. In: *Seed Ecology,* edited by W. Heydecker. Butterworths & Co. (Publishers) Ltd., London. pp. 347–366.

Nordine, R. M. 1952. Collecting, storage and germination of Maple seed. *Proc. Pl. Prop. Soc.* **2**: 62–64.

———. 1962. Propagation of Oaks by seed. *Comb. Proc. Pl. Prop. Soc.* **12**: 166–168.

Pinney, T. S., Jr. 1957. Propagation of *Picea* by seed. *Proc. Pl. Prop. Soc.* **7**: 33–38.

———. 1973. Seedbed management. *Comb. Proc. Inter. Pl. Prop. Soc.* **23**: 276–280.

Reisch, K. W. 1962. After ripening as related to germination and seedling growth. *Comb. Proc. Pl. Prop. Soc.* **12**: 150–154.

Schneider, G. 1960. Production of rootstocks for ornamental trees in the container nursery. *Comb. Proc. Pl. Prop. Soc.* **10**: 282–286.

Sherlock, J. 1983. *Selection and Propagation of Candidate Woody Plant Species for Erosion Control in British Columbia.* Unpubl. M.Sc. Directed Studies Report, Dept. of Plant Science, Univ. of British Columbia, Vancouver, B.C.

Shugert, R. 1968. Seedling propagation. *Comb. Proc. Inter. Pl. Prop. Soc.* **18**: 188–192.

———— . 1981. Seedling production in the eastern U.S.A. *Comb. Proc. Inter. Pl. Prop. Soc.* **31**: 78–81.

Steavenson, H. 1973. Seedling propagation—solving the seed source problem. *Comb. Proc. Inter. Pl. Prop. Soc.* **23**: 281–284.

Taylor, R. L. & S. Taylor. 1979. *Pinus contorta* D. Douglas ex Loudon (Shore Pine, Lodgepole Pine). *Davidsonia* **10**: 75–83.

Thomas, T. H. 1981. Seed treatments and techniques to improve germination. *Sci. Hort.* **32**: 47–59.

U.S. Department of Agriculture, Forest Service. 1974. *Seeds of Woody Plants of the United States.* USDA Forest Service, Agriculture Handbook No. 450.

Vanstone, D. E., W. G. Ronald & H. H. Marshall. 1982. *Nursery Propagation of Woody and Herbaceous Perennials for the Prairie Provinces.* Publication 1733E, Agriculture Canada, Ottawa.

Vertrees, J. D. 1978. Notes on propagation of certain *Acers*. *Comb. Proc. Inter. Pl. Prop. Soc.* **28**: 93–97.

Wood, A. T. 1979. Nursery production in England. *Comb. Proc. Inter. Pl. Prop. Soc.* **29**: 54–59.

———— . 1982. Propagation from seed. *Proc. 17th Refresher Course for Nurserymen.* Pershore College of Horticulture, Pershore, Worcs., U.K. pp. 17–21.

Chapter 2

PROPAGATION FROM SEED
Greenhouse Production

During the last decade there has been considerable interest in the technique of growing woody plants from seed under glass- or plastic-covered greenhouses. A considerable amount of the technology used has come from both the forestry and the bedding plant industries. The advantages to be gained by growing seedlings in a greenhouse are:—

(i) It provides an alternative facility if open ground conditions are not conducive to good seedling development.

(ii) It is a more suitable facility for small quantities of small seeds and small quantities of plants. For example, species of *Eucalyptus, Gaultheria* (Wintergreen), *Kalmia* (American Laurel) and *Rhododendron* spp.

Figure 2-1.
A flat of young *Rhododendron molle* (Chinese Azalea) seedlings successfully raised from seed.

(iii) It allows the propagator to have much greater control over the environment. For example, increased temperature, increased light intensity and more precise irrigation allow better control of the growth in order to shorten production cycles or to germinate seed at times of the year other than those used for open-ground seed crops.

(iv) It can provide both more crop uniformity and greater crop flexibility.

(v) It enhances the growth and development of seedlings.

However, capital costs for facilities and equipment are higher, as are labor costs, compared to a similar area of land used for open-ground production.

The systems used for raising seedlings of woody ornamentals in a greenhouse may be divided into three categories:—

(i) Floor level beds

(ii) Flats, pots and containers

(iii) Specialized containers

Figure 2-2. Cold frames can be used successfully to raise pot-grown liners from seed. These liners are Snake Bark Maples (e.g., *Acer capillipes; A. davidii,* David Maple; and *A. grosseri* var. *hersii,* Hers' Maple). (Oakover Nurseries, Ashford, Kent, U.K.)

Figure 2-3. Young pot-grown seedlings of Snake Bark Maples. Note the flat used to retain the pots for easier handling. (Tom Wood, Oakover Nurseries, Ashford, Kent, U.K.)

Figure 2-4. Pot-grown liners of *Hamamelis virginiana* (Common Witch Hazel) (left) and *Rhododendron ponticum* (Pontic Rhododendron) (right) for sale as rootstocks for bench grafting.

FLOOR LEVEL BEDS

The first time that I saw walk-in (quonset-type) polyethylene tunnels being used for seedling propagation was in Europe to supplement open-ground production. A group of these structures clad with polyethylene film was being used for seedlings where conventional open-ground techniques produced unsatisfactory results. The seed beds in the houses were designed in a fashion similar to those used in open-ground production. Two specific uses were:—

(i) To increase growth from late sowings of *Gleditsia triacanthos* (Honey Locust), *Liriodendron tulipifera* (Tulip Tree), *Pterocarya fraxinifolia* (Caucasian Wingnut), and *Taxodium distichum* (Common Bald Cypress).

(ii) To sow seed of short viability received from seed houses during the summer, e.g., *Acer rubrum* (Red Maple) (see also p. 62). This was done because the open-ground facility did not have irrigation installed to provide conditions for even germination at this time of year.

There are limitations to this system, including:—

(i) Shoot growth is softer (less lignified) because of the warm humid atmosphere, resulting in insufficient ripening of the wood prior to winter. Seedlings of *Liquidambar styraciflua* (American Sweet Gum) and *Gleditsia triacanthos* (Honey Locust) are particularly prone to die-back in more northerly climates. This problem can be largely overcome by using ventilation in the fall to ensure correct hardening-off.

(ii) There is a greater tendency to induce secondary dormancy into seeds of some species because of the rapid rise in daytime temperatures.

(iii) Mechanization is severely curtailed, e.g., for undercutting and lifting the crop.

(iv) There is often less root development compared to open-ground seedlings, resulting in a lower success rate in subsequent establishment after harvesting.

Some of these problems can be solved by covering the structures with one of the woven polypropylene shade cloth materials rather than with polyethylene film. These woven materials provide much better ventilation and reduce air and soil temperatures, while still providing the desired protection.

Oakover Nurseries, Ashford, Kent, England, are among the nurseries that have used this form of structure very effectively to produce container-grown liners of choicer Maples (e.g., *Acer capillipes* and *Acer grosseri* var. *hersii*, Hers' Maple, of the "Snake Bark" group), *Quercus robur* (English Oak) for amenity planting, and seedling rootstocks for bench grafting (e.g., *Hamamelis virginiana*, Common Witch Hazel).

The maple seeds are germinated in a cold frame, the seedlings potted into 9 cm (3½") pots, packed in trays and then set down in the shade cloth-clad structure. Other species such as *Hamamelis virginiana* (Common Witch Hazel) and *Ginkgo biloba* (Maidenhair Tree) are chitted and sown one seed per 9 cm (3½") pot for growing-on to produce a saleable rootstock to be used for grafting the following January.

The oaks are potted into 7.5 cm (3") peat pots, which are then subsequently plunged into spent hops (a waste by-product from brewing beer) inside the structure. The secret for good root and shoot growth using this system is to ensure that the peat pots are thoroughly soaked with water and that root growth develops as far as possible through the peat pot and into the surrounding spent hops. This is encouraged by covering the structure with polyethylene film for the first six weeks to raise the temperature and humidity. Ample irrigation is provided to promote these conditions. The polyethylene film is removed when the roots have broken through the peat pots, leaving only the shade cloth. The seedlings are then later re-potted into 10 cm (4") diameter × 12.5 cm (5") deep pots ("Long Toms") or 13 cm (5") diameter containers.

FLATS, POTS AND CONTAINERS

The greenhouse propagation of seedlings germinated in various types of flats, pots and containers is particularly useful for:—

(i) Large-scale production of species for ground cover production, e.g., *Gaultheria procumbens* (Creeping Wintergreen).

(ii) Small quantities of a wide range of species for the smaller specialist nursery, plant collector, or botanical garden. Propagators of alpine plants, for example, use a combination of greenhouse and cold frames to raise their seedlings.

(iii) One-year production systems for pot-grown rootstocks, e.g., *Betula pendula* (European White Birch) and *Alnus glutinosa* (Black or Common Alder) (see p. 525). This is a convenient technique that can provide a large number of straight-stemmed rootstocks as compared to the conventional two-year cycle following sowing in an open-ground seed bed (i.e., potting one-year open-ground seedlings for a further season of growth prior to grafting).

Seed Sowing Media

There is a wide range of recommended seed sowing media to be found in various books. Many propagators make their own adaptations to these to specifically suit certain species. The propagator should, however, try to standardize the media as much as possible, so that a minimum of changes have to be made for various species of plants.

A standard seed sowing medium formula that has proved successful at the University of British Columbia (UBC) Botanical Garden, Vancouver, is as follows:—

1 part—Sieved Sphagnum Peat Moss
1 part—Perlite
1 part—Sterilized Loam

To each m³ (cu. yd.) of the above add:—

1160 g (31.2 oz) Superphosphate
 580 g (15.6 oz) Dolomitic Limestone
 110 g (2.9 oz) Ethazol (Truban®)

NOTES:

(i) Ethazol (Truban®) is used to prevent damping-off disease infection. It should be thoroughly mixed with the superphosphate and dolomitic limestone before incorporation with the three bulk components to ensure that it is evenly mixed in the medium.

(ii) A nitrogen-based fertilizer is not incorporated into this medium. Rapid-growing seedlings are pricked out shortly after germination. Slower-growing seedlings are watered every two weeks with a soluble fertilizer containing a 20-20-20 ratio at half the recommended rate.

There are two modifications to this basic formula that may be made for ericaceous species and plants that are prone to damping-off:—

(i) Add an extra part of milled sphagnum moss to the basic constituents.

(ii) Place a 6 mm (¼″) layer of milled sphagnum moss on top of the medium in the flat or container and sow the seed onto this.

The benefits of the sphagnum moss are two-fold. Firstly, it acts as an inhibitor to the development of damping-off diseases and, secondly, it helps to retain moisture around the seed.

Types of Flats and Containers

It is best to use conventional seed flats with a minimum depth of 7.5 cm (3″). A successful method for deeper-rooting species with a tendency to produce a tap root (for example, *Magnolia grandiflora*, Southern Magnolia, and *Camellia japonica,* Common Camellia) is to increase the depth of the flat to 10–12.5 cm (4–5″) and replace the wooden base with a copper gauze sheet. Four or five wooden slats are attached under the copper gauze to raise the flat about 1.3 cm (½″) above the bench. This air space encourages air pruning (see p. 91), which helps the formation of lateral roots. I have seen this type of tray with a depth of 7.5 cm (3″) used very successfully as a standard flat for propagating tree, shrub and conifer seeds on nurseries. Other types of sowing containers include half-flats and 10.0 cm (4″) square pots—the latter being particularly useful for the numerous small amounts of different types of seeds received at the UBC Botanical Garden nursery.

Figure 2-5. Deep flats are suitable for raising many species of woody trees and shrubs.

Figure 2-6. Seedlings of *Camellia japonica* (Common or Japanese Camellia) show a strong tendency to produce a dominant tap root which must be pruned in order to encourage the development of lateral roots.

Procedures for Sowing

Procedures for sowing seed in flats are well-documented, with recommendations ranging from those for nurseries producing large quantities of bedding plants to ones for those specializing in alpines. However, it is worth itemizing the main points of the procedures used.

1. Ensure that the medium is firm at the corners and sides of the flat. Overall firming should be gentle.

2. The surface of the medium must be level.

3. Allow for sufficient watering space between the top of the flat and the surface of the medium.

4. Water the flats and allow to drain for at least two hours before sowing to bring the medium up to field capacity.

5. Make a visual assessment of the amount and size of seed before sowing to save any embarrassment in seed sowing rates—especially when sowing from seed packets.

6. Sow the seed evenly. It is better to under-sow than over-sow. Work as near to the surface of the medium as practical when sowing.

7. Mix very small seed with a small quantity of dry sand to make sowing easier.

8. Use a fungicidal seed dressing if damping-off diseases are a problem.

9. Standardize the method of sowing so that the quality of the end result is improved. This can be done in one of the following ways:—

(i) Sow from a packet, using the first and second finger to gently tap the seeds from the open end.

(ii) Place the seeds in the palm of one hand, pick them up with the thumb and first two fingers of the other hand and broadcast over the surface of the medium. Larger seeds can be space-sown—the seeds are placed an equal distance apart, for example, 9 × 7 giving a total of 63 seeds in a medium-sized flat.

(iii) Place the seeds in the palm of the open hand and gently tap one side of the hand with the fingers of the other, so the seeds slowly fall onto the medium.

10. Cover the seed to a depth of about twice its diameter. The covering can be applied evenly by passing the medium through a hand sieve.

11. Leave small seeds such as *Eucalyptus* and *Rhododendron* uncovered.

12. Label the flat with the name of the plant, the date of sowing, and any other information dictated by nursery policy.

Figure 2-7.
Well-labelled pots containing small quantities of woody plant seeds sent to a plant collector from different regions of the world.

Aftercare

The medium should not dry out and any covering material used to cut out the light should be removed as soon as the seedlings break the surface of the medium. The flats or containers should be lightly misted after sowing, placed in a greenhouse with the air temperature set at around 16°C (60°F). The seed can be covered with a pre-cut section of shade cloth to cut out the light and reduce the water requirements. Another method is to use a sheet of glass that is, in turn, covered by a sheet of brown paper. The containers should be checked once or twice daily for watering needs and signs of damping-off diseases, with the appropriate action taken to remedy these problems should they arise.

Two excellent booklets describing seed sowing and pricking-off procedures, although orientated to bedding-plant production, are the trainee guides *Sowing Seed into Seed Boxes* and *Pricking-off into Containers* (Agricultural Training Board, 32-34 Beckenham Road, Beckenham, Kent, BR3 4PB, England).

SEED SOWING PROCEDURES AT THE UNIVERSITY OF BRITISH COLUMBIA BOTANICAL GARDEN

The following description of the procedures used at the University of British Columbia Botanical Garden relates specifically to woody plants, and is intended to provide information particularly for botanical garden propagators and the "plantsman nurseryman". The procedures are those currently used by Charles Tubesing, Propagator at the UBC Botanical Garden Nursery.

Accession of Seed Received

Seed is received from collectors and botanical gardens throughout the world, especially Asia. Numerous small quantities arrive throughout the year so it is vital to have a systematic accession procedure by plant species.

The first procedure when the seed arrives at the Nursery is to complete a Plant Accession form to feed information to the computerized B.G.A.S. (Botanical Garden Accession System) terminal.

This format can be simplified and adapted to other botanical garden and nursery situations where appropriate. The card or form should have sufficient space to make notes on the overall handling, pre-sowing treatment(s) and germination success. This type of input form provides an invaluable long-term record—particularly for rare and/or relatively unknown plant material.

TABLE 2-1. Example of Plant Accession Form Used at the University of British Columbia Botanical Garden, Vancouver, B.C.

BOTANICAL NAME	*Ampelopsis vitifolia*					v.	FAMILY NAME	*VITACEAE*

GEOGRACODE (ORIGIN)					REC'D. AS SEED	QUANTITY 8	DAY / MONTH / YEAR 13 / 8 / 82	PRESENT LOCATION 8	WANTED FOR AREA 3a

SOURCE 0 5 2 — Botanical Garden of Duschanbe Karamova, USSR

OTHER NUMBERS

NO. OF LABELS 2

MAXIMUM QTY. REQUIRED 3

ACCESSION NUMBER 30002 - 052 - 82

EX.

PROPAGATION:

sown 1 Nov. 82 — cold frame
germinated 11 Apr. 83 — 5 seedlings total
4 pricked out 25 Apr. 83

1

Handling of Seed

The seed is re-packed properly in a Ziploc® moisture-tight polyethylene bag if not received from the sender in this manner. To save re-sorting at sowing time, these small packets of seed are grouped together into larger polyethylene bags for fall or spring sowing, or when a specific pre-sowing treatment is required. Seed that is not to be sown immediately is stored in a refrigerator set at 5°C (41°F).

Sowing

All seeds are sown in either 45 × 30 × 10 cm (18 × 12 × 4″) flats or 10 cm (4″) square containers. Some species are sown in the fall and the flats or containers placed down in a cold frame to over-winter. Fall sowing is used for species that require a short-term cold stratification period, e.g., *Sorbus reducta*.

Seed sown in the spring is kept in the greenhouse for germination. Spring sowing is used for:—

(i) Those species that require a more specific treatment to overcome dormancy, e.g., *Cornus* (Dogwood) and *Magnolia*.

(ii) Those that have few or no dormancy requirements, e.g., *Buddleia* (Butterflybush), *Hydrangea, Sorbaria* (False Spiraea), *Spiraea* (Spirea) and *Schizophragma* (Hydrangea Vine).

Sowing Medium and Covering of Seed.

The seed sowing medium used is that recommended on p. 84.

Two methods are followed after the flats or pots have been filled with the seed sowing medium. A thin layer of milled sphagnum moss is placed over the regular sowing medium for ericaceous and other non-dormant small seeds. The seeds are sown directly onto the milled sphagnum moss and are not covered with medium. A pane of glass is placed over the top of the pot or flat to retain moisture. It is important to keep the surface moist until germination occurs.

Larger seeds are sown onto the medium, covered with a sifting of the medium, and then top-dressed with a 1.5 mm (1/16″) layer of coarse silica sand. This top-dressing helps to protect the surface of the medium from disturbance (rain splash) as well as deterring the growth of mosses and liverworts. This method is used for all seeds except those sown on top of sphagnum.

Labelling

Each flat or pot is labelled as soon as it is sown. Two types of labels are used—a record label and an information label. The record label is inserted in every container, with the information label sometimes being used as well.

(i) Record Label—This is color coded to the garden area in which the plant is to be used (e.g., Orange is Asian Garden and Yellow is Alpine Garden). On the label is written the sowing date and botanical name of the plant. The number of plants required is indicated on the reverse side of the label. The germination date and total number of seedlings obtained are also recorded on the reverse of the label for later transference to the permanent record card.

(ii) Information Label—This label is green and is used only when it is necessary to include information pertinent to the care of the plant, e.g., Half-hardy (requires frost protection), ericaceous medium, etc.

Aftercare

The containers are placed on the bench in a greenhouse with a minimum air temperature of 16°C (60°F). Seed covered with a sheet of glass or polyethylene is shaded to avoid temperature build-up. The containers are checked twice daily and watered with a hand-regulated pressure fogging nozzle as necessary.

A series of high-pressure sodium lamps are installed above the benches and are used if necessary to both increase the intensity of light and extend the day length as required to encourage increased growth of the seedlings.

Figure 2-8. A (left). A section of a well-equipped botanical garden propagation unit showing the metal bench installation and high pressure sodium vapor lamps used for initial growing-on of the many species of plants received from different countries. (Charles Tubesing and Elaine LeMarquand, University of British Columbia Botanical Garden, Vancouver, B.C., Canada) B (right above). Small square pots retained in flats are ideal for raising small quantities of seed. Note the coarse sand (grit) used to cover the seed and the recently germinated *Clethra* sp. seedlings. C (right below). Ericaceous species are raised successfully by sowing onto milled sphagnum moss without covering the seed afterwards. Note the use of shade cloth to cover the newly germinated seedlings and the systematic labelling of each pot.

Seeds that have not germinated after the expected time lapse following sowing are moved from the greenhouse to the cold frame. They remain in the cold frame for up to two subsequent winters. The container is then discarded if no seedlings have germinated during that period. The traditional practice of placing seed in cold frames should not be forgotten as the natural cold and warm temperature cycle during the year can sometimes result in ultimate success. When germination occurs, the container is brought immediately into the greenhouse or adjacent polyethylene structure so that a closer watch can be kept on the seedlings for water requirements and damping-off diseases.

INTENSIVE CONTAINER SEEDLING PRODUCTION
(ACCELERATED GROWING)

Intensive container seedling production is the production of seedlings under a partially or fully controlled environment, where temperature, humidity, light intensity and day length can be regulated. The level of carbon dioxide is also increased in some instances. The saleable product is a small seedling with the root system retained in and around a "plug" of growing medium.

Scandinavia and North America have led the field in developing the technology necessary for the intensive production of seedlings in containers. The system has been adopted for the production of large quantities of forest trees for re-forestation programs in the Northern Hemisphere. It is currently being effectively used in western Canada for *Thuja plicata* (Western Red Cedar), *Pseudotsuga menziesii* (Douglas Fir), *Abies grandis* (Grand Fir), *Tsuga heterophylla* (Western Hemlock), *Picea sitchensis* (Sitka Spruce), and *Picea glauca* (White Spruce).

There is limited published information on the practical procedures used for intensive container seedling production of ornamental and native plants compared to published material on conifers and some deciduous trees. Therefore, a system used to raise coniferous seedlings in a forest nursery will be outlined. This will help you to understand the basic principles and techniques, and provide a basis on which to commence growing ornamentals, rootstocks and native plants in a similar fashion. *Betula* spp. (Birch), *Alnus* (Alder), and some *Acer* (Maple) and *Quercus* (Oak) have been particularly responsive to accelerated growing.

Figure 2-9. Many native species of Alberta and British Columbia are successfully raised for planting in reclamation sites by adopting the principles used for the production of coniferous trees for reforestation. (Reid Collins Nurseries, Aldergrove, B.C.)

This section is based very largely on techniques and procedures used by Reid Collins Nurseries, Aldergrove, B.C., and on those documented in publications from the British Columbia Ministry of Forests. However, the individual approach to intensive container seedling production is likely to vary from nursery to nursery. Reid Collins Nurseries have produced millions of seedlings for the forestry industry. They have also successfully adapted the system to grow both ornamental and native plants in multi-bay, environmentally-controlled greenhouses clad with polyethylene film.

A research program investigating intensive seedling production was carried out at the Forestry Department, Michigan State University, East Lansing. They subsequently termed this method of growing seedlings of woody plants as Accelerated-Growth (A/G). They found that growth rates could be dramatically improved by using suitable seed provenances and by manipulating temperature and light. For example, seedlings of *Betula pendula* (European White Birch) reached a height of 1 m (40″) and *Juglans nigra* (Black Walnut) reached 1.17 m (46″) within ten weeks of sowing. The extended daylength period was altered according to the species.

The benefits of increased growth rate must be evaluated against costs, compensating natural dormancy requirements, and establishment and growth following planting out before using the system on the nursery.

The advantages of intensive container seedling production over bare-root (open-ground) production are:—

(i) Greater control of the growth rate of the seedlings resulting in more uniform shoot and root systems. Dormancy problems relating to shoot and root growth are more easily overcome.

(ii) The production period is very much shorter than conventional open-ground techniques. It is even possible to produce two crops per year in the same greenhouse because saleable crops can be produced within six months versus one to two years in open ground.

(iii) The containers result in the root system forming a "plug" with the surrounding growing medium and it is possible to both extend the planting season and improve establishment success rates. The root system is protected during the handling stages from the nursery to the planting site.

There are disadvantages of intensive container seedling production, three of which are:—

(i) The initial capital investment for structures, benching, and control mechanisms is high.

(ii) Staff have to be re-trained to adapt to a new production system.

(iii) There is greater susceptibility to, and rapid spread of, certain diseases.

In reality, the nursery owner will probably find that the first two disadvantages will present few problems. The existing propagation or production greenhouses can often be utilized with little modification and an already trained staff person will adapt easily to the new system.

Pre-Germination Treatments

Seed dormancy and techniques used to overcome germination problems have already been explained (see p. 32). However, some nurseries use specific procedures on forest seed for container-grown seedlings.

A good example of this are the recommendations issued by the Ministry of Forests in British Columbia. Each seed lot that is sent out by the Ministry is labelled with basic data to assist the nursery operators. These data include source, species, weight of seed, sowing rate (number of seeds per cavity), any pesticide treatment, and the period of stratification where applicable. However, in some cases the stated percentage germination rate is not attained under greenhouse conditions.

It is advisable to carry out a germination test for each batch of seed by sowing a sample in flats kept in a greenhouse for 21–24 days. The appropriate stratification treatment should be given to the sample prior to testing.

If time does not allow germination test before the crop is sown, then sow three Styroblocks (or similar cavity container) with one seed only per cavity. The subsequent germination test can then be checked against the viability stated by the supplier.

The following procedure is advised if the seed arrives dry and unstratified:—

1. Soak the seed for 24 hours by placing it in a polyethylene bag containing water.

2. Drain the water from the bag and surface dry the seed on a mesh screen or a moisture-absorbent paper such as blotting paper.

3. Place the seed back into the polyethylene bag, insert a 6 mm (¼″) diameter plastic tube into the bag to ensure aeration, and tie the neck of the bag tightly. A short length of the tube should extend out of the bag. Place the bag and contents in a refrigerator at 2°C (35°F), and turn the seed each day.

4. Recommended stratifying periods by the British Columbia Ministry of Forests are 21 days for *Pseudotsuga menziesii* (Douglas Fir) and *Picea* spp. (Spruce); 28 days for *Pinus contorta* var. *latifolia* (Lodgepole Pine), *P. ponderosa* (Ponderosa Pine), *Tsuga heterophylla* (Western Hemlock) and *T. mertensiana* (Mountain Hemlock); and 60 days for *Abies* spp. (Fir). Seed of *Thuja plicata* (Western Red Cedar) requires no stratification.

5. Condensation may form on the inside of the polyethylene bags after removal from the refrigerator, resulting in too much moisture on the seed coat surface. The seed must be re-dried on a mesh screen or moisture-absorbent material.

TABLE 2-2. Pre-Sowing Cold Moist Stratification Periods for Coniferous Species.

SPECIES	STRATIFICATION PERIOD (DAYS)
Abies grandis (Grand Fir) (eastern form)	30
Abies grandis (Grand Fir) (western form)	60
Abies procera (Noble Fir)	30
Picea abies (Norway Spruce)	21
Picea glauca (White Spruce)	21
Picea omorika (Serbian Spruce)	14–28
Picea pungens (Colorado Blue Spruce)	14–28
Pinus contorta var. *latifolia* (Lodgepole Pine)	21–28
Pinus mugo var. *mugo* (Mugo Pine)	21
Pinus mugo var. *pumilio* (Shrubby Mugo Pine)	21
Pinus nigra (Austrian or Black Pine)	21–28
Pinus sylvestris (Scots Pine)	7–21
Pseudotsuga menziesii (Douglas Fir) (coastal B.C. provenances)	21
Pseudotsuga menziesii (Douglas Fir) (interior B.C. provenances)	30
Sequoia sempervirens (Coast Redwood) (coastal U.S. provenances)	21
Sequoiadendron giganteum (Giant Sequoia) (interior U.S. provenances)	28
Tsuga canadensis (Canadian Hemlock)	60
Tsuga heterophylla (Western Hemlock)	28

Source:—Reid Collins Nurseries, Aldergrove, British Columbia, Canada.

Unit Containers (see also Chapter 5)

There is a wide selection of containers available, differing in price, design and durability. Various trade names are given to the type of container, such as Leach Tube®, Multipot®, Styroblock®, McConkey Deepot®, Spencer-Lemaire®, and Paperpot. Several of these products also have a number of accessories to make handling and marketing more efficient—such as trays, seed sowing machines and block loaders. (Chapter 5 on Unit Containers provides information on these and other types of containers suitable for seed propagation.)

Some nurseries market seedlings based on the container production system implemented at that nursery. Two examples are A/G Plants (A/G meaning Accelerated-Growth) marketed by Van Pines Inc., West Olive, Michigan, and Gro-Plugs®, a registered name for the plants sold by Evergreen Nursery Co. Inc., Sturgeon Bay, Wisconsin. The Gro-Plug® system differs from the other systems in that the seeds are germinated in flats and then transplanted into the cavity of the container, rather than being sown directly into the container.

The aim of all these containers is to produce a stable "plug" of growing medium and roots that does not break up when handled, thus ensuring effective establishment of the transplanted seedlings.

Most of these containers or blocks are designed to control root system development. They are normally tapered and have vertical ribs or grooves on the inside to direct the root system vertically down the plug of growing medium. There is an opening at the base of the container to:—

(i) Facilitate drainage.

(ii) Encourage the roots to shrivel as they emerge through the base of the container. This is usually referred to as "air pruning". "Air pruning" promotes secondary root growth and reduces the incidence of root spiralling (root curl or root circling), which develops when the root system builds up in a circular fashion at the base of the container. This deformity of the root system may cause instability of the trees in subsequent years.

"Air pruning" is further encouraged by standing the sets or blocks of containers on a galvanized wire mesh bench or by raising the blocks at least 15 cm (6") above the surface of a solid bench.

(iii) Encourage good aeration of the growing medium.

There is a wide range of products available, and it is therefore strongly recommended that samples of the different containers be obtained and tested to determine which one is best suited for your own requirements. The following points can help in determining the container to choose:—

1. Market outlet for the crop (customer requirements).

2. Plant species being grown.

3. Cost and availability.

4. Storage space. Some containers are shipped flat and are expanded as required, while others are rigid and can take up a considerable amount of storage space.

5. Durability. Some containers, e.g., Paperpot, must be re-purchased for each crop, while others, e.g., Spencer-Lemaire Rootrainer® and Styroblock®, can be re-used for two to four years. Rigid plastic containers such as the Can-Am®, Hiko®, Leach Tube® and McConkey Deepot® should last for many years.

6. Ease of handling on the nursery, and the degree of mechanization required for the production system.

Figure 2-10. Can-Am® (top left) and Hiko® (bottom left) multipots being used to grow quality seedlings of *Picea glauca* (White Spruce) and *Thuja plicata* (Western Red Cedar). *Gleditsia japonica* var. *koraiensis* seed germinated successfully in McConkey Deepots® (right).

Types and Uses of Containers

The types and uses of unit containers for intensive seedling production can be illustrated by outlining three different types popular in Canada. Moulded plastic unit containers are popular in many areas of the United States.

Rootrainer® and Rootmaster® (Spencer-Lemaire Container)

This container, sometimes referred to as a "book planter", was designed by Hank Spencer of Spencer-Lemaire Industries Ltd., Edmonton, Alberta, and has been very successful for growing seedlings for re-forestation programs. The use of Rootrainers® has been extended to native plant production, establishment of plant material from micropropagation laboratories, propagation of exotic greenhouse plants, and the rooting of hardwood and softwood cuttings of ornamental shrubs.

Rootrainers® are designed to interlock at the top when assembled, providing a single row of individual cavities. The assembled containers are first packed vertically into a deep-sided plastic tray. The growing medium is then placed into the cavities and the seed is sown. The trays are then placed directly onto the greenhouse bench. The seedlings are removed by taking the container from the tray and simply spreading it open. It is important to remove the growing medium from around the edges of the retaining trays to prevent build-up of mosses and lichens.

Figure 2-11. *Picea Pungens* (Colorado Spruce) growing in Rootrainers® held in a rigid plastic flat.

Figure 2-12. The root system development of *Thuja plicata* (Western Red Cedar) grown in Rootrainers®. Note the air space at the base of the cavity to encourage air pruning of the roots.

They are particularly useful in British Columbia for *Thuja plicata* (Western Red Cedar) and *Chamaecyparis nootkatensis* (Yellow Cedar) because the vigorous root systems of these plants will actually grow into retaining walls made of soft material, thus making it difficult to extract the plugs. A distinct advantage of the Spencer-Lemaire container is that the "book" can be opened at various phases during the production cycle to assess root development and moisture content.

Good air pruning does not always occur with *Thuja plicata* (Western Red Cedar) in Rootrainers® because roots form at the base of the container and travel from one cavity to another.

Styroblock®

The Styroblocks that are currently widely used in British Columbia resulted from a research program initiated in the 1960s to provide increased numbers of coniferous seedlings for re-forestation programs. The block development program was initiated jointly by the Canadian Forestry Service, B.C. Ministry of Forests and the University of British Columbia. The annual production of plug seedlings was estimated to be 70 million in 1985. A blueprint publication, *Seedling Production for Crown Lands in British Columbia—Guideline for Commercial Container Nurseries* by Glen Matthews, is available from the B.C. Ministry of Forests. Nursery operators wishing to use or adapt the Styroblock system are well advised to refer to this publication before making any decisions.

Styroblocks are approximately 30 × 60 cm (1 × 2′) rectangular polystyrene (Styrofoam®) containers with a set number of tapering cavities in which the seedlings are grown. A widely-used specification recommended for conifer species is P.S.B. 313 (4A) which has a cavity diameter at the surface of 2.7 cm (1/12″), tapering to a 1.3 cm (½″) space at the base. The depth of cavity is 13.3 cm (5¼″), and there are 198 cavities in the block.

Styroblocks are preferred to Paperpots in British Columbia because the plug is longer and therefore gives better establishment, particularly in drier exposed areas. They are easy to use because there is no assembly necessary to form the unit, but they do take up considerable storage space. Temperature variation within the block is kept low because the Styrofoam® insulates the growing medium and reflects light.

Figure 2-13. A well-grown crop of *Tsuga heterophylla* (Western Hemlock) germinated in a Styroblock®.

Figure 2-14. The plug and root system development of *Thuja plicata* (Western Red Cedar) seedling germinated in a Styroblock®

Paperpot

The concept of biodegradeable Paperpots was developed in Japan for the sugar beet industry. Since then, there has been diverse use and application in both horticulture and forestry. Finland adapted the technique for its forest industry, with many millions of seedlings now being raised annually in them. They are satisfactory in eastern Canada for re-forestation with *Picea mariana* (Black Spruce) and *Pinus banksiana* (Jack Pine). They have not always been satisfactory in the drier areas of British Columbia because the paper has not degraded properly, thus restricting the development of the root system following outdoor planting. They are very suitable for raising native plants and ornamentals from seed—particularly for container production. They are also used successfully for rooting softwood, semi-ripe wood and evergreen and deciduous hardwood cuttings.

The Paperpots are formed by expanding "flat-sets" to produce a series of bottomless containers with a retaining wall of paper. Each hexagonal unit is sealed with insoluble glue while the adjoining unit is attached by a water-soluble glue. The use of the water-soluble glue means that each unit separates under the moist conditions in the propagation area.

They are available in three grades of biodegradable paper. The grade used depends on the required propagation period. Paper grades are as follows:—

Grade B—Prevents inter-rooting for 4–6 weeks

Grade V—Prevents inter-rooting for 6–12 weeks

Grade F—Prevents inter-rooting for 9–12 months

Figure 2-15. *Picea pungens* (Colorado Spruce) germinated in the biodegradable Paperpot.

Grade F is used for forestry. The hexagonal units are available in a variety of sizes. One popular size is 408—each individual unit is 3 cm (1¼") wide and 8 cm (3") deep, with a total of either 192 or 336 units in each set.

The expanded sets are placed either in pre-fabricated plastic trays or home-made trays of galvanized mesh with wooden sides, and are held in position with clips. The trays are taken to the greenhouse after the seed is sown. The degree of sophistication attained with the Paperpot system largely depends on the capital available and the volume of production. The ancillary equipment includes automated filling and seed sowers, conveyors, and handling and planting gear. As with Styroblocks, one advantage of these Paperpots is that they can be conveniently carried in a basket with a shoulder strap for planting with a Pottiputki planting tube, a foot-operated planting unit.

A recent product is the P.S. Paperpot which is currently being evaluated in commercial nurseries in North America. This Paperpot is designed for seedlings that must remain in the nursery for more than one year. The P.S. Paperpot is made of a thin plastic which is peeled off when planting or packing the seedlings for shipment. A thin copper strip is impregnated in the plastic to deter the seedlings from rooting through to the adjacent cell during the nursery production phase.

Growing Medium and Nutrition

It is important to obtain advice from the local extension service before formulating the growing medium for seedlings. A small error in the formulation and application of the nutritional levels can be extremely detrimental to the young soft seedlings growing in a container where root development is restricted.

There are ready-mixed, commercial growing media that are specifically formulated for intensive container seedling production of conifers. It may be more convenient for a nursery beginning intensive production to simply purchase one of these media.

If you wish to mix your own medium, a successful formulation used in British Columbia for conifer seedlings is described below.

> 3 parts—Sphagnum Peat Moss
> 1 part —Vermiculite

To each m³ (cu. yd.) of the above add:—

> 3.5–4.0 kg (6–7 lb)—Osmocote 18-6-12
> 3.0　　kg (5 lb)　—Dolomitic Limestone (100% thro #12 mesh) (for Ca and Mg)

For convenience, proprietary liquid feed fertilizers are to be recommended, particularly for the beginner. For example, Peters® Conifer Grower formulations which contain major, minor and trace elements and sold as Conifer Starter (7-40-17), Conifer Grower (20-7-19) and Conifer

Finisher (4-25-35). The timing of changing from one formulation to the next largely depends on the stage of crop growth, the species and the location. It is advisable to do a routine foliar analysis in early to mid-summer to check the nutritional status of the crop.

Nurseries have successfully used liquid feeding programs in which the fertilizer is injected into the irrigation supply. Compounds with ratios of 10-52-17 and 20-20-20 (trace elements incorporated) and ferrous sulfate have been used. The 10-52-17 compound is used at 625 g/1000 l (25 oz/300 U.S. gal) in spring and fall, while the 20-20-20 is used at 500 g/1000 l (20 oz/300 U.S. gal) in summer. Three to four applications a week are advised. Slower-growing species requiring a boost in the summer are given a twice weekly feeding of ammonium sulfate (21-0-0) at 325 g/1000 l (13 oz/300 U.S. gal). Ferrous sulfate can be applied twice weekly at 150 g/1000 l (6 oz/300 U.S. gal) to help maintain foliage color. It is essential to determine the nutritional status of the seedlings and the salt concentration of the growing medium at weekly intervals.

Seed Sowing

The cavities in the Styroblocks are filled with the growing medium which is then lightly firmed to leave a space of 1.0 cm (⅜") to accommodate the seed and sand cover.

For large-scale production, precision sowing is carried out using a vacuum-type seed sowing apparatus that can drop either individual or multiple seeds into each cavity. One such machine has a series of inter-changeable revolving drums for different seed sizes. The filled containers are placed on a conveyor and move under the drum to receive the seed.

A convenient sowing method for smaller operations is to use manually-operated shutters made of wood or plexiglass (a clear, strong, rigid plastic). These shutters have a series of inter-changeable plates, and are capable of seeding 100,000 cavities per day.

It may be necessary to hand sow seeds that are irregular in shape (e.g., *Thuja plicata*, Western Red Cedar) to ensure accurate sowing rates.

It is important to know the viability of the seed at the time of sowing, particularly when sowing one seed per cavity, otherwise there could later be a number of empty cavities. Sowing 2–4 seeds per cavity does help to prevent wasted space, but extra labor is needed later to reduce the number of seedlings to one per cavity.

The table has been adapted from one issued in 1986 by the British Columbia Ministry of Forests and provides guidelines with relation to percentage viability and the number of seeds to be sown per cavity.

TABLE 2-3. Container Sowing Rates (1986)

GERMINATION	SOWING FACTOR (# seeds per cavity)	CORRECTION FACTOR (# cavities sown)
100–96	2	1.25
95–93	2	1.30
92–90	2	1.35
89–86	2	1.40
85–81	3	1.30
80–76	3	1.35
75–71	3	1.40
70–66	3	1.45
65–61	4	1.50
60–56	4	1.55
55–51	4	1.60
50–46	4	1.65

Source: Silviculture Branch, B.C. Ministry of Forests, Victoria, B.C.

After sowing the seeds are covered by washed coarse sand (grit). The sand cover holds the seed in place, ensures adequate aeration during germination, and helps to reduce the formation of mosses and liverworts on the surface of the medium. A seed cover of 1 cm (⅜") should be used for large seeds, reducing the depth to 6 mm (¼") for small seeds.

Figure 2-16. Conifer seed being deposited into the cavities of a manually-operated plexiglass shutter unit.

Figure 2-17. Seed being sown into a Styroblock® using a manually-operated plexiglass shutter unit.

Figure 2-18. A crew hand-sowing seed of *Thuja plicata* (Western Red Cedar) into Styroblocks®. (Reid Collins Nurseries, Aldergrove, B.C., Canada)

Figure 2-19. A simple method of hand-sowing the optimum number of *Thuja plicata* (Western Red Cedar) seeds into each cavity of the Styroblock®.

Figure 2-20. A hand dispenser for covering hand-sown seed with coarse sand (grit).

Figure 2-21. Newly-germinated conifer seedlings growing in a well-designed polyethylene greenhouse. (Reid Collins Nurseries, Aldergrove, B.C., Canada)

Irrigation

The containers are placed end to end on greenhouse benches after the seed is sown, and then misted. The source of water must be free of harmful salts and diseases. A chemical and disease analysis must be carried out if there is any doubt, and the pH level of the growing medium should be monitored. Irrigation water should be tested weekly for both salts and pH levels.

Water requirements are high after germination. For example, a Styroblock® tray of seedlings may need 2.25 l (0.5 U.S. gal) up to 4 times per week in summer. Determining the optimum frequency and duration of irrigation requirements needs considerable experience as the seedlings are extremely subject to checks in growth caused by stress from lack of water.

The correct irrigation regime should be related to individual species. Excessive watering will encourage weak top growth instead of balanced stem and root growth in some species, e.g., *Pseudotsuga menziesii* (Douglas Fir), *Picea sitchensis* (Sitka Spruce), *Larix* (Larch) and *Thuja plicata* (Western Red Cedar), while *Tsuga heterophylla* (Western Hemlock) is very prone to crop damage in an excessively dry irrigation regime.

Instead of permanent irrigation lines, large-scale operations sometimes install a moving overhead irrigation gantry over the beds to automate watering. An example of such a system is the Travelling Irrigator supplied by Growing Systems Inc., 2950 North West Street, Milwaukee, Wisconsin, 53212, U.S.A., which is available in either manually or electronically operated versions. It produces either fine moist water droplets for the early stages of crop growth (normally up to when the seed coats fall off the young seedlings) or larger droplets for normal irrigation. Large water droplets or excess water pressure dislodge the sand cover. Exposure of the growing medium facilitates the spread of mosses and liverworts. Pesticides and fertilizers can also be applied with the boom.

Figure 2-22. Uneven distribution of water from the misting system can dislodge the coarse sand cover, resulting in variable seedling growth.

Figure 2-23. An automatic overhead boom moves down the greenhouse to irrigate the conifer seedlings.

Thinning

Each tray must be carefully examined 4–8 weeks after germination and the number of seedlings in each cavity reduced to one. Early thinning could lead to a repeat operation due to late germinating seeds.

Moss and Liverwort Control

Moss and liverwort build-up in the cavities impedes successful crop growth because of competition for water and nutrients. Spread is accentuated in greenhouses due to overhead irrigation, high humidity and increased day length.

The coarse sand layer over the seed helps to prevent the establishment of mosses and liverworts. However, moss and liverwort establishment is encouraged if the sand is not allowed to dry because of excessive irrigation.

Before sowing, a thorough greenhouse sanitation and clean-up program using bleach is necessary. Benches, floor areas, pathways and sides of greenhouses are sprayed to prevent the spread of mosses and liverworts.

Care should be taken when chemicals are used to control mosses and liverworts because young seedlings, particularly *Tsuga heterophylla* (Western Hemlock), are very sensitive to foliage and stem damage. It is strongly recommended that some initial trials are carried out at the nursery to assess crop sensitivity. A chemical program should be implemented as a preventative measure rather than to control established moss and liverwort. A useful preventative spray program has been carried out using dodine acetate (Cyprex®) at 2 gm per litre (0.26 oz/1 U.S. gal) every 2–3 weeks following germination.

Figure 2-25. Development of moss is encouraged by water droplets that are too large or if there is insufficient coarse sand cover around the perimeter of the cavity. The coarse sand cover is dislodged and the growing medium exposed in such situations.

Figure 2-24. Thinning each Styroblock® cavity to one seedling. Accurate assessment of viability and precision sowing will significantly reduce the need to thin.

Figure 2-26. Severe competition to the *Picea pungens* (Colorado Spruce) seedlings is caused by allowing excessive development of liverworts. This should be controlled during the early stages of development.

Shading

Shading is essential when sowing a crop in mid- or late summer, otherwise the seedlings will become severely scorched. A woven shade cloth with a 40–50% shade factor should be adequate. Clear polyethylene can be sprayed with a proprietary shading compound if shade cloth is not installed.

Extending Day Length

The provenance of the seed can have a direct effect on the seedling's response to day length. In British Columbia, seedlings of *Abies lasiocarpa* (Alpine Fir), *Picea* spp. (Spruce) and *Pseudotsuga menziesii* (Douglas Fir) grown in the south from seed collected in either northern or high latitude areas develop a dormant terminal bud due to the shorter daylength before and after mid-summer in southern coastal regions of the Province. This dramatically reduces the growth, but can be prevented by installing lamps, e.g., high pressure sodium (H.P.S.), in the greenhouse to give a light reading for Spruce between 130–165 Lux (12–15 ft. candles) at seedling height. Increasing the duration of light to 18 hours per day allows the crop to continue growing while temperatures are warm as it prevents the formation of dormant terminal buds.

Figure 2-28. Burners to produce CO_2 are sometimes installed in the greenhouse in order to increase seedling quality during the early stages of development under poor light conditions.

Figure 2-27. High-pressure sodium lamps may be used to extend the daylength in order to prevent the early development of dormant terminal buds. (Hybrid Nurseries, Pitt Meadows, B.C., Canada)

Pests and Diseases

In British Columbia, government services must be consulted regarding plant quarantine regulations that make it mandatory to ship plants only within or to specific regions, or to carry out mandatory pesticide application. For example, it is necessary in some regions of British Columbia to spray for Balsam Woolly Aphid (*Adelges piceae*), and true firs may only be propagated and shipped by permit within a restricted area. Similar regulations may be in operation in other localities and must be checked. Particular pests to check are red spider mites, aphids, springtails, root weevils, cutworms and European Pine Shoot Moth (*Rhyacionia buoliana*).

Diseases can present the greatest problem to the nursery because the enclosed environment is ideal for their growth and spread. *Botrytis cinerea* (Gray Mold) can be prevalent, especially on *Thuja plicata* (Western Red Cedar), *Tsuga heterophylla* (Western Hemlock) and *Pseudotsuga menziesii* (Douglas Fir), if there is inadequate ventilation and excess humidity, particularly when combined with low temperatures. Alternating sprays of benomyl (Benlate®) and chlorothalonil (Daconil®) or captan and glycophene (Rovral®) applied at four-week intervals should serve as a good preventative measure. Other diseases affecting seedlings are Sirococcus Blight (*Sirococcus strobilinus*), damping-off diseases (*Fusarium, Pythium* and *Rhizoctonia*), and rusts.

Detailed information on some of these pests and diseases can be obtained from the excellent British Columbia Ministry of Forests publication *Diseases and Insect Pests in British Columbia Forest Nurseries* by J. R. Sutherland and E. van Eerden.

Marketing

Intensive container seedling production in British Columbia is normally done on contract to the provincial government, which has strict specifications as to crop quality. It is essential to carry out daily checks on the crop as lack of water or disease can quickly reduce the growth. A sample of the crop should be measured once a month for height and stem caliper, plus an evaluation of root system development. The seedlings are removed from the cavities in the late fall and winter, gathered into "25-tree units" and wrapped in polyethylene film. The bundles are then packed tightly in strong waxed cardboard boxes and cold stored at −2° to +2°C (28–35°F) until shipping in the spring.

Figure 2-29. The production crop should be assessed monthly for height, caliper and root development. (Reid Collins Nurseries, Aldergrove, B.C., Canada)

Figure 2-30. A quality crop can be produced after one growing season only by daily inspection of the seedlings and quick resolution of any potential problem(s). (Reid Collins Nurseries, Aldergrove, B.C., Canada)

Figure 2-31. A high-quality crop of *Picea glauca* (White Spruce) near the end of the growing season. (Reid Collins Nurseries, Aldergrove, B.C., Canada)

REFERENCES AND SUGGESTED SOURCES FOR FURTHER READING

Gaggini, J. B. 1975. Plastic structures and seedling production. *Nurseryman and Garden Centre*, April 3, 1975, pp. 529–603.

Hanover, J. W., E. Young, W. A. Lemmien & M. van Slouten. 1976. Accelerated-optimal-growth: A new concept in tree production. In: *Mich. Agric. Exp. Sta. Res. Rpt. 317.*

Huber, R. F., Compiler. 1982. Proceedings of the 1981 Intermountain Nurserymen's Association Meeting. *Information Report NOR-X-241*, Northern Forest Research Centre, Canadian Forestry Service, Environment Canada.

Matthews, G. 1982. *Seedling Production for Crown Lands in British Columbia—Guidelines for Commercial Container Nurseries.* Mimeographed Report. British Columbia Ministry of Forests, Victoria, B.C.

Pinney, T. S., Jr. 1980. Gro-Plug® systems and their practical application in growing ornamentals. *Comb. Proc. Inter. Pl. Prop. Soc.* **30**: 312–318.

Spencer, H. 1982. Rootrainers®—"Way to Grow". *Prairie Landscape Magazine* 5(4): 2–3.

Sutherland, J. R. & E. van Eerden. 1980. Diseases and Insect Pests in British Columbia Forest Nurseries. *Joint Report No. 12*, British Columbia Ministry of Forests and Canadian Forestry Service, Victoria, B.C.

van Slooten, M. 1977. Accelerated growth of conifers. *Comb. Proc. Inter. Pl. Prop. Soc.* **27**: 374–377.

Wells, P. 1977. Seedling oak production in containers. *Comb. Proc. Inter. Pl. Prop. Soc.* **27**: 75–78.

Witte, W. T., P. A. Cope and G. S. Smith. 1982. Rapid growth of tree seedlings in bottomless containers under continuous light. *Comb. Proc. Inter. Pl. Prop. Soc.* **32**: 423–427.

SECTION B

Figure 3-1.
Heavily shaded bell-jars
used for winter grafts of
Picea (Spruce) and *Pinus*
(Pine). (Orleans region,
Loire Valley, France)

Figure 3-2. Rooting of *Helianthemum* sp. (Sun or Rock
Rose) under a bell-jar. Note that the handle has been
removed and that a small block of wood is used to tilt
the bell-jar for ventilation. (Orleans region, Loire
Valley, France)

Figure 3-3. Traditional glass lanterns being used for
rooting *Cytisus* (Broom) cuttings.

Chapter 3

PROTECTED PROPAGATION FACILITIES

There have been considerable advances over the last 50 years in the development of protected propagation facilities, ranging from simple adaptions for existing cold frames to sophisticated equipment for dispersing very small particles of water. Today's propagator is able to take full advantage of modern technology (for example, energy saving) to ensure that the facility is both efficient and successful.

There are two fundamental points that the propagator must appreciate initially. Firstly, that it is all very well to carry out the correct procedures for sowing seed, preparing cuttings and grafts but the end result depends on the propagator's ability to fully understand all the aftercare requirements—and this is only learnt by *practical* experience. Secondly, that new sophisticated equipment is not necessarily the best. The simpler facilities used over many decades will often achieve the most successful and economic result. Therefore, this chapter will describe the principles and uses of different protected facilities and the associated equipment that have been and are currently used in propagation of woody ornamental plants.

TRADITIONAL FACILITIES

BELL-JARS

Bell-jars were the traditional method used in some parts of Europe for propagating small quantities of shrubs, conifers, herbaceous perennials and even some alpines. I visited the nursery area in the Loire Valley near Orleans, France, in 1973 and was fascinated to see neat rows of bell-jars still being used on one nursery to root cuttings and to callus conifer grafts.

Bell-jars were made of glass and were round at the base, varying in height up to around 60–75 cm (2–2½'). Thus, they were small enough to be conveniently handled by one person. There was usually a knob on the top of the bell-jar, but this was often removed because it acted as a lens in bright sun, making the cuttings prone to leaf scorch. Traditionally, a 1.3 cm (½") layer of silver sand was placed on top of the rooting medium before the cuttings were stuck. Each bell-jar acted as an individual greenhouse in that the environment around the cutting could be partially controlled. The glass was shaded with whitewash on all but the north-facing side in late spring and summer. Ventilation was provided after rooting by placing a small block of wood under the bottom edge to tilt the bell-jar. A layer of reed mats supported by wire or wood was often placed over the whitewashed bell-jars if extra shading was required for grafts. Some nurseries placed their bell-jars so that they received full sun in the morning and partial shade during the afternoon.

These bell-jars involved considerable hand labor, but provided a useful propagation facility for the small family nursery. A bell-jar, if you can find one, is certainly worth keeping for historical interest.

GLASS LANTERNS

Glass lanterns had metal or wooden frames that held a number of small panes of glass. The lanterns could be circular, square, conical or pyramidal in shape. They were used in a similar fashion to the bell-jars.

BURLAP CLOUD METHOD

The Burlap Cloud method was developed by the respected Canadian propagator Leslie Hancock of Woodland Nurseries, Mississauga, Ontario, based on observations he made in China during the 1920s. It was essentially built of 3.6 m (12') lengths of portable frames covered with burlap (hessian) cloth placed over softwood cuttings stuck in raised beds filled with sifted soil. The sifted soil was saturated with water just before sticking, creating what is best described as a "slurry". Following sticking, the burlap (hessian) was secured across the top of the wooden frames. The burlap cloth was regularly hand-watered to keep it moist and thus create a humid and cooler environment around the cuttings. The frequency of spraying varied according to weather conditions, with the optimum being around six times per day. The burlap was removed after rooting had occurred and was replaced with wooden slatted sections to provide shading.

I visited this nursery in 1968 and was very impressed with the consistent results obtained in rooting many thousands of cuttings using the Burlap Cloud technique. Today, the Burlap Cloud method is still very much an integral part of the production system at Woodland Nurseries.

Figure 3-4. A (Left). The successful results obtained by rooting softwood cuttings using the Burlap Cloud method. B (Right). Note the use of wooden slats in some locations after the removal of the burlap (hessian). (Reproduced by courtesy of Woodlands Nurseries, Mississauga, ON, Canada)

BOLIVAR PIT

The Bolivar Pit technique evolved in the West Indies for rooting cuttings of tropical crops but was considered to have potential uses in more temperate regions. The method involved the construction of a pit some 50 cm (20") deep and up to 6 m (20') wide. A 15–25 cm (6–10") layer of coarse gravel was placed at the bottom of the pit, followed by the rooting medium. The cuttings were stuck and then covered by cotton or burlap (hessian) cloth supported on wires. An overhead water sprinkler was then installed and turned on every two or three hours to keep the cotton or burlap constantly moist. The shade, humidity and reduced air temperatures kept the cuttings turgid and encouraged rooting.

COLD FRAMES

Cold frames have been an important facility for many decades in producing a wide range of crops in the horticulture industry, particularly out-of-season salad and vegetable crops. Cold frames are labor-intensive, but a number of nurseries still use them today for the propagation of woody ornamentals as they provide an excellent, simple, low-cost facility—especially for a small intensive nursery. There have been modifications in design over the years, and propagators have also made their own modifications based on need, so that cold frames can be utilized effectively for an increasing range of plants and types of propagation techniques.

The uses of cold frames for woody ornamentals can be summarized as follows:—

(i) To carry out cold stratification of seed to break seed dormancy (p. 37).

(ii) To germinate seeds of trees, shrubs and conifers. It is particularly useful for small mixed quantities of seedlings intended for rootstock and ornamental use providing that they do not grow too large.

(iii) To root softwood, semi-ripe wood, evergreen hardwood and deciduous hardwood cuttings.

(iv) To harden-off flats of cuttings in a facility adjacent to the propagation greenhouse.

(v) To bed out rooted cuttings to provide bare-root liners or to act as a facility for newly potted cuttings in pot-grown liner production.

(vi) To hold pot-grown rootstocks for subsequent bench grafting in the greenhouse. In addition, they provide an excellent facility for hardening-off bench grafts from the greenhouse prior to planting out in open ground. Cold frames are also useful for over-wintering summer bench grafts, thus enabling the greenhouse to be utilized for late fall to spring propagation. They have proved to be a reliable facility to encourage the union between scion and rootstock following bench grafting.

Figure 3-5. A frame yard with double-span cold frames provides a low-cost facility for pot-grown rootstocks and liners. (W. R. Crowder & Sons, Horncastle, Lincolnshire, U.K.)

Figure 3-6. Utilization of a cold frame for *Camellia* grafts. Note the bamboo rolls for shading. (Angers, France)

Cold frames provide a low-cost, intensive facility, but do have drawbacks. For example, labor intensity, automation and access are sometimes problems; their restricted height limits both the range of plants and the length of time that crops can be grown in them; and they do not provide a convenient walk-in facility like a greenhouse.

Design and Construction of Cold Frames

The traditional cold frame is a brick or wooden rectangular framework around and over an unheated soil base. The removable cover or light is made of panes of glass fitted into a rectangular wooden framework that fits the opening. The lights are made to a standard measurement for simplicity, for example, the traditional "English" light is 180 cm (72") long and 120 cm (48") wide, although there are variations to these dimensions. These "English" lights are heavy to handle, and individual broken panes of glass must often be replaced. Ventilation is provided by placing a wooden block or upturned pot under the edge of the light, or by simply pushing the light back along the wooden runner that it lies on so that it protrudes from the back of the frame. Shading is provided by whitewash, wooden or bamboo cane laths, reed mats or burlap (hessian)—the latter two are also used for providing additional winter protection. "French" lights were similar in construction to the "English" lights but had dimensions of 135 cm (53") × 120 cm (48") or 137 cm (54") × 127 cm (50").

Figure 3-7.
A traditional frame yard with cold frames constructed of brick and designed to accommodate "English" lights. (Maidstone, Kent, U.K.)

A cold frame can be one individual frame or a continuous multiple of up to twenty or more. A single row is referred to as a single-span while an immediate adjoining double row is a double-span. Cold frames are best sited in an east-west orientation to take advantage of maximum sunlight. The lights may be sloped, in which case they should be sloped to the south side.

Figure 3-8.
A section of a double-span cold frame showing the attractively-designed wooden slats for shading. (Exbury Gardens, Exbury, Hampshire, U.K.)

There have been a series of adaptations to the traditional cold frame over the years. These adaptations have developed from the need to encourage more efficient horticultural production. Individual nursery propagators have made further changes to suit their particular requirements. The following comments review the adaptations that were and are currently used in the nursery industry.

Cold Frame Adaptations

(i) Height Reduction

The overall height of the cold frame has been reduced to lower construction costs and to allow additional light to reach the plant material. For example, the front and back of the frame are reduced from 45 cm (18") to 20 cm (8") and 60 cm (24") to 30 cm (12"), respectively.

(ii) Nearing Propagating Frame

The Nearing Propagating Frame was developed by Guy Nearing, a New Jersey nurseryman, during the 1920s and was subsequently patented in 1932. His objective was to create a low-cost, reliable propagation facility that could be used for both summer and fall cutting propagation of a wide range of species. He achieved this by ensuring that the frame faced exactly due north and by creating a reflective inner surface to reflect the maximum light in the absence of direct sunlight.

The base of the frame is sloped either side from the centre. The back of the frame is angled to provide an overhang for the cuttings while the front of the frame is protected by glass. Maximum reflection is achieved by installing corrugated aluminum onto the overhang and painting the remainder of the inner surfaces white.

Many species have been successfully rooted in Nearing Propagating Frames—including *Acer palmatum* (Japanese Maple), *Pieris* and *Rhododendron*. The normal procedure for rhododendrons was to stick the cuttings in mid-September and then remove them the following August.

Figure 3-9. A (Left above) Front view of a series of Nearing Propagating Frames. B (Left below). Rear view of a series of Nearing Propagating Frames. C (Above). New growth on *Rhododendron* cuttings inside a Nearing Propagating Frame in early summer. These cuttings were stuck the previous September. (Reproduced by courtesy of Hall Rhododendrons, Junction City, OR, U.S.A.)

(iii) Dutch Lights

A major modification for salad and vegetable crops was developed in Holland earlier this century and then was introduced into other regions of Europe. It uses a single pane of glass that can be slipped into an outer wooden framework. This light is both smaller and lighter in weight than the "English" light and can be conveniently lifted and handled by one person. The dimensions of Dutch light frames vary slightly according to design and manufacture, although most have overall measurements of 150 cm (59″) × 81 cm (31¾″). They all take a standard-size glass sheet measuring 142 cm (56″) × 73 cm (28¾″). Cold frames built to accommodate Dutch lights are those normally used in nurseries today. The most efficient design for nursery propagation is a double-span Dutch light which has the lights hinged in pairs along one side for easy access and ventilation.

Figure 3-11. A simple Dutch light cold frame constructed with railway ties. Note the planting board and spacer rod to aid the sticking of cuttings.

Figure 3-10. Dutch light cold frames accommodate the smaller and more manageable single pane lights. The photograph shows an excellent crop of conifers stuck in the previous fall. (Pinneberg area, West Germany)

Dutch lights are more easily maintained; allow more incoming light; and are more flexible because the lights can be used to cover a simple but effective greenhouse for propagating and growing-on container crops.

(iv) Double-Glass

A double-glass cold frame is one in which an additional layer of glass lights is placed between the cuttings and the outer lights. This provides a more precise environment around the cuttings because both temperature and humidity can be increased. Water droplets form on the underside of the inner lights, so it is important that the inner lights are level to prevent the water droplets accumulating and dripping from the lowest point. The two panes of glass, and the continuous water droplets diffusing the light, results in reduced incoming light levels received by the cuttings. However, it is very important to provide additional shading in spring and summer otherwise the cuttings may deteriorate at the higher temperatures of 26°C (79°F) or more combined with humidity levels of 98% or less.

Double-glass frames provide greater flexibility in both the type of cuttings and the range of plants that can be rooted because the humid environment prevents wilting of the cuttings and the basal heat of the rooting medium is increased. I have seen excellent quantities of softwood and

Figure 3-12. A typical double-glass cold frame. Note the formation of water droplets on the underside of the inner glass and the wooden slats used to provide shading on the outside.

evergreen hardwood cuttings rooted in double-glass frames—including softwood cuttings of deciduous azaleas, *Cotinus coggygria* 'Royal Purple' (Purple Smoke Tree), miniature roses, *Acer palmatum* cvs. (Japanese Maple), *Syringa vulgaris* cvs. (Common or French Lilac) and *Magnolia* × *soulangiana* (Chinese or Saucer Magnolia); and evergreen hardwood cuttings of evergreen azaleas, *Cotoneaster, Ilex aquifolium* (English Holly), evergreen *Berberis* (Barberry), *Skimmia* and many ornamental conifers.

Softwood cuttings are best rooted in flats. Fall-rooted coniferous and broad-leaf evergreen hardwood cuttings can be stuck either in flats or *in-situ* in the frame bed, left to over-winter and potted-up the following spring.

The cuttings should be drenched with a fungicidal solution after sticking as the high humidity encourages the spread of diseases. The high humidity reduces the need for additional watering but it is still necessary to check for dry areas, particularly during the summer. Ventilation is best carried out by first removing the inner lights and then opening up the outer lights.

(v) Polyethylene Film Cover

An efficient adaptation of the double-glass system for softwood and evergreen hardwood cuttings in Holland is to replace the inner layer of glass with a continuous layer of thin polyethylene film simply laid over the cuttings and tucked in around the sides. An additional seal is provided by wrapping polyethylene around the Dutch lights and the wooden laths laid on the outside for heavy shading. Many deciduous azaleas, *Magnolia, Acer palmatum* cvs. (Japanese Maple) and ornamental conifers are effectively rooted using this method.

Figure 3-13. A modified double-glass cold frame in which polyethylene film laid directly over the cuttings and tucked in around the sides forms the "inner" layer of glass. Heavier-grade polyethylene is used to cover the Dutch light to produce a better seal. (Boskoop, Holland)

(vi) Basal Heat

The "hot-bed" was traditionally used in horticulture to increase basal heat beyond that obtained from sunlight. "Hot-beds" were used largely to provide out-of-season salads and vegetables. They were prepared by placing a thick layer of fermenting horse manure over a layer of

Figure 3-14. Heaps of fermenting horse manure ready for spreading to provide basal heat and a rich organic growing medium into which rooted cuttings and seedlings can grow. (Pinneberg area, West Germany)

plain straw on the bottom of the frame. Basal heat was provided by the continuing fermentation of the horse manure. I saw this technique being used as recently as 1967 in West Germany to raise seedlings and root cuttings for nursery stock propagation. An excellent root system was produced in this rich organic medium.

Today, basal heat is provided by electrical cables or hot water circulating through rigid plastic or metal pipes (see p.127). Frames with basal heat provision are used sometimes to callus grafts or to accelerate the rooting of cuttings.

(vii) Mist Propagation

A standard mist propagation unit (see p. 140) can be installed in a cold frame by increasing the height of the frame to accommodate the misting equipment and then providing basal heat.

GREENHOUSE FACILITY

A greenhouse clad either with glass or plastic is the basis of most facilities used today for vegetative propagation, and sometimes for seed propagation. The remainder of this chapter is mainly devoted to greenhouse facilities, particularly focusing on the following 3 features:—

(i) Factors involved in siting, selecting and designing the basic layout for a greenhouse to be used for propagation.

(ii) Methods used for energy saving.

(iii) Equipment designed for mist propagation, fogging and propagation under polyethylene films, and an explanation of their use.

The type and size of greenhouse selected will largely depend on the capital available, the nursery production schedule, the propagation method to be used and the materials handling system.

When planning the propagation component of the nursery, it is important not to fall into the trap of making it over-complicated and of purchasing sophisticated equipment that will be little used. The idea should be to keep it simple and not to over-stretch your financial resources with unnecessary capital expenditures. The propagation sector of the nursery industry is a good example of where low capital expenditure has achieved excellent results. Important fundamental aspects are to make the greenhouse energy-efficient and to design and site it so that it forms an integral part of the nursery operation.

Capital Cost

Assuming that both capital and experience are limited, history has shown that there is certainly no need to initially install an expensive new propagation facility. Extra capital expenditure will be better utilized at a later date when you have greater financial resources and practical experience. If you are starting a new nursery, you should consider a second-hand greenhouse, a pre-fabricated kit such as the popular walk-in tunnel (quonset) covered with polyethylene, or simply buying lumber and building it yourself. The main objective should be to produce sufficient well-graded, quality plant material as economically as possible in order to provide a good, profitable return. The danger is falling into the trap of spending too much time and money on gadgets and gimmicks at the expense of propagating and properly maintaining plant material.

Siting and Utilities

As with other nursery facilities, it is important to check with the local municipality regarding building regulations. [For example, greenhouses in the United Kingdom are classed as "Agricultural Buildings" and must conform with the British Standard 5502 code of practice for the design of buildings and structures for agriculture.]

Shelter from wind is important to reduce both heat loss from the greenhouse and physical damage to the structure. Manufactured (artificial) windbreaks are particularly useful if suitable living plant material is not established or immediately available (see p. 57). The windbreaks must be sited so that they will provide maximum protection to the greenhouse without casting shade over it. A useful "rule of thumb" for siting windbreaks relative to a greenhouse are to allow:—

(i) A permeability factor of 50%.

(ii) An optimum height of two-thirds the height of the greenhouse ridge.

(iii) An optimum distance of 3× the height of the shelter between the greenhouse and the windbreak.

The quality of the water supply must be carefully checked, particularly for misting and fogging systems. Tests should be made for pathogens, pH and impurities. The impurities to specifically check are, firstly, sodium salts that will cause major damage to plants by scorching the leaves, stems and roots, and secondly, iron content—this is a common cause of nozzle blockage. Water to be used in fogging systems should be checked against local health and safety requirements if treated mains water is not used.

Water with a high pH is often detrimental to rooting because it raises the alkalinity of the rooting medium, and also causes hard calcium carbonate deposits in and around misting nozzles. Rain water should be trapped and collected in areas of high pH water. It may be collected from the gutters on the greenhouse roof and piped to a butyl-lined storage tank with a tight-fitting cover to eliminate light and debris. Mains or well water will have to be used if rainwater collection is not possible.

Equipment to reduce the pH and to purify the water by eliminating harmful salts is available but it is expensive.

Salts may be removed from water by reverse osmosis or by ion exchange resin filters. Such equipment is high in capital cost and relatively complex to operate and maintain. It is generally supplied by companies specializing in water treatment for industry and not specifically for horticulture.

More recently, the pH of water for use in nursery stock production has been controlled by the injection of nitric acid. Reliable application and control equipment for both small- and large-scale application is available, and this method of controlling pH is likely to replace reverse osmosis and ion exchange for this application. Nitric acid application does not remove salts but it is the most effective method of controlling pH to the desired level. Aklaline carbonates are turned into soluble nitrates which the rooted cutting can use. This equipment is made and supplied by T.T.S. Baggaley Ltd., Mead Lane, Lydney, Gloucestershire, U.K.; Flowering Plants Ltd., 55 Well Street, Buckingham, U.K.; and Stapley Contracts Ltd., High House Farm, Ashford, Kent, U.K.

Metal pipework, particularly galvanized steel pipe, should not be used when water is treated in this way due to the action of the treated water on metals. Rigid plastic pipe should always be used in this situation. (Note that galvanized piping can also be attacked by water with a pH level below 6.)

Power for normal lighting and basal heating will be needed. Power and the appropriate fittings must also be installed if, for example, an air heating system, fan and pad ventilation, and high intensity lights are to be used.

General Layout

Obtain expert advice on the correct choice of materials and equipment to use *before* making any purchases. This will help to ensure that the objectives of the business are met. Consult, in person, with local extension officers during the planning stage—particularly those with a good

Figure 3-15.
The propagation department should be integrated with the growing-on, shipping and office facilities of the nursery, with good access for mechanization, transportation and general communication. (Monrovia Nursery Inc., Azusa, CA, U.S.A.)

specialist knowledge of such matters as greenhouse design, heating, water sources and propagation equipment. High capital investment justifies the provision of extra funds in the budget to hire a private consultant with a good track record in horticultural engineering and operation. A consultant can be particularly useful in providing advice on integrating the whole nursery complex. Specialist knowledge can, and should be, obtained on electronics, work flow programs and materials handling. Last but not least, visit other nurseries, both locally and some distance away, to learn about new equipment and ideas, and to benefit from their experiences so that the same mistakes are not made twice.

Greenhouses are essentially laid out in one of three ways:—

1. Single-span greenhouses with a propagation bench or floor bed on either side of a central aisle (pathway).

Figure 3-16. A single-span polyethylene-clad greenhouse for the winter propagation of *Taxus* (Yew) in floor-level propagation beds. Note the polyethylene ducting for air heating. (Sheridan Nurseries, Oakville, ON, Canada)

2. Wide single- or twin-span greenhouses with benches or floor beds for propagating, often with additional space for hardening-off, liner production and perhaps a work area.

3. Multi-span greenhouse complex with carefully planned integration of propagation, liner production and work areas.

All three categories must have sufficient space to allow for future expansion. A common afterthought is "I wish I had retained a greater or more suitable area for expansion." Businesses often tend to expand faster than envisaged once they have become established.

The planning stage of a multi-span greenhouse complex should include special consideration of the maximum utilization of the available space. Some guidelines to consider when planning the general layout of a multi-span greenhouse complex are as follows:—

1. Include a work area for mixing the rooting medium and filling flats, and a bench area for staff to carry out the propagation work. These benches should be mobile so that the floor area can be rearranged and used for other purposes as needed—for example, mixing rooting medium or to accommodate additional benches during peak work periods. I have noted some excellent working areas, but also many that leave a lot to be desired—all the result of either careful planning or the lack of it. An uncomfortable work area cluttered with unnecessary materials will significantly lower morale and output. The area should be well ventilated and well lit, with back-up fluorescent lighting if there is insufficient natural light. Sliding doors not only allow easy movement of materials but also increase light and ventilation when required. There should be adequate heating, with heat loss reduced by insulating the walls and roof if necessary. Fans or other cooling methods will be required to reduce temperatures in hotter climates.

2. Allow sufficient space for access around the outside and inside of the greenhouse. The roadways must be sufficiently wide and strong enough for the use of pallet trucks. The usual layout inside the house is to have a wide central pathway for tractors or fork-lifts, with aisles to the propagation beds or benches coming off at right angles.

3. Design the bed or bench layout around an integrated materials handling system—manual or mechanized.

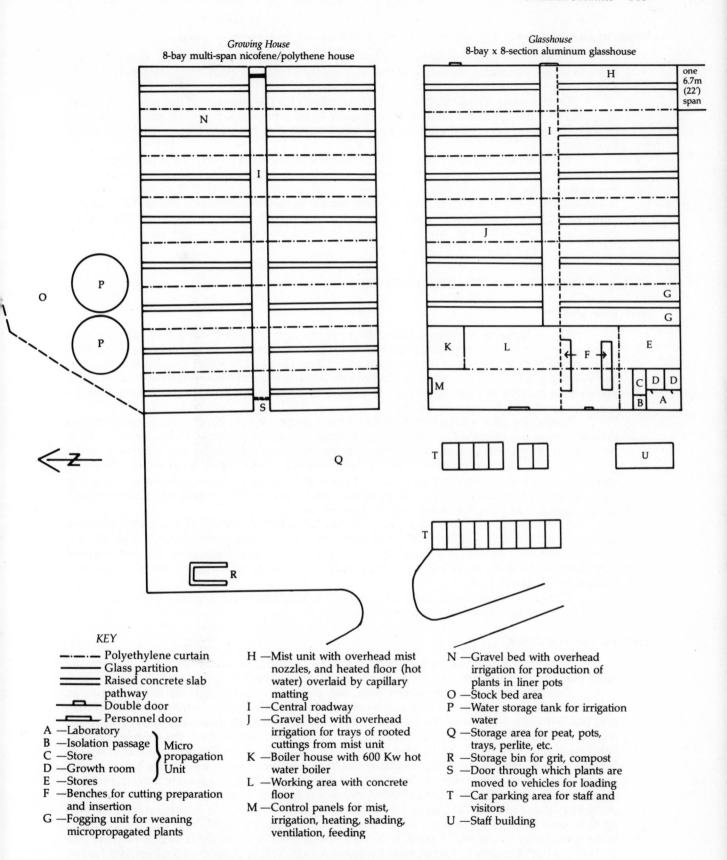

Growing House
8-bay multi-span nicofene/polythene house

Glasshouse
8-bay x 8-section aluminum glasshouse

one
6.7m
(22')
span

DIAGRAM 3-1. A Successful Nursery Lay-out Using Multi-Span Greenhouses

KEY

—·—·— Polyethylene curtain
———— Glass partition
════ Raised concrete slab
        pathway
— Double door
— Personnel door
A —Laboratory
B —Isolation passage ⎫ Micro
C —Store   ⎬ propagation
D —Growth room   ⎭ Unit
E —Stores
F —Benches for cutting preparation
    and insertion
G —Fogging unit for weaning
    micropropagated plants

H —Mist unit with overhead mist
    nozzles, and heated floor (hot
    water) overlaid by capillary
    matting
I —Central roadway
J —Gravel bed with overhead
    irrigation for trays of rooted
    cuttings from mist unit
K —Boiler house with 600 Kw hot
    water boiler
L —Working area with concrete
    floor
M —Control panels for mist,
    irrigation, heating, shading,
    ventilation, feeding

N —Gravel bed with overhead
    irrigation for production of
    plants in liner pots
O —Stock bed area
P —Water storage tank for irrigation
    water
Q —Storage area for peat, pots,
    trays, perlite, etc.
R —Storage bin for grit, compost
S —Door through which plants are
    moved to vehicles for loading
T —Car parking area for staff and
    visitors
U —Staff building

Reproduced by permission of Notcutts Nurseries, Woodbridge, Suffolk. U.K.

Types of Greenhouses

Greenhouse engineering technology has led to significant advances in increasing light input to plants, automatic controling of the environment, utilizing space more effectively, and the ability to plant, grow and harvest the crop more efficiently.

Greenhouses can be categorized into two groups for the purposes of this text. Firstly, glass, rigid plastic or fiber glass panels fixed to a metal or wood framework. Secondly, polyethylene film or related material supported on a series of metal or wooden hoops to form a "walk-in" tunnel (quonset).

When starting a small nursery, it is probable that restricted capital will mean that the first greenhouse purchased for propagation will be a single-span unit to which others will be added as business dictates. A series of single-span greenhouses can provide excellent independent control of various crops, because each can house plants similar in their requirements and for the length of time needed to successfully regenerate. However, a multi-span unit has the advantage of providing greater overall flexibility and can utilize propagation and growing space more effectively.

GLASS AND RIGID PLASTIC GREENHOUSES

Structural Design

The remarkable success achieved by growers over the years using a diverse range of propagation structures is surprising. These include the traditional "lean-to" greenhouse adjoining a south-facing brick wall and the narrow span (3.7–4.3 m/12–14') Lee Valley cucumber house (the Lee Valley is just north of London, U.K., and was an important greenhouse production area). I have even seen a nursery that converted a shed into a mist propagation house by increasing window space and installing fluorescent lighting.

Today, the most satisfactory module for both single- and multi-span greenhouses is considered to have a width of 6.7 m (22'). The greenhouse should be an optimum height of 2.9–3.7 m (9½–12') at the gutters, with no support bracing or ventilation equipment below the level of the gutter. This height allows sufficient room for the installation of shading material, overhead misting and irrigation equipment and for movement of the staff. Overhead shading, misting and irrigation equipment are all attached to the longitudinal and cross supports of the house, which must be both strong enough and of sufficient number to bear the weight.

A "double" Venlo greenhouse, each section 3.2 m (10½') wide to give a 6.4 m (21') clear module, is a good, and possibly less costly, alternative. If a shading screen is to be installed, it is necessary to have a secondary support system underneath the shading support for irrigation and mist lines. This can be provided by a lattice girder or by cross tubes below the roof truss and secured to the gutter posts.

The greenhouse should have an east-west orientation in areas where it is necessary to obtain the maximum benefit from solar radiation.

Heating and Ventilation

Modern greenhouses are designed to take full advantage of solar heat, which will provide more than the required daytime needs during much of the year.

Propagation in the greenhouse does not generally require high air temperatures, an optimum night air temperature being in the range of 10–12°C (50–54°F). Temperatures lower than this, but 1–2°C (2–4°F) above freezing, have been quite satisfactory for many species, although rooting is usually slower. The temperature interacts with other conditions in the greenhouse (e.g., light, humidity, wetness of the rooting medium, etc.) so that, in reality, it is hard to define an "optimum" temperature range. For example, too high a temperature in a relatively low humidity propagation system can be devastating due to drying of the cuttings. The same temperature in a high humidity system (e.g., contact polyethylene) would be considerably less damaging. Generally, providing other conditions are taken care of, rooting reacts positively to increasing temperatures up to around 25°C (77°F). In practice, it is just not economic to maintain these high temperatures in the greenhouse as a whole. A small area can be partitioned or a tent made of polyethylene film (p. 164) if a high temperature is required for some reason. This is cheaper and easier than raising the temperature throughout the greenhouse. However, it is generally the temperature of the rooting medium which is more important than the air temperature.

Greenhouses may be heated by direct warm air heaters fired by light oil or gas, circulated hot water, or steam from boilers fired by oil, gas or solid fuel. In the context of nursery stock production, the choice is likely to be between air heaters and circulated hot water.

Warm air heaters are relatively low in capital cost but tend to give poor uniform temperature distribution and large vertical gradients unless they are fitted with correctly designed and positioned perforated polyethylene ducting to "carry" the warm air. The ducting should be placed low down in the greenhouse and this frequently means that it causes an obstruction.

Hot water systems are higher in capital cost but temperatures can be controlled more accurately and the pipes can be arranged to give good uniform temperature distribution with only small gradients. There are systems that combine warm air and hot water heat exchanges.

In general, it would be better to select warm air heating for small operations, while larger operations would obtain greater benefits from circulated hot water. Small operations that do not have a permanent heating system installed will find that portable unit heaters are particularly useful as a temporary measure during periods of severe cold weather.

Interest has recently developed in the use of radiant heaters for the production of greenhouse crops. Heat is lost in conventional heating systems by conduction through the structure and by air leakage. This loss can be reduced by installing high temperature radiators close to the roof in the greenhouse and directing the radiant heat with suitable reflectors so that it heats the plants and soil rather than the structure. Heat loss from the greenhouse is reduced because the infra-red radiation does not directly heat the air. The radiators operate at a temperature of about 500°C (932°F), and the equipment available for horticultural use normally consists of steel tubes heated by a series of gas burners. The products of combustion pass along the tubes from the burners and then out to the atmosphere.

Radiant heaters have limitations in that only those plants that intercept the radiation are treated and therefore the crop tends to be heated unevenly. The system has possibilities for low-growing horticultural crops and there have been some promising trials at the Glasshouse Crops Research Institute, Littlehampton, U.K.

Humidity and the excess temperature from solar gain in the greenhouse are controlled by bringing in air from outside and exchanging it with the inside air—i.e., by ventilation. Ventilation efficiency is a particularly important point to check when purchasing a greenhouse and related equipment. A good "rule-of-thumb" is that the ventilator area should not be less than one-sixth of the floor area. Ventilation in smaller greenhouses can be carried out manually by opening and shutting ridge and/or side vents and entrance doors. Larger greenhouses should have a thermostatically-controlled automatic system installed to control the opening and closing of the ridge vents.

Electrically-powered fans provide an alternative method of ventilating greenhouses. They create positive air movement compared to hinged ventilators, which depend on natural convection and wind effects, and they are therefore more advantageous under still, calm conditions. However, they are costly to run and there are often marked horizontal temperature gradients from inlet to outlet.

Figure 3-17. Electrically-powered extractor fan installed at one end of a polyethylene-clad greenhouse for ventilation.

The fans used in greenhouses are normally of the extractor type. The fans may be installed in the sides or ends of the greenhouse, depending on the shape and size of the house or complex. Air inlets must be provided at the opposite side or end to the fans. These air inlets should be suitably louvered or draft-proofed so that the greenhouse is sealed when the fans are not operating. A heating engineer must be consulted to determine the size and number of fans required in relation to the size of the greenhouse and the correct rate of air movement necessary for efficient use.

The cooling efficiency of the fans can be increased in areas with hot dry weather by using wet pads or spinning disk humidifiers in the air inlet. These provide evaporative cooling in addition to the cooling provided by simple air exchange.

A convenient method to improve the ventilation of polyethylene-clad hoop "walk-in" greenhouses (quonsets) is to partially or completely replace the sides with shade cloth. However, this can create problems with uneven air currents during windy conditions—for example, by creating uneven distribution of water droplets from the misting nozzles.

Finally, I strongly advise consultation with a horticultural engineering specialist *before* installing any heating or ventilation system—specialist knowledge is required to determine what is best for your particular needs.

Shading

Shading is important to reduce stress to plant material by lowering the air temperature and transpiration and by helping to retain the optimum relative humidity levels.

The average propagation house is likely to require anything from 0–80% shade during the 12 months of the year, depending on the weather, location of the nursery and the propagation system used.

Such a wide range of shading is not easily achieved, but reasonable versatility is possible by using a proprietary liquid shading compound applied to the outside of the glass in combination with a shade fabric installed inside the greenhouse. The shade fabric (cloth) can be mounted either above the individual benches or floor beds or as a "false ceiling" over the whole area. In either case, it should be supported over strong, tight wires so that it can be withdrawn with minimum effort when the weather is dull. Muslin or thin burlap (hessian) fabrics can be used but are prone to deterioration. It is better to use one of the woven polyester fabrics which contain stabilizers to inhibit deterioration due to ultra-violet light.

It is certainly worthwhile to consider the use of a fabric that has both the properties of shading and of reducing heat loss from the greenhouse (p. 134). Automatic shading can be installed, using a sensor that responds accurately to changes in temperature or light level.

The greatest cooling effect is achieved by installing shading outside the greenhouse, ideally with a gap between the shading material and the roof of the house. More heat is absorbed when the shading material is dark and thick, e.g., wooden laths.

Cladding (Covering) Materials

There are a variety of rigid materials used for cladding greenhouses, each of which has its virtues and shortcomings. It is important to relate the strength of the supporting structure to the cladding material. Generally, the supporting structure is less costly for rigid plastics than for glass, but there are sometimes problems with attaching the plastic and with expansion and contraction of the materials.

(a) Glass

Glass has been the universal cladding material for many decades, but can be replaced by plastic-based materials. A greenhouse clad with glass still provides one of the best propagation structures because the glass provides excellent light transmission, and is long-lasting and easy-to-clean. It is heavy, so requires strong structural support and must be installed into wood or metal glazing bars to give a tight seal. One problem with older greenhouses is that the panes of glass slip and break, resulting in additional heat loss from the greenhouse. A polyethylene liner fixed to the inside of the greenhouse can help to reduce heat loss in these circumstances (p. 132).

A double layer of polyethylene installed over the outside of an existing glass-clad greenhouse and then inflated provides very good heat conservation. The cost involved can be justified in very cold climates.

(b) Fiber Glass

Fiber glass has been used as an alternative to glass for a number of years. It is available in flat or corrugated sheets that are convenient and easy to install. One problem with fiber glass is that it deteriorates in time, causing it to take on a "cloudy" appearance, particularly if scratched. This reduces light transmission. Fiber glass attracts dust as it becomes electrically positively charged. It is also very flammable. Some materials have a polyvinyl fluoride compound bonded to the fiber glass during the manufacturing process to reduce surface deterioration and to lessen the adhesion of dirt in exposed fibers. Corrugated sheets have around 13% more surface area than flat sheets, and this means that there is increased heat loss.

(c) Polyvinyl Chloride

These are clear, rigid, non-plasticized, light-weight materials containing a stabilizer to prevent deterioration caused by ultra-violet (UV) light. Longevity is increased by applying an acrylic coating during the manufacturing process to the side exposed to the weather. They seem to be satisfactory for 8–10 years. Novulox® is one type of polyvinyl chloride that is manufactured as rigid corrugated sheets with a visible light transmission value of 87%.

(d) Twin-Walled ("Double Skin") Rigid Plastics

These proprietary materials are designed with a narrow space of 6–12 mm (¼–½") between two sheets of rigid plastic. This acts as an insulation to reduce heat loss while giving good light transmission. The major types are described below.

(i) **Acrylic**—Plexiglas® is an acrylic-based material that has been well tested and has 92% light transmission value compared to glass. Heat loss from inside the greenhouse is 50% of that transmitted by a single sheet of 3 mm (⅛") glass. Acrylic materials weather well with little deterioration, but are considerably more costly than glass. They seem to have a satisfactory life span of at least 12 years.

(ii) **Polycarbonate**—Sheets made from polycarbonate are cheaper than glass but tend to become brittle. They generally have 88% light transmission and 50% heat loss from inside the greenhouse compared to a single sheet of glass. The sheets should be coated with acrylic to lengthen their life. They are generally unreliable without such a coating.

(iii) **Polypropylene**—Polypropylene sheets are cheaper than glass but are prone to degrading in sunlight. These materials generally have a light transmission value of around 85% and a 50% heat loss compared to a single sheet of glass.

Experiments have shown that acrylic, polyvinyl chloride and polycarbonate materials are more suitable than polypropylene because they do not degrade as quickly.

(e) Film Plastics—The horticultural industry has found film plastic cladding materials to be a cheap and successful way to provide temporary protection for many flower, fruit and vegetable crops. A similar transition has occurred in the nursery stock industry where plastic, particularly polyethylene film, is installed over metal or wooden structures to control the environment for encouraging crop growth during the growing season and to provide winter protection. Polyethylene-clad houses also have a use for propagation.

Film plastics are probably best used for either a static or movable temporary house (p. 173) where the floor bed area contains large quantities of cuttings requiring similar environmental conditions for rooting—for example, direct sticking (Chapter 13). Glass or rigid plastics are most likely to meet the requirements of a permanent propagation house utilized for propagating a variety of species by differing methods. Unfortunately, film plastics must be replaced after two or three years due to deterioration.

The roof of a single- or multi-span structure to be clad with a film plastic is often best designed with an arch shape rather than a regular hoop. The arch generally provides better ventilation space and causes condensation to run down along the inside of the plastic to the edge of the floor rather than dripping directly onto the plant material. Condensation droplets held by surface tension on the film plastic of regular hooped houses usually drip onto the plant material and aisles, particularly in the early evening after warm daytime temperatures. This problem can be reduced by ventilation and also by physically vibrating the film plastic or by applying a proprietary compound such as Sunclear® which reduces the surface tension when sprayed on the film plastic. This causes the droplets to form a thin film of water which runs down the plastic to the edge of the floor bed area.

Figure 3-18.
A series of single-span polyethylene-clad propagation greenhouses to be used for direct sticking. Note the arch design of the structure. (Christie's Nurseries, Pitt Meadows, B.C., Canada)

Ventilation can be a problem in the typical film plastic propagation house. It is necessary to exchange the warm moisture-laden air with cooler outside air. This will reduce the formation of water droplets due to condensation. The methods used for ventilating include the ones outlined below.

1. Open the doors or ends of the structure. Check to ensure that this does not create air currents which will cause uneven misting patterns or dislodge polyethylene covers laid over cuttings. Air flow is more easily controlled when a woven plastic fabric is used to replace the film at the doors or ends.

2. In warm climates, install a continuous panel about 1.0 m (3'3") above the ground along the side of a well-anchored structure. Roll up the film plastic from the base and fix to the panel. A continuous length of woven plastic fabric is then fastened into place to replace the film plastic. The film plastic is let down over the woven plastic fabric when temperatures drop later in the year. This dual system can be re-used the following year. Alternatively, a series of individual panels of woven plastic fabric can replace rectangular sections of the film plastic. Some manufacturers of hoop houses have special extrusions on the side section of the greenhouse so that both the fabric and film plastic can be securely held in place. Ventilation can be controlled more accurately by installing either a manual or automatic "roll blind" system to cover the open or shade cloth sections.

Greenhouse engineers have also designed roof and side ventilation systems for greenhouses clad with film plastic.

3. Install inlet and extractor fans that can be operated by a time clock. The time clock can also be linked to a "fogging" unit so that humidification occurs while the extractor fans are working.

Types of Film Plastics

Film plastics are bought in "made-to-measure" lengths and widths and custom-fitted to different designs of greenhouse structure. They come in a range of thicknesses, normally expressed as gauge, mil, ins, μm (micrometers), microns, μ or mu (the last 4 are different ways of writing the same measurement). Two popular thicknesses for polyethylene for cladding greenhouse structures are 4 and 6 mil. Approximate equivalents are 4 mil ≡ 400 gauge ≡ 100 microns (μ or mu) ≡ 0.1 mm ≡ 0.004", and 6 mil ≡ 600 gauge ≡ 150 microns (μ or mu) ≡ 0.15 mm ≡ 0.006". (This is based on 0.25 mm (0.01") = 250 microns or 10 mil or 1000 gauge.)

TABLE 3-1. Conversion Table for Film Plastic Thickness.

TO CONVERT	TO	METHOD	EXAMPLE
mil	gauge	× 100	4 mil = 400 gauge
mil	inches	÷ 1000	4 mil = .004 inches
mil	μm	× 25 (approx)	4 mil = 100 μm
gauge	μm	÷ 4 (approx)	400 gauge = 100 μm

Metric Units — microns (μ) = micrometers (μm)
Imperial Units — gauge.
[The approved international unit is now the micrometer (μm)]

There is a knack in cladding the greenhouse so that the film is really tight. Therefore, try to obtain the help of an experienced person when you are doing it for the first time. Cladding needs to be carried out on a still day and the plastic film must be sufficiently warm to stretch. This will make it tighter when the temperatures cool, particularly with polyethylene. The film is battened down with wood or batten tape or fixed into place with a proprietary fixing strip such as Grip-Strip®. Alternatively, the film can be secured by burying it in the soil along each side of the house.

Polyethylene is particularly prone to degradation when in direct contact with a metal framework. It hardens at these "hotspots" and later tears. A proprietary tape can be fixed onto the metal to form a "sandwich" between the metal and polyethylene if this is a problem. It is useful to have some clear poly-mending tape on hand in case the film should tear as you are putting it on. This tape is also useful to quickly repair damaged areas of the film later.

Two proprietary tapes that have been used successfully in Britain are firstly, Sellotape 4327®, an anti-hot spot foam tape. This is a closed-cell P.V.C. foam/polyester laminate coated with a pressure-sensitive adhesive. Secondly, Sellotape 1433® (All Weather Tape), a repair tape for torn covers or to reinforce fold lines. It is clear and UV stabilized and has a polyethylene base. Black tape absorbs heat and will therefore damage both the repair itself and the immediate surrounding film area. It is recommended that 7.5 cm (3") width clear tape be used to repair clean cuts and small holes as this will normally allow a sufficient bonding area around the damage.

The two types of film plastics are summarized below.

(i) **Polyethylene**—Polyethylene is the most widely used film plastic cladding in Europe and North America, largely on the grounds of cost. It is often referred to as polythene. Clear polyethylene film transmits 89% of incident light. It is stabilized by the incorporation of ultra-violet (UV) inhibitors, which will normally give it a 2-year life span. There is a tendency for "temperature inversions" to occur on clear, cold, still nights due to the permeability of polyethylene to long-wave radiation.

Opaque or "milky" polyethylene film is also available but this reduces incoming light to around 50%, thus slowing down the build-up of the air temperature within the structure.

Films made from a copolymer of polyethylene and ethyl vinyl acetate (E.V.A.) are now generally available. These are sometimes referred to as E.V.A. films. The amount of E.V.A. in the film varies from 4–18%. The addition of E.V.A. increases the cost (depending on the amount added), but it can improve the qualities of polyethylene by:—

(a) Increasing elasticity and strength, and overcoming the problem of "edge fold" weakness.

(b) Reducing the transmission of long-wave radiation so that, like glass, potential damage to plants by radiation frosts is reduced.

Film plastics containing 18% E.V.A. are popular in Scandinavia where the improved elasticity makes it easier to clad structures in very cold temperatures. Conversely, these high E.V.A.-content films are not suitable for hot climates. Most of the polyethylene films now used for cladding greenhouses contain E.V.A. but the amount does not usually exceed 4%. This level improves the handling properties of the film but does not materially affect the transmission of long-wave radiation.

(ii) Plasticized Polyvinyl Chloride (PVC)—Plasticized polyvinyl chloride, normally referred to as PVC, is not so widely used as polyethylene film because it is considerably more expensive. However, it is more effective in reducing heat loss. It tends to build-up static electricity, thus attracting dirt particles on the surface and reducing light transmission.

PVC is now the major film plastic used in Japan for cladding greenhouses, as researchers there have overcome the problems associated with the electrostatic attraction of dust particles.

Benches Versus the Floor Area—Basic Design and Method of Heating

You will have to decide whether to install benches or utilize the floor area for rooting cuttings and callusing grafts in a greenhouse propagation unit. This section describes some of the criteria necessary to make this decision and explains basic designs. It is based on the assumption that most greenhouse propagation units will use either overhead misting or a closed case system in which the plant material is covered by glass or polyethylene.

Benches

Benching is the traditional facility for propagating and growing-on plants, and still has a firm place on the nursery today. The main advantage of benches is that they provide a permanent structure on which to place down, maintain and easily observe plant material. Human nature makes it more likely that staff will look more closely at the crop if they do not have to bend down to inspect it. I would recommend benching for grafted stock where regular inspection, both from above and from the sides, is vital.

There are other factors to be considered for cuttings before making the final choice. Benching allows a greater flow of air around the plant material due to the gap between the base of the bench and the floor. Do *not* be tempted to use this space for storage because it is more than likely that unwanted utensils, plants and debris will accumulate there, thus providing a ready source of disease infection.

The main limitation of benches is their degree of permanency which reduces flexibility within the greenhouse. Handling of materials over floor beds is much easier than having to work around benches. Benches are more costly to install than a similar area of floor bed propagation area.

The following criteria should be kept in mind when designing and installing benches:—

(i) They must be a convenient height and width at which to work. A common mistake is to make them too high or too wide, causing that annoying situation of "not quite being able to reach" so that the work is not carried out efficiently. Benches at around 75 cm (30") are generally a convenient height for many people. Side benches should be sufficiently narrow for a person to stretch across to lift plants from the back. Center benches are wider and should be accessible from both sides.

(ii) Bench width is often designed around the selected flat size if they are to be used for cuttings rooted in flats to ensure a tight fit and full utilization of the space. However, this statement requires qualifying as "today's flat may be tomorrow's reject", thus making it better to select the best aisle (path)/bench/handling combination.

(iii) Benches must be sufficiently strong to support the weight of rooting medium, flats or pots and heating pipes, as well as the added weight of water if mist propagation is used. The legs of the bench should be braced where necessary to provide additional strength and the lumber should be pressure-treated to resist decay.

(iv) Provision for drainage must be made, especially when mist propagation is used.

(v) Benches used for cuttings rooted in medium placed directly into the bench or for grafts callused in pots plunged at a 45° angle in peat moss should have the sides 15–21 cm (6–8") deep. A low retaining wall of 2.5–5 cm (1–2") used to be popular for benches utilized for cuttings rooted in flats. [Additional depth will be required if the bench is insulated with polystyrene sheets (p. 138) on the base and sides.] Some propagators today generally prefer sideless benches for cuttings and seedlings in flats, and removable sides for bench grafting.

(vi) Costs can be reduced by using second-hand materials, especially for metal benches. Good buys can often be made when another nursery is modernizing or closing.

Bench Design—Several bench designs that could be adapted to suit your specific requirements are described below.

1. A traditional method was to use corrugated asbestos sheets supported by a metal or wooden framework for the base of mist or closed case beds. A 6 mm (¼″) diameter hole was made at the base of each "trough" to provide drainage and some aeration. A flat surface was made by filling the troughs with sand, electric heating cables placed on top of the sand and covered with a 2.5–5 cm (1–2″) layer of coarse sand. The flats of cuttings were placed on this layer. The sides of the bench were either wood or asbestos, or even metal if only a low retaining wall was required. Asbestos is now regarded as a hazardous material for health reasons and its use is prohibited in many countries.

Manufacturers of asbestos sheets have undertaken research into substitute products—one example being Masterboard® (Cape Board & Panels Ltd., Iver Lane, Uxbridge, England). These fire- and moisture-resistant sheets are manufactured with a calcium silicate matrix reinforced with cellulose. Other substitute products for asbestos include Masterclad®, Supalux® and Unicem Cement-Corrugated®.

2. Corrugated fiber glass, corrugated zinc-coated steel sheeting or a series of wooden slats spaced 2.5 cm (1″) apart can be used. A metallic or robust plastic fabric should be placed over the wooden boards to prevent sand and/or rooting medium falling through the slats.

3. The base of the bench can be made of weld mesh lined on the inside with expanded polystyrene sheets (Styrofoam®) wrapped in polyethylene.

4. A recent innovation in nurseries is the concept of roller benches, based on those used in the greenhouse pot plant industry. The benches are constructed on rollers so that they can be easily pushed together or separated. It is difficult to achieve more than 70% space utilization with fixed benches, but roller benches can increase this up to 95%. This system has been utilized for intensive greenhouse production of conifer seedlings, cuttings and bench grafts.

5. I have noted two-tier bench/floor bed combinations being used in France to increase available space. This system was largely used for callusing conifer grafts. The light over the middle and lower beds must be supplemented with either fluorescent tubes or tungsten filament light bulbs.

Figure 3-19. Roller benches can significantly increase the area of available bench space. Note the manual operation of the rollers to separate or close up adjacent benches. (Philip McMillan Browse, Saratoga Horticultural Foundation, CA, U.S.A.)

Figure 3-20. A propagation house installed with a custom-made combination of benches and beds to provide 2-tiered propagation space. Note the lighting fitted under the benches to provide increased illumination to the floor bed and the use of polyethylene to cover the bench grafts. (Minier Nurseries, Angers, France)

Bench Heating—The heating cables must be evenly spread down or across the base of the bench to encourage even heat distribution and be placed as close to the ends and sides of the benches as is practical. One useful method is to attach the cables in a series of loops to a continuous roll of chicken wire so that each cable is about 15 cm (6″) from the adjacent one. The chicken wire keeps the cables in place and the wire and cables can be simply rolled up and moved from the bench when it needs cleaning. Alternatively, the cables can be attached to either continuous or sectional pieces of weld mesh netting, which can also be moved in and out of the bed as required.

There has been interest recently in propagation mats where the cables are permanently fixed inside a sealed protective covering. They are available in various lengths but are most useful for small propagation areas or temporary propagation beds and benches. The manufacturer usually sets the electric cables into a heavy-duty rubber mat or a temperature-resistant, moisture-proof "jacket". The mats are simply plugged in when required and are easily removed and stored after use.

Figure 3-21.
An Agritape® root zone heater is a convenient method of providing basal heat to flats of cuttings.

One method that has been creating interest is a low voltage system that uses only 12–14 volts to heat the rooting medium. This is called the Charlton Thermosystem® (Charlton Thermosystems, Romsey, Hampshire, U.K.) and consists of a transformer connected to a length of 2.5 cm (1″) low-resistance steel rope or cable placed in sand at the base of the propagation bed. It is easy to move the equipment to another propagation bed. The claimed energy saving benefits require assessment of further experimental data before definite conclusions can be formulated.

Aisles (Pathways)—About 27–30% of the total floor area of a large greenhouse is likely to be taken up by aisles, both narrow and wide. This figure could be reduced to about 25% for a smaller single-span greenhouse.

The benches should be located so that there is maximum use of space for benches over aisles. The mistake sometimes is to take this too far and make the pathways too narrow. This causes frustration because handcarts or barrows barely fit and staff graze the backs of their hands against the benches. Aisle floors should provide a firm slip-proof footing for staff. They should be designed so that water drains away readily and the material should be easily cleaned. A rough-finish concrete is a good surface and is made by brushing the concrete with a stiff brush while it is still "green". Porous building blocks have been found to be very effective as water drains away and the surface provides a good "grip" for footwear. Some propagators prefer concrete floors or soil covered with rounded pea gravel because these surfaces retain humidity levels after damping-down.

Floor Area

Today's trend in cutting propagation is to place the beds directly on to the greenhouse floor. The floor area has been successful for grafted stock. There are essentially two ways to utilize floor space. Firstly, by installing a series of individual beds, and secondly, by using all the floor space with no pre-designated beds.

The advantages gained by using the greenhouse floor are that there is generally less cost involved compared to benches and there is considerably more flexibility to implement an effective materials handling system.

A disadvantage is that it could encourage bringing soil-borne diseases such as *Phytophthora cinnamomi* (Root Rot) and *Rhizoctonia* spp. (Damping-off) (see Chapter 12) into the actual propagation area on footwear. (A natural stance when discussing propagation with fellow enthusiasts seems to have one foot at the edge of the propagation bed!) It can be helpful to consider issuing instructions that all staff and visitors walk through a tray containing a pad of disinfectant at all entrances to the propagation house (p. 378). A further disadvantage is that element of human nature which makes it less likely to attend to the aftercare of cuttings when bending down is required.

(a) Individual Floor Beds—A series of individual beds can be conveniently constructed at right angles to a central or side pathway in the greenhouse. A convenient bed width is around 1.8 m (6'). The beds are separated by 45–60 cm (1½–2') wide pathways which allow access to either side of the bed and along which flats can conveniently be hand-carried. Four flats 45 cm (18") square conveniently fit across a 1.8 m (6') bed. Two rows of flats can be placed down or removed by staff working from opposite sides of the bed.

A well-tested bed design uses a concrete base with a 10 cm (4") retaining wall. Pairs of 1.3 cm (½") wide drainage holes are made at 1 m (3') intervals down the bed. A 5 cm (2") layer of sand is placed on the concrete, then the heating cables or pipes, followed by a further 1.3 cm (½") layer of coarse sand. The flats are placed directly on the coarse sand. The sides of the bed will need to be raised to 15–21 cm (6–8") if cuttings are to be stuck directly into the beds or grafts callused by plunging into peat moss.

Figure 3-22. A well-designed propagation unit with overhead misting lines installed above individual floor-level beds. Note the ample access around the beds and the false ceiling of shade cloth. (Blakedown Nurseries, Kidderminster, Worcestershire, U.K.)

Figure 3-23. A floor-level concrete propagation bed. This method of attaching the heating cables to chicken wire can be adapted for use on a bench. Note the drainage holes for removal of excess water. (Hadlow College of Agriculture & Horticulture, Tonbridge, Kent, U.K.)

Wider beds up to 2.75 m (9') with 38 cm (15") pathways make better utilization of space, but some form of overhead gantry system for handling materials is advisable to provide access to all the propagation material for maintenance. An overhead gantry is also useful if there is a risk of damaging the beds by staff walking on them.

A unique bed design was implemented by Notcutts Nurseries Ltd., Woodbridge, Suffolk, England, in conjunction with horticultural engineering consultant G. F. Sheard (formerly Deputy Director of the Glasshouse Crops Research Institute, Rustington, Sussex, England). Instead of using conventional heating pipes, a series of hollow polypropylene panels are placed down to cover the complete area of the bed. The panels were originally designed as solar collectors for heating swimming pools. In a propagation facility, their role is reversed from gathering heat to dispensing it. Each panel is approximately 3 × 1.25 m (10 × 4') and they are connected in groups of five. Each layout requires some special design work to fit the greenhouse and to ensure a uniform flow of water through all panels. These panels provide a very uniform distribution of heat.

Essentially, the bed is constructed by placing and levelling a layer of sand, followed by 5 cm (2″) thick expanded polystyrene (Styrofoam®) sheets wrapped in polyethylene film for insulation. The polypropylene heating panels are laid on top of these sheets and the sheets are then covered with Lantor® capillary irrigation matting fabric. The flats or trays of cuttings are placed directly on to the matting fabric.

Figure 3-24.
A polypropylene heating panel can be used to provide basal heat with hot water. Note the matting fabric on to which the flats are stood down and the 5 cm (2″) thick Styrofoam® sheet wrapped in polyethylene beneath the heating panel for energy saving. (Notcutts Nurseries, Woodbridge, Suffolk, U.K.)

(b) Open Floor—The heated open floor space of the greenhouse provides greater flexibility as there is no fixed bed and pathway system. An overhead mist propagation system can be fixed to cross supports in the roof of the greenhouse to give overall coverage, or alternatively the whole greenhouse or section of floor space can be used for propagation under polyethylene film. Open floor facilities are useful for greenhouses that have a fogging system installed. Materials handling can be implemented by using fork-lifts to transport flats or pallets to and from the greenhouse.

Earlier floor designs had the heating cables or pipes laid in solid concrete. The flats were then placed directly onto the concrete surface. Sloping beds or narrow surface drainage channels leading to a central drain could be made to remove surface water. Hillier Nurseries (Winchester) Ltd., England, decided to provide a completely porous base

Figure 3-25.
A wide-span greenhouse with an open floor bed for propagation. Note the maximum use of space and the use of the roof structure to support the misting lines.

rather than one of solid concrete. This porous base is made by mixing cement with 10 mm (⅜″) grade of gravel aggregate with no fine particles. The mixture, known as "no-fines" concrete, is used to form a 15 cm (6″) deep floor. There is a definite knack in knowing how to prevent the cement smearing, which would cause uneven drainage. The mixture for the floor base is installed by pressing it into place with a hand-pulled garden roller. Plastic water pipes, 1.3 cm (½″) in diameter, are sandwiched in during the construction of the floor base so that they are 10 cm (4″) deep and 15 cm (6″) apart. [The water temperatures should be controlled to a maximum of 40.5°C (105°F) to prevent the plastic water pipes from breaking down too quickly.]

Reduced misting cycles and the very effective floor drainage may result in a lack of humidity in the greenhouse during the winter. (Flats may also dry out too quickly.) This is best overcome by brushing a light covering of coarse sand over the floor and into the floor crevices as soon as the cement has dried. This will partially inhibit drainage and so ensure that humidity levels rise in the greenhouse.

Heating with Hot Water

Basal heat provided by hot water heated by gas-, oil- or coal-fired boilers and circulated by pipes, tubes or panels is usually favored for larger propagation areas due primarily to the lower energy costs. The response to changes in temperature requirements pre-set on the temperature control unit will not be as rapid as with electricity. However, this response can be improved by installing a modulating mixing valve. Systems have been designed using a combination of hot water pipes and electric cables. The hot water pipes provide the basic heat regime while the electric cables can provide a "boost" if necessary.

An excellent heat source can be provided at a relatively low cost by purchasing a second-hand boiler, ensuring that both it and all exposed piping are sound.

The conventional means of distributing the heat is to use 1.3 cm (½″) rigid plastic or polyethylene pipes. However, Biotherm Engineering, Petaluma, California, has developed a system that passes hot water through a series of narrow, 0.75 cm (0.3″) diameter, synthetic rubber pipes. This system is called Biotherm® Bottom Heating pipes. A life expectancy of 20–25 years before deterioration caused by hot and cold temperatures and corrosion is claimed. The pipes can be sandwiched in a cement/gravel aggregate base, in the rooting or plunging medium itself, or simply just laid under the flats.

Figure 3-26.
Synthetic rubber pipes can be used to conduct hot water for heating a floor-level bed.

Controlling the Basal Heat Temperature

Basal heat temperature in the propagation bench, bed or open floor is controlled in one of the following ways, irrespective of whether electric or hot water heat is used.

Thermostat—The rod thermostat is the standard method used for controlling temperature. This is a 45–60 cm (18–24") long, horizontal rod containing a bi-metallic strip and attached to a control box that contains a dial for pre-setting the temperature and also a switch mechanism. The rod is placed through a hole made at the side of the bench or bed so that it is at the average level of the base of the cuttings. The rod of the thermostat must always be kept covered by the rooting medium or flats.

A good rod thermostat should have a differential of about 0.6–0.8°C (1–1.5°F) each side of the pre-set temperature. Differentials larger than this result in higher energy costs because a greater temperature lift is required to bring the temperature to the desired level. The thermostat should be calibrated before installing—the dial may read, for example, 21°C (70°F) but the switching mechanism may be operating a few degrees higher or lower. It is also recommended that they be re-calibrated annually as part of the regular maintenance cycle. A couple of spare thermostats should be kept on hand in case of failure.

Electronic Pulse Ratio Controller—Electronic pulse ratio controllers are able to maintain the basal temperature at a steady value without the "saw-tooth" overshoot and undershoot associated with thermostat controllers. The control system manufactured by Nobel Engineering (Goring-by-Sea, Worthing, Sussex, England) is now standard equipment on many British nurseries. The required temperature, for example, 21°C (70°F), is set on the control box and a series of heat pulses (about 80 per hour) is initiated when the temperature of the rooting medium, measured by a sensor in the medium, falls below this set value. It is recommended that the sensor temperature probes be placed in several different locations in the bench or bed. The control box then works out the averages of the signals from the probes.

Figure 3-27. Electronic pulse ratio controllers provide accurate basal temperature control. Note that the read-out on the panel is above that on the dial setting due to solar heat build-up during the day.

The advantages of electronic pulse ratio controllers over traditional thermostats are:—

(i) "Tighter" temperature control around the set value at the base of the cutting.

(ii) Computation of an average reading, thus eliminating misleading temperature recording in "hot and cold" areas of the bench or bed.

(iii) Energy costs are lower due to the reduced overshoot above the set temperature.

(iv) Greater reliability and less frequent calibration needed than rod thermostats.

(v) Easily fitted with display meters, so that staff can read the basal temperatures at a glance.

Materials Handling

It is essential that some method of materials handling system be dovetailed into the over-all planning of both large and small propagation operations. This may vary from just a simple system of hand trailers and trays to a more sophisticated one using an electrically-powered gantry to span floor propagation beds.

The materials handling system should be simple, flexible and robust. Over-planning of long-term objectives should be avoided—it is surprising how quickly some equipment can become obsolete. One theory is to build large, wide-span, open propagation structures for the long-term while choosing equipment, etc. to "furnish" them with fairly short-term expectations.

The different types of materials handling aids can be grouped within the categories below.

Trays and Flats

There is a wide range of trays and flats from which to select. Trays can be used for handling cuttings during preparation, to hold polyethylene bags of cuttings during cold storage, to transfer flats or containers to and from the propagation benches or beds, or for direct rooting when the containers remain in the tray while the cuttings root. Trays can be expensive, therefore it certainly pays to seek second-hand trays that, for instance, may have been used in the bakery, fruit or vegetable industries. The criteria to use when selecting a tray for the propagation area are:—

(i) Cost and availability.

(ii) That it is sufficiently robust to withstand continual use.

(iii) That the tray size be standardized to one suitable for the majority of requirements.

(iv) That it is suitable for use in either a present or projected mechanized carrying system—for example, tiered trailers.

(v) That it is convenient for one person to carry when filled with plant material and rooting/growing media.

(vi) That trays used for direct sticking will firmly hold multiples of the pot sizes used. Trays for this purpose may be non-segmented and the containers packed into place, or segmented and without a base so that the container is retained at the rim within each segment of the tray—for example, the Empot® handling system manufactured by Moulded Plastics (Birmingham) Ltd., Lovell, Tamworth, Staffordshire, U.K. The Empot® trays are particularly useful with capillary watering systems as there is no solid barrier between the underside of the pots and the capillary watering base.

Figure 3-28. A (left). A segmented carrying tray to facilitate the handling of small container pots. The extrusions around each segment hold the container near its rim. B (right). The "Carri-Aid" attachment to facilitate the carrying of the tray when filled with pots. (Both reproduced by permission of Empot®, Moulded Plastics (Birmingham) Ltd., Tamworth, Staffordshire, U.K.)

Pallets

Moving materials on pallets is widely used in larger nurseries. Palletized handling systems use devices ranging from hand-operated units, fork-lift units fitted on to either the front or rear of tractors to fork-lift trucks.

Pallet systems can be conveniently divided into three groups:—

(i) Single pallets.

(ii) Multi-tiered pallet units with a series of interchangeable shelves. More material can be moved at one time and the number of tiers can be varied for different sized material.

(iii) Pallet bins to move such materials as mixed rooting medium into the propagation area.

Figure 3-29. A propagation greenhouse installed with palletized propagation beds. This system provides considerable flexibility as the pallets can be moved easily to the potting shed with fork-lift (pallet) trucks. (Bruce Briggs, Briggs Nurseries, Olympia, WA, U.S.A.)

Figure 3-30. A multi-tier pallet specifically custom-designed for moving pallets and containers with a fork-lift (pallet) truck. (Reproduced by courtesy of Notcutts Nurseries, Woodbridge, Suffolk, U.K.)

The small, narrow-wheelbase tractors and fork-lift (pallet) trucks designed for use in vineyards are becoming favored for material handling in some propagation areas because they are maneuverable in a restricted area. The greenhouse floor must be sufficiently strong to stand the extra weight. It is important that the driver of the truck or tractor is fully trained because of the restricted enclosed area, and the overall care required with plant material. [Unfortunately, there is a too frequent tendency on some nurseries for equipment to be handled incorrectly by an over-confident driver who can easily damage plants and equipment and who is often unaware of common-sense safety procedures.]

Trailers and Carts

Hand- or tractor-pulled trailers and carts are the basic units for moving plants around on nurseries. They are suitable for most requirements because of the various types and sizes available. It is particularly useful when a series of small individual trailers can be hooked up to each other to form a train of "tracking trailers".

An idea that I noted in Holland is a self-steering "two-way" tiered trailer in which the wheels can be moved and fixed at right angles. Normally the wheels are in line with the direction of the pathway, but can be turned 90 degrees and locked in place when the selected propagation bed is reached. The trailer is then pushed by hand so that it straddles the bed with its wheels on the pathways on each side. The flats or containers can be set down exactly where desired.

Flat-Decked Trucks

Small battery-powered flat-deck trucks have been used successfully in and around propagation areas. The truck may have a multi-shelved unit fitted to the deck to increase the quantity of material transported at one time.

Gantries

A considerable amount of work has been carried out over the last decade at the National Institute of Agricultural Engineering (N.I.A.E.), Silsoe, Bedfordshire, England, on the design and use of a crop-spanning gantry system for low-growing horticultural crops. The basic principle of the system is that a hand-operated or electrically-powered metal framework travels on rails over the crop or bed so that the operator(s) can sit and work over the plants. The gantries designed so far have varied in width from 2.0 m (6'6") to 6.5 m (21'6"). The gantries do not necessarily use up floor space because the heating pipes just above the crop can serve as the rail system, providing they have sufficient strength. There has been interest in using square heating pipes to give increased stability to the gantries. Gantries are very useful for wide beds that normally require the worker to stretch with difficulty. In addition, it is easier to spot problems, and thus rectify them quickly, when working over the bed and looking down on the plants.

Some gantries are sufficiently light in weight to be manually lifted from one bed to the next. Heavier gantries require the use of a transfer carriage that is sited in the central pathway and has a pair of rails that line up with the gantry wheels.

The first gantry system that I saw in use was at Notcutts Nurseries, Woodbridge, Suffolk, England, where it travelled over the propagation and adjacent liner beds using the heating pipes as rails. Two operators could sit on it. It was used very successfully for moving plants, trays, maintaining cuttings and grafts, and pruning liner stock. This gantry system was adapted from the N.I.A.E. design to provide a simple, manually operated, low-cost inspection and materials handling system.

Figure 3-31. A custom-designed gantry mounted on the heating pipes to allow two operators to move and implement necessary maintenance procedures for cuttings and liners. (Reproduced by courtesy of Notcutts Nurseries, Woodbridge, Suffolk, U.K.)

The design and installation of a gantry system requires specialized knowledge. Outside advice must be sought when planning to use gantries because of the specialized knowledge and capital expenditure required. Comparisons should be made with alternative systems (e.g., ones built around tractors, trailers or fork-lift trucks) before finally deciding on a gantry system.

DEVELOPMENTS IN ENERGY-SAVING TECHNOLOGY

The O.P.E.C. oil crisis in 1973 caused a rapid escalation in fuel prices. Since then, both public and private research organizations have directed a considerable amount of their resources to seeking out new, and to improving existing, methods of increasing energy efficiency in industry. The greenhouse has been one of the prime targets for reducing energy costs because of its high fuel requirements for crop production. The ideas and materials used for energy saving include modification of covering materials, utilization of waste heat, accurate electronic sensors for temperature control, and insulation with expanded polystyrene. This section will review the different methods that can be used to reduce energy costs in the propagation greenhouse.

Research on energy saving has been carried out in a number of centers in North America and in Europe—including the Ohio Agricultural Research and Development Center, Wooster, U.S.A.; the National Institute of Agricultural Engineering, Wageningen, Holland; and the National Institute of Agricultural Engineering, Silsoe, Bedfordshire, England. More specific to the plant propagation facility is the experimental work carried out by Margaret E. Scott at the Efford Experiment Horticulture Station (Efford E.H.S.), Lymington, Hampshire, England, and by J. G. D. Lamb and J. C. Kelly at the Agricultural Institute, Kinsealy Research Centre, Dublin, Ireland.

Figure 3-32.
A major priority of the nursery stock program at the Efford Experimental Horticulture Station has been to evaluate and develop innovative methods in energy-saving technology for the plant propagator. (Reproduced by courtesy of Efford Experimental Horticulture Station, Lymington, Hampshire, U.K.)

For convenience, this section on energy saving can be divided into three parts:—

(i) External Factors.

(ii) Greenhouse structure and control of the environment.

(iii) Propagation bed (floor or bench).

External Factors

The importance of site and protection from wind has been explained on p. 112. However, it must be emphasized that increasing wind speed can dramatically increase heat loss due to the large surface of the greenhouse. Wind is a more important factor in heat loss than temperature difference. Heat loss doubles as the wind speed increases from calm to 15 knots. It has been estimated that a 10% energy saving can be achieved by reducing the wind speed by 30%.

Artificial (manufactured) windbreaks are more costly but give an immediate effect, maintain a constant filter factor and take up less space. Living windbreaks initially cost less but are slow to establish so do not give an immediate effect and have a variable filter factor which decreases with age (thinning required) (see p. 51).

Greenhouse Structure and Control of the Environment

Structural Maintenance

Most of the heat is lost from the greenhouse structure and it is, therefore, imperative that the structure be well-maintained. This is particularly true with older greenhouses where the structural strength has begun to deteriorate. Broken, cracked and slipped panes of glass must be repaired or replaced, while any tears in polyethylene should be fixed with a weatherproof sealing tape. A weatherproof transparent polyethylene film-coated tape with a good adhesive seal (e.g., Sylglas Tape®) is particularly useful for repairing cracked glass or plastic. It has been stated that between 5–7% fuel savings can be achieved by sealing glass panes with a proprietary sealing compound (e.g., Dow Corning 781 Silicone Seelant). Roof and side ventilators should fit snugly against the surrounding framework. Insulating the gutters with an expanded polystyrene (Styrofoam®) molding will reduce heat loss through the gutter section by two-thirds.

Double Lining

It is well-known that lining the inside walls and roof of an existing greenhouse will reduce energy costs. This has been very useful for the propagator wanting to create a more controlled environment in an older greenhouse, either to conserve heat or to create a more humid environment. Modern technology has introduced more sophisticated and different methods of double lining a greenhouse.

Figure 3-33.
Installing polyethylene to double line the inside of an existing greenhouse prior to winter to conserve energy.

(a) Bubble Polyethylene—The inside walls of the greenhouse can be lined with an ultra-violet light resistant "bubble polyethylene" material—e.g., Pillo-Sol®. This light-weight material has been claimed to be effective in providing up to 50% in energy savings. The bubbles are essentially created by pockets of "dead air" between two layers of polyethylene film. The material comes in rolls, which are cut into appropriate lengths with a knife or scissors and then fixed in place with a special screw plug called the Alliplug®. An air gap of 2.5 cm (1″) should be left between the glass and the bubble polyethylene during installation to provide maximum insulation.

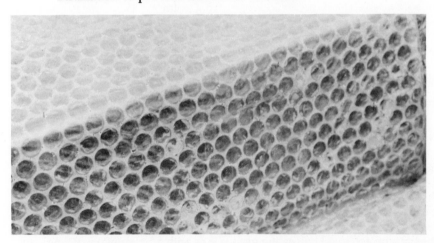

Figure 3-34.
Bubble polyethylene is a useful material for insulating greenhouses and for covering winter propagation beds and frames.

(b) Double Layer or Double Skin of Polyethylene—This is a structure covered with two layers of 125 μm (500 gauge) polyethylene. A small electric fan unit is installed in the center of the structure to continuously blow air between the two layers so that they are kept about 15 cm (6″) apart. The air blown between the two layers of polyethylene film is taken from inside the greenhouse. Thus, it encourages condensation to form on the inside of the outer layer instead of on the inner layer. An additional benefit of the double layer is that the inner film deteriorates less rapidly where it contacts the metal hoop structure that supports it.

Figure 3-35.
A propagation facility installed in a greenhouse clad with the energy-conserving feature of two layers of polyethylene kept separated by continually blowing air from an electric fan.

This modification should give up to 30% saving in energy costs for heating floor level propagation beds. There is approximately 15% loss of incoming light as compared to a single layer of polyethylene film. Compared to a single layer of polyethylene film, the additional frost protection provided by the double layer has been quoted at 5°C (9°F).

[Considerable interest has been raised in the European greenhouse industry by a highly transparent polyester film with insulation properties of up to 30% when it is used to totally line the greenhouse. It is known as Melinex 071® (made by ICI Petrochemical and Plastics Division, Wilton, Middlesborough, U.K.) and contains an ultra-violet light inhibitor (U.V.I.). The material is claimed to transmit more light than glass and to result in a 4–6% reduction in light transmission when installed as an inner lining to the glass structure. There is currently some doubt regarding its usefulness to the nursery industry because of the high expense.]

Figure 3-36. A vertical mobile plastic screen for energy conservation between sections of a greenhouse. This method can be useful to section off the propagation area from the growing-on area in a large greenhouse, and allows flexibility for materials handling. (Reproduced by courtesy of Notcutts Nurseries, Woodbridge, Suffolk, U.K.)

Thermal Screen

A thermal screen is generally a woven or spun-bonded polyester fabric (sometimes film plastic) that is drawn across the crop at night to serve as an insulation layer between the plants and the roof of the greenhouse. It is more effective if it also drapes down the sides of the greenhouse.

Thermal screens have been particularly successful in the floriculture and pot plant industries, but have been adapted recently to woody ornamental plant propagation and liner production—particularly in multi-span greenhouses. In these cases, it serves as both shading and a thermal screen.

Figure 3-37.
A spun-bonded thermal screen fabric (Floratex®) that also provides about 50% shade capacity during the day. Note that it is both drawn across the ceiling and drapes down the sides of the greenhouse.
(Reproduced by courtesy of G.F. Sheard, Arundel, Sussex, U.K.)

Research institutions in North America and Europe have evaluated a number of different materials for their effectiveness in reducing heat loss through radiation. The selection of a thermal screen should be based not only on the energy saving capacity, but also on the ability to withstand ultra-violet light degradation and the provision of shade requirements. Thermal screens alone are not generally cost effective for nursery stock, but dual purpose screens for thermal and shading are. For nursery stock, some of the heat saving must be sacrificed because a porous screen is necessary.

Examples of manufactured spun-bonded polyester fabrics suitable for nursery stock are Reemay 2016®, Fibertex® and Floratex®. These can all be suitably used as a thermal screen at night and shading material during the day. Energy savings of around 25% have been achieved with these types of fabrics.

Air Temperature Control

While the air temperature in a nursery stock propagation house can be considerably lower than for most greenhouse crops, it is still very important to use accurate, well-maintained equipment linked to the heating system to control the air temperature.

Figure 3-38.
A simple aspirated screen suspended in the greenhouse to provide greater accuracy of air temperature control.

An aspirated screen is a considerable improvement over the conventional rod thermostat for regulating air temperature. This screen is essentially a small hollow tube that hangs inside the greenhouse. An electrically-powered fan at one end of the tube draws in a sample of the air and directs it over a sensing element near the other end of the tube. The screen is protected to eliminate inaccuracies caused by radiation and variation of air currents within the greenhouse. Some aspirated screens are box-shaped so that a thermograph can be placed inside them to make continual checks on the accuracy of the automated heating and control system.

It is sometimes necessary to check the uniformity of air temperature distribution within a greenhouse. This is especially useful for a larger greenhouse to check the efficiency of the air heating system. [One method is to use a number of simple integrating jars (1 kg/2 lb jam jars) or bags distributed throughout the greenhouse. These units are made by covering the outside of the jars or bags with aluminum foil and then filling them with water. A drop of oil is placed on the surface of the water to reduce evaporation and the jar or bag is sealed with a cork or 1.3 cm (½″) expanded polystyrene plug. A thermometer is inserted to half its length through a hole in the cork or plug. The temperature on the thermometer is recorded just before or at sunrise. The temperatures for several days or weeks are used to determine the average temperature for the one and a half hours immediately preceding the time of record-taking.]

Heating System Maintenance

The heating system, and its associated control instruments, is like a car—it must be maintained correctly on a regular basis to make maximum use of fuel. Check boilers equipped with an oil-fired burner by measuring the amount of carbon dioxide in the flue gases. Excess air, the optimum being 20% excess, is required to ensure complete combustion of the oil. This is indicated by a measurement of 13% carbon dioxide in the flue gases. Fuel is wasted when there is too much air, indicated by a low carbon dioxide content. Too little air causes incomplete combustion and is indicated by a high carbon dioxide content. (It also wastes oil, and causes smoke and smuts to be produced.) Simple boiler testing kits to evaluate boiler efficiency by measuring the contents of smoke, flue gas temperature and carbon dioxide level are available. Routine inspections for heaters circulating warm air include mechanical and electrical checks on the burner and fan and the percentage of carbon dioxide in the flue gas.

The boiler house, boiler, pipes distributing heated water, flanges and hand wheel valves should all be insulated. Temporary repairs can be done by packing fiber glass around the area and covering with black polyethylene tied into place firmly with polypropylene twine.

Specific details on maintenance procedures, insulation and repair of heating systems should be obtained from the manufacturer of the equipment or an extension officer specializing in heating engineering.

Propagation Bed (Floor or Bench)

This section largely reviews the research carried out by Margaret E. Scott at Efford Experimental Horticulture Station (Efford E.H.S.). The nursery industry in Britain has been quick to use the findings of her research because much of it is relatively inexpensive, and straightforward and cost effective to install. The results of her work to reduce energy costs for propagation are included among the following suggestions.

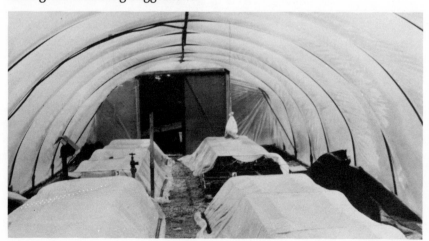

Figure 3-39.
An energy-saving propagation greenhouse for winter propagation. Features include the double-skin greenhouse, beds lined at the sides and bases with 5 cm (2″) thick expanded polystyrene (Styrofoam®) sheets covered with polyethylene film, thermal covers, and reduced basal and air temperatures. (Efford Experimental Horticulture Station, Lymington, Hampshire, U.K.)

Unheated Propagation Facility

Cold frame (p. 106) and low polyethylene tunnel propagation (p. 166) are two very effective facilities in situations where the plant being propagated requires no additional basal heat. There are a substantial number of relatively easy-to-root ornamentals that can be rooted successfully in such an unheated propagation facility. Installing basal heat does provide flexibility for propagating bench-grafted plants and rooting the more difficult-to-root evergreen and deciduous shrubs, trees and conifers in such relatively simple facilities.

Hot Water Heat Instead of Electricity.

When the scale of operation is sizable and capital/running costs are correctly evaluated, the circulation of hot water is generally a cheaper source of heating. The method of providing the hot water need not involve excessive capital expenditure—for example, a second-hand boiler may be installed (p. 127).

Duration of Basal Heat

In certain situations (e.g., rooting cuttings), savings in heating costs can be realized by supplying basal heat for an overnight period of 8 hours instead of the full 24 hours. Solar radiation can be relied on to provide sufficient basal heat for many plants for the remaining portion. Costs can be lowered still further if the local electricity price structure provides reduced "off-peak" rates during the night. Research on a range of plants rooted in low polyethylene tunnels sited in a greenhouse at Efford E.H.S. has shown that basal heat for the 8 hours from 11:00 p.m. to 7:00 a.m. resulted in rooting equivalent to that obtained when the heat was used for the full 24 hours. There was a delay in rooting with some slower-to-root evergreen shrubs, such as *Camellia*.

Research at Kinsealy Research Centre, Dublin, Eire, showed a similar benefit when basal heat is provided during the daytime only and switched off at night.

Control of Basal Heat

Considerable reductions in costs can be obtained by replacing the typical thermostat-controlled system with an electronic pulse ratio controller (see p. 128). The latter provides a more accurate and faster response to heat demand, resulting in energy savings.

Replacement of Mist Propagation with a Polyethylene Film Covering for Fall and Winter Propagation of Cuttings.

Each burst of mist cools the leaf tissues as well as the rooting medium. This cooling effect on the medium is minimal in the summer because solar radiation quickly reverses such reductions. However, the cooling effect lasts longer in the lower night temperatures of fall and winter. Rooting under a polyethylene film covering, either laid directly over the leaf surface of the cuttings (contact polyethylene) or supported on a hoop slightly above the cuttings, reduces heating costs because it helps to retain heat from the base and there is no overhead water application except to correct the occasional drying out of the rooting medium or to apply a fungicidal drench or spray. Experiments at Luddington Experimental Horticulture Station, Stratford-upon-Avon, Warwickshire, England, demonstrated that cuttings being rooted during August and September required 36 units of heat under polyethylene for every 100 units under mist propagation.

Measurements comparing the differences in heat units when rooting cuttings in a greenhouse under mist propagation and polyethylene film at the Glasshouse Crops Research Institute, Rustington, U.K., are tabulated below.

TABLE 3-2. Relative Power Usage in Different Propagation Systems

	OPEN MIST	POLY-ENCLOSED MIST [Polyethylene Tunnel enclosing mist line]	CONTACT POLYETHYLENE
December 1980	100	75	52
January 1981	100	56	31
Mean	100	66	42

Expanded Polystyrene (Styrofoam®) Insulation of Beds

Lining the base and sides of the bed, bench or cold frame with sheets of expanded polystyrene (Styrofoam®) is one of the most effective methods for reducing energy costs. Expanded polystyrene is very resistant to moisture, and gives long-term insulation because of its "closed cell structure".

Experiments have been carried out during March and April on the use of these sheets on propagation beds with the basal temperature set at 18°C (64°F). Expanded polystyrene sheets 2.5 cm (1″) thick provided 32% saving in electricity consumption when installed on the base of the bed and a 49% saving when installed on the base and sides. The use of 5 cm (2″) thick sheets provided a 42% saving when installed at the base alone and 53% on both the base and sides.

Expanded polystyrene sheets are installed as follows:—

1. Wrap the sheets in clear or black polyethylene film to prevent water penetration and to provide a further insulating layer.

2. Make the sides of floor beds very slightly lower than the center. The slight camber thus created will assist in drainage.

3. Adjacent sheets on the benches should fit loosely so that water can percolate through.

4. If mist propagation is used, lay a plastic pipe drilled with holes on top of the sheets down the center of the bed (two for wide beds) to remove excess water. The pipe should be wrapped with a capillary irrigation matting fabric to prevent clogging of the holes by the 7.5 cm (3″) layer of sand that is used between the top surface of the expanded polystyrene sheet and the base of the flats.

Thermal Covers (Thermo-blanket)

For the purposes of this text, a thermal cover is an energy-saving material placed directly over the propagation bed or bench to distinguish it from a thermal screen which creates a false ceiling beneath the roof of the greenhouse. Research at Efford E.H.S. has shown that the use of thermal covers produces significant energy savings. The initial trials were with two materials covering a propagation bed insulated with 5.0 cm (2″) thick sheets of expanded polystyrene inside a "walk-in" tunnel clad with both a single and a double layer of polyethylene. The cuttings were covered with polyethylene supported on hoops. The two thermal cover materials used were bubble polyethylene and aluminized polyester. Microfoam® is one material that has been used successfully in North America for the winter protection of nursery stock.

(a) **Bubble Polyethylene (e.g., Pillo-Sol®)**—This thermal covering material produced 15% energy savings for a double-clad tunnel. It was left on for 24 hours a day, but it has not yet been established whether the reduced light level during the winter is detrimental to rooting of the cuttings.

(b) **Aluminized Polyester**—This material produced a 10% energy saving figure in a double-clad tunnel, but it must be removed during the daytime to allow light to reach the cuttings.

Reducing Temperature Levels

Air and basal temperatures can be reduced without damage to many species, resulting in energy savings.

(a) **Basal Temperature**—The optimum basal heat used for propagation is usually considered to be 18–21°C (65–70°F). Efford E.H.S. experiments have shown clearly that these levels are not necessary for many easy-to-root species. Energy savings can be achieved by using a 12–15°C (54–59°F) regime with virtually no detrimental effects on the speed of rooting or the quality of roots formed. Rooting was actually improved in some cases. There was less *Botrytis* (Gray Mold) infection to the cuttings at this lower basal temperature regime.

(b) **Air Temperature**—A night air temperature of between 10–12°C (50–54°F) is generally considered to be the optimum range for the typical propagation greenhouse. Experiments with rooting cuttings under polyethylene film at a night air temperature of 5°C (41°F) showed very comparable, and in some cases, better results.

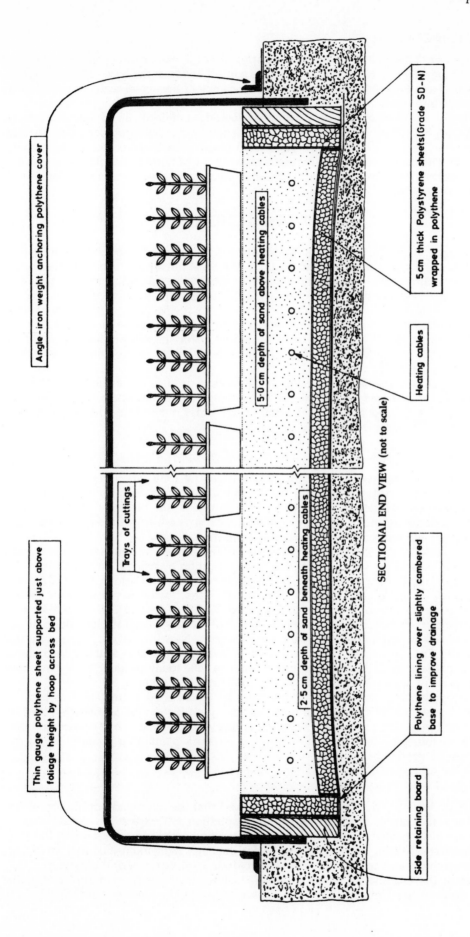

Angle - iron weight anchoring polythene cover

Thin gauge polythene sheet supported just above foliage height by hoop across bed

Trays of cuttings

5·0 cm depth of sand above heating cables

2·5 cm depth of sand beneath heating cables

5 cm thick Polystyrene sheets(Grade SD–N) wrapped in polythene

Heating cables

Polythene lining over slightly cambered base to improve drainage

Side retaining board

SECTIONAL END VIEW (not to scale)

DIAGRAM 3-2. Construction of an Insulated Propagation Bed

Reproduced by courtesy of Efford Experimental Horticulture Station, Lymington, Hampshire, U.K.

Type of Flat or Unit Container

Two criteria are important for good heat transfer from the basal heating cables or pipes to the base of the cuttings. Firstly, there should be a firm contact between the base of the flat or container and the sand base. Secondly, the heat transfer efficiency of the actual material used for the flats or containers is important.

Three types of rooting retainers were evaluated at Efford E.H.S.—a polystyrene (Styrofoam®) flat, a polystyrene moulded unit container tray and a polypropylene flat. The aim was to determine how much electricity was required to obtain a continuous root zone temperature of 21°C (70°F). The best heat transfer was achieved with the polypropylene flat while the least efficient was the polystyrene flat for which it was not possible to raise the temperature above 17.5°C (63.5°F).

MIST PROPAGATION

Mist propagation, in which very small water droplets are sprayed through the atmosphere and on to the cuttings to keep them cool and turgid, is the most universally used method for the propagation of leafy cuttings. Mist propagation also raises the relative humidity of the surrounding atmosphere. There has been considerable research devoted to equipment, methods of installation, correct facility, and on its use with rooting cuttings of numerous species. This work has resulted in a considerable number of research papers and popular articles, and even books devoted specifically to mist propagation. This section provides a brief history of mist propagation, followed by an explanation of the principles involved, the equipment needed and the practical considerations of day-to-day maintenance.

Mist propagation is a well-proven method for rooting cuttings but it should not be considered as providing the answer to all situations. Recent research has shown that other propagation methods are preferable under certain situations. These other methods include fogging and a cover of polyethylene film over the cuttings.

History of Mist Propagation

The first documented use of mist propagation was in 1936 when researcher G. E. L. Spencer attempted to root cuttings of the tropical plant *Theobroma cacao* (Cacao) under mist. Research continued in other locations during the 1940s, but with little publicity. This early work depended upon a continuous application of mist over the cuttings which resulted in a cold, often waterlogged, medium and tended to leach nutrients from the cuttings.

The real breakthrough came in 1953 when H. Templeton, a Tennessee nurseryman, devised a method to control the frequency of the mist application by using a twin-electrode controller. This was called the Phytotector System or "intermittent mist". Both researchers and nursery operators were quick to realise and develop the potential of the Phytotector System for rooting cuttings of many species. Two prominent researchers were W. E. Snyder and C. E. Hess, then both at Cornell University, Ithaca, N.Y., and they provided much of the physiological explanation of mist propagation. They later moved to Rutgers—the State University, New Brunswick, N.J., and Purdue University, Lafayette, Ind., respectively, continuing their research programs at those institutions. The basic concept of the original Phytotector System remains valid today although there have been modifications to parts of it, mainly in nozzle design and control equipment.

Mist propagation has also been used successfully to aid seed germination of bedding plants and greenhouse pot plants, and to improve the germination of *Sciadopitys verticillata* (Japanese Umbrella Pine). Other uses have been in grafting certain species, in establishing rooted air layers, and in encouraging new growth to develop on stock plants in a greenhouse so that earlier cuttings can be obtained.

Physiological Principle of Mist Propagation

Research by W. E. Snyder and C. E. Hess showed that the overhead application of fine water droplets keeps the cuttings turgid by reducing transpiration and respiration, and also that the cell tissues are essentially cooled by the subsequent evaporation of the film of water that forms on the upper leaf surfaces. Misting allows rooting under the high light intensities that encourage maximum photosynthesis and so build up the carbohydrate food reserves of the cutting.

K. Loach at the Glasshouse Crops Research Institute recently re-examined this earlier research work done in the United States, and subsequently reached some interesting conclusions:—

(i) Accurate measurements showed that leaf temperatures of misted cuttings remained within ±1°C (1.8°F) of the surrounding air over a wide range of light levels. In comparison, cuttings under a polyethylene tent were considerably warmer than the surrounding air (4°C/7.2°F greater at high light levels). This confirms the ability of mist to effectively lower leaf temperatures.

(ii) Variations occur in the humidity levels of the air surrounding the cuttings. The humidity level drops considerably between each mist burst and water vapor is then lost from the cuttings, mainly from the stomata on the under surface of the leaf which is not covered by a film of water. This loss of water stresses the cuttings and reduces rooting. The rooting of summer softwood cuttings can be improved by enclosing the propagation bench or floor bed with supported polyethylene to form a low tunnel or tent so that the humidity level is kept much more constant between mist bursts (p. 142).

(iii) The concept of providing maximum light intensity for carbohydrate production in the cuttings is not beneficial in practice. Rooting is seldom limited by carbohydrate shortage and, in fact, there is some evidence that too high a carbohydrate accumulation can reduce root initiation. More importantly, reducing the light helps to avoid water stress in the cuttings. The shading required depends on geographical location, time of year and weather—for example, ranging from no shade in mid-winter to 80% shade in summer (p. 118).

To summarize, the two essentials for successful use of mist propagation are firstly, to reduce leaf tissue temperatures, and secondly, to raise the humidity levels of the air surrounding the cuttings.

TYPE OF FACILITY SUITABLE FOR INSTALLATION OF A MIST PROPAGATION SYSTEM

A mist propagation system can be installed in any of the following facilities.

1. Outdoors

Open-air beds with a mist system have been used successfully in the eastern United States and in California for rooting cuttings—particularly in locations with high summer temperatures. Capital costs are reduced because there is no permanent covering structure. Wind protection must be provided along each side of the beds to prevent wind drift of the fine water droplets. Humidity levels around the cuttings are considerably less than in an enclosed area, therefore outdoor beds would not be suitable for thin-leaved *Acer palmatum* cvs. (Japanese Maple). Increased misting is necessary in hot weather to keep the cuttings turgid, therefore drainage of the bed and aeration and drainage of the rooting medium must all be efficient. Shade cloth supported by wire and posts is helpful in lowering the temperature and reducing the frequency of misting. Open-air floor-level beds lend themselves to materials handling systems.

Figure 3-40. A (left). An outdoor mist propagation area in southern California for large-scale propagation of cuttings. B (right). Shade fabric installed over an outdoor mist propagation area. (Both reproduced by courtesy of Monrovia Nursery Inc., Azusa, CA, U.S.A.)

2. Cold Frames

Mist units have been successfully installed in single- and double-span cold frames. They must be of a sufficient height to ensure good distribution of the misting pattern. The frames may be left open with the lights removed or covered with shaded glass, wooden laths or shade cloth when using a mist system.

Figure 3-41.
Cold frames designed for overhead misting. Note the extra height of the sides to allow better distribution of the water droplets. (Angers, France)

3. Polyethylene Tunnels (Sun Tunnels)

A mist line covered by polyethylene supported on hoops was the basis of the original Phytotector System. This system created the basis of today's low polyethylene tunnels or sun tunnels for rooting cuttings with essentially little modification from the original design.

4. Lath or Shade Houses

Traditional lath or shade houses have been successfully used for mist propagation. The houses reduce lateral wind movement and provide overhead shade. Additional protection by installing a windbreak fabric on the side(s) of the shade house may be necessary in windy sites.

5. Greenhouses

Glass or plastic-covered greenhouses are the most widely used type of facility in which mist systems are installed, either over a bench or floor area. The merits, limitations, modifications, and design of bench and floor areas in greenhouses are described on pp. 122–127.

A very successful system that I saw on propagation nurseries in West Germany is the enclosure of floor mist beds in a 1.2 m (4') high continuous tunnel made of milky polyethylene. Research by K. Loach has demonstrated that a combination of mist propagation and supported clear polyethylene with additional shading, sometimes referred to as closed mist, offers a number of advantages, including:—

(i) Considerably less variation in humidity levels because the resulting polyethylene tunnel ensures that the level drops slowly.

(ii) Lower frequency of misting required, reducing the likelihood of water saturation of the rooting medium and loss of soluble nutrients from the leaves of the cuttings.

(iii) Improved turgidity of very soft leafy cuttings.

(iv) Less need to shade.

Types of cuttings that K. Loach found to respond especially well to the closed mist system are:—

(i) Softwood cuttings of large-leaved species, e.g., *Corylus maxima* 'Purpurea' (Purple Giant Filbert), and thin-leaved species with slender stems, e.g., *Acer palmatum* 'Atropurpureum' (Red Japanese Maple).

(ii) Softwood cuttings of high-value species taken shortly after bud burst, e.g., deciduous azaleas and *Parrotia persica* (Persian Parrotia).

(iii) Cuttings with soft immature tips which are especially prone to disease attack, e.g., *Cotinus coggygria* 'Royal Purple' (Purple Smoke Tree).

(iv) Broad-leaf evergreen species taken in late summer/early fall as opposed to more conventional late fall and winter propagation, e.g., *Garrya elliptica* (Coast Silk-tassel).

So far, K. Loach has found that this system is not suitable for conifers—they have simply failed to root and the reason has not yet been determined.

WATER SOURCE

The quality of the water used for mist propagation is very important. Provision for collecting and storing rain water is certainly advantageous (p. 113). The optimum pH level sometimes recommended for a mist propagation water source is 5.8.

The water source should be tested for the following in particular:—

1. Disease pathogens and algae.

2. Mineral impurities, particularly iron which causes nozzle blockage.

3. High salt levels, which can be damaging to foliage and the developing root system.

4. High pH levels, which can result in calcium carbonate deposits causing a hard encrusted layer over the leaf surface of cuttings, increased alkalinity of the rooting medium, and increased frequency of maintenance for some types of mist control systems.

REVIEW OF EQUIPMENT

There are numerous designs and suppliers of mist propagation equipment, so it pays to thoroughly investigate the various alternatives relative to their suitability for your situation. Besides cost, two particularly important aspects are the efficiency of the mist nozzles in providing a fine and even distribution pattern, and the efficiency of the automatic control system that controls the amount and frequency of misting over the cuttings.

The basic elements of a mist propagation system are a control box, pump, solenoid valve, pipework and nozzles [Layout/design and installation details may be obtained from the manufacturers.]

Control Box

The control boxes should be enclosed to make them waterproof if they are in a humid greenhouse or if there is any chance that water droplets may drift onto them. They should be installed in a location where they are not liable to damage from hand trucks and where unauthorized personnel can be discouraged from meddling with them.

There are two types of control boxes.

(a) Mist Control Box—This is basically an on/off mechanism and relays the "message" from the automatic or manual control system to the solenoid valve that, in turn, allows water to pass through the misting nozzles.

(b) Weaner Control Box—Some manufacturers provide an optional additional control unit to harden-off the cuttings following mist. This is usually referred to as the weaner unit, and is used when there are two or more benches or beds. Weaner control boxes are now little used in commercial practice. [The weaner unit, if used, must be co-ordinated with the mist control box because the frequency of misting is reduced at pre-set intervals on one bed while operating normally on the other. A series of weaner control boxes can be installed if there are more than two beds.]

The frequency of misting to harden-off the cuttings in single beds or benches can be controlled manually or by a time clock (p. 147).

Pump

The optimum water pressure should be 34.5 Newtons per cm² (50 psi). Mains water pressure is often sufficient to provide this requirement, thus eliminating the need to install a pump. The need for a pump is determined by the existing water pressure, nozzle design and by the size of the area to be covered by the mist propagation system. If the pressure is too low, the water droplets may be too coarse so that coverage over the cuttings is incomplete. Conversely, very high water pressure produces very small droplets that are extremely prone to movement caused by air currents, again resulting in dry areas.

A piston or centrifugal pump that builds up pressure in a pressurized "holding" tank is recommended for achieving the instant pressure response required by mist systems.

Solenoid Valve

A solenoid valve is required to open and close the supply of water to the misting nozzles. The mechanism is operated automatically from the mist control unit. It is advisable to install a filter on the water source side of the solenoid valve to reduce the risk of debris clogging the nozzles. The action of the solenoid valve must be very precise as a faulty valve leads to uneven misting at the beginning and ending of the misting cycle, resulting in large water droplets dripping onto the cuttings.

Pipework

The piping is usually 1.3 cm (½") diameter copper, galvanized iron or rigid plastic. Durable rigid plastic pipes capable of withstanding high water pressure are now preferred. Copper is too costly, while galvanized piping can cause zinc toxicity in the water and also give rise to scale after a time, resulting in blocked nozzles (remember that galvanized pipes deteriorate in low pH water).

Valves (stopcocks) should be installed at each bench or bed so that the system can be turned off as necessary.

Two systems are basically used when installing the pipework to the misting nozzles:—

(a) Lay the pipes just below or directly on top of the bench. Riser (upright) pipes are placed at set intervals depending on water pressure, nozzle size and width of bench and the mist nozzles are screwed into these. Riser pipes do not give as much freedom of movement within the bench or bed area, but any drips from the nozzles will run down the riser pipe and not onto the cuttings.

Most layouts run one pipe down the center of the bench. An alternative is to run the pipe down one side with angled risers to site the nozzles over the center of the bench. Wider benches will probably require two equidistant sets of pipes and risers.

Figure 3-42. A floor bed mist propagation unit with durable rigid plastic risers. Note the plastic deflection (anvil) nozzles and the shade cloth fabric suspended above to provide a false ceiling. (Hadlow College of Agriculture & Horticulture, Tonbridge, Kent, U.K.)

Figure 3-43. A greenhouse propagation facility with suspended mist lines installed over and down the benches. The mist lines must be level to avoid dripping and uneven spray patterns. (Sheridan Nurseries, Oakville, ON, Canada)

(b) Suspend the pipes above the bench or floor bed facility, thus eliminating the risers. Less pipe is required for an overhead system as there are no risers. This system permits a free working area, and is therefore particularly useful for floor bed and open floor facilities. The pipework must be absolutely level, otherwise drip problems and uneven mist spray patterns will result. This system is also flexible in that the bench or bed can be easily adapted during the winter to a closed case facility for cuttings and flats. The misting lines can remain, be taken down and utilized elsewhere, or simply moved to one side of the bed if attached to a series of metal swing-arm units.

Nozzles

The correct choice of nozzle is very important for the success of a mist propagation system. Try to obtain samples of different nozzle types and, if possible, install them in an existing system to assess their suitability. Alternatively, visit other nurseries in the area to learn the merits and limitations of the nozzles that they are using.

The important points to consider when selecting a misting nozzle are:—

1. Cost—For convenience, nozzles can be divided into two groups. Firstly, more expensive ones that can be adjusted and maintained so that they can be used successfully for many years. Secondly, low-cost products that are simply removed and replaced with a new one when the nozzle becomes worn or severely clogged.

2. Size of Droplet and Amount of Water Used—Nozzles that produce a very fine mist droplet using little water are preferable. The droplets should hang as a "cloud" for a few seconds immediately after misting before falling down onto the cuttings. One mistake sometimes made is to install a system using a nozzle that is designed for overhead mist irrigation which produces too coarse a droplet and uses too much water.

Figure 3-44.
A floor-level greenhouse mist installation at the peak of the misting burst. Note the "suspension cloud" of mist droplets. (Hillier Nurseries (Winchester) Ltd., Romsey, Hampshire, U.K.)

3. Spray Pattern—The spray pattern is generally circular and the distance between the nozzles down the bench or bed should be such that there is not an excessive overlap. Some degree of overlap is necessary for the perimeter ("tails") of the misting pattern from adjacent nozzles to "reinforce each other" and so ensure even coverage over the cuttings. Too much overlapping results in over-wet areas and wastes water, while too small a spray pattern results in insufficient coverage and allows the cuttings to dry out. The distance between the nozzles is largely determined by the type of nozzle and by the bench or bed width.

4. Filtering—Nozzles containing a removable filter are preferable as they reduce the possibility of blockages.

5. Maintenance and Replacements—Permanent nozzles should be easy to clean and dismantle, and the local supplier should be able to ensure the availability of replacement parts. Always keep a few spare nozzles or replacement parts at the nursery for immediate repairs (see also p. 150).

There are basically two fundamental types of nozzle—the deflection nozzle and the oil burner nozzle.

(a) **Deflection or Anvil Nozzle**—Deflection nozzles are the most widely used. The nozzle contains a flat surface, the anvil, which produces a fine mist spray when a pressurized stream of water is deflected from it. An example is the well-known Macpenny® Atomiser Jet, which has proved to be reliable over many years of use. As with some other nozzles, there is a removable filter at the base to catch any debris that could clog the nozzle itself. The water is deflected by hitting the base of a vertical stainless steel pin. An adjustable screw at the top of the nozzle alters the amount of water being deflected from minus to plus 25%. A small piece of rubber (or a piece of disused plastic credit card) can be secured between the orifice and base of the deflection pin if individual nozzles need to be cut off. Other makes of deflection nozzles can also be adjusted, but some are fixed and cannot be altered. Most nozzles are virtually self-cleaning providing there is sufficient pressure and aperture space.

Figure 3-45.
The Macpenny®
Atomiser Jet deflection or
anvil nozzle for mist
propagation. Note the
filter at the base of the
nozzle which can be
easily slipped off, cleaned
to remove any debris and
then replaced.

(b) **Pressure Jet or Whirl Nozzle**—The pressure jet or whirl nozzle has a number of grooves set at different angles so that a very fine mist is produced when water enters the nozzle under pressure. The earlier designs were effective only under high water pressure, and were prone to blockage and dripping. Improved designs operate under lower water pressures, and are self-cleaning and non-dripping.

Pressure jet nozzles have a number of curved internal channels. Water is forced through these channels under pressure and the impact at the orifice of the nozzle then breaks up the water flow into small droplets.

Mist Frequency Control Systems

Some means of controlling the frequency and length of misting is necessary. However, there is no foolproof system available—each has both its merits and limitations. Whichever system is selected, it is important to remember that it will take a few weeks to become fully acquainted with its use. The instructions provided with an automatic system should be treated as a guideline only—you will need to make further adjustments, and sometimes extra calibrations, for different weather conditions. The success of a mist control system depends on the ability of the user. The main fault of some mist control systems is that they allow the application of too much water—particularly during low light intensity periods and at night. Therefore, adjustments are often necessary for these periods. The need to mist the cuttings will rapidly increase during hot dry periods. Under these circumstances, it is better to set the control system for short, very frequent bursts of mist rather than using long, less frequent applications.

The main mist control systems used by nursery operators are explained below.

1. Manual Operation

A manually-operated mist control unit is normally used to over-ride an automatic system. A manual over-ride is particularly useful in more northerly climates when propagating broad-leaf evergreen and conifer cuttings during the shorter days and lower light intensities of the fall and winter. Automatic systems frequently apply too much water under these circumstances. A manual control is used also when a time clock has not been installed for turning off the mist at night.

2. Time Clock

Time clocks are a reliable and virtually maintenance-free method to control misting. Time clocks that control both the frequency and the length of the misting cycle are available. A second time clock can be installed to automatically switch off the system at dusk and re-start it at dawn, thus eliminating the need to re-set the time clock every evening. The optimum frequency of misting can be varied from 1–60 minutes and the optimum length of the misting period from 4–75 seconds. Time clocks are best suited to propagation units in areas where the weather conditions are relatively constant.

Figure 3-46.
A control center for a large outdoor mist propagation unit. Note the series of time clocks to individually control misting frequency of different bed areas. (Reproduced by courtesy of Monrovia Nursery Inc., Azusa, CA, U.S.A.)

Time clocks have two disadvantages. Firstly, they do not respond to varying weather conditions and must be re-set to compensate for this to avoid too much or too little water. Secondly, it can be more difficult to expect substitute staff to appreciate the necessity to re-set and to initiate the required setting. The skill of using time clocks correctly develops with experience.

3. Balance

The balance system works on the principle that water droplets from the misting nozzles fall onto a metal plate, screen or pad that moves downward under the weight of the water. The plate, screen or pad then rises as the water evaporates until it reaches a pre-determined point when a "message" is relayed, either directly or indirectly through a control box, to the solenoid valve. This "message" causes the valve to open and misting to occur. The downward movement caused by the increasing weight of water causes the solenoid valve to close. Balance systems require some maintenance, but have proved to be reliable and to take variable weather conditions into account.

Figure 3-47.
A misting control unit. The metal plate is kept in a downward position by the weight of the water droplets, thus causing the solenoid valve to close.

Figure 3-48.
A Mist-A-Matic® balance control for controlling misting frequency. Note the fine mesh stainless steel screen at the front and the screw device at the back for adjusting misting frequency and duration.

I have seen a very successful balance system used in Holland and Belgium in which the water falls onto a metal plate. A popular balance in North America is the Mist-A-Matic®, in which water droplets fall onto a fine stainless steel screen. The screen must be kept free of slime and other deposits or inaccuracies will occur. It may be cleaned by using a small hard brush and then dipping the screen into a proprietary algicide such as Algimine®, Algofen® (dichlorophen) or Cyprex® (dodine acetate).

4. "Electronic Leaf" (Artificial Leaf)

The term "electronic leaf" arose following the availability of an electronic control system developed in 1948 by H. Templeton, Winchester, Tennessee. The term is often used today to describe a mist control system that essentially "mimics" the rate of water evaporation from the leaves of the cuttings. The following systems are used:—

(a) Two carbon electrodes set in a small circular ebonite block supported on a short length of cane so that the upper surface of the block is just above the level of the cuttings. A thin film of water lying between the two electrodes causes a low electrical current to flow between them. The resistance between the electrodes increases as the water evaporates and the solenoid valve is energized at a pre-set value. This information is relayed to the control unit which opens the solenoid valve to allow misting to occur. Misting continues until a film of water has formed again between the two electrodes. This system was incorporated in the original MacPenny mist propagation system, and has proved to be very satisfactory in many countries.

Figure 3-49.
"Electronic leaf" (artificial leaf) with the two carbon electrodes set in a carbonite block. Note the beginning of calcium carbonate deposits (from the water) over the surface of the "leaf." This will require removal to ensure accuracy.

Inaccuracies will occur if deposits are permitted to build up between the two electrodes. It is important to check that the electronic leaf is not causing excessive misting. One electronic leaf, the Aquamonitor®, claims to overcome this problem by having an adjustable air gap between the two electrodes.

The following points will prove useful when using this type of electronic leaf mist control system:—

(i) The frequency of misting can be regulated in part by the position of the electronic leaf in the bench or bed. Less misting will occur if it is sited in the center of the bed where there is an overlap of misting patterns. Increased misting will occur if it is placed at the front or back of the bench so that it is just covered by the perimeter of the misting pattern.

(ii) The surface of the ebonite block must be horizontal and the support cane securely positioned. Even a slight dislodgement will result in considerable inaccuracies.

(iii) Do not allow people to test or play with the leaf. Touching with the fingers leaves a film of grease on the electrodes, resulting in uneven evaporation of water.

(iv) The upper surface of the electronic leaf must be regularly maintained by removing slime, calcium carbonate, grease and other deposits. An effective method of cleaning is to slowly rotate the surface over sand or glass paper placed on a hard surface. One problem specific to high pH water sources is the build-up of calcium carbonate deposits on the upper surface. This can be removed by dipping the top 1.3 cm (½″) into a 10–20% solution of hydrochloric acid until effervescing ceases. The block is washed well in running tap water to remove all traces of the acid before re-installing amongst the cuttings.

(b) A method using Monel metal bars developed by E. C. Geiger of Harleysville, Pennsylvania, works essentially on the same principle as the previous method. Two Monel metal bars are set in parallel within a rectangular block.

(c) A very sensitive method of measuring the degree of evaporation has been achieved by placing either a strip or a circular piece of filter paper between two electrodes. The filter paper is changed at regular intervals to ensure accuracy. The EDAC controller was designed about 1958 at Massey University, New Zealand, and was noted for its accuracy. It worked on the basis of changes in the resistance across the filter paper as it dried out.

Figure 3-50. A mist control system using two parallel metal bars to control the frequency of misting.

Figure 3-51. The sensitivity of the mist control system has been increased in this design by using a piece of filter paper placed between the two electrodes to monitor the degree of evaporation. (Manufactured by Dansk Gartneri-Teknik, 2660 Brøndby Strand, Egeskovvej 6, Denmark)

5. Photoelectric Cell

The principle of using a photoelectric cell to control the misting frequency is based on the direct relationship between the rate of transpiration and the amount of incoming solar radiation. The cell integrates the incoming solar radiation and, at a pre-determined point, triggers a mechanism that causes the solenoid valve to open. The greater the amount of solar radiation, the greater the frequency of misting. Some of the newer mist systems now use photoelectric cells. The MacPenny Solarmist® system has an adjustment for increasing or decreasing the frequency of misting to give a greater amount of flexibility. One problem that is sometimes experienced with photoelectric cell controllers is that excessive misting occurs during dull weather, and even at night. If necessary, a time clock can be installed to over-ride the photoelectric cell at night and thus control the frequency of the mist bursts more accurately.

A photoelectric cell should be installed where it receives a similar amount of light to the cuttings, but away from the mist lines so that it does not become covered with water. One manufacturer recommends that their product be sited on a south-facing wall or post 90 cm (3') above the mist propagation bench or bed.

MANAGEMENT OF MIST PROPAGATION UNITS

Modern equipment is becoming increasingly sophisticated, but it is still essential to carefully monitor the cuttings during their aftercare. I have noticed that unsuccessful results are often more attributable to neglect in effective maintenance of the cuttings and equipment or to insufficient shading than to the time of year, incorrect rooting hormone or rooting medium. Important management guidelines are outlined.

Aftercare of cuttings

Daily inspection should be made for both over-dry and over-wet areas, particularly where the foliage covers the surface of the rooting medium. The effects of stress on broad-leaved evergreens and conifers show up several days or weeks later, therefore an initial complacent attitude will mean financial losses later. Dry areas can be corrected by watering with a hand-regulated pressure spray attachment on a hose or a watering can with a fine rose attachment. Dry spots will normally be found at the perimeter of the bench or bed. Over-wet areas indicate that the mist control equipment, misting pattern and the components of the rooting medium should all be checked immediately to determine the reason, and corrections undertaken to rectify the problem(s). A major cause of cutting deterioration following sticking is to allow far too excessive misting—particularly during the fall and winter.

Dead leaves, dead cuttings and other debris should be removed during each daily inspection. Weeds should be removed to prevent them from seeding and competing with the cuttings. Weeds often grow from seeds left in the corners and edges at the base of the benches and beds if they have not been thoroughly cleaned before use.

Any form of overhead water application, particularly in enclosed areas, encourages the development of mosses and liverworts. A preventative spray with the algicides Algofen® or Algimine® or with the fungicides carbendazin/maneb (Delsene M®) or dodine acetate (Cyprex®) should keep moss and liverwort development in check. The source of water used for misting should be checked if mosses and liverworts are a serious problem. Procedures for disease control (Chapter 12) and the importance of providing shading (p. 118) are described in the respective sections in the text.

Finally, designate a staff member to specifically check the propagation area first thing every morning. This will ensure that the above operations are carried out daily. The checks should be undertaken twice daily during hot weather.

Equipment Maintenance

The main filter ahead of the solenoid valve should be removed and thoroughly cleaned in water every month. Note that the cleaning may need to be carried out more frequently if there is a large amount of debris in the water supply.

The mist nozzles should be removed once every month or two months. The small detachable filter should be cleaned with a fine brush and clean water (a toothbrush is excellent for this purpose). A blocked orifice can be conveniently cleaned with a piece of fine wire. The gap between the base of the deflection pin and orifice should be adjusted according to the manufacturer's instructions. Fixed adjustment nozzles that are designed to be disposable should be replaced as necessary. Always keep a stock of mist nozzles and parts on hand for emergency replacements.

Depending on its source, low pH water can give rise to slime and iron deposits over the mist nozzles. These are best removed by allowing the deposits to dry and then brushing with a wire brush. Encrusted deposits of calcium carbonate can build up under high pH water conditions. These can also be removed with a wire brush. However, it is sometimes more effective to place the nozzles in a 10–20% solution of hydrochloric acid until effervescing ceases, using a container made of acid-resistant material. The nozzles must be thoroughly washed with clean water to remove all traces of the acid.

The pipework forming the uprights for the mist nozzles must also be cleaned occasionally.

Further guidelines to the maintenance of mist control systems can be found by referring to the appropriate sections on pp. 143–150.

Leaf Drop and Nutrient Mist

The prime causes of stress to cuttings leading to leaf drop of evergreens and premature leaf drop of deciduous cuttings have been explained (p. 118). One is the leaching of soluble nutrients from the leaves caused by overhead misting. The problem usually arises when the cuttings take a long time to root, especially when there is excessive misting.

Research carried out in the 1960s by H. B. Tukey and J. A. Wott showed that the application of a soluble compound fertilizer through the mist lines improves stem and foliage quality, root system development and subsequent establishment after initial potting. The process of applying fertilizers in this manner is sometimes referred to as "nutrient mist". Leafy softwood cuttings of *Philadelphus* (Mock-orange) and *Ligustrum* (Privet) have responded well to nutrient mist, while deciduous azaleas showed adverse effects.

The fertilizer used must be one formulated for foliar application if nutrient mist is to be successful. The fertilizer is applied either through a proportional injector in the mist line or separately through a pressurized sprayer. Nutrient mist may be applied at every misting provided that the fertilizer is at very low concentrations. It is preferable to apply higher concentrations no more than twice weekly in the evening and then turn off the mist line until the following morning.

Problems experienced with nutrient mist have arisen when it is used incorrectly. These problems include leaf scorch, damage to the root system due to salt build-up, and encouraging the development of mosses and liverworts over the surface of the rooting medium.

Species which do not respond to nutrient mist are likely to give better results when a liquid feed is used after the cuttings have rooted or when a controlled-release fertilizer is incorporated in the rooting medium.

Hardening-Off (Weaning-Off) and Maintaining the Quality of Cuttings

Cuttings should be removed from the mist unit when they are well-rooted. A major reason for rapid deterioration of cuttings after rooting is because they remain in the mist propagation facility for too long. Cuttings of *Acer* (Maple), *Betula* (Birch), *Daphne, Cotinus coggygria* cvs. (Smoke Tree), *Prunus glandulosa* cvs. (Dwarf Flowering Almond) and climbing *Lonicera* (Honeysuckle) are among those that are particularly prone to deterioration. The cuttings should be kept shaded as necessary.

Figure 3-52.
The cuttings must not be put under stress during the hardening-off period. Additional shading may well be needed.

Hardening-off is important for two reasons. Firstly, the dryer regime encourages the development of secondary roots—the root system under mist is often rather fleshy with few secondary roots. Secondly, it helps to firm up the leaf and stem tissues.

The following procedures are successfully used for hardening-off cuttings:—

(i) Reduce the frequency of misting by manual operation or time clock (or a weaner control unit, p. 143).

(ii) Remove the flats to a heavily shaded area covered by polyethylene.

(iii) Remove the flats or containers onto adjacent pathways so that they benefit from some of the humidity arising from normal misting of the beds.

(iv) Remove the flats or containers to a separate area equipped with a mist line operated by a time clock control unit.

It is important to check the water requirements of the cuttings frequently during the hardening-off period because they must not be allowed to dry out. The cuttings may show signs of nutrient deficiency during this period, so a liquid feed may be applied to rectify this problem. This will also stimulate root development and help establishment after the initial potting. This procedure is also beneficial to cuttings left to over-winter in flats if the time of potting has been delayed.

Trials at Efford E.H.S. have demonstrated that there are considerable benefits to a nutritional program for the cuttings from hardening-off until potting if a controlled-release fertilizer was not incorporated in the rooting medium. The cutting quality was maintained and improved and there were also improvements in establishment after potting.

Trials were also carried out on fall-stuck cuttings kept under polyethylene-covered beds for potting in late spring. The liquid feed was applied every 1–2 weeks following hardening-off, using two alternative regimes:—

(i) 50 ppm N + 50 ppm K_2O

(ii) 50 ppm N + 50 ppm P_2O_5 + 50 ppm K_2O (This regime encouraged early growth of the cuttings in the flats so that the potting date had to be brought forward.)

The frequency of liquid feed application must be reduced if there is a danger of the rooting medium becoming water-logged—especially in the winter.

The trials were carried out on cuttings being rooted under polyethylene film, but it is reasonable to assume that a similar liquid feeding program would be beneficial for cuttings being rooted under a mist or fogging system.

Establishment can be improved by using unit containers (Chapter 5), extended daylength (pp. 251–52), and by delaying the potting-up of deciduous cuttings rooted late in the season until the following spring.

Carbonated Mist

Research has shown that the percentage rooting and root system quality of some woody plants can be improved by injecting carbon dioxide (CO_2) into the water in the mist lines. Levels between 900–1800 ppm CO_2 have been used in tests—these compare with average mains water levels of between 200–400 ppm. Some *Magnolia*, *Rhododendron*, *Ilex* (Holly) and *Pseudotsuga menziesii* (Douglas Fir) are among those species that demonstrated a beneficial response. Carbonated mist is rarely used on nurseries today, mainly because problems due to the unreliability of the injection equipment have been experienced under commercial nursery conditions.

FOGGING

Despite its universal use, mist propagation is by no means a foolproof system for rooting all cuttings. This is a prime reason behind the renewed interest in the principles and application of fogging systems in plant propagation facilities. Increased knowledge of plant physiology and improved technology in nozzle design, control equipment and the method by which the very small droplets can be distributed has resulted in the availability of some excellent equipment for fogging.

First, what do we understand by fogging and how does it essentially differ from mist propagation?

Figure 3-53. The effect on cutting quality by incorporating a controlled-release fertilizer (Osmocote® 18-10-10) at 1 kg per m³ (27 oz/1 cu. yd.) into a rooting medium of 3 parts peat moss and 1 part coarse sand (grit). The cuttings of *Hydrangea* 'Mme. J. de Schmedt' were stuck in May. Left — Osmocote® incorporated into the rooting medium. Right — control with no fertilizer; (Reproduced by courtesy of Efford Experimental Horticulture Station, Lymington, Hampshire, U.K.)

Figure 3-54. Improved establishment and increased, earlier growth resulting from the incorporation of a controlled-release fertilizer into the rooting medium. The cuttings of *Rhododendron* 'Vuyks Rosyred' were stuck in August in a 1:1 peat moss/bark mix and then potted in the following February (photographed in June). Left — control with no fertilizer; Center — Ficote® 16-10-10 controlled-release fertilizer added at 1 kg per m³ (27 oz/1 cu. yd.); Right — Osmocote® 17-10-10 controlled-release fertilizer added at 1 kg/m³ (27 oz/1 cu. yd.). (Reproduced by courtesy of Efford Experimental Horticulture Station, Lymington, Hampshire, U.K.)

Figure 3-55. Maintaining cutting quality by liquid feeding. A (left). Rooted cuttings of *Viburnum* × *burkwoodii* (Burkwood Viburnum) in June after sticking the previous October in a rooting medium of 3 parts peat moss to 1 part coarse sand (grit). Left — control with no feeding; Center — nitrogen (N) and potash (K₂O) added; Right —Nitrogen (N), Phosphate (P₂O) and potash (K₂O) added. B (right). Root development of *Abelia* × *grandiflora* (White Abelia) in June after sticking the previous October in a 3:1 peat moss/coarse sand (grit) rooting medium. Left —control with no feeding; Center — nitrogen and potash added; Right — nitrogen, phosphate and potash added. (Reproduced by courtesy of Efford Experimental Horticulture Station, Lymington, Hampshire, U.K.)

Principle of Fogging

Fogging is best described as the distribution of very small water droplets to create a constant humidity level of between 93–100%. These air-borne water droplets are minute—down to 10 microns* in size or less, or equivalent to one-tenth the diameter of human hair. The dispersal of these droplets increases the humidity level of the atmosphere until there is an excess of water droplets suspended in the air. Like a sea mist, they move very slowly but are extremely sensitive to movement and drift easily in the slightest air currents.

Figure 3-56.
A fog of minute water droplets suspended in the air gradually forms as it is produced by a ventilated high humidity unit installed at one end of the greenhouse.

The water droplets are suspended in the air and are therefore able to create and maintain a very thin film of water over both the upper and lower surfaces of leaves, buds and stem tissues. The water particles cool the surrounding air as they evaporate which, combined with the slow evaporation of the film of water covering the plant tissues, keeps the cuttings turgid. The flow of water particles is not necessarily directed at the bench or bed, but rather the entire propagation house is humidified with an equal distribution of water particles. This means that the moisture content of the rooting medium can be kept virtually constant, thus overcoming the problems that can result from increasing the wetness of the rooting medium. This, combined with a warm constant humidity, produces less water stress on the cuttings compared to mist propagation. However, fogging relies on tiny particles of water drifting around the propagation facility so "dry and wet spots" can still occur in the rooting medium. Also, coalescence of droplets and consequent fall-out seems to occur fairly readily in areas where the droplets are densest (e.g., near the nozzle). Some authorities feel that this distribution problem is the most important difficulty faced by any fine water droplet system. Systems that have nozzles at frequent intervals in the supply line give a better chance of providing a well-distributed fog compared to individually mounted fan units.

Comparison With Mist Propagation

Mist propagation (p. 140) differs from fogging in that misting produces droplets with a considerably greater size range in which most are larger than 50 microns. Water particles above 50 microns in size lose their suspension properties and quickly fall. The particles are forced from the nozzle for a short distance and then drop down on to the surface of the cuttings and surface of the rooting medium. Evaporation of water from the wetted leaf surface cools the leaves and reduces transpirational loss of water. However, over-wetting of the rooting medium can easily occur and cause problems. Moreover, the cuttings can become water stressed if the water film on the foliage is incomplete and the humidity drops between mist bursts due to convective air currents.

---

* 1 micron (also written 1 μ or 1 μm) = 0.001 mm (0.00004").

Merits and Limitations of Fogging

Merits

The merits claimed for fogging compared to conventional mist propagation may be summarized as follows:—

NOTE:—The benefits gained from fogging are very likely to depend very much on the geographical location of the nursery.

(i) Larger cuttings may be successfully rooted—particularly those with large soft leaf laminas. Cuttings can continue to grow during the rooting process. A "water-soaked" appearance may occur on the leaves of the new growth and terminal die-back develop during misting unless the frequency is carefully controlled. Fogging has been found to keep cuttings in better condition until rooting has occurred.

(ii) Cuttings can be taken earlier in the season because the high humidity makes it easier to keep them turgid.

(iii) Rooting is sometimes faster, with a higher percentage success rate.

(iv) Less premature leaf drop caused by leaching of nutrients and stress to the cuttings.

(v) Reduced waterlogging of the rooting medium with consequent reduction in disease problems.

(vi) Significantly less water is required. Quoted figures state that a mist nozzle will use up to 25 times more water compared to a modern fog nozzle.

(vii) More even dispersion of water particles.

(viii) High humidity provides an excellent environment in the greenhouse for establishing new plants from the micropropagation laboratory to wean them to a more normal regime. Fogging should also be ideal for rooting the small thin shoots after they have been severed from the differentiated tissue removed from the test-tube (see p. 623).

Limitations

The limitations of fogging as compared to conventional misting may be summarized as follows:—

(i) The water particles are not dispersed directly onto the cuttings so there is less flexibility in the use of the propagation greenhouse. This is particularly important for the smaller nursery wanting to graft, propagate under polyethylene film and grow-on liners in the same facility. Partitioning the house with a polyethylene curtain can help to overcome this problem. A gap should be left between the top of the curtain and the roof of the greenhouse to allow for ventilation of the hot humid air. Alternatively, the fogging area can be restricted by installing it inside a polyethylene tent.

(ii) The high humidity, especially when combined with a high air temperature, may make the environment less comfortable to work in. This is especially true during the summer months when temperatures up to 46°C (115°F) may be reached. This is one reason why systems which draw in and distribute air from outside the greenhouse are advantageous during the summer. (Those systems producing droplets of around 10 microns in size create a "dry" fog which makes the environment more comfortable for work.)

CHOICE OF EQUIPMENT

The Defensor® unit manufactured in Switzerland was the main fogging system used in Europe during the 1950s and 1960s. This unit was a circular, electrically-powered machine that drew water from a reservoir dish. The water was then atomized and dispersed through a fan at the apex of the unit. Units were small enough to be moved to different areas. They were stationary when in use, and therefore were unable to evenly distribute water droplets over any area of large size. Distribution was improved by mounting the fogging units onto mono-rails located on each side of the propagation bench. These two units slowly moved in opposing directions up and down the greenhouse. One initial problem with these units was that the float control system for the water level was not very dependable in practice, and it also had a relatively low fog capacity output.

Examples of newer equipment based on three different methods of creating the fog are described below.

Figure 3-57. A Defensor® fogging unit uses a fan at the apex of the equipment to disperse the very small water droplets.

Figure 3-58. A pair of Defensor® fogging units mounted on opposite sides of a propagation bench, These units move down the bench in opposing directions, dispersing the fog as they move.

1. High Pressure Fogging

The Mee Industries Fog System is popular in many areas of the United States and operates as a series of atomizing nozzles embedded in 1.3 cm (½") pipes with the water particles distributed upwards as a "symmetrical cone". The water must be thoroughly filtered and under a pressure of 345 Newtons per cm^2 (500 psi) for the system to operate adequately. Water is forced through a minute opening and the cylindrical water pattern that is created hits an "impact pin". This impact produces air-borne water droplets of which 95% are less than 20 microns in size, thus forming a dense fog. The coverage by each nozzle is estimated to be in the region of 7 m^2 (80 sq. ft.). Chlorine is added at 0.5 ppm if there is any chance that the water supply contains algae and/or bacteria. It is important to install an inlet fan to draw in and distribute air from outside the greenhouse in order to reduce the air temperature inside the house.

Figure 3-59. A greenhouse installed with a high pressure fogging system (Mee Industries) and used for the direct sticking of cuttings. Note the vertical dispersal of the water particles as a "symmetrical cone". (Christie Nurseries, Pitt Meadows, B.C., Canada) *Note:* the "dry fog" produced from this system has proved excellent for rooting individual shoots (micro-cuttings) produced from micropropagation.

The main items of equipment used in the system are:—

(a) High pressure pump and motor capable of producing a water pressure of around 345 N/cm^2 (500 psi), plus pipework capable of withstanding these high pressures. Equipment that will produce a water pressure of 690 N/cm^2 (1000 psi) is now available.

(b) Where mains water is not used, a chlorine injector unit is installed to kill and prevent growth of algae, bacteria and any slime in the water.

(c) Sand filter to collect precipitates from the chlorine treatment and to remove any debris.

(d) High and low pressure line filters and regulator manifold for final clean-up of the water to reduce blocking of the nozzles.

(e) Fogging nozzles and control equipment.

In addition to propagation, the Mee Industries Fog System has also been used successfully for cooling plants in shade structures, frost protection and for insecticide and fungicide application. For further information contact Mee Industries, Inc., 1629 South Del Mar Avenue, San Gabriel, CA 91776.

2. Ultrasonic Humidifier Nozzle

This type of fogger is sometimes referred to as a siphon nozzle, one of which is the Sonicore® system that has been used successfully in industry for dust suppression, air conditioning and odor control. It is based on the principle of ultrasonics with the water being accelerated by compressed air.

Figure 3-60. The Sonicore® ultrasonic humidifier nozzle showing the fog dispersal. (Reproduced by permission of Glasshouse Crops Research Institute, Littlehampton, Sussex, U.K.)

This unique ultrasonically-operated nozzle has been successfully used in propagation. Compressed air is directed against a cup-shaped resonator located in front of the nozzle outlet so that the water passes through a very sensitive sound energy field between the resonator and the nozzle. This causes the water to disperse as extremely small particles of 10 microns or less (even down to 1 micron), thus producing an extremely fine, dry fog. There must be adequate compressor capacity to ensure intermittent operation without overheating.

This system has several advantages:—

(i) Water enters under low pressure thus reducing installation costs. However, the capital cost of a large air compressor partially offsets this advantage.

(ii) The nozzle orifice is larger and not as easily blocked by impurities in the water.

(iii) It is virtually self-cleaning and there is an absence of moving parts meaning that it is maintenance-free for long periods. Also, there is no drip after the water is cut off.

The basic items of equipment making up this system are:—

(a) Filter and compressor.

(b) Solenoid valve for control of the air supply valve.

(c) Nozzles.

(d) Air and water pipes.

(e) Spring-loaded valve which opens to take in water when the air pressure is greater than two atmospheres.

Further information may be obtained from Ultrasonics Ltd., Otley Road, Shipley, West Yorkshire, U.K.

3. Ventilated High Humidity

This type of fogger differs from the previous two types in that it consists of a self-contained unit which generates water particles that are then, in turn, forced by a fan and mixed into a stream of cool air for distribution into the greenhouse. The cool air is drawn into the propagation facility from outside or produced by a refrigeration unit. The mixture of water droplets and cool air is directed through the cuttings so that the entire leaf, bud and stem surfaces are "bathed" in moisture and the relative humidity of the house is raised and maintained at virtually 100%. The moisture content of the air is continually replenished and therefore ventilation is possible. The combination of ventilation and drawing in cool air means that the ambient temperatures in the greenhouse can be substantially lowered. Some propagators using ventilated high humidity equipment have experienced over-watering of the rooting medium around the area where the water droplets are dispersed into the greenhouse.

Pioneer research on ventilated high humidity for propagation by D. C. Milbocker, Virginia Truck and Ornamental Research Station, Virginia Beach, has led to the development of the Agritech® fogging unit, which has found acceptance by propagators in both North America and Europe. The Agritech® unit is mounted at the side of the greenhouse and swivels through a 90–120°C arc, although units are now available that will turn through a 360°C arc. Air is forced through water being ejected from a spinning nozzle. This causes the water to atomize into particles 30 microns in size which are then forced into a cool air stream through the greenhouse by a fan fixed at the rear of the unit. The most recent version of the machine has the capacity to produce fog from 38–190 l (10–50 U.S. gal) of water per hour. The units are virtually maintenance-free because the nozzle orifice is relatively wide and there are few moving parts apart from the fan. However, there have been problems in practice with the motor and some other parts that have been attributed to corrosion and rusting.

Commercial nursery experience in England has found that the Agritech® system can be difficult to manage in the unstable climate in that country. Ideally, a climate control computer should be used if available and if it can be justified on a large installation. This is thought to produce the best system to reduce water stress in leafy cuttings, especially when combined with suitably treated water (pure, low pH, etc.). It is the opinion of some propagators that the development of ventilated high humidity is the most significant development in propagation equipment since the introduction of mist.

An improved model of the basic Agritech® machine has a pressurized hub assembly fitted to it. The water is injected into the machine under pressure, producing a finer fog containing water droplets 20–30 microns in size. The water pressure at the nozzle is increased to 207 N/cm² (300 psi) instead of the previous 138 N/cm² (200 psi).

Each unit will humidify around 93 m² (1000 sq. ft.) of floor space with a stream of air 9–12 m (30–40′) long. Humidity and cooling levels will not be adequate if the amount of water in the air stream is too low, so cuttings at the periphery (more than 9 m (30′) from the unit) of the distribution area will wilt. Conversely, excess water in the stream will result in the rooting medium near the unit becoming saturated due to the collision and joining up of small water particles to form larger ones which then fall on to the medium. Further information may be obtained from Agritech Inc., Box 33083, Raleigh, N.C. 27606.

A more recent machine is the Humidifan® which has a single motor but no nozzle to become blocked. It disperses fog-sized droplets in an air stream, as does the Agritech® unit, but the droplet sizes are smaller, particularly at low rates of dispersal. This results in better distribution and water saturation near the unit. The Humidifan® is currently being manufactured for commercial use. A ventilated fogging system for greenhouse propagation that is being supplied in Britain is the Mellor Bromley equipment (Mellor Bromley Air Conditioning Services Ltd., 5 Morris Road, Clarendon Industrial Estate, Leicester, U.K.).

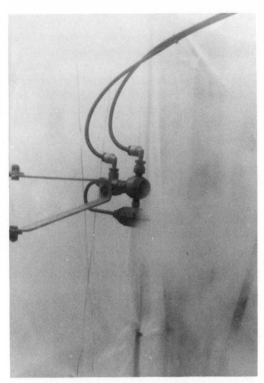

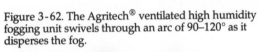

Figure 3-61. A (Left). The Macpenny® fogging nozzle installed inside a greenhouse. (Cameron, Harwood Industrial Estate, Littlehampton, Sussex, U.K.) B (Right). The fog produced by the Macpenny® fogging nozzle results from a mixture of compressed air and water. Adjustments can be made to this system to produce droplets ranging from less than 10 microns to 30 microns, thus providing the propagator with a choice between a "dry" and a "wet" fog.

Figure 3-62. The Agritech® ventilated high humidity fogging unit swivels through an arc of 90–120° as it disperses the fog.

Figure 3-63. A spinning disc humidifier installed at one end of a propagation greenhouse. (Reproduced by courtesy of Paul Labous, Merrist Wood Agricultural College, Worplesdon, Surrey, U.K. and of Mellor Bromley Air Conditioning Services, Leicester, U.K.)

CONTROL SYSTEMS

Different methods of control systems have been used. Firstly, a time clock unit that provides continuous ventilation for 8–12 hours (e.g., the Agritech® and Humidifan® systems). Secondly, an interval controller which humidifies the air for 30 seconds at a time. This system has a sensor at the level of the cuttings to accurately sense the falling water droplets. Thirdly, some systems use a humidistat, e.g., the Mee Industries Fogging System.

Nobel Engineering Ltd., Worthing, Sussex, England, have recently developed an aspirated humidity controller suitable for the different fogging systems described. This controller is unaffected by ambient temperature changes and has a graduated relative humidity setting scale for between 90–100%.

SHADING

A greenhouse equipped with a fogging unit does not require as much shading because the vast quantity of water particles diffuse incoming light. Nevertheless, it is still advisable to shade up to a 50% level in summer, removing the shading as soon as light levels begin to drop in early fall. [Some propagators in the United States have experienced good results with no shading when using some fogging systems.]

CLOSED CASE PROPAGATION

A closed case is traditionally a brick or wooden cold frame structure inside a greenhouse. Basal heat is provided through electrical cables or hot water pipes. The overhead protection of the glass lights, and the glass of the greenhouse itself, allows greater control of the environment around the cuttings or grafts. They are sometimes called "grafting cases" as they are very useful for callusing bench grafts (p. 514).

Closed cases are effective not only for grafts but also for rooting evergreen hardwood cuttings of broad-leaved evergreens and conifers. It is possible to root softwood cuttings in them, but heavy shading is necessary and also sometimes two layers of glass (p. 110) to give better control of the humidity.

There have been a number of variations in the design of closed cases. The glass and wooden lights originally used to cover the cases (a frame-like structure) were sometimes quite large and heavy so that it was necessary to suspend chains from the roof of the greenhouse to hold the lower end of the lights open at different heights for ventilating the cuttings and grafts.

The advent of polyethylene film has made it possible to introduce a considerable amount of flexibility in both the design and use of closed case propagation. This section will explain the principles and variations in design and uses of closed case propagation when polyethylene is used to cover the cuttings or grafts.

Figure 3-64.
A traditional closed case propagating frame. Note the depth of the frame on the left, which makes it ideal for bench grafts, and the use of chains to hold the frames open for ventilation. (Exbury Gardens, Exbury, Hampshire, U.K.)

USE OF POLYETHYLENE FILM

Mist propagation was the most widely used greenhouse propagation system during the 1960s and 1970s. The last five years has seen a considerable interest in and use of polyethylene covers over cuttings placed in the bench, floor bed or open floor facility. I first saw polyethylene film being used in 1966—a continuous roll of the material was laid over cuttings stuck directly into the propagation bench so that it was in direct contact with the upper surface of the leaves.

The Proefstation voor de Boomkwekerij (Research Station for Nursery Stock Production), Boskoop, Holland; Agricultural Institute, Kinsealy Research Centre, Dublin, Ireland; Glasshouse Crops Research Institute, Rustington, Sussex, England; and Efford Experimental Horticulture Station, Lymington, Hampshire, England, have all played a significant role in demonstrating the benefits gained by rooting cuttings under polyethylene film.

Mist propagation is an excellent method for rooting cuttings but does not meet all the propagator's requirements. Rooting under polyethylene film has solved some of these shortcomings.

Advantages and Disadvantages Over Mist Propagation

The advantages of rooting cuttings under polyethylene film instead of mist propagation are as follows:—

(i) It is simple, cheap and fast to install. Costs are reduced because there is no need for pipework, mist nozzles and much of the ancillary control equipment. Additional areas in the propagation house can be easily installed to meet increasing production needs.

(ii) It is readily adaptable for cuttings and grafts in both greenhouses and cold frames.

(iii) There is minimal leaching of nutrients and subsequent leaf drop caused by the frequent overhead application of water droplets.

(iv) The cuttings are much less liable to stress caused by excess water being retained in the rooting medium. [Although a well-equipped mist system with well-designed and maintained nozzles plus the correct rooting medium should present few problems.] Evergreen cuttings requiring a high peat ratio content in their rooting medium are better rooted under polyethylene than mist propagation.

(v) There is a significant reduction in unsightly deposits of calcium carbonate on the leaf surfaces.

(vi) Less energy is required to heat the rooting medium because there is no overhead misting, except during necessary maintenance, to lower the temperature.

NOTE:—An excellent adaptation for softwood cuttings and broad-leaf evergreens is to install a mist line inside a polyethylene tunnel (mist tunnel) (see p. 166).

As with any other system, there are some problems when rooting cuttings under polyethylene film.

(i) The stress during high summer temperatures can cause the cuttings to wilt and deteriorate, particularly if there is insufficient shade and humidity.

(ii) Diseases can develop and spread rapidly, especially when the cuttings become saturated with water droplets.

(iii) There is sometimes less of an inclination to inspect the cuttings regularly, making it more difficult to correct problems.

However, the last two problems also occur in a mist propagation facility, so both are clearly a matter of properly understanding the different propagation regimes involved. In the final analysis, sound knowledge and careful attention to good management will produce excellent results with either system.

Principle of Propagating Under Polyethylene Film

There has not really been any thorough fundamental research on the physiological aspects of rooting cuttings under polyethylene film until recently. The major research has been carried out by K. Loach at the Glasshouse Crops Research Institute, Littlehampton, Sussex, England. His program has produced a far better understanding of the differences in the physiology of cuttings propagated under polyethylene and under mist.

Polyethylene film allows some movement of gases such as carbon dioxide and oxygen but inhibits the movement of water vapor. This enables humidity levels to increase in order to keep the cuttings turgid. There has to be a correct balance between air temperature, leaf temperature of the cutting, humidity levels and shade for cuttings to root. As the air temperature rises due to solar radiation, so will the temperature of the plant tissues. The humidity and shade levels must be increased as required to prevent wilting of the cuttings.

The conclusions of K. Loach's research program include the following:—

(i) Leaf tissue is not readily cooled. This is due, firstly, to the lack of air movement (minimum "convective cooling"), and secondly, to the absence of overhead misting (minimum "evaporative cooling").

(ii) Leaf tissue is kept cooler when the polyethylene is in direct contact with the upper surface of the leaf than when there is an air space between the cuttings and the polyethylene film supported on a metal or wooden framework. This is because a very thin film of water develops between the leaf surface and polyethylene in the former situation.

(iii) It is important to provide heavy shading to avoid stress, particularly during the summer months when up to 80% shade is necessary (p. 118).

Depending on the geographical location of the nursery, research has demonstrated that a useful guideline for rooting cuttings under polyethylene film is to provide:—

(i) An optimum of 70% shade in summer, increasing to 80% during very sunny weather.

(ii) An optimum of 50% shade in spring and fall, increasing to 70% on bright sunny days.

(iii) Around 40% shade on the brightest days in winter.

Based on the climate of southern England, K. Loach suggests that the ideal cycle of rooting cuttings is to provide mist propagation during the summer and to root under polyethylene film in the fall and winter. The concept has certainly worked in commercial practice, especially in temperate climates where there are low light and temperature levels. I have obtained excellent results with this philosophy and have no hesitation in recommending it.

Methods of Rooting Cuttings Under Polyethylene Film

There are fundamentally three methods used to cover the cuttings with polyethylene within a modified closed case facility. These are referred to as "contact polyethylene", "supported polyethylene" forming a tunnel or tent, and polyethylene drape.

1. Contact Polyethylene

A continuous roll of very thin 20 μm (1 mil/80 gauge) film is used. This is similar to the grade used by dry cleaners for clothes bags or to cover the spawn in commercial mushroom enterprises. I have heard Dutch nurserymen use the expression "it should be so thin that it breathes". The weight of a heavier grade will cause the cuttings to bend over, although 38 μm (1.5 mil/150 gauge) grade is satisfactory for the thicker leaves of broad-leaved evergreens such as

Figure 3-65.
An example of the use of contact polyethylene for large-scale propagation of broad-leaved evergreen cuttings.

Figure 3-66. Sticking cuttings of deciduous azaleas under 20 μm (1 mil/80 gauge) polyethylene film. (Proefstation voor de Boomkwekerij, Research Station for Nursery Stock Production, Boskoop, Holland)

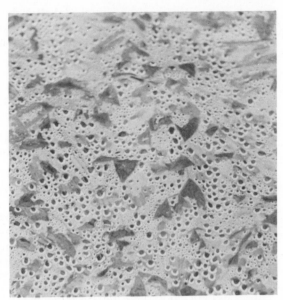

Figure 3-67. Very high humidity is encouraged by the formation of numerous condensation droplets on the underside of the plastic film—particularly during the summer months.

Rhododendron, Viburnum, Skimmia and *Prunus laurocerasus* cvs. (Cherry Laurel). Contact polyethylene is not as convenient for cuttings with spines on the stems or leaves because the spines catch in the polyethylene and the cuttings are dislodged when the polyethylene is disturbed.

Humidity levels can be increased still further by replicating the double-glass facility used for cold frames (p. 110). This is achieved by covering the contact polyethylene with shaded glass or milky polyethylene supported by strips of wood at 1.0 m (39″) intervals, leaving a space of 10–15 cm (4–6″) between the two layers.

The cuttings can be immersed in fungicide before being stuck in the rooting medium and/or drenched with a fungicide (p. 375). The leaf surfaces should be misted lightly with water if they are dry. This overhead misting is not necessary if the cuttings are to be given a fungicidal drench immediately after sticking.

Lay the polyethylene directly over the cuttings, beginning from one end of the bench or bed and ensuring that it is in direct contact with the upper surface of the leaves. Tuck it in around the edges of the bench or bed if the whole area is covered. If only part of the area is to be covered, a 2.5 × 2.5 cm (1 × 1″) strip of wood can be laid across the end of the polyethylene to secure it until the remainder of the cuttings are stuck.

Condensation droplets will quickly form after placing the polyethylene over the cuttings. One can see an erratic combination of small areas of green leaf tissue and numerous particles of water on the underside of the polyethylene film. It is likely that the polyethylene will have to be removed to prevent excess condensation, to provide some aeration, and to allow inspection of cuttings for any necessary maintenance procedures.

Two different systems which are used for handling the polyethylene film in the fall and winter after the cuttings have been stuck in a greenhouse are as follows:—

(a) Remove the polyethylene once a week in the evening and replace the following morning to allow air to circulate around the cuttings overnight.

(b) Remove the polyethylene twice a week for 1 or 2 hours, turning the film so that it is replaced with the dry outer surface in contact with the cuttings.

The polyethylene film should be removed once or twice a week during the summer, shaken to remove condensation droplets, turned and replaced within a few minutes to prevent the cuttings from wilting. If excess condensation droplets form suddenly, lift the polyethylene carefully from the cuttings at the center of the bench so that the droplets will move down along the underside of the film to each side of the bench.

When the polyethylene film is removed, carefully inspect the cuttings for disease, remove any damaged tissue, apply fungicidal drenches or sprays as necessary and check the rooting medium for dry spots, particularly around the edges of the bed or bench. Note that insufficient shading is a primary cause of failures when using contact polyethylene.

2. Supported Polyethylene

In this case, the polyethylene film is supported by some form of metal or wooden framework so that there is an air space between it and the top of the cuttings. I have noted several support systems used successfully:—

(a) A series of metal or wooden hoops permanently fixed to the sides at 1.2 m (4') intervals down the bed or bench to formulate a tunnel.

(b) Removable hoops with a heavy flat metal base at either end, so they can simply be placed down on the sides of the bench or bed when required, removed and stored after use.

Alternatively, conventional hoops fixed into a socket or clamp at either side of the bench can be used. This procedure is particularly useful when the area is to be used for open mist propagation during the summer and the hoops have to be removed. [The hoops and polyethylene are sometimes retained and a mist line installed down the centre of the tunnel to imitate a low polyethylene tunnel (p. 166).]

(c) For a floor bed, make a series of holes, 5.0–7.5 cm (2–3") in diameter and 0.9–1.2 m (3–4') apart, in the floor of the propagation house. Pre-made hoops can then be simply slotted into the holes when required. This approach is particularly useful in cases where there are no permanently installed sides or ends to the floor beds.

Cuttings can be easily inspected under supported polyethylene by simply lifting up the sides. Some propagators prefer to use supported polyethylene because the increased air circulation reduces disease in cuttings and grafts. Humidity levels are lower than under contact polyethylene so particular care must be given to shading. Milky opaque polyethylene should be used during the summer as it will reduce the air temperature by around 5°C (9°F) as well as reduce the intensity of the incoming light. Shading should be provided by installing it on the outside of the greenhouse or by building a false ceiling with shade fabric (cloth). This is more effective than simply placing the shade fabric directly over the polyethylene tunnel. Remove the polyethylene when the cuttings have rooted or the grafts have callused, leaving the shade cloth. Thermacover material can be placed over the hoops to save energy (p. 138) when rooting during the winter.

For summer propagation, I would recommend a "hybrid" combining supported polyethylene and mist propagation. A mist line is installed down the center of the bed (p. 142).

Maintenance is similar in principle to that with contact polyethylene, except that it is not usually necessary to remove the film at regular intervals. Ventilation, spraying and watering are done by lifting the sides as needed. Hardening-off is simply a matter of gradually raising the sides of the polyethylene until it is finally removed, and, where applicable, by reducing the frequency of misting.

3. Polyethylene Drape

Polyethylene drapes allow a greater air space around the cuttings than either of the methods just described. There are basically two designs used:—

(a) The polyethylene is secured down the inside of the greenhouse roof and allowed to drape down along the sides of the propagation bench or floor bed. This method is useful if the propagation area is along the sides of the greenhouse and for greenhouses that are narrow and have low eaves.

(b) A false ceiling can be created in wider greenhouses by suspending a layer of polyethylene across the greenhouse, supporting it on tight wires. The polyethylene is draped down on four sides to form a tent over the propagation bench or floor beds. Such an arrangement allows staff to walk into the area to maintain plants. It is also a useful means of making older greenhouses more energy efficient (p. 132) and to partition off the propagation area from other areas of the greenhouse.

Overhead mist lines should be installed to increase humidity and lower the temperature during summer propagation. A fogging unit can be installed as an alternative to mist if the tent area is sufficiently large. It is essential to provide shading from late spring to the early fall.

The innovative researcher C. E. Whitcomb, Oklahoma State University Horticulture

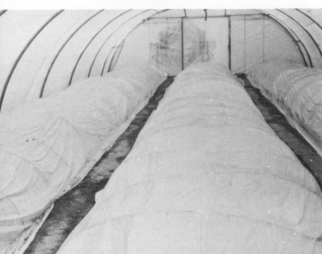

Figure 3-68. A (above left). A section of a wide-span greenhouse with beds fitted with metal hoops and cross wires to support polyethylene, thus forming a series of tunnels. B (above right). A simple but very effective floor-level facility used for rooting deciduous softwood cuttings in the summer and broad-leaved evergreen and conifer cuttings in the fall and winter. Note the installation of a spray line for summer propagation, the use of a shade cloth over the bed on the right for species sensitive to excessively high temperatures and humidity, and the false ceiling of shade cloth. (Westham Island Nursery, Delta, B.C., Canada). C (left). A simple facility of 3 m (10′) wide tunnels installed inside a polyethylene greenhouse. A mist line is normally installed for summer propagation.

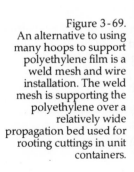

Figure 3-69. An alternative to using many hoops to support polyethylene film is a weld mesh and wire installation. The weld mesh is supporting the polyethylene over a relatively wide propagation bed used for rooting cuttings in unit containers.

Figure 3—70. A simple tent facility in a narrow greenhouse with low eaves in which the polyethylene is secured to the inside of the roof, leaving sufficient length to form a drape. This facility is being used for bench grafts.

Figure 3-71. A high humidity tent formed by a false ceiling of polyethylene with drapes on opposite sides of the bench. Note the installation of a mist line for summer propagation.

Department, Stillwater, undertook an evaluation of a wet tent system used by a forestry research organization in France. The fabric forming the sides of the tent fits into a continuous grooved slit in a 5.0 cm (2″) diameter pipe around the top of the tent. This pipe is connected to a hose with a flow control valve to allow water to flow through the pipe and seep into the fabric to keep it moistened. Increased amounts of water evaporate from the fabric as the air temperature rises during the day. The moistened fabric keeps the humidity and air temperature levels more constant. Results so far have been very promising—good rooting, reduced leaf drop and no saturation of the rooting medium. An overhead mist line was necessary on some sunny days to retain the 98–100% humidity levels. More research is required to further test the system and to establish the best type of fabric.

LOW POLYTHENE TUNNELS (SUN TUNNELS)

The concept of outdoor, low polyethylene tunnels, often referred to as sun tunnels, was initially developed in the United States and Denmark to provide a low-cost propagation facility for rooting softwood cuttings, but they have also been found to be useful for evergreen hardwood cuttings of broad-leaf evergreens and conifers. I have noted that some deciduous shrubs root more successfully in a low polyethylene tunnel than in a conventional greenhouse mist propagation unit. These tunnels provide a very flexible alternative to a conventional greenhouse mist unit because they can be easily constructed as a temporary or semi-permanent facility. Rooted cuttings can be left in the tunnel for one growing season after rooting, thus providing a low-cost method of producing quality liners.

The low cost means that tunnels are particularly useful for a new nursery with limited capital. In an established operation, they save tying up more valuable greenhouse space for the production of large quantities of easy-to-root cuttings.

The low polyethylene tunnel is simply a continuous tunnel 1.0 m (3′3″) high and 0.9–1.2 m (3–4′) wide supported by a wood and metal framework. The concept of the tunnels as originated in Denmark was to completely enclose the cuttings with milky polyethylene film without an internal misting line. The design from the United States, and the one most often used in England, has a mist line running longitudinally down the tunnel.

The principle is that high temperature and humidity levels are allowed to develop within the tunnels during the summer, providing that the incoming light intensity is reduced by at least 50%. The cuttings will rapidly wilt and deteriorate if the humidity levels drop or if there is insufficient shading.

Three important aspects in their use—site preparation, design and construction, and procedures for sticking and aftercare—are described.

Figure 3-72.
A well-managed low polyethylene tunnel (sun tunnel) enterprize to provide liners for open-ground and container production. (Coles Nurseries (Thurnby) Ltd., Leicester, U.K.)

Figure 3-73. A (left). Low polyethylene tunnels without mist lines for rooting ground covers. Note that the soil has been back-filled to secure the polyethylene. (Denmark). B (right). A low polyethylene tunnel enterprize before and after sticking. Note the opaque film used to cover the beds. (Hillier Nurseries (Winchester) Ltd., Romsey, Hampshire, U.K.)

SITE PREPARATION AND ROOTING MEDIUM

A level, well-drained, open site free of perennial weeds is the basic necessity. It is important to provide shelter (an artificial (manufactured) windbreak can be particularly useful) for two reasons. Firstly, to prevent wind from causing physical damage to the tunnel, and secondly, to prevent excessive drift of water droplets from the misting or overhead irrigation nozzles after removal of the polyethylene. An ample supply of clean water is required for the misting lines, particularly when a series of tunnels requires misting at the same time.

The beds should be 0.9–1.2 m (3–4') wide, and raised to a height of 15 cm (6'') above the ground to encourage better drainage and aeration. There should be sufficient cross aisles (pathways) to allow easy access to the cuttings. Peat moss and lime-free coarse sand are incorporated into the soil base of the bed to give an approximately 1:1:1 ratio by volume. The beds can be raised in a similar fashion as for open-ground seed beds by using two potato ridgers and a levelling board mounted on the rear of a tractor (see p. 56). The beds can be fumigated prior to sticking the cuttings to remove soil-borne pests and diseases. Dazomet (Basamid®) can be incorporated, ensuring that the same depth is used on the cultivator when opening up the beds so that untreated soil is not brought up to the surface (p. 57). Methyl bromide is more costly but is reliable and has the advantage that the cuttings can be stuck a few days after application compared to the longer time lapse necessary for Basamid®.

Traditionally, a 5.0 cm (2'') deep layer of sand is spread over the top of the fumigated bed to support the cuttings and provide the necessary aeration and drainage. The developing root systems will grow down into the loam/peat moss/sand base to provide well-rooted cuttings or liners. Recent trials have demonstrated that a 1.0 cm (⅜") depth of sand provides better growth in tunnels sited on light soil than does the deeper 5.0 cm (2") layer.

However, recent experimental work at the Efford Experimental Horticulture Station, Hampshire, England, has shown that a better quality liner is obtained by incorporating a controlled-release fertilizer (e.g., Osmocote®, 16-9-9, 16–18 month) at 1 or 2 kg per cubic meter (1.7–3.4 lb/1 cu. yd.) to a depth of 26 cm (10¼") in the loam/peat moss/sand base. The layer of sand is reduced to a depth of only 1.0 cm (⅜") instead of the standard 5.0 cm (2"). The spacing of the cuttings at sticking time must be increased to compensate for the additional shoot and root growth (see p. 170). Trials demonstrated that the cuttings went into dormancy earlier with some premature leaf fall when a controlled-release fertilizer was not incorporated into the bed.

Instead of rooting directly in prepared beds, cuttings can be rooted in flats in the tunnels and then removed. This involves more handling, but it is possible to obtain two crops of softwood cuttings from one tunnel. However, it is generally not possible to obtain such a substantially rooted cutting or liner compared to sticking directly into the beds unless one direct sticks into a liner pot.

DESIGN AND CONSTRUCTION

Tunnel designs can be varied as necessary—for example, increased strength of the hoops for exposed sites or where cuttings have to be over-wintered under polyethylene or thermal blankets.

1. One of the most orderly, well-managed and effective set-ups that I have seen was at Coles Nurseries (Thurnby) Ltd., Leicester, England, where they have designated a 0.4 ha (1 acre) component for low polyethylene tunnel propagation to produce both container and open-ground liners. The area consists of a series of 1.0 m (3'3") beds with 45 cm (18") pathways. The facility has a degree of permanence in that the sides of each bed are made of 15–10 cm (6–8") high wooden boards.

One successful design is to use wooden posts, 5.0 × 2.5 cm (2 × 1") thick, placed at 1.5 m (5') intervals down the center of each bed so that they project to a height of 1.0 m (3'3") above ground level. A galvanized wire hoop (8 gauge) is fixed over the top of each post, being secured to the sides of the bed. A mist line is then firmly secured to one side of each central upright so that it is approximately 25 cm (10") above the soil surface. The mist line must be level so as to deliver an even distribution of water droplets.

Figure 3-74. A (above). A simple low tunnel installation during various stages of preparation. Opaque polyethylene has been battened down on the softwood cuttings that have already been stuck. B (right). A close-up of the support system using a central wooden post and bent heavy gauge cross wires. (Coles Nurseries (Thurnby) Ltd., Leicester, U.K.)

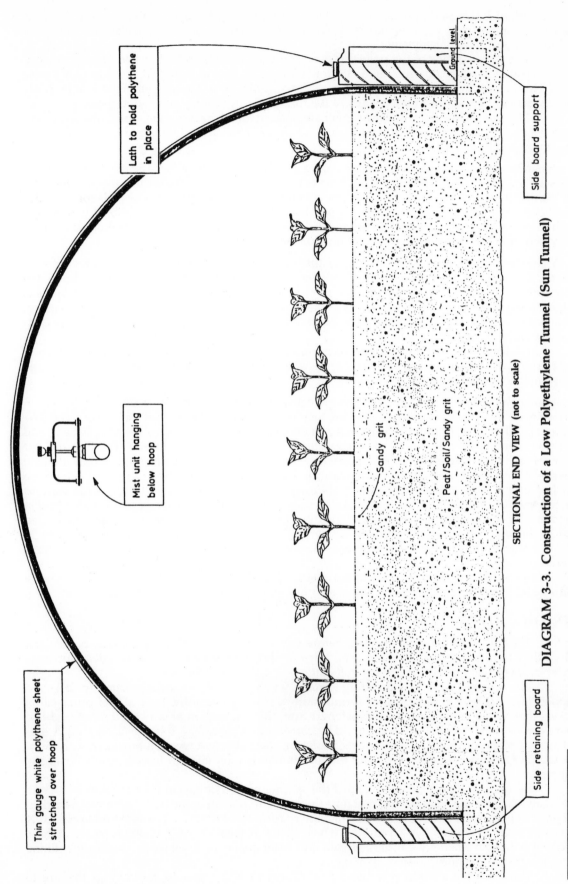

Lath to hold polythene in place

Thin gauge white polythene sheet stretched over hoop

Mist unit hanging below hoop

Sandy grit

Peat/Soil/Sandy grit

Ground level

Side board support

Side retaining board

SECTIONAL END VIEW (not to scale)

DIAGRAM 3-3. Construction of a Low Polyethylene Tunnel (Sun Tunnel)

Reproduced by courtesy of Efford Experimental Horticulture Station, Lymington, Hampshire, U.K.

Efford E.H.S. design their tunnels using 6 mm (¼") galvanized water pipes to form the hoops, spacing them at 3 m (10') intervals. Two plastic hoops between each galvanized wire hoop help to support the polyethylene.

The specifications of the polyethylene often used for this and other low tunnel propagation is opaque ("milky" or white) film, 38 μm (1.5 mil/150 gauge), supplied in 2.0 m (6'6") wide rolls. This film reduces the light intensity by approximately 50%. The polyethylene is kept firmly taut by stapling on to the wooden sides of the tunnels or by nailing to wooden battens.

This type of low polyethylene tunnel can be used for fall propagation, unless there are very high winds or heavy snow loads. If necessary, 1.3 cm (½") galvanized tubing can be used to form the hoops to provide extra stability.

2. Hillier Nurseries (Winchester) Ltd. have used a similar layout very successfully, except that the beds are 1.2 m (4') wide with 30 cm (12") wide pathways to allow a tractor to pass over the beds for lifting. Increased stability is given to the wooden sides by using railway ties (sleepers). Thick bamboo canes were originally used to support both the mist line and the galvanized wire hoops, with the latter also being secured to the railway ties. An irrigation pipe at one end of each tunnel provided both a water outlet and a mist line for the tunnel.

3. A simple but effective design is to substitute sections of weld mesh for the galvanized wire hoops. The sections are cut so that they can be bent to form a 1.0 m (3'3") diameter hoop, the protruding wire at each end of the hoop is then pushed firmly into the soil. A 60 cm (2') space is left between each hoop to provide access to the cuttings. The mist line is supported by a series of wire hooks suspended from the arc of the hoop. The polyethylene is secured by burying the ends and the sides in the soil.

A facility of this kind can be erected quickly. The weld mesh gives a good degree of support in contrast to galvanized wire hoops which tend to keel over in windy weather if the polyethylene is very tight.

4. Another design is based on the low polyethylene tunnels used to produce early season strawberries. Lengths of galvanized wire are bent on a jig to form hoops that will make a bed 0.6–1.0 m (2–3'3") wide. A loop or eyelet is made on each side of the hoop as the wire is bent, and polypropylene twine then threaded through these to secure the polyethylene. The first and last hoop of each row require strengthening to withstand the pressure exerted by the taut polyethylene cover—1.3 cm (½") galvanized piping can be substituted for these two. The wire hoops are pushed into the soil at 45 cm (30") intervals down the length of the raised bed. It is not usual to place a mist line down this type of tunnel. The polyethylene cover is attached to a wooden post at each end of the row or the edges are buried in the soil. The sides of the tunnel are not buried unless the site is very windy so that it can be easily lifted to inspect or ventilate the cuttings. A trickle irrigation line is installed down the center of the tunnel to provide for water requirements within the bed.

Although this system is simple to construct and dismantle, I would much prefer to use a more solid construction with a mist line down the tunnel as used in the previous designs.

STICKING OF CUTTINGS

The mist lines must be checked before use for cracks and blocked nozzles, particularly when they have been stored and not used since the previous season. An uneven distribution of water droplets will quickly cause very soft cuttings to wilt and deteriorate.

The appropriate softwood cutting is made, immersed in a fungicidal solution (p. 291) and dipped into a 0.3–0.5% IBA powder formulation of rooting hormone. Low tunnel propagation means that the cuttings have to be transferred from the preparation area to the tunnel, and it is therefore essential that they are kept turgid by correct handling followed by quick sticking. A useful aid is a plastic or polystyrene domestic cooler or, alternatively, a wooden box lined with moist burlap (hessian) can be used, ensuring that the burlap is long enough to completely cover the cuttings.

Research at Efford E.H.S. evaluated the spacing of the cuttings in the tunnel in relation to the plant being rooted and the length of time they were to remain in the bed. There was a marked increase in both shoot and root growth when the spacing was increased from the traditional 5.0 × 5.0 cm (2 × 2") to either 7.5 × 7.5 cm (3 × 3") or 10.0 × 10.0 cm (4 × 4"). Cuttings rooted at these wider spacings gave better establishment and improved quality material for marketing after lifting from the frames for open-ground planting.

The guideline advised is to use 7.5 × 7.5 cm (3 × 3") spacing for cuttings that are to

Figure 3-75. Sticking of *Weigela florida* 'Variegata' (Old-fashioned Weigela cv.) softwood cuttings in a tunnel bed. (Hillier Nurseries (Winchester) Ltd., Romsey, Hampshire, U.K.)

remain in the bed for 6–8 months and 10.0 × 10.0 cm (4 × 4") for cuttings that are to remain for 14–16 months. (However, these distances may have to be either reduced or increased according to the species being rooted.)

As each section between the hoops is filled, the cuttings are watered in with a fungicide solution (p. 291) and the opaque polyethylene is pulled taut and secured with wooden battens, staples, polypropylene twine or simply by covering with soil, according to the design of the tunnel.

AFTERCARE OF CUTTINGS

The cuttings can be kept misted by manually turning the water on 3–4 times a day for about 3 minutes at a time. Depending on the weather, this is reduced to twice a day after 2–3 weeks. The length of each mist burst is reduced to one minute after 4–5 weeks. It is difficult to be dogmatic about these misting schedules, because the frequency and burst length depends so much on the prevailing weather conditions and the geographical location of the nursery. A time clock and solenoid valves to automatically mist the cuttings at pre-set intervals should be installed when a series of tunnels is used. More accurate control of misting can be achieved by installing a time clock to provide a short mist application at 30–60 minute intervals. A pre-set frequency used by one nursery is a 1-minute burst every 1 or 2 hours, gradually reducing over the next 4–5 weeks. An "electronic leaf" control system has also been successfully used.

High temperatures build up during the daytime within the tunnels so, where feasible, it is important that the cuttings are checked regularly for dry areas and for development of fungal diseases. In practice, it is difficult to carry out many of these checks in most of these closed tunnel systems. Plants such as *Cotinus coggygria* cvs. (Smoke Tree), *Clematis*, *Prunus* × *cistena* (Purple-leaf Sand Cherry) and *Rosa* spp. (Rose) rapidly deteriorate if affected by disease, so a weekly fungicidal spray application through the mist lines until rooting commences will be helpful. The fungicidal spray is best applied in the evening, turning off the mist lines until the following morning.

Ventilation should begin about 4–5 weeks after the cuttings have been stuck, as this is when the root system should have begun growing down into the sand. Premature leaf drop may occur if misting is excessive and if the polyethylene is left on too long without adequate ventilation. Shrubs such as *Cotinus coggygria* (Smoke Tree), dwarf *Prunus* (Cherry) and *Rosa* spp. (Rose) are particularly susceptible.

Low polyethylene tunnels are ventilated by:—

(i) Slitting the polyethylene with a knife. The polyethylene will tend to tear later using this method.

(ii) Cutting circular holes in the polyethylene with a knife. The polyethylene can be completely removed about 3–4 weeks later, either with this or the previous method.

(iii) Lifting the polyethylene from one side first and then from both sides. This is best done where polypropylene twine is used to secure the polyethylene over the supporting hoops. The polyethylene can be re-used the following year.

(iv) Removing the polyethylene and immediately replacing with a woven shade cloth having a 40–60% shade value. The shade cloth can remain in place until the fall. Like method (iii), the polyethylene can be re-used the following year. The added advantage of this technique is that the shade cloth reduces water requirements and also wind drift of the mist water droplets.

The cuttings are generally left *in-situ* to over-winter in the beds. The beds can be covered in very cold weather with burlap (hessian) cloth or a thermal blanket, if the hoops are strong enough. The cuttings are lifted and graded in the spring and then containerized or planted out in open ground. There are two ways to ease the work schedule in areas where there is strong possibility of winter damage:—

(i) Completely lift all cuttings from the beds in the fall, grade and bundle for cold storage at 1°C (34°F) until the following spring. Shoot growth must be well-ripened in this case— this can be induced by applying a high potash fertilizer in August. Cuttings with a poor root system and a low carbohydrate reserve will not cold store successfully.

(ii) Lift the cuttings in late summer to early fall, and immediately pot up into liner pots to allow new root development prior to the onset of winter. The liners are then over-wintered in a frost-free protected structure. However, some species have not responded well to this system, including *Cornus alba* 'Sibirica' (Siberian Dogwood) and many variegated plants.

A convenient method for lifting cuttings from a series of beds without fixed wooden sides is to use a tractor-drawn, rear-mounted horizontal under-cutting blade as used in seedling tree production (p. 54). Sun tunnels with fixed wooden sides do not permit this method of lifting.

If the cuttings are to be grown-on *in-situ* for a further growing season, the late winter/early spring shoots should be pruned back to encourage side shoots and the beds top-dressed with a 10-10-10 fertilizer. The soft growth from these developing liners has been used for softwood cuttings for the next crop to be propagated in the tunnels and has performed well for some species. However, it is better to obtain cuttings from stock plants or, if necessary, from larger production stock as this will normally produce an improved quality rooted cutting.

Figure 3-76. A successful rooting of deciduous softwood cuttings left *in-situ* from propagating the previous summer. (Hillier Nurseries [Winchester] Ltd., Romsey, Hampshire, U.K.)

LATE SUMMER AND FALL ROOTING OF CUTTINGS

A number of ornamental conifers will root well in low polyethylene tunnels in late summer or fall. The tunnels must obviously be strengthened and, in addition, there are six other important provisos:—

(i) The site must be extremely well-drained to remove winter rainfall.

(ii) The cuttings should be grouped in different beds according to their ease of rooting if at all possible.

(iii) The optimum time for sticking is late August through to late September, depending on locality and species. Root development normally takes place prior to the onset of winter. However, it is acceptable in some climates to have cuttings callused by November/December. These will then root in the following spring.

(iv) A mist line is used until early October, after which it should be removed. The frequency of misting should be roughly one-third to one-half of that used for softwood cuttings.

(v) Opaque or clear polyethylene should be used for covering the cuttings, depending on the locality. Shade cloth or whitewash can be used to cover the tunnels during late summer and early fall when clear polyethylene is used.

(vi) The polyethylene film must remain over the tunnels until the following spring, when the rooted cuttings should be gradually ventilated. Well-rooted cuttings can be lifted and potted in late spring, but are often best left *in-situ* until the following fall to encourage better root and shoot development.

MOBILE WALK-IN POLYTUNNELS

Mobile walk-in polytunnels made by welding conventional polyethylene tunnels on to 5.0 cm (2") square sections which are then placed on the rollers and dollies of a conventional mobile greenhouse have been used successfully at Hillier Nurseries (Winchester) Ltd., England. Cuttings in the tunnels are kept turgid by installing mist lines suspended from the metal hoop framework, using a fogging system or covering with contact polyethylene.

These mobile walk-in polyethylene tunnels have recently been utilized very successfully for direct sticking (Chapter 13).

Figure 3-77. A (left). A mobile walk-in polyethylene tunnel used for softwood cutting propagation in pots or beds. Note the suspended mist lines and the rollers installed on concrete blocks. B (right). A tractor is used to move the mobile walk-in house on to the adjacent bed.

REFERENCES AND SUGGESTED SOURCES FOR FURTHER READING

Albright, L. D. 1983. New double-layer thermal curtain reduces fuel waste. *Amer. Nurseryman* **158**(10): 81–85 (November 15, 1983).

Bailey, L. H. 1907. 11th ed. *The Nursery-book. A Complete Guide to the Multiplication of Plants.* The Macmillan Company, New York.

Baldwin, I. & J. B. Stanley. 1983. Innovative heating techniques can save money for growers. *Amer. Nurseryman* **157**(2): 35–36 (January 15, 1983).

Bock, R. F. 1982. Propagation under poly film—no mist. *Comb. Proc. Inter. Pl. Prop. Soc.* **32**: 444–446.

Chadwick, L. C. 1951. Controlled humidification as an aid to vegetative propagation. *Proc. Pl. Prop. Soc.* **1**: 38–39.

Deen, J. L. W. 1971. Rooting cuttings under polyethylene tunnels. *Comb. Proc. Inter. Pl. Prop. Soc.* **21**: 248–252.

———, Chairman. 1972. Propagation under polyethylene tunnels—Discussion Group report. *Comb. Proc. Inter. Pl. Prop. Soc.* **22**: 264–266.

———. 1982. Add up your savings. *GC & HTJ* **192**(18): 37–38 (October 29, 1982).

———. 1983. Doing it their way. *GC & HTJ* **194**(16): 35–38 (October 14, 1983).

Dempster, C. D. 1973. The propagation of Holly (*Ilex aquifolium*) under double glass. *Comb. Proc. Inter. Pl. Prop. Soc.* **23**: 191–193.

Efford Experimental Horticulture Station. 1981. Hardy Nursery Stock: Fuel Economy in the Plant Propagation Bench. *Efford Experimental Horticulture Station Review for 1980,* pp. 14–27.

Electricity Council, U.K. no date. Ventilation for Greenhouses. *Electricity Handbook No. 3.* Electricity Council, London, U.K.

———. no date. Fan Ventilation. *Techn. Infom. Leafl.* Electricity Council, London, U.K.

Fuller, A. S. 1897. *The Propagation of Plants.* Orange Judd Company, New York.

Gaddy, B. 1982. My experience with high humidity propagation. *Comb. Proc. Inter. Pl. Prop. Soc.* **32**: 446–448.

Gillette, R. 1984. Fog. De-mist-ifying propagation. *Grower Talks* **47**(9): 56, 58, 60, 62, 64. (Reprint available from: Mee Industries Inc., 1629 South Del Mar Ave., San Gabriel, CA 91776.)

Gordon, I. 1983. Mechanical aids to plant propagation. *Comb. Proc. Inter. Pl. Prop. Soc.* **33**: 182–185.

Gouin, F. R. 1980. Vegetative propagation under thermo-blankets. *Comb. Proc. Inter. Pl. Prop. Soc.* **30**: 301–305.

Hall, C. G. 1982. High humidity propagation. *Comb. Proc. Inter. Pl. Prop. Soc.* **32**: 448–450.

Hancock, L. 1953. Shrubs from softwood cuttings. *Proc. Pl. Prop. Soc.* **3**: 151–164.

———. 1959. The burlap cloud method of rooting softwood summer cuttings. *Proc. Pl. Prop. Soc.* **9**: 165–167.

Hartmann, H. T. & D. E. Kester. 1983. 4th ed. *Plant Propagation: Principles and Practices.* Prentice-Hall, Inc., Englewood Cliffs, N.J.

Heuser, C. W. 1981. How propagators can reduce energy needs. *Amer. Nurseryman* **154**(5): 135–138 (September 1, 1981).

James, B. L. 1980. Propagation without mist. *Comb. Proc. Inter. Pl. Prop. Soc.* **30**: 473–475.

Kains, M. G. & L. M. McQuesten. 1946. Rev. ed. *Propagation of Plants.* Orange Judd Publishing Company, Inc., New York.

Labous, P. 1983. The fog factor. *GC & HTJ* **194**(14): 25–26 (September 30, 1983)

———. 1983. A clear choice? *GC & HTJ* **194**(16): 33–34 (October 14, 1983).

Lamb, J. G. D. & J. C. Kelly. 1980. Reducing costs in plant propagation. *Comb. Proc. Inter. Pl. Prop. Soc.* **30**: 190–198.

Leach, D. G. 1957. The Nearing Propagating Frame. *Proc. Pl. Prop. Soc.* **7**: 141–145.

———. 1961. *Rhododendrons of the World.* Charles Scribner's Sons, New York.

Loach, K. 1977. Leaf water potential and the rooting of cuttings under mist and polyethylene. *Physiol. Plant* **40**: 191–197.

———. 1979. Mist propagation—past, present and future. *Comb. Proc. Inter. Pl. Prop. Soc.* **29**: 216–229.

———. 1980. Shading success. *GC & HTJ* **187**(15): 21–24 (October 10, 1980).

———. 1981. Propagation under mist and polyethylene—history, principles and developments. *Proc. 21st Askham Bryan Hort. Techn. Course.*

——— & A. P. Gay. 1979. The light requirements for propagating hardy ornamental species from leafy cuttings. *Scientia Hortic.* **10**: 217–230.

Macdonald, A. B. 1981. Propagation—reducing heating costs. *Dig This* (B. C. Nursery Trades) **6**(2): 6–7 (March/April 1981).

Milbocker, D. C. 1977. Propagation in a humid chamber. *Comb. Proc. Inter. Pl. Prop. Soc.* **27**: 455–461.

———. 1980. Ventilated high humidity propagation. *Comb. Proc. Inter. Pl. Prop. Soc.* **30**: 480–482.

———. 1983. Ventilated high humidity propagation. *Comb. Proc. Inter. Pl. Prop. Soc.* **33**: 384–387.

Ministry of Agriculture, Food & Fisheries, U.K. 1979. *Economies in Greenhouse Heating.* Agricultural Development and Advisory Service (A.D.A.S.), Mechanization Department, West Midland Region, Ministry of Agriculture, Fisheries & Food, London, U.K.

———. no date. *Mist Propagation of Softwood Cuttings of the Hop.* Agricultural Development and Advisory Service (A.D.A.S.), Ministry of Agriculture, Fisheries and Food, London, U.K.

O'Flaherty, T. & J. C. Kelly. 1983. Evaluation of the Charlton Thermosystem base heating apparatus. *Comb. Proc. Inter. Pl. Prop. Soc.* **33**: 295–298.

O'Rourke, F. L. 1955. The Bolivar Pit method of rooting softwood cuttings. *Proc. Pl. Prop. Soc.* **5**: 54–55.

Press, T. F. 1983. Propagation: Fog not mist. *Comb. Proc. Inter. Pl. Prop. Soc.* **33**: 100–109.

Regulski, F. J. 1983. Circulated groundwater heating improves quality of cuttings. *Amer. Nurseryman* **158**(10): 59–63 (November 15, 1983).

Roller, J. B. 1959. The polyethylene tent. *Proc. Pl. Prop. Soc.* **9**: 89–91.

Rowe-Dutton, P. 1959. Mist Propagation of Cuttings. *Digest No. 2.* Commonwealth Agricultural Bureaux, East Malling, Maidstone, Kent, U.K.

Scott, M. A. 1982. Fuel economy in the propagation bench. *Comb. Proc. Inter. Pl. Prop. Soc.* **32**: 275–283.

———. 1983. Using low air temperatures and insulated propagating beds results in better fuel economy. *Amer. Nurseryman* **158**(10): 54–57 (November 15, 1983).

Sharp, J. R. no date. The Design of Gantry Systems for Protected Crops. *Report No. 41.* National Institute of Agricultural Engineering, Silsoe, U.K.

Sheard, G. F. 1979. Planning a place to propagate in? *GC & HTJ* **185**(7): 29–31 (August 10, 1979).

Sheat, W. G. 1948. *Propagation of Trees, Shrubs and Conifers.* Macmillan & Co. Ltd., London.

Short, T. H. & J. Huizing. 1983. Movable energy screens with inflated tubes bring together the best of US and Dutch designs. *Amer. Nurseryman* **158**(10): 77–79 (November 15, 1983).

Shugert, R. 1980. A racking and conveyor system for increased efficiency. *Comb. Proc. Inter. Pl. Prop. Soc.* **30**: 300–301.

Snyder, W. E. 1965. A history of mist propagation. *Comb. Proc. Inter. Pl. Prop. Soc.* **15**: 63–67.

Stanley, J. B. 1980. Costly materials. Handling nursery materials. *GC & HTJ* **188**(8): 23, 25 (August 22, 1980).

Starkey, N. G. 1983. Installation of Melinex 071 Secondary Glazing. *Techn. Note No. 83* (July 1983). South Coast Glasshouse Advising Unit, Agricultural Development and Advisory Service (A.D.A.S.), U.K.

Stoltz, L. P., J. N. Walker & G. A. Duncan. 1977. Mist nozzles. *Comb. Proc. Inter. Pl. Prop. Soc.* **27**: 449–453.

Tacchi, R. B. 1982. Cost effective propagation using polyethylene structures. *Comb. Proc. Inter. Pl. Prop. Soc.* **32**: 167–171.

Templeton, H. M. 1953. The Phytotektor method of rooting cuttings. *Proc. Pl. Prop. Soc.* **3**: 51–56.

———. 1965. Mist systems and their controls. *Comb. Proc. Inter. Pl. Prop. Soc.* **15**: 67–71.

van der Giessen, P. 1979. Propagation in unheated houses. *Comb. Proc. Inter. Pl. Prop. Soc.* **29**: 436–438.

van der Staay, R. 1979. Setting up a mist propagation system. *Comb. Proc. Inter. Pl. Prop. Soc.* **29**: 558–561.

van Hof, M. 1958. Rooting under plastic. *Proc. Pl. Prop. Soc.* **8**: 168–169.

Ward, W. F. 1954. Mist propagation in open frames. *Proc. Pl. Prop. Soc.* **4**: 109–113.

Welch, H. J. 1970. *Mist Propagation and Automatic Watering.* Faber and Faber Ltd., London.

Weller, H. A. 1959. Outdoor mist propagation. *Proc. Pl. Prop. Soc.* **9**: 168–170.

Whitcomb, C. E. 1982. Rooting cuttings under a wet tent. *Comb. Proc. Inter. Pl. Prop. Soc.* **32**: 450–455.

Worrall, R. J. 1983. Evaluation of commercial mist control units. *Comb. Proc. Inter. Pl. Prop. Soc.* **33**: 176–181.

Wott, J. A. & H. B. Tukey. 1967. Influence of nutrient mist on the propagation of cuttings. *Proc. Amer. Soc. Hort. Sci.* **90**: 454–461.

Chapter 4

TOOLS AND MATERIALS FOR THE PROPAGATOR

The correct choice, use and maintenance of tools are all essential for successful propagation. Unfortunately, these criteria can be easily overlooked, so that hand equipment is cumbersome to handle and poorly maintained, thus making it unsuitable for the purpose for which it was intended. This chapter describes the range and uses of tools available and then sets some guidelines by which some of the common errors can be corrected.

HAND TOOLS

Hand tools for cutting stems, leaves and roots can be placed into two categories:—

(1) Knives, which either have:—
   (a) Folding blade
   (b) Fixed blade
   (c) Disposable blade

(2) Hand pruners (secateurs).

KNIVES

Types of Knives

There are three main types of knives used in propagation. These are described below.

(a) Folding Blade Knives

The three basic uses for propagating knives are taking cuttings, grafting and budding—and not for cutting string, tape, paper or other items. The average, small pocket knife, whether it is single- or multiple-bladed, is not suitable for plant propagation. The unsuitable features of such a knife include the blade design, the method of attachment to the handle, the size and shape of the handle, and the impermanence of a suitable cutting edge.

Folding blade knives are the type most commonly used by propagators. They are safer when not in use because the cutting edge is protected, which also means that it is less exposed to physical damage. A wide range of knives is available throughout the world. Some of the most widely used are manufactured in Switzerland (Victorinox) and in West Germany (Tina, Freunde, Kamphaus and Kunde), while the Saynor range is a well-known British brand. Propagators' knives are modified in the design of both the blade and handle.

Irrespective of the variations, there are a number of fundamental guidelines to consider when choosing a folding blade knife:—

(i) Determine the primary use of the knife. I recommend that one knife should be kept solely for grafting and a different knife used for cuttings.

(ii) Determine which members of staff will use the knife. There is little point in purchasing a high-quality small grafting knife for use by unskilled labor taking softwood cuttings.

(iii) The blade should be of high-quality steel that will keep its cutting edge for a long time. Stainless steel is often used on knives in the lower price range.

(iv) The blade should be set well down into the handle and riveted firmly. The blade on cheaper knives can become loose after a relatively short period of use. This results in poor carpentry, and allows the blade to bend backwards when cutting through hard wood, thus increasing the likelihood of personal injury. When purchasing a knife, I always check the way in which the blade is set into the handle, whether it can be physically moved, that it has a firm sprung action when folding the blade back, and that the blade rests in the handle without the tip exposed.

(v) Determine whether the blade is "single-angled" or "double-angled" (bevelled or ground on one or both sides of the blade). The majority of specialist knives, except T- (shield) budding knives, are single-angled. A single-angled blade has one side of the blade sloped (indicated by the bevel at the base of the blade) while the other side is flat. When using the knife, the flat surface is against the stem being cut to ensure a flatter, straighter surface—particularly important when grafting. Some specialist knives are designed so that there is a choice for right- or left-handed users. Single-angled blade knives should always be purchased as right- or left-handed models and used appropriately.

(vi) The overall weight of the knife should be located in the handle, so that more hand pressure can be put into making cuts, as well as allowing more efficient work over a long period. This is common with many of the knives with wooden handles, but those with composition handles are generally of lighter weight. A good test is to open the knife and place it carefully over two fingers to determine the point of equilibrium.

(vii) The design of the handle is important, particularly for grafting and when cutting ripened tissue for long periods. Many of the specialist knives with wooden handles are contoured so they fit into the hand, and some are widened and lengthened for large hands. The size and weight of the handle should increase with the size of the blade. [One large pruning knife has a combined blade and handle length of up to 20 cm (8″) and weighs 200 g (7 oz).]

(viii) Cost is an important consideration, particularly when making a multiple purchase for a large number of employees. However, cost should be of secondary importance for the skilled propagator. It is more important to purchase a high-quality knife that will last for many years if maintained correctly, for example, the Tina range. The lower price range of folding knives or small fixed blade tools would suffice for relatively unskilled staff mainly involved in preparing soft material.

(b) Fixed Blade Knives

Fixed blade knives are generally more popular in North America than in Europe, particularly for T- (shield) budding open-ground roses. The blades are similar to those of folding blade knives, but the range offered for sale is considerably smaller. The simpler design means that they are generally cheaper.

Their main feature is that the blade is permanently fixed about 3.5 cm (1½″) into the handle and is held rigidly in place by two or three metal rivets. This means that there is negligible risk of blade movement when cutting through hard stems. Although the handles are contoured, they are lighter than most folding blade knives. A disadvantage of these knives is safety. Unless they are placed in a sheath after use, the open blade can quickly cause injury to the unwary operator. It is easier to train a person to fold a blade into the handle than to place a knife in a sheath each time and the latter itself may be easily misplaced.

(c) Disposable Blade Knives

These are fixed blade knives in which either the blade or the knife itself is thrown away when the cutting edge becomes dull. Included in this category are the single-edged razor blades used for softwood cuttings of plants such as *Clematis*. Alternatively, there are types available at hardware stores in which the blade is pushed out from the handle and locked in place by a small catch. When the cutting edge becomes blunt, it is broken off and another section is pushed out. These are effective and safe for relatively inexperienced labor in the preparation of softwood, semi-ripewood and many evergreen hardwood cuttings when conventional knives are not used.

Classification of Knives

Knives can be classified by the primary use for which they were originally designed. However, one cannot be dogmatic—some propagators prefer to use their budding knife for

Figure 4-1.
A convenient tool for taking many types of cuttings is a knife in which the blade is extended and secured in place by a locking device in the handle. The blade is broken off when it becomes blunt and a new "piece" pushed out and secured.

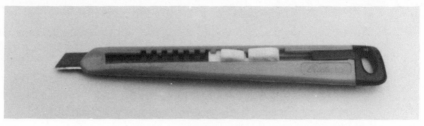

Figure 4-2.
Two types of Victorinox cutting and grafting knives. Top—Victorinox 475 H: Rosewood Handle. Note how the blade is set well into the handle and secured with a sturdy rivet, and the contoured handle to fit the hand. Bottom— Victorinox 247 I: Composition Handle.

Figure 4-3.
Two types of Tina cutting and grafting knives. Top—Tina 605 (left-handed). Bottom—Tina 606. Note the thin point to the blade of the Tina 606 to enable precision work, e.g., for wounding and preparing thin caliper scions for bench grafting.

cuttings. The choice should be made on personal preference based on experience.

A selection of folding knives is summarized below. The first number is the manufacturer's list code, while the second normally indicates the length of handle.

Cutting and Grafting Knives

Victorinox 247 I: Composition Handle—Single-angled stainless steel folding blade with light handle. More suitable for cuttings than grafting. A good, low cost, general purpose knife.

Victorinox 475 H: Rosewood Handle—Single-angled stainless steel folding blade with heavier, contoured handle. Low cost knife suitable for both cuttings and grafting.

Tina 605; Kamphaus 953: 10 cm (4″)—Single-angled folding blade with heavier contoured wooden handle. Excellent high-quality general purpose knife for both cuttings and grafting. Also available with a longer 11 cm (4¼″) handle. A larger bladed version (Tina 600 and 600A) is also available. Some propagators prefer these larger bladed versions for grafting as they find it easier to produce straighter cuts.

Tina 606; Kamphaus 943: 10 cm (4″)—Single-angled thin-pointed folding blade used for cuttings. I find this an excellent knife for bench grafting, and the blade design permits precise wounding and leaf removal to be carried out when preparing cuttings. The pointed tip is prone to break if dropped onto a hard surface.

Tina 607—Single-angled curved folding blade similar to Tina 606.

Tina 640—Single-angled folding blade with non-contoured wooden handle. General purpose knife that may be used for budding as the upper end of the blade has been flattened and extended so that it can be used to lift rind from the rootstock. (The extension of the blade can make it uncomfortable to carry around in pockets.)

Tina 685—Single-angled fixed blade knife with the blade held firmly in place by three metal rivets. Similar in design and use to the Tina 605.

["**Locked Blade**"—Folding grafting knives are available in which the blade is tightly locked after opening, thus giving the blade greater support when in use.]

Figure 4-4.
A French-made Opinel knife that is occasionally used for grafting. Note the metal ring at the top of the handle which is turned to lock the blade in position.

Pruning Knives

These traditional double-angled knives have been in use in the nursery trade for many decades for de-heading or snagging-back rootstocks and for tree training. They are a heavier knife with a curved blade and a contoured handle to give the operator maximum pressure when cutting the stems. The handle is distinctly curved on the larger knives to give greater support to the operator. The smaller pruning knives are used for heading back rootstocks preparatory to open-ground whip and tongue grafting and also to make cuts on thick caliper material. The curvature of the blade helps to ensure longer flatter cuts, but more skill is needed to effectively sharpen the blade.

Tina 620/10; Kamphaus 842: 11 cm (4¼")—A curved blade knife for heading back and for outdoor grafting of larger caliper stems.

Figure 4-5.
Tina 620/10 pruning knife (left-handed). Note the curved blade and the contoured handle.

Budding Knives

The budding knife must allow dexterity of movement. Of all the specialist horticultural knives, this is probably the one having the widest range of design over the years, all aimed at enabling the budder to speedily remove the bud from the scion and lift the rind for T-budding. The earlier budding knives had handles of ivory or bone but many are available today with high-quality plastic handles.

An early budding knife was described in 1897 by Arthur S. Fuller in his book *The Propaga-*

tion of Plants. The "Yankee Budding Knife", as it was called, had a rounded tip to the blade that was used to lift the rind away from the rootstock so that the bud could be slipped into place.

Modern budding knives generally have a "two-angled" blade with the tip rounded so that the rind can be lifted with less risk of cutting into the wood compared to a pointed knife. The handles are slimmer and lighter than a grafting knife, thus allowing greater dexterity. The end of the handle may be flattened to form a spatula to lift the rind—the knife is reversed after the T-cut is made so that this spatula can be used. This can take longer compared to the use of the blade for lifting the rind. Other knives have a spatula designed as a separate component that is firmly riveted onto the end of a conventional rounded handle. Depending on the manufacturer, this extended spatula may fold down into the handle.

The range of budding knives available includes:—

Tina 650 E: 10.5 cm (4.2″)—A high-quality knife with flattened plastic handle that tapers to a pointed spatula.

Tina 650 S: 10.5 cm (4.2″)—Similar to the 650 E except that the spatula is contoured, making it flatter and rounded, and curved in the opposite plane to the knife blade.

Tina 650 E8—A small knife with a 3.5 cm (1½″) blade compared to the conventional 6.0 cm (2½″). It is suitable for small nimble hands. In use, it is often held well into the palm of the hand with the forefinger over the top of the blade to give direction and pressure.

Freunde 218—A single-angled blade with a rounded plastic handle to which a fixed rounded metallic spatula is firmly attached with two rivets.

Fiqure 4-6. A range of Tina budding knives. Top—Tina 650 S with contoured spatula. Center—Tina 650 E with pointed spatula. Bottom—Tina 650 E8, a smaller knife. Note the rounded tips to the blades to assist in making incisions in the rootstock and the flattened ends of the handles that form spatulas to assist in lifting the rind.

Figure 4-7. The Freunde 218 budding knife with a flat metallic spatula riveted into the end of the handle.

Saynor—A well-tried knife, popular in Britain for many years, with a molded spatula tapering from the end of the handle.

Two-Edged "Mexican" Knife—This is described by R. J. Garner as a knife with a fixed blade that has two distinct cutting edges and is wider at the end than at the base. This chisel-like sharpened end is pushed into the rootstock for T-budding and the knife manipulated so that the rind is lifted away from the wood on the vertical cut. Very high rates of budding have been achieved with roses (up to 4,000 per day) as there are fewer movements involved compared with the conventional budding knife.

Kunde 35 st—A double-angled blade which becomes rounded towards the tip giving, essentially, two sharpened sides. The additional sharpened side can be used to make the vertical cut of a T-incision on the rootstock and for lifting the rind. This design shows similarities to the two-edged "Mexican" budding knife.

Tina 670 (Folding Blades), Tina 671 (Fixed Blades): Twin (Double-Bladed) Knives—A specialist twin-bladed knife designed for patch budding, and available with either folding or fixed blades. The fixed blade design has the twin blades securely fixed into the handle with screws (to allow removal of the blades if necessary) and rivets so they are set permanently 2.5 cm (1″) apart. A metallic spatula is attached to the opposite end of the handle.

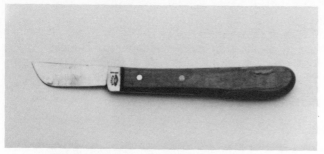

Figure 4-8. The Kunde 35 st budding knife. A fixed blade, double-angled knife with a conventional contoured handle.

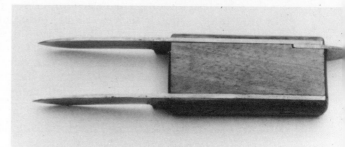

Figure 4-9. Tina 671 twin-bladed budding knife with fixed blades and a metal spatula at the end of the handle. This specialist knife is designed for patch budding.

Knife Sharpening

There are many myths about knife sharpening and the ancillary equipment necessary. Once a specialist knife has been obtained, the first priority is to keep it in prime condition and this can only be achieved by methodical maintenance. I have seen a number of good knives ruined by carelessness, either when sharpening or during use and/or storage. This section will provide some guidelines on the correct usage and maintenance of knives.

Sharpening Aids

The two basic sharpening aids are special stones and pieces of leather. Depending on the structure of the stone, it can be covered with a thin layer of oil (oilstone) or water (whetstone or wetstone) in order to smooth the traction of the knife during sharpening.

Carborundum—Carborundum is an artificial hard substance that is even harder than quartz. The surface of the stone may be coarse and it should then be used only on a blade that is in poor condition and very blunt as a fine edge cannot be obtained. The coarse-graded stones will scratch the surface of the blade.

Sandstone and Siltstone—Sandstones are made of grains of sand that are naturally or artificially cemented together. Very fine-grained stones can be derived from silt and are sometimes referred to as "siltstones". The fine texture of sand- and siltstones means that there is very little risk of scratching the blade when sharpening.

They are available commercially as either whetstones or oilstones and in a range of sizes. A small whetstone, 7.5 × 2.0 × 1.3 cm (3 × ¾ × ½″), is excellent to keep in the pocket for maintaining the sharp edge of a budding knife during use. A convenient stone for the propagation shed is an India Oil Sharpening Stone, 20 × 5 × 2.5 cm (8 × 2 × 1″), which is large enough to accommodate most straight bladed knives. Some of these are available in a combination form, with the two flat 20 × 5 cm (8 × 2″) surfaces of different textures.

Popular oil- and whetstones used in North America are the Arkansas (pronounced "Arkansaw") stones which are shaped from naturally-occurring stone quarried around Hot Springs, Arkansas. These stones are sold in three grades:—

(i) Soft Arkansas for general purpose use.

(ii) Hard Arkansas for finishing and touching-up.

(iii) Black Hard Arkansas for blades which are already very sharp.

The stones are brittle and are easily broken if dropped onto a hard surface. It is advisable to mount the larger stones within a wooden box, ensuring that the stone is set above the top of the box for ease of sharpening. Any oil spillage is encouraged to flow into the box. The box should have a lid that is closed when not in use to prevent damage and to keep the stone clean. Short nails at each of the corners will prevent movement of the box during knife sharpening.

A stone with a rounded upper surface is often recommended for curved blade grafting and pruning knives.

Belgian Brocken—Belgian brocken is a naturally occurring, impure limestone—the impurities being mainly silt and mud. It makes an extremely fine stone with a silky texture to the sharpening surface. Useful for finishing off after using a fine stone or for "touching-up" the knife to keep the cutting edge sharp.

Leather Strop—A leather strop is a useful aid for completing the final sharpening. A used or unused barber's strop is ideal or, alternatively, a pre-cut piece of leather with an optimum size of 10 × 30 cm (4 × 12″). The leather strop must be kept taut during use;

(a) By hooking one end onto a nail in the wall,

(b) By attaching a small strap to the base, forming a loop that can go over one's foot, or

(c) Cementing the strop to a wooden block with a handle at one end so that it can be easily carried around.

Figure 4-10. A piece of Belgian brocken is excellent to carry around to keep a sharp edge to the blade of a knife.

Figure 4-11. Left—a section of leather strop cemented onto a wooden block. This is used to keep a fine sharp edge to the knife. Right—a fine-grade sandstone (oilstone) for knife sharpening.

Method of Sharpening

There are many variations in sharpening procedures, but all should achieve the desired result. The best publication at present is *Care, Maintenance and Use of Knives—Trainee Guide HCA 6-A-5* (Agricultural Training Board, Beckenham, Kent, U.K.). The following comments are based on this publication. The best way to learn is to be shown by a competent knife sharpener. If this is not possible, a recommended procedure is outlined below.

(1) The surface of the stone is cleaned, using water for a whetstone and kerosene (paraffin) for an oilstone.

(2) A thin layer of oil or water, according to the type of stone, is applied and spread over the surface.

(3) The side (or sides) of the knife to be sharpened is determined. A single-angled blade is sharpened on *one* side only (where the notch is) while a double-angled blade is sharpened on *both* sides. Sharpening a single-angled blade on both sides will cause the blade to bow in the middle and produce an uneven and short-lasting cutting surface.

(4) Hold the handle of the knife with one hand, placing the thumb and first 2 or 3 fingers of the other on the back of the blade, which is facing towards you. Hold the cutting edge at an angle of 20–25° to the stone, then use a constant, steady forward movement to push it away from you along the length of the stone. Raise the cutting edge and return to the starting position. This is continued until the knife is sufficiently sharpened.

(5) Gently move the knife over the stone 2 or 3 times on each side, then remove debris and oil by wiping the blade with a cloth.

Figure 4-12.
A single-angled blade is
sharpened on the sloping
side only. Note that the
thumb and fingers are
held at the back of the
blade so that the operator
can hold the blade at a
constant angle of
between 20–25° and
move it with a constant
forward movement. Note
also that the stone being
used has two layers—
coarse-grained below and
fine-grained above.

(6) A leather strop may be used to finish off both sides of the blade, holding each side in turn flat against the leather surface. If the leather is dry, it may be soaked in mink oil about 24 hours before use.

(7) Clean the knife blade again, and test its degree of sharpness by seeing if the complete length of the cutting edge will cut through paper without tearing it. If it does tear, the knife is not yet sharp enough.

If the blade is longer than the width of the stone, the above instructions can be modified by:—

(a) Directing the forward movement of the blade so that it is slightly across the stone, or

(b) Using a circular movement—anti-clockwise for a right-handed knife, clockwise for a left-handed one.

Both these methods are also suitable for a slightly curved grafting knife, but some propagators find that it is best if the stone itself is slightly curved.

For a curved budding knife, a small circular movement is often used. This action is particularly useful when using small pocket fine stones to maintain the cutting edge when budding in the field.

Storage of Knives

Knives should be personally identified and kept in a safe place. It is best to use one's own knife rather than relying on those used by others. A good way to ensure permanent identification is to ask a jeweler to engrave the owner's name along the spring of the knife.

After use, the blade should be wiped clean and both it and the spring folding mechanism should be given a coating of light oil if the knife is not to be used in the near future.

If a knife mechanism is badly corroded, apply a penetrating lubricant (e.g., W.D.40®) to the spring folding mechanism and gradually work it in. I find the following procedure useful to clean a rusted or badly stained blade. Obtain one of the proprietary biochemical rust removing gels and apply a liberal coating over the blade. Then place the knife into a polyethylene bag to prevent the gel from hardening. Three to four hours later, remove the gel under running water, and polish the blade with chrome cleaner. This should return the blade to almost "new" condition.

Use of a Knife

Considerable skill is needed to develop the correct procedures and an economic work rate. It is often not easy to comprehend from a textbook the precise movements involved, so the best advice that I can give is to make every attempt to be shown what to do by a competent expert. Nursery operators' workshops and employee training sessions provide excellent opportunities for this.

Safety

Some fundamental safety procedures are essential to encourage a safe work place. Injuries are generally caused through lack of concentration, faulty and/or poorly maintained tools, incorrect storage, poor instruction, and both over- and under-confidence. Therefore, it is helpful to set up some safety guidelines for the beginner. Those listed below should provide a good basis.

(1) Do not use a knife for an operation for which it was never intended.

(2) Work on a clean and well laid-out work bench.

(3) Repair or discard knives that are faulty.

(4) Keep knives well maintained with a sharp cutting edge. Blunt knives often cause more accidents than sharp ones.

(5) Keep the blade of a folding knife closed when not in use. An open knife blade on a bench is easily forgotten, particularly if it is hidden by plant material. A knife blade may be effectively closed either by using the palm of an open hand or a thumb and bent forefinger. In both cases, continue the pressure until the blade is well set into the handle. Do not close the blade by placing the thumb along the back of the blade.

(6) Ensure that fixed blade knives are placed in a sheath when not in use or, where appropriate, retracted into the handle.

Figure 4-13. Serious injuries occur easily when the knife blade is not folded into the handle after use—particularly if the open blade is covered by plant material on the bench.

Figure 4-14. Two methods of closing a folding knife. A (left). Push gently down with the palm of the hand. B (right). Hold the back of the blade with the thumb and index finger and ease the blade into the handle.

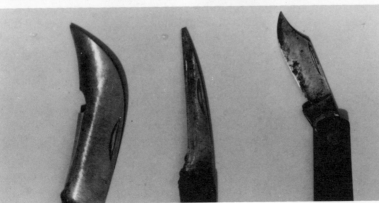

Figure 4-15. Examples of poor maintenance and careless use of knives. Left and center—Broken blades caused by dropping the knife onto a cement surface. Right—A corroded folding mechanism prevents the blade from opening fully. Note also the ingrained debris on the blade.

Holding a Knife

Both geographical area and tradition have caused many variations of knifemanship, but all have resulted in an excellent finished product. The type of plant, method of cutting, and graft preparation have meant that a considerable number of techniques have evolved over the years. One develops a "feel" for which particular aspects should be stressed when teaching nursery employees, and university or college students. It should be impressed on everyone that only continual practice and experience will ensure competence. The following advice may prove helpful when teaching other people:—

(1) Explain the fundamentals of a knife, its care and maintenance.

(2) Identify correct and faulty practices, particularly in relation to safety.

(3) Instill confidence in the trainee, with encouragement to develop a rhythmical movement, and ensure that ample follow-up is allowed. Jerky movements slow down the work rate and tire the propagator, resulting in a poor-quality finished product.

Some examples of procedures are outlined below.

(a) **Cuttings**—The cutting is held between the thumb and knife so that the thumb will support the cutting when the cut is made. Attempt to work with the thumb and knife in parallel. The movement should be away from the body; i.e., for a right-handed person the movement is offset to the right side of the body.

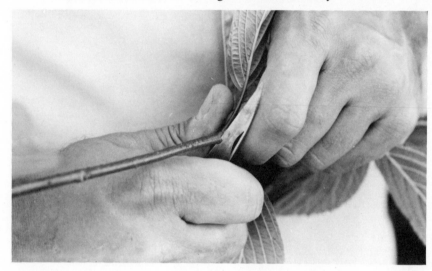

Figure 4-16. Preparing a nodal softwood cutting of *Viburnum × bodnantense* 'Dawn' (Bodnant Viburnum cv.). Note that the thumb is used to support the stem. Essentially, the thumb and knife work in parallel and the cutting movement is away to the side of the operator's body. (To reduce the possibility of injury, the blade and thumb must not be "pushed" directly towards each other.)

Figure 4-17. Open-ground grafting often requires long even flat cuts which are encouraged by simultaneously moving both elbows in an outward direction.

Figure 4-18. Preparing scions of *Campsis × tagliabuana* 'Madame Galen' (Madame Galen Trumpet Vine) for grafting onto root pieces of *C. radicans* (Common Trumpet Creeper). Note the position of the operator's elbows as she whip grafts. (Angers, France)

(b) Whip and Whip and Tongue Grafting—The aim in these grafts is to obtain a long, flat even cut with one movement. One method to achieve this is by moving both elbows in a straight, outward direction when making the cut. Short, rounded and uneven cuts are the result when the elbows move round the side of the body. Another method is to "lock" the elbow to the side of the body. This makes it easier for some grafters to return the knife to exactly the same place on the scion when further cuts have to be made.

Some propagators hold the scion so that its base faces away from them when grafting, thus making the cuts away from the body. I have never found the degree of control necessary to make a satisfactory cut surface when cutting this way.

(c) Bench Grafting—Bench-grafting thin caliper material requires more precise cuts and more support of the scion. One method is to hold the scion over the tips of the fingers and prevent it from moving with the thumb. This stops the scion bending when the cut is made. The movement of the knife is towards the body, enabling one to make the necessary shallow precise cuts.

Confidence can be instilled in trainees by allowing them to use softer wood for practice. A technique that I find helpful when teaching cutting propagation in the fall is to use stems of a plant such as *Escallonia,* hand-stripping all leaves and removing any side branches. The trainee can begin with the softer tip growth, working down the stem and gradually getting into the more ripened wood. This allows them to develop rhythm and to begin to make precise cuts at the nodes and on individual cuttings as their confidence increases.

Aesculus (Buckeye) and *Alnus rubra* (Red Alder) wood is excellent for practicing some methods of grafting—avoid the much harder, rounded wood of *Acer* (Maple). Impress on the trainees that the knife should not be forced through the material when grafting or budding. For example, if the knife blade "sticks" behind the bud when chip budding (p. 478), remove the blade from the cut and re-position it so that the bud is nearer the handle. In most instances, the blade will then easily pass under the bud to the pre-cut veneer. The Trainee Guides produced by the Agricultural Training Board (ATB) (Beckenham, Kent, U.K.) admirably break down the more commonly used techniques into their different components so that the trainee can practice each step.

Young and re-trained people are a major factor in the long-term success of the nursery stock industry, thus it is important that skills are communicated and practiced. The nursery trade has a history of sometimes allowing only a very few senior staff to graft or bud, and I feel strongly that opportunity should be given to newcomers. Time and money is well spent by encouraging "hands-on" training which is helped by lining out additional rootstocks in the open ground or providing additional pot-grown stocks for bench grafting. In this way, the trainee can carry out the complete process, as well as understand the importance of correct aftercare procedures.

PRUNERS (Secateurs)

There are essentially two reasons why pruners (either hand or tree pruners) are now more commonly used for propagation. Firstly, their design and precision has greatly improved, and, secondly, the development of large nurseries with sizable teams of semi-skilled staff carrying out the propagation has made it necessary to resort to cutting tools other than knives.

They are used to prune established plants thus improving the quality, to take hardwood and evergreen hardwood cuttings—particularly of evergreen shrubs and conifers—and to head-back rootstocks for grafting. There are numerous types on the market, with the well-known brands including Felco, Leyat, Wilkinson, Modena, Corona, Tina and Rolcut. However, even the most expensive models cannot cut as cleanly as a really sharp knife. This can sometimes be demonstrated by cutting a well-ripened stem with both a knife and a pruner and then closely examining the cut surfaces. The surface cut with the pruners has a "whitish" appearance while the knife cut is a clean-cut green. The difference is insignificant when taking many cuttings, but it is important when preparing a scion or rootstock.

Points to consider when purchasing pruners for propagation are:—

(1) Determine the specific purposes for which they are to be used, considering both staff and cost.

(2) They should be comfortable in the hand and easy to manipulate. Models are available with plastic-covered metallic handles, with revolving lower handles to make it easier when continuously pruning heavier stems, and with shorter handles for smaller hands. Power-assisted pruners are available for field pruning of trees and rootstocks.

(3) There should be no lateral movement of the blades. The tips should completely adjoin and not leave a gap when the blades are closed. The release catch should hold the blades in this position when the pruners are not in use.

(4) They should be easy to take apart for repair, replacements and sharpening.

Figure 4-19. Power-assisted pruners being used to head-back rootstocks to just above the bud. Note the steel-mesh safety glove worn by the operator. (Reproduced by permission of GC/HTJ, Haymarket Publishing, Twickenham, Middlesex, U.K.)

Types of Pruners

Based on their design, pruners can be placed into three groups which are outlined below.

(a) Scissors (Snippers)

These are essentially designed along a similar line to ordinary kitchen or dressmaking scissors. The long-pointed blades make them suitable for softwood cutting work or for trimming the soft tips from bundles of prepared cuttings. They are not suitable for larger caliper, harder wood.

(b) Anvil ("Parrot Bill")

One blade is rounded but with a straight cutting edge while the other is a flat metal anvil. During use, the anvil is under the stem and the cutting blade above. Hand pressure on the handles brings the blade down into contact with the anvil after the stem has been cut through. These types are losing their popularity—their main disadvantage is a tendency to crush and subsequently bruise the stem. However, there is a modified design available, the Modena (from S. Gobbi, Torino, Italy), which gives a very precise clean cut.

(c) Bypass

This type has two curved blades whose cutting surfaces glide past (by-pass) each other when cutting through stems. Modern design has resulted in these being the most satisfactory type for propagation. Generally, they can be quickly dismantled when required. The model that I find to be excellent for cutting preparation is the Felco #6. This model has a small handle and cutting head, which means that it can be more easily manipulated for the detailed work of cutting preparation, including wounding thicker stemmed evergreens. The narrow thicker blade should be kept under the stem when cutting.

Maintenance

A leather or plastic holster is useful to ensure that the pruners are not damaged or mislaid when carried around. The principles involved in the maintenance of pruners are similar to those for a knife in that only the sloping side of the blade is sharpened. If the blade is not or cannot be

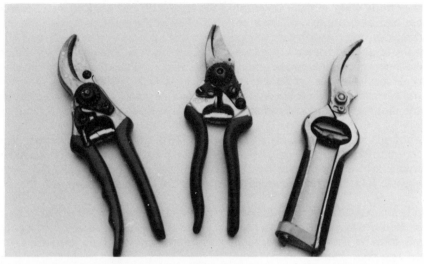

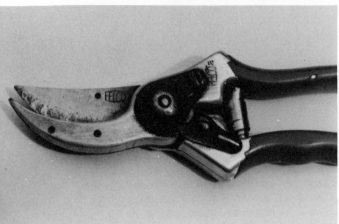

Figure 4-20.
Three models of bypass
pruners used successfully
for cutting propagation.
Left—Corona #850.
Center—Felco #6.
Right—Zenith.

Figure 4-21. Two examples of poor maintenance and incorrect usage of pruners. A (left). Incomplete closing of the blades when the catch is in place indicates that the pruners must be dismantled and the blades re-set. B (right). These pruners have been used for a purpose for which they were not intended. Note the damage to the upper blade which was probably caused by cutting wire.

removed, the pruners are opened fully with the handles parallel with or away from the body. The sharpening stone is then moved in a circular fashion along the length of the blade. Alternatively, the blade can be removed and held in a vise and a hand-held stone used for sharpening.

A common reason for pruners not cutting effectively, besides a blunt blade, is that they have been used to cut too large a stem and have been twisted by excessive hand pressure. In this case, the pruners must be dismantled and the blade re-set. It is useful to keep a quantity of spare springs as they can sometimes accidentally fall out of the handles. Details of dismantling the pruners are normally given on the packaging box. As with knives, all moving parts should be regularly oiled. The procedures described on p. 184 can be used for corroded metal. One of the penetrating aerosol lubricants (e.g., W.D.40®) can be recommended for coating blades for off-season storage and rust prevention.

Further details on maintenance are well described in Trainee Guide No. HCA 6-A-6 *Care, Maintenance and Use of Secateurs* published by the Agricultural Training Board (Beckenham, Kent, U.K.).

SEALING COMPOUNDS FOR GRAFTS

Grafting waxes, rubberized-latex and bitumastic emulsions are the major materials used for sealing grafts. Their primary role is to seal the graft effectively in order to reduce water loss from the cut surfaces at the apex of a prepared scion and/or around the cut surfaces at the graft. A secondary effect is to reduce the incidence of subsequent disease infection starting at the cut surface.

Some of the compounds were initially developed for arboricultural work to seal the cut surfaces of tree limbs that had been removed. They are also used in the nursery to seal the cut surface of a budded rootstock during the dormant season, either after it has been cut back to a 10–15 cm (4–6") snag above the scion or flush with the scion the following year. However, their major use in the nursery is to seal open-ground dormant grafts, e.g., the whip and tongue graft, while also being effectively used in certain instances for bench grafting, for example, cold grafting of *Betula* (Birch), *Fagus* (Beech) and *Hamamelis* (Witch Hazel). There is little or no control of the environment in either of these situations so that a localized application of a sealing compound can have a considerable impact.

Historically, compounds to seal a graft union have been used since the 19th century, and even earlier. One such compound was a mixture of clay, fresh cow manure and fine hay, straw or cow hair which was formed into a thick paste by adding water. A small amount of salt was sometimes added to the paste to make the subsequent seal over the graft site more effective in reducing water loss.

Today, compounds are available as proprietary products that can be purchased either as a solid to be heated and melted down for application with a brush in the liquid state, or as a cool liquid for immediate application by brush. Essentially, the compounds most widely used are:—

(a) Those applied as a cool liquid.
    (i)   Bitumastic emulsions
    (ii) Cold resin-based waxes
    (iii) Rubberized-latex compounds
(b) Those applied as a soft wax.
    Hand mastics
(c) Those applied as a hot liquid.
    (i)   Hot resin-based waxes
    (ii) Paraffin wax

BITUMASTIC EMULSIONS

These compounds are water emulsions that were developed primarily for the arboricultural profession. Sometimes they have a fungicide incorporated in them. They are dark brown to black in color and tend to be sticky. Thinning the compound with water may be necessary if it should develop a very thick consistency in storage. The thin surface layer present in a new tin should not be used as it will "run" and more easily penetrate the cut surfaces.

I have effectively used this material for open-ground dormant whip and tongue grafting of *Prunus*, *Tilia* (Linden), *Robinia* (Locust) and *Sorbus* (Mountain Ash), with a satisfactory seal resulting. However, bitumastic emulsions are not advised under the following circumstances:—

(i) Open-ground grafting when heavy rain occurs or is expected within 24–36 hours after application. The rain dilutes the emulsion, causing it to run. Re-application will be necessary.

(ii) Open-ground grafting during continuous periods of mild, warm weather.

(iii) Bench grafting

I learned about (ii) and (iii) the hard way when grafts suddenly began to deteriorate after the initial flush of growth from the buds. These compounds harden from "outside-to-in"—the outer surface exposed to the air hardens first while the protected layer adjacent to the stem hardens last. This time gap, which is lengthened by increasing temperatures, can allow the emulsion to penetrate between and into the cut surfaces. This was very apparent in some *Prunus* bench grafts when the scion and rootstock were separated—the stained tissue in and around the cambium could be clearly seen. (see also p. 515)

COLD RESIN-BASED WAXES (COLD BRUSH WAXES)

These are not widely used in nurseries—the hot waxes are more common. They are largely resin-based and may also have beeswax, talc and methylated spirits added—the latter evaporates after application to harden the material. A small stiff brush is used to apply the wax.

RUBBERIZED-LATEX COMPOUNDS

A relatively new range of materials is having considerable success in the Pacific Northwest region of North America, and is marketed in the Farwell Tree Doc® range by Farwell Products, East

Wenatchee, Washington. They are latex-based, waterproof materials initially formulated for tree surgery, although the "Yellow Cap" formulation is specifically designed for both open-ground and bench grafting. It is bright yellow in color and is applied over the union and other relevant cut surfaces to a thickness of about 1.6 mm (1/16"). It dries within 30 minutes, and is then unaffected by rain. The material has a reasonable amount of elasticity so that it will expand slightly without cracking, and has performed well in both warm and cold temperatures.

HAND MASTICS

The three major components of soft waxes are resin, beeswax and tallow mixed in an optimum ratio of 5:4:1. The consistency may be altered by adjusting the ratio levels—for example, resin will increase the wax's hardening properties while tallow will make it more supple. A thin covering of light oil or grease on the hands will make the application of the wax to the grafts easier. The disadvantages of these compounds are that they are less convenient and slower to apply than the brush-applied liquids or dips. To avoid covering the cut surfaces of the grafts, it is best to have an additional person other than the grafter to apply these materials.

HOT RESIN-BASED WAXES

The additional equipment required when applying hot liquid materials is some form of container in which the solid material may be heated to form a liquid. These containers are sometimes referred to as "wax pots". They can either be purchased pre-made or, as in many cases, constructed in the nursery. The basic criteria when selecting or making a wax pot are as follows:—

(i) It should be stable so as to avoid spillage of fuel and wax.
(ii) It should be easily movable by the grafter.
(iii) It should hold sufficient liquid wax to avoid continuous melting of more solid.

Some designs are quite elaborate, while others are based on a small portable camping stove to which is fixed a framework to securely hold the wax pot as required. The source of fuel may be methylated spirits, gas or electricity.

There are a number of different formulae for making one's own resin-based hot wax, most of which are very satisfactory. One recommended by R. J. Garner is as follows:—10 parts Resin, 3¼ parts Burgundy Pitch, 2½ parts Tallow, 2½ parts Paraffin Wax and 3 parts Venetian Red. The mixing procedure and other formulations are well documented in his book *The Grafter's Handbook*. However, it is more convenient to purchase ready-made blocks for melting down.

These hot waxes are excellent sealing compounds for open-ground grafting and are also very satisfactory for bench grafting. They do give off a considerable amount of heat, so they should be allowed to cool a little before application, particularly for thin-barked plant material.

The different formulations can directly affect the ability of the liquid to harden, therefore consideration must be given to methods of re-melting the wax during grafting.

PARAFFIN WAX

Paraffin wax may be purchased in solid rectangular blocks. Domestic candles may be used if these are not available. This material has proved to be excellent for bench grafting of ornamental trees, shrubs and conifers. It is not as suitable as the hot resin-based waxes for outside work because extreme and varied weather conditions can crack and loosen the paraffin wax, thus lifting it away from the stem surface. Paraffin wax has been effectively used for covering the union and scion for bare-root grafts of deciduous trees and shrubs to be cold stored at 1°C (34°F) for 3 to 4 months. Different colored dyes can be mixed with the wax to make subsequent identification of the grafts easier, using a different color for each plant grafted.

There are two methods for applying paraffin wax to bench grafted stock:—

(i) Use a brush to paint the liquid around the union and, where necessary, the cut terminal surface of the scion. The molten wax needs to be just below boiling point because it quickly thickens if left to cool beyond this, making it difficult to apply evenly with the brush.

(ii) Invert the graft and dip both the scion and union into the liquid for 1 or 2 seconds. This method is suitable for some deciduous trees and shrubs. Damage can occur to buds with naturally thin outer protective coverings. The scion and union can be dipped into a container of cold water after removal from the molten wax to reduce the temperature and harden the wax more quickly.

In both cases, the subsequent cracking of the wax around the union is a good indicator of callus formation activity at the graft union.

Figure 4-22.
A good indication of active callus formation occurring between the scion and rootstock of a bench graft is when the wax begins to crack.

TYING MATERIALS

The type of tying material adopted during the earlier days of nursery development was largely traditional, using natural plant-based materials or localized alternatives. Today it is more sophisticated, with far more thought and emphasis being given to the correct tying material and to the method by which it is secured. There are essentially three reasons for this. Firstly, the development of new, and the refinement of traditional, grafting and budding techniques; secondly, the development of large nurseries where speed and efficiency are paramount to reduce production costs; and, thirdly, the greater world-wide use of plastics.

Selection of a tying material involves the following criteria:—

(a) It should be readily available at an economic price.

(b) It should be easy to manipulate with the fingers under the different temperatures likely to be experienced in one's locality at the time of grafting or budding. A simple dispenser for rolls of tapes can be constructed to make handling easier.

(c) It must exert sufficient tension without breaking prematurely until the scion and rootstock have formed a union.

(d) Whether costs can be lowered by using a tie that effectively breaks down when it has achieved its purpose, thus reducing the necessity of physically removing it.

(e) The ties must not deteriorate quickly during storage, which should be in a cool dark place. The materials that degrade in sunlight *must* be stored in the dark.

(f) The material should "flow well" if designed for use with a specific tying machine.

Tying materials can be grouped into two categories:—

(i) Natural Plant-based Materials

(ii) Manufactured Materials—plant-derived and synthetic.

NATURAL PLANT-BASED MATERIALS

(1) Raffia

Raffia is derived from the leaf cuticle of *Raphia farinifera*, the Raffia Palm, which grows in countries such as Mauritius and Madagascar. This has been the standby material for nurseries over the decades, both for propagation and for tying-up plants in the production areas. It is both strong and flexible, although it has the disadvantage of tending to roll in the hand when dry. However, the handling of raffia can be improved by immersing it in a bucket of water for 1–2 hours. Other techniques used are to leave it on grass overnight so that overnight humidity will dampen it, or to wrap it in moist burlap (hessian) and leave the bundle for a few hours in a cool place.

Plastic materials have largely replaced raffia. It is, however, occasionally used in bench grafting as an alternative to waxed cotton when a tie of thin width is required—for example, with *Clematis* and *Daphne*.

(2) Bass

Bass is derived from the inner bark of *Tilia americana* (American Linden or Basswood) and was once popular in North America. It is made by stripping the bark from trees in the spring and soaking it in water for 2–4 weeks. Soft strands are later developed from the mucilaginous material that separates from the bark. Unlike raffia, it does not have a tendency to roll when handled.

(3) Reed

A traditional material that I have seen used in Belgium is prepared from a local reed, *Juncus inflexus*. The reeds are cut in July and dried, after which they can be successfully stored for many years. Prior to use, the dried reeds are soaked in either cold water for 24 hours or hot water for 1 hour. They are then used for tying-in open-ground late winter grafts, remaining intact until October. However, there is no stem constriction as the technique used to secure the reed when tying-in allows the knot to untie itself as the caliper of the stem expands. Some nurseries still prefer to use reed as a tying-in material, mainly because there is no need to remove and dispose of the ties as has to be done with plastic materials.

MANUFACTURED MATERIALS—PLANT-DERIVED AND SYNTHETIC

Plant-Derived

(1) Cotton

This is a traditional material that is still effectively used for bench grafting ornamentals. It has also been popular for growers specializing in miniature roses. A knot is not always necessary as one end can be pressed onto the stem of the plant so that it adheres, or the two ends can be quickly twisted together. One specification that is advised is to use No. 20 knitting cotton. Waxing gives the cotton longer life. The complete spools are immersed in molten wax for 15–30 minutes to ensure an adequate covering. Additional materials, such as linseed oil and tallow, are sometimes added to make the cotton more supple, and also to improve the penetration of the molten wax into the spool.

(2) Fillis String

This soft string can be used successfully for larger caliper grafts, such as bare root grafts of *Malus, Prunus* and *Sorbus* (Mountain Ash). Like cotton, it can be waxed to improve its longevity. The main disadvantage is that it does not expand when tying, making it more difficult to obtain enough tension.

(3) Paper Tape

A paper tape is widely used in Wetteren, Belgium, for open-ground grafting. The two major reasons for its popularity are that, firstly, it is not necessary to remove the tape later in the growing season and, secondly, it provides protection against wind damage.

Synthetic

(1) Adhesive Tapes

These tapes have one side coated with an adhesive compound and are purchased in rolls. The tape is tightly wrapped around the union. They are used for both greenhouse and open-ground grafting, but not for budding. Two disadvantages of these tapes are that it can be difficult to get enough tension to give a tight seal, and that wet weather can reduce the adhesive properties, thus causing the tape to unwind.

(2) Rubber Strips or Bands

These popular pre-cut strips are purchased in bulk, normally by weight in either 1 kg or 1 lb bags. They are available in a variety of colors ranging from white to gray, pink and blue. They are widely used for bench grafting and are popular in some areas of North America for tying-in T-buds in the open-ground production of trees and roses. The advantages include their ability to expand when tying-in so giving excellent tension between scion and rootstock; they are held securely by a simple half-hitch knot at the end of the tying sequence; and, unless there is the likelihood of a constriction forming, they can be left to deteriorate slowly and snap off when the caliper around the union increases. The rubber strip normally has to be physically removed if it is beneath peat moss or soil to avoid constriction.

They are usually available in two widths—3 mm (⅛″) for bench grafting and 6 mm (¼″) for budding. The narrow, and often thinner, grade makes it easier to use for a wide variety of bench grafted subjects. The strips are also available in different lengths, for example, 10.0 cm (4″), 12.5 cm (5″) and 15.8 cm (6¼″) for bench grafting and 12.5 cm (5″), 15.8 cm (6¼″) and 21 cm (8¼″), thus making them useful for a wide range of caliper sizes when budding. A new supply of ties should be ordered if they begin to snap when tying-in. Rubber ties and strips should be kept in a refrigerator where it is dark and cool for long-term storage.

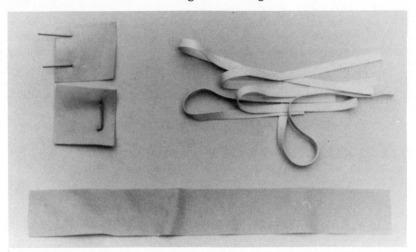

Figure 4-23. A selection of synthetic tying-in materials. Upper left—rubber patches for open-ground rose budding. Note the staple for securing the patch around the hypocotyl of the rootstock to keep the patch under tension. Upper right—rubber strips or bands for bench grafting. Bottom—Rapidex® degradable tie formulated for chip budding.

(3) Sunlight Degradable Ties

Degradable ties are purchased in bulk by weight, and are off-white in color and partially translucent. They are quick to tie on, being fixed either by a knot or, alternatively, by a small metallic staple. Their objective is to apply sufficient tension for a satisfactory union to develop between scion and rootstock before they snap off due to deterioration caused by the ultra-violet light spectrum in sunlight. These ties need to be stored in a dark cool cupboard or refrigerator to retain their effectiveness.

There are different designs of degradable ties currently available on the market:—

(a) Rubber Patches (Fleischhauer®, Okulette® and Speedeasy®)—These ties are actually a square rubber patch with a staple through one side. They are very popular for roses because they are extremely easy and quick to fix. The patch is held under tension by securing the staple through the other edge, ensuring that it is on the opposite side to where the scion bud was inserted. The patches normally disintegrate over 3–4 weeks.

(b) Ties (Rapidex®)—These ties are supplied with Rapidex Products, Knutsford, Cheshire, England, and each consists of a strip with an enlarged area in the center that completely covers the bud and two narrow ends that are securely tied by hand. Different sizes are available, designed for both roses and trees.

A more recent development has been the formulation of a degradable strip tie designed specifically for chip budding. The objectives were, firstly, to have a tie that would provide sufficient tension to hold the scion chip firmly into the rootstock, and, secondly, one that would degrade within 4–6 weeks after budding to prevent constriction in the stem (see also p. 482).

(4) Polyvinyl Chloride (PVC) Tape or Strips

There are a number of brands of thin polyvinyl chloride materials, normally green in color, that are used to tie in the scion when T-budding trees. I find that some snap easily when applying tension, while others have proved to perform well. The bud is left exposed when tying-in, and the ties are secured with a half-hitch knot. They are purchased in reels, removing a sufficient amount for each stock as required. [There have been occasional problems with damage to plant tissues by the chemicals present in the PVC.]

Robert J. Garner at East Malling Research Station showed me a budding tape that was interesting because it was ribbed so that the fingers gripped it more easily. It is excellent for field grafting of large rootstocks when really firm ties are needed. It is bright orange, making it highly visible, and excellent tension could be applied as it showed good elasticity properties. R. J. Garner recently wrote to me, "Its bright orange colour in the field rows gives much encouragement to the keen grafter."

(5) Polyethylene Tape

The use of polyethylene has made a considerable impact in grafting and budding, as in many other areas of propagation. It is used for tying-in dormant open-ground grafts and for spring and summer chip budding. It is normally purchased in rolls as clear tape, but milky polyethylene is also available. The latter makes the ties more visible in the rows, and tends to have greater elasticity. It is available in two widths, 1.3 cm (½″) or 2.5 cm (1″).

The 2.5 cm (1″) tape is normally favored for open-ground grafting. It gives an excellent waterproof seal with excellent tension, thus minimizing the need for subsequent waxing around the union. It also performs exceedingly well for chip budding as a good seal results and considerable tension can be applied both above and below the exposed bud. However, the 1.5 cm (½″) width tape is particularly useful for budding as it is easier to work around the bud, making it more popular with many propagators. The disadvantage of polyethylene tape is that it can quickly bite into the stem as the caliper increases thus causing a constriction, therefore it has to be removed at the correct time. Polyethylene tapes that are degradable in sunlight have so far met with little success.

The 1.3 cm (½″) tape has also been successfully used in bench grafting conifers, for example, Pines, but it does take practice to tie effectively as there is a tendency for the finished tie not to have sufficient tension.

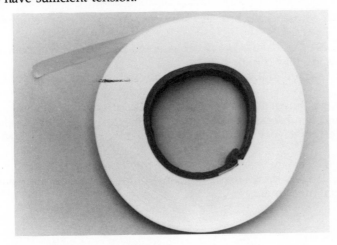

Figure 4-24. A roll of polyethylene tape. This material is manufactured in 1.3 cm (½″) and 2.5 cm (1″) widths and is ideal for both open-ground grafting and chip budding. It must be released at a later date to avoid the development of a constriction in the stem tissue.

MACHINES FOR BENCH GRAFTING AND OPEN-GROUND BUDDING

The development of these machines was very largely due to the need to overcome the infection of fruiting vines by the destructive root aphid *Phylloxera,* which was a particular problem in both France and California. Resistant rootstocks were developed but it was necessary to graft the scions in large quantities, using largely unskilled labor. This meant that the operation had to be mechanized and subsequently a large number of machines were developed—particularly in France, Austria, Germany and the United States.

Although the great majority of grafting and budding machines were developed for the vineyard and orchard industries, I decided that it would be useful to include a section reviewing their use so that the propagator can assess their potential application for a particular situation. Some of these machines have been successfully used for *Corylus* (Filbert), *Hibiscus,* ornamental *Malus* (Crab Apple) and roses.

Mechanized grafting and budding must *not* be used simply as an excuse for not trying to learn and use the conventional manual skills. The need for machines and the equipment involved should be carefully considered by the nursery management so that mechanization can be success-fully "dovetailed" into the nursery production program.

MERITS OF MACHINE GRAFTING/BUDDING

These can be summarized as follows:—

(1) To increase output and reduce labor costs in the propagation department by using largely unskilled labor. A three-person crew may produce up to 2,500 grafts per 8-hour day. Quoted figures state that labor costs are between 12–16% of the total costs.

(2) To simplify the grafting procedure—for example, staples are used to tie in the scion to the rootstock, or it may not be necessary to use a tie at all as in some wedge grafts. A hard resin-based hot wax has been used to unite the stock and scion.

(3) A varying range of aftercare facilities can be used—cold stores, the floors of nursery sheds, and both heated and unheated propagation greenhouses.

(4) Suitable for plants whose wood does not bruise easily with a relatively crude cut but that are traditionally whip, splice or wedge grafted, e.g., *Hibiscus* and miniature roses.

(5) Encourages specialization so that one or two propagation nurseries can perfect the technique and economically supply a number of larger producers.

LIMITATIONS OF MACHINE GRAFTING/BUDDING

There are several limitations to the use of grafting machines and these can be summarized as follows:—

(1) Not suitable for plants whose wood bruises easily, e.g., *Prunus.* The bruising of tissue delays subsequent callusing.

(2) Not successful for plants that have a heavy sap rise and need to be side-grafted, e.g., *Acer palmatum* (Japanese Maple) and *Pinus* (Pine).

(3) Some machines have resulted in unsightly unions after callusing and in splitting of the rootstock when growth begins.

(4) Some nursery trials have shown that some plants, e.g., *Malus,* have a lower success rate in open-ground establishment and a subsequent lower grade product at the point of sale. This could have been caused by the inefficiency of the carpentry and/or an unsuitable aftercare procedure.

(5) Many of the cuts made by machine are inferior to the traditional grafter's hand knife.

(6) Some machines are relatively inexpensive, but some of the larger and more sophisticated ones can require high capital investment.

GRAFTING PROCEDURE

The procedure can be broken down into the following elements:—

(i) Collection of scion wood and availability of correct rootstock. The wood must be fully dormant to reduce tissue damage.

↓

(ii) Grading of scion and rootstock so that they are of similar stem caliper.

↓

(iii) Where appropriate, disbudding of rootstock with a hand knife to reduce subsequent sucker growth.

↓

(iv) Prepare scion and rootstock on machine.

↓

(v) Tie, staple or interlock scion and rootstock.

↓

(vi) Place in designated aftercare facility.

The team of operators needs to be well organized, otherwise any labor reduction advantages are lost. The personnel need to operate smoothly without waiting periods at any stage in the procedure.

TYPES OF MACHINES

The types of machines available and their performance was well documented by the late C. J. Alley of the University of California, Davis, as part of his research program on the propagation of vines (see References).

Whip/Splice Graft Machine

These were largely developed by the French company of A. Lozevis, Place Pelletan, Lot-et-Garron. Their range of machines can be operated either by hand lever, foot pedal or electricity, depending on the user's requirements. The blades on the Lozevis models are able to produce a whip graft with an optimum length of 2.5–3.5 cm (1–1½") and to produce a precise and clean cut. The larger Ultra Rapide model is said to have an output of 5,000 grafts in an 8-hour day. Difficulty has been encountered with tying-in, as there is no pre-made cut to hold the stock and scion together during this stage. In addition to vines, the machine has been used for *Hibiscus* and roses.

One procedure that has been developed in Europe is the storage of the grafts in boxes stacked on a pallet at 21°C (70°F) for 2–3 weeks until a union develops, followed by cold storage at 1–3°C (34–38°F) until the time of potting or lining out.

Whip and Tongue Graft Machine

This is another Lozevis machine that I have seen demonstrated by R. J. Garner. It is portable and can be placed on the bench when in use. A single smooth movement of the arm makes both the splice and the tongue. Subsequent tying-in is much easier.

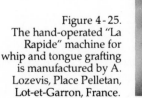

Figure 4-25.
The hand-operated "La Rapide" machine for whip and tongue grafting is manufactured by A. Lozevis, Place Pelletan, Lot-et-Garron, France.

Mortice and Tenon (Tongue and Groove) Graft Machine

Machines that cut out a mortice and tenon pattern have essentially a series of rotating saw blades separated by spacers, not a single fixed blade. The cuts tend to be rougher, but some designs do produce cuts that interlock securely enough to make additional tying-in materials unnecessary. Safety is important when operating these electrically-powered machines because of the high-speed rotating parts.

Three examples of these machines are as follows:—

(i) Long Ashton Grafting Machine

This machine was developed by G. S. Coles and C. G. Thomas of Long Ashton Research Station, Bristol, England, for the bench grafting of fruiting *Malus*. It has a good safety feature in that it is only possible to remove the guard covers when the power supply is turned off. There are three sites on the machine for cutting the wood. Firstly, a single rotating blade makes the initial horizontal cut on the rootstock and scion stem; secondly, a single "wobble blade" makes the mortice (groove) in the rootstock; and, thirdly, a double "wobble blade" makes the tenon (tongue) on the scion. The advantage of these "wobble blades" is that there is some lateral movement to enable wider cuts to be made.

The grafts are tied with conventional polyethylene grafting tape or, alternatively, with a metal staple. The percentage success rate of producing a satisfactory union has been in the region of 95%. This machine was found to be excellent for unskilled labor, but the rate of output was not significantly faster than a skilled knifesman could attain.

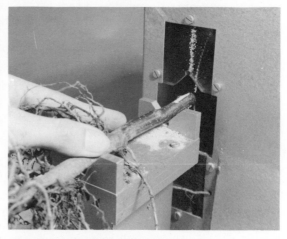

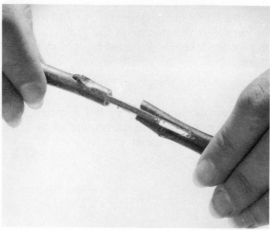

Figure 4-26. A (upper left). The Long Ashton Grafting Machine developed by G. S. Coles and C. G. Thomas for use in bench grafting fruiting *Malus*. B (upper right). Making the mortice (groove) cut on the rootstock. C (left). Interlocking the scion into the rootstock. (Reproduced by permission of C. G. Thomas, East Malling Research Station, Maidstone, Kent, U.K.).

(ii) Karl Fischer R.H.52

This machine is sold by the Karl Fischer Company, Vienna, Austria. It produces a larger cut surface than the Long Ashton Grafting Machine because there are 2 mortices and 2 tenons that firmly interlock, making it unnecessary to use tying-in materials. The machine is capable of producing about 400–600 grafts per hour, using a three-person crew. One operator prepares the rootstock, the second prepares the scion, and the third interlocks the cut surfaces of scion and rootstock, placing them on a flat for carrying to the grafting case.

Hillier Nurseries (Winchester) Ltd. used this machine to graft a wide range of plant material, but two problems occurred, due mainly to the large area of cut surface (up to 6.5 cm/2½") and the grafting pattern. Firstly, some soft dormant tissue was bruised, and, secondly a roundish unsightly union quickly began to form on liner plants.

Figure 4-27. Bench grafting trials being undertaken using a Karl Fischer R.H.52 grafting machine. The operator has just prepared the rootstock (foreground) on the adjacent cutting blade unit and is now preparing the scion using the cutting blade unit to the right.

(iii) Pfropf-Star

The German-manufactured Pfropf-Star (E. & H. Wahler, 7056 Weinstadt-Schnait, Buchhaldenstrasse 21, West Germany) has been successfully used in many areas of the world— e.g., by John Harper, Langley, British Columbia, as an integral part of his former business propagating grapes for vineyards. The scion and rootstock are first soaked in water for 12 hours followed by a further 12-hour soak in a fungicide. The machine is operated by a foot pedal that has two actions. It cuts the scion first and then the rootstock, interlocking the omega-shaped cuts on the scion and rootstock at the same time as the second cut is made. Two people could make up to 600 grafts in an 8-hour day, while four persons can make up to 2,000 grafts. The grafts are packed into "sweat-boxes" for callusing and remain at 29°C (85°F) for 3 weeks before hardening-off.

A pneumatic-powered version of this machine was recently made available. The significant features of the new version are the replacement of the foot lever with a compressed air cylinder to make the work more comfortable for the operator and the use of compressed air to remove any small pieces of wood or debris from the cut surfaces.

Figure 4-28. A (left). The Pfropf-Star machine forms omega-shaped cuts on the scion and the rootstock. B (right). A series of Pfropf-Star machines installed on a propagation bench. Note the pipes leading from the bench into a basket under the bench. Small pieces of wood and debris are carried down these pipes away from the working area. (Reproduced by courtesy of E. & H. Wahler, 7056 Weinstadt-Schnait, West Germany)

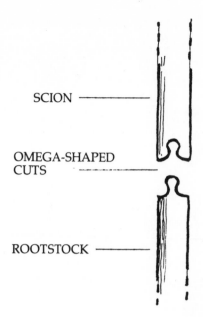

SCION ————————

OMEGA-SHAPED
CUTS ————————

ROOTSTOCK ————————

Diagram 4-1. Matching omega-
shaped cuts on scion and
rootstock made by the Pfropf-
Star grafting machine.

Wedge Graft Machine

A reliable hand-operated device was originally developed by Ulysse Fabre, Vaison-Vaucluse, France and is now sold in North America by J. E. Heitz (436 St. Helena Highway S, St. Helena, California) as the Heitz Grafting Tool. The machine can be bolted down onto the propagation bench or fixed to a heavy wooden block so that it can be moved to other areas of the nursery as necessary. The cutting knives are available in four sizes—22 mm (ca. ⅞"), 25 mm (ca. 1"), 30 mm (ca. 1-1/5") and 40 mm (ca. 1⅔"). The size chosen depends on the length of cuts required to make the wedge and on the caliper size of the rootstock. Best results are obtained when the scion and rootstock have the same diameter. It was originally manufactured for propagating grapes but has recently been used successfully for bench grafting *Corylus* (Filbert) at Holden Wholesale Nurseries Inc., Silverton, Oregon. These grafts were subsequently callused in a hot callusing pipe system (p.536).

The Raggett Grafting Machine is manufactured in New Zealand and sold in Australia by U.R. Machinery (Sales) Pty. Ltd. (63 Eighth, Mildura, Victoria 3500). It may be bench-mounted or hand-operated in the open ground. The operator uses a simple hand lever to produce a clean-cut wedge graft. The Raggett Grafting Machine was initially developed for the dormant grafting of

Figure 4-29. A (left). Robert J. Garner demonstrates an original foot-operated Ulysse Fabre wedge grafting machine to the author's young daughters. B (right). A close-up view showing the working mechanism of the Ulysse Fabre machine.

grape vines but has subsequently been used successfully for apples, pears and plums. (A Raggett device is also available for chip budding.)

Modified Wedge Graft Machine

This European machine has been useful for medium to larger caliper rootstocks. The scion is tapered to a point (like a pencil point) which fits tightly into the rootstock with a matching wedge. This method has been found to give a very strong union, but the rootstock sometimes splits when scion growth begins.

Figure 4-30. A (left). This graft was callused in a hot callus pipe and then potted. A Grow-Straight® shoot guide was then placed next to the scion in order to encourage vertical growth. B (right). Maiden growth of the potted *Corylus* in the September following machine grafting. (Verl Holden, Holden Wholesale Growers, Silverton, OR, U.S.A.).

MECHANICAL AIDS FOR BUDDING

There are various mechanical aids for budding which can reduce labor costs and increase output (plus, in some cases, make the budder more comfortable, e.g., handcarts). Some of these are summarized below.

BUD STICK DEFOLIATOR

One type of bud stick defoliator is a simple gadget which precisely removes the leaf lamina and shortens the petiole to complete the prepared bud stick. It essentially consists of a small metal tube within which are revolving blades powered by a battery.

Long Ashton Research Station, University of Bristol, England, developed an electrically-powered "de-leafing" machine. The cutting blade was installed onto a nylon core. The protected blade was driven at 3000 rpm from a belt drive and the nylon core could be changed to accommodate significant variations in bud wood caliper.

LILIPUT BENCH AND FIELD BUDDING TOOL

This device has been successfully used for many years in the United States and Europe for propagating grapes. It is simple to operate and is quickly adopted by unskilled operators. As the name implies, it can be operated on a bench or by open-ground budding. The Liliput Bench and Field Budding Tool is available from J. E. Heitz (436 St. Helena Highway S, St. Helena, California).

FURNESS CHIP BUDDER

This successful Australian-made device was also originally designed for propagating grapes at the bench or by open-ground budding. Two jaw-clamps prevent the wood from moving while the operator uses both hands to draw together two arms that make the precision cuts. Simple adjustment mechanisms are attached to the tool to ensure the correct depth of cuts, irrespective of the shape of the wood. The Furness Chip Budder is manufactured by Keith Furness Pty. Ltd. (5 Yalanda Street, Eden Hills, South Australia 5050).

Figure 4-31. A (left). The hand-operated Furness Chip Budder for bench or open-ground use. B (right). Matching the scion chip into the rootstock. (Reproduced by courtesy of Keith Furness Pty. Ltd., Eden Hills, S.A., Australia)

BUDDING GUN

An interesting innovation was designed during the 1970s by L. Pettifer at the University of North Wales, Bangor, U.K., to mechanize the traditional T- or shield-budding of roses. His award-winning prototype machine was called the Budding Gun. He had three fundamental objectives:—

(i) To encourage contract budding due to the decreasing number of skilled nursery employees.

(ii) To enable budding to be carried out both in the open ground and at the bench using unskilled labor.

(iii) To increase output and reduce labor costs.

The budding gun is small enough to comfortably fit into the palm of the hand. The first stage is to select a dormant bud on a well-matured bud stick of the current season's growth (cold-stored material selected for early season budding has been found to be ideal). A core, containing the bud and rind plus a small amount of woody tissue, is taken by pushing the gun barrel into the stem past the bud and rind and squeezing the trigger. The core is held in the gun, taken to the stock and released into the rind with the aid of a fixed cutting blade at the tip of the barrel and a plunger. The core is then tied in with a conventional rubber degradable budding patch.

Further trial work by L. C. Pettifer was directed to the budding gun's possible role for bench work on bare root ⅝ mm grade Laxa rose seedling rootstocks. Initial experimental work was carried out with summer bench grafting but it was later moved to fall grafting. The completed bud grafts could be plunged into flats containing peat moss for 2–3 weeks in a high humidity grafting case at 17–19°C (63–66°F). Experimental success rates of 75–80% were achieved within 14 days after placing in the flats.

Modifications were later made to the original (Mark I Model) and these resulted in a small number of further prototypes (Mark 2 Model) being used for evaluation in commercial nurseries. Unfortunately, there are still difficulties with the gun's operational efficiency and the budding gun is not yet recommended for manufacture and nursery use until these problems are resolved.

TROLLEYS AND HANDCARTS

Information on the use of these budding aids may be found in the section on open-ground rose budding on p. 468.

REFERENCES AND SUGGESTED SOURCES FOR FURTHER READING

Agricultural Training Board, U.K. 1979. *Care, Maintenance and Use of Knives.* Trainee Guide No. HCA.6-A-5, Agricultural Training Board, Beckenham, Kent, U.K.

_____ . 1979. *Care, Maintenance and Use of Secateurs.* Trainee Guide No. HCA.6-A-6, Agricultural Training Board, Beckenham, Kent, U.K.

Alley, C. J. 1960. Machine grafting and preplanting techniques for Grape benchgrafts. *Comb. Proc. Pl. Prop. Soc.* **10**: 239–246.

_____ . 1965. Materials and equipment used in grafting and budding. *Comb. Proc. Inter. Pl. Prop. Soc.* **15**: 275–278.

_____ . 1970. Can grafting be mechanized? *Comb. Proc. Inter. Pl. Prop. Soc.* **20**: 244–248.

Bailey, L. H. 1907. 11th ed. *The Nursery Book. A Complete Guide to the Multiplication of Plants.* The Macmillan Company, New York.

Boye, D. 1977. *Step-by-Step Knifemaking.* Rodale Press, Emmaus, PA.

Cole, B. 1984. Hand operated grafting machines—a review. *Austral. Hortic.* **82**(9): 27–29 (September, 1984).

Coles, J. S. 1971. The Long Ashton Grafting Machine. *Comb. Proc. Inter. Pl. Prop. Soc.* **21**: 254–257.

Fuller, A. S. 1897. *The Propagation of Plants.* Orange Judd Co., New York.

Gaggini, J. B. 1974. Knifesmen still have the edge but machines are coming. *Nurseryman and Garden Centre,* February 28, 1974, pp. 340–342.

Garner, R. J. 1979. 4th ed. rev. *The Grafter's Handbook.* Faber & Faber Ltd., London.

Gilbert, D. 1977. The Bangor Gun: on target. *Nurseryman and Garden Centre,* August 27, 1977, pp. 13–15.

Howard, B. H. 1982. Plant propagation reports—Degradable rubber ties for chip buds. *Rep. E. Malling. Res. Stn. for 1981,* pp. 68–69.

Kershaw, G. 1960. Machine grafting of fruit trees. *Comb. Proc. Pl. Prop. Soc.* **10**: 249–250.

Law, J. B. 1977. Manual grafting versus machine grafting. *Comb. Proc. Inter. Pl. Prop. Soc.* **27**: 368–369.

Pettifer, L. 1974. The Budding Gun. *Proc. 9th Refresher Course for Nurserymen,* Pershore College of Horticulture, Worcs., U.K., pp. 32–33.

Thomas, C. G. 1972. The Long Ashton Budwood De-leafing Machine. *Comb. Proc. Inter. Pl. Prop. Soc.* **22**: 230–232.

Chapter 5

UNIT CONTAINERS

Essentially, a unit container is a cavity, cube, block, pellet or pot in which the root system of a seedling or cutting develops in complete or partial isolation from adjacent seedlings or cuttings. Today, suppliers are able to offer a very wide range of products, which can vary considerably in design and materials used in their manufacture. Additional accessory equipment to improve the subsequent handling of the unit containers is also offered by some suppliers.

Benefits and Limitations of Unit Containers

Benefits gained from using unit containers for propagation can be summarized as follows:—

(i) Reduction in disturbance and damage to the roots at the time of potting, resulting in improved establishment of the subsequent crop. Plants that particularly benefit from having their root system retained within a unit container include *Ceanothus* (California-lilac), *Cornus florida* cvs. (Eastern Flowering Dogwood), *Dipelta*, *Fremontodendron* (Fremontia), *Garrya elliptica* (Coast Silk-tassel), *Magnolia*, *Metasequoia glyptostroboides* (Dawn Redwood), *Stewartia* and *Styrax* (Snowbell).

(ii) The opportunity to adopt cost reduction procedures because container-handling techniques can be improved.

(iii) Production of a crop to marketing stage over a shorter period of time. Three systems of achieving this are as follows:—

    (a) Increasing the size of cutting.

    (b) Rooting vigorous growing plants in unit containers and then potting directly into 15 cm (6") diameter containers within one growing season, thus eliminating the need for traditional liner pots. This procedure is suitable for plants such as *Buddleia* (Butterflybush), evergreen *Ceanothus* (California-lilac), hardy *Fuchsia* and *Potentilla fruticosa* (Shrubby Cinquefoil).

    (c) Direct sticking single or multiple cuttings into a 6–10 cm (2¼–4") liner pot or 15 cm (6") diameter container.

(iv) Elimination of the traditional rooting media with some types of unit containers—for example, cubes of artificial substrates, and dry pellets of peat that expand when moistened.

(v) Production of a quality rooted cutting by the specialist propagation nursery. The rooted cuttings are more "substantial" because either the roots are embedded into a substrate such as peat, or a surrounding rooting medium is encouraged to adhere to the root system. This can also help to make the cuttings easier to handle and ship.

There are also several disadvantages to the use of unit containers, as indicated below:—

(i) Considerably more propagation space is required compared to rooting cuttings in a flat. This, in turn, means that it is important to keep wastage to a minimum by achieving a high percentage of rooting.

(ii) The initial capital and material costs are higher than for a traditional system, particularly when accessories to mechanize the system are purchased.

(iii) Some products will require considerable storage space before use, e.g., artificial substrate cubes.

(iv) The cost of the final product to the customer will be increased in some instances.

SELECTION OF UNIT CONTAINERS

There are many different types of unit containers on the market. A number of useful guidelines on which to base the decision on the type(s) to choose are summarized below.

1. Select three or four different products that seem suitable for your own particular requirements and then carry out some initial trials on the nursery. These trials should particularly evaluate:—

(a) The percentage rooting success for important crops on the nursery.

(b) The drainage of the substrate or rooting medium, particularly for units where the roots are required to penetrate into a compressed material. The amount of water saturation at the base of the unit must be checked when overhead misting is used for propagation. Conversely, some products can present a problem in re-moistening satisfactorily if allowed to dry out.

Drainage and root system development are also influenced by firstly, the size and type of drainage hole, and secondly, the depth of the cavity into which is placed the rooting medium. The general rule is that the greater the depth of the cavity, the better the drainage.

(c) That the root system is not prone to spiraling at the base of the unit. Some units are specifically designed to avoid this problem by tapering to the base, having molded parallel ridges on the inside of the unit, and/or providing an open space at the base to facilitate air pruning (see p. 91).

Figure 5-1.
Spiraling of the root system can occur at the base of the plug in a unit container. Modern cavity design and the provision of an air space at the base significantly reduces this problem.

(d) That cuttings intended for removal with the rooting medium surrounding the root system can be easily removed from the container so that the root system is kept intact.

2. Determine the purchase cost of the unit containers and of additional accessory equipment (e.g., automated seed sowing and rooting medium filling machines). Quotations for the lowest price and a reliable delivery date must be obtained if there is more than one supplier of the selected product. Do not pay high costs for a new product before it has been thoroughly evaluated and tested, as it may ultimately prove to be a gimmick that results in financial loss.

3. Determine the shelf life of the unit containers, as far as is possible—particularly when they are intended for re-use.

4. Select an economical tray to retain individual units, especially pots, or thin and weak containers that require additional support. This will save labor in both handling and marketing.

5. Carefully calculate the amount of additional propagation space that will be necessary to produce the required quantity of rooted cuttings. It is important to include these additional production costs in the selling price of the end product.

6. Contact both local nursery operators and extension officers who may have used the same product(s) for information and advice. A number of the manufacturers produce some excellent technical brochures which should also be requested.

TYPES OF UNIT CONTAINERS

The range of materials used to manufacture unit containers is considerable, ranging from peat moss, cellulose fibre, polyurethane, polystyrene and plastics to paper. These can all be essentially categorized into two groups:—

(i) Those that have a retaining wall into which the rooting medium is placed.

(ii) Those that consist of a pre-made block, cube, or expanded pellet with a hole, into which the cutting is placed thus making it unnecessary to add a conventional rooting medium.

The types of unit containers that have been used for rooting cuttings are now reviewed, emphasizing their design, handling and uses.

Compressed Peat

1. Molded Peat Strips

These compressed molded peat strips consist of a series of multiple units into which a pre-mixed rooting medium is placed. Each individual unit is square with a tapering base. The strips are shipped from the supplier with each strip interlocked into the adjacent one, and can be difficult to separate from each other. This is assisted by laying the pack of strips on their side, applying pressure down onto the pack with one hand and separating them with the other.

Wet strips are liable to collapse and therefore have to be carefully handled. More stability can be provided by placing them in a flat or, for large areas, by laying them on a sheet of polyethylene on the floor of the greenhouse. The dry strips should readily take up moisture. However, it is advisable to pre-moisten them prior to adding the rooting medium to encourage the roots to penetrate the walls. Each individual unit is simply pulled away from the strip when the cuttings are well-rooted and ready for potting. Specialized hand forks are sometimes used to make it easier to handle the strips of rooted cuttings when they are not kept in a flat for support.

2. Peat Pots

These are available as round or square pots and may be purchased in a range of sizes. They serve as a cheaper alternative to the traditional rigid pot, and have been very successfully used for "in-company" liner production. Some products have nutrients added to the compressed peat to aid plant growth. Cuttings are direct stuck into a rooting medium placed in the pot. The compressed peat pots do not have the physical strength of rigid plastic pots, therefore care is needed in handling to prevent them from collapsing—particularly when the root system of the cutting has not sufficiently penetrated into the wall to hold the pot together.

3. Peat Pellets

A commercially available pellet (Jiffy 7®) has been successfully used for some years for plant propagation in the greenhouse industry. They have also been successfully utilized for some easier-rooting woody ornamental plants. The Jiffy 7® is a compressed peat pellet (with added nutrients) encased in a thin plastic net to provide stability. This extra stability makes it particularly useful for shipping the rooted cuttings. The pellets can be kept in a flat or placed directly on the propagation bench, using a hand-operated tool to speed up the dispensing procedure.

The pellets are best expanded the day before the cuttings are stuck. This is conveniently done by overhead misting for 10–20 minutes every hour for 4 hours. Alternatively, they can be expanded by placing them onto a synthetic capillary mat. The pellets can be also purchased with pre-made holes for the cuttings. If necessary, aeration and support for cuttings, e.g., conifers, can be improved by placing a small amount of sand in the hole prior to sticking.

Figure 5-2.
Cotoneaster × *watereri* cv.
(Waterer Cotoneaster)
successfully rooted in a
medium retained in a
peat pot.

Figure 5-3.
× *Cupressocyparis leylandii*
(Leyland Cypress)
cuttings stuck into an
expanded Jiffy 7® pellet.

Figure 5-4. *Buddleia davidii* 'Harlequin' (Butterflybush cv.) well-rooted in peat blocks.

Figure 5-5. Deep pre-molded, Hiko® rigid plastic unit trays designed especially for larger seedlings and cuttings.

Figure 5-6. Sticking cuttings into a peat moss/perlite rooting medium in a rigid pre-molded plastic unit tray.

Figure 5-7. Some manufacturers supply a peg board that is placed under the unit tray to aid the removal of rooted cuttings.

Peat Blocks

Solid peat blocks have been successfully used for easy-to-root cuttings. They can be purchased ready-made as a commercial product with nutrients incorporated with the peat moss and with a pre-made hole. The alternative is to make fertilized peat blocks in the nursery, thus adapting the technique successfully used for vegetables in the European greenhouse industry. The blocks can be made by either using a hand-operated device or an electrically-powered machine. It is important to add sufficient water to the peat moss when making the blocks to obtain the correct consistency and strength.

Experience has shown that it is advisable to fill the pre-made holes with sand or a fine, well-aerated rooting medium for shrubs and conifers. Summer-propagated cuttings in peat blocks are best placed under mist propagation or foggers after sticking, while it is preferable to cover fall- and winter-propagated evergreen cuttings with polyethylene film. The aim should be to encourage the cuttings to root as quickly as possible and to prevent the blocks from becoming either too dry or too wet. Difficulty in re-wetting can arise if they become too dry, while excess moisture will encourage stem rots.

Experiments have shown that fertilized peat blocks promote earlier growth, improve establishment following potting, and reduce the length of the production period of the crop.

Plastic Pots and Trays

Plastic unit containers can be conveniently divided into three categories.

1. Rigid Plastics

These are the conventional round or square pots for container growing which, if economically viable, can be cleaned and re-used. This is one product where it pays to shop around for the best price because of the number of different manufacturers. The 6 cm (2¼") pot to 15 cm (6") diameter container sizes have been successfully used in production systems for the direct rooting of cuttings. Re-usable plastic trays to retain small pots are available in different designs.

2. "Vacuum-molded" Plastics

These are supplied as individual pots or as pre-molded trays and provide a much cheaper alternative to the rigid pot. They are treated as disposable units and are rarely used more than once.

Their reduced strength makes it necessary to place both the pots and trays in a flat for support. They are used extensively for the bedding plant trade but are suitable for easy-to-root species—especially quick turnover nursery stock such as some ground covers.

Rootrainers® (or Rootmaster®), sometimes referred to as "book planters", were developed by Spencer-Lemaire Industries in Edmonton, Alberta, for forest seedling production (see p. 93), but they have also been successfully used for deciduous hardwood and evergreen hardwood cuttings. Their design encourages the roots to grow down the parallel grooves on the inside of the container. Formation of a spiral root system is prevented by an air space at the bottom for air pruning. The containers are packed in a specially designed tray for support. The rooted cuttings are released by opening up the "book planter" at potting time.

Figure 5-8. *Betula glandulosa* (Glandular Birch) seed germinated in Rootrainers® for subsequent sale for use in land reclamation projects in western Canada. (Reid Collins Nurseries, Aldergrove, B.C., Canada)

Figure 5-9. *Populus* × 'North West' cuttings direct stuck into Rootrainers®. (Reid Collins Nurseries, Aldergrove, B.C., Canada)

3. Netted or Mesh Pots

The principle of netted or mesh pots is that the root system is encouraged to develop through the spaces of the pot wall. They have been extensively used in the foliage plant industry, partly because they encourage an increased root system on the cutting—the netted pot being retained when potting. There is a risk that the retention of the netted pot may constrict the base of the stem of woody ornamentals.

I have seen excellent results in France where *Syringa* (Lilac) and *Magnolia* were propagated from hardwood cuttings, with the wide mesh netted pots being plunged into a well-drained medium so that the rim of the pot was completely covered by the medium. A well-developed root system formed and the plastic net was carefully slipped off when potting, resulting in minimal root damage. The root system should not be permitted to develop too extensively or excessive root damage will occur. Plunging deep into the medium will allow the roots to develop over the rim of the pot.

Plastic pre-molded trays are available for use with netted pots, and are designed so that a small pot fits into each unit. Different designs are available, for example, with the pots protruding above the tray for easier removal or with an air space between the plastic net and the retaining wall of the tray.

Perforated Polyethylene Film

A product occasionally used in Europe for rooting cuttings was a continuous strip of 25–50 very thin polyethylene film units, perforated at the base for drainage. The units were joined at the side by heat sealing. Rooting medium was placed in each unit, the cuttings stuck, and the units were then rolled up to utilize space more efficiently and to make handling easier. At potting time, the individual units were simply torn off and the polyethylene film was slit to remove the rooted cutting and rooting medium.

Polyethylene Tape

An interesting innovation, the Bloxer system, was developed some years ago by J. H. Beacon, Eckington, Worcestershire, England. It was originally developed for the local vegetable plant raising industry, but was subsequently found to be very adaptable for smaller nursery stock producers. We found it to be very successful at Hadlow College of Agriculture and Horticulture, Kent, England, for many species which benefited from the lack of root disturbance when potting.

A continuous strip of polyethylene tape is fed through a series of upright pegs on a template on a small aluminum jig. A standard size flat, $35 \times 21 \times 91$ cm ($14 \times 8\frac{1}{2} \times 36''$), is placed over the pegs and tape, the flat and jig are turned over, and the rooting medium is fed through the holes of the jig to fill the unit. The jig is removed and the cuttings are then stuck. It takes a little practice to perfect the procedure so that the polyethylene tape is correctly fed in and is not dislodged when removing the jig.

The cuttings root within each individual unit or cell, and then the tape is gently pulled out at potting time, leaving the rooted cutting and a small amount of rooting medium. Different widths of the polyethylene tape and templates with differing peg arrangements are used for varying depths of flats and sizes of cuttings.

Melfert® System

The Melfert® unit container, developed in France by the Association Fôret Cellulose, has created considerable interest in the European forestry and nursery stock industries as an alternative to the traditional pot liner container for seedlings and rooted cuttings. The Melfert® unit container is essentially a "padded envelope". The "padding" is a well-aerated growing medium of a mix containing pine bark, peat moss, lignite and controlled-release fertilizer. A thin woven fabric is used as the outer covering to the "envelope" to retain the growing medium.

Investigations have shown that the Melfert® unit containers can also be used for rooting cuttings. They have been used to root many coniferous species and some broad-leaf evergreen and deciduous species, including *Actinidia*, *Clematis montana* (Anemone Clematis) and *Hibiscus*

Figure 5-10. *Pieris japonica* 'Forest Flame' (*P.* 'Forest Flame') rooted in a medium retained in perforated polyethylene.

Figure 5-11. In the Bloxer system, the empty flat is inverted over an aluminum jig with polyethylene tape fed through a series of pegs.

Figure 5-12. Softwood cuttings of *Picea glauca* 'Conica' (Dwarf Alberta Spruce) stuck in flats prepared by the Bloxer system.

Figure 5-13. The Nisula® system for growing-on forestry seedlings, in which the seedlings are machine-rolled in a growing medium sandwiched between layers of rolled polyethylene, has occasionally been adapted for deciduous hardwood and softwood cuttings. The above illustration shows the production of *Philadelphus* 'Madame Lemoine' in an adaptation of the Nisula® system in which the rolls have been hand-rolled.

prepared as winter hardwood cuttings.

The prepared cuttings are rolled up individually in the padded envelope, packed into flats and taken to the propagation facility. The rooted cutting and "padded envelope" are ready for potting or planting out into open ground when roots being to emerge through the woven fabric. Custom-designed flats called "Stamp" flats have been designed for use with the Melfert® unit containers, and a machine is being developed to both wrap the "padded envelopes" and pack them into the flats. (Source of Melfert® unit containers:—Fertil, 33 Avenue du Maine, Case postale 28, 75755 Paris Cedex 15, France.)

Expanded Polystyrene (Styrofoam®)

Molded expanded polystyrene trays are made in a range of sizes and can be successfully used for a variety of cutting sizes and seedlings. They are generally available in a range of 24 7.5 cm (3″) diameter cells per tray down to 40 6.0 cm (2¼″) per tray. The Styroblocks® used for forestry seedlings provide up to 240 units per tray and therefore could be used for very small cuttings (see p. 93). Removal of the rooted cuttings from some designs of molded trays can be made easier by pushing the tray down over a pegboard to raise the surface of the rooting medium above the tray. One problem when using some types of these trays for rooting cuttings is that there is poor transmission of basal heat from the heating cables or pipes through the polystyrene into the rooting medium.

Figure 5-14. A greenhouse filled with *Alnus viridis* ssp. *fruticosa* (American Green Alder) (often known as *A. crispa*) germinated in Styrofoam® blocks. (Reid Collins Nurseries, Aldergrove, B.C., Canada)

Figure 5-15. Close-up of individual Styrofoam® block with *Alnus* seedlings. (Reid Collins Nurseries, Aldergrove, B.C., Canada)

Paperpots

The Paperpot, now widely used for raising forest trees, has been successfully adapted for woody ornamental cuttings. They are received as compressed folded "flats" that are expanded to form a series of hexagonal units when required for use. The expanded sets are secured with metal clips to the sides of a heavy-duty plastic flat or to the sides of a wooden flat with a chicken-wire mesh base and then filled with rooting medium. The specification for size and paper type will depend on the size of the cuttings and the length of time they remain in the Paperpots before potting. Inter-rooting (roots growing into adjacent containers) occurs if the rooted cuttings remain in the Paperpots too long, and the individual units then become more difficult to separate at potting. The glue holding the hexagonal units together is water-soluble and therefore they are easily separated when the cuttings have rooted.

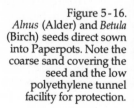 

Figure 5-16. *Alnus* (Alder) and *Betula* (Birch) seeds direct sown into Paperpots. Note the coarse sand covering the seed and the low polyethylene tunnel facility for protection.

A mold that turns from white to brown may sometimes develop under high moisture/low temperature conditions. It is not directly harmful to the cuttings, but aeration of the rooting medium is reduced if it should develop into a thick layer. Difficulty also occurs with re-watering if it should dry out to form a surface cap. Reducing the humidity and decreasing overhead misting will deter development of the mold. If necessary, it can be effectively removed by using a fungicide such as benomyl (Benlate®).

Refer to p. 94 for further details on specifications, accessories and uses of Paperpots.

Synthetic Foam Cubes

There has been varying success with synthetic cubes, some of which are made from polyurethane or urea formaldehyde. Some products have nutrients impregnated into the foam. These foam products are light and clean to handle, and have been found particularly useful for fast-rooting softwood cuttings. Problems experienced with some products in the past have been three-fold.

(i) The low compressive strength can make them friable and liable to break up when handled.

(ii) They are difficult to re-wet if allowed to dry out.

(iii) They can easily become saturated with water at the base when cuttings are slow to root in a mist propagation unit, causing cuttings to rot. This problem may usually be solved by placing the cubes on a layer of sand and by ensuring that the cuttings are not placed too deeply in the cube.

Figure 5-17.
A *Juniper* cutting being rooted in a synthetic foam cube.

Recently, modifications have been made in the design of foam products specifically for rooting cuttings; e.g., to improve drainage, strength, cutting support, and to stabilize the pH level. An example of this work is the development of the Oasis® Rootcubes® by Smithers-Oasis (P.O. Box 118, Kent, Ohio, USA), which have been used successfully for the large-scale rooting and marketing of Poinsettia cuttings. Another example of their use is for the successful rooting of 12.5 cm (5″) long cuttings of miniature roses. In this instance, a 2.5 cm (1″) layer of the subsequent potting mix is placed on the base of the flat holding the 2.0 cm (¾″) cubes. The cuttings are inserted in the cubes, watered in with both a fungicide and fertilizer, and then root from the cubes into the potting mix layer below. This provides a "heavy" rooted cutting for potting up. Rootcubes® must be thoroughly saturated and leached prior to sticking cuttings.

Rockwool (Mineral Wool)

Rockwool was initially developed as an insulation material. It is made in Denmark from a rock known as diabas, which is mined and exported by Sweden. The crushed rock is mixed with coke and limestone and heated to approximately 1600°C (ca. 2900°F). A bonding resin is added to the molten compound which is then spun into threads, cooled, and finally compressed into cubes. A wetting agent is added to encourage uptake of water. It is an inert material and therefore provides no nutrients. Rockwool cubes achieve 97% aeration and are capable of absorbing 80% of water applied.

Rockwool has given rise to a unique system of growing nursery stock, usually referred to as the Grodan® system, in which the propagation cube just slots into a pre-made hole in a larger cube. Despite its success, reservations have developed about the stability of plants on the container ground, establishment of the plants in their final planting site, and acceptance of the final product by retail outlets. Rockwool has become popular in Europe for the soilless culture of greenhouse crops.

The standard size propagation cubes are supplied in 30 × 30 cm (12 × 12″) sheets. A container with 1,000 3 × 3 × 4 cm (1¼ × 1¼ × 1½″) cubes will cover a propagation bench area of 1 m² (1.2 sq. yd.). Individual cubes with an outer covering of black polyethylene are also available, and the larger sizes of these are useful for heavier cuttings. More than one cutting can be placed in the larger cubes, which is particularly useful for some deciduous hardwoods, e.g., *Platanus* × *acerifolia* (London Plane), and easy-to-root shrubs, e.g., *Cornus alba* 'Sibirica' (Siberian Dogwood). The blocks can be cut into two for growing-on in a conventional pot. If the cuttings are to be potted into a larger container with a conventional growing medium, it is important that firstly, the cube is well covered, and secondly, that watering requirements are carefully checked to ensure successful establishment.

Figure 5-18. Three softwood cuttings of *Forsythia* rooted in a rockwool cube. The cube will be cut into 3 individual units for potting into conventional pots.

The cubes must be thoroughly moistened before use and liquid fertilizer application begins as soon as rooting commences. The management of the crop differs from conventional production systems. Further information on the use of the cubes and the required nutritional regime should be obtained by reference to the technical literature available from: Grodania A/S, Hovedgaden 483, Hedehusene DK 2640, Denmark; Growool, C.S.R. Bradford Insulation, 7 Percy Street, Auburn, N.S.W. 2144, Australia; or Clovis Lande Associates Ltd., Gaza Trading Estate, Hildenborough, Kent TN11 8PL, England.

Vermiculite Cubes

These cubes are made by compressing micaceous minerals comprising aluminum and hydrous silicates. They are light, readily hold water, and have been successfully used in the greenhouse industry. Sand placed in the pre-made hole will improve cutting support.

Cellulose Pulp Fiber Cubes

These are made by combining a resin with cellulose fibers from the pulp paper industry. Experience has shown that they, firstly, hold water to saturation point causing cuttings to deteriorate, and secondly, present subsequent handling problems.

REFERENCES AND SUGGESTED SOURCES FOR FURTHER READING

Allred, R. R. 1977. Miniature roses by Oasis Rootcubes. *Comb. Proc. Inter. Pl. Prop. Soc.* **27:** 474–477.

Attenburrow, D. C. 1980. Propagation of shrubs using Blocking Composts. *Comb. Proc. Inter. Pl. Prop. Soc.* **30:** 249–255.

Gaggini, J. B. 1974. Rockwool—a remarkable propagation technique used in Denmark. *Nurseryman & Garden Centre,* September 12, 1974, pp. 293–294.

_____. 1974. Rockwool—the culture of the future. Part 1: What it is, how it works. *Nurseryman & Garden Centre,* September 19, 1974, pp. 331, 333.

_____. 1974. Growing trees in rockwool under glass. *Nurseryman & Garden Centre,* September 26, 1974, pp. 367–368.

Jones, J. B. 1982. The development of foam propagating systems. *Comb. Proc. Inter. Pl. Prop. Soc.* **32:** 271–275.

Stanley, J. & A. Toogood. 1981. *The Modern Nurseryman.* Faber & Faber Ltd., London, U.K.

Verwer, F. L. J. 1974. Rockwool as a growing medium opens up new possibilities for crop mechanization. *The Grower,* February 9, 1974, pp. 270, 275.

SECTION C

Chapter 6

PRINCIPLES OF VEGETATIVE PROPAGATION, CLONAL SELECTION AND STOCK (MOTHER) PLANTS

Vegetative propagation serves as the primary method to reproduce ornamental plant material for commercial production on the majority of nurseries. Methods vary considerably from the traditional methods of layering in the open ground to the sophisticated method of micropropagation in the laboratory.

The major methods used for woody ornamental plants are:—

> Cuttings from stems and roots
> Grafting and budding
> Layering
> Division
> Micropropagation

The actual size and part of the plant used for vegetative propagation is largely dependent on three factors. Firstly, the genus, species and, sometimes, the cultivar of the plant; secondly, the propagation facility available; and thirdly, the inbuilt skill of the propagator. The aim of the following chapters is to outline the principles and reasons why certain procedures are used and to describe how the different techniques are actually carried out.

Uses and Merits of Vegetative Propagation

Vegetative propagation is essentially the reproduction of plant material so that the offspring will contain the exact characteristics of the parent material with regard to genotype and health status. Examples of the subsequent use of vegetatively-propagated plants are indicated in the table below.

Specimen Trees	*Acer platanoides* 'Drummondii'
	    (Silver Variegated Norway Maple)
	Gleditsia triacanthos var. *inermis* 'Sunburst'
	    (Sunburst Honey Locust)
	Sorbus 'Joseph Rock'

Specimen Shrubs	*Hamamelis mollis* 'Pallida '
	    (Chinese Witch Hazel cv.)
	Rhododendron racemosum 'Rock Rose'
	    (Mayflower Rhododendron cv.)
	Viburnum × *bodnantense* 'Dawn'
	    (Bodnant Viburnum cv.)

Specimen Conifers	*Chamaecyparis lawsoniana* 'Pembury Blue' (Lawson Cypress cv.) *Picea pungens* 'Hoopsii' (Hoops Blue Spruce) *Taxus baccata* 'Semperaurea' (Evergold English Yew),
Climbing Plants	*Clematis armandii* 'Snowdrift' (Evergreen Clematis cv.) *Hedera colchica* 'Dentata Variegata' (Colchis or Persian Ivy cv.) *Lonicera* 'Dropmore Scarlet' (Red Dropmore Honeysuckle)
Ground Covers	*Euonymus fortunei* 'Emerald 'n Gold' (Winter Creeper Euonymus cv.) *Pachysandra terminalis* 'Variegata' (Variegated Japanese Pachysandra) *Vinca minor* 'Variegata' (Variegated Common Periwinkle)
Hedging Plants	*Ligustrum ovalifolium* 'Aureum' (Golden California Privet) *Prunus laurocerasus* 'Rotundifolia' (Cherry Laurel cv.) *Thuja occidentalis* 'Pyramidalis' (Pyramidal Arborvitae)
Rootstocks	Malling Merton 106 Myrobalan B *Prunus* 'Colt'

Figure 6-1. Vegetative propagation of crops, e.g., *Clematis armandii* cvs. (Evergreen Clematis) enables a nursery to produce a very uniform, quality crop. (Homestead Nurseries, Clayburn, B.C., Canada)

Figure 6-2. An open-ground crop of *Picea pungens* 'Fat Albert' (Colorado Spruce cv.) rooted from cuttings but showing complete uniformity in color and habit compared to a crop raised from seed. (Iseli Nurseries, Boring, OR, U.S.A.)

Other advantages of vegetative reproduction, in addition to reproduction of the exact genetical characteristics, are:—

(i) The ability to obtain a high degree of crop uniformity. This is particularly important in reducing crop wastage and in encouraging high quality of the final product at the point-of-sale.

(ii) The opportunity to overcome complex dormancy problems, low seed viability and difficulty in procedures dependent upon seed propagation.

(iii) The encouragement of both flowering and more consistent flowering of some plants during the cycle of crop production. Some plants raised from seed can go through a lengthy juvenile (non-flowering) stage. For example, *Wisteria sinensis* (Chinese Wisteria) propagated from seed may take up to 7 years before flowering satisfactorily, while a plant grafted with mature (flowering stage) wood is able to flower satisfactorily after only one or two years from grafting.

(iv) The ability to perpetuate both pest- and disease-resistant forms of certain plants by using breeding programs. It is also possible to perpetuate certain plants that have been freed from virus infection—for example, rootstocks of *Prunus* 'Colt' versus *P. avium* (Mazzard) which can transmit viruses via the seed.

Limitations of Vegetative Propagation

The limitations of vegetative propagation include:—

(i) Transmission of plant viruses by vegetative propagation. The effects of some of these viruses cannot always be seen, which makes it difficult for the propagator to appreciate that stock may be deteriorating in quality. Programs to ensure plant material free from all known viruses have made a major contribution to ensuring that true-to-name healthy plants are available.

(ii) Lowered disease resistance. Some environmentalists feel that it is better to use material raised from seed because there can be a greater chance of natural disease resistance than with clonally-produced material.

However, the nursery operator growing native trees from seed will sometimes find that genetical variation can lead to varying quality. A more uniform product can usually be obtained by vegetatively propagating a selected form. Today, the "straight" species of trees offered for sale are sometimes, in fact, budded—e.g., *Fraxinus excelsior* (European Ash) budded onto seedling *F. excelsior* rootstocks.

(iii) Reduced vigor. Some plants are able to exert more vigor in their growth when raised from seed ("seedling vigor") compared to plants raised vegetatively. This is mainly due to the influence of juvenility (see p. 263).

(iv) Cost. More sophisticated propagation facilities are usually required for vegetative propagation compared to crops raised from seed. However, an exception is the greenhouse production of seedling trees in unit containers.

(v) Low productivity. Some methods of vegetative propagation techniques result in a low productivity of plants, e.g., layering.

SOURCES OF PLANT MATERIAL FOR VEGETATIVE PROPAGATION

The initial selection of material to use as stock plants is vital to successful vegetative propagation. The selection will have a direct influence on propagation and growing-on, as well as a direct effect on marketing.

Four terms require explanation before proceeding further:—

Clone—The plant that is vegetatively propagated so that the resulting progeny is genetically identical to the original parent material.

Clonal Material—The progeny that has been vegetatively propagated from the parent plant.

Cloning—The process by which clonal material is bulked up by vegetative propagation techniques—for example, cuttings, grafting, and micropropagation.

Clonal Selection—The evaluation of two or more clones of the same species for such characteristics as disease resistance, ease of propagation, hardiness or flower and fruit color, with selection of the best of these clones for further propagation and distribution. This process should result in a uniform and distinct clone.

Clones have played a major role over the decades in improving the productivity of various food crops, such as tree fruits. However, it is perhaps only in the last decade that the importance of improving and selecting clones has been fully acknowledged in a number of other nursery areas. With this in mind, it is important to explore more fully the principles involved and the benefits that are currently being obtained by the industry. It is vital that the plant propagator should appreciate this aspect, and not dismiss the subject as of concern only to the growing-on and marketing aspects of the business.

CLONES, CLONAL MATERIAL AND CLONING

The following story can be cited to illustrate the definitions given above for these terms. J. Henry Eddie was a nurseryman who played a major role in the early development of the nursery industry in British Columbia. He emigrated from Scotland to Canada in 1910 and, after a number of ventures in rose bush and fruit tree production, eventually established his nursery at Sardis in the Lower Fraser Valley region. One of his major interests was the breeding of azaleas, rhododendrons, roses and dogwoods. During the early 1940s, Mr. Eddie began a hybridization program to combine the best qualities of *Cornus nuttallii* (Western Flowering Dogwood) and *C. florida* (Eastern Flowering Dogwood). Tragically, almost all his promising seedlings were lost during 1948 when the Fraser River burst its banks, resulting in the nursery being under 4.25 m (14′) of water for several weeks. Fortunately, one particular seedling that had shown considerable promise had already been propagated by grafting and budding onto *C. florida* (Eastern Flowering Dogwood) and the progeny had already been planted out in an area near the site of what is now the Vancouver International Airport. These plants were not lost in the floods, and the selection was later named *Cornus* 'Eddie's White Wonder'. This award-winning plant is now highly desired in many areas of North America and Europe.

Figure 6-3. A well-grown specimen of *Cornus* 'Eddie's White Wonder' established as a street tree in Vancouver, B.C., Canada.

Figure 6-4. Close-up of the profuse flowers of *Cornus* 'Eddie's White Wonder'—a cultivar bred by Henry Eddie by hybridizing *C. nuttallii* (Western Flowering Dogwood) and *C. florida* (Eastern Flowering Dogwood).

To relate this back to the original terms, it can be summarized as shown in the diagram below:—

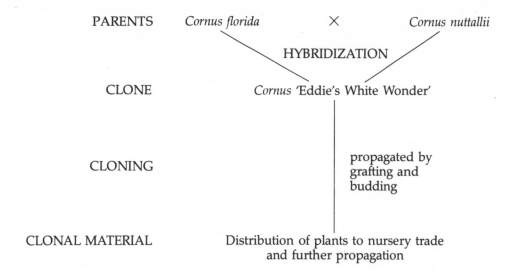

PARENTS   *Cornus florida*   X   *Cornus nuttallii*

HYBRIDIZATION

CLONE   *Cornus* 'Eddie's White Wonder'

CLONING   propagated by grafting and budding

CLONAL MATERIAL   Distribution of plants to nursery trade and further propagation

The advantage of using clonal material is that one is propagating from a known entity because the material is genetically identical to the parent plant. This reliability is not seen with many seed-raised plants because of cross pollination. For example, stock plants of clonal *Berberis thunbergii* 'Atropurpurea' (Red Barberry) will be identical while seed-raised progeny will yield a range of different colors from green to purple and variation in habit.

In practice, however, the appearance of clones can change. Among the reasons for this deterioration are:—

(i) **Plant Viruses**—Virus infection can alter both the visual appearance and reduce quality, therefore affecting the nursery's financial revenue. The build-up of viruses in plants can sometimes present difficulties in propagation, e.g., reduced "bud take" in ornamental *Prunus* (Cherry). Some viruses, such as the Cucumber Mosaic Virus infecting *Daphne cneorum* (Garland Flower), are insect-transmitted which can result in a relatively fast build-up of infection. This is a major reason why this plant can quickly lose vigor and deteriorate. Other viruses are slow to build-up in the plant and the symptoms are often masked so that immediate visual identification is not apparent. For example, the vegetatively-transmitted viruses infecting *Malus* (Apple) and *Prunus* (Cherry). The role of programs for grafted and

Figure 6-5. Severe virus infection of a red-flowered *Camellia japonica* cv. (Common or Japanese Camellia) has resulted in yellow mottling of the foliage and white marbling on the petals.

budded trees in different parts of the world is to produce clones that are both free from all known viruses and true-to-name—for example, the E.M.L.A. Scheme in Britain (see also p. 454). [A characteristic of virus-infected clones of *Prunus serrulata* 'Kwanzan' (Kwanzan or Kanzan Cherry) was the "vase-shaped" head to the trees, while virus-free clones show a strong tendency to develop a dominant leader.]

A program was recently begun at Massey University in New Zealand, through the co-operation of research workers and the nursery trade, to produce virus-free clones of *Daphne* spp. These clones are referred to as "high health" plants and are free of known viruses. The cultivars of "high health" plants already distributed for bulking-up are *Daphne odora* 'Alba' (White Winter Daphne), *D. odora* 'Rubra' (Red Winter Daphne), *D. odora* 'Aureo-marginata' (Pink Winter Daphne), *D.* × *burkwoodii* 'Somerset' (Somerset Daphne) and *D.* × *burkwoodii* 'Somerset Variegata' (Variegated Somerset Daphne).

(ii) Genetical Variations—Mutations or sports caused by a sudden and permanent change within the reproductive cells of the plant can change the appearance of a shoot or flower. This can be beneficial because a new clone can originate from the sport—for example, flower color in roses. Conversely, it can be undesirable because an inappropriate habit may result.

Plant chimeras (in which two or more tissues of different genetical makeup exist within the plant) can develop as a result of mutation. The stability of these plants is largely dependent on the type of chimera. A number of variegated forms are plant chimeras, and some of these are prone to reverting to a green-leaved shoot or, on occasion, to an "all-gold" leaf.

Propagating from unstable plants can result in greater variability of the subsequent crop compared to the original clone. Among plants prone to reverting that I have particularly noted are many of the variegated forms of *Acer negundo* (Box Elder or Manitoba Maple), *Elaeagnus pungens* (Silverberry or Thorny Elaeagnus), *Ilex aquifolium* (English Holly) and *Aucuba japonica* (Japanese Aucuba).

Figure 6-6 (left). A clone of *Hebe cupressoides* reverting to a more vigorous upright growth habit.

Figure 6-7 (right). Some variegated cultivars of *Acer negundo* (Box Elder) are relatively unstable. Note the all-gold and all-green shoots arising from a tree of *A. negundo* 'Aureo-marginatum' (a.k.a. 'Elegans').

Figure 6-8 (left). A shoot of *Aucuba japonica* 'Picturata' (Japanese Aucuba cv.) showing considerable variation in the variegation.

Figure 6-9 (right). Note the difference in habit and variegation on two plants which are both being grown as *Ilex aquifolium* 'Argenteo-marginata' (Broad-leaved Silver Holly).

(iii) Environment—Modern nursery production has resulted in a greater dependence on increased protection of plants to improve quality and shorten the production cycle. In many areas of the world this has led to more plants being grown under polyethylene and glass. This change of environment can result in plants being more susceptible to disease— for example, *Pestalotiopsis (Pestalotia)* spp. on *Camellia* and *Rhizoctonia* on *Calluna* (Heather). Reliance on the production crop as the source for future cuttings will quickly result in deterioration of the clone if disease and quality control programs are not successfully implemented.

CLONAL SELECTION

Clonal selection is now playing a major role in improving the overall knowledge and quality of woody ornamental crops. These programs are sometimes carried out by individual nurseries—for example, Darthuizer Nursery, Leersum, Holland, introduces plants aimed particularly at highway and municipal planting. Useful plants that they have introduced include *Physocarpus opulifolius* 'Dart's Gold' (Eastern Ninebark cv.), *Rosa* 'Smarty' and *Thuja occidentalis* 'Wintergold' (Eastern Arborvitae cv.). This company has a forward-looking breeding program to provide plants for specific purposes, particularly for the landscape industry. However, the majority of long-term clonal selection schemes are carried out by institutions that are wholly or partially public-funded.

Clonal selection programs are usually carried out with one of the following three objectives in mind:—

(i) To select the best clones resulting from plant breeding programs, discarding the inferior clones.

(ii) To select one clone that is true-to-name from a group of clones submitted for evaluation, all of which are being or have been sold under the same cultivar name. In other words, schemes based on the selection of "sub-clones" from within a clone with the objective of distinguishing between clones.

(iii) To select and recommend the best clone for a particular purpose from a range of different species or named cultivars. For example, the best red-berried *Pyracantha* (Fire Thorn) for highway planting in a certain geographical location.

[*NOTE:*—Ease of propagation should be a major criterion with all three of the above objectives.]

Two fundamental reasons for the importance of clonal selection are as follows:—

(i) Plant Naming—Incorrect initial identification, a low standard of plant naming in the nursery (often based solely on assumption) and a lack of labelling during the production stages have been the prime reasons for incorrectly named plants being sold in the trade. This situation has not been helped by an over-emphasis in some countries on the use of common names for plants, which can ultimately lead to different plants being sold under the same common name.

Regrettably, even today, it is only too frequent that we see the same plant being sold under different names. For example, the Proefstation voor de Boomkwekerij (Research Station for Nursery Stock Production), Boskoop, Holland, found during their heather clone evaluation that the popular purple-red *Erica cinerea* 'C. D. Eason' (Bell Heather cv.) was being produced and sold under 15 different names. Understandably, this can happen accidentally but it is not always helped by patenting, trademarking and naming a plant for convenience without thoroughly checking to see if it really is "different". Clonal selection schemes provide the industry with the opportunity to sort out these existing problems and to ensure that plants are correctly named.

I make a strong plea to ensure that a systematic labelling system is set up in the nursery, and that plants are not given names where there is no justification. The plant propagator has a major responsibility in ensuring that the plant material selected for propagation is true-to-name.

(ii) Improvement of the Landscape—Long-term clonal selection is particularly beneficial because clones suitable for different sites can be evaluated, selected and recommended, while discarding inferior ones. Clones can be recommended for hardiness, soil type, desired habit and disease resistance. What is perhaps not so much appreciated is the necessity to disseminate this information to both the grower and the user of the plants to ensure that the results of the work can be fully utilized.

[A nurseryman who had the foresight in 1946 for the need to select particular clones of trees for the landscape was Edward H. Scanlon (Founder of the International Plant Propagators' Society). A Shade Tree Selection Committee was initiated following a National Shade Tree Conference. The City of Cleveland Shade Tree Division planted up one of the first selections in 1952. Clones were selected for the urban environment, based partially on habit in relation to adjacent buildings and overhead wires, soil type, tolerance to industrial pollution, and, where applicable, good fall color. These "tailored trees" are sometimes referred to as the "Scanlon Selections". The growth habits of the selections he made varied from oval to pyramidal, conical, upright, and globe-shaped. Three specific trees that met Scanlon's requirements were the conical *Pyrus calleryana* 'Chanticleer' (Callery Pear cv.) and *Fraxinus oxycarpa* 'Flame' (Pointed-fruit Ash cv.), and the globe-shaped *Acer pseudoplatanus* 'Tilford' (Sycamore Maple cv.).]

Clonal Selection and Plant Introduction Programs

A. Government and Industry Supported

Some of the various programs undertaken by both industry- and government-sponsored organizations around the world are described below. The results achieved by these programs have or will be making an impact on the nursery industry by improving the quality of clonal material. (See Appendix for addresses of some organizations involved in clonal selection.)

(1) Oregon State University and Oregon State Extension Service, United States

During the last two decades members of the Department of Horticulture at the Oregon State University, Corvallis, have worked on dwarf *Pinus mugo* (Mugo Pine) cultivars. They have carefully selected and evaluated some 100 selected seedlings out of large batches of many thousands of seed-raised plants. Among the criteria for selection were dwarf and compact habit, needle color and the ability to root successfully from cuttings. The European selections are traditionally bench-grafted in order to be propagated successfully. The Oregon program resulted in the release during 1977 of six named clones which, depending on the selected cultivar, had the ability to provide 60–90% rooting success in either June or January. These cultivars include *Pinus mugo* 'Green Candle', 'Oregon Jade', 'Oregon Pixie' and 'Alpenglow'—the latter being capable of producing 80–100% rooting success.

R. J. Ticknor of the North Willamette Experimental Station, Oregon, has made a significant contribution to introducing improved cultivars of *Pieris japonica* (Lily-of-the-Valley Bush). Three of the main objectives in his breeding program were pink to red flower color, early flowering, and a compact habit for container production. Cultivars resulting from the program are *P. japonica* 'Valley Rose' and 'Valley Valentine'.

Figure 6-10. *Pieris japonica* 'Valley Valentine' (Lily-of-the-Valley Bush cv.) is one example of the popular cultivars bred by Robert J. Ticknor at the North Willamette Experimental Station, OR, U.S.A. (Reproduced by permission of Robert J. Ticknor)

Figure 6-11. The Saratoga Horticultural Foundation has played an important role in developing or selecting plants primarily suited for the dry arid conditions found in California. (Philip D.A. McMillan Browse, Director, Saratoga Horticultural Foundation, San Martin, CA, U.S.A.)

(2) Saratoga Horticultural Foundation, California, United States

One of the main aims of the work carried out by the Saratoga Horticultural Foundation is. to recommend and introduce material for both urban and re-vegetation sites in California. Emphasis on ability to survive water stress is a major consideration. The three selections of *Liquidambar styraciflua* (American Sweet Gum)—'Burgundy', 'Festival' and 'Palo Alto'—represent a good example of the Saratoga Horticultural Foundation Introductions. These clones have a "tailor-made" habit for urban planting and the foliage is highly colored in the fall. It is important to remember that these clonal features are likely to change in a high rainfall climate.

The award-winning selection *L. styraciflua* 'Palo Alto' was made in 1954 by the former director, M. van Rensselaer, with the assistance of G. Kood.

The Saratoga Horticultural Foundation is also noted for selecting and introducing clones of *Magnolia grandiflora* (Southern Magnolia), e.g., 'Russet' and 'Samuel Sommer', and for the *Ginkgo biloba* (Maidenhair Tree) selection 'Autumn Gold'.

(3) Clonal Selection Scheme, England (formerly the Long Ashton Clonal Selection Scheme)

The nursery industry in Britain recognized that a major reason for variable quality in plants was the differing clones being sold under the same name. This contributed to the fact that plants were not being sold true-to-name. Variations could occur in habit, flower and/or leaf color, and in the ability to propagate successfully.

Industry pressure resulted in a program being started in 1975 at the Long Ashton Research Station, Bristol, to carry out an on-going clonal research program to select commercially important plants. Fourteen different plants were originally selected by a committee representing different sections of the nursery stock industry. Future projections to 1986 are aimed at clonally selecting up to 100 different items. This program was moved in 1983 to East Malling Research Station in Kent and current information is available from there.

In outline, the program is formulated as follows:—

(a) The Clonal Selection Committee meets to decide on the plants to be chosen for the program.

(b) Individual nurseries, botanical gardens, horticultural colleges, etc. are encouraged to contribute propagating material of their clone of the selected plant to the center that is to carry out the clonal selection work. Horticultural colleges, botanical gardens and government experimental stations are among the sites for the subsequent evaluation of the material.

(c) The plants are later assessed by the committee for specific features, including:—trueness-to-name; habit and growth characteristics; flowers, fruit and foliage; plant health; recommended use for the plant; and ease of propagation.

(d) The superior clone is given a code—for example, *Forsythia* × *intermedia* 'Lynwood' LA79 (Lynwood Forsythia). LA means Long Ashton, and the number represents the year of release.

(e) The nursery that submitted the selected clone bulks up the material and makes it available for sale to the wholesale and retail trade.

The work so far has demonstrated the need for clonal selection because of the considerable variability of some plant material submitted, e.g., *Cornus alba* 'Spaethii' (Yellow-edge Dogwood).

This program also provides the opportunity to identify plant viruses and to assess if they are a major factor in giving rise to poor-quality growth. The success of this and other similar programs requires keen industry support.

(4) Plant Introduction Scheme, University of British Columbia (UBC) Botanical Garden, Vancouver, Canada (P.I.S.B.G.)

Roy L. Taylor, then Director of the UBC Botanical Garden, initiated a cooperative program with the British Columbia Nursery Trades Association (BCNTA) and the British Columbia Society of Landscape Architects (BCSLA) in 1980. The objective is to use the Botanical Garden collections as a resource for providing new and recommended material to the nursery industry. This program also provides a facility for the initial bulking-up of material for distribution. In addition, it acts as a center for displaying improved clones from other organizations and provides facilities for clonal selection of native plants.

The stages of the Scheme are summarized as follows:—

(a) A general committee, assisted by research, introduction and release, and publicity sub-committees, makes specific recommendations on possible introductions. These committees are composed of representatives from all sectors of the industry, from growing, retailing and research to landscaping.

(b) A selected evaluation panel is invited to appraise these possible introductions and/or specific plants from the collections at the Botanical Garden that are suitable for inclusion in the Scheme.

(c) The introduction and release sub-committee determines the final selection of the introductions.

(d) The Botanical Garden Nursery bulks up the introductions to provide between 500–1000 individual stock plants to the participating nurseries that are responsible for further bulking-up.

(e) Plants are sent to 13 Research Institute Test Stations in different geographical areas of North America for hardiness testing.

(f) The participating nurseries are under contract to the Botanical Garden to bulk-up an agreed number of plants by the chosen release date. Royalties are collected through the Canadian Ornamental Plant Foundation (COPF).

(g) The introduction is released to the wholesale and retail trade, with a picture-tag label for retail sales to identify both the plant and the Scheme.

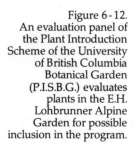

Figure 6-12.
An evaluation panel of the Plant Introduction Scheme of the University of British Columbia Botanical Garden (P.I.S.B.G.) evaluates plants in the E.H. Lohbrunner Alpine Garden for possible inclusion in the program.

Subsequent to distribution of the stock plants by the Botanical Garden, the first four introductions were made available for general release by the 18 participator nurseries in 1985. These introductions, namely *Arctostaphylos uva-ursi* 'Vancouver Jade' (Kinnikinnick cv.), *Genista pilosa* 'Vancouver Gold' (Vancouver Gold Broom), *Microbiota decussata* UBC Clone 12701 (Russian Cypress) and *Rubus calycinoides* 'Emerald Carpet' (Taiwan Creeping Rubus), quickly found a heavy demand in the domestic and international wholesale and retail nursery industries. The compact, free-flowering and easy-to-root *Viburnum plicatum* 'Summer Snowflake' was released in 1986. An important goal of this program was to undertake clonal selections of certain British Columbian native species. This initially resulted in interesting selections of *Ribes sanguineum* (Red-flowering Currant) and *Vaccinium ovatum* (Evergreen Huckleberry).

This Canadian plant introduction scheme demonstrates the role that a botanical garden can play in co-ordinating industry cooperation, increasing plant sales and in the ultimate improvement of the landscape. It has also stimulated the concept of similar introduction programs in eastern Canada, the United States and Scotland.

CHART TO SHOW PROCEDURES TO INTRODUCE PLANTS THROUGH THE UNIVERSITY OF BRITISH COLUMBIA BOTANICAL GARDEN PLANT INTRODUCTION SCHEME

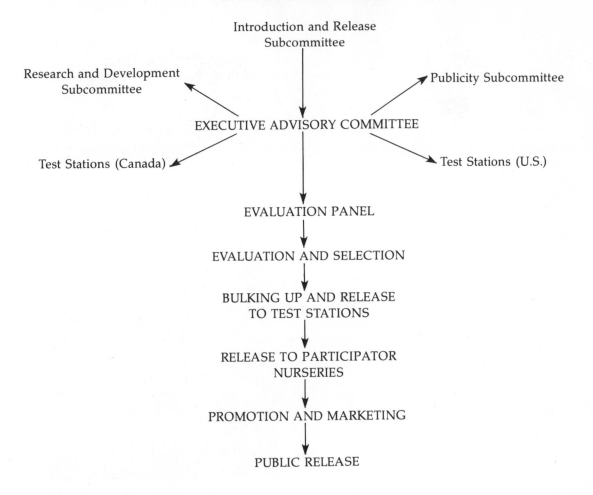

Introduction and Release
Subcommittee

Research and Development
Subcommittee

Publicity Subcommittee

EXECUTIVE ADVISORY COMMITTEE

Test Stations (Canada)

Test Stations (U.S.)

EVALUATION PANEL

EVALUATION AND SELECTION

BULKING UP AND RELEASE
TO TEST STATIONS

RELEASE TO PARTICIPATOR
NURSERIES

PROMOTION AND MARKETING

PUBLIC RELEASE

Figure 6-13 (left). After the final selection by the introduction and release sub-committee of the P.I.S.B.G., the plant is bulked-up to 500–1000 stock plants by the UBC Botanical Garden Nursery for distribution to the participator nurseries. *Rubus calycinoides* 'Emerald Carpet' (Taiwan Creeping Rubus cv.) just prior to distribution. (Ron Rollo, Nursery, UBC Botanical Garden, Vancouver, B.C., Canada)

Figure 6-14 (right). *Arctostaphylos uva-ursi* 'Vancouver Jade' is a successful introduction through the P.I.S.B.G. program.

Figure 6-15. *Genista pilosa* 'Vancouver Gold' (Vancouver Gold Broom) has been successfully introduced by the P.I.S.B.G. program.

Figure 6-16. *Viburnum plicatum* 'Summer Snowflake' is another recent introduction from the P.I.S.B.G. program.

Figure 6-17. *Kalmia latifolia* (Mountain Laurel) is a species that has benefited greatly from systematic hybridization carried out by Richard A. Jaynes, formerly of the Connecticut Experimental Agriculture Station. Right—one of the banded selections. (Reproduced by courtesy of Richard A. Jaynes and Broken Arrow Nursery, Hamden, CT, U.S.A.)

Figure 6-18. Two notable introductions bred by Felicitas Svejda are the following. A (left). *Rosa* 'John Cabot'. B (right). *Weigela* 'Rumba'. (Reproduced by permission of the Agriculture Canada Research Station, Ottawa, ON, Canada)

(5) Connecticut Experimental Agriculture Station, New Haven, United States

An ericaceous shrub native to eastern North America is the magnificent summer-flowering evergreen *Kalmia latifolia* (Mountain Laurel). The flower color varies in the wild from virtually white through to shades of rose pink. Traditionally, it has been a plant where only limited quantities have been available on the market, chiefly because there is a lengthy time to the point-of-sale when propagated from seed and it is both slow and inconsistent in rooting from cuttings.

The nursery trade today has benefited from the excellent research (and publication of the results) carried out by Richard A. Jaynes, former Associate Geneticist attached to the Connecticut Experimental Agriculture Station. His deep understanding of the genus has allowed him to develop a greater range of size and color in both the unopened flower buds and the flowers themselves, plus the fact that some of his selections have shown much improved rooting from cuttings.

However, it was largely the resourcefulness of the pioneers of woody ornamental micropropagation techniques in the Pacific Northwest that allowed these new clones to be so effectively bulked-up and sold in the nursery trades of North America and Europe. Among these notable clones of *Kalmia latifolia* are 'Freckles', 'Goodrich', Ostbo Red', 'Sarah', Shooting Star', 'Silver Dollar' and 'Stillwood'.

(6) Institute of Landscape Plants, Hornum, Denmark

The nursery trades, landscape industry and the government in Denmark realized the value of a clonal selection program for plants used in the landscape. There was a problem with confusion over the naming of plants and the selection of the appropriate species or cultivars to withstand the rigors of some areas of the windswept Danish landscape.

Recommendations for plants to be put through the program are made either to the Institute of Landscape Plants or to the Plant Control Commission. These recommendations are then considered by the Committee for Clone Source, which consists of experts from the landscape and nursery industries and relevant government departments. Plants that rate highly for the program are those that are long-lived and able to be used for a specific purpose, such as street trees, ground covers and hedgerows.

The collection and distribution of the selected clones is summarized as follows:—

(a) Nurserymen are invited to send in their clone of the selected plant. Other clones are sometimes collected from abroad.

(b) Initial screening is carried out to eliminate obviously unsuitable material.

(c) The remaining material is first evaluated by the station staff and then, over the next 3–4 years, by an evaluation committee and experts on that particular group of plants.

(d) Final evaluation and selection of a clone for a specific purpose is made.

(e) A new clonal name is registered if necessary, and the plant is sent for bulking-up at the Plant Propagation Station under the auspices of the Danish Association of Horticultural Producers. Virus identification and testing is carried out at the same time.

(f) The plant material is sold to the nursery trade either as a "DG" plant, confirming that it is a uniform and correctly-named clone, or as a "DP" plant, confirming that it is free of certain named pathogen(s).

(g) Subsequent plant health inspection is carried out annually and re-distribution of the original clone is carried out in future years as necessary.

(7) Agriculture Canada Research Station, Ottawa, Ontario, Canada

Felicitas Svejda has developed an interesting breeding program at the Agriculture Canada Research Station in Ottawa. The main objectives of the program are winter hardiness, disease resistance and ornamental attributes, such as flowering and foliage color. The four genera that have received most attention are *Forsythia*, *Philadelphus* (Mock-orange), *Rosa* (Rose) and *Weigela*. The cultivars currently available are well-illustrated in a recent publication, *New Winter-hardy Roses and*

Other Flowering Shrubs (Canada Department of Agriculture Publication No. 1727). These plants include *Forsythia* 'Northern Gold', *Philadelphus* 'Buckley's Quill', *P.* 'Snowbelle', *Rosa* 'David Thompson', *R.* 'Henry Hudson', *R.* 'John Cabot', *R.* 'John Franklin', *R.* 'Martin Frobisher', *Weigela* 'Minuet', *W.* 'Rumba', *W.* 'Samba' and *W.* 'Tango'.

(8) Agriculture Canada Research Station, Morden, Manitoba, Canada

A valuable breeding, selection and introduction scheme is carried out at Morden Research Station (Zone 3b—USDA), largely pioneered by former staff members W. A. Cumming, W. G. Ronald and H. H. Marshall. It has played a major role in increasing the range of ornamentals suitable for the Prairie provinces. Evaluation through the Prairie Regional (Zonation) Trials for Woody Ornamentals establishes data on performances on the prairies. This area in Canada means that the material has to withstand extreme cold and exposure. The program has helped to upgrade the quality of nursery stock for the region and, as these introductions are registered through the Canadian Ornamental Plant Foundation (COPF), it has also meant that some of the plants have been successful in the United States and Europe.

Four examples of clones produced by this breeding and selection work are as follows.

(i) *Salix* 'Prairie Cascade'

This very hardy Willow was selected following crosses between *S. pentandra* (Bay or Laurel Willow) and *S.* × *sepulcralis* (Salamon Weeping Willow). It is noted for its weeping habit, glossy leaves and golden stems, and represents the first weeping willow to be considered as hardy in this region.

(ii) *Populus canescens* 'Tower' (Tower Poplar)

This hybrid was the result of a controlled cross between *P. alba* (White Poplar) and *P. tremula* 'Erecta' (White Trembling Aspen). It is significant for its extreme columnar habit, hardiness, disease resistance, and its ability to propagate easily by root cuttings. It serves as an alternative to the less hardy poplars such as *P. nigra* 'Italica' (Lombardy Poplar), and is now becoming popular in both the United States and Europe.

(iii) *Ulmus japonica* 'Jacan' (Jacan Japanese Elm) (= *U. davidiana* var. *japonica* 'Jacan')

This clone was selected for its resistance to Dutch Elm Disease (*Ceratocystis ulmi*), its vase-shaped crown, and its suitability as a shade tree. This hardy elm represents a promising species with Dutch Elm Disease resistance for planting in colder regions since earlier, conventional resistant clones from eastern North America and Europe are not adapted for these areas. It has been propagated by grafting onto seedlings of *U. pumila* (Siberian Elm).

(iv) *Fraxinus nigra* 'Fallgold' (Fallgold Black Ash)

This seedless clone of *F. nigra* is noted for its excellent foliage and fall color, and has proven to be an excellent tree for the prairie region. This cultivar is propagated by budding on to seedlings of *F. pennsylvanica* var. *lanceolata* (Green Ash).

Figure 6-19.
Fraxinus nigra 'Fallgold' (Fallgold Black Ash) is a good example of a tree introduced for the very cold and exposed Canadian prairie landscape. (Reproduced by permission of Agriculture Canada Research Station, Morden, MB, Canada)

Other notable selections introduced by the Morden Research Station include *Rosa* 'Adelaide Hoodless', *R.* 'Morden Cardinette', *R.* 'Prairie Dawn', *Caragana arborescens* 'Walker' (Walker Siberian Pea Shrub), *Lonicera* 'Miniglobe', *Juniperus horizontalis* 'Prince of Wales' (Prince-of-Wales Juniper), *Crataegus* × *mordenensis* 'Toba' (Toba Hawthorn), *Syringa* × *prestoniae* 'Coral', 'Minuet', and 'Royalty' (Preston Lilac cvs.), and *Malus* 'Almey' and 'Selkirk'.

(9) Proefstation voor de Boomkwekerij (Research Station for Nursery Stock Production), Boskoop, The Netherlands

The Research Station for Nursery Stock Production for the Boskoop nursery industry is actively supported through contributions from the government, nursery operators and plant sales. A major part of their work is a planting area for the establishment of plants to be evaluated. A committee first chooses a genus where it is felt that there is a need to assess the performance of one cultivar against another and/or where there is a need to determine whether cultivars are true-to-name.

The plants being evaluated during a recent visit to Boskoop included the cultivars and hybrids of *Pieris japonica* (Lily-of-the-Valley Bush). Growers are invited to send in their own selection of this, and other chosen plants, for evaluation while the research station locates additional selections from overseas from time to time. A committee consisting of ornamental woody plant growers, ornamental woody plant authorities, members of the Royal Boskoop Horticultural Society and, sometimes, Station personnel evaluates the plants over a 2–3 year period.

The results are brought to the attention of nursery operators in two ways. Firstly, through the annual publication *Dendroflora* (which contains an English summary for each article). The text is written by members of the committee (largely by Harry van de Laar and Richard van Gelderen). Secondly, through publications and field days at the Research Station.

Figure 6-20. The committee of the Royal Boskoop Horticultural Society judges a collection of *Pieris japonica* cvs. (Lily-of-the-Valley Bush) at the Research Station for Nursery Stock Production. (Reproduced by courtesy of the Proefstation voor de Boomkwekerij, Boskoop, The Netherlands)

The plants are assessed on a merit star system outlined as follows:—

***—Excellent	S—Special purposes
**—Very good	O—Not worthy of cultivation
*—Good	

The table shows the merit star system used in a recent issue of *Dendroflora* for *Potentilla fruticosa* cvs. (Shrubby Cinquefoil).

TABLE 6-1. Summary of the Report of the 1979 Judging Committee of the Royal Boskoop Growers Association on *Potentilla fruticosa* cultivars

The recommended *Potentilla fruticosa* cultivars in this report are:

***   'Abbotswood'—rather tall, bushy habit; leaves deep bluish-green; flowers pure white, large, numerous, May–October.

s   'Beesii' ('Nana Argentea')—low, spreading habit; leaves grayish-green with silvery hairs; flowers deep yellow, small, June–September.

**   'Dart's Golddigger'—low, spreading habit; leaves grayish-green; flowers deep yellow, very large, June–October.

*   'Elizabeth' ('Arbuscula' Hort.)—low, spreading habit; leaves bluish-green; flowers bright yellow, very large, June–October.

***   'Goldfinger'—tall and bushy habit; leaves fresh green; flowers deep yellow, very large, numerous, June–October.

*   'Goldstar'—tall habit with spreading and upright branches; leaves bluish-green; flowers deep yellow, very large, June–October.

**   'Goldteppich'—low, spreading habit; leaves bluish-green; flowers deep yellow, large, June–October.

*   'Klondike'—tall, rather bushy habit; leaves green, small; flowers deep yellow, large, June–October.

**   'Kobold'—low and dense, bushy habit; leaves green, small; flowers bright yellow, small to large, June–October.

**   'Longacre'—low, extremely spreading habit; leaves grayish-green; flowers bright yellow, large, May–October.

*   'Maanelys' ('Moonlight')—very tall, upright habit; leaves bluish-green; flowers light yellow, small, May–October.

s   'Manchu' ('Manshurica' Hort.)—low to very prostrate habit; leaves bluish-to grayish-green; flowers pure white, small, May–September.

**   'Primrose Beauty'—rather tall, spreading habit; leaves bluish-gray; flowers creamy-white, yellow-centered, large, June–October.

**   'Red Ace'—low, bushy habit; leaves green, small; flowers bright (orange-) red, fading to light orange, reverse yellow, small, June–October.

s*   'Royal Flush'—low, bushy habit; leaves green, small; flowers bright pink, fading to pale pink, reverse yellow, small, June–October.

*   'Snowflake' ('Hersii')—very tall, upright habit; leaves dark green, very large; flowers white, small, June–September.

***   'Sommerflor'—low, bushy habit; leaves bluish-green; flowers deep yellow, large, numerous, June–October.

*   'Tangerine'—tall, bushy habit; leaves light grayish-green, small; flowers orange-yellow to yellow (when sunny and warm), large, May–October.

s   'Vilmoriniana'—tall, upright habit; leaves bluish-gray with silvery hairs; flowers creamy-white, small, June–September.

Cultivars submitted for examination	62	Cultivar names identified as synonyms	16
Recommended for cultivation	19	Cultivars not tested and known only	
Not recommended for cultivation	27	from literature	49

Reproduced from *Dendroflora* Nr. 19 (1982) by permission.

(10) U.S. National Arboretum, United States Department of Agriculture (USDA), Washington, D.C., United States

The U.S. National Arboretum has played a major role in North America in the selection and introduction of woody plant material to the nursery trade for subsequent use in the home and public landscape. It is also one of the centers that has developed a well-defined breeding program. Perhaps the best known plants, resulting from the work of D. Egolf, are the Scab and Fireblight resistant clones of *Pyracantha*—*P.* 'Mohave', *P.* 'Navaho' and *P.* 'Teton'. However, there has recently been some doubt in Europe as to the resistance of *P.* 'Mohave' to Fireblight. Viburnums have also received priority and the clones bred by D. Egolf, including *Viburnum* 'Chesapeake' and 'Eskimo', are excellent examples of the U.S. National Arboretum's breeding work.

A program to breed Mildew-resistant *Lagerstroemia* (Crape Myrtle) with colored bark, floriferousness and defined habits has been successful with the introduction of *L.* 'Natchez' and *L.* 'Tuscarora'.

The policy of the National Arboretum has been largely to collect wild, documented material in specific regions of Japan and China that could result in subsequent successful adoption in the eastern United States.

A new phase of the exploration and collection policy began in 1984 with the aim of concentrating on specific regions of Korea. The plan is to travel in early summer when many plants will be in flower and to tag particularly good wild specimens. The seed will then be collected in the following fall. This more precise system will reduce the variations resulting from one-time mass collections of seed with the aim that superior material will ultimately be available for introduction.

Figure 6-21 (left). *Hibiscus syriacus* 'Helene' is a good example of important cultivars introduced by the U.S. National Arboretum. (Reproduced by permission of the U.S. National Arboretum, Washington, D.C., U.S.A.)

Figure 6-22 (right). *Pyracantha* × 'Mohave' is another important introduction from the U.S. National Arboretum. (Reproduced by permission of the U.S. National Arboretum, Washington, D.C., U.S.A.)

Figure 6-23 (below). *Viburnum* × *rhytidophylloides* 'Alleghany' was introduced by the U.S. National Arboretum. (Reproduced by permission of the U.S. National Arboretum, Washington, D.C., U.S.A.)

Figure 6-24 (above). *Lagerstroemeria* 'Natchez' (*L. indica* × *L. fauriei*) was introduced by the U.S. National Arboretum. (Reproduced by permission of the U.S. National Arboretum, Washington, D.C., U.S.A.)

The chart below outlines the various stages of the U.S. National Arboretum Introduction Program from selection to general public release.

CHART TO ILLUSTRATE FORMAT OF THE U.S. NATIONAL ARBORETUM INTRODUCTION PROGRAM

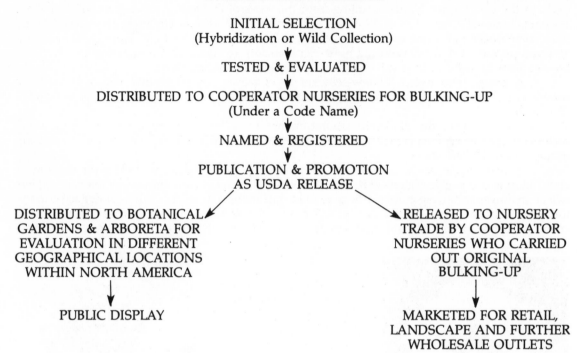

INITIAL SELECTION
(Hybridization or Wild Collection)
↓
TESTED & EVALUATED
↓
DISTRIBUTED TO COOPERATOR NURSERIES FOR BULKING-UP
(Under a Code Name)
↓
NAMED & REGISTERED
↓
PUBLICATION & PROMOTION
AS USDA RELEASE

DISTRIBUTED TO BOTANICAL GARDENS & ARBORETA FOR EVALUATION IN DIFFERENT GEOGRAPHICAL LOCATIONS WITHIN NORTH AMERICA
↓
PUBLIC DISPLAY

RELEASED TO NURSERY TRADE BY COOPERATOR NURSERIES WHO CARRIED OUT ORIGINAL BULKING-UP
↓
MARKETED FOR RETAIL, LANDSCAPE AND FURTHER WHOLESALE OUTLETS

(11) Texas Agricultural Station, The Texas A & M University System, College Station, Texas, United States

An interesting scheme initiated at the above center was set up to promote the nursery production and landscape use of Texan native plants. The selected plants had to meet certain criteria in their evaluation—including drought resistance, low maintenance, ease of propagation and sales appeal when marketed.

Four clones were released during 1981 to the nursery trade as a 'Texas A & M Resource Efficient Plant'. These native sub-shrub selections (suitable for USDA Plant Hardiness Zones 10a–8b) are briefly described.

Leucophyllum candidum **'Silver Cloud'**—A deep purple-flowered selection of the Violet Silver-leaf. Grows as a dense bush to a height of up to 1.0 m (3').

Leucophyllum frutescens **'Green Cloud'**—A purple-violet flowered selection of the Texas Silver-leaf. Grows to a height of 2.5 m (8').

Leucophyllum frutescens **'White Cloud'**—An intense white-flowered selection similar in habit to the above.

Salvia regla **'Mount Emory'**—A vermilion-red flowered selection of the Mountain Sage. Grows as a multi-stemmed plant to 2.5 m (8').

B. Commercial Nurseries

Selection for clones with attributes such as habit and color has been carried out on a range of economically important crops by many leading nurseries. The nursery operator's enthusiasm and discerning eye has resulted in many of the excellent cultivars now in commerce. History has shown that many of these selections have been, and will be, listed in nursery catalogues for many

Figure 6-25. Stan Sorenson with one of his unnamed, floriferous, deciduous azaleas that resulted from hybridizing a unique red-flowered form with a selected superior commercial cultivar. (Homestead Nurseries, Clayburn, B.C., Canada)

Figure 6-26. Enthusiastic plantsmen/nurserymen such as Jean Iseli have played important roles in the introduction of some excellent selections of conifers into commerce. (Iseli Nurseries, Boring, OR, U.S.A.)

Figure 6-27. Cultivars of *Picea pungens* (Colorado Spruce) are normally bench grafted. This clone, *P. pungens* 'Fat Albert', roots readily from cuttings and was introduced by Iseli Nurseries. (Iseli Nurseries, Boring, OR, U.S.A.)

Figure 6-28. *Acer rubrum* 'Red Sunset' (Red Maple cv). is an example of how a nursery can evaluate, select and introduce an important shade tree cultivar into commerce. (Reproduced by permission of J. Frank Schmidt & Son Nursery, Boring, OR, U.S.A.)

decades. For example, the late British nurseryman Rowland Jackman, owner of the former nursery George Jackman & Son, Woking, Surrey, England, selected and introduced to the trade the excellent fall-colored form *Liquidambar styraciflua* 'Worplesdon' (American Sweet Gum cv.) and the excellent urban tree *Sorbus aucuparia* 'Sheerwater Seedling' (European Mountain Ash or Rowan cv.). We have been very fortunate that nursery operators have been so dedicated with respect to their breeding and/or selection programs.

Another recent example is seen at Homestead Nurseries, Clayburn, British Columbia, where Stan Sorenson has been hybridizing deciduous azaleas for many years. His hybridization program crossed a unique red-flowered form that he had raised previously with well-known azalea cultivars such as 'Strawberry Ice', 'Whitethroat Cynthia' and 'George Reynolds' and resulted in his new introductions. These introductions include 'Dawn Chorus', 'Cheerful Giant' and 'Rapunzel'. This is another example of the potential rewards to the nursery and the landscape industries from selection programs.

A further example of nursery contributions is in the glaucous forms of *Picea pungens* (Colorado Spruce). The standard cultivars, which are still grown in certain locations, were *P. pungens* 'Koster' (Koster Blue Spruce) and 'Moerheimii' (Moerheim Blue Spruce). Many wholesale nurseries and garden centers are now increasingly carrying two other most attractive, glaucous, silvery-blue cultivars—*P. pungens* 'Thomsen' (Thomsen Blue Spruce) and 'Hoopsii' (Hoops Blue Spruce)—despite the fact that these were raised as far back as 1928 and 1956 respectively. Two more recent Blue Colorado Spruce cultivars from Oregon that are likely to have an impact are *P. pungens* 'Iseli Foxtail', raised by Iseli Nurseries, and the compact 'Baby Blue Eyes' from Verl Holden of Holden Wholesale Growers.

Similarly, *Acer palmatum* 'Atropurpureum' (Red Japanese Maple) was the accepted purple-foliaged form of the Japanese Maple, despite its variability when grown from seed and the fact that it has to be rogued for color. Selected clones of the purple-leaved forms are generally superior in form and keep their leaf color better, e.g., *A. palmatum* 'Bloodgood'.

There are now numerous selections available in the two genera *Picea* and *Acer*, so the nursery owner should resist the temptation to grow many different cultivars. Advice should be sought from all possible sources, including botanical gardens, other nurseries, research workers and landscapers, to determine the best two or three clones that will grow well and sell best in a specific geographical area. Then, having made the selection, continue to look elsewhere in case there are improved clones available for replacement. If there are no local clonal selection schemes available, be prepared to do it yourself on the nursery.

J. Frank Schmidt & Son Nursery, Boring, Oregon, have made very significant contributions to the shade tree industry through clonal selection and evaluation programs at their nursery. Three of their successful introductions are *Acer rubrum* 'Red Sunset' (Red Maple cv.), *Prunus cerasifera* 'Mt. St. Helens' (Myrobalan Plum cv.) and *P. × cistena* 'Big Cis' (Purple-leaf Sand Cherry cv.).

The late Sir Harold Hillier and the staff at Hillier Nurseries (Winchester) Ltd., England, have made a major contribution in the introduction of plants into the nursery trade. This feat has been celebrated with the publication of a booklet, *The Hillier Hundred*, which lists and describes the plants acquired by Sir Harold Hillier or raised and introduced either from one of the Hillier nurseries or the 44.5 ha (110 acre) Hillier Arboretum. Among the introduced plants are *Acer* 'Silver Vein', *Cistus* 'Silver Pink', *Corylopsis willmottiae* 'Spring Purple', *Ilex × altaclerensis* 'Silver Sentinel' (= 'Belgica Aurea'), *Pinus parviflora* 'Adcock's Dwarf', *Potentilla fruticosa* 'Elizabeth', *Prunus × hillieri* 'Spire', *Quercus castaneifolia* 'Green Spire', *Sorbus* 'Wilfrid Fox' and *× Stranvinia dummeri* 'Redstart' (*Photinia × Stranvaesia* hybrid).

One problem that is sometimes met when growing standard trees from unworked seedlings is poor caliper and somewhat crooked stems. Hillier Nurseries (Winchester) Ltd. have assisted in overcoming this problem by selecting a range of seedlings and then budding them onto other seedlings of the same species, e.g., *Fraxinus excelsior* (European Ash) onto *F. excelsior*, just as one would do with a cultivar. These worked forms are evaluated for caliper and quality of stem, documented, and given a number. The purchaser still obtains trees with genetical variation as the selections can be randomly budded or mixed after lifting.

COLLECTING FROM PRIVATE GARDENS

The horticultural industry is indebted to many private, keen, enthusiastic individuals who build up personal collections of plants in their gardens. These collections can vary from a relatively wide range of plants to just a single genus. Private collectors normally obtain these plants by exchange or purchase from other collectors or specialist nurseries. However, one important source is the collection of native plants from the wild, where variations can occur in habit, leaf/flower/fruit color, and hardiness. For example, valuable collections have been made in the mountainous regions of the Pacific Northwest of North America where different habitats have resulted in interesting forms of plants.

One problem that can occur when obtaining stock from private gardens is that the initial material may lack vigor and be of poor quality. It will need careful handling and good cultural conditions after the initial propagation to ensure that vigorous, disease-free material is available for subsequent commercial use.

CONCLUSIONS

(1) Carry out market research on the potential demand for the plants you wish to grow, particularly when specializing in a crop or group of plants. This entails visiting possible customers, talking to fellow nursery operators, and contacting your local nursery specialist extension officer.

(2) Make every endeavour to obtain plants that are true-to-name. Keep plants well-labelled and documented at all stages from propagation to marketing.

(3) Do not grow poor forms of plants if there are superior forms available. Adjacent nurseries may grow the same form(s) because of convenience. However, market demand can restrict the form of plant grown even though superior ones are available.

(4) Carefully observe your plants for changes in habit, hardiness, pest and disease susceptibility, etc., and discard those plants found to be inferior. This is particularly important when purchasing plants from a southerly climate for growing in a more northerly situation.

(5) Make sure that you are on the mailing list of organizations that specialize in new and improved material of plants in which you also wish to specialize.

Figure 6-29. The Savill Gardens is an excellent example of a garden that has selectively exchanged material with North American institutions in order to improve the respective plant collections. (John Bond, Curator, Savill Gardens, Windsor, Berkshire, U.K.)

Figure 6-30. A primary objective of the plant collections at the University of British Columbia Botanical Garden is to ensure that new and improved plant material is distributed into the nursery trade. (University of British Columbia Botanical Garden, Vancouver, B.C., Canada)

(6) Get to know your local botanical gardens and take an interest in their activities. Plant specialists work in these gardens, and it is unusual for a botanical garden not to encourage the distribution of at least some of their collections. The Royal Horticultural Gardens, Wisley, England, have promoted the sales of many plants grown in their Garden by contracting with local nurseries to grow materials in containers, using stock plants supplied by the Garden. These plants are then sold through the garden center located near the entrance of the Gardens.

(7) Avoid selling plants if there is doubt over correct identification. There is already enough confusion with many plants. If in doubt, contact a botanical garden, arboretum, reliable nursery operator or a private individual with a specialist knowledge of that plant.

(8) If a disease problem is present in your area, emphasis should be given to disease-free clones; for example, the Dutch Elm Disease resistant clone introduced into commerce as *Ulmus* 'Sapporo Autumn Gold' (Sapporo Autumn Gold Elm). This tree resulted from the work started in 1958 by E. Smalley at the University of Wisconsin in hybridizing *U. pumila* (Siberian Elm) with *U. japonica* (Japanese Elm) (= *U. davidiana* var. *japonica*). Seed for the female parent, *U. pumila,* was sent from the Botanical Garden of Hokkaido University, Sapporo, Japan. This tree is now propagated under license in the United Kingdom by Crowders & Sons Nurseries Ltd., Horncastle, Lincolnshire.

Figure 6-31.
Ashley Stephenson, Bailiff of the Royal Parks, David Shreeve of the Conservation Foundation, Prof. Eugene Smalley of Wisconsin University and Robert Crowder, Managing Director of Crowder Nurseries, examine the Hyde Park (London) 'Sapporo Autumn Gold' elm tree. (Reproduced by permission of W. Crowder & Sons Nurseries, Horncastle, Lincolnshire, U.K.)

SITING, PLANNING AND MAINTENANCE OF STOCK (MOTHER) PLANTS TO PROVIDE STEM CUTTINGS

The method of obtaining cutting material in the nursery can be subdivided into four categories:—

A. Cuttings obtained from the container production crop (and, where applicable, the open-ground production crop).

B. Cuttings obtained from permanent stock plants in the open ground without overhead protection.

C. Cuttings obtained from permanent stock plants in the open ground with overhead protection.

D. Cuttings obtained from specific container-grown plants grown under protection.

A. CONTAINER PRODUCTION CROP

The liner and "growing-on" container stages can provide an excellent source of cutting material. This method is convenient because the plants are at hand and additional space is not required in another area on the nursery. However, there are three points that need to be made:—

(i) Good supervision of staff taking the cuttings is vital to avoid mixing of species and cultivars. This is particularly important with crops such as *Clematis* where similarity in growth between two or more cultivars, and the possibility of growth falling over into adjacent rows, means that it is easy to make a mistake.

(ii) Clear and reliable labelling of the crops is essential.

(iii) Deterioration of a clone or mixing of a crop is more difficult to detect because the propagator is not returning to a permanent stock plant area each time cuttings are required. It is therefore advisable to plant out in the nursery one or two labelled, permanent plants of each of the lines being grown and sold so that checks can be made at periodic intervals.

The cuttings come essentially from two phases of the container production cycle, as follows.

(1) Liners

Container-grown liners that have been over-wintered under glass or polyethylene can provide a considerable quantity of softwood cuttings—particularly from deciduous plants. The new growth arising from the dormant buds is soft and vigorous and should root very successfully if handled correctly. The main criterion for this technique is that the pruning back of the soft growth does not detract from the ultimate quality of the crop. In practice, it is very beneficial from many crops as it encourages side branching at an early stage and discourages "leggy" plants. The plants are normally re-potted into a larger container after the shoots have been pruned back for cuttings. A careful watch needs to be maintained for aphids and mildew when the growth is at this stage.

For practical purposes we can divide the liners into 3 groups for their suitability to this technique.

(a) Climbing Plants—e.g., *Clematis, Lonicera* (Honeysuckle), *Parthenocissus* (e.g., *P. quinquefolia,* Virginia Creeper), *Vitis* (Grape).

Climbing plant liners are over-wintered under protection and the buds will then break during early March, producing strong vigorous shoots. The shoots are pruned back either to one or two single or to a pair of buds above the surface of the container medium. The length of shoot reached before pruning back depends largely on the growth habit. About 30–45 cm (12–18") is allowed to develop on *Clematis* before pruning back. There are two options with *Lonicera* (Honeysuckle)—the shoots can be pruned back when 7.5 cm (3") long to provide nodal tip cuttings or left to grow to 30–45 cm (12–18") to provide a series of single node bud cuttings (see p. 294).

The timing of pruning can be critical—the shoots will fall over and inter-twine if they are allowed to grow too long. This will lead to bruising when handled.

(b) Deciduous Shrubs Producing Multiple Shoots—e.g., *Caryopteris* (Bluebeard), *Ceratostigma, Fuchsia, Spiraea* × *bumalda* cvs. (Bumalda Spirea).

Numerous nodal tip cuttings can be obtained by pruning back shoots when there has been about 10.0–12.5 cm (4–5") of new growth. These plants readily develop new and additional side shoots. It also helps to prevent the plants becoming too "leggy" early in the season. Rooting of these cuttings early in the season will allow them to develop sufficiently to provide further liners and more softwood cuttings later in the same year.

(c) Evergreen Shrubs Producing Multiple Shoots—e.g., *Hebe, Escallonia,* evergreen Azalea.

These plants normally come into growth after the deciduous shrubs, and the optimum time for rooting is May. The shoots should be allowed to harden up very slightly before cuttings are taken. This technique offers an alternative method to the traditional period of taking cuttings later during the growing season. It is useful for quickly bulking-up some multi-shooted dwarf evergreen shrubs that are easy to root.

(2) "Growing-on Stock" (Gallon Containers and Larger)

The practice of taking cuttings from plants being grown-on for sale is more common in North America than in Europe. The advantages of this are that it can be dove-tailed with the regular pruning operations in the nursery so that the pruned stems, usually vigorous shoots of the current season's growth, are used for cuttings. However, pest and disease problems can easily be re-cycled through the propagation stages if care has not been taken with their control on the crop. Lack of experience can easily ruin a crop intended for sale if sufficient growth cannot be re-furnished in time.

To re-emphasize a point made earlier, I would strongly advise that a specimen plant of each line grown is maintained to ensure that the characteristics are not masked and that the true clone is kept in production.

Figure 6-32.
The production crop is the primary source of cutting material on many nurseries.

B. PERMANENT OPEN-GROUND STOCK PLANT BEDS WITHOUT OVERHEAD PROTECTION

The best system to use as the major source of cuttings is permanent stock plants grown in the open ground, provided that sufficient land is available. Extra labor will be necessary to manage the plants. However, the costs of land and labor involved are very likely to be more than returned to the business in the long term.

The advantages gained from open-ground stock beds are:—

(i) There is a greater opportunity to keep the plants true-to-name as the propagator can return to the initial clonal material each time cuttings are required. The continual removal of cuttings from the production areas can allow confusion over correct naming to creep in—especially when some of the growth characteristics of similar cultivars may be masked in the production stage.

(ii) Uniform growth of cuttings is encouraged as systematic pruning, fertilizing, pesticide application and removal of cutting material can be practiced. Uniform cuttings mean less grading is required before sticking, more even rooting and an improved grade of product at the point-of-sale.

(iii) It is relatively easy to "manipulate" the plants to improve the number of cuttings at the desired stage of growth by using specific pruning techniques, growth regulator applications or the decrease or increase of light. The material removed for cuttings can have a greater ability to root due to increased vigor.

(iv) It encourages the keeping of accurate records on the performance of the stock plants, and thus aids in the determination of when new or replacement clonal material is required.

(v) Unskilled labor, properly supervised, can often be used to collect the cuttings.

Planning

The actual area of land required for the stock plants largely depends on plant habit, degree of mechanization and the number of potential plants required for sale. Economic reality means that there will be a strong possibility. that cuttings will have to be taken from the production crop during the early period of stock plant development.

Information is scarce on the number of plants required to provide a known quantity of cuttings. Estimates must be made from whatever published figures are available, and from the propagator's intuition. The planting of stock plants well beyond expected requirements must be avoided—particularly for the easy-to-root softwood deciduous shrubs.

Land should be designated as a stock plant growing area as the nursery expands and possibly diversifies. Forward planning is greatly helped by keeping good records. A file should contain information on:—

(i) The source of the clone. Stock plants developed from this original source should all come from one plant to ensure that the material is truly clonal.

(ii) The date the clone was obtained by the nursery

(iii) The date when planted out in the stock plant bed.

(iv) Location in the stock plant area.

Site and Soil Preparation

The temptation to establish stock plants on land that has not been properly prepared must be resisted. One only has to see the poor growth and high plant losses that occur on poorly prepared landscape sites to realize the importance of good soil preparation. It must be remembered that these plants are to provide the foundation for economic revenue in the years ahead.

The site should not be in a frost pocket or there will be damage to new growth. Fencing against vermin is necessary—for example, rabbits eat stems and foliage of their favorite plants and their surface burrows dislodge newly planted material. Windbreaks may be necessary to ensure shelter to prevent damage to shoots and foliage (see p. 51). Facilities for either overhead or trickle irrigation will assist in establishment and also provide water needs during a dry spring and summer.

The topsoil should be of good depth and any soil pan broken up by sub-soiling. Good drainage is also a necessity. The pH and soil type will depend on the plant material being grown—a "brick earth" or sandy loam with a pH of around 6.0 provides an optimum guideline.

Attention must be given to control of perennial weeds to prevent problems in future years. General-purpose translocated herbicides for perennial grasses and broad-leaved plants, such as glyphosate (Round-up®), are particularly useful for this purpose, while oxadiazon (Ronstar®) sprays are excellent against Field Bindweed (*Convolvulus arvensis*).

A heavy dressing of well-decomposed steer (farmyard) manure is advised—a recommended rate is 150.5–175.5 metric tons per hectare (60–70 long tons/acre) spread over a grass ley. This will introduce weed seeds so peat can be used if economically viable. The grass ley should be deeply ploughed and the soil subsequently cultivated ready for planting when weather conditions are suitable. It may be necessary in smaller areas to raise the soil level by bringing in topsoil.

A soil analysis for pH and nutritional status is required so that any imbalances can be corrected with a base dressing. Soil fumigation using metam (Vapam®), chloropicrin, methyl bromide or dazomet (Basamid®) is advised on sites where there could be possible soil-borne disease infection and soil pests to affect the new plants. Costs can be reduced by treating only the sections where the plants are to be grown and not the whole area. However, it is certainly worthwhile to completely treat smaller areas that are to be intensively planted with plants prone to soil-borne diseases, for example, dwarf rhododendrons, dwarf conifers and heathers.

[*NOTE:*—Refer to Chapter 1 on open-ground seed propagation for further details on land preparation procedures and soil fumigants.]

Design Layout

Careful thought should be given to the design layout for the stock plant beds. Haphazard arrangements cause frustrations, which include maintenance problems. The most convenient method is to use a hedgerow system because this allows more efficient maintenance operations and thus uniform cutting material. The following comments will prove helpful:—

(i) The rows should be orientated north to south to reduce the incidence of shading by the plants.

(ii) Plants should be grouped either by broad types as evergreen shrubs, deciduous shrubs and conifers, etc., or according to particular soil or shelter requirements. Within this major grouping, plants of similar height (following pruning) and habit should be planted adjacent in the row. Shelter can also be provided by planting taller conifers next to rows of lower-growing evergreen shrubs.

(iii) Sufficient space should be allowed between different cultivars in the row so that the identification labels can be clearly seen when collecting cuttings.

(iv) Cultivars with similar foliage should be separated by cultivars of different color or habit, where applicable.

Figure 6-33. The long-term benefits of established open-ground stock plants can suit a diverse range and size of plants. A (top left). This nursery provides an excellent example of the importance of correct planning and maintenance of stock plants for a specialist heather nursery. Note the conspicuous labels for correct identification, and the variable flower or foliage color to allow early distinguishing of adjacent cultivars in the row. (John Hall, Windlesham Court Nurseries, Sunningdale, Surrey, U.K.) B (top right). A diverse range of choice and unusual species for the "plantsman/woman" nursery. (Peter Catt, Liss Forest Nurseries, Petersfield, Hampshire, U.K.) C (center left). Well-maintained hedges of *Ilex aquafolium* cvs. (English Holly) can provide an abundance of cuttings for early fall propagation. (Chris Lane, Hadlow College of Agriculture & Horticulture, Tonbridge, Kent, U.K.) D (center right). A high-density area of different dwarf *Picea abies* cvs. (Norway Spruce) to provide late summer and early fall cuttings, as well as scion wood for bench grafting. (Boskoop, Holland). E (bottom left). Extensive hedges of *Juniperus* (Juniper) and *Picea* (Spruce) cultivars for large-scale container production. Note the pathways for easy access to the hedges for taking cuttings. (Pinneburg area, West Germany) F (bottom right). This extensive nursery in California provides an excellent example of the efficient utilization of space for growing stock plants. Note that the stock plants are being established on the slopes above the flat area used for container production beds. (Monrovia Nurseries, Azusa, CA, U.S.A.)

(v) Collecting time can be reduced by siting plants requiring frequent pruning closer to the propagation house or pick-up point.

(vi) Try to project a rotation system for those plants that need frequent replacing. For example, a grower of heathers should try to design his stock beds on a four-year rotation. The stock plants are discarded on completion of the fourth year following establishment, and the ground is prepared and fumigated for re-planting.

Planting

Fall planting, depending on climate, should give better establishment, unless the winter temperatures are extremely cold or exposure will cause problems with evergreen plants. A very general guideline for planting distances used at Efford Experimental Horticulture Station, Hampshire, England, when the stock plant beds were established was:—

	BETWEEN PLANTS IN ROW	BETWEEN ROWS
Vigorous plants	1.8–2.0 m (6–7′)	1.8 m (6′)
Medium vigor	0.9–1.2 m (3–4′)	1.2 m (4′)
Slow growing	0.7–0.9 m (2½–3′)	0.9 m (3′)

[*NOTE:*—Plant habit will also influence spacing.]

It may be more convenient to have a fixed spacing between the rows, irrespective of the vigor of the plants, to assist mechanization.

Heathers can be planted in rows 0.4–0.5 m (15–18″) apart and 0.9 m (3′) between rows, or bedded out in raised beds at 0.4–0.5 m (15–18″) square spacings. Young rhododendron plants establish better if they are planted in close proximity to each other, and are best spaced to allow for two seasons' growth before adjacent stems will make contact. They can then be thinned at the end of this period by removing alternate plants. Hedges for hardwood cuttings are conveniently planted with 0.3–0.5 m (12–18″) between the plants within the row and 1.8 m (6′) between the rows.

There are many variables to consider when evaluating the planting distance, such as plant habit and the methods used for maintaining the stock beds, but a uniform planting pattern should be maintained whenever possible.

Climbing plants present a problem because their characteristic growth is rampant, making them difficult to manage. Many nurseries use the liner crop as a source for softwood cuttings (see p. 241). However, there are two ways to handle climbing plants in an outdoor stock bed. The first technique is to use 10 cm (4″) thick wooden stakes, placed 1.8 m (6′) apart, with 2.4 m (8′) of stake above soil level. Vines such as *Parthenocissus* (Woodbine) are self-clinging, while *Lonicera* (Honeysuckle) will require tying-in to the stakes. The second technique is to use a trellis and train the growth along it.

Extra cuttings can be obtained during the early years of the stock bed by doubling the intensity of planting within the row. Alternate plants are removed after three years.

Irrigation should be available during the establishment stages, particularly after spring planting. An alternative is to plant through black polytheylene laid down along the designated rows. The edges of the polyethylene must be held down by covering over with soil. This not only acts as a mulch, but also keeps weeds down around the base of the plants.

Figure 6-34. Planting the stock plants through a strip of black polyethylene is helpful for weed control and maintaining soil moisture content. (Reproduced by courtesy of Efford Experimental Horticulture Station, Lymington, Hampshire, U.K.)

Weed Control

Weeds, especially when they get out of control, can severely affect the quality and number of cuttings by competing for water, nutrients and light. Some time ago I saw how Chickweed (*Stellaria media*) had been allowed to smother rows of horizontally growing junipers—the effect was dramatic because only about 10% of the material would provide suitable cuttings.

Alternatives to mulching with polyethylene are leaf mold, peat moss or bark. These are particularly good for small, intensively planted stock beds. Bark is sometimes mixed with an equal volume of peat moss to improve its structure and lessen the risk of nitrogen deficiency.

Chemicals can be used for weed control. The soil is lightly cultivated after planting and a residual herbicide such as simazine (Princep®) applied at a rate of 2.24 kg active ingredient per hectare (2 lb a.i./acre) when the soil is moist. An alternative for simazine-sensitive plants, such as *Syringa* (Lilac) and *Cornus alba* cvs. (Red-bark Dogwood), is lenacil (Venzar®). Fall application of napropamide (Devrinol®) is also recommended for established plantings. There may be concern that residual herbicides will harm growth during the year following planting and, in this case, the area around the plants may be hand-weeded or carefully sprayed with the contact herbicide gramoxone (Paraquat®). An application in early spring of a mixture of gramoxone and simazine is effective for annual weeds that have over-wintered. The use of alternative herbicides will be needed if a resistant weed population develops. Fluazifop-butyl (Fusilade®) should be a useful herbicide for controlling perennial grasses in established stock plant areas.

As the stock bed becomes established, dichlobenil (Casoron®) can be applied during December/January at a rate of 123 kg per hectare (110 lb/acre) to kill both annual weeds and the early development of perennial weeds. A natural "crust" may form on the soil surface after about three seasons, and this itself deters the germination of weeds. Spot treatments with translocated herbicides are necessary to prevent zoning of perennial weeds. Particular care should be taken with chemicals such as glyphosate (Round-up®) to prevent contact with the stems of the stock plants. Pronamide (Kerb®) is very useful for controlling perennial grasses in and among established stock plants. It is usually used during November/December as this allows the winter rains to carry it down to the grass roots.

Pest and Disease Control

There are three stages where this can be effectively implemented:—

(i) Soil fumigation against soil-borne pests and diseases (many weed seeds are also killed).

(ii) Routine sprays for the normal pests and diseases affecting the stock plants. For example, aphids, red spider mites, caterpillars and mildew. The build-up of chemical resistance by the pest or pathogen can be avoided by rotating the chemicals used. A spray program should be implemented at the beginning, and reviewed each year.

(iii) "Trouble shooting sprays" for a sudden localized build-up of a pest or disease—for example, Leaf Miner on Hollies (*Ilex*).

Scale insects may become a problem on evergreen shrubs, and a program of both winter petroleum oil and summer sprays will be necessary if this occurs.

In recent years diseases caused by *Pseudomonas* spp. and *Coryneum* spp. have been a problem, giving typical "shot hole" symptoms on *Prunus laurocerasus* 'Otto Luyken' (Cherry Laurel cv.). Stem die-back and defoliation have been caused in some localities by *Glomerella cingulata* (Glomerella Blight) on *Berberis julianae* (Wintergreen Barberry) and *Pseudomonas syringae* on *Magnolia* × *soulangiana* (Chinese or Saucer Magnolia).

Nutrition

A soil analysis prior to planting the stock beds will allow adjustments to be made to correct major deficiencies in pH and mineral elements. A regular program of top-dressing with fertilizers is necessary to ensure vigor and to encourage balanced growth for the correct quality of cutting material. A 14:6:20 ratio fertilizer applied at 336–448 kg per hectare (3–4 cwt/acre) during February to early March should suffice for the season. A ratio that has been successfully used for rhododendrons is 10:10:10 applied at a rate of 112 kg per ha (1 cwt/acre).

Foliar feeding is used to counteract isolated deficiencies or when a quick response is required. Soluble sequestrene chelated iron will be useful for ericaceous plant cuttings where increase of pH is a problem. [Also, I have noted that it is very useful to apply this compound to

heathers to bring back the color of the shoots before cuttings are taken or the crop is marketed.]
Some deciduous *Prunus* are susceptible to magnesium deficiency, but one or two applications of
magnesium sulfate at 2% concentration should quickly solve the deficiency.

Labelling

A well-managed stock plant area must be clearly and accurately labelled. As a safety
measure, there should be two copies of a plan documenting the layout and the individual species
and cultivars. A clearly visible, well-secured label should be placed in front of each different plant
in the row. Two effective ways are, firstly, paint the plant name in black on a white-painted, 1.2 m
(4') tall stake, or secondly, fix an engraved or photofoil, 10 × 5 cm (4 × 2") label to a 1.2–1.5 m (4–
5') tall post. The label should not overlap the edge of the stake, otherwise it is likely to be broken
off.

Confusion at collecting time due to dislodged or broken labels can often be prevented by
securely attaching a small permanent label to one of the conspicuous main branches on the first
plant in the sequence. This can be a photofoil, engraved or "surface scratch" label.

Pruning

Pruning of the stock plants is necessary for the following reasons:—

(i) It encourages vigor, thus improving rooting (p. 266), and increases the number of
cuttings. The development of flowering wood and fruits is not helpful as this can significantly limit the amount of vegetative growth for cuttings, e.g., *Callicarpa* (Beautyberry),
Pyracantha (Fire Thorn) and *Stranvaesia*.

(ii) It regulates the growth and encourages the cuttings to be at the correct stage for collection.

(iii) It allows manipulation of "flushes" of growth.

(iv) It shapes the plants so that it is easy to collect cuttings and to maintain the area.

Therefore, the plants have generally to be treated very differently from those grown in a
display garden. Pruning is essentially carried out when the cuttings are collected, while a heavier
pruning may be needed either during the summer and/or winter. This heavier pruning is mainly
carried out to keep the more vigorously growing plants in shape, as well as retaining vigor and
increasing the number of potential cuttings.

The method of pruning may be categorized as follows:—

(i) Stooling of all shoots to virtually ground level.

(ii) Heavy annual pruning to a foundation framework.

(iii) Annual winter, spring or summer pruning of all shoots to half their length. Sometimes
two or three prunings are carried out, e.g., spring and summer.

(iv) Replacement procedures in which shoots from the base of the plant are removed
every 3–4 years, thus allowing younger shoots to act as replacements.

(v) Shearing of growth to remove all shoots to just below the previous season's growth.
This is useful for plants that produce large numbers of annual shoots, e.g., *Berberis*
(Barberry), *Cotoneaster*, and many conifers grown as hedges.

Figure 6-35. Pruning stock plants is a useful means of
manipulating a flush of growth so that the correct type
of material is selected and provides easy access for
collection. Left—new flush of growth on *Cotoneaster
franchetii* (Franchet Cotoneaster) following shearing in
February. Right—plants left unpruned from the
previous year. (Hadlow College of Agriculture &
Horticulture, Tonbridge, Kent, U.K.)

There are some fundamental practices that need to be carried out whichever method is used:—

(i) Removal of all diseased and dead material. The crown of stool plants and the framework of heavily pruned plants must be checked for canker and stem decay.

(ii) Removal of stems with foliage that has reverted from the true variegation, e.g., in the evergreen *Elaeagnus pungens* 'Maculata' (Golden Elaeagnus) and the deciduous *Cornus alba* 'Elegantissima' (Silverleaf Dogwood). This will discourage clonal variability.

(iii) Removal of flower buds on plants such as hardy hybrid *Rhododendron, Skimmia* and *Kalmia* (American Laurel) to encourage vegetative growth.

(iv) Removal of all prunings to discourage infection of the stock plants with diseases such as Coral Spot (*Nectria cinnabarina*).

Outlines of specific techniques used in pruning stock plants are:—

(1) (a) Deciduous Hardwood Plants—Stooling

e.g., *Viburnum carlesii* (Korean Spice Viburnum), *Ribes sanguineum* cvs. (Red-flowering Currant), *Cornus alba* cvs. (Red-bark Dogwood), *Philadelphus* (Mock-orange).

These plants receive an annual pruning when the cuttings are collected as hardwood cuttings. Some "tidy-up" pruning will be necessary after collection of the desired number of shoots.

If it is estimated that hardwood cutting requirements have been met, excess shoots can be tipped in mid-June if softwood cuttings are required. Removal of the apical dominance of the shoot will cause side shoots to arise, thus providing excellent cuttings for later in the summer.

Figure 6-36. The removal of reverted shoots from a stock hedge of the variegated *Elaeagnus pungens* 'Maculata' (Golden Elaeagnus) to discourage clonal variability can be undertaken more efficiently in designated stock plant locations in the nursery.

Figure 6-37. A well-managed stock plant hedge of *Platanus* × *acerifolia* (London Plane) in August. This hedge will provide deciduous hardwood cuttings during late fall and winter. (Hadlow College of Agriculture & Horticulture, Tonbridge, Kent, U.K.)

(b) Deciduous Hardwood Plants—Foundation Framework

e.g., Quince, Myrobalan B, *Prunus* 'Colt', *Prunus cerasifera* 'Nigra' (Black Myrobalan Plum), *Platanus* × *acerifolia* (London Plane).

This is a very useful method devised by East Malling Research Station, Kent, England, for providing cuttings of tree rootstocks and of some ornamental trees (see p. 327).

The technique is based on maintaining a main stem up to a height of approximately 0.6–1.2 m (2–4') with evenly spaced main branches 7.5–10 cm (3–4") long. The annual growth is pruned back to this foundation framework each winter when the cuttings are collected.

The deciduous *Metasequoia glyptostroboides* (Dawn Redwood) can be treated in a similar fashion, with the foundation framework being allowed to reach a height of around 1.5 m (5').

(2) Conifers

e.g., *Taxus* (Yew), *Juniperus* (Juniper), *Chamaecyparis* (False Cypress), *Thuja* (Arborvitae).
These can be pruned by shearing. Pruning is also carried out when using hand pruners for removing individual shoots for cuttings. Excessively heavy pruning on conifers can decrease the number of subsequent cuttings and encourage stem dieback.

(3) Heathers

The flower heads should be sheared on completion of flowering, and the prunings removed from the foliage.

(4) *Garrya elliptica* (Coast Silk-tassel)

This species should be pruned heavily every two years to 0.6 m (2′) above ground level in March, then the tips are removed from the leader shoots during the subsequent mid-summer. Numerous side shoots arise that can be used for nodal tip or heel cuttings in the subsequent fall. The plants are left virtually untouched in the second year except for a light pruning in March, and will produce numerous cuttings for the next fall.

(5) Rhododendrons

The removal of shoots for cuttings is normally sufficient pruning for rhododendrons. Past experience in New Jersey, USA, has shown that a major factor contributing to the number of suitable possible cuttings that should be removed for rooting is the number of growth flushes which take place on the stock plant. Plants that have only one flush of growth should have not more than 50% of potential cuttings removed, while up to 100% of the second flush can be removed from plants with two growth flushes. The subsequent vigor of the plants will be reduced, with possible loss, if excess cuttings are removed year after year when there is just the one flush of growth. This is because subsequent growth is dependent on buds from older wood.

Flower bud formation on the terminals of shoots after one growth flush has been deterred by removing the terminal bud and/or applying a foliar feed containing chelated iron in a liquid fertilizer with nitrogen at a strength of 30 ppm.

(6) Other Plants

The following comments summarize some of the pruning treatments carried out at the Efford Experimental Horticulture Station, Hampshire, England.

(a) *Hydrangea* and *Senecio* 'Sunshine'—The plants are stooled back to virtually soil level during March, because winter damage to the crown of the plants can result from fall pruning.

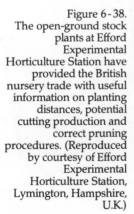

Figure 6-38.
The open-ground stock plants at Efford Experimental Horticulture Station have provided the British nursery trade with useful information on planting distances, potential cutting production and correct pruning procedures. (Reproduced by courtesy of Efford Experimental Horticulture Station, Lymington, Hampshire, U.K.)

(b) *Berberis* × *stenophylla* **(Rosemary Barberry)**—A good flush of cuttings in July/August was obtained by shearing back the previous season's growth in February/March. A second shearing was carried out during June of the same year if cuttings were not required until October/November. The overall total number of cuttings was increased by this second shearing operation.

(c) *Deutzia scabra* **(Fuzzy Deutzia)**—Shoot growth was reduced by half each year through pruning. Summer cuttings were best after a spring pruning while cuttings required later were better from a June pruning.

(d) *Viburnum* × *bodnantense* **(Bodnant Viburnum)**—Annual spring pruning that reduced shoot growth on the stock plants by half produced good quality summer cuttings. Increased cutting numbers with shorter internodes resulted from a subsequent June pruning.

(e) *Pyracantha* **'Orange Glow'**—Increased numbers of longer ripened cuttings resulted from a spring pruning compared to a June pruning.

C. PERMANENT OPEN-GROUND STOCK PLANT BEDS UNDER PROTECTION

A very effective method for establishing stock plants is to house them in a greenhouse, polyethylene structure or shade house. These can be in a separate area or a continuation from the unprotected open-ground stock plant area.

Some specific examples are:—

(a) Climbing Plants and Semi-hardy Shrubs—A method that we found effective at Hadlow College of Agriculture & Horticulture, Kent, England, for a number of climbing plants was to plant them in the inside beds adjacent to the pathway down one side of the greenhouse, and then to train them up the side to the eaves. This method is useful in two respects. Firstly, where there is a need for a small amount of cuttings annually from plants that are liable to be killed off during a harsh winter, e.g., *Azara* (Boxleaf) and *Pittosporum*. Secondly, for weaker-growing plants or where there is unreliability in rooting and subsequent over-wintering as liners, e.g., *Actinidia kolomikta* (Kolomikta Actinidia).

Summer as well as some winter pruning will be necessary if the plants become vigorous. Also, a careful watch needs to be kept on these plants to ensure that they do not harbor pests and diseases which could, in turn, infect the production crop.

Admittedly, this method can reduce the floor space of the greenhouse but well-labelled plants add interest to the area, both for the staff at a nursery and for students at an educational establishment.

Figure 6-39. The establishment of stock plants of climbing plants in a raised bed adjacent to one side of the greenhouse is a useful method of providing cuttings of some of the more tender species.

Figure 6-40. New growth arising from a spring-pruned stock plant of *Clematis armandii* (Evergreen Clematis).

(b) Deciduous Shrubs (plus some trees and climbing plants)—A protected structure over certain shrubs planted in a series of beds is an excellent way to provide the source of cutting material—particularly in north temperate regions where there is a shorter growing period. In warmer areas with longer growing periods, cuttings from the production crop and open-ground stock will be suitable. This technique, with modifications based on experience, has been found to be extremely useful for the commercial production of container plants. Crops for which it can be effective include deciduous Azalea, *Cornus florida* cvs. (Eastern Flowering Dogwood), *Acer palmatum* cvs. (Japanese Maple), *A. rubrum* cvs. (Red Maple), *Corylopsis* spp. (Winter Hazel), *Magnolia, Hamamelis* (Witch Hazel) and *Viburnum carlesii* (Korean Spice Viburnum).

Some large-leaved trees can also be rooted by this technique. Fully expanded shoots of *Catalpa bignonioides* 'Aurea' (Golden Indian Bean) are large and difficult to handle as cuttings. An effective alternative is to have stock plants pruned annually to a framework, allow the shoots to grow to about 7.5 cm (3") and then cut them off just above the previous season's growth for subsequent rooting.

The climbing plant *Hydrangea anomala* subsp. *petiolaris* (Climbing Hydrangea) can be a problem to root when the wood has ripened. Shoots with pre-formed root initials can be obtained by planting up stock plants in a border to grow as a shrub. This encourages vigorous non-flowering shoots to break near the soil and these then readily root.

Figure 6-41.
Pruning stock plants of *Hydrangea anomala* subsp. *petiolaris* (Climbing Hydrangea) will encourage the formation of root initials along the stem of vigorous non-flowering shoots.

Benefits of a Protected Structure

For the groups of plants indicated, the benefits gained by a protected structure to accommodate the stock plants are:—

(i) There is little risk of the soft leaf and stem tissue being damaged by wind. *Acer palmatum* cvs. (Japanese Maple) and many climbing plants are particularly prone to wind damage of the leaves because of the thin leaf lamina. This damaged tissue then provides a source of fungal infection during propagation.

(ii) It may provide an alternative technique for the bench grafting of plants—e.g., *Acer palmatum* cvs. (Japanese Maple) and *Hamamelis* cvs. (Witch Hazel).

(iii) It provides the opportunity, firstly, to take cuttings earlier in the season and, secondly, to extend the season for taking cuttings, compared to outdoor stock plants.

A problem with normal summer rooting of these shrubs and their over-wintering as liners is that losses often occur by the following spring. The liner is more prone to deterioration due to low temperatures and excess moisture levels in the potting mix unless it has a well-developed shoot and root system. Also, plants such as deciduous azaleas can readily form a dormant bud in the stem apex as the summer progresses after the longest day. This, in turn, restricts further shoot development.

Figure 6-42.
A simple extended day-length installation to grow deciduous azalea liners obtained by rooting softwood cuttings from stock plants forced under polyethylene. This treatment encourages growth to remain in the vegetative phase and thus increases the number of axillary buds, carbohydrate levels and root system development, reducing crop losses over the winter. Hadlow College of Agriculture & Horticulture, Tonbridge, Kent, U.K.)

This problem can be reduced for species that are daylength-responsive by taking cuttings early in the season and then providing an extended daylength treatment (using either fluorescent tubes or tungsten filament light bulbs) following potting in June or early July. This will help to keep the growth in the vegetative phase and so prevent the formation of dormant vegetative or flower buds. The increase in the number of axillary buds, carbohydrate content of the stem and development of the root system will help to ensure successful over-wintering of the liner. The extended daylength treatment in the liner house should be discontinued by late September so that the plants can harden off and go through the natural dormancy process—otherwise growth will be affected the following spring.

If these facilities are not available and there is doubt as to whether the rooted cuttings will over-winter as liners, then it is best to have the well-rooted cuttings remain in flats, potting early the following year shortly before they break into growth. This is the safest way for the vast majority of species.

Type of Protected Structure

A conventional greenhouse clad with glass is an expensive investment for this purpose, unless part of an existing greenhouse can be sectioned off. A structure clad with polyethylene or shade cloth fabric is more practical.

Polyethylene Cladding (Cover)

There are two ways in which this type of protection can be used. Firstly, as a permanent cover and replacing the polyethylene when it has deteriorated. Secondly, as a temporary covering during the period from March until sufficient cuttings have been taken from the plants.

Ventilation may be a problem, and the high air temperatures and humidity during the day can result in extensive, and sometimes unwanted, growth. Therefore, some later spring and summer pruning may be necessary. Irrigation facilities are essential. The use of a small heating unit is necessary as a protection against spring radiation frosts, otherwise there will be severe damage to the soft stem growth. I can recall seeing a sorry sight in early May where temporary frost protection had not been provided—the growth that was to provide potential cuttings was ruined by mid-day of the day following a spring radiation frost.

Shade Cloth Cladding (Cover)

A woven polypropylene fabric that allows about a 40–50% shade factor is an excellent alternative to a polyethylene cover—especially for broad-leaved evergreens. It allows air circulation from outside and does not create high air temperatures, and therefore the cutting material is available only about 2–3 weeks before open-ground material. This means that the full advantages gained by taking cuttings early in the season cannot be achieved. I prefer this system as the cutting material is still protected against wind and there is also slight frost protection. The plants receive natural rainfall, and ventilation problems do not occur. The current year's growth is well-ripened later in the year if scion material is required for bench grafting. This method is useful for providing some protection for those evergreens in which the new growth is susceptible to radiation frosts— e.g., *Pieris japonica* cvs. and hybrids (Lily-of-the-Valley Bush).

Figure 6-43. Covering stock plants in open-ground beds with a polyethylene greenhouse has been used successfully to promote bud break to provide early softwood cuttings of many deciduous species, e.g., *Acer palmatum* cvs. (Japanese Maple), deciduous azaleas, *Cornus florida* cvs. (Eastern Flowering Dogwood), *Corylopsis* spp. (Winter Hazel) and *Magnolia*.

Figure 6-44. Shade cloth fabric provides an excellent cover for open-ground stock plants to protect the stems and foliage from direct sun and wind, in addition to providing slight frost protection. Note the newly established hedge of × *Cupresso-cyparis leylandii* (Leyland Cypress) to provide additional wind protection. (Hadlow College of Agriculture & Horticulture, Tonbridge, Kent, U.K.)

Figure 6-45. Blackened growth on the shoot terminals of *Pieris japonica* cv. (Lily-of-the-Valley Bush) caused by a late spring frost. The risk of frost damage to *P. japonica* cultivars and hybrids can be reduced by using shade fabric covers.

Another type of fabric used goes under the trade name of Paraweb® (Fordingbridge Engineering (Barnham) Ltd., Barnham, Bognor Regis, West Sussex, England). It is a reinforced alkathene sheath which is both strong and extremely durable. A structure clad with Paraweb® provides an excellent site for stock plants of high-value evergreens such as *Camellia* and *Rhododendron*. This material is particularly useful in regions with snowfall problems. An alternative to Paraweb® is Tensar® Shelter Shading (Netlon Ltd., Blackburn, England).

Figure 6-46. A (left). A structure covered with Paraweb® provides an excellent environment for stock plants of *Camellia* and *Rhododendron*. B (right). Rows of *Camellia* stock plants growing inside the Paraweb®—covered structure. This encourages vigorous undamaged shoot growth. (Reproduced by courtesy of Efford Experimental Horticulture Station, Lymington, Hampshire, U.K.)

Lath House

A wooden lath house is the traditional structure to provide protection for crops requiring protection from direct sun and wind. It can also provide an alternative facility for the growing of protected stock plants. There is the problem of deterioration and subsequent replacement, especially if the wood has not been treated with a preservative. The modern plastic-based materials such as Paraweb® and Tensar® are better long-term products.

Figure 6-47.
A traditional wooden lath house provides an excellent environment for numerous *Rhododendron* species and cultivars. (Reproduced by courtesy of the Proefstation voor de Boomkwekerij, Boskoop, Holland)

Site and Plant Establishment

The following procedure may be used as a guideline for site and plant establishment.

1. Choose a level site near the propagation house where irrigation facilities can be provided.

2. Treat the area with herbicides if perennial weeds are a problem, otherwise weed growth will become rampant.

3. Deeply cultivate the soil with the addition of well-decomposed bulky organic manure. This will encourage the stock plants to develop the well-developed root systems that are essential if they are to provide a plentiful supply of cuttings every year.

4. It will be advantageous to fumigate the soil with metam (Vapam®), dazomet (Basamid®) or methyl bromide.

5. It is preferable to plant in the fall, as this allows better establishment of the stock plants. The optimum spacing for deciduous azaleas, *Magnolia* and *Hamamelis* (Witch Hazel) is between 1.2–1.5 m (4–5') square.

6. Shortly before the buds begin to swell, cover with shade cloth or polyethylene to protect the new growth. Only limited cuttings should be taken the season following planting.

7. Carry out routine maintenance for weeds, pests and diseases. Check regularly for irrigation needs.

8. A plentiful supply of cuttings should be available by the second season after planting.

Pruning

Five guidelines to pruning are:—

(i) Removal of diseased or broken stems and those that cross over into paths and other plants.

(ii) Reduction of approximately two-thirds of the previous season's growth. Remember that it is non-flowering vegetative growth that is required and not flowering wood.

(iii) A 3–4 year program of renewal of the main shoots will ensure a prolific number of cuttings is retained each year. A winter wash with a petroleum oil is advised if there is a build-up of lichens and mosses on the stems.

(iv) Some plants may become "leggy"—especially deciduous azaleas. If this happens, they should be pruned hard back to about 23–30 cm (9–12") above soil level. This will encourage shoots to break from the basal framework again.

(v) Sucker growth on plants that were originally grafted should be removed below soil level.

Pruning can be carried out at different times of the year, as indicated below.

(a) Winter

Late November or early February are two convenient periods for pruning. Pruning in late November means that all the old leaves and prunings can be raked up at the same time, thus lessening the risk of the carry-over of disease and red spider mites.

(b) Late Winter/Early Spring

Flower buds should be removed wherever possible, as flowering can delay the break of side shoots on the stem. Also, the flower buds of some plants—for example, *Camellia*—can provide a source of infection for *Pestalotiopsis (Pestalotia)* spp. and *Monochaetia* spp. to the shoots and leaves (see p. 372). However, plants should be allowed to partially flower in the first 1–2 years to ensure that they are true-to-name.

(c) Summer

Summer pruning is carried out only to prevent the plants from becoming overcrowded with shoots. The removal of cuttings earlier in the season will reduce the need for summer pruning. Sucker growth on grafted plants should be removed as it develops.

D. CONTAINER-GROWN STOCK PLANTS UNDER PROTECTION

This technique provides considerably more flexibility than permanent stock plants in the soil border. It is much easier to move plants around and to discard unwanted or diseased plants. It is a useful method for the smaller nursery growing a wide range of plant material. This method can also act as a "back-up" to open-ground stock beds in cases where there is a risk of the plants suffering from difficulties with irrigation and/or pest and disease control.

It provides a useful compromise should the propagator not wish to obtain cuttings from the production crop or has not the facilities for open-ground stock beds. In addition, the plants can be used to provide excellent specimens to exhibit at wholesale or retail shows.

Three examples of the different ways in which the plants can be used and/or "manipulated" are as follows:—

(i) To reduce the risk of mixing cuttings of cultivars with similar foliage and stem features—e.g., golden cultivars of *Calluna vulgaris* (Scotch Heather), and evergreen azaleas.

(ii) To increase the extension growth of slower-growing rhododendrons that require grafting to improve the quality of scion—e.g., *Rhododendron yakusimanum* (Yakusima Rhododendron).

(iii) To provide an early source of cutting material—e.g., softwood cuttings of *Metasequoia glyptostroboides* (Dawn Redwood) and some dwarf *Picea* cvs. (Spruce).

Figure 6-48.
Growing stock plants of *Clematis* in large containers and training them on trellises slotted inside the containers has proved to be a useful method for one specialized Clematis grower. (Fred Wein, Clearview Horticulture Products, Aldergrove, B.C., Canada)

Figure 6-49.
Growing heather plants in large-sized containers provides a quality retail sales product and also a flexible method of growing additional stock plants under protection or in outside beds. (John Hall, Windlesham Court Nurseries, Sunningdale, Surrey, U.K.)

Figure 6-50. Young liners of *Rhododendron yakusimanum* (Yakusima Rhododendron) propagated by bench grafting.

Figure 6-51. Container-grown stock plants of *Picea glauca* 'Conica' (Dwarf Alberta Spruce) can be forced in a greenhouse to provide softwood cuttings.

APPENDIX

A Selected List of Institutions That Carry Out Plant Introduction and/or Clonal Selection Proqrams for Ornamental Woody Plants

NORTH AMERICA

CANADA
Agriculture Canada Research Station
Morden, MB
R0G 1J0

Agriculture Canada Research Station
Central Experimental Farm
Ottawa, ON
K1A 0C6

Canadian Ornamental Plant Foundation
    (COPF)
P.O. Box 725
Durham, ON
N0G 1R0

Royal Botanical Gardens
P.O. Box 399
Hamilton, ON
L8N 3H8

University of British Columbia Botanical
    Garden
6501 NW Marine Drive
Vancouver, BC
V6T 1W5

UNITED STATES

The Arnold Arboretum
The Arborway
Jamaica Plain, MA 02130

Chicago Botanical Garden
P.O. Box 400
Glencoe, IL 60022

Connecticut Experimental Agriculture
    Station
P.O. Box 1066
New Haven, CT 06504

Iowa State University
Ames, IA 50010

North Dakota State University
Department of Agriculture & Applied
    Science
Fargo, ND 58102

North Willamette Experimental Station
Oregon State University Extension
    Service
15210 NE Miley Road
Aurora, OR 97002

Saratoga Horticultural Foundation, Inc.
15185 Murphy Avenue
San Martin, CA 95046

The Texas Agricultural Station
The Texas A & M University System
College Station, TX 77843

United States National Arboretum
Washington, DC 20002

University of Minnesota Landscape
    Arboretum
3675 Arboretum Drive
Chaska, MN 55318

EUROPE

East Malling Research Station
East Malling
Maidstone, Kent ME19 6BJ
England

Efford Experimental Horticulture Station
Lymington, Hampshire
England

Institute of Landscape Plants
Hornum, DK-9600 Ars
Denmark

Proefstation voor de Boomkwekerij
Valkenburgerlaan 3
2771 CW Boskoop
The Netherlands

H.A.P.I.E. (Plant Introduction
    Programme)
c/o The North of Scotland College of
    Agriculture
Aberdeen AB9 1UD
Scotland

REFERENCES AND SUGGESTED SOURCES FOR FURTHER READING

Agriculture Canada. 1977. *Hardy Fruits and Ornamentals from Morden, Manitoba.* Canada Department of Agriculture, Ottawa, Ontario.

Anderson, D. 1976, Hardy ornamental stock beds. *Comb. Proc. Inter. Pl. Prop. Soc.* **26**: 136–139.

Baldwin, I. & J. Stanley. 1981. How to manage stock plants. *Amer. Nurseryman* **153**(8): 16, 74, 76, 78, 80 (April 15, 1981).

Brander, P. E. no date. Investigation concerning clone selection of trees and shrubs for ornamental landscaping purposes. *Report No. 1599.* Danish Research Service for Plant and Soil Science.

Campbell. A. I. & R. A. Goodall. 1980. Clonal selection in nursery stock. *Comb. Proc. Inter. Pl. Prop. Soc.* **30**: 204–211.

East Malling Research Station. no date. *Propagation of Clonal Fruit Rootstocks by Hardwood Cuttings.* Techn. Leafl. M.P. 85. East Malling Research Station.

Egolf, D. R. 1972. New cultivars from the US National Arboretum. *Amer. Nurseryman* **136**(1) (July 1, 1972). (Reprint available from Horticultural Research Institute, Washington, D.C.)

Gaggini, J. B. 1972. Think carefully before siting and planning your stock plants. *Nurseryman & Garden Centre,* November 29, 1972, pp. 718–721.

Garner, R. J. 1944. *Propagation by Cuttings and Layers. Recent Work and Its Application, With Special Reference to Pome and Stone Fruits.* Techn. Comm. No. 14. Imperial Bureau of Horticulture and Plantation Crops, East Malling. Kent, England.

Gilbert, D. 1983. Stock under control. *GC & HTJ* **194**(25): 12–13 (December 16, 1983).

Goodall, A. R. & S. Gundry. 1981. Best of the bunch—progress of the Long Ashton Clonal Selection Scheme. *GC & HTJ* **189**(19): 20, 21, 23 (May 8, 1981).

Humphrey, B. E. 1980. Clonal selection scheme. *Comb. Proc. Inter. Pl. Prop. Soc.* **30**: 211–216.

Jaynes, R. A. 1975. *The Laurel Book. Rediscovery of the North American Laurels.* Hafner Press, New York.

Macdonald, A. B. 1982. New plants for old—new plant selection at Saratoga. *GC & HTJ* **191**(19): 21, 23, 24, 26 (May 7, 1982).

Roberts, A. N. 1977. Six dwarf mugo pine cultivars released. *Ornamentals Northwest,* December 76/January 77, pp. 1–3.

Ronald, W. G. 1977. Nursery plant introductions from Manitoba. *Comb. Proc. Inter. Pl. Prop. Soc.* **27**: 494–495.

———. 1982. Tree breeding and evaluation—Morden Research Station 1980–1981. *Proc. 18th Meeting, Canad. Tree Improvement Assoc., Part 1,* pp. 109–111

Rumbal, J. P. 1974. Cutting selection in conifers. *Comb. Proc. Inter. Pl. Prop. Soc.* **24**: 286–287.

Scott, M. A. 1979. Taking stock—management of stock blocks. *Comb. Proc. Inter. Pl. Prop. Soc.* **29**: 233–241.

———. 1980. *Stock Beds for Hardy Nursery Stock. A Review of the Beds Set Up at Efford E.H.S. 1974–1979.* Techn. Leafl. 79/31/a. Efford Experimental Horticulture Station, Lymington, Herts, U.K.

Simpson, B. J. 1983. Native release program introduces drought-tolerant plants to Texas landscapes. *Amer. Nurseryman* **158**(10): 90–93 (November 15, 1983).

Svejda, F. 1982. *New Winter-hardy Roses and Other Flowering Shrubs.* Publ. No. 1727. Agriculture Canada, Ottawa, Ontario.

Sweet, J. 1980. The world's best—high health daphne plants. *GC & HTJ* **188**(15): 31 (October 20, 1980).

van de Laar, H. J. 1982. *Potentilla fruticosa. Dendroflora* **19**: 29–44.

Vanderbilt, R. 1960. The establishment and maintenance of a stock block of hardy hybrid rhododendrons. *Comb. Proc. Pl. Prop. Soc.* **10**: 99–100, 103–104

Vanderbrook, L. 1960. Establishment and maintenance of stock blocks for propagation. *Comb. Proc. Pl. Prop. Soc.* **10**: 96–98, 101–104.

SECTION D

Chapter 7

FACTORS AFFECTING THE ROOTING OF CUTTINGS

There are several factors that affect the successful rooting of cuttings. They can be divided into two major groups—those factors occurring before the cuttings are taken (pre-removal) and those occurring afterwards (post-removal).

One of the classic publications on the principles of vegetative propagation of woody plants is *Propagation by Cuttings and Layers* by R. J. Garner, which was published in 1944 but contains much information that is still relevant today.

A. PRE-REMOVAL

PLANT JUVENILITY

Scientists at many international conferences and symposia have critically discussed the anatomical and physiological aspects of plant juvenility. It is not intended to summarize these discussions, but rather to explain the importance of plant juvenility to the practicing plant propagator.

It is convenient to divide juvenility into three categories for the purposes of the plant propagator.

1. (True) Plant Juvenility

Plant juvenility is the pre-flowering stage of plant growth, covering the period between seed germination and the ability to flower. The plant then enters the adult, mature or flowering stage. The juvenile stage is one of the four basic phases of plant growth summarized in the table below.

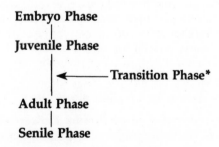

Embryo Phase

Juvenile Phase

Transition Phase*

Adult Phase

Senile Phase

*Transition Phase = the period between the juvenile and adult stage. The period can be quick and sudden or exist over a period of 10–15 years or more.

A long period from the juvenile stage to flowering can be a problem for some plant breeding programs. In addition, a retail customer buying a seed-raised *Wisteria* or *Magnolia* may not know that flowering will take up to 7 and 15 years respectively.

The term "seedling vigor" is sometimes used to describe the growth of seedlings, generally in a seed bed, while in the juvenile stage. Cuttings taken from these plants (bearing in mind the possibility of seedling variation of the progeny) show distinct advantages in their ability to root, e.g., *Acer griseum* (Paperbark Maple).

Changes in Visual Features

The juvenile plant can differ from the adult form in leaf shape and color, stem color and the overall habit of the plant. Juvenile features may be present on the same plant as the adult features during the transition phase. These differences provide a wider range of plants to sell because the juvenile stage can often be more attractive for retail sales—for example, the feathery foliage of *Cupressus macrocarpa* 'Goldcrest' (Monterey Cypress cv.) compared to the more rounded foliage of *C. macrocarpa* 'Lutea' (Golden Monterey Cypress). Other recognizable features of juvenility are late abscission (and even the retention of leaves for much of the winter on *Fagus sylvatica,* European Beech) and the intensified fall color on some Maples.

Figure 7-1. The bright yellow, feathery foliage of *Cupressus macrocarpa* 'Goldcrest' (Monterey Cypress cv.) provides the retailer with an attractive, saleable product.

Figure 7-2. The retention of leaves towards the center of the tree is considered to be a characteristic of juvenility in some species.

Hedera helix (English Ivy) is the example most often quoted in text books. The juvenile stage of English Ivy has adventitious roots along the stem, lobed alternate leaves, and no flowers. The adult form has few or no roots along the stem, virtually entire, spirally arranged leaves, and flowers. In nature, the juvenile form twines, trails and climbs until it reaches more light and little further support for climbing. It then develops a shrubby habit for flowering. Growers have taken advantage of this in various ways—for example, I noted containerized, hardy, adult plants of the variegated forms of *Hedera* offered for sale as shrubs in Denmark.

Further specific examples of plant juvenility shown in woody ornamentals are:

(i) *Malus* (Apple)—*Malus* seedlings show the characteristics for thorniness and hairy leaves which decline in the adult phase.

(ii) *Passiflora caerulea* (Blue Passion Flower)—The juvenile phase is distinguished by cordate leaves while the leaves of the adult phase are strongly divided.

(iii) *Gleditsia triacanthos* cvs. (Honey Locust)—Seedling forms of *G. triacanthos* are very thorny on the stems as a means of repelling grazing animals. However, the adult *G. triacanthos* var. *inermis* (Thornless Honey Locust) and its cultivar 'Sunburst' (Sunburst Honey Locust) carry few if any thorns, thus making them easier to handle during propagation and growing-on.

(iv) Conifers—Conifers provide many of the best examples of juvenility, and fall into two categories. Firstly, those with "fixed juvenility" where the plant seldom changes into adult foliage—e.g., *Chamaecyparis pisifera* 'Boulevard' (Boulevard Cypress) and *Cryptomeria*

Figure 7-3. Visual distinction between adult and juvenile phases of *Hedera helix* (English Ivy). A (left). Lobed leaves and root initials along the stem of the juvenile phase. B (right). Virtually entire leaves of the adult phase.

Figure 7-4. Two examples of "fixed juvenility" in conifers in which the plant seldom changes into adult foliage are shown above. A (left). *Chamaecyparis pisifera* 'Squarrosa' (Moss Cypress). B (center). *Cryptomeria japonica* 'Elegans' (Plume Cryptomeria). C (right). Typical needle-like (awl-shaped) juvenile foliage on *Juniper* sp. (left) and the more rounded and "scale-like" adult foliage on *J. chinensis* cv. (Chinese or Pfitzer Juniper).

japonica 'Elegans' (Plume Cryptomeria). Secondly, those with "non-fixed juvenility" where the plant takes on adult foliage characteristics as it develops—e.g., *Pinus sylvestris* (Scots Pine) and *Cryptomeria japonica* (Japanese Cedar). These feathery-foliaged juvenile conifers are generally much easier to root than the adult forms. Some of the juvenile forms of conifers will suddenly develop a shoot with adult foliage, e.g., some dwarf *Cryptomeria* cvs. These shoots must be removed. Also, some of the juvenile forms of *Cupressus macrocarpa* (Monterey Cypress) have a tendency to develop adult foliage 5–6 years after planting out.

Junipers are variable because some forms have all juvenile foliage (feathery and needle-like), e.g., *J. communis* 'Depressa Aurea' (Common Juniper cv.), while others will have both the juvenile and the more rounded adult foliage—e.g., *J. chinensis* 'Pfitzerana Aurea' (Golden Pfitzer Juniper).

Some cultivars of *Chamaecyparis lawsoniana* (Lawson Cypress) show some of the classic features.

e.g., *Feathery Foliage*—'Ellwoodii' (Ellwood Cypress); Very Easy to Root
   Intermediate Foliage—'Fletcheri' (Fletcher Cypress); Easy to Moderate
   "Flat" Foliage—'Allumii' (Pyramidal Blue Cypress); Moderate to Difficult

In addition to improved rooting, the production period of plants propagated from juvenile material can sometimes be reduced compared to the use of adult material.

2. Adventitious Buds

(a) Sphaeroblasts

Some hardwood cutting hedges demonstrate the formation of sphaeroblasts. A sphaeroblast is a "round body" found in the outer region of the rind of many woody plants. Each contains a wood center, cambium and rind and is able to form shoot buds. Sphaeroblasts show strong characteristics similar to (true) juvenility. They only form when normal axillary shoots are constantly removed, and appear to be isolated from the vascular system of the plant after formation. If a branch is severely pruned, the sphaeroblasts may grow into shoots and then make connection with the branch vascular system. [The sphaeroblasts can be "dug out" and "germinated" like seeds.]

(b) Root Cuttings

Occasionally, plants that can form adventitious buds on the roots are encouraged to develop stems. Root pieces are taken during December/January and placed in a greenhouse as for rooting cuttings. The numerous shoots that arise are "juvenile-like" and should root readily. Alfred J. Fordham, the former plant propagator of the Arnold Arboretum, has recorded this technique for three trees that are normally difficult to root from stems:—*Picrasma quassioides* (India Quassiawood), *Albizia julibrissin* (Silk Tree) and *Elliottia racemosa* (Georgia Plume).

3. "Vegetative (Non-Flowering) Shoots By Manipulation or Conditioning"

This is where the plant propagator is able to "manipulate" or "condition" mature stock plants to produce vigorous, non-flowering vegetative shoots. It is not true juvenility but the use of cultural practices to develop some of the advantages of juvenility.

The benefit of these practices is to increase vigor with subsequent improved rooting. There are essentially two ways by which this can be achieved.

(a) Specific pruning treatments to manipulate the plant to increase its vigor by:—

(i) Hard pruning to encourage basal or adventitious buds to break on an established root or shoot system and thus induce vigorous, non-flowering vegetative shoots.

(ii) Shearing and light pruning of conifers and evergreen shrubs such as *Berberis* (Barberry).

(b) The replacement of stock plants. Many plants reach an optimum stage for rooting effectively, after which the percentage success rate drops and the plants' vigor declines. An example of this is X *Cupressocyparis leylandii* (Leyland Cypress) as shown by the work done by Brian Halliwell at the Royal Botanic Gardens, Kew, England. He obtained 94% rooting success from a 5-year-old tree, 34% from a 20-year-old tree and only 5% from a 50-year-old tree. All the rooted cuttings were potted and grown-on. Cuttings taken from these plants at 2-years old gave 100% success regardless of the age of the original tree.

The techniques described for pruning and maintenance of stock beds (pp. 247–250) will induce vigorous, non-flowering vegetative shoots and reduce the need for replacement.

CARBOHYDRATE AND NITROGEN LEVELS WITHIN THE STOCK PLANTS

The carbohydrate and nitrogen levels within the stem are referred to as the carbon/nitrogen ratio (C:N ratio) or the "condition" of the wood. This level or ratio is particularly important with many evergreen and deciduous hardwood cuttings where it is necessary to have a high level of manufactured foods (through photosynthesis taking place) and a low level of free or soluble nitrogen. The firmness of growth due to the build-up of food storage products should not be confused with the hardening of growth due to the thickening of cell walls within the stems.

There are two major facets of the carbohydrate and nitrogen ratio that should be appreciated.

(1) Nutrition—Fertilizer Program

It is often very difficult to show the effects that the nutrition of the stock plants has on the rooting of cuttings. However, the fertilizer program should ensure that the plant receives a balanced fertilizer (see p. 246) and that excess nitrogen fertilizers are not applied towards the end of the growing season. Nitrogen is required at the beginning of the season to encourage maximum shoot growth, or in early summer to give support to growth that tends to flush rather than grow continuously. However, it should be remembered that rooting could be inhibited if the nitrogen levels are too high. Emphasis should be placed on potassium towards the latter part of the growth cycle.

Hardy hybrid *Rhododendron* cuttings taken from production crops are likely to be unsuitable if fertilizers and irrigation have been regularly applied. The cuttings are vigorous, but too "fleshy and pithy", which encourages the leaves to turn a brown-black color and fall off, thus increasing disease susceptibility. The best type of cuttings are those which are thinner and woodier. These are found towards the center of the stock plants where pruning to encourage shoot development has been done (see p. 247).

(2) Light

Light is required for the manufacture of carbohydrates through the process of photosynthesis. In practice, shading is necessary for some plants because excess light intensity is detrimental to plant growth.

LOCATION (SITE) OF SELECTION OF CUTTINGS ("POSITIONAL EFFECT")

The location from which the cuttings are taken can influence the overall quality of the cutting, its ability to root and the subsequent growth habit. The plant "juvenility factor" is strongest towards the center at the base of the stock plants. Cuttings from this region will root more easily. However, the quality of these cuttings may be poor due to possible overcrowding and lack of light, especially in some conifers. In addition, cuttings taken from very near soil level are more prone to infection with soil-borne diseases because of rain splash.

A most marked effect which depends on the location from which cuttings are taken is sometimes seen in the change of habit of certain plants resulting from the growth pattern following rooting. The phenomenon is sometimes referred to as "topophysis".

Examples of the effect of the cutting removal location where the topophysis effect is seen are described below.

(i) *Sequoia sempervirens* 'Aptos Blue' (Coast Redwood cv.)—The selection site of the cuttings shows a dramatic effect on growth habit in *Sequoia sempervirens* (Coast Redwood). A cutting rooted from a vertical shoot will grow vertically, while a cutting from a shoot growing horizontally will continue to grow horizontally after rooting. This horizontal habit gives a ground cover appearance. This effect is perhaps only of academic interest, because *Sequoia sempervirens* is normally raised from seed. However, it is important if one is propagating the clones of *Sequoia sempervirens* and a quality crop of liners is desired.

Figure 7-5. A (left). A liner of *Sequoia sempervirens* 'Aptos Blue' (Coast Redwood cv.) showing horizontal growth. The horizontal shoot should be pruned-back to the upright shoot at the crown of the plant in order to ensure vertical growth of the plant. B (right). A display of some excellent specimens of *S. sempervirens* 'Aptos Blue' propagated from cuttings. (John Farmer-Bowers, Skylark Nurseries, Santa Rosa, CA, U.S.A.)

(ii) × *Cupressocyparis leylandii* (Leyland Cypress) —This bigeneric conifer is popular as a fast-growing hedging plant and can show the effect of the site of cutting removal, particularly on stock plants that are not pruned annually. Differences are seen not only in subsequent growth habit but also in the potential to root successfully.

This crop is sold by height so that an even growth pattern is desired. The significance of cuttings taken from the flatter lower shoots of the stock plants is that they root more easily but have difficulty in developing a terminal leader and so lack vigor. They thus produce a lower grade crop. Subsequent caning is normally necessary to support the growth, together with pruning to encourage a strong terminal shoot to develop. A useful method to utilize these plants is to grade the liner crop, prune the substandard plants to encourage a terminal leader, and then line them out in the open ground. This encourages them to develop a dominant, "forked" root system similar to that of one of the parents, *Cupressus macrocarpa* (Monterey Cypress). A strong leader shoot develops and the foliage takes on a brighter green, three-dimensional appearance. The crop can later be sold as sturdy open-ground grown plants.

Figure 7-6. The different growth habits of × *Cupressocyparis leylandii* (Leyland Cypress). Left—an undesirable "flatter" shoot removed from the base of a stock plant. Right—a desirable, vigorous shoot with a 3-dimensional growth habit taken from further up the plant. Cuttings should be made from this type of shoot. Vigorous terminal shoots are encouraged by annual pruning (trimming) of the stock plants.

The importance of the site of removal of shoots from stock plants was brought home to me some years ago when I was with the eminent English nurseryman, Douglas Weguelin of Barters Farm Nurseries. Robert J. Garner (formerly of East Malling Research Station) noticed an unusual characteristic in some of the well-established conifer stock plants of *Chamaecyparis lawsoniana* 'Ellwoodii' (Ellwood Cypress) in D. Weguelin's garden. The trees narrowed very noticeably at the height where staff had regularly taken cuttings. Cuttings from the lower level developed into rounded plants, those from the central region were true-to-type, and the ones from the upper region (which were out-of-reach and normally not used) were more upright in habit with more adult foliage. This example shows how topophysis can affect the appearance of the market product.

The site of removal of shoots from the stock plants is also beneficial to rooting in some types of cuttings where topophysis is not subsequently exhibited. Examples include:—

(a) Deciduous Hardwood Cuttings—Following heavy annual pruning during the dormant period, many hardwood cuttings root best when taken at the point just above the site of the previous season's growth. Some plants swell at the stem base, e.g., *Malus*, *Prunus* and *Crataegus* (Hawthorn). This swollen base contains numerous compressed nodes and should be taken with the cutting whenever possible as the bud sites present at these nodes are favored places for rooting. There is possibly a natural accumulation of both food storage products and natural auxins (growth regulators) at this point, which assist in rooting of the cutting.

(b) Heel Cuttings

(i) Evergreen *Cotoneaster* for Rooting in Cold Frames—Cuttings should be taken from the severed branches so that each cutting has a small amount of ripened wood of the previous season's growth. The heel is trimmed and prepared in the normal fashion (p. 303). These heel cuttings perform better in unheated cold frames, compared to nodal stem cuttings, because the heel contains the favored basal nodes and helps to prevent the cuttings dying during the low-light, cold winter period.

(ii) *Cotinus coggygria* 'Royal Purple' (Purple Smoke Tree) Rooted Under Mist—This plant can be unreliable in its ability to root successfully from softwood cuttings under mist. Firstly, the waxy nature of the cuticle may cause excess water droplets to accumulate on the leaves, thus encouraging damping-off. Secondly, the stems seem to "bleed" when the young stems are severed. The latter problem sometimes can be prevented by taking the cuttings with heels and leaving them untrimmed. The heel cuttings are given an application of 0.5% IBA in talc and then stuck in flats. The frequency of misting should be reduced, especially at night and on dull days (see p. 140).

Figure 7-7.
Cuttings of *Cotinus coggygria* 'Royal Purple' (Purple Smoke Tree) prepared for sticking with untrimmed heels can improve rooting.

ETIOLATION (EXCLUSION OF LIGHT)

It has been known for many years that rooting of stem cuttings can be improved by taking them from shoots that have been grown in darkness. Various anatomical and physiological reasons have been advocated to explain this phenomenon. New interest in the technique has recently revived, particularly in the way it can be exploited and handled by the commercial nursery operator.

Plants are by no means universal in their response to etiolation. The four benefits obtained by etiolation in some species of woody ornamentals have been:—

(i) Increased number of cuttings available.

(ii) Increased percentage of rooting.

(iii) More root initials produced per cutting.

(iv) Greater extension growth on the cutting/liner, resulting in fewer losses during subsequent over-wintering.

Research at East Malling Research Station, Kent, England, involving the use of a wooden framework clad with black polyethylene showed that etiolation increased the percentage of rooting of cuttings of the apple rootstock Malling 9 from 11% to 78%. This research was then taken a stage further by the Agriculture Extension Service (Ministry of Agriculture, A.D.A.S., Cambridge) through a series of nursery trials to see if it could be exploited on ornamental nursery stock.

The technique requires a wooden framework clad with 5 mil (500 gauge) black polyethylene. A removable panel is placed on the north-facing side of the framework. A useful framework length is 1.0 m (3'). This can be extended to cover a long stock bed, or, alternatively, a series of 1.0 m (3') frameworks can be used.

Note that problems likely to result from the etiolation of shoots under these frameworks include temperature and heat build-up, susceptibility to leaf scorch, and losses due to fungal and pest attack.

The wooden framework is placed over the stock plant(s) or hedge just prior to bud break in the spring. The removable panel on the north side is taken out when the shoots are about 8.0 cm (3") long. The possibility of wind scorch to the soft etiolated shoots can be reduced by replacing this panel with one clad with shade cloth, rather than just leaving an opening. Exposure to light "greens" the stems by allowing some chlorophyll to form and helps firm up the cuttings. Most shoots will rapidly deteriorate in the propagation unit if this is not done. The etiolated cuttings are removed from the stock plants about 7–10 days after re-exposure to light.

Results so far have shown etiolation to be beneficial for a number of *Syringa vulgaris* cultivars (Common or French Lilac), e.g., 'Charles Joly'—the number of available cuttings was increased, rooting improved, and subsequent extension growth was greater. The limited tests carried out did not show positive results with *Corylus maxima* 'Purpurea' (Purple Giant Filbert) and *Cotinus coggygria* 'Royal Purple' (Purple Smoke Tree).

As previously indicated, problems have occurred when the wooden framework is placed over the shoots, including infection of the etiolated shoots by *Botrytis* mold, and aphid attack in some cases. It is advisable to spray with benomyl (Benlate®) or orthocide (Captan®) before the frameworks are placed over the beds, repeating the spray at 10–14 day intervals. Excessive temperature build-up and ventilation problems can be partly alleviated without detriment to the etiolation process by removing the north-facing panel for up to 5 minutes per day.

The results to date have been inconsistent, so the propagator should be prepared to try the procedure on a trial basis. Further developmental work is required to perfect the technique before etiolation becomes a standard procedure for certain plants that show difficulty in rooting.

Research at East Malling Research Station has also indicated that ultra-low light levels (i.e., some light is present) are sufficient to improve rooting. The stock plants have been sited in walk-in tunnels (quonsets). The new growth produces shoots that show "juvenile-like" characteristics. The shoots are green so that the "greening-up" period is not required before they are removed as cuttings.

[*TAPING STEMS:*—A narrow band of black tape is sometimes placed around the base of a shoot until the tissues have become pale. The tape is then removed, the shoot severed in that area and then stuck in the normal way. Because the tape is placed around a green shoot to exclude light, this method is called "blanching" (as in stooling or mound laying) not etiolation in which light is excluded from shoot growth following bud break. Blanching is only practiced when a very limited number of cuttings is required.]

Figure 7-8.
Opening-up a simple etiolation box clad with black polyethylene. Note the side panels on the open side which can be replaced with shade fabric for ventilation.

TIME OF YEAR

A frequent round-table question at meetings of propagators is "What is the best time to root a certain species of cultivar?". It is likely that a variety of answers will be given for some plants. This is fundamentally why propagating woody ornamentals is so challenging, because "you cannot know it all". Sound principles can be laid down, but very often the best time to successfully propagate a difficult-to-root shrub is based on the propagator's own ingenuity or intuition, the growing method(s) or the locality of the nursery.

There are essentially four criteria that determine the correct time to root cuttings.

(a) Genus, Species and Cultivar

Cultivars of *Potentilla fruticosa* (Shrubby Cinquefoil) and *Spiraea* × *bumalda* (Bumalda Spirea) show little or no variation in their ability to root, while there are marked differences between the cultivars of both hardy hybrid *Rhododendron* and *Juniperus scopulorum* (Rocky Mountain Juniper). Then there are those "classics" that have been notoriously difficult to propagate from stem cuttings—for example, *Populus lasiocarpa* (Chinese Poplar), *Prunus tenella* 'Firehill' (Dwarf Russian Almond cv.), *Kalmia latifolia* (Mountain Laurel), and *Lapageria rosea* (Chilean Bellflower).

Some plants can be rooted virtually the year round, e.g., the evergreen ground cover *Rubus calycinoides* (Taiwan Creeping Rubus) and the juvenile forms of *Hedera helix* (English Ivy). Some deciduous shrubs, such as *Ribes sanguineum* 'Pulborough Scarlet' (Red-flowering Currant cv.), readily root from softwood, semi-ripe wood and hardwood cuttings. The ability of a species to initiate pre-formed root initials reduces the significance of the season. Other plants will root best over a short period during the spring flush of growth, e.g., *Syringa vulgaris* cvs. (Common or French Lilac).

The reason why certain plants do not root readily is essentially genetical, subsequently linked to differences in anatomy and physiology. The provision of a different environment (increased light or increased temperature) can both bring forward and extend the propagation period.

(b) Geographical Location of the Nursery

A nursery in California has a greatly extended period for propagation compared to a nursery on the north-eastern seaboard of the United States. Thus, timing should be linked to the actual condition of the potential cuttings—their firmness and growth pattern—rather than to the calendar week. This, and other texts, should be viewed only as providing guidelines, because weather patterns from year to year will finally determine the exact time when cuttings are taken.

(c) Propagation Facility

The propagation facility available also influences the timing of cutting preparation, especially when a nursery is only geared to one particular type of facility—for example, a low-cost facility consisting of cold frames and low polyethylene tunnels. The use of fogging equipment now allows slow-rooting species the potential to survive for a long enough period to root in large numbers from leafy cuttings.

(d) Crop Growing System

The production system used for different crops will determine the time of year in some instances. A nursery with ten financially rewarding crops will give these priority over propagation space for their less remunerative crops. In this hypothetical instance, the less remunerative crops will be given second priority for propagation and pushed back further into the growing season when rooting could be less predictable.

Finally, it is difficult to be dogmatic about correct times for rooting as there are other constraints to consider. This is considered in further detail under the sections dealing with types of cuttings (Chapters 8, 9, and 14). The recommended time of year for a wide range of common and rare woody ornamental plants will be found in Volume 2 of this text.

B. POST-REMOVAL

HANDLING OF CUTTINGS

Three important criteria when handling cuttings are to ensure that:—

(i) There is minimum water loss from stems and leaves so that the cuttings are kept turgid.

(ii) The tissues are not bruised as the damaged area is a source of disease infection. Note that softwood cuttings are particularly easily bruised.

(iii) The cuttings are handled efficiently to reduce costs and avoid unnecessary repetition of movement during collection and preparation.

Particular care has to be taken with softwood cuttings. Collection of the cuttings must be carried out in the early part of the day during warm weather, cold or cool storage should be available to hold the cuttings if they are not to be stuck immediately, and there should be no unnecessary delay between cutting preparation and placing in the propagation facility. The mist propagation facility must be checked to ensure that the misting nozzles are distributing an even water application and that air currents are not forcing the water droplets to fall away from the cuttings. Carelessness can spell disaster on a hot day!

Cuttings must not be taken from certain species that have received a heavy frost, particularly *Ceanothus*. If the shoots are covered in frost, they should be placed in polyethylene bags and left for up to 24 hours in a frost-free shed. This gentle thawing-out will prevent damage to the plant tissue when handled later.

The terminal cut surface of hardwood cuttings is the region from which excessive water loss occurs in exposed sites. It acts as a "wick" in the sense that water lost from the cut surface is replaced from reserves further down the cutting. Dipping the tip to 1.0 cm (⅜") in hot paraffin wax or petroleum jelly may help in some instances. The establishment of cuttings stuck in open-ground beds will be helped by the construction of a low polyethylene tunnel.

These procedures and others are dealt with in more detail in Chapters 8 and 9.

POLARITY

Polarity simply means that the cuttings (both shoot and root cuttings) have to be the correct way up, whether being stuck in flats or lined out in the open ground. The base of a stem cutting is referred to as the proximal end (closest to the root) while the upper part is called the distal end (furthest from the root).

Cuttings with leaves on have an obvious right and wrong direction for sticking. However, problems can occur with deciduous hardwood cuttings—particularly when using unskilled labor with inadequate supervision. In such situations, cuttings should be prepared with the upper cut surface sloped away from the terminal bud while the basal cut is horizontal (see also p. 311).

TYPE OF CUTTING USED

The type of cutting used essentially depends on four criteria:—

(i) Genus, species and cultivar being propagated.

(ii) Time of year the cutting is taken.

(iii) Quantity of cuttings required.

(iv) Propagation facility available.

The procedures used, and the reasons for using different types of cuttings, are described in the section dealing with softwood, semi-ripe wood, and evergreen and deciduous hardwood cuttings (Chapters 8 and 9).

WOUNDING OF TISSUE DURING PREPARATION OF CUTTINGS.

Additional procedures may be used to prepare the typical types of cuttings. These are:—

(i) "Wounding of Cuttings", a term used to describe techniques that either remove tissue or make incisions at the bottom 2.0–3.0 cm (¾–1¼") of the cutting.

(ii) Removal of terminal flower buds, vegetative buds or shoot tips.

(iii) Reduction in size of the leaf lamina ("leaf blade").

(iv) Removal of basal leaves.

1. Wounding of Cuttings

The benefits obtained by wounding the base of cuttings have been known for many years, and is a standard procedure used on nurseries. It was particularly exploited by the Boskoop nurserymen during the 1930s and 1940s, and was seen there by James S. Wells of Red Bank Nursery, New Jersey, during a visit in 1946. He carried out trials on his return, and passed on the information to other nursery operators on the east coast of the United States.

The benefits gained by wounding cuttings are:—

(i) An increase in the quantity and quality of roots. Sites for root initiation are encouraged to develop when stems are wounded. Maximum benefit from wounding is obtained by subsequently treating the cuttings with a rooting hormone, e.g., indole-3-butyric acid (IBA). [Wounding enhances the uptake of the rooting hormone.]

(ii) An increase in water uptake by the cuttings from the rooting medium. This is particularly useful for large-leaved softwood cuttings, such as *Magnolia*, to help keep them turgid.

(iii) It encourages roots to develop further up the stem in the event that roots at the basal cut surface are lost because the rooting medium is too wet. However, wounding may increase basal rotting in some instances.

Over the decades nursery propagators have developed a number of differing techniques for wounding cuttings. Recently, research by B. H. Howard and R. S. Harrison-Murray at East Malling Research Station, Kent, England, has shown a significantly better understanding of the anatomical and physiological processes which take place within the cutting following wounding. They have also shown that actual splitting of the stem base of the cutting could offer advantages over other techniques.

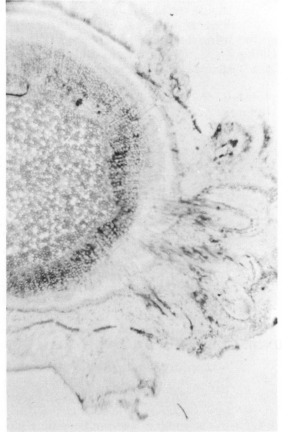

Figure 7-9. A (above). Many broad-leaved evergreen cuttings benefit from wounding. Note the high density of emerging roots resulting from a single slice wound near the base of the cutting. B (right). A cross-section of a single node cutting of *Mahonia japonica* (Japanese Mahonia) which was given a single slice wound. Note the emergence of root initials arising from the vascular tissue and growing through the callus tissue which developed at the site of wounding. (Reproduced by permission of B. E. Humphrey, Hillier Nurseries (Winchester) Ltd., Romsey, Hampshire, U.K.)

Wounding Techniques

(a) Stripping Off Lower Stems by Hand—Small lower stems have to be removed from many conifer cuttings to provide a 2.5–5.0 cm (1–2″) area of clear main stem before sticking in the rooting medium (see p. 278). This process is often referred to as "stripping" and effectively wounds many conifers, e.g., *Chamaecyparis* (False Cypress), *Juniperus* (Juniper) and *Thuja* (Arborvitae).

These small branches should be removed with a knife if the stems tear badly. Removal of the branches with a knife is best carried out by holding the base of the cutting upwards and removing the stems nearest to the basal cut first.

(b) Scraping—Occasionally propagators scrape the base of the stem with a knife blade, or even with a potato peeler, to assist rooting. This method of abrasing the plant tissue is sometimes used for cuttings when it is difficult to either remove a slice of tissue or to penetrate into the stem with a knife blade.

(c) Slice Wound—A slice wound is the removal of one or two 2.0–3.0 cm (¾–1¼″) long, shallow slivers of tissue from the base of the stem with a knife or blade of a hand pruner. I prefer a knife blade because it provides greater precision. The depth of wounding depends largely on the species, degree of lignification, thickness of the rind and the overall stem caliper. In some instances, heavy wounding is carried out by removing up to about one-fifth of the tissue. Care should be taken as heavy wounding on some plants can actually inhibit rooting.

Research has shown the cambium must be penetrated for shallow wounding to be effective, and that shallow wounding is then generally superior to heavy wounding. One reason suggested for this is that, proportionately, shallow wounding exposes more cortex and phloem than xylem tissue compared to heavy wounding. Roots arise from cortex and phloem tissue rather than the xylem in cuttings of woody plants.

Wounding must be carried out quickly and precisely. One useful way to train staff to familiarize themselves with the movement is to practice on firm, larger caliper stems, gradually building up the precision needed for softer, thinner stems. The cutting should be held by the thumb and index finger and laid across the finger tips for support. A thinner sliver of tissue can be removed more easily and more accurately by using the tip of the knife blade.

There are three techniques used to slice wound, based on the number of slivers removed and on the position of removal.

(i) Single Slice Wound—The removal of a single sliver of tissue is the most common of all wounding techniques, and is particularly helpful with semi-ripe wood of *Elaeagnus*, *Ilex* (Holly), *Skimmia*, *Osmanthus* × *burkwoodii* (often called × *Osmarea burkwoodii*) (Burkwood Osmarea), *Osmanthus* and evergreen *Viburnum*. Rooting is encouraged particularly around the edge of the wounded tissue and roots should later emerge from around the remaining area of stem.

Large evergreen cuttings prepared by using pruners are easier to wound with the pruner blade. I have also used pruners effectively for promoting extra root development on late-stuck *Prunus laurocerasus* 'Rotundifolia' (Cherry Laurel cv.) cuttings in cold frames.

(ii) Double Slice Wound—The removal of two opposite slivers of tissue is useful for plants that do not root readily around the stem, such as some *Rhododendron* forms. Plants that root on one side only are liable to have the roots broken when transplanting from the flats. I have even seen this occur on such plants when lifted from the open ground some five years after planting out.

(iii) Modified Slice Wound—This is a technique in which the cut is made further up the stem, leaving the bottom 1.0 cm (⅜″) unwounded. It has been successful for evergreen hardwood cuttings in which stem rot or poor rooting occurs at the base of the cutting, especially when there is a likelihood of the rooting medium becoming too wet.

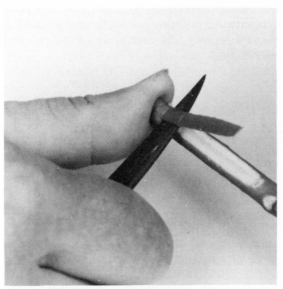

Figure 7-10. (left). Making a heavy single slice wound at the base of a broad-leaved evergreen cutting.
B (right). Making a shallow single slice wound at the base of a *Garrya elliptica* (Coast Silk-tassel) cutting.

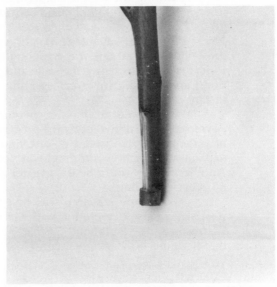

Figure 7-11. Making a double slice wound at the base of a *Rhododendron* cutting (the knife has been removed for clarity).

Figure 7-12. A modified slice wound at the base of a broad-leaved evergreen. A short cut was made about 1.0 (⅜″) above the stem base and the second cut was then brought down to meet it.

(d) Incision Wound—No tissue is removed in an incision wound, but the tip of the knife is drawn down the basal 2.0–3.0 cm (¾–1¼″) of stem so that it penetrates to the xylem wood. Sometimes up to three incision wounds are made on each cutting. It is not easy to carry out incision wounding unless the cutting is supported. The cutting should be held down on a flat surface with one hand while making the incision wound.

This technique was traditionally used for thinner stem cuttings of *Cupressus* (Cypress), *Juniperus* (Juniper) and *Taxus* (Yew) where slice wounding is difficult.

Research at East Malling Research Station on dormant hardwood cuttings of the apple rootstock Malling 26 has demonstrated that two incision wounds per cutting is optimum and there is little advantage gained by increasing this number. Anatomical studies have also shown that the callus which develops following incision wounding is derived mostly from the cortex. A new cambium differentiates within this callus tissue adjacent to the original cambium, thus forming a cambial bridge. Closer examination has shown that this callus is laid down as an outward pointing salient (protuberance). It is at this salient that a new root initiates and develops. The formation of this cambial bridge does not develop following slice wounding.

Figure 7-13. The tip of a knife blade being used to make an incision wound at the base of a cutting.

(e) Split Wound—This differs from the previous methods described in that the stem base is actually split up the center to a depth of around 1.0 cm (⅜"). Research at East Malling Research Station on rooting dormant winter cuttings of Malling 26 apple rootstocks in heated or callus bins (p. 321) demonstrated that incision wounding was superior to slice wounding and that an even greater improvement was achieved by split wounding the stems. This benefit was even greater on cuttings prepared from inter-nodal and non-basal wood collected from hardwood cutting hedges, compared to grade I cuttings with a swollen stem base.

A further advantage to splitting the stem at the base of the cutting is that there is a better survival rate if the rooting medium should remain too wet. This is because roots develop further up the stem and not just at the stem base where the wetter conditions are found. However, splitting may actually increase basal rotting in some instances.

Compared to incision wounding, split wounding allows more callus to develop. A line of two outward pointing salients later differentiate to provide a source of potential roots instead of one line as in incision wounding. This could possibly explain why split wounding was found to be superior over incision wounding. Another reason could be the greater ability for IBA uptake from split wounding over incision wounding.

While the research was first done on Malling 26 apple rootstocks, positive results have also been found with *Malus* 'Purple Wave', *Acer platanoides* 'Crimson King' (Crimson King Maple) and *Castanea sativa* (Spanish Chestnut). The evidence indicates that it would be worth evaluating the technique on other woody ornamentals.

Figure 7-14. A (left). The tips of pruner blades can be used to make a split wound at the base of a deciduous hardwood cutting. B (right). A young liner of *Edgeworthia papyrifera* (Paperbush, Mitsumata) which was initially split wounded at the base of the cutting. Note the callus formation along the stem and the well-developed root system. (Some roots have been removed at the site of the split wound for clarity.) University of British Columbia Botanical Garden, Vancouver, B.C., Canada).

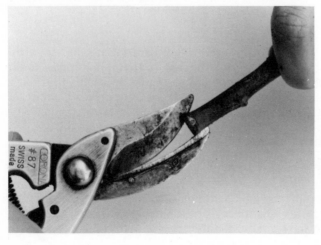

2. Removal of Shoot Tips, Flower Buds and Vegetative Buds

The removal of shoot tips and buds is carried out for the following reasons:—

(i) To promote side shoots during the early production stage.

(ii) To standardize the shape and sizes of cutting batches for handling and rooting. A good example is with conifers where I have noted a major difference between the North American and European procedures. The cuttings for most *Juniperus* (Juniper) and *Thuja* (Arborvitae) are sheared horizontally across the top to remove any dominant leader in North America, while the normal European practice is to retain the leader shoot. The sheared cuttings are important in production as the first pruning builds up a good liner. The plants will develop a leader if desired.

Unsheared cuttings of some conifers such as × *Cupressocyparis leylandii* (Leyland Cypress) tend to lean over to one side after sticking, but the upright sheared cuttings will ensure better air circulation and allow water droplets from mist propagation to fall through the cuttings, thus reducing the risk of unforeseen drying out of the rooting medium.

(iii) To lessen the risk of stem die-back from soft and immature growth at the top of the cutting. This is particularly important when over-wintering cuttings of *Cotoneaster* and deciduous *Berberis* (Barberry) stuck in an unheated cold frame during the previous fall.

(iv) Terminal flower buds on the large-leaved species of *Rhododendron* are thought to actually inhibit rooting. Also, the warm conditions present when rooting under mist propagation, fogging system or polyethylene film encourage the bud scales to break and thus expose the petals. The petals are then susceptible to fungal attack, risking infection to the rest of the cutting.

The buds are easily removed with the thumb and finger. Flower and vegetative buds are also removed to encourage side shoots.

Figure 7-15. Terminal flower buds of *Rhododendron* should be removed during cutting preparation.

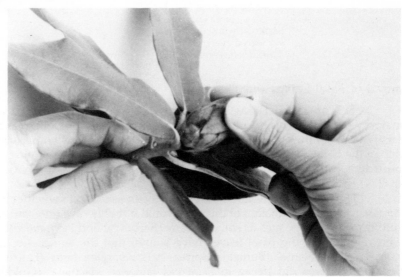

3. Reduction in Size of Leaf Lamina

This procedure is often carried out on the larger-leaved evergreen and deciduous shrubs for three reasons:—

(i) To reduce transpiration (water loss) from the cutting.

(ii) To handle the cuttings more easily.

(iii) To enable the propagator to stick more cuttings in a given area. Overlapping of leaves allows water to accumulate on the upper leaf surface, prevents water from mist propagation reaching the rooting medium thus drying out the cuttings, shades the lower leaves, and increases stress to the cuttings.

There is one major disadvantage of reducing the leaf lamina (particularly with some broad-leaf evergreens, such as *Camellia* and *Rhododendron*) in that the exposed cut surface is susceptible to fungal infection, e.g., *Monochaetia karstenii* (see p. 372). Research has indicated that reduction of the leaf lamina may have to be re-assessed when using fogging equipment—the leaves are less stressed in this situation and can photosynthesize better when not reduced in size.

If leaf lamina reduction is used, the aim should be to reduce it by about one-third to one-half. This can be done simply by holding the cutting(s) in the hand, drawing the leaves together in one plane and cutting with a pair of pruners. Alternatively, a knife can be used. If the leaves tear when using a knife or if the cuts are uneven, the cutting should be laid on the bench, held in place with the hand and then the leaf lamina cut through with a knife.

Figure 7-16. Although there are advantages to reducing the area of the leaf lamina when preparing cuttings, the exposed cut surface is susceptible to disease infection (e.g., by *Monochaetia karstenii*)— particularly in some broad-leaved evergreens, e.g., *Rhododendron* and *Camellia*.

4. Removal of Basal Leaves and Thorns

This procedure is usually referred to as "stripping" the cutting, and is standard for the great majority of plants prior to cuttings being stuck. There are several reasons for "stripping" cuttings. Firstly, it makes the sticking operation easier as the leaves will otherwise resist the downward motion of the hand. Secondly, the leaves below the surface of the rooting medium tend to decay, thus providing a source of fungal infection to the cutting. Thirdly, it can assist in wounding the cutting (p. 274).

However, the question has recently been asked as to whether it is necessary to remove the basal leaves. The elimination of this step would not only save time, but also make it easier to handle cuttings with thorns, such as some *Berberis* (Barberry) and *Pyracantha* (Fire Thorn). The initial trials with retention of the basal leaves have shown that the leaf tissue did not decay on *Spiraea* × *bumalda* 'Gold Flame' (Bumalda Spirea cv.), *Viburnum tinus* (Laurustinus) and *Hebe* 'Eversley Seedling'. Leaves did decay in *Elaeagnus pungens* 'Maculata' (Golden Elaeagnus), *Erica carnea* (Spring Heather) and *Pernettya mucronata* (Chilean Pernettya), although it was not carried over to the stem. It was also noted that the improved aeration around the base of the cutting could prove advantageous in aiding rooting. Leaving the cuttings of larger leaved species untrimmed can result in the need for more propagation space.

C. PROPAGATION FACILITY

Information on the appropriate propagation facilities may be found in Chapter 3.

REFERENCES AND SUGGESTED SOURCES FOR FURTHER READING

Argles, G. K. 1969. Root formation by stem cuttings. 2. The effect of pH and calcium. *Nurseryman & Garden Centre,* July 17, 1969, pp. 61–65.

Beakbane, A. B. 1969. Relationships between structure and adventitious rooting. *Comb. Proc. Inter. Pl. Prop. Soc.* **19**: 192–201.

Chadwick, L. C. 1955. The choice of shoots: A consideration of the influence of source factors on regeneration. *Rep. XIVth Inter. Hort. Congr.,* pp. 215–222.

Fordham, A. J. 1969. Production of juvenile shoots from root pieces. *Comb. Proc. Inter. Pl. Prop. Soc.* **19**: 284–287.

Garner, R. J. 1944. *Propagation by Cuttings and Layers. Recent Work and Its Application, With Special Reference to Pome and Stone Fruits.* Techn. Comm. No. 14. Imperial Bureau of Horticulture and Plantation Crops, East Malling, Kent, England.

Halliwell, B. 1970. Selection of material when propagating Leyland Cypress. *Comb. Proc. Inter. Pl. Prop. Soc.* **20**: 338–340.

Harrison-Murray, R. S. 1981. Etiolation of stock plants for improved rooting of cuttings: I. Opportunities suggested by work with Apple. *Comb. Proc. Inter. Pl. Prop. Soc.* **31**: 386–392.

Hartmann, H. T. & D. E. Kester. 1983. 4th ed. *Plant Propagation: Principles and Practices.* Prentice-Hall, Inc., Englewood Cliffs, N.J.

Herman, D. E. & C. E. Hess. 1963. The effect of etiolation upon the rooting of cuttings. *Comb. Proc. Pl. Prop. Soc.* **13**: 42–62.

Howard, B. H. 1968. Effects of bud removal and wounding on rooting in hardwood cuttings. *Nature* **220**: 262–264.

_____. 1971. Nursery experiment report: The response of cuttings to basal wounding in relation to time of auxin treatment. *Comb. Proc. Inter. Pl. Prop. Soc.* **21**: 267–274.

_____, R. S. Harrison-Murray & C. A. Fenlon. 1983. Effective auxin treatment of leafless winter cuttings. *IN: Growth Regulators in Root Development,* edited by M. B. Jackson & A. D. Stead. Monograph No. 10, British Plant Growth Regulator Group, pp. 73–84.

_____ & K. A. D. Mackenzie. 1984. Rooting responses to wounding winter cuttings of M.26 apple rootstock. *J. Hort. Sci.* **59**: 131–139.

Hudson, J. P. 1956. The art and science of plant propagation. *Gardeners Chronicle & Gardening Illustrated,* April 21, 1956, p. 421.

Humphrey, P. 1983. Effects of wounding combined with growth substances on semi-hardwood cuttings of some hardy deciduous woody plants. Unpubl. mss., Hillier Nurseries (Winchester) Ltd., England.

James, R. 1975. Light in propagation. *Comb. Proc. Inter. Pl. Prop. Soc.* **25**: 242–245.

Kester, D. E. 1976. The relationship of juvenility to plant propagation. *Comb. Proc. Inter. Pl. Prop. Soc.* **26**: 71–84.

Lamb, J. G. D., J. C. Kelly & P. Bowbrick. 1975. *Nursery Stock Manual.* Grower Books, London, U.K.

Maronek, D. M., D. Studebaker, T. McCloud, V. Black & R. St. Jean. 1983. Stripping vs. nonstripping on rooting of woody ornamental cuttings—grower results. *Comb. Proc. Inter. Pl. Prop. Soc.* **33**: 388–396.

Rowell, D. J. 1981. Etiolation of stock plants for the improved rooting of cuttings. II. Initial experiences with hardy ornamental nursery stock. *Comb. Proc. Inter. Pl. Prop. Soc.* **31**: 392–397.

Schonbeck, H. 1982. Is stripping of cuttings necessary? *Comb. Proc. Inter. Pl. Prop. Soc.* **32**: 199–200.

Stoutemyer, V. T. 1961. Light and propagation. *Comb. Proc. Pl. Prop. Soc.* **11**: 252–260.

Wells, J. S. 1955. *Plant Propagation Practices.* The Macmillan Company, New York.

_____. 1962. Wounding cuttings as a commercial practice. *Comb. Proc. Pl. Prop. Soc.* **12**: 47–55.

Chapter 8

SOFTWOOD, SEMI-RIPE WOOD AND EVERGREEN HARDWOOD CUTTINGS

Propagation by cuttings is the most widely used vegetative method for propagating woody ornamental plants in nurseries. It is usually a very predictable method because many species present few problems in rooting. However, some plants are unpredictable and thus present a constant challenge to the dedicated propagator.

There are essentially three types of cuttings based on the stage of stem growth development:—

(i) Softwood cuttings

(ii) Semi-ripe wood (semi-hardwood) and evergreen hardwood cuttings.

(iii) Deciduous (leafless) hardwood cuttings (see Chapter 9).

In the next two chapters, methods are suggested for obtaining maximum efficiency from employees, and the techniques used to prepare cuttings and the critical aftercare procedures required are explained.

Repetition of principles and items discussed in detail in other chapters is avoided by cross-references to those sections, and the reader is urged to follow up this suggestion. Specific details for the propagation of individual plants will be found in Volume 2 of this text.

Topics suggested for cross reference are as follows:—

Stock Plants and Cutting Collection	p. 240–p. 256
Time of Year	p. 271
Wounding	p. 272–p. 276
Rooting Hormones	Chapter 10
Disease Control	Chapter 12
Rooting Media	Chapter 11

PLANNING AND PREPARATION FOR PROPAGATION

Only recently has there been careful study of methods to improve both the output and the quality of work by nursery employees making cuttings. A study was done in Britain by B. J. W. Morgan and R. Menneer of the Agriculture Development Advisory Service (ADAS), Ministry of Agriculture. They used well-tried work study procedures to examine the methods involved in the handling and preparation of certain types of softwood, semi-ripe wood and evergreen hardwood cuttings. The results showed that savings in cutting preparation costs of up to 50% could be made. The Agricultural Training Board (ATB), whose directive is to train horticultural employees, subsequently produced an excellent booklet, *Nursery Stock Propagation—Preparation of Cuttings* (Agricultural Training Board, Beckenham, Kent, U.K.).

Before describing the recommended techniques in detail, I think that it would be helpful to mention a few of the points that the propagator should consider when planning and undertaking cutting propagation work.

1. Training Staff

Hands-on training in the use of tools is required for quality of work, speed and safety (see

Chapter 4). Cutting propagation is often carried out by unskilled staff, but it is no use expecting good results unless they are properly trained. Unskilled does *not* then mean un-trained. The supervisors themselves must be trained properly, and be able both to communicate instructions and to train effectively. Further, supervisors must thoroughly understand that routine quality control checks are vital and that low quality output must be sorted out immediately, not left until the next day or the next week.

Today, unskilled propagators often use pruners or hardware knives with disposable blades rather than true propagating knives. I still believe that it is important for employees to be equipped with, and instructed in, the proper use of propagating knives (p. 184), particularly when they are likely to be on long-term employment.

The initial problem is that people are afraid of knives, so they try to sever a cutting by pressing and bending it over the blade, resulting in a break rather than a cut. The possibility of self-injury is markedly increased using this method.

I find that confidence in using a knife for taking cuttings can be built up by commencing training with soft-stemmed evergreen material such as *Escallonia* or *Ligustrum* (Privet) (see Chapter 4). The leaves are stripped from a 45 cm (18") long piece of stem, the cutting held in one hand, and the knife drawn from left to right (or vice versa) across the soft tip. This practice allows the trainee to get the feeling of "cutting through butter" rather than snapping at it with the knife. The easy cutting of the softer wood at the tip builds up confidence before working down to the riper, harder wood.

[All staff working on the nursery should be encouraged to have tetanus injections, and to maintain the protection with booster shots as required.]

2. Facilities and Equipment

Inside work with cuttings should be carried out in a well-lit room with a comfortable working temperature and shading to encourage maximum output. Adjustable chairs should be provided, both for support and to reduce fatigue. A clean bench at the correct height for working is vital. A successful bench design to improve efficiency reported from New Zealand was based on the ADAS potting system developed by the Ministry of Agriculture, U.K. A semi-circle was cut out on the side of the bench where the operator was to sit and there was also a hole in the bench so that waste material could be brushed down into a bin below.

The basic equipment that should be supplied are pruners, knives, sharpening aids, flats for sticking, a cleaning cloth, and solvent to wipe cutting blades. A waste receptacle is required for discarded plant material. Two useful additions are, firstly, a hand-operated misting sprayer to damp down softwood material. This can be either a plastic cannister or a permanent attachment fitted to the bench and supplied with water piped from a central source. Secondly, a small plastic dish containing a damp sponge for moistening the base of cuttings is useful if rooting hormone powders are used and stems of the cuttings are dry. This is more convenient than dipping or spraying the stem base with water prior to rooting (p. 340).

Optional items are a rubber thumb pad to protect against knife cuts and a tough but flexible glove to wear when holding cuttings with sharp thorns. The latter will also be a protection against infection(s) that may develop from skin punctures.

3. Bench Layout for Equipment and Cuttings

Equipment, unprepared and prepared cuttings should not be piled haphazardly on the bench, but rather placed at each work station in an orderly fashion so that the employee can comfortably carry out the minimum number of movements necessary for the operation.

Common mistakes are to clutter the bench surface with excess unprepared cuttings and waste material. This causes both employee frustration and lower output. These extra materials cover flats and equipment and must constantly be pushed out of the way. Begin with a clean work surface and reduce the amount of equipment and plant material to the minimum necessary for sustained output.

Illustrated opposite are suggested bench layouts of equipment and material for cuttings of specific plants as recommended in the ADAS study and outlined in the Agricultural Training Board (U.K.) booklets (ATB, 32-34 Beckenham Road, Beckenham, Kent BR3 4PB, U.K.).

(a) **Conifers**

(b) **Large-leaved Broad-leaved Evergreens, e.g., Rhododendrons**

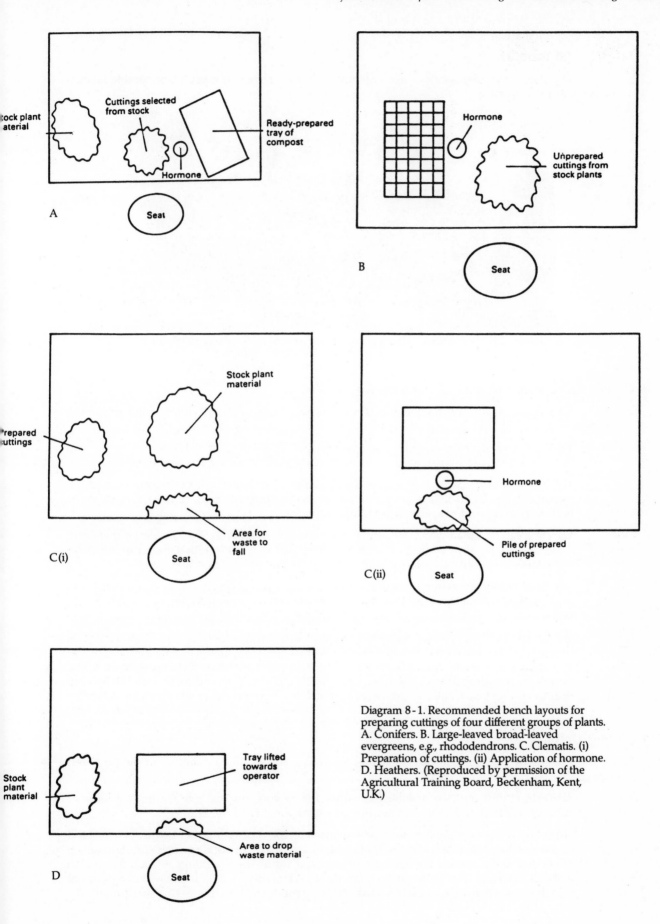

Diagram 8-1. Recommended bench layouts for preparing cuttings of four different groups of plants. A. Conifers. B. Large-leaved broad-leaved evergreens, e.g., rhododendrons. C. Clematis. (i) Preparation of cuttings. (ii) Application of hormone. D. Heathers. (Reproduced by permission of the Agricultural Training Board, Beckenham, Kent, U.K.)

(c) Clematis

(d) Heathers

The thoughtful manager can use ingenuity and experience to design comparable layouts for other plant materials.

Figure 8-1. The efficiency of the operators preparing cuttings is reduced significantly when the work bench is cluttered with cuttings, trays and baskets.

4. Cutting Preparation and Rooting Hormone Application

Employees should be trained to carefully observe the following steps when preparing cuttings:—

(a) Cuttings must be graded by size and grouped by these grades. Employee output will be greatly reduced by having to work with constantly changing measurements.

(b) Stems with multiple side shoots should have all potential cuttings removed and the remainder discarded before preparing individual cuttings. It is an unnecessary waste of time to remove and prepare each cutting individually.

(c) Time can be saved when preparing larger evergreen cuttings, e.g., *Skimmia, Prunus* and *Rhododendron,* by slice wounding with the sharp pruning blade rather than putting aside the pruner and using a knife for each cutting. This technique needs practice.

(d) Basal leaves are generally best removed before making the basal cut just beneath the node, rather than afterward. This makes it easier for the operators to see what they are doing.

(e) Preparation of cuttings not prone to bruising can be speeded up. Each cutting is prepared with a knife and then gathered into one hand until there is a small bundle of 10–15 cuttings. The lower cut surfaces should be kept level as the cuttings are gathered. The bundle is then dipped with the basal ends of the cuttings placed directly into the rooting hormone. [Very soft cuttings prone to bruising are best placed neatly in clean flats after preparation.]

5. Sticking Cuttings

The following suggestions will increase the rate of the sticking operation for the prepared cuttings.

(a) Instruct the employees to use two hands for sticking, not just one. Gather a bundle of cuttings together and then transfer one at a time directly to the flat.

(b) If unit containers are not used, a template with fixed pegs (marker board) can be used to pre-mark or make holes in the rooting medium for faster sticking. This simple practice eliminates inconsistency in spacing and incorrect numbers of cuttings in each flat. It also helps the sticking of cuttings with weaker stems. Alternatively, a template with longitudinal thin metal plates fixed to it can be used. Pressing the metal into the rooting medium marks

Figure 8-2. Greater efficiency is achieved by removing all potential cuttings from a stem with multiple shoots, then preparing each cutting individually. The photograph shows *Cotoneaster horizontalis* (Rock Cotoneaster or Rockspray) cuttings being torn off the main stem for subsequent preparation as heel cuttings.

Figure 8-3. A crew preparing and sticking heather cuttings. Note that the flats are angled towards the operator and that the cuttings are stuck from left to right, commencing with the first row at the top of the flat. (Windlesham Court Nurseries, Sunningdale, Surrey, U.K.)

the row spacing, but not the distance between the cuttings. A light scattering of sharp sand on the surface of the medium will help to make the marks more visible.

(c) Sticking a flat of small cuttings, such as heathers, is made easier by placing a block of wood under the far end of the flat so that the surface slants towards the operator.

(d) Three methods used for sticking are:—

(i) Stick from left to right, beginning with the row furthest away and working towards the operator. For example, heathers.

(ii) Stick diagonally across the flat from the top left-hand corner (particularly useful for large flat modules). For example, conifers.

Diagram 8-2. An efficient method to stick conifer cuttings in a flat is illustrated below. A. Begin at the top left- (or right-) hand corner, holding a bunch of cuttings in one hand while sticking with the other. B. Continue sticking on a diagonal across the flat. (Reproduced by permission of the Agricultural Training Board, Beckenham, Kent, U.K.)

A

B

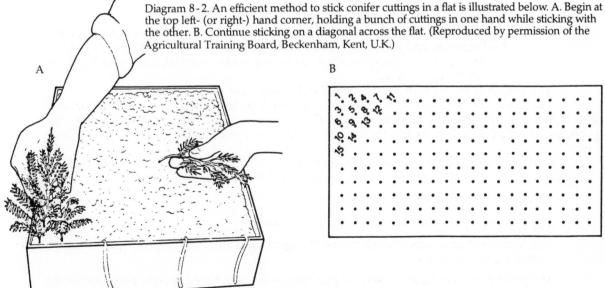

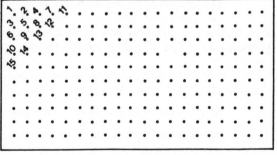

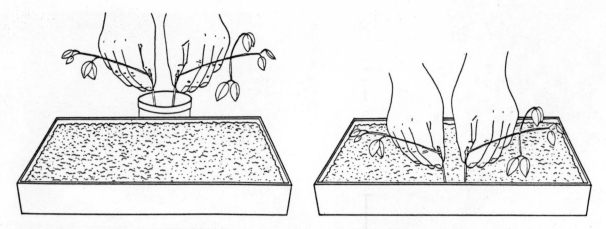

Diagram 8-3. Both hands can be used to simultaneously dip (left) and stick (right) two cuttings at a time. Note that sticking begins at the center of the flat and then proceeds outwards to the two sides. (Reproduced by permission of the Agricultural Training Board, Beckenham, Kent, U.K.)

(iii) Stick with both hands simultaneously, beginning with the two center rows of the flat and then working outwards to the sides. For example, clematis.

(e) Hand-mist the prepared flat if there is any risk of the cuttings being stressed due to loss of water.

6. Movement of Cuttings to Propagation Facility

Ensure that the cuttings are moved to the propagation facility as soon as they are stuck. Softwood cuttings can quickly deteriorate if allowed to stand too long in the propagation shed.

A convenient method is to have one employee responsible for supplying fresh materials to employees at the bench, removing waste material, and collecting and taking completed flats to the propagation facility.

7. Crew Tasks

Larger propagation units often use a crew of employees in order to achieve maximum output. I was impressed with the planning and excellent team work that the Darby Nursery Stock Ltd., Methwold, Norfolk, U.K., had used to achieve an efficient flow.

The crew consisted of 8 employees whose tasks were as follows:—

4—Grading, sorting, preparing cuttings and applying hormones
1—Preparing and sticking cuttings
1—Sticking
1—Labelling, recording and transporting trays of cuttings to propagation facility
1—Preparing and filling flats with rooting medium, transporting cuttings stuck in flats to the propagation shed, removing waste materials, and sticking if not otherwise occupied.

The output achieved with this plan nearly doubled their previous rates.

The most effective work is obtained from a crew if their work is coordinated to prevent interruptions in the flow due to lack of materials or a delay in moving completed flats to the propagation facility. The diagram illustrates a layout and crew duties used at Darby Nursery Stock Ltd.

Assuming one operator carries out the cutting preparation (using a knife) and the sticking, the normal outline procedure for the ADAS method of cuttings is as follows:—

(i) Remove leaves from pre-cut stem.

(ii) Sever cutting at the base and wound if applicable.

(iii) Move cutting into the angle between the thumb and forefinger, repeating until there is a small bundle of cuttings.

(iv) Press base of cuttings on sponge pad moistened with liquid rooting hormone or dip into rooting hormone powder.

Diagram 8-4. A. Layout for an 8-person crew for preparing and sticking cuttings. B. Bench for cutting preparation. (Source: Darby Nursery Stock Ltd., Methwold Hythe, Thetford, Norfolk, U.K.)

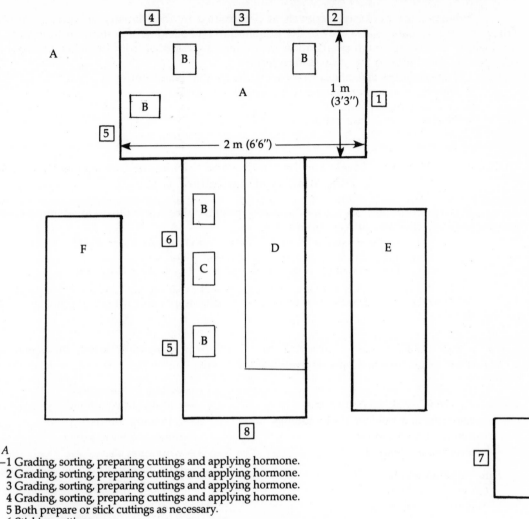

Key for A

Crew—1 Grading, sorting, preparing cuttings and applying hormone.
      2 Grading, sorting, preparing cuttings and applying hormone.
      3 Grading, sorting, preparing cuttings and applying hormone.
      4 Grading, sorting, preparing cuttings and applying hormone.
      5 Both prepare or stick cuttings as necessary.
      6 Sticking cuttings.
      7 Labelling, recording, transporting cuttings to propagation facility.
      8 Preparing and filling flats with rooting medium; also transporting cuttings to propagation house; sticking cuttings if required.
A—unprepared cuttings brought from nearby cold store.
B—prepared cuttings in flats.
C—flats of stuck cuttings.
D—flats filled with rooting medium.
E—cart (trolley) to bring rooting medium-filled flats from nearby potting shed.
F—cart (trolley) to take flats of stuck cuttings to propagation house.

NOTE:—The work rate over a 2-week period for an 8-person crew each of whom had at least one full season's propagation experience averaged 22,080 cuttings (prepared and stuck) in a 6-hour day.

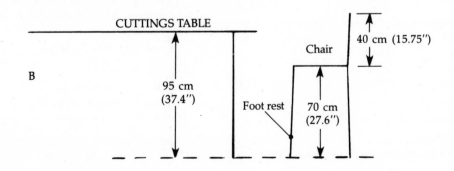

(v) Stick cuttings.

(vi) Transport to propagation facility.

Tabulated are performance levels as determined by the Ministry of Agriculture (ADAS). This performance data relates only to the preparation and sticking of cuttings as indicated. It does not include collection, rough preparation (i.e., removing cuttings from branches in the shed), or transporting filled flats to the propagation facility.

1. *Chamaecyparis lawsoniana* cvs. (using disposable blade knife)
2. *Hypericum calycinum* (using disposable blade knife)
3. *Berberis* (using pruners)
4. *Rhododendron* (using pruners)

TABLE 8-1. Performance Levels For Preparation and Sticking of Cuttings as Determined by the Ministry of Agriculture, U.K.

These performance figures are those determined by the Agriculture Development Advisory Service (ADAS), Ministry of Agriculture, U.K.

Good—Average of best 25% of workers in good conditions
Typical—Average worker in average conditions
Poor—Average of worst 25% of workers in poor conditions

NOTE: Working conditions are the responsibility of the management and are not under the control of the worker (e.g., a good worker under poor conditions may only manage a typical overall time for the job).

A. To prepare 1000 conifer (*Chamaecyparis lawsoniana* cvs., Lawson Cypress) cuttings by:

—removing basal leaves by hand
—gathering and holding 10–15 cuttings
—dipping into hormone
—inserting in compost

Time required will be:—
Good   —70 mins.
Typical   —90 mins.
Poor   —140 mins.

B. To prepare 1000 *Hypericum* (St. John's-wort) tip cuttings by:

—cutting stem
—removing basal leaves by hand
—bunching and holding 15 cuttings
—dipping into hormone
—inserting in compost

Time required will be:—
Good   —50 mins.
Typical   —60 mins.
Poor   —100 mins.

C. To prepare 1000 *Berberis* (Barberry) cuttings by:

—cutting below a node
—cutting above a node
—removing thorns
—removing basal leaves
—wounding stem
—bunching and holding 5–8 cuttings
—dipping into hormone

Time required will be:—
Good   —150 mins.
Typical   —280 mins.
Poor   —380 mins.

D. To prepare 1000 large-leaved *Rhododendron* cuttings by:

—removing basal leaves
—cutting stem
—wounding
—removing flower bud
—cutting leaves across to reduce area
—dipping individual cuttings into hormone
—inserting into compost

Time required will be:—
Good   —180 mins.
Typical   —270 mins.
Poor   —420 mins.

Reproduced by permission of the Agricultural Training Board, Beckenham, Kent, U.K.

SOFTWOOD CUTTINGS

Softwood cuttings are selected from the current season's growth before extensive lignification has occurred. Softwood cutting propagation is a very useful method to quickly bulk-up easy-to-root material. Those cuttings that are fast rooting can very often be potted-up soon after rooting and grown under protection to provide a further source of softwood cuttings—for example, *Caryopteris* (Bluebeard), *Fuchsia* and many *Spiraea* (Spirea). Some evergreens can be successfully rooted from softwood cuttings, particularly when the stock plants or production crops are grown under protection, for example, *Erica* (Heath), *Escallonia*, *Hebe* and *Ceanothus* (California-lilac). However, many evergreens, such as *Ilex* (Holly), *Camellia*, *Osmanthus* and *Photinia* are unpredictable as softwoods so should be tackled as evergreen hardwood cuttings.

Using the soft growth by taking nodal tip and/or single node ("leaf bud") cuttings is a rapid way to root climbing plants—examples being *Actinidia*, *Clematis*, *Celastrus* (Bittersweet), *Lonicera* (Honeysuckle) and *Vitis* (Grape).

Certain conifers are also suitable for rooting as softwood cuttings if container-stock plants are forced into growth early in the season, for example, *Metasequoia glyptostroboides* (Dawn Redwood) and *Picea glauca* 'Conica' (Dwarf Alberta Spruce). However, difficulties in subsequent establishment after potting into liner pots can occur with these conifers when softwood cuttings are used.

Trees are often thought of as being propagated only by seed, budding or grafting, but considerable success has been obtained by using softwood cuttings of *Alnus glutinosa* 'Imperialis' (Black or Common Alder cv.), *Betula pendula* 'Dalecarlica' (Cutleaf Weeping Birch), *Prunus padus* 'Watereri' (European Bird Cherry cv.) and *Liquidambar styraciflua* 'Worplesdon' (American Sweet Gum cv.). Softwood cutting propagation eliminates buying rootstocks and thus reduces overall propagation costs. When considering cutting propagation of trees that are normally grafted or budded, it is important to remember that there must be a high rooting percentage and that the time period of production ideally should not be lengthened. Grafting or budding onto an established rootstock has the great advantage of producing a "thrust" of maiden growth in the following year. Trees from cuttings do lend themselves particularly to container production.

Softwood cuttings are normally taken from shoots soon after growth breaks from the bud in late spring and early summer, which means that the shoots are in an active state of growth and therefore careful, rapid handling is required during their collection, preparation and aftercare. Close supervision is required to ensure that the cuttings are not subject to stress and begin to deteriorate.

Time of Year

Softwood cuttings can be categorized into two groups based on the time period when they will successfully root and over-winter. The time period for rooting of both these groups can often be brought forward and extended by growing stock plants or production crops under protection with higher air temperature. In addition, provision of artificial lighting to extend the day length is useful for specific plants, e.g., deciduous azaleas.

1. Cuttings Which Root Over a Short Period in Spring or Early Summer

These cuttings have an initial short growth period from bud burst until hardening of the shoot. They should be rooted just as the base of the new shoot has started to become firm. Thus, the propagator has 4–6 weeks after bud burst during which these cuttings root best. This earlier rooting helps the cuttings or liners to over-winter more successfully because there has been a longer growth period for shoot and root development before leaf fall compared to taking cuttings in mid-summer.

EXAMPLES:—

Azalea—deciduous
Acer palmatum cvs. (Japanese Maple)
Cornus florida cvs. (Eastern Flowering Dogwood)
Corylopsis spp. (Winter Hazel)
Cotinus coggygria cvs. (Smoke Tree)
Fothergilla major (Large Fothergilla)
Hamamelis (Witch Hazel)
Magnolia (deciduous spp.)

Stewartia spp.
Syringa vulgaris cvs. (Common or French Lilac)
Viburnum carlesii (Korean Spice Viburnum)

2. Cuttings Which Root Within a Period of 12 Weeks from Bud Burst

These are also generally successful as semi-hard wood cuttings following ripening of shoot growth.

EXAMPLES:—

Buddleia davidii (Butterflybush)
Deutzia gracilis (Slender Deutzia)
Forsythia × *intermedia* (Border Forsythia)
Hypericum patulum 'Hidcote' (Goldencup St. John's-wort cv.)
Kolkwitzia amabilis (Beautybush)
Lonicera tatarica 'Arnold Red' (Tatarian Honeysuckle cv.)
Philadelphus cvs. (Mock Orange)
Physocarpus opulifolius cvs. (Eastern Ninebark)
Potentilla fruticosa cvs. (Shrubby Cinquefoil)
Ribes alpinum (Alpine Currant)

Collection of Cuttings

Cuttings are collected from true-to-name stock material permanently sited in open ground, in a protected structure, or from the production crop. It is important that the stock material be well-watered prior to collection to ensure that the shoots are turgid—this is particularly important when collecting from container plants. They should not be collected during the warm part of the day because water is too easily lost from the tissues. Ideally, collection should be done on dull days, in the early morning, or late afternoon/evening. Preferably, either polyethylene bags containing a few water drops or moist burlap (hessian) sacks should be used to contain the cuttings as they are collected. Avoid clear and black plastic bags as they absorb more heat. Using a cold store or refrigerator set at 3°C (38°F) to temporarily hold the cuttings is useful when collecting late in the day for the following day or to take out the "field heat" if they are collected during warm weather. A couple of hours in cold storage at 1–3°C (34–38°F) helps to restore turgidity.

Stems of climbing plants, especially *Clematis* and *Lonicera* (Honeysuckle), grow very rapidly so it is important to gather them before they have started to intertwine. Twining of the stems both reduces the number of cuttings and leads to damage while untangling them.

Depending on the plant species, there are several ways to remove the cuttings—these include individual soft tips, single shoots from which two or more cuttings can be made, or stems with multiple side shoots.

Figure 8-4. Collecting shoots of a golden *Erica cinerea* cv. (Bell Heather) from the stock beds. These will be prepared as softwood cuttings. (Windlesham Court Nursery, Sunningdale, Surrey, U.K.)

Handling and Disease Protection

It is important to prevent bruising, tearing and water loss, both to keep the cuttings turgid and to reduce the risk of subsequent disease infection. It is essential to have a hand-operated misting unit to spray over the prepared and unprepared cuttings when working in warm temperatures. A short spray every few minutes will reduce the chance of wilting. The prepared cuttings can be immersed in a fungicidal solution, and the cuttings and rooting medium should be drenched with a fungicide when sticking is completed. This will help to prevent rotting of leaves, stems and particularly of the developing roots (see p. 337). This initial drench should be followed with back-up drenches or sprays during the aftercare. [*NOTE:* There have been instances of staff developing skin irritations after immersing cuttings in a fungicide solution. In this case, supply the staff with thin rubber gloves or, if this is not effective, omit the immersion procedure and rely on fungicidal drenches after sticking.]

Figure 8-5.
It is important to ensure that softwood cuttings are kept turgid from collection until rooting. A suspended hose with a fine rose attachment and connected to a main water line is one convenient way to re-wet the rooting medium, prepared and unprepared cuttings during warm weather. (Monrovia Nursery, Azusa, CA, U.S.A.)

Propagation Facility and Immediate Aftercare

The key to success in rooting softwood cuttings is keeping them turgid during the period from collection until they are well rooted in the propagation facility. The main types of facilities for rooting softwood cuttings are cold frames, mist propagation units, fogging systems, low polyethylene tunnels, and closed cases with glass or polyethylene coverings (see Chapter 3). However, it is attention to detail during aftercare that will finally count, no matter how simple or sophisticated the type of facility used. Guidelines for aftercare are:—

1. The optimum rooting medium temperature should run at 18–21°C (65–70°F). Air temperatures in excess of 30°C (86°F) should be avoided wherever possible. However, these high temperatures can be tolerated providing that high humidity is maintained around the cuttings. Higher temperatures can also cause greater disease risks. In warmer climates, it may be necessary to force air through cooling pads. A rise in temperature without a corresponding increase in humidity causes desiccation of the cuttings and thus places them under severe stress. A good propagator will know the signs of such stress just by the appearance of the cuttings—there is often a subtle change of color and they look limp. Regular checks need to be made to monitor the cuttings and the equipment—for example, the distribution pattern of water droplets from the misting nozzles.

It may become necessary to adapt the existing propagation facility. For example, the enclosure of mist propagation beds with polyethylene supported on hoops to form a low tunnel (see p. 166). This is a very satisfactory means to overcome problems such as reduced humidity or dealing with air currents which cause uneven dispersal of water droplets to the cuttings.

It is critical that precise instructions be given to weekend staff—24 hours can undo all the correct procedures of the previous six days. It is essential to check the cuttings *after* working hours during hot weather and the long summer days.

2. The full light intensity of the summer is counter-productive. A shading value of up to 70–80% is an optimum level for many facilities in mid-summer (p.118). The overall degree of error is lessened by reducing both light intensity and air temperature.

3. All flats should be checked daily to remove dead leaves and cuttings to reduce possible sources of re-infection. It is easy to say "I will leave it until tomorrow", but that is often too late and it is all too likely that other tasks will divert attention.

4. Contingency plans should be made to replace cuttings that have failed to root. These can include modifying the propagation program, or obtaining rooted cuttings or liners from another source.

Reference should be made to Chapter 3 on propagation facilities for a more detailed account of specific aftercare and maintenance procedures.

Types of Cuttings

The type of cutting prepared at the bench is largely governed by the plant being rooted and by the propagation facility available. It is also related to the length of individual shoots, the distance between each node (called the internode) and the number of cuttings required. The optimum length for a cutting is between 2.5–12.5 cm (1–5"), e.g., 2.5 cm (1") for *Calluna* (Heather) and 10 cm (4") for *Cornus alba* cvs. (Red-bark or Tatarian Dogwood).

Reducing the leaf lamina by trimming during preparation is now falling out of favor because it provides an easy entry point for disease infection. However, it is unavoidable with some foliage, but it is better to remove whole leaves where possible so that leaf trimming is kept to a minimum (see Chapter 12).

NODAL CUTTING

Examples: *Abelia, Cornus* (Dogwood), *Deutzia, Prunus* and *Viburnum.*

This is the most common technique and refers to the cutting of the soft shoot tip just beneath a node. These cuttings are sometimes referred to as shoot tips as well as soft tip nodal cuttings. This method is used particularly for the new growth of shoots following bud burst—particularly when taking cuttings from production crops. Some plants, e.g., *Trachelospermum* (Star Jasmine), exude a sticky latex when cut and the knife blade will need wiping regularly with a rag or pad soaked in a proprietary alcohol-based solvent.

The soft tip of the cutting is often removed for other reasons, including:—

(i) It is susceptible to disease infection.

(ii) It contains flower buds.

(iii) To encourage early side shoot development following rooting.

Figure 8-6.
A (left). Prepared softwood cuttings of *Weigela florida* 'Foliis Purpureis' (Old-fashioned Weigela cv.) (left) and *Deutzia* sp. (right). B. (right). Prepared softwood cuttings of *Forsythia* × *intermedia* cv. (Border Forsythia) (left) and *Spiraea* × *vanhouttei* (Bridal-wreath Spirea) (right).

Procedure

1. Where required, strip or cut off potential cuttings from a shoot and discard remainder.

2. Make a clean cut just beneath a node and remove the soft tip if required.

3. Remove sufficient leaves so that the lower leaves are not in contact with the rooting medium after sticking. (Note that this is not always possible with some larger-leaved cuttings.)

NOTE:—It is generally best to reverse steps 2 and 3 when wounding of the cuttings is carried out.

4. Wound difficult-to-root cuttings and reduce the leaf lamina area if necessary (remembering that cut leaf surfaces can encourage disease pathogens).

5. Apply rooting hormone, stick and move to aftercare facility as soon as possible.

BASAL CUTTING

Practical experience has shown that many species taken as softwood cuttings survive and root better if they are prepared as basal cuttings. The very base of the cutting is firm and lignified but the cutting itself has not entered the semi-ripe wood phase (p. 297). The shoot is severed flush with the older wood on the adjoining stem. Every attempt should be made to include the closely packed nodes at the base of the young shoot. A hard-trimmed heel cutting would give a similar result. Species that benefit from the use of basal cuttings include *Acer palmatum* cvs. (Japanese Maple), deciduous Azalea, *Cornus* (Dogwood), *Exochorda* (Pearlbush), *Prunus* (Cherry, etc.) and *Viburnum*.

Figure 8-7. A (left). Removal of a basal softwood cutting from a stem of *Acer palmatum* 'Shindeshojo' (Japanese Maple cv.). B (right). Prepared cutting of *A. palmatum* 'Shindeshojo'. Note the region of compressed nodes at the stem base (indicated by the arrow).

INTERNODAL CUTTING

Internodal cuttings are used under the following circumstances:—

(i) Where the plant is so easy to root that it makes no difference whether or not it is cut at a node. For example, *Hydrangea macrophylla* subsp. *macrophylla* (Hortensia or Garden Hydrangea) and *Rubus calycinoides* (Taiwan Creeping Rubus).

(ii) For cuttings with extremely short internodes and numerous leaves so that it is just not practical to locate the node each time a cutting is made. Some cuttings will be severed at a node as they are cut or pinched at random; for example, heathers.

Procedure

Make a clean cut between two nodes and then proceed as for nodal cuttings.

Procedure for Heathers

1. Use finger and thumb of either one or both hands to sever 2.0–2.5 cm (¾–1″) long cuttings from non-flowering shoots on stock material and place into collection bag.

2. Stick cuttings into the flat without further preparation.

Alternatively, remove short multiple shoots and prepare individual cuttings from these in the propagation shed.

SINGLE NODE ("LEAF BUD") CUTTING

Single node cuttings are particularly useful when a maximum number of cuttings are required from the propagation material available, or where the cuttings are too large if taken by other techniques. Nodal cuttings of *Magnolia* × *soulangiana* cvs. (Chinese or Saucer Magnolia) can be impractical to handle when there are long internodes and large leaf laminas. This makes single node cuttings a useful alternative. However, they can be difficult to over-winter unless rooted early in the season. This may result in a smaller liner.

Single node cuttings consist of a stem section and a single or double pair of buds and leaves. The stem must be of sufficient length to anchor the cutting into the rooting medium. Therefore, species with medium to long internodes are most suitable for this technique. The prepared cutting should have a minimum stem length of 2.5 cm (1″) to avoid dislodgement while rooting. Medium to heavy pruning of stock plants will help to ensure the maximum number of cuttings with good internodes.

It is vital that the axillary bud or buds are kept alive for this technique to be successful. If the bud dies, the cutting will fail to grow, even though it has rooted, unless an adjacent bud is present. Therefore, particular care should be given during the aftercare period to prevent disease infection (see p. 378). *Clematis* is particularly prone to damping-off and decay of the buds, so care is needed to prevent excess water build-up if using mist propagation. Avoid overlapping of the leaves when sticking. Not only do the cuttings look tidier if all the leaves are in one plane, but it can also reduce the possibility of water collecting between the overlapping leaves and around the buds. Cuttings of *Parthenocissus* (Woodbine) should be checked to ensure that the buds in the leaf axils are not "blind", otherwise shoots will not grow away after rooting.

There are two types of single node cuttings.

1. Cuttings Containing a Single Bud

This type of single node cutting contains a stem section, a single bud and a leaf. Examples include species and cultivars of *Actinidia, Ampelopsis* (Pepper Vine), *Campsis* (Trumpet Creeper), *Magnolia, Passiflora* (Passion Flower) and *Vitis* (Grape).

Procedure

1. Make a sloping cut just above an axillary bud and an internodal cut about 2.5–3.0 cm (1–1¼″) below the base of a leaf petiole.

2. Repeat this procedure along the stem, discarding any surplus stem sections.

3. Discard the soft growing tip.

4. Wound the cuttings on the side opposite to the bud, if applicable.

5. Reduce the leaf area (e.g., *Magnolia*) or the number of leaflets (e.g., *Campsis*, Trumpet Creeper), if required.

6. Apply rooting hormone, stick and move to aftercare facility as soon as possible.

2. Cuttings Containing Two Opposite Buds

This type of single node cutting includes a stem section with a pair of opposite buds and a pair of leaves. The leaf may be reduced during preparation. Examples include *Clematis* and *Lonicera* (Honeysuckle). Additional cuttings may be made by splitting them down the center, but remember that they will then be more prone to damping-off.

Figure 8-8. A (left). Prepared softwood cuttings of *Erica carnea* cv. (Spring Heather). B (right). Prepared softwood cuttings of *Calluna vulgaris* cv. (Scotch Heather).

Figure 8-9. A (left above). Prepared single node cuttings of *Ampelopsis vitifolia* (left) and *Parthenocissus henryana* (right). B (left below). Prepared single node cuttings of *Rubus tephrodes* (left) and *Stauntonia hexaphylla* (right). C. (right above). Rooted single node cutting of *Actinidia kolomikta* (Kolomikta Actinidia).

Procedure

1. Begin from the base of the shoot, making a horizontal cut just above a pair of buds and an internodal cut about 2.5–3.0 cm (1–1¼") below the base of the leaf petioles. A very short length of stem can be left above the buds to reduce damage to the bud tip while making the horizontal cut.

2. Repeat the procedure up the shoot, discarding any surplus stem sections.

3. Discard the soft growing tip, except with species, e.g., *Lonicera* (Honeysuckle), in which it may be used as a soft tip nodal cutting.

4. Wound the cuttings if required—it is not necessary to wound *Lonicera* (Honeysuckle), and *Clematis* only if they have previously been found to be difficult to root.

5. Reduce the leaf area or number of leaflets if required.

6. Apply rooting hormone, stick and move to aftercare facility as soon as possible.

DOUBLE NODAL CUTTING

The basal cut is made just beneath a node instead of between the nodes, so that each cutting will have two pairs of opposite buds. This technique has been found successful with *Clematis* and climbing *Lonicera* (Honeysuckle) as it encourages two shoots to arise below ground level. These can act as a back-up if buds fail to grow away from the upper pair, and a multi-stemmed plant is encouraged earlier in the production cycle if all four break.

Figure 8-10. Prepared double node cutting (with 2 opposite buds) of a large-flowered hybrid *Clematis* cv. (left) and of *Lonicera tragophylla* (Chinese Honeysuckle) (right).

HEEL CUTTING

Traditionally, a heel cutting is formed when the basal part of the cutting contains a small section (the "heel") of older wood. This older wood is normally from the previous season's growth. The technique is useful under the following circumstances:—

(i) When numerous shoots of roughly the same length arise from a stem. This is occasionally useful for shoots between 5–10 cm (2–4") in length. For example, *Abelia* and *Symphoricarpos* (Snowberry).

(ii) For softwood cuttings that are particularly prone to rotting off at the base (see p. 269). For example, soft nodal cuttings of *Cotinus coggygria* 'Royal Purple' (Purple Smoke Tree) tend to bleed after preparation.

(iii) For shoots with very large leaf laminas that are clumsy to handle if taken as nodal tip cuttings. For example, *Catalpa bignonioides* 'Aurea' (Golden Indian Bean) and *Actinidia chinensis* (Kiwi Vine or Chinese Gooseberry).

(iv) To encourage additional shoots to arise from the base of plants that have small dormant accessory buds around the main axillary bud. I find this method to be particularly useful when propagating Hybrid Tea, Floribunda and species roses from cuttings. It will produce an attractive container plant with basal shoots forming early in the production cycle. [The root system is considerably more fibrous compared to plants budded or grafted onto seed-raised rootstocks.]

Procedure

The different methods used to prepare heel cuttings are as follows.

Method I

e.g., roses, dwarf *Picea* (Spruce)

See section on heel cuttings of semi-ripe wood and evergreen hardwood (p. 303) as the method used is more widely used for evergreen shrubs and conifers. It is particularly important with roses to remove the soft tip as this portion is susceptible to damping-off diseases.

Method II

e.g., *Cotinus coggygria* 'Royal Purple' (Purple Smoke Tree)

Carefully strip the leaves from the cuttings, leaving the heels untrimmed, prior to sticking. The leaves should be removed with a knife if there is any risk of damage to the stem tissue. This method should be tried only if both Method I and nodal cuttings have been found to be unsatisfactory.

Method III

e.g., *Actinidia chinensis* (Kiwi Vine or Chinese Gooseberry), *Catalpa bignonioides* 'Aurea' (Golden Indian Bean)

The young shoots arising in late spring from the older wood are removed when they are about 10 cm (4") long, well before the leaves are fully developed. The cuttings are severed with a hard-trimmed heel from the stock plant.

This method has the disadvantage with some species that it may remove buds surrounding the axillary bud in the leaf axil, unless there are other latent buds on the stems. It is, therefore, important to later encourage replacement shoots on the stock plants.

The details for removing basal leaves, wounding, sticking and moving to the propagation facility are as for nodal cuttings.

Figure 8-11. This stage of growth is a convenient time to make softwood heel cuttings of *Actinidia chinensis* (Kiwi Vine or Chinese Gooseberry).

SEMI-RIPE WOOD AND EVERGREEN HARDWOOD CUTTINGS

The shoot passes from the softwood phase into the semi-ripe wood phase as the tissues become lignified and summer dormancy commences. The term semi-ripe wood (or semi-hardwood) is used for cuttings propagated at this stage. The use of semi-ripe wood and evergreen hardwood cuttings is an important propagation method for many conifers and broad-leaved evergreens, while semi-ripe wood cuttings also serve as a useful back-up method for many easy-to-root deciduous shrubs normally propagated by softwood cuttings.

Semi-ripe wood cuttings can be subdivided into two groups based on the degree of lignification:—

1. Soft semi-ripe wood—Summer dormancy has not begun so that the shoot is still growing, but the lower region of the stem is becoming lignified. For example, *Cotinus coggygria* cvs. (Smoke Tree) in early July.

2. Firm semi-ripe wood—The shoot has virtually stopped growing following the onset of summer dormancy and the whole stem is undergoing varying stages of lignification. For example, *Buddleia* spp. (Butterflybush) and *Rhododendron* in mid-August.

The wood becomes much firmer and is usually virtually fully lignified by late fall and winter. Evergreen cuttings are best referred to as evergreen hardwood cuttings at this phase (as distinct from deciduous hardwood cuttings (Chapter 9) which are leafless at this time of year). This type of cutting is the primary method used for conifers and broad-leaved evergreens.

Semi-ripe wood and evergreen hardwood cuttings have been merged into the same section for the purposes of this text. This is because the methods of preparing the cuttings for sticking are usually identical and they normally have similar propagation facility and aftercare requirements.

Time of Year

1. Deciduous Shrubs

The easy-to-root softwoods, such as *Forsythia, Deutzia, Philadelphus* (Mock-orange), *Physocarpus* (Ninebark), *Kolkwitzia* (Beautybush) and *Weigela*, are simple to root as semi-ripe wood cuttings during the summer. They are deciduous and therefore it is not advisable to continue rooting after late August/first week in September because their chances of successfully overwintering are reduced due to insufficient root development occurring prior to leaf fall.

2. Evergreen Shrubs and Conifers

Most evergreen shrubs and conifers are considerably more flexible in the time during which they can be rooted than are those species propagated from softwood cuttings. Some *Chamaecyparis* (False Cypress), *Juniperus* (Juniper), evergreen *Prunus, Skimmia* and *Aucuba* can be successfully rooted from September to February as semi-ripe wood or evergreen hardwood cuttings. On the other hand, some are much more specific, for example, *Osmanthus, Garrya* (Silktassel), *Laurus* (Laurel), *Ilex* (Holly) and some *Rhododendron* species and hybrids. I have found that these root better as firm semi-ripe wood cuttings in late August to early October when the wood has not fully ripened.

A problem with some evergreen shrubs is that they are subject to leaf drop during the rooting process, thus severely reducing the overall success rate. The reasons for this are:—

(i) Stress caused by high air temperatures and reduced humidity. This can occur frequently under mist propagation.

(ii) Air temperature becoming excessively high, even though there is high humidity. Evergreen *Ceanothus* (California-lilac) are particularly prone to these conditions when rooting under a polyethylene film covering in a closed case facility. The leaves turn partially yellow and drop off. Shading will assist in reducing air temperatures and help to maintain optimum relative humidity levels.

(iii) Excessive overhead misting, which encourages leaching of nutrients from the leaves (see p. 150) and waterlogging of the rooting medium.

(iv) Cuttings prepared from shoots collected from stock plants that have received a prolonged period of cold weather. Some natural leaf fall occurs in spring following a period of extended cold weather and this leaf drop effect is re-created in the "artificial" propagation environment. *Ilex* (Holly), *Elaeagnus* and *Osmanthus* are particularly prone to this. Correct timing of collection virtually ensures that this problem is avoided with these three species. On the other hand, some propagators have found that rooting of *Juniperus* (Juniper) and *Taxus* (Yew) cuttings is improved in January/February after some prolonged cold weather.

Some evergreens rooted in the fall or winter sometimes show delayed and/or erratic bud break in the following spring. For example, leaf bud cuttings of *Mahonia* spp. (Oregon-grape) and *Clematis armandii* (Evergreen Clematis). Two possible reasons for this are, firstly, the time of year that the cutting is rooted, and secondly, absorption of the rooting hormone into the axillary bud. Nurseries in British Columbia have experienced this problem when direct sticking *Prunus laurocerasus* 'Otto Luyken' (Cherry Laurel cv.). They found that rooting this cultivar in September/October results in a pronounced delayed bud break, while normal bud break occurs after rooting in late December. A likely explanation for this is that the cuttings rooted in early fall did not receive a sufficient cold period because they were over-wintered in a protected structure, while the cuttings prepared in late December were collected from outdoor stock plants that had already received a sufficiently long cold spell to prevent bud break delay. [*Prunus laurocerasus* 'Otto Luyken' is one of the broad-leaved evergreen shrubs that will root without basal heat when stuck in September/October in a low polyethylene tunnel sited within a polyethylene-clad greenhouse.]

Finally, the comments below may prove helpful when propagating from semi-ripe wood and/or evergreen hardwood cuttings:—

1. Standardize treatments given to cuttings of different species, and aim for a through-put of two crops of cuttings through the facility during fall and winter. (Some species will only allow one crop of cuttings during this period.)

2. Advance the propagation dates by up to 6–8 weeks (see p. 271) for cuttings that present difficulty in producing roots or suffer from leaf drop problems. Late August to early October has proved an excellent time for propagating *Elaeagnus pungens* 'Maculata' (Golden Elaeagnus), *E.* × *ebbingei* (Ebbinge's Silverberry), *Osmanthus delavayi* (Delavay Osmanthus), *Garrya elliptica* (Coast Silk-tassel) and many cultivars of *Camellia* and *Ilex aquifolium* (English Holly).

3. If late summer and early fall rooting proves difficult, success is sometimes achieved by rooting in January/February or even just a few weeks before bud break. Also, remember that summer softwood cuttings are feasible for some evergreens.

4. Increasing the hormone concentrations and/or changing the rooting medium components and ratios may help.

5. If erratic and/or delayed bud break occurs, it is important to keep the rooting medium dry following rooting and to maintain the over-wintering air temperature in the region of 4°C (40°F) for as long as possible. This will help to ensure that the rooted cuttings receive a "winter chill". Early propagation helps to ensure that this can be carried out with minimal risk to the cuttings. Spraying the cuttings with gibberellic acid (GA$_3$) does offer a solution for very difficult species, but no positive recommendation can currently be given. Reducing the strength of the rooting hormone and using powders instead of solutions have also been suggested as methods to overcome this problem.

Collection of Cuttings

Ideally, cuttings are selected from permanent stock plants in open ground or under protection. Remember that broad-leaved evergreens can be particularly susceptible to wind and exposure, which damages leaf tissue and reduces growth. Shade house protection is particularly useful for *Camellia, Rhododendron, Pittosporum, Photinia, Pieris* and *Mahonia japonica* forms (Japanese Mahonia). Regular checks need to be made to ensure that the wood and leaves are free from scale, red spider mite and mealy bug. Shoots of variegated plants that have reverted should be rejected.

A more recent problem has been the increasing infection by a bacterial disease caused by *Pseudomonas* spp. and *Coryneum* on *Prunus laurocerasus* 'Otto Luyken' (Cherry Laurel cv.) under high rainfall and overhead irrigation conditions, causing "shot-hole" on the leaf lamina and stem die-back. This problem is aggravated by taking cuttings from a production crop grown under overhead irrigation. The problem can be reduced by taking cuttings from open-ground stock plants or from well-grown crops grown on capillary sand beds. *Glomerella cingulata* (Glomerella Blight) has recently become a problem on *Berberis julianae* (Wintergreen Barberry), causing shoot die-back and defoliation. Infection has been reduced by spraying in summer with prochloraz (Sportak®) at an optimum of 500 ppm and by ensuring that there is good drainage during the winter to keep the root system healthy.

Semi-ripe wood and evergreen hardwood cuttings are less apt to show visible signs of lack of turgidity compared to softwood cuttings, but it is wrong to assume that the collection and handling can be carried out more casually—many broad-leaved evergreens are particularly prone to suffer from desiccation. Rapid collection, careful handling and speedy sticking must be practiced. If frosted material must be collected, put the shoots in bags and place them in a cool structure to thaw out slowly before preparing the cuttings. Cuttings are best collected in polyethylene bags or moist hessian sacks, and stored in cool or cold storage facilites if it is necessary to hold them over.

Figure 8-12. Maintaining cutting quality during selection, preparation and aftercare is a primary factor in producing a well-graded, uniform conifer crop. (Reproduced by courtesy of Efford Experimental Horticulture Station, Lymington, Hampshire, U.K.)

Handling and Disease Protection

The same principles of handling softwood cuttings to prevent disease infection and loss of cuttings also apply to semi-ripe wood and evergreen hardwood cuttings, even though water loss is slower. Removal of damaged or diseased material during cutting preparation, drenching the cuttings and rooting medium with fungicide immediately after sticking, and back-up fungicidal drenches of both cuttings and rooting medium during aftercare should all be among the routine practices and subject to constant quality-control supervision.

Propagation Facility and Immediate Aftercare

Soft semi-ripe wood cuttings are conveniently rooted in mist, fogging or closed case facilities. Firm semi-ripe wood and evergreen hardwood cuttings are usually rooted in cold frames, mist or closed case facilities. Recently, there has been renewed interest in modifications to the traditional closed case facility for use in rooting broad-leaved evergreens and conifers. Polyethylene film is either laid in direct contact with the upper leaf surface or supported on a wooden or metal framework so that it lies a few centimeters above the cuttings (see p. 261).

Guidelines for the aftercare of the cuttings are:—

1. The optimum rooting medium temperature for mist and closed case facilities is between 15–21°C (59–70°F), depending on the species, ripeness of wood and health status. However, many easy-to-root species will root equally well at a lower range of 12–15°C (54–59°F) (see p. 138). Cold frames are normally left unheated. Recent research has shown that many species show considerable tolerance of reduced basal temperature. This reduction reduces energy costs while yielding very satisfactory rooting results. The air temperature can be reduced down to 2–5°C (35–41°F), which is still high enough to prevent the cuttings of many species from becoming frosted.

2. Avoid stress to the cuttings caused by variations in air temperatures and humidity levels. Such variations will lead to leaf drop and subsequent deterioration of the cuttings. A further reason for stress, particularly with mist propagation, is excessive overhead application of water droplets through the misting nozzles. This leads, firstly, to leaf drop caused by the leaching of nutrients from the cuttings, and secondly, encourages rotting of the cuttings due to water-logging of the rooting medium. Shading is also important—particularly in sunny weather when rooting under polyethylene film (see p.162).

3. Check frequently for fungal diseases, taking routine precautions—particularly for diseases where infection enters through severing of the leaf lamina (p. 277 and p. 377). One problem that may arise with × *Cupressocyparis leylandii* (Leyland Cypress) and other species when high ratios of peat moss are used in the rooting medium is damage caused by sciarid fly larvae (fungus gnats). The larvae of this pest enter through the basal cut surface and then burrow up the cuttings. Subsequent fungal infection is encouraged, resulting in rotting of the cuttings.

4. As described under softwood cuttings, mist propagation units must be checked daily for dry areas within the rooting medium, dead leaves and debris. Closed case and cold frame systems should be inspected at least once or twice a week.

A more detailed account of aftercare and maintenance procedures is described in the relative sections dealing with propagation facilities (Chapter 3).

Types of Cuttings

The procedures for preparing most deciduous semi-ripe wood cuttings are fundamentally the same as for softwood cuttings. Refer to the section on softwood cuttings (p. 289) for further detailed information.

The general rules for preparing evergreen shrub and conifer cuttings include:—

(i) Compared to softwood cuttings, more emphasis is placed on wounding cuttings because the stem has a greater physical resistance to the emergence of roots.

(ii) Precision-made pruners are an excellent alternative to a knife for many large-leaved evergreens, particularly when the wood is very hard and thorns must be removed.

(iii) Unripened shoot tips should be removed, especially when a cold frame is used as the propagation facility.

(iv) Flower buds should be removed where practical (see p. 277).

(v) Many evergreens lend themselves to stripping of the leaves with the thumb and first finger. However, the stripping should be done with a knife or pruners if there is any risk of tearing the stem.

(vi) Do not reduce the leaf area of plants susceptible to *Pestalotiopsis (Pestalotia)* and *Monochaetia* whenever possible, because the cut surface provides an initial infection source.

NODAL CUTTING

Deciduous and Broad-leaved Evergreens

Procedure

1. Where required, strip off or cut potential cuttings from shoots and discard remainder.

2. Remove sufficient leaves so that the lowest leaves will not be in contact with the rooting medium when stuck. Snap off or rub out flower buds with the thumb and first finger. Alternatively, cut off with a knife or pruners.

3. Make a clean cut just beneath a node.

NOTE:—Depending on the plant being propagated, it is generally preferable to reverse the order of steps 2 and 3 if wounding is not carried out, e.g., *Hypericum calycinum* (Aaron's-beard).

4. Wound cutting and reduce leaf lamina area depending upon species and nursery policy on disease control.

5. Apply rooting hormone, stick and move to aftercare facility as soon as possible.

Conifers

European nurseries tend to use shorter cuttings (light cutting) than is the common practice in North America. The optimum length for a vigorous *Chamaecyparis* (False Cypress), *Juniperus* (Juniper) and *Thuja* (Arborvitae) cutting in Europe is between 10–12.5 cm (4–5″), while in North America it is often between 12.5–17.5 cm (5–7″). Three reasons for the larger cutting (heavy cutting) used in North America are the larger and deeper flats that are traditionally used, the wider use of direct sticking, and the emphasis on obtaining a heavy liner in one growing season after propagation.

North American propagators often prepare cuttings by pruning them to remove the leader (p. 277). This practice allows better penetration of overhead misting or watering to the flats, reduces overlapping of foliage, and is, in fact, the first pruning which, combined with the large cutting, promotes a quality liner. Leader shoots will develop later. This pruning procedure is particularly effective for × *Cupressocyparis leylandii* (Leyland Cypress), *Juniperus* (Juniper) and *Thuja* (Arborvitae).

Either one of two types of conifer nodal cuttings is normally used.

(a) "Light" Cutting

An excellent rule of thumb is to allow for 1.3 cm (½") of ripened wood at the base of the cutting. This is the area where the stem color is normally yellow-brown—i.e., the halfway stage between the green and the fully brown wood. This distance is usually roughly equivalent to the length of 2 scales down the stem in × *Cupressocyparis leylandii* (Leyland Cypress) and many *Chamaecyparis* (False Cypress), *Thuja* (Arborvitae) and *Juniperus* (Juniper). This procedure helps to standardize the length of cuttings and promotes more even rooting.

(b) "Heavy" Cutting

The longer, heavy cutting often means going into well-ripened wood of the previous season's growth, and even occasionally into three-year-old wood. This procedure is satisfactory for the easier-to-root conifers, but variable results are much more likely to occur on the difficult-to-root forms, with excess callusing and uneven rooting—e.g., *Juniperus scopulorum* cvs. (Rocky Mountain Juniper). Results can be improved by wounding and applying higher hormone concentrations.

Favorable climates, such as that of west coast North America, combined with the heavy pruning techniques used on the production crops does mean that there is often sufficient extension growth to take a heavy cutting with a minimum of ripened wood at the base.

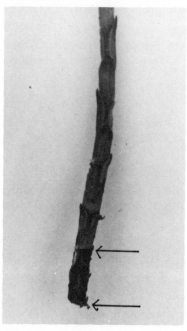

Figure 8-13.
Close-up of the stem base of a conifer cutting showing about 1.3 cm (½") of ripened wood (indicatd by the arrows).

Figure 8-14.
Prepared cutting of a conifer. Note that this "heavy" cutting has a considerable amount of the previous year's wood at the base.

Procedure

The sequence is similar to that for broad-leaved evergreen nodal cuttings, but the additional comments below will be useful:—

1. Pruners are particularly useful for heavier cuttings. A horizontal cut is made across the tip to remove about 1/4–1/5 of the total length of the stem and foliage.

2. Stripping the leaves normally causes sufficient wounding on easy-to-root cultivars, except when the cutting is made from old wood. It is beneficial to slice (heavy wound) or incision wound (light wound) *Taxus* (Yew), *Juniperus virginiana* cvs. (Eastern Red Cedar), *J. scopulorum* cvs. (Rocky Mountain Juniper), *Cupressus macrocarpa* cvs. (Monterey Cypress) and × *Cupressocyparis leylandii* (Leyland Cypress).

HEEL CUTTING

Heel cuttings of semi-ripe wood and evergreen hardwood are useful for many evergreen shrubs and conifers, particularly those in which the growth habit produces a series of side shoots along the stem. In practice, it is usual to augment heel cuttings with nodal cuttings for some species. Shoots that are too long for a heel cutting are made into a nodal cutting. Similarly, a long, vigorous, vegetative side shoot can be made into, for example, three nodal cuttings of which the lowest one will be a heel cutting. Heel cuttings are very useful for cold frame propagation. Evergreens that lend themselves to heel cuttings include *Cotoneaster, Pernettya, Myrtus* (Myrtle), *Pittosporum, Ilex crenata* cvs. (Japanese Holly), dwarf *Picea* (Spruce) and *Taxus* (Yew), as well as *Chamaecyparis pisifera* cvs. (Sawara Cypress).

Procedure

Method I

1. Pull off all side shoots from stems so that a heel remains attached to the base of the cutting.

2. Strip off lower leaves with thumb and first finger. Use a knife or pruners if the stem tissue tears.

3. Cut through the heel with a knife so that there is a smooth cut across the entire stem base. A common fault is to just trim off the thin end of the heel, leaving the remainder untrimmed. This can encourage basal stem rots—particularly in cold frame propagation. Unskilled staff should be trained to cut the entire heel cleanly. Thumb pads are advised if the heels are tough to cut through—for example, *Cotoneaster microphyllus* (Small-leaved or Rockspray Cotoneaster or Rockspray).

4. Wound cutting and remove unripened tip, if required.

5. Apply rooting hormone, stick and quickly move to aftercare facility.

Figure 8-15.
Prepared heel cuttings of *Arctostaphylos uva-ursi* 'Vancouver Jade' (left), *Microbiota decussata* (Russian Cypress) (center) and *Hebe pimeleoides* 'Quicksilver' (right).

Figure 8-16.
An incorrectly prepared heel cutting. Note that only the end of the heel was trimmed during preparation. The knife *must* be taken right through the stem base.

Method II

This method is appropriate if the sideshoots grow in a symmetrical pattern—e.g., *Cotoneaster horizontalis* (Rock Cotoneaster or Rockspray) and *C. microphyllus.*

The side shoots are not removed as heels and then prepared individually. Instead, the base of the shoot is held away from the operator who works the knife up the stem, removing each shoot with a small, rounded, prepared heel.

SINGLE NODE ("LEAF BUD") CUTTING

Single node cuttings provide a very useful procedure for propagating specific evergreen shrubs, such as *Camellia* and *Mahonia* (Oregon-grape). Pruners are ideal for preparing *Mahonia* cuttings. However, it is essential to ensure that the maximum extension growth of the current year's shoots is obtained. This is achieved by heavy pruning of stock plants grown in a shade house (p. 255). Another technique for *Camellia* is to cut back the current year's growth on the liner crop to 2 or 3 buds above soil level. This does, however, mean that it is likely that the crop will require a further year in the production cycle.

However, *Camellia* single node cuttings should only be used as an alternative method during periods of scarce stock material. Single node cuttings can produce poorly-branched plants that will take one or more seasons longer to develop to saleable quality than vigorous nodal stem cuttings with 3–4 leaves.

Procedure

1. Make a sloping cut just above the axillary bud and an internodal cut about 2.5–3.0 cm (1–1¼") below the base of the leaf petiole. It is not always possible in evergreens to obtain the required length of internode, therefore care is needed not to dislodge the cuttings when sticking and handling.

2. This procedure is repeated along the stem, discarding any surplus stem sections.

NOTE:—The stem tip is made into a nodal cutting. A nodal cutting with 2 fully expanded leaves is used for *Camellia,* while the leaf area is reduced for *Mahonia.* The larger cuttings of *Mahonia* are ideal for direct sticking into a liner pot.

3. The cuttings are wounded on the opposite side to the bud.

4. The number of leaflets is reduced to 2 pairs where required, e.g., *Mahonia.*

5. Apply rooting hormone (not always necessary with *Mahonia*), stick and quickly move to the aftercare facility.

Figure 8-17. Prepared single node cutting of *Camellia.* Note that the cutting has been slice wounded on the side opposite to the bud.

Figure 8-18. Prepared mallet cutting of a *Berberis* sp. (Barberry).

MALLET CUTTING

The mallet cutting is a traditional method of propagation for evergreen or deciduous hardwood material that has now been largely superceded by heel and nodal cuttings. However, the method is still occasionally used and so a brief explanation is necessary. A number of propagators find that the preparation of mallet cuttings significantly reduces the output compared to nodal and heel cuttings.

Mallet cuttings are prepared so that the base contains a complete "section" of the previous season's growth rather than just a sliver of older tissue as in a heel cutting. It is important that the stock plants are pruned back heavily each winter to obtain quality mallet cuttings. They are particularly useful when rooting deciduous and evergreen *Berberis* (Barberry) in cold frames because the extra amount of ripened wood contains increased food reserves and thus helps to keep the cutting alive during the winter. It is also a technique used as a back-up to summer propagation of deciduous *Berberis* (Barberry) if further cuttings are required to meet target production figures. The long, vigorous vegetative shoots of *Berberis* × *ottawensis* 'Superba' and *B.* × *stenophylla* (Rosemary Barberry) provide enough stem length to enable nodal cuttings to be taken from the area above the mallet cuttings. The shorter shoots of *Berberis thunbergii* 'Rose Glow' (Japanese Barberry cv.), *B. darwinii* (Darwin Barberry) and *B. verruculosa* (Warty Barberry) will make excellent mallet cuttings but less material is left over for nodal cuttings.

The preparation of mallet cuttings should be carried out with sharp pruners—ones with thin pointed cutting blades are ideal. The work requires a reasonable amount of dexterity. It is helpful to have a tough glove on one hand when making cuttings from this thorny material.

Procedure

1. Reduce the length of the shoot to 10.0–12.5 cm (4–5").

2. Cut a mallet, 1.3 cm (½") long, from the previous season's wood. Make one cut flush with the stem to ensure that there is not a snag; otherwise, die-back can occur.

3. Remove 3–4 basal sets of leaves and thorns.

4. Wound the cuttings, either underneath the mallet or down one side of the stem and mallet.

5. Mallets that are too large in diameter can be split in two.

6. Apply rooting hormone (it is advantageous to add fungicide to powders), stick and quickly move to cold frame aftercare facility.

REFERENCES AND SUGGESTED SOURCES FOR FURTHER READING

Agricultural Training Board, U.K. no date. *Nursery Stock Propagation—Preparation of Cuttings.* Trainee Guide NSP.1.A.12/TA. Agricultural Training Board, Beckenham, Kent, U.K.

———. no date. *Nursery Stock Production—Softwood and Semi-Mature Cuttings.* Trainee Guide NSP.1.A.12/1. Agricultural Training Board, Beckenham, Kent, U.K.

———. no date. *Nursery Stock Production—Leaf-Bud Cuttings.* Trainee Guide NSP.1.A.12/2. Agricultural Training Board, Beckenham, Kent, U.K.

———. no date. *Nursery Stock Production—Heeled Cuttings.* Trainee Guide NSP.1.A.12/3. Agricultural Training Board, Beckenham, Kent, U.K.

Agriculture Canada. 1982. *Nursery Propagation of Woody and Herbaceous Perennials for the Prairie Provinces.* Publication No. 1733 E. Agriculture Canada, Ottawa, Ontario.

Alberta Agriculture. 1980. *Propagation and Production of Woody Ornamentals in a Small Nursery.* Alberta Agriculture, Edmonton, Alberta.

Baldwin, I. & J. Stanley. 1983. Going native. *GC & HTJ* **194**(26): 12, 14 (December 23/30, 1983).

Hartmann, H. T. & D. E. Kester. 1983. 4th ed. *Plant Propagation: Principles and Practices.* Prentice-Hall, Inc., Englewood Cliffs, N.J.

Lamb, J. G. D., J. C. Kelly & F. J. Nutty. 1972. 5th ed. *Propagation of Trees and Shrubs at Kinsealy.* An Foras Taluntais, Dublin, Eire.

———, J. C. Kelly & P. Bowbrick. 1975. *Nursery Stock Manual.* Grower Books, London, U.K.

Macdonald, A. B. 1973. Production of climbing plants. *Nurseryman & Garden Centre,* April 19, 1973, pp. 584–587.

———. 1974. A programme for rooting cuttings under mist. *Nurseryman & Garden Centre.* July 11, 1974, pp. 44–45; July 25, 1974, pp. 104–105; August 8, 1974, pp. 158–159; August 22, 1974, pp. 211–212; September 5, 1974, pp. 263–264.

———. 1974. Demand increase for conifers. *Gardeners Chronicle/HTJ* **176**(8): 24–27 (August 23, 1974).

_____. 1979. Propagating climbers. *Gardeners Chronicle/HTJ* **185**(21): 14–17 (May 25, 1979).

_____. 1980. Guide to success. *Gardeners Chronicle/HTJ* **187**(24): 19–22 (June 13, 1980).

_____. 1980. Conifers by cuttings. *Gardeners Chronicle/HTJ* **187**(25): 31–33 (June 20, 1980).

_____. 1980. For all seasons. *Gardeners Chronicle/HTJ* **188**(2): 33–34 (July 11, 1980).

_____. 1980. Getting it right. *Gardeners Chronicle/HTJ* **188**(3): 15–16 (July 18, 1980).

McMillan Browse, P.D.A. 1979. *Plant Propagation.* The Royal Horticultural Society's Encyclopaedia of Practical Gardening. Mitchell Beazley Ltd., London, U.K.

_____. 1981. *The Commercial Production of Climbing Plants,* Grower Books, London, U.K.

Ministry of Agriculture, Fisheries & Food, U.K. no date. *The ADAS Potting System.* The ADAS Nursery Stock Group. Ministry of Agriculture, Fisheries and Food, London, U.K.

_____. 1983. *Guide to Pest Control on Hardy Ornamental Trees and Shrubs.* Booklet 2368(83). Ministry of Agriculture, Fisheries and Food, London U.K.

Sheat, W. G. 1957. *Propagation of Trees, Shrubs and Conifers.* Macmillan Ltd., London, U.K.

Wasley, R. 1979. The propagation of *Berberis* by cuttings. *Comb. Proc. Inter. Pl. Prop. Soc.* **29**: 215–216.

Wells, J. S. 1955. *Plant Propagation Practices.* The Macmillan Company, New York.

Chapter 9

DECIDUOUS (LEAFLESS) HARDWOOD CUTTINGS

Hardwood cutting propagation is carried out during the fall and late winter/early spring when growth has ceased and the tissues are ripened. The cutting is thus dormant and secondary thickening is complete.

The range of species successfully propagated by deciduous hardwood cuttings is less than that for either softwood or semi-ripe wood cuttings, but this method plays an important role in the production of ornamentals. The table of specific examples below shows the groups of plants successfully propagated using this technique.

Specimen Trees	*Laburnum* × *watereri* 'Vossii' (Voss' Long-cluster Golden-chain Tree) *Platanus* × *acerifolia* (London Plane) *Populus balsamifera* 'Aurora' (Balsam Poplar cv.) (syn. *P. candicans* 'Aurora') *Prunus cerasifera* 'Atropurpurea' (syn. 'Pissardii') (Purple-leaf Plum) *Salix matsudana* 'Tortuosa' (Corkscrew or Dragon-claw Willow)
Shrubs	*Atriplex halimus* (Mediterranean Saltbush, Sea Orach) *Buddleia davidii* cvs. (Butterflybush) *Cornus alba* cvs. (Red-bark or Tatarian Dogwood *Cornus stolonifera* 'Flaviramea' (Yellow-twig Dogwood) *Deutzia scabra* 'Plena' (Double Rose Deutzia) *Euonymus europaea* (European Spindle Tree) *Forsythia* spp. and cvs. (Forsythia) *Hibiscus syriacus* cvs. (Rose-of-Sharon) *Hypericum patulum* 'Hidcote' (Goldencup St. John's-wort cv.)

	Kerria japonica 'Pleniflora'
	  (Double Japanese Rose)
	Philadelphus × *virginalis* 'Virginal'
	  (Double Mock-orange cv.)
	Physocarpus opulifolius 'Luteus'
	  (Golden Ninebark)
	Rosa rugosa cvs.
	  (Rugosa Rose)
	Sambucus canadensis cvs.
	  (American Elder)
	Sambucus nigra cvs.
	  (European Elder)
	Spiraea × *vanhouttei*
	  (Bridal-wreath Spirea)
	Symphoricarpos spp. and cvs.
	  (Snowberry, Coralberry)
	Tamarix spp. and cvs.
	  (Tamarisk)
	Weigela spp. and cvs.
	  (Weigela)

Conifers	*Metasequoia glyptostroboides* (Dawn Redwood)

Windbreaks	*Populus* × *canadensis* 'Robusta'
	  (False Lombardy Poplar)
	Salix alba 'Drakenburg'
	  (White Willow cv.)

Hedging	*Ligustrum ovalifolium*
	  (California Privet)
	Prunus × *blireiana*
	  (Blireiana Plum)
	Prunus × *cistena*
	  (Purple-leaf Sand Cherry)

Rootstocks	Malling Merton 111 (M.M.111) *Prunus* 'Colt' *Prunus* 'Myrobalan B' *Prunus* 'Pixie' *Prunus* 'St. Julien A' Quince C *Rosa rugosa* 'Scherpe Boskoop' (a.k.a. *R.*. 'Hollandica')

Climbers	*Clematis montana* var. *rubens*
	  (Pink Anemone Clematis)
	Lonicera periclymenum var. *belgica*
	  (Dutch Woodbine or Honeysuckle)
	Polygonum aubertii
	  (Chinese Fleece Vine, Silver Lace
	  Vine)
	Vitis coignetiae
	  (Crimson Glory Vine)
	Vitis vinifera cvs.
	  (Wine Grape)

Deciduous hardwood cuttings are useful both to lighten the summer propagation workload and as a "back-up" in the event of partial failure of summer propagation. The material is dormant and there is therefore considerably more flexibility with its handling—for example, cold storage of unrooted and callused material. This greater flexibility should not be taken to extremes, however, because poor timing and carelessness in handling procedures, which result in losses from desiccation and bud development before planting leading to water stress, will significantly lower the rooting potential. Cuttings can conveniently be prepared in a covered shed as part of the winter work schedule when outdoor work is held up due to bad weather. A further advantage is that relatively unskilled labor can be used to prepare the cuttings. Deciduous hardwood cutting propagation is particularly useful for nurseries with limited propagation facilities because many species propagated in this way root successfully without artificial basal heat.

Production trends during the last decade that have encouraged the growing of nursery stocks from deciduous hardwood cuttings are:—

1. Widening and increasing demand for specific windbreak, hedging and highway material. Ornamental shrubs marketed as pre-packs can be conveniently produced from hardwood, as well as softwood, cuttings.

2. Increased knowledge resulting from research into physiology and rooting hormones, and the sophistication of specific propagation facilities.

3. The technique lends itself to mechanization for preparing cuttings, planting in open ground and for palletizing the actual propagation facility.

4. The move away from the traditional layer bed to more intensive propagation facilities for specific rosaceous rootstocks. This both intensifies propagation and reduces the risk of build-up of soil-borne diseases, e.g., Specific Replant Disease of *Prunus* (Cherry) and Crown Gall (*Agrobacterium tumefaciens*). The collection of "aerial" cuttings breaks the chain in soil-borne diseases if they are then planted in sterilized soil.

5. Large cuttings can be prepared and direct stuck into the selling container, thus shortening the production cycle (see Chapter 13).

FACTORS THAT PROMOTE SUCCESSFUL ROOTING

The following factors are specific for successful rooting of deciduous (leafless) hardwood cuttings.

1. Permanent stock plants, ideally as hedges, should be used to provide cutting material rather than taking cuttings from the production crop.

2. The cuttings should be prepared from well-ripened vigorous wood of the current season's growth that contains a high level of food reserves. The stock plants should be pruned back hard every winter to maintain vigor and cutting quality. In the nursery situation, cuttings from well-established hedges have rooted better than ones removed from hedges during the early years of establishment.

3. The cuttings should be long enough to provide economical use of the shoots, easy handling, and possess sufficient food reserves to support rooting, establishment and production of a plant of the desired shape and quality. The length of the cuttings will be determined largely by the propagation facility, the species/cultivar being rooted, and the nursery's mechanized equipment.

4. As a general rule, time of year plays a major role in success as difficulty in rooting increases. Many easy-to-root species, e.g., *Ribes sanguineum* cvs. (Red-flowering Currant), are very flexible with regard to the time for rooting during the dormant period. Research on more difficult-to-root species has shown that the peak times to encourage rooting are around leaf fall and a few weeks prior to bud burst. The wood is not sufficiently ripened if propagation is carried out too early, while the buds swell and shoot before there is a sufficient, established root system to support them if the cuttings are taken too late.

5. Cold storage facilities are very useful to hold unrooted and callused cuttings before they are next handled. Cold storage is particularly advantageous during the turn of the year because it keeps buds dormant, thus slowing down the loss of food reserves. There is evidence to suggest that a period of longer than about 4 weeks between cutting collection and rooting causes loss of rooting potential or loss of cuttings in subsequent establishment. Storage of rooted cuttings can result in losses from molds and desiccation, even in a well-managed cold store facility.

6. Rooting hormones and their method of application, particularly when applied in solution, can significantly improve results.

7. Fungicides applied to the base of the cutting, with or without hormones, can improve results when rooting in the open ground or in cold frames by reducing losses due to basal stem rots.

8. The aftercare in the propagation facility should provide good aeration to the base of the cutting, while the air temperature should be kept cool to delay bud break. The degree to which this can be done will depend on the propagation facility.

9. Minimize water loss from the cuttings by providing protection, waxing exposed areas or minimizing the length of cutting remaining above soil level. This is particularly important for species that have hollow stems.

10. Continual and detailed attention must be given to the unrooted or callused cuttings in the open ground or containers following lining out or potting. Timing, avoidance of damage to roots, and irrigation all contribute to successful aftercare.

[East Malling Research Station, Kent, England, are now establishing hardwood cuttings of fruit tree rootstocks intensively in raised beds containing the rooting medium with excellent results. The cuttings can be planted in the beds at any time, even after prolonged rain (see p. 333).]

TECHNIQUES USED TO PROPAGATE DECIDUOUS HARDWOOD CUTTINGS

The technique selected for propagating deciduous hardwood cuttings is based essentially on the type of facility selected for aftercare.

OPEN GROUND

The planting of unrooted or callused cuttings in the open ground is the most widely used technique. It is simple and economical, and mechanical aids can be used both in cutting preparation and planting out. Ornamentals successfully raised in the open ground include those tabulated below:—

> *Cornus alba* (Red-bark Dogwood)
> *Forsythia* (Forsythia)
> *Deutzia* (Deutzia)
> *Lonicera* (Honeysuckle)
> *Symphoricarpos* (Snowberry, Coralberry)
> *Spiraea* (Spirea)
> *Sambucus* (Elder)
> *Salix* (Willow)
> *Populus* (Poplar)
> *Ribes* (Flowering Currant)
> *Rosa multiflora* (Baby or Japanese Rose)
> *Rosa rugosa* (Rugosa Rose)
> *Weigela* (Weigela)

Time of Year

Hardwood cuttings of these species will root successfully from late fall until early spring, but the best period is from November through to February. Timing of cutting collection largely depends on the method of subsequent handling of the prepared cuttings.

Preparation of Cuttings

The cuttings are taken from stock plants grown as hedges or stools, selecting well-ripened, vigorous, one-year-old shoots. Traditionally, the cuttings were between 25–30 cm (10–12″) long or even more, but this length can create problems today. The optimum length of cutting should be 15 cm (6″). This shorter length yields more cuttings from each shoot, they are easier to handle and to plant out, and less stem is below soil level so that tractor-drawn undercutting blades can be used more readily. The final grade of the plant relates directly to the caliper and quality of the cutting.

Figure 9-1.
Hardwood cuttings of
many deciduous shrubs
are obtained by pruning
back the hedge to ground
level. Note the uniformity
of the developing shoots.

However, there is no point in taking small cuttings high up a shoot if it has rooting potential only at the base. Numerous small cuttings can only be made in very free-rooting species.

Procedure

1. Discard weak and bent shoots, and remove the unripened tip.

2. Begin from the top of the shoot, using sharp pruners to prepare 15 cm (6″) long cuttings by making a sloping cut away from the tip bud and a horizontal nodal (or internodal) cut to form the base. Make all cuttings of a particular species to a uniform length to expedite subsequent operations. An alternative method is to hold the shoot near the top with one hand and make the respective cuts progressively up the stem from the base, allowing the cuttings to fall into a container below.

The basal cut should be made at a node if the stems are hollow or if rooting has been variable. Anvil (parrot-bill) pruners should not be used as they tend to crush the stem base.

If necessary, the apex of the cutting can be dipped into a dye to indicate the correct polarity for lining out.

Two other methods are sometimes employed to increase output:—

(a) Fix a wooden or solid plastic strip down the length of bench, setting it 15 cm (6″) in from the front edge. The top of the shoot is fed up to the solid strip and held in place. The operator cuts the shoot flush with the edge of the bench. The shoot is fed again and the process repeated until all suitable cuttings have been made from the shoot. Alternatively, hold the shoot or bundle of shoots over the surface of the bench (or flat) in one hand and make the cuttings progressively down the stem. A flat can be placed on the bench so that the cuttings fall directly into it after preparation. Marks can be made on one side of the flat so that the length of cutting can be checked initially, if required.

(b) Install a power-driven bandsaw with a fine cutting surface or a sharp guillotine blade to cut precisely through bundles of shoots. This is a cruder method with less precision, but is successful with very easy rooting plants. It is essential that both hand- and power-driven machines are operated in accordance with local safety regulation requirements.

It is not always feasible to obtain the sloping cut at the tip of the cutting with these methods, therefore both cuts will be horizontal.

3. If the plant species being propagated is to be used as a rootstock and is known to sucker freely (e.g., *Rosa rugosa*, Rugosa Rose), then all buds except the upper two are cut out. This will help to reduce problems of "sucker shoots" arising from below soil level in subsequent years.

[One practice used in British Columbia to provide rootstocks of the thornless *Rosa multiflora* 'Inermis' (Baby or Japanese Rose) is to remove pencil-thickness caliper stems (ca. 6 mm/¼") in late fall and cool store them until February when 25 cm (10") long cuttings are made. All the buds except the top two are removed. The cuttings are dipped in liquid rooting hormone and then planted out in open ground from March through to early April.]

Rooting Hormone Application

It should not be necessary to use a rooting hormone except when unsatisfactory results are obtained when direct-lining cuttings outside or when pre-callusing specific plants (see below). A strength of 0.8% IBA in talc is sufficient.

Subsequent Handling

There are basically two methods of handling the prepared cuttings.

(i) Fall Planting

The cuttings are immediately lined out in the open ground (see p. 314 for procedure). This technique is normally used for easy-to-root material—some of which have pre-formed root initials, e.g., *Salix* (Willow) and *Populus* (Poplar). Other appropriate plants include those tabulated below.

> *Symphoricarpos* (Snowberry, Coralberry)
> *Ribes sanguineum* (Red-flowering Currant)
> *Rosa rugosa* (Rugosa Rose)
> *Rosa multiflora* (Baby or Japanese Rose)
> *Tamarix* (Tamarisk)

Cornus alba cvs. (Red-bark or Tatarian Dogwood) and some *Ligustrum* (Privet) can be added to this list in sheltered or warmer locations.

Fall planting is quite successful providing that the soil is suitable and is prepared for planting, and that sufficient time remains for the cuttings to callus before heavy frosts occur and subsequently to root before bud burst in the next spring. Soils prone to frost heave should be avoided. Forward planning is necessary to ensure that the land is prepared for planting.

(ii) Pre-callusing Prior to Planting Out

The prepared cuttings are pre-callused, to stimulate the early stages of rooting, in a frost-free building prior to planting out in the open ground in the following spring. This technique is superior to direct lining out in the fall under the following circumstances:—

(a) Provides greater flexibility because the cuttings may be held over for planting out until the following year when weather conditions may be better.

(b) Successful establishment is often higher and more consistent because all the cuttings are pre-callused before planting out. Cuttings that are not suitable for planting out can be discarded. Also, the cuttings are not subject to the adverse weather conditions of some locations.

(c) There is never sufficient soil warmth available for some species to root. Basal heat achieves a "threshold stimulus" that is the difference between success and failure.

(d) The range of species suitable for subsequent direct sticking can be increased as the cuttings are not over-wintered in the open ground. The table below tabulates a selection of trees and shrubs successfully propagated by this technique. The species tabulated in the previous list can also be grown using this method.

> *Cornus alba* 'Elegantissima' (Silverleaf Dogwood)
> *Cornus stolonifera* 'Flaviramea' (Yellow-twig Dogwood)
> *Deutzia scabra* 'Plena' (Double Rose Deutzia)
> *Forsythia* × *intermedia* 'Lynwood' (Lynwood Forsythia)
> *Kerria japonica* 'Pleniflora' (Double Japanese Rose)
> *Philadelphus* × *virginalis* (Double Mock-orange)
> *Potentilla fruticosa* cvs. (Shrubby Cinquefoil)
> *Ribes sanguineum* cvs. (Red-flowering Currant)
> *Sambucus canadensis* 'Aurea' (Golden American Elder)

Spiraea × *vanhouttei* (Bridal-wreath Spirea)
Symphoricarpos orbiculatus cvs. (Indian-currant Coralberry)
Weigela florida cvs. (Old-fashioned Weigela)

Pre-Callusing Methods—Three different methods of pre-callusing cuttings to stimulate the early stages of rooting are described below.

Boxes and Flats—The prepared cuttings are tied into bundles of 20–30, with the basal cuts all level, and labelled. Boxes or flats deep enough to hold the cuttings vertically are lined with perforated polyethylene if necessary, and a 2.5 cm (1″) layer of slightly moist peat moss placed along the bottom. The labelled bundles of cuttings are packed vertically into the box, with more peat moss worked in between the bundles as the packing proceeds. Alternatively, cuttings can be laid horizontally to form two layers, again being well-packed with peat moss.

The boxes are then stacked in an unheated building. Good air circulation is provided by placing the bottom row on blocks to raise it above the floor. The air temperature of the building should remain below 3°C (38°F) even if outside temperatures rise.

Faster callusing can be achieved by putting the cuttings into flats which are then placed on a bench or floor area with basal heat at 18°C (65°F) for 3 weeks. The flats are then transferred to an unheated building.

Pits and Floor Beds—Covered pits and floor beds are useful for larger quantities of cuttings. The cuttings are bundled and labelled as previously described and then packed into a medium of either pure sand, bark, sawdust, or a mixture of equal parts of peat moss and sand or peat moss and perlite. A layer of the medium is placed at the base of the pit or on the floor bed. The bundles of cuttings are placed on the medium and additional medium is worked in amongst the bundles as the packing proceeds. The top of the bundles should be just covered by the medium. The moisture content of the medium should be kept very low. Excessive moisture content, such as would occur if the beds are open to the rain, will lead to rotting at the bases of the cuttings.

[One modification occasionally used was to reverse the polarity of the bundles so that the basal cuts were uppermost. A suggested reason for this practice was to delay possible bud break by keeping the tops of the cuttings cooler and at the same time to provide better aeration to the base of the cuttings. The cuttings were planted the right way up after callusing. However, commercial experience in England has shown that excessive die-back from the buried tip of the cutting is likely to occur with this method.]

Straw Bale Bin—This method is particularly useful if there is no shed or other suitable covered area in which to over-winter the cuttings. The straw bale bins are simple and economical to construct. They can, in fact, provide better insulation than many buildings, so the range of species successfully callused this way is relatively extensive. This type of facility helped to contribute to the conception of the modern-day heated bin (see p. 321).

The table below lists additional species found to callus successfully in a straw bale bin.

Holodiscus discolor (Creambush)
Jasminum nudiflorum (Winter Jasmine)
Rhodotypos scandens (Jetbread, White Kerria)
Ribes aureum (Golden Currant)
Sorbaria aitchisonii (Kashmir False Spiraea)
Spiraea × *bumalda* 'Anthony Waterer' (Dwarf Pink Bridal-wreath Spirea)

The bins are constructed with a square of straw bales to give a depth of 60 cm (24″). Wooden panels supported by posts are placed inside the bins to give a degree of permanence, and better insulation is achieved with a 10 cm (4″) thick sheet of polystyrene wrapped in polyethylene between the wood and rooting medium (see also p. 321). The bales can be wrapped in polyethylene as a protection from rain and snow as the bales lose their insulation properties when wet, and to lessen the risk of mice sheltering in the straw.

The shoots are cut to give approximately 15 cm (6″) long nodal cuttings and 0.8% IBA powder applied. The addition of a fungicide to the powder (p. 337) is beneficial.

The cuttings are bundled, labelled, stacked into the bin, and packed vertically into a medium of equal parts of peat and coarse sand. About 1.3 cm (½″) of the cuttings should remain above the medium surface. The medium is again kept on the dry side.

Traditionally, a 5 cm (2″) thatched mat was placed over the bin to keep the contents dry.

Today, a wooden lid insulated on the inner side with expanded polystyrene (Styrofoam®) sheets or "bubble polyethylene" would be a good alternative. The outside of the lid could be covered with polyethylene to shed water.

The cuttings should be checked regularly, particularly for damage by mice which should be poisoned or trapped.

Planting Unrooted and Callused Cuttings In Open Ground

Site, Soil, and Soil Preparation

The site should be well-drained, level and protected against wind, so the provision of shelter will be beneficial to reduce desiccation—particularly following planting and as the new growth breaks. Sites prone to frosts are a problem, particularly for fall planting, because frost heave lifts the cuttings thus causing them to dry out. A good overhead irrigation system is necessary to aid cutting establishment.

The soil should be a well-drained sandy loam that will warm up quickly in the spring and is easily worked—particularly when mechanization is involved. A pH between 5.5–6.5 is suitable for most species.

Perennial weeds must be eliminated, therefore adequate time should be allowed to treat the soil with translocated herbicides (p. 54). A dressing of well-decomposed farmyard manure, up to 75 metric tons per hectare (30 tons/acre), is sometimes used to increase the organic content of the soil and to retain moisture if necessary. This is ploughed in and the land cultivated ready for planting. However, there are likely to be subsequent problems with weeds and increased basal rotting of the cuttings. The incorporation of peat moss is an excellent alternative, if economically possible. Nutritional and pH deficiencies should be rectified with a base dressing.

The timing of planting is often spoiled by soil being too wet. East Malling Research Station have demonstrated that one way to overcome this problem for high value crops is to plant intensively in raised beds filled with a medium consisting of equal parts by volume of peat moss, bark, and fine and coarse sand. A controlled-release fertilizer is incorporated into this medium.

Planting

There are essentially two systems for planting out the cuttings. Firstly, the single row system with the cuttings spaced 7.5 cm (3") apart in 0.8–1 m (28–36") wide rows. This is convenient for both hand planting and inter-row cultivators. Secondly, there is the bed system, which is more efficient because it increases intensity and lends itself to mechanization. Models of tractors, planters, cultivators and lifting equipment are available with the wheels set wide enough apart to straddle over the bed (see p. 56).

A well-tested system used by E. R. Johnson (Nurseries) Ltd., Whixley, York, England, is to plant four-row beds where the cuttings are placed 7.5 cm (3") apart in rows 30 cm (12") apart. This spacing will give approximately 222,000 cuttings per hectare (90,000 per acre). The cuttings are planted by machine at the rate of 6,000 cuttings per hour. They use the hardwood cuttings as a "cleaning crop" for the land as it is very easy to remove the weeds by side-hoeing between the rows. The new growth from the cuttings will later develop over the bed and smother the second crop of weeds.

Three methods of planting are employed, depending on the size of area to be planted and on the equipment available:—

(i) Line and spade—the operators work in pairs with one making the slit while the other plants and firms the cuttings.

(ii) A machine makes the slit or groove in the soil with a sufficient number of rows for each bed, while the operators follow behind to plant and firm in by hand.

(iii) A planting machine both makes the slit and plants, with operators riding on the machine to feed the cuttings into the planting mechanism. Longer cuttings may need adjusting vertically and a final firming by hand.

Problems may arise in determining the polarity of the cuttings, particularly when they are mechanically prepared. (The tips of the bundles can be dipped into a dye that will adhere to the bark, as previously described to deal with this problem.)

The depth to which the cuttings are planted is important for establishment and plant quality. Plant the cuttings so that only 1.3 cm (½") remains above soil surface, both to reduce desiccation and to encourage buds to break from below the soil level. Cuttings planted with half

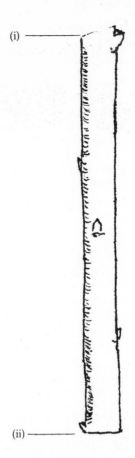

Figure 9-2. Hand planting of open-ground cuttings can be speeded up by planting in slits or grooves made by a tractor-drawn machine.

Diagram 9-1. Diagrammatic representation of a typical deciduous hardwood cutting of a shrub. Note (i) the cut at the apex slopes away from the bud; (ii) the horizontal cut at the base.

the cutting or less below the soil level have a tendency for buds to break just above the surface, thus resulting in a "leggy" plant. However, it is desirable to have a "longer leg" on cuttings planted out as rootstocks as this will allow for budding later.

Heavier soils with a high water content may present a problem with aeration. One suggested technique to help to rectify this problem is to run a layer of sand along the bottom of the planting slit—this is an extra cost but it will improve cutting development. However, experience has shown that this may create a "drain" and so lead to free water remaining around the cutting base for long periods.

Aftercare

Irrigation is necessary after planting to prevent drying out of the cuttings, particularly in the spring. It also helps to firm the soil around the cuttings. The crucial stage is when the shoots break on cuttings that have little or no root system. Cuttings that have been previously cold stored and planted late into the season have to be watched with particular care due to the rapidity of shoot growth.

Weeds compete with the cuttings and will become a problem if left unattended—especially where the bed system is used. Reducing weeds can be tackled in three ways:—

(i) Inter-row cultivators.

(ii) Application of paraquat (Gramoxone®) or phenmedipham (Betanal®) as a contact herbicide, using shielded spray nozzles to avoid drift and damage to other plant material.

(ii) Applications of chlorthal-dimethyl (Dacthal®), oryzalin (Surflan®) or napropamide (Devrinol®) have been successfully used as residual herbicides for open-ground hardwood cuttings. Devrinol® has been particularly effective and seems to be very safe for a wide range of species. Simazine at a rate of 840 g active ingredient per hectare (12 oz a.i./acre) has been used successfully but there is a risk of damage with some species on different soil types. It is very important that residual herbicides be washed in with irrigation following their application—particularly when using Devrinol®.

[Note:—Fumigating the beds with chemical soil-sterilants for soil-borne pests and diseases will also control many weed seeds.]

A top dressing of a 12-8-18 compound fertilizer can be applied in May at a rate of 336 kg per hectare (3 cwt per acre) to encourage growth after the cuttings have rooted. It can also be beneficial to apply a top dressing of fertilizer in June when the new shoot growth is 30–45 cm (12–18") long.

Additional protection may have to be provided on exposed sites to prevent desiccation of the cuttings. Methods that have been used are as follows:—

(i) Dipping the top 2.5 cm (1") of the cutting in molten paraffin wax or petroleum jelly before planting out. Do not allow the temperature of the wax or jelly to exceed 60°C (140°F) or the buds and stems may be damaged.

(ii) Constructing a low, opaque (milky) polyethylene-covered tunnel over the beds as described on p.168. This system is much more appropriate for smaller intensive areas where the beds are less wide. Ventilation can be a problem with tunnels, so film with pre-made holes should be used if possible. It is advisable to run an irrigation line down the length of the tunnel. The polyethylene should be removed when the cuttings are well rooted, otherwise shoot growth will be too soft. (This method is also successful for October-stuck evergreen cuttings such as *Laurus,* Laurel, and *Vinca,* Periwinkle.)

(iii) Constructing a low tunnel using a polypropylene woven shade cloth. This will give better ventilation and allow natural rainfall to reach the cuttings. This method is not appropriate for fall-planted cuttings.

(iv) Fall-planted cuttings requiring winter protection can be covered with straw, and heavy wooden frames made of slatted wood laid on top. Stability can be provided by running two sets of wire over the slats, tying them tightly to a post at each end of the bed. Ensure that precautions are taken against damage by mice.

The usual procedure is to allow the cuttings to remain in the ground for one growing season, and then to prune the shoots back hard near to the crown of the liner. The plants are then undercut and lifted for re-planting out or containerizing. Each shrub liner should have a minimum of three shoots to provide the initial branch framework.

Figure 9-3. Beds of recently planted open-ground hardwood cuttings. Note the use of overhead irrigation to improve establishment. (Denmark)

Figure 9-4. A (left). Rows of *Populus* (Poplar) in the August of the year following sticking of the cuttings in the open ground. (Oakover Nurseries, Ashford, Kent, U.K.) B (right). Open-ground beds of ornamental shrubs lend themselves to mechanized procedures. (H. Clasen Nursery, Pinneberg, West Germany)

COLD FRAMES

Cold frames provide an excellent low-cost facility for rooting leafless hardwood cuttings. Compared to rooting cuttings in the open ground, the added protection results in less risk of desiccation, frost heave or rotting at the base of the cutting. A wider range of deciduous plants can therefore be successfully rooted. The design of cold frames can be found on p. 107.

The table lists a selection of species successfully rooted in cold frames.

> *Buddleia davidii* (Butterflybush)
> *Cornus alba* (Red-bark or Tatarian Dogwood)
> *Deutzia* (Deutzia)
> *Forsythia* (Forsythia)
> *Holodiscus* (Oceanspray)
> *Hypericum patulum* (Goldencup St. John's-Wort)
> *Kerria* (Japanese Rose or Kerria)
> *Leycesteria formosa* (Himalaya Honeysuckle)
> *Metasequoia glyptostroboides* (Dawn Redwood)
> *Philadelphus* (Mock-orange)
> *Physocarpus* (Ninebark)
> *Platanus* × *acerifolia* (London Plane)
> *Potentilla fruticosa* cvs. (Shrubby Cinquefoil)
> *Rubus* (Bramble)
> *Spiraea* (Spirea)
> *Stephanandra* (Stephanandra)
> *Symphoricarpos* (Snowberry, Coralberry)
> *Tamarix* spp. and cvs. (Tamarisk)
> *Viburnum farreri* (Fragrant Viburnum)
> *Weigela* (Weigela)

Frame Bed Preparation

The time for preparation of the frame beds will largely depend on the cropping plan carried out at the nursery. The beds are hand dug or mechanically cultivated from late summer through to early fall, incorporating peat moss and coarse sand so as to provide a rooting medium of approximately equal parts of peat moss, sand and loam. The bed is brought to a tilth and, if desired, can be treated with a soil fumigant such as methyl bromide (see p. 58) to eliminate pests, diseases and most weed seeds. If dazomet (Basamid®) is used, sufficient time must be left to open up the treated beds to release the gas prior to sticking (see p. 57). The loam in the medium may cause aeration and drainage problems—this may be corrected by first spreading a 15 cm (6") deep layer of a pre-mixed rooting medium consisting of equal parts of peat moss and coarse sand over the bottom of the cultivated bed. It may be necessary to deepen the bed by removing some of the base material in order to accommodate the peat/coarse sand mix.

Finally, the beds are leveled and slightly firmed. Frames in cool wet localities should be covered with the lights if the cuttings are not to be stuck immediately. This will keep out rain and raise the temperature of the rooting medium.

Preparation of Cuttings, Hormone Application and Sticking

The cuttings are best made around the time of leaf fall, i.e., from late October through to early November. They are prepared from one-year-old vigorous shoots collected from pruned hedges or stools.

The cuttings should be about 15 cm (6") long, with the basal horizontal cut just beneath a node and a slanting cut (away from the bud) at the apex of the cutting.

A rooting hormone of 0.8% IBA is applied as a powder to the base of the cutting. The risk of basal stem rot can be reduced by incorporating a fungicide such as captan or benomyl (Benlate®) with the rooting powder (see p. 337). The moisture content of the rooting medium can be a critical factor so it should be checked just prior to sticking; it is better to have the medium slightly on the dry side rather than too wet. Work from each side of the frame, or use a planting board, and simply push the cuttings into the frame bed in pre-marked rows. The cuttings should be 5 cm (2") apart within the rows, with 5 cm (2") separating each row. The top 1.3 cm (½") of the cutting should project above the surface of the rooting medium. Use a permanent marker to label each batch of cuttings with name and date of sticking. It is advisable to draw up a plan of the frame bed if there are a number of different cultivars of the same species in it. This will reduce the risk of misidentification.

Aftercare

The cuttings are lightly watered in and the lights placed over the frame. Prolonged periods of sunshine can occur in the fall, therefore it is advisable to spray the glass lights with a shading compound or to secure a length of shade cloth over them. Also, it is important to check regularly for watering needs.

It is vital to check that the rows of lights are firmly secured, otherwise the glass may break when they are lifted. One or two lines of wire fastened to a hook at each longitudinal end of the frame should be sufficient.

Additional protection can be provided during freezing weather by covering the lights with a roll of heavy-grade burlap (hessian) or a proprietary thermal cover product.

The cuttings will likely show some activity by March of the following year, with the buds beginning to swell. It is important not to encourage a flush of growth before sufficient roots have formed. The cuttings should be ventilated during the day, with gradual increase of ventilation during both day and night until the lights are completely removed by late April/early May.

The soft growth after bud break is very susceptible to sun scorch, which quickly causes deterioration of the cuttings. It is therefore advisable to re-shade the cuttings just before bud break. The water requirements of the cuttings will increase as day length increases. A convenient method is to secure an overhead irrigation spray line inside the cold frame. An oscillating spray line or rotating sprinklers can be used to irrigate the frame yard once the lights are removed. This practice eliminates the need to have individual spray lines for each length of cold frame.

The cuttings are allowed to grow for a full growing season in the frames. They are lifted in the fall, and cold stored ready for lining out in the open ground or containerizing the following spring. The majority of ornamental shrubs normally require only one further growing season before selling.

GREENHOUSE FACILITY

As long as shoot growth does not advance too quickly, another method of rooting hardwood cuttings is in a greenhouse with basal heating facilities. This is a convenient method for some ornamental shrubs, e.g., *Euonymus europaea* (European Spindle Tree) and *Hypericum patulum* 'Hidcote' (Goldencup St. John's-wort cv.), and specific deciduous conifers as well as for a number of the climbing vines including *Clematis montana* cvs. (Anemone Clematis), *Lonicera* (Honeysuckle), *Parthenocissus* (Woodbine), *Polygonum* (Fleece Flower), *Vitis* (Grape) and *Wisteria*. Generally, green-

Figure 9-5. A (left). Successful rooting of *Lonicera periclymenum* cvs. (Woodbine) stuck in wooden flats in the greenhouse in December. B. (right). Liners of *Parthenocissus quinquefolia* cvs. (Virginia Creeper) rooted from hardwood cuttings.

house propagation of hardwoods serves as a back-up method for summer softwood propagation.

The hardwood cuttings are rooted from late December through to mid-February. The basal heat should be 18–21°C (65–70°F), and the air temperature can be allowed to rise to 15–18°C (59–65°F). However, the lower the air temperature the greater is the possibility of the buds remaining dormant. The aim is to encourage relatively fast root initiation and development to support new shoot growth breaking from the dormant buds.

There are essentially three ways in which the cuttings can be handled after preparation:—

(i) Direct stick into liner or 21 cm (8″) diameter pots.

(ii) Stick into flats of sufficient depth so that at least half of the cutting is below the surface of the rooting medium. Deep flats with a wire mesh base are very suitable for hardwood cuttings.

(iii) Stick the cuttings directly into 1.0 m (3′) wide floor-level beds with a solid surround and containing a pre-mixed rooting medium of equal parts of peat and coarse sand or peat and perlite. I noted this method used successfully in West Germany for large-scale propagation of ornamental shrubs.

Cold storage facilities can be used to extend the period of rooting to give up to three crops of cuttings during the dormant season.

Nodal cuttings, 15 cm (6″) long, are prepared, bundled and the bases dipped into 0.8% IBA powder. One modification that has been successfully used to increase the number of cuttings is to reduce the length to 8.5 cm (3½″).

Three specific examples of propagating plants by hardwood cuttings are outlined below to demonstrate different methods and/or systems of handling cuttings to be rooted in greenhouses.

1. *Vitis* (Grape)—Vine Eyes

A successful alternative to softwood single node ("leaf bud") cuttings (p. 294) for propagating ornamental *Vitis* and *Parthenocissus* (Woodbine) is to use a type of cutting called a Vine Eye. This consists of an axillary bud with a short length of stem taken from ripened one-year-old wood during the period from late December through to February. The stock plants can be grown in a greenhouse, if there is sufficient room, and will then produce an abundance of suitable wood.

Pruners are used to prepare the vine eye cuttings in one of two ways:—

(a) Make a sloping cut away from and just above an axillary bud. Then make a horizontal internodal cut 4.0 cm (1½″) below the axillary bud. The cutting can be wounded on the side opposite the bud.

Diagram 9-2. Diagrammatic representation of two methods for preparing dormant hardwood "vine eye" cuttings. A. Vertical cutting with a slice wound on the side opposite to the bud. B. Horizontal cutting with a centrally located bud and a slice wound along the entire length of the lower surface of the stem.

(b) Make horizontal cuts 2.0 cm (¾") above and below the axillary bud. The cutting can be wounded on the underside of the stem opposite the axillary bud.

The cuttings are then dipped into 0.8% IBA powder to promote rooting and stuck individually into liner pots, 7.0–7.5 cm (2½–3") size, or in rows in flats. The axillary bud should be just visible above the level of the rooting medium. A suitable rooting medium is equal parts of peat and coarse sand or peat and perlite.

The cuttings are lightly watered in and placed on a bench or floor-level bed, with 18–21°C (65–70°F) basal heat provided to give a closed case or mist environment. Check for watering requirements regularly as the rooting medium must be kept relatively moist. Particular care should be taken not to dislodge the cuttings and that the rooting medium does not become excessively dry near the surface. The vine eyes are removed from the propagation facility when they are well rooted.

2. *Metasequoia glyptostroboides* (Dawn Redwood)

Hardwood cuttings can be conveniently taken in January, using well-ripened wood from previously pruned stock plants grown in containers or the open ground. Buds may break before a sufficient root system has formed if cuttings are taken later than this, resulting in subsequent deterioration of the cuttings.

Nodal cuttings, 15 cm (6") long, are made, avoiding thin tips and weak shoots, and 0.8% IBA powder applied to the base of the cuttings. The root system of *Metasequoia* is brittle so it is best to stick the cuttings directly into a liner pot or some type of unit container supported in a flat. This will prevent the roots growing into each other, resulting in damage when potting. A rooting medium of equal parts of peat and coarse sand or peat and perlite is satisfactory.

The cuttings are placed in a closed case or a mist propagation bed with a base temperature of 21°C (70°F). A mist unit is useful to keep the soft growth turgid once the buds have broken. This new growth is susceptible to scorch; therefore shading will be required as the light intensity increases.

3. *Polygonum baldschuanicum* (Bukhara Fleece Flower or Russian Vine).

This vigorously growing, deciduous climbing vine can be produced to a saleable size from hardwood cuttings in 4–5 months by rooting cuttings directly into 4 l (1 gallon) pots. Double node cuttings are prepared in January/February, 0.8% IBA applied, and 3–4 cuttings are stuck into each container. The cuttings should be stuck to half their length. The containers are placed in a greenhouse with an air temperature of 10–15°C (50–59°F). For quick rooting, the containers can be placed on a heated bed with a base temperature of 18°C (65°F), providing the space is not required for the propagation of more important plant material. The new shoot growth, normally beginning before rooting, needs to be sheared back when it is around 30 cm (12") long to encourage basal breaks and to prevent the shoots from becoming excessively tangled with growth from adjacent pots.

Figure 9-6. Successful rooting of *Polygonum baldschuanicum* (Bukhara Fleece Flower or Russian Vine) following direct sticking in a greenhouse during January.

HEATED BINS

The pioneer of the heated bin was R. J. Garner of East Malling Research Station, Kent, England. He began to modify the traditional straw bale bin (p. 38) during the 1950s so that it would be a more permanent and reliable facility for rooting cuttings of fruit tree rootstocks. B. H. Howard, who joined him in 1962, has improved and extended the system by combining fundamental research in physiology with modern control equipment. This section is largely based on the work from East Malling Research Station and F. P. Matthews Ltd., Tenbury Wells, U.K., a specialist commercial producer of virus-tested fruit tree rootstocks.

The procedure for rooting dormant deciduous cuttings in heated bins essentially proceeds in three phases:—

(i) The pre-conditioning of one-year-old shoots arising from a heavily pruned stock hedge.

(ii) The provision of an environment to minimize stem rotting to promote the development of root initials and discourage the vegetative buds on the shoot from breaking into growth.

(iii) The encouragement of the successful establishment of the cuttings in the open ground or into containers.

Uses of Heated Bins

The uses for heated bins today are essentially three-fold:—

1. Rootstocks for Fruit and Ornamental Trees

Heated bins are now a standard facility for raising specific clonal rootstocks of apple, pear, cherry and plum. The main reason for its wider use is that it is an economically viable, far more intensive alternative to open-ground layering under certain circumstances. Also, subsequent growth is not inhibited by build-up of specific replant diseases occurring in the layer beds. However, apples are still mainly layered due to efficient mechanization and the easy working of already-established stool beds.

Heated bins are particularly useful for propagating plum rootstocks as they are generally shy-rooting when stooled or propagated by other layering techniques. Apple rootstocks are more commonly propagated by stooling, and it is often necessary to bed out apple rootstocks for a further year to build up the root system before they can be planted out in open ground for budding. Up to 100% rooting can be achieved with the apple rootstocks Malling Merton 106 and Malling Merton 111. [A reduced optimum rooting of 70% has been experienced for M.26 in the nursery.] The dwarfing Malling 9 is particularly shy with a success rate of between 50–60% being obtained. Malling 9 often produces excessive callus which, in turn, inhibits rooting. The table below lists some fruit tree rootstocks successfully rooted in a heated bin:—

Apple	M.27, M.26, M.M.106, M.M.111
Cherry	*Prunus* 'Colt', *P.* 'Cob'
Pear	Quince A, Quince C
Plum	Brompton, Myrobalan B, St. Julien A, Pixie

There is considerable potential for research programs to evaluate different clones of ornamental tree rootstocks for their ease of rooting in heated bins. Encouraging results have been shown with clonal selections of *Tilia cordata* (Little-leaf Linden) and *T.* × *europaea* (European Linden) (syn. *T.* × *vulgaris*) at East Malling Research Station.

2. Ornamental Trees and Shrubs

Heated bins have not been as widely used for propagating woody ornamentals when compared to raising fruit tree rootstocks. However, they have been exploited successfully in the last few years for some specific ornamentals.

The heated bin is an alternative to conventional budding and grafting for most trees—the cost of the rootstock is eliminated because the tree is allowed to grow on its own roots. A high rooting percentage must occur in the heated bin, followed by successful establishment in the open ground or in the container, to make it a viable technique. The growth rate should compare favorably with budded or grafted rootstocks. The range of trees propagated in heated bins includes those that are largely to be sold for hedging—for example, *Prunus* × *blireiana* (Flowering or Blireiana Plum) and *P. cerasifera* 'Nigra' (Black Myrobalan Plum). Standard trees of *Laburnum* × *watereri* 'Vossii' (Voss' Long-cluster Golden-chain Tree), *Malus* 'Golden Hornet' (Golden Hornet Crab Apple), *Prunus padus* 'Watereri' (European Bird Cherry cv.), *P. serrulata* 'Kwanzan' (Kwanzan Cherry), *P. subhirtella* 'Autumnalis' (Autumn Flowering Higan Cherry), and *Platanus* × *acerifolia* (London Plane) have been found to be particularly responsive to rooting in heated bins. However, some nurseries have experienced heavy establishment losses of the cuttings following removal from the bin, thus making heated bin propagation an economically non-viable alternative to budding and grafting.

Research on propagating ornamentals in heated bins has also been carried out by D. N. Whalley at the Glasshouse Crops Research Institute, Rustington, U.K. His work has led to some adjustments to the recommendations for propagating rootstocks, particularly in relation to rooting hormone concentrations, moisture content and basal temperature of the rooting medium. Ornamentals are generally more sensitive in open-ground establishment if the roots of the cuttings have been damaged. The variation of rooting in ornamentals is demonstrated below, adapted from a table by D. N. Whalley (1979) in which he grouped the plants into four categories based on successful rooting in a heated bin. This work clearly demonstrates that heated bins have considerable potential for specific plants, while others are best left to propagation by conventional methods.

(1) High Percentage Rooting

Platanus × *acerifolia* (London Plane)
Ulmus × *hollandica* 'Commelin' (Dutch Elm cv.)
Laburnum × *watereri* 'Vossii' (Voss' Long-cluster Golden-chain Tree)
Viburnum × *bodnantense* 'Dawn' (Bodnant Viburnum cv.)
Cotoneaster bullatus 'Firebird' (Hollyberry Cotoneaster cv.)
Hibiscus syriacus 'Woodbridge' (Rose-of-Sharon cv.)
H. syriacus 'Hamabo'
H. syriacus 'Blue Bird' (= 'Oiseau Bleu')
Cornus alba 'Spaethii' (Yellow-edge Dogwood)
C. alba 'Variegata'
Rosa rugosa (Rugosa Rose)

(2) Variable Rooting

Acer platanoides (Norway Maple)
A. platanoides 'Drummondii' (Silver Variegated Norway Maple)
A. saccharinum (Silver Maple)
A. saccharinum 'Pyramidale' (Pyramid Silver Maple)
Betula pendula 'Youngii' (Young's Weeping Birch)
Sorbus intermedia (Swedish White Beam)
Corylus maxima 'Purpurea' (Purple Giant Filbert)

(3) Heavy Callusing, No Rooting

Crataegus laevigata 'Rosea' (Single Pink English Hawthorn)
C. laevigata 'Coccinea Flore Pleno' (Paul's Scarlet Hawthorn)
C. monogyna 'Stricta' (Single-seed Hawthorn cv.)
C. × *prunifolia* (Plum-leaf Hawthorn)

(4) Rooting Exceptionally Difficult

Betula pubescens (Downy Birch)
Acer platanoides 'Crimson King' (Crimson King Maple)
Syringa × *hyacinthiflora* 'Esther Staley' (American Lilac cv.)
Corylus avellana 'Aurea' (Golden European Filbert)
Sorbus aria 'Lutescens' (White Beam cv.)
Tilia × *euchlora* (Crimean Linden)

3. Direct Rooting of Ornamental Shrubs

A more recently developed technique in which easy-to-root deciduous shrubs are callused in a heated bin and then directly stuck into 15 or 21 cm (6 or 8") diameter containers has been found to be very successful. The cuttings range in size from 15 cm (6") to 30 cm (12") long, depending on the species. The small 15 cm (6") cuttings should be potted so that only 1.3 cm (½") is above the level of the potting mix. Experience has shown that the potting mix should contain little or no fertilizer, relying on liquid feeding during the early stages of development and then applying a top dressing of a controlled-release fertilizer later.

The table lists a range of shrubs that have been successfully direct-rooted in the selling container and marketed after one season of growth. The costs of the liner pot and of the subsequent potting are thus eliminated.

Cornus alba 'Spaethii' (Yellow-edge Dogwood)
Leycesteria formosa (Himalaya Honeysuckle)
Ribes sanguineum (Red-flowering Currant)
Symphoricarpos × *doorenbosii* 'Magic Berry'
Tamarix tetrandra (Four-stamen Tamarisk)

Research by D. N. Whalley and K. Loach at the Glasshouse Crops Research Institute has investigated the establishment in containers of ornamental deciduous hardwood cuttings—some of which have been unpredictable in rooting and establishment. The experiments carried out in 1981 and 1982 attempted to synchronize root and bud growth and to place cuttings directly into the final container from the heated bin. The containerized plants were then placed in a polyethylene hoop tunnel with 40% shade and a mist line suspended 1 m (3') above the ground and controlled by a time clock. The mist was turned on when the cuttings had reached the stage of leaf expansion. The treatments were aimed at maximizing early leaf and root growth and reducing stress to the plants to a minimum by reducing the leaf temperature with the cooling effect of mist. A comparison was also made by using a shaded polyethylene tent without mist. The two species tested responded quite differently—the survival values of *Acer saccharinum* (Silver Maple) were 25%, 27% and 60%, whilst those for *Platanus* × *acerifolia* (London Plane) were 78%, 94% and 94%.

As a general rule, it is possible to use a heated bin for this production system to stimulate the early stage of rooting. The subsequent rooting, growth and management of the cuttings may be aided by the limited use of mist at an early stage of growth. The time of transfer from the protected environment to the open ground must be carefully judged in order to obtain the highest quality plants.

Design of Heated Bins

The bins are best sited in a cool insulated building with limited temperature variation and air movement. A barn, a well-constructed shed or a similar type of outbuilding is ideal. A very successful facility used by F. P. Matthews Ltd. is their cold store building where temperature and humidity can be controlled and there is no air movement. A layer of polyurethane compound was sprayed on the surface of the inner wall to improve insulation. The construction of a cold storage facility to house the bins is costly, but a cheaper alternative recently designed at the new plant propagation facility at East Malling Research Station is to pre-cool the air and then continually cycle it over the cuttings to maintain a constant temperature between 5–10°C (41–50°F).

If there is no room in an existing building, the heated bins can be constructed outside so that they adjoin the north-facing side of a building. They must be under a lean-to roof to keep out rain and snow, and surrounded by a woven plastic shade cloth windbreak to reduce air currents and keep out debris. However, a cool insulated building is much preferable to this method, especially since a relative humidity of 90% seems to be the optimum level.

1. East Malling (Static) Bin

This type of bin is the standard recommended design, although various improvements have been made over the years. The diagram shows the main features of the standard heated bin.

A convenient width is 1.2 m (4'), with the length varying according to the area available. Greater flexibility is achieved by having a series of smaller bins, each with its own individual temperature control, rather than a smaller number of larger bins. A maximum of between 4,000–5,000 cuttings can be accommodated in a bin with a floor area of 1.2 × 1.2 m (4 × 4').

The main components of the bin are:—

(i) A shallow bed of sand spread over a sloping, drained floor. The sand layer should be sufficiently deep to draw the water away from the rooting zone, thus eliminating excessive moisture build-up at the base of the cuttings.

(ii) A wooden retaining wall, 1.0 m (3') high, on all four sides.

(iii) A single layer of insulation bricks is used to hold the rooting medium to a depth of 35 cm (14"). The bricks should be painted with a bitumastic paint to retain insulation, and, if the bins are sited outdoors, water should be prevented from entering the aggregate to avoid cracking of the bricks due to frost. Insulation can be improved by lining the inner walls and floor with 5 cm (2") thick expanded polystyrene (Styrofoam®) sheets wrapped in polyethylene.

Diagram 9-3. East Malling cuttings bin. *NOTE:* This diagram shows the East Malling bin before modifications made to reflect recent research recommendations. (Reproduced by permission of East Malling Research Station, Maidstone, Kent, U.K.©)

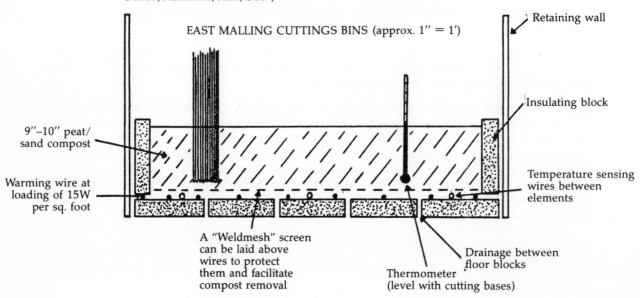

Figure 9-7.
A series of East Malling bins installed in a cool insulated building. Note that each bin has its own individual temperature control unit on the wall above the bin. In the foreground are bundles of callused cuttings with newly emerged roots. (Reproduced by permission of East Malling Research Station, Maidstone, Kent, U.K.©)

(iv) Heating cables are attached to a grid, thus making it easy for the bin to be cleaned out and sterilized after the propagation season has finished. The cables are attached to the underside of the metal grid so that it protects the heating cables. Electrical cables should be self-earthed and a layer of plastic windbreak material (e.g., Netlon®) sandwiched between the grid and heating cables for added safety. Sand should be brushed through the mat to improve drainage of the rooting medium.

(v) Electronic controllers are recommended as these give greater stability, flexibility and accuracy. Such controllers normally rely on a remote temperature sensor that is placed alongside the bundles of cuttings in the rooting medium. Typical sensors are platinum resistance thermometers, thermistors, thermocouples and semiconductor diodes. An alternative approach is one in which a resistance thermometer is made from 20 m (65′) of PVC-covered copper wire (0.6 mm/¼″ diameter) and placed at the base of the bins (East Malling Misc. Publ. 138, 1975). The use of a number of sensors minimizes temperature gradients as compared to the use of a single rod thermostat.

2. Palletized Bins

An interesting modification to the East Malling bin was recently developed by F. P. Matthews Ltd. The dimensions are 1.2 × 2.6 m (4 × 8′6″) and 76 cm (30″) deep, to fall into line with the standard-size pallet. The main advantages are:—

(i) It is more flexible because the bin containing the rooted cuttings can be easily moved by fork-lift trucks to the planting site or cold store building for holding until planting conditions are correct. The bins can also be stacked on top of each other if space is limited.

(ii) Establishment of the cuttings is improved because they are not disturbed until the time of actual planting in open ground. Taking the cuttings to the planting site in the bin results in exposing the root system to the air for a maximum of 15 minutes. There is considerably less breakage and drying-out of the roots than when they are removed from the medium, bundled and cold stored until planting out.

As the diagram shows, 10 cm (4″) thick sheets of expanded polystyrene (Styrofoam®) are laid over the floor of the bin and on the sides of the retaining wall to improve insulation. The bin is connected to the electrical system after the rooting medium and cuttings are in place. The bin is moved out after the cuttings have rooted and hardened off and is replaced with another bin con-

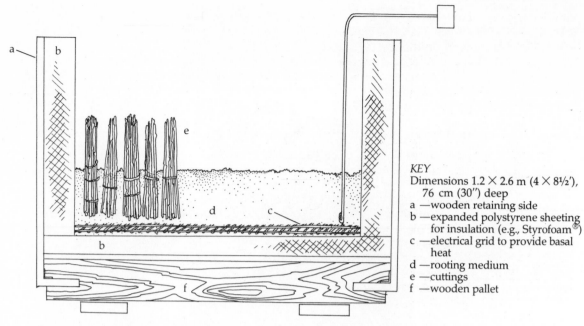

Diagram 9-4. A palletized heating bin. (Formulated from information received from N. Dunn, Frank P. Matthews Ltd., Tenbury Wells, Worcestershire, U.K.)

KEY
Dimensions 1.2 × 2.6 m (4 × 8½'),
    76 cm (30") deep
a —wooden retaining side
b —expanded polystyrene sheeting
    for insulation (e.g., Styrofoam®)
c —electrical grid to provide basal
    heat
d —rooting medium
e —cuttings
f —wooden pallet

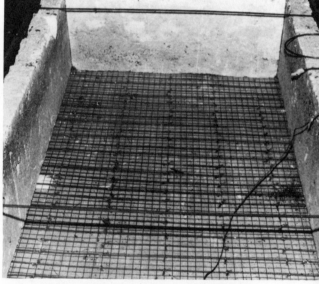

Figure 9-8. A (above left). Cuttings stuck in palletized heated bins in a cold storage facility. Note that polyurethane has been sprayed on the inner walls of the building to improve the insulation. B (above right). An empty palletized heating bin showing the grid heating panel and the expanded polystyrene (Styrofoam®) used for insulation inside the bin. (Both reproduced by courtesy of F. P. Matthews Ltd., Tenbury Wells, Worcestershire, U.K.)

Figure 9-9. A palletized heated bin stuck with a range of ornamental deciduous shrubs being moved to the potting bench. (Homestead Nurseries, Clayburn, B.C., Canada)

taining unrooted cuttings. The type of construction materials leads to easy construction and dismantling of the bins. The main problem is ensuring correct drainage because of the solid expanded polystyrene (Styrofoam®) floors.

This palletized system has also been adopted successfully at Homestead Nurseries, Clayburn, B.C., for rooting ornamental shrubs and climbing vines, e.g., *Spiraea* (Spirea), *Potentilla* (Cinquefoil), *Sambucus* (Elder) and *Weigela*. This nursery pots the rooted cuttings directly after removal from the palletized bins.

Stock Hedges as Cutting Source

Cuttings to be rooted in heated bins should be taken from stock hedges. The reasons for stock hedges and their role in providing vigorous material to improve rooting had been previously explained (p. 243).

The plants to form the stock hedge should be obtained from a virus-free source (not available for ornamentals other than fruit-related species) and planted in rows 2 m (6') apart with 30 cm (1') between each plant in the row. The height is reduced to 60 cm (2') at the time of planting. The sequence diagrams illustrate the initial and subsequent pruning regime.

More recently, it has been found that potential rooting of apple rootstocks is higher from those shoots that arise closest to the ground in the hedge framework. Hard annual pruning effectively encourages these basal breaks.

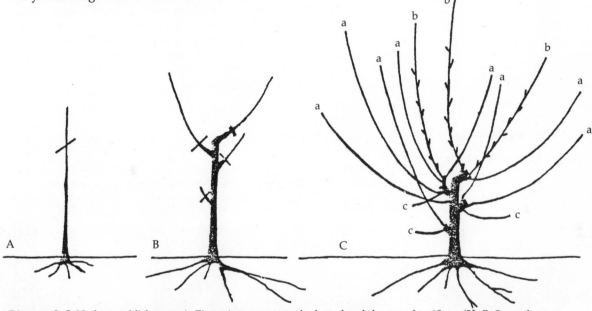

Diagram 9-5. Hedge establishment. A. First winter—rootstock planted and shortened to 60 cm (2'). B. Second winter—growth pruned to 2–4 buds or bent down. A few cuttings can be taken. C. Types of shoots on a young hedge plant a few years later: a—to be taken as basal cuttings; b—coarse feathered shoots, bent down (*NOTE:* these shoots are removed today as this method of layering is rarely used); c—small shoots, cut to 1–2 buds. The last two types of shoots (b and c) are used to provide further framework of the mother plant in the hedge. (Reproduced by permission of East Malling Research Station, Maidstone, Kent, U.K., but original (Technical Leaflet M.P. 85) modified by the author for this text.)

Figure 9-11. Collecting hardwood cuttings from a plum rootstock hedge in the fall. (Reproduced by permission of East Malling Research Station, Maidstone, Kent, U.K.©)

Selection and Removal of Cuttings

The shoots should be removed with pruners, ensuring that each has a swollen shoot base and does not include any two-year-old wood. This swollen base occurs where the current year's growth adjoins wood of the previous season. The swollen shoot base assists rooting because multiple nodes are compressed together in this region and it possibly contains higher levels of natural auxin. Many shoots, particularly plums, will have the potential to provide 2 or 3 cuttings, but only one will have the swollen stem base. Cuttings prepared from the mid- and upper-sections of the shoot must be cut at a node. It is advisable to wear gloves, particularly when taking cuttings from Myrobalan B and ornamental plums, because the spines on the shoots can be a hazard.

Side shoots arising from the leader are prone to forming in dry summers when more irregular growth patterns occur. Such shoots should not be used to provide cuttings as the removal of the feathers will leave exposed areas that will encourage water loss. However, this will not be a problem if the cuttings are rooted in an indoor bin with very high relative humidity.

A problem that may occur when collecting cuttings in the fall is that the leaves can be retained on the shoots. For example, apples can retain leaves into early December. The leaves can be removed mechanically with power-driven rotating leather flails as long as the shoot itself is not damaged. Alternatively, defoliants can be sprayed onto the leaves three weeks before the cuttings are to be taken. A mixture of 10 kg (20 lb) copper oxychloride and 1 kg (2 lb) of ammonium sulphate added to 1000 l (200 Imp. gal) of water and then sprayed to run-off is effective on apples and pears. A test area should be sprayed first when using ammonium sulphate to see if there is any risk of scorch to the stems and buds of the shoots. The spraying equipment must be thoroughly cleaned with water as ammonium sulphate is very corrosive to metallic parts. Chelated copper (Cu.EDTA) has also been found to be very successful. Cuttings collected when about 50% of the leaves have fallen can be easily stripped of the remainder by hand.

Figure 9-10 section of a *Prunus* 'Colt' hedge for production of hardwood cuttings showing the pre-formed root initials at the bases of the annual shoots. (Reproduced by permission of East Malling Research Station, Maidstone, Kent, U.K.©)

Figure 9-12. Pruners are used to collect deciduous hardwood cuttings with slightly swollen shoot bases from the hardwood cutting hedge. (Reproduced by permission of East Malling Research Station, Maidstone, Kent, U.K.©)

Figure 9-13. A close-up of a hardwood basal cutting just removed from a hardwood cutting hedge. (Reproduced by permission of East Malling Research Station, Maidstone, Kent, U.K.©)

Time of Year

Timing is more critical when using heated bins than for the other methods of hardwood cutting propagation. The two peak periods for rooting are October/November and February/March. Between these two peaks there is a trough when rooting is considerably slower.

1. October/November

This is a particularly useful period for the plum rootstocks Brompton, Myrobalan B, St. Julien A and Pixie. It is also a convenient time for *Prunus* 'Colt' (Cherry rootstock) cuttings that do not have pre-formed root initials. October/November propagation ensures that the buds are dormant, as there is a risk that the buds will have already swollen by February/March.

The cuttings can be planted out into open ground after 3–4 weeks in the bin. Root development is then able to continue before the onset of winter. Two problems that must be considered with propagation at this time of year are that it may be difficult, firstly, to get the soil into the correct condition for planting due to increased rainfall, and, secondly, that frost heave may dislodge the cuttings in colder climates.

[The fruit tree rootstocks mentioned above can all be planted directly into the open ground in the fall in some localities.]

2. February/March

This period is preferable for apple rootstocks because the buds break later in the season than do those of plums and cherries, the leaves will have fallen, and they root better. In addition, commercial experience has demonstrated that the plum rootstock St. Julien A roots well in February if the shoots are removed from the hedges in December and then cold stored prior to sticking. These cuttings are re-cut at the base, liquid rooting hormone applied, and placed into the bins. Commercially, *Prunus* 'Colt' has been unpredictable in rooting in heated bins during March.

The East Malling Research Station has been investigating the reason why February/March is the best time for rooting apple rootstocks. It is believed to be due to the increased level of a naturally-occurring compound, best described as a co-factor, which results from a reaction between a phenolic sugar compound (phenolic glycoside phloridzin) and an enzyme (polyphenol oxidase). Further research is in progress to see if it is possible to induce this co-factor to form in apples between the two peak periods for rooting, and to fully identify it. This will be followed by experiments to see if it is possible to make a synthetic version that could be applied to the base of cuttings to improve root promotion.

Preparation of Cuttings

Success in establishment depends on the size of the cutting, (i.e., the available food reserve). For rootstocks, it is also important to determine the stem caliper required at the time of budding. The optimum lengths of cutting used are 60 cm (24") for rootstocks, 45 cm (18") for ornamental trees, and 15–30 cm (6–12") for ornamental shrubs.

Grade the cuttings at the time of preparation, with grade 1 for cuttings with swollen stem bases and grade 2 and grade 3 for cuttings with nodes at the base but prepared from progressively further along the stem from the base.

A horizontal cut is made at the base of the cutting and a sloping cut away from a bud at the tip. Wounding at the base of the cutting is beneficial for rooting. This is achieved by making 2 or 3 incision wounds 2.5 cm (1") long with a knife or pruner blade, or alternatively by splitting the stem base with pruners. (Further details and benefits gained are explained in Chapter 7.)

Rooting Hormone Application

The cuttings are best dipped into a liquid rooting hormone containing IBA the day after collection and preparation as this assists the capillary uptake of the liquid. However, good results have also been achieved by dipping just a few hours after cutting preparation. The quick dip method is used to apply the rooting hormone (p. 342). This means that only the basal cut surface is dipped (not exceeding a depth of 1 cm/⅜") for five seconds. It is important that the basal cuts are at the same level when bundles of cuttings are dipped into the rooting hormone. The solvent is allowed to evaporate for 20–30 minutes, after which the cuttings can be stuck in the rooting medium in the bin. [Commercial practice has shown that there is little or no detrimental effect in some instances if the prepared cuttings are dipped in liquid hormone one month in advance of sticking.]

A useful guideline for the concentration of IBA is as follows:—

Quince — 1,000 ppm IBA
Apple   — 2,500 ppm IBA
Plum   — 2,500 or 5,000 ppm IBA*

*Dependent on ease of rooting

The table below documents specific treatment for different rootstocks as recommended by the East Malling Research Station.

TABLE 9-1. Specific Hormone Treatments For Rootstocks*

CLONE	COLLECT	ppm IBA	BASAL TEMPERATURE
Myrobalan B plum	mid-Nov.	2,500	plant directly in field
St. Julien A plum	early Nov.	2,500	15°C (60°F) 3–4 weeks
Brompton	late Oct.	5,000	15°C (60°F) 3–4 weeks
Colt (having pre-formed roots)	before spring	none	plant directly in field
Colt (not having pre-formed roots)	before spring	1,000	15–18°C (60–65°F) 2 wks
Quince A or C	late Oct.	1,000	15–21°C (60–70°F) 2–3 wks
M.27	early Jan.	2,500	21°C (70°F) 3–4 wks
MM.106	early Feb.	2,500	21°C (70°F) 2–3 wks
MM.111	early Feb.	2,500	21°C (70°F) 2–3 wks
M.26	early March	2,500	21°C (70°F) 2–3 wks

* Reprinted by permission of East Malling Research Station, Maidstone, Kent, England.

For ornamental shrubs and trees, first try 2,500 ppm IBA, reducing it to 1,000 ppm if the previous concentration should prove to be too strong. Powders can be made more effective if the cuttings are pre-dipped in 50% acetone, rubbing alcohol or methylated spirits before dipping them in the powder. This pre-treatment improves the uptake of IBA (see Chapter 10).

Rooting Medium and Aftercare Requirements

1. Constituents and Moisture Level

Good drainage, aeration and moisture level of the rooting medium are vital for success. An open medium containing equal parts of coarse peat moss and 5 mm (1/5″) coarse sand (grit) should provide the necessary requirements. Perlite can be substituted for the coarse sand (grit). The components are thoroughly mixed and then placed into the bin to a depth of 25–30 cm (10–12″).

It is important to place the rooting medium into the bin 4–5 days before sticking the cuttings as this gives time to make adjustments to the moisture content and for calibration of the temperature control equipment. Over-watering cannot be corrected except by slow drying out.

The cuttings are packed tightly into the bins so that half the stem length is covered by the rooting medium. The base of the cuttings should be 2.5–5.0 cm (1–2″) above the heating grid. Care should be taken to ensure that the medium is in close contact with the cuttings so that the centers of the bundles do not dry out.

Recent research at East Malling Research Station by B. E. Howard and colleagues has achieved excellent results by replacing the peat and coarse sand (grit) mix with a 7.5 cm (3″) layer of granulated bark over a bed of sand. The cuttings are bundled with the bases level and then wrapped in polyethylene film with the top open to reduce lateral desiccation. The base of the cuttings are worked into the bark to a depth of about 3.5 cm (1½″).

The cuttings should have a slightly dry moisture regime. Do not be misled into thinking

Figure 9-14.
Bundles of cuttings wrapped in polyethylene film to reduce lateral desiccation and then stuck into a 7.5 cm (3") deep layer of granulated bark. Recent research has shown that this system gives excellent results. (Reproduced by permission of East Malling Research Station, Maidstone, Kent, U.K.©)

that the cuttings need watering just because the surface of the rooting medium is dry—it is important to check the medium at the base of the cuttings to assess whether any additional watering is required. Too much moisture, particularly around the cutting base, is a primary reason why cuttings fail to root satisfactorily. If the rooting medium requires additional water, the basal heat should be turned off three days beforehand and not switched on again until at least one week later. However, commercial practice has shown that it is not necessary to turn off the heating when watering provided that the electrical connections are waterproofed.

Under experimental conditions, injection of oxygen into the rooting medium from a conventional pressurized oxygen cylinder has been found to be beneficial in reducing basal rotting of the cuttings if the moisture level of the medium is too high. A five-second burst of oxygen into the rooting medium was given every two to three days to improve aeration. However, these beneficial results have been difficult to repeat subsequently.

2. Basal Temperature

An optimum basal temperature of 21°C (70°F) is recommended for most rootstock cuttings, reducing it to 15–18°C (60–65°F) for *Prunus* 'Colt', plum rootstocks and ornamental plums. [Difficult-to-root apple scions such as 'Cox' require 30°C (86°F).]

The most important aim of the propagation cycle in heated bins is to callus the cuttings and develop root initials as quickly as possible. Leaving the cuttings in the bins too long at these high temperatures causes deterioration and excessive root development, resulting in reduced establishment as food reserves are used up and roots become damaged. Two to three weeks is normally sufficient to develop callus and root initials. Although hardening-off (weaning) is not always essential, the cuttings can be hardened-off if desired when there are signs that the root initials are well developed, either by swelling or actual root emergence. [Hardening-off is best carried out in stages by lowering the temperature 5°C (9°F) every two days. The heat is turned off after two weeks. The cuttings may be cold stored or planted out when hardening-off is completed.]

3. Air Temperature

The air temperature should be kept constantly cool (5–10°C/41–50°F) to delay bud break on the cuttings. A cold storage facility used to house the bins has been beneficial in commercial practice as the temperature can be kept to a constant 2°C (35°F), although there is a risk that the lower temperature in "direct-cooled" storage will dry out the air too much.

Figure 9-15. *Prunus* 'Colt' cuttings removed from a palletized bin and ready for open-ground planting. (Reproduced by permission of F. P. Matthews Ltd., Tenbury Wells, Worcestershire, U.K.)

Figure 9-16. A jacketed (indirect) cold store provides an excellent environment for holding cuttings (and layers) until open-ground planting. Note the easy access to the portable metal shelving units and the use of wooden pallets for holding the plant material. (Reproduced by permission of East Malling Research Station, Maidstone, Kent, U.K.©)

Figure 9-17. A (left). Plum rootstocks stuck in raised beds containing a medium composed of equal parts of peat moss, bark, and fine and coarse sand (grit) plus the incorporation of a controlled-release fertilizer. This is a very useful alternative for the establishment of cuttings when open-ground soils are too wet. B (right). *Tilia cordata* (Little-leaf Linden) clones established on raised beds. Successful establishment of the plants on the left followed a 14-day period in a heated bin at 20°C (68°F) basal heat. The plants on the right show poor establishment caused by excessive rooting and loss of carbohydrates due to spending 35 days in the bin at 20°C (68°F). (Both reproduced by permission of East Malling Research Station, Maidstone, Kent, U.K.©)

4. Cold Storage Humidity

If the cuttings are being rooted in heated bins in a cold storage facility, atmospheric humidity can be maintained by hand-misting the cuttings and watering the floor area every two days. There is little drying out of the rooting medium over a period of six weeks compared to having the bins installed on a north-facing wall.

Establishment

The rooted cuttings are planted out 37.5–45 cm (15–18″) apart in the row. Budding can be done in the summer of the same year for easy-to-root rootstocks such as plum. However, apple rootstocks do not establish regularly enough to guarantee direct planting from the bin and should be bedded out for one season before planting for budding. The spacing can be reduced to 5 cm (2″) apart if the stem caliper will not be sufficient at the time of budding or if a further season is required to build up the root system before open-ground planting. The cuttings should be firmed well after planting.

Following are several suggestions that can help to improve establishment.

1. Avoid breaking the root system when handling the cuttings.

2. Do not allow the root systems to dry out—cover the bundles of cuttings with moist burlap (hessian) sacking while awaiting planting.

3. If there is a risk of planting being hindered by over-wet soils, plant in specially-prepared raised beds that will allow free drainage. East Malling Research Station have demonstrated successful establishment in over-wet soils when the cuttings are planted out in raised beds containing equal parts by volume of peat moss, bark, fine and coarse sand (grit) into which has been incorporated a controlled-release fertilizer.

4. Remove all used rooting medium from the bins and use to backfill the trench prior to planting. This improves aeration around the base of the cutting and helps to prevent the trench from opening up as the soil dries out. This method is likely to be too expensive for commercial operations.

5. Plant the cuttings through a black polyethylene mulch. This will keep the weeds down and conserve moisture. This practice is particularly useful where overhead irrigation is not available.

6. Overhead irrigate within 24 hours after planting and subsequently as required to maintain the soil at field capacity.

7. Provide a temporary artificial windbreak in exposed sites so that drying winds cannot desiccate the cuttings and rapidly reduce soil moisture.

NOTE:—All the above suggestions are useful crop husbandry practices, but it is much more important to have adequately stimulated the cuttings towards rooting without any rotting; i.e., conditions within the bin are of primary importance.

Figure 9-18.
These well-established deciduous hardwood cuttings of *Malus* rootstocks resulted from the application of the correct principles and practices. (Reproduced by permission of East Malling Research Station, Maidstone, Kent, U.K.©)

REFERENCES AND SUGGESTED SOURCES FOR FURTHER READING

Agricultural Training Board, U.K. 1978. *Ornamental Hardwood Cuttings (Dormant Deciduous)*. Trainee Guide 8NSP 1.A.11, Agricultural Training Board, Beckenham, Kent, U.K.

Clayton, N. & J. Richardson. 1977. Hardwood cuttings—field production. *Comb. Proc. Inter. Pl. Prop. Soc.* 27: 64–67.

Dunn, N. D. 1979. Commercial propagation of fruit tree rootstocks. *Comb. Proc. Inter. Pl. Prop. Soc.* 29: 187–190.

East Malling Research Station. no date. *Propagation of Clonal Fruit Rootstocks by Hardwood Cuttings*. Technical Leaflet M.P.85, East Malling Research Station, Maidstone, Kent, U.K.

———. 1975. *Resistance Thermometer*. Technical Leaflet M.P. 138, East Malling Research Station, Maidstone, Kent, U.K.

Hatcher, E. S. J., S. de Boer & R. J. Garner. 1955. The influence of soil environment on the behaviour of apple and plum cuttings. *Jour. Hort. Sci.* 30: 268–281.

Howard, B. H. 1975. Improved rooting of cuttings by diffusion of oxygen through the rooting medium. (Research Note). *Jour. Hort. Sci.* 50: 173–174.

———. 1978. Field establishment of apple rootstock hardwood cuttings as influenced by conditions during a prior stage in heated bins. *Jour. Hort. Sci.* 53: 31–57.

———. 1981. Propagation by leafless winter cuttings. *The Plantsman* 3: 99–107.

———. 1981. Propagation of fruit and other broadleaved trees. *Jour. Royal Agric. Soc. England* 142: 110–127.

Lohnes, J. P. 1985. Hardwood rooting method shows promise at Lohnes. *Amer. Nurseryman* 161(7): 42–50 (April 1, 1985).

Macdonald, A. B. & R. J. Kempton. 1969. Chemical defoliation of deciduous nursery stock. *Rep. Glasshouse Crops Res. Inst. 1968*, pp. 133–141.

Rigby, B., Chairman. 1981. Discussion Group Report—Hardwood cuttings. *Comb. Proc. Inter. Pl. Prop. Soc.* 31: 403–406.

Stanley, J. & A. Toogood. 1981. *The Modern Nurseryman*. Faber & Faber Ltd., London. Pp. 109–128.

Vanderbrook, L. C. 1953. Hardwood cuttings of deciduous shrubs. *Proc. Pl. Prop. Soc.* 3: 133–137.

Whalley, D. N. 1972. The propagation of certain deciduous plants by hardwood cuttings. *Comb. Proc. Inter. Pl. Prop. Soc.* 22: 304–318.

———. 1979. Propagation of ornamental trees and shrubs by dormant leafless (hardwood) cuttings. *Arboric. Jour.* 3: 499–512.

——— & K. Loach. 1981. Rooting of two genera of woody ornamentals from dormant, leafless (hardwood) cuttings and their subsequent establishment in containers. *Jour. Hort. Sci.* 56(2): 131–138.

——— & K. Loach. 1982. Establishment in containers of woody ornamentals propagated from dormant leafless cuttings. *Comb. Proc. Inter. Pl. Prop. Soc.* 32: 186–199.

——— & R. E. Randall. 1976. Temperature control in the rooting medium during propagation. *Ann. Appl. Biol.* 83: 305–309.

Chapter 10

ROOTING HORMONES

Rooting hormones are synthetic growth substances applied to the base of cuttings to aid rooting. They are derivatives of growth substances or regulators that occur naturally in living plants. The plant propagator is principally concerned with the auxins and particularly with their physiological activity on root formation, which is only one of their varied functions.

A very important discovery was made in 1934 by F. W. Went at the University of Utrecht when he isolated and identified indole-3-acetic acid (IAA) as a naturally occurring auxin in fungi and then found it to be a compound of primary importance in the rooting of cuttings. Shortly afterwards, chemists began to synthesize this and other related compounds which were subsequently made available commercially.

Further information on the physiological aspects of naturally occurring growth regulators can be found in *Plant Propagation: Principles and Practices* by H. T. Hartmann and D. E. Kester (1983, 4th Edition, pp. 246–257).

Reasons for Using Rooting Hormones

The four major advantages for using rooting hormones are to:—

(i) Increase overall rooting percentages

(ii) Hasten root initiation

(iii) Increase the number and quality of roots

(iv) Encourage uniformity of rooting.

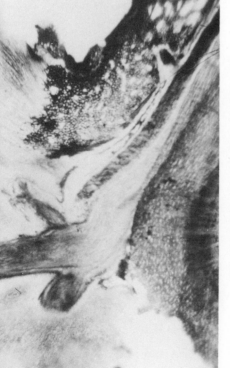

Figure 10-1.
Rooting hormones are particularly valuable for encouraging rooting of difficult-to-root species. This longitudinal section of a *Rhododendron* stem shows the development of root initials from the vascular tissue and entering the callus tissue following the application of a rooting hormone. (Reproduced by courtesy of B. E. Humphrey, Hillier Nurseries (Winchester) Ltd., Romsey, Hampshire, U.K.)

Figure 10-2.
Well-rooted cuttings of *Taxus* (Yew) showing how the emergence of the roots has been significantly increased by the application of a rooting hormone.

It is important to remember that the effect of these compounds varies considerably between genera, species and, in many cases, cultivars. Also, the effect can vary from year to year—this can be very frustrating when you think that you have solved the problem of rooting a difficult plant, only to find that exactly the same treatment gives a different result 12 months later. There have been numerous experiments on this phenomenon by both scientists and the nursery industry, and many reports have been published on their observations.

One fault with some propagators is the over-use of rooting hormones. Little or no hormone is required at certain times of the year, e.g., shortly after bud break of some deciduous shrub species. It is a fallacy to think that rooting hormones are always the answer to success by believing that the higher the strength of rooting hormone the better will be the rooting. Severe damage and loss of cuttings often occur in situations where high strengths of rooting hormone are used. Rooting hormones are a very useful aid for the plant propagator, but their merits and limitations must be clearly understood.

The aim of this section is to explain the practical application of rooting hormones, the correct storage procedures necessary, and to indicate the various products currently available for the plant propagator.

Figure 10-3. Excessive distortion of tissues at the base of the cutting and stem necrosis on softwood cuttings may be a sign of the application of too much rooting hormone.

CONSTITUENTS OF A ROOTING HORMONE COMPOUND

Fundamentally, each rooting compound, whether bought as a commercial product or made by the propagator, contains the following group of constituents:—a root promoter, a "carrier", and optional additives.

(1) Root Promoter

This is the active ingredient that promotes root formation. Three compounds are generally used:—

(a) Indolebutyric Acid (IBA)

This is a stable compound and is the one most widely used by nursery operators. It is effective for a wide range of plants, and is the most common compound found in commercial preparations.

(b) α-Naphthaleneacetic Acid (NAA)

This is a relatively stable compound, and is a good alternative to IBA although it is not so widely used.

(c) Indole-3-acetic Acid (IAA)

This is the least stable and therefore has a shorter shelf-life than IBA and NAA. It has a tendency to break down in sunlight and to attack by micro-organisms.

A preparation may contain a single root promoting compound or a combination of two or more. They may have greater overall effect when applied in combination than singly (known as synergism or "synergistic effect").

It is important to remember that only a very small amount of the root promoting substance is required and that the concentration and method of application, particularly for solutions, has to be precise. Excessive concentrations will cause damage and distortion of stem tissue, leading to discoloration and death of the cutting.

Levels of Active Ingredient—The concentration is expressed either as a percentage or in parts per million (ppm)—for example, 1% IBA or 10,000 ppm IBA. In general, the rooting hormone in talcs or powders is expressed as a % while solutions are usually expressed as ppm. A percentage can be converted to ppm by multiplying by 10,000, e.g., 0.5% ≡ 5,000 ppm, 1% ≡ 10,000 ppm, etc.

The pure synthetic products are available from most laboratory chemical suppliers. However, there has been some difficulty reported in obtaining IBA for nursery use in the United States. These products are usually used in gram lots, and a container will last a long time on the average nursery. Costs can be reduced by buying the "horticultural grade" if available. The substance comes in a brown bottle that should be kept in a refrigerator at all times, re-sealing after use. The potassium salts of these compounds are now recommended because of their greater solubility, which makes easier the task of making up the formulation.

Other Substances—Other growth regulators are occasionally used for rooting cuttings. Firstly, solutions containing a very low concentration of a translocated herbicide (phenoxy compounds) have been used. Good results have been obtained by using 2-(2,4,5-Trichlorophenoxy)propionic acid (2,4,5-T) at a strength of 0.12–0.15% (1,200–1,500 ppm) combined with 0.8% (8,000 ppm) IBA and applied as a powder for rooting junipers. There are, however, some problems with these substances. They should be used very carefully, both from the safety aspects of handling them and to prevent possible contamination of the bench, tools and other plant material. It has been found that subsequent shoot growth may be delayed by the compounds being carried within the stem to the vegetative buds. There have also been reports that cuttings treated with these phenoxy compounds lack a fibrous root system, developing instead a large quantity of short roots at the base of the cutting and many of these roots are fused. Secondly, substances largely used in the greenhouse industry for growth regulation and bud initiation, such as B-Nine®, Cycocel® and Ethrel®, have been reported by research workers to promote root activity in cuttings. However, they have not been explored sufficiently to become a widely-used recommended product for this purpose.

(2) The "Carrier" or Dispersal Agent

The rooting hormone has to be dispersed evenly and accurately at the base of the cutting. This is done by mixing it evenly with a material such as finely ground talc to form a powder or by dissolving it in an organic solvent for application as a solution. Further details can be found under the section on Methods of Application.

(3) Optional Additives

The synthetic rooting hormone and carrier are the two basic constituents, but some compounds do have additional materials. These are not an absolute necessity but have been found to be very helpful in improving the overall quality of rooting in certain instances.

(a) Fungicides

Fungicides are sometimes incorporated in the powders. They may also be either included in solutions or applied to the cuttings after dipping when the solvent has evaporated. In the latter case, they should be applied just before sticking in the rooting medium.

Fungicides can help in two ways. Firstly, they can prevent loss of the cuttings due to stem rots during the rooting process, thus helping to keep cuttings alive. Secondly, they can help to obtain a better quality root system.

Captan® is the most widely used fungicide and has the advantage of remaining stable for a long period. Research work in Boskoop, Holland, has claimed that Captan® also helps in root initiation, but this does not necessarily seem to be confirmed by work elsewhere. Captan® appears to have its best effects under low temperature conditions. Dutch growers have found that dipping in Captan® is particularly useful for rooting deciduous (leafless) hardwood cuttings in the open ground. Other fungicides successfully used as additives are benomyl (Benlate®), Thiram® and ferbam (Fermate®). Dichlone (Phygon®) has been mixed with rooting hormones used for propagating rhododendrons. The addition of the Phygon® is reported to encourage rooting with very little or no visible callus forming at the base of the cutting. It does stain the exposed cut surface black but no damage to stem tissue has been reported.

A fungicide is a standard ingredient in a number of commercial powder and some liquid preparations available today. Alternatively, they can be mixed into the standard product on the nursery (see p. 339 for mixing details). The amount of fungicide is expressed as a percentage of the total, and falls into an optimum range of 4–15%. There have been reports of phytotoxicity when Benlate® is incorporated in talc preparations. For this reason, some propagators reduce the strength of Benlate® from 5% to 2.5%.

The addition of a fungicide to the rooting compound does *not* mean that general hygiene procedures in the propagation facility can be relaxed, or that necessary fungicidal drenches or sprays to the cuttings can be omitted.

(b) Boron

A very small amount of boron (optimum concentration 40–70 ppm) is included in some compounds principally to aid root development. Research on the rooting of *Ilex aquifolium* (English Holly) indicates that increased rooting is promoted through a synergistic relationship with IBA.

(c) Plant Extracts

Researchers have experimented with natural extracts from woody plants that root easily, such as *Hedera helix* (English Ivy) and *Salix* (Willow), to assist the rooting of more difficult species. Although not repeated consistently, positive results have been observed—for example, a willow extract combined with IBA showed a synergistic effect on rooting *Betula alleghaniensis* (Yellow Birch). In 1962, Charles Hess isolated compounds, referred to as rooting co-factors, from the juvenile wood of *Hedera helix* (English Ivy). When combined with IAA, they were found to have a synergistic effect in aiding rooting of cuttings.

To date, the use of natural plant extracts has not been developed commercially.

METHODS OF APPLICATION

The two main methods by which rooting hormones are applied are either powders or solutions. Other techniques used in the past included the dispersal of the rooting hormone in a paste of lanolin—the hormone was first dissolved in alcohol and this was then mixed with warm lanolin. Another method was to inject the rooting hormone into the stem base. Neither of these former techniques is now recommended.

Powders (Talcs or Dusts)

This popular method is based on the principle of dispersing the rooting hormone (IBA, NAA or IAA) evenly through a carrier of talc or ground charcoal. Talc is the most convenient material to use. A dye is sometimes added so that the different strengths of the same brand of product can be easily distinguished, e.g., gray, white, pink.

The advantages of powders are:—

(i) They are convenient because commercial products of different strengths are easily obtainable.

(ii) They are simple to use, and a large quantity of cuttings can be treated quickly.

(iii) They are generally safe to use on a wide range of plants.

(iv) They are ready to use without further preparation.

The disadvantages of powders are:—

(i) It can be difficult to make up the talcs accurately in the nursery.

(ii) Variable amounts of rooting hormone adhere to the base of the cutting.

Mixing Powders

Nursery operators rarely mix their own powders, except where a fungicide needs to be added or to combine two strengths of the same commercial product to make an intermediate strength, e.g., mixing 0.3% and 0.8% IBA to make approximately 0.5% (a useful concentration for semi-ripe wood cuttings). This is because of the convenient and widespread availability of commercial products and because it is rather a time-consuming process to accurately mix the basic ingredients. A good, accurate, metric weighing balance is required. However, there are times when a specific strength is required and must be mixed on the nursery because a commercial product cannot be obtained. It may be worth contacting a local laboratory to see if they would be able to do the preparation for a small fee. An outline for preparing the powder is provided in case it is not possible to have it made elsewhere.

Note that the measurements are given in metric and must not be converted to other systems.

(i) Rooting Hormone and Talc

Example:—To obtain a 1% IBA powder

A 1% strength powder of IBA requires the accurate weighing out of 1 g IBA and 99 g of talc (1% = 1 in 100). A solution is made by dissolving the IBA in a small quantity of organic solvent (e.g., acetone or isopropyl alcohol). The talc is placed into an electric blender and the IBA solution is then poured and spread over the surface of the talc. A small amount of solvent is swirled around the utensil in which the IBA solution was made so that all traces of the hormone are removed and an accurate concentration obtained. This is then added to the blender. The mixture is stirred, adding further solvent as necessary to give a soft-textured liquid. The blender is then switched on for 5 minutes, at the end of which time the mixture is poured evenly over an evaporating dish (a concave glass or ceramic dish). It is then left until the solvent has evaporated and the mixture is completely dry. This dry powder is ground with a pestle and mortar to restore the original fine texture of the talc. If the procedures are carried out correctly, the result will be 100 g of powder containing a 1% concentration of IBA.

Further details on the above procedures and on how to mix in additional compounds, e.g., boron, can be found in the paper *Mixing Rooting Hormones* by John Machen of Mobjack Nurseries, Virginia, U.S.A. (Vol 27, Comb. Proc. Inter. Pl. Prop. Soc.).

(ii) Addition of Fungicide

A fungicide can be added to a powder formulation of known concentration, whether made up in the nursery or purchased. Note that some commercial preparations already contain a fungicide. One procedure to use is outlined in the following example.

A procedure to mix a fungicide with hormone powder formulation

Note that mixing the fungicide with a commercial talc preparation will reduce the concentration of the hormone by 50%, i.e., a preparation containing 0.8% IBA will contain 0.4% IBA after addition of the fungicide.

Mix 25 g (1 oz) benomyl/50% WP (Benlate® 50% WP) with 100 g (4 oz) talc and combine with 125 g (5 oz) 0.8% IBA commercial talc preparation. This produces a mixture containing 5% benomyl and 0.4% IBA.

A suggested alternative method is to add 1 part Benlate® 50% WP to 19 parts Seradix® #3 to give a mixture containing 2.5% Benlate® and 0.76% IBA, which is very close to the strength of the original preparation.

(iii) Other Additives

As previously stated, boron is sometimes added in the form of boric acid, primarily to assist root development. The optimum strength is in the region of 40–70 ppm.

Procedure for Application to Cuttings

(1) Transfer sufficient powder for a maximum of half-a-day's work from the stock container into a smaller dish. Excess powder causes wastage and over-filled dishes make the work bench messy. Do not dip the cuttings directly into the stock container—moisture and pieces of

plant tissue will be deposited and the powder will deteriorate.

(2) The base of the cutting should be moist so that the powder will adhere. Many evergreen shrubs and conifers will retain sufficient moisture on the stem surface if collected under moist conditions in the winter. Some cuttings, such as *Fremontodendron californicum* (Flannelbush or California Fremontia), have a sufficient number of small hairs on the stem to retain the powder. Others will have to be pre-moistened.

An excellent method to moisten the stem is to use a small rectangular sponge (obtainable from any drug store). The sponge is dampened and placed snugly into a plastic or wooden tray. The cuttings (in bundles where feasible) are pressed lightly onto the sponge so that they are moistened at the base.

(3) The cuttings are dipped in the powder to a depth of 5–10 mm (1/5–3/8″). The cut surfaces of cuttings that have been wounded (p. 273) are also normally covered with the powder. However, some propagators have obtained better results when only half the wounded area is covered with the powder.

(4) Excess powder is removed by lightly tapping the cuttings on the side of the dish.

(5) The cuttings are stuck into the rooting medium

(6) Any excess powder left in the dish is discarded, *not* replaced in the stock bottle. The dish should be washed and dried for future use.

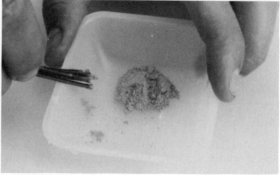

Figure 10-4. A (above). Transferring the rooting hormone powder from the stock container to a small dish. B (top right). Lightly pressing the bases of the cuttings onto a moist sponge. C. (middle right). Dipping the bases of the cuttings into the powder to a depth of 5–10 mm (1/5–3/8″). D (below right). Lightly tapping the cuttings onto the side of the dish to remove excess powder.

Storage Procedures

Correct storage procedures are vital if rooting hormones are to perform correctly. Carelessness and untidy work habits during and after using rooting hormones will quickly reduce their beneficial effects. The following guidelines should prove helpful.

(i) It is advisable not to purchase a large container of a commercial preparation unless it will be used within 18–24 months. It is better to purchase small quantities more often, especially if the numbers of cuttings to be treated are small. It is a mistake to buy the largest size (hoping to save money in the long term) and have the same tin still in use for the next 3–4 years, because the strength of the rooting hormone will have broken down.

I have seen situations where old tins have been left around on window ledges, shelves and benches and are useless in their activity because the cuttings are dipped in talc only, the hormone(s) having broken down.

(ii) The date of purchase should be marked on each container as soon as it arrives or is formulated. Alternatively, a number code may be used, in which a number on the tin refers to the purchase or formulation date recorded in a book.

(iii) Containers should be kept sealed and in a refrigerator when not in use. This should preserve the activity of the hormone for 2–3 years.

(iv) Contaminated powders should be discarded, as should those where there is doubt over effectiveness due to incorrect storage. A simple test sometimes used to determine if a rooting hormone is still active is to dip the petioles of Chrysanthemum or Tomato leaves in the powder or solution. Dipped and undipped leaves are then placed in a facility such as a warm mist propagation unit to encourage a quick result. The difference in root activity will show whether the preparation is still effective.

(v) Do not return excess amounts of powders used for dipping cuttings to the stock container.

Acetone Pre-Dipping

One technique to improve the performance level of powders that has caused interest recently is to pre-dip the base of the cutting in a solution of 50% acetone.

I believe this technique was first recorded in 1976 during B. H. Howard's work on the rooting of fruit tree rootstocks at the East Malling Research Station, England. Development work has since been carried out in England on woody ornamentals at the Efford Experimental Horticulture Station, Lymington, and at Hadlow College of Agriculture and Horticulture in Kent, where we found it was particularly useful for a number of broad-leaf evergreen cuttings taken in early fall.

The principle behind this technique is as follows. Acetone is a solvent for IBA, so dipping the base of the cutting first in acetone and then into the powder causes the immediate dissolving of the IBA, thus helping it to penetrate more quickly into the tissues. One plant with which we had excellent response was the rooting of *Ilex aquifolium* (English Holly) cultivars. Rooting at that time

Figure 10-5.
The effect of applying an acetone pre-dip followed by 0.8% IBA rooting hormone powder to a cutting of an *Ilex aquifolium* cv. (English Holly). Note how the acetone pre-dip has encouraged root development to occur up the stem of the cutting.

was often erratic, and water-stress problems also developed as the leaves were dropping prematurely from the stems of the cuttings. Pre-dipping resulted in the emergence of roots after 3–4 weeks, and roots also developed some 2.5 cm (1″) or more up the stem. The cultivar that showed the greatest effect was *I. aquifolium* 'Ferox Aurea' (Gold Hedgehog Holly). Cultivars of *Juniperus scopulorum* (Rocky Mountain Juniper) and × *Cupressocyparis leylandii* (Leyland Cypress) also responded to this technique, but less dramatically.

It must be noted that not all plant species respond to acetone pre-dipping and that it is, in fact, counterproductive for some species and cultivars.

Solutions

Solutions are based on the dispersal of the rooting hormone within an organic solvent. This solution is then applied to the base of the cutting. This method has gained popularity in the last five years for three reasons:—

(i) More published information is now available on the exact concentration of rooting hormone to use.

(ii) A wider range of commercial preparations is now available, and propagators have had good results with them.

(iii) A wider range of specific concentrations can be more quickly formulated on the nursery.

There are two methods by which rooting hormones are applied in solution:—

(i) quick dip (concentrated solution method)

(ii) soak (low-concentration solution method).

Compounds to aid penetration of the rooting hormone have been used in commercial preparations. Dimethyl sulfoxide (DMSO), an organic solvent, was used but is not now recommended due to the potential health problems. It is now replaced as a penetrant by another organic solvent, dimethylformamide (DMF). Rubber gloves should be worn when handling preparations containing a penetrant.

Quick Dip Method

Quick dips are generally more widely used than the soak technique, except in some European countries such as Holland. The procedure involves dipping the base of the cutting for only 3–5 seconds. The advantages for a quick dip are as follows:—

(i) It is quick, simple and economical to use.

(ii) It is precise and more accurate with relation to the amount of rooting hormone entering the stem tissue compared to powders.

(iii) The solutions can be stored for long periods under the correct conditions.

The disadvantages of a quick dip are:—

(i) There is little room for maneuvering if the precise concentration is not known. I observed that the base of hardwood cuttings of *Cotoneaster* × *watereri* hybrids (Waterer Cotoneaster) will quickly deteriorate if treated in the fall with solutions containing more than 500–1000 ppm IBA and then placed in a heated bin with a basal heat of 18°C (64°F). Efford Experimental Horticulture Station, England, have noted that *Berberis* (Barberry) cuttings are particularly prone to deteriorate if the IBA concentration is too high.

(ii) Fewer commercial preparations are available compared to powders.

Formulation of Stock Solution

The procedures are straightforward providing that an accurate metric weighing balance and basic laboratory glassware are available at the nursery. The alternative is to ask a local pharmacist to make the solution.

Note that these measurements should always be done in metric, do not attempt to convert to other systems.

Example:—To obtain 500 ml of a 5,000 ppm IBA stock solution.

Accurately weigh out 2.5 g IBA and dissolve in 250 ml full strength acetone. Ethyl alcohol may be used as the organic solvent instead of acetone. Make this solution up to 500 ml using pure distilled water. It is important to use full strength organic solvents so that the crystals of IBA will dissolve quickly. Also, the final stock solution must contain at least 50% of the organic solvent; otherwise, there is a risk that the IBA will crystallize out. If the stock solution is diluted to a lower strength, 50% acetone, alcohol or other organic solvent must be used or crystals will form. A few drops of ammonium hydroxide will disperse the crystals if they should form. Note that the potassium salts of IBA and NAA may be dissolved in water (preferably distilled).

The stock solution is placed in a stoppered brown bottle, labelled, dated and placed in the refrigerator. Again, it is stressed that the formulation must be done accurately because the rooting of cuttings is likely to be very unreliable if the initial stock solution is at the wrong concentration and used for many months afterwards.

[Note that 100% alcohol absorbs water from the atmosphere as soon as the seal is removed, stabilizing at about 98%. Do not purchase in larger quantities than needed for short-term use.]

A stronger stock solution can be made and then diluted to provide lower concentrations. For example, if the stock solution is 10,000 ppm ($\equiv$ 1%), the following concentrations can be made by diluting as indicated:—

5,000 ppm	— 1 pt stock solution + 1 pt 50% acetone or alcohol
2,500 ppm	— 1 pt stock solution + 3 pts 50% acetone or alcohol
1,000 ppm	— 1 pt stock solution + 9 pts 50% acetone or alcohol
500 ppm	— 1 pt stock solution + 19 pts 50% acetone or alcohol

Quick identification of the solutions that are to be stored can be achieved by adding a different, specific color dye to each dilution in addition to labelling the bottles or flasks. This is a particularly useful method for directing staff to the concentration to use if there is a communication problem due to language difficulties. Instructions are thus given based on a color code system instead of on concentration.

Concentrations

The optimum concentrations for application using the quick dip method are 250–10,000 ppm (0.025–1%). A guideline on concentrations to use is as follows:—

(i) Softwood cuttings, and easy-to-root semi-ripe wood, evergreen hardwood and deciduous hardwood cuttings—500–1,000 ppm (0.05–0.1%) IBA.

(ii) Moderate-to-root semi-ripe wood, evergreen hardwood and deciduous hardwood cuttings—2,000–2,500 ppm (0.2–0.25%) IBA.

(iii) Difficult-to-root semi-ripe wood, evergreen hardwood and deciduous hardwood cuttings—5,000–7,500 ppm (0.5–0.75%) IBA.

These figures provide a basis on which to begin; adjustments should be made with experience. Remember that other factors, such as time of year and wounding, also determine the degree of rooting.

Procedure

(1) Place the solution in a clean dish, using only a sufficient quantity for up to 2–3 hours as organic solvents can quickly evaporate.
(2) Dip the cutting to a depth of 5 mm (1/5″) for 3–5 seconds.
(3) If bundles of cuttings are dipped, ensure that the basal ends are even to obtain a uniform depth of dipping.
(4) Allow the solvent to evaporate from the stem of the cutting.
(5) Stick cuttings into the rooting medium.
(6) Discard any remaining solution as it will be contaminated with plant material.

Variations to the Standard Procedure

(i) Deciduous (Leafless) Hardwood Cuttings (Chapter 9)—Research work at East Malling Research Station, Kent, England, has shown that it is advantageous to dip only the basal cut surface of deciduous hardwood cuttings (see also p. 329). Traditionally, dipping to 2.5 cm (1″) has been found to inhibit rooting as the IBA can be "locked" in the external woody tissue and does not penetrate into the stem. Root emergence is reduced because this "IBA barrier" hinders development following initiation.

Dipping the basal cut surface means that the rooting hormone is drawn up into the internal tissues where root initiation takes place. Absorption of the IBA solution may be improved by storing the prepared cuttings overnight in a cool shed before dipping as this increases the capillary effect.

The principle of shallower dipping can also be extended to softwood and semi-ripe wood cuttings.

(ii) Rhododendrons—A technique used successfully at Hillier Nurseries (Winchester) Ltd. to root shy-rooting rhododendrons, such as *R.* 'Britannia', 'Doncaster' and 'Purple Splendour', and *Syringa vulgaris* cvs. (Common or French Lilac) is to use a higher than normal concentration of IBA so that the basal tissues of the cutting are killed. This shock treatment later begins to show on the propagation bench when the tissues turn first yellow, then brown and finally black. The rooting hormone travels up the stem during this period and rooting begins just above the dead tissue and new callus. The strength of the IBA has been reduced by this point to that suitable for optimum rooting.

Concentrations of up to 20,000 pm (2%) IBA have been used for this technique with rhododendrons. An optimum strength of 5,000 ppm (0.5%) IBA has been used for successful rooting of *Syringa vulgaris* cvs. (Common or French Lilac). These strong solutions may need to be slightly warmed to ensure that the IBA is dissolved, but this must be done with great care as

Figure 10-6. The application of a 3–5 second dip with a 2,500 ppm IBA liquid rooting hormone to the basal cut surfaces of *Malus* (Apple) rootstock cuttings. Note the well-labelled brown bottle containing the liquid hormone, measuring cylinder, timer, use of a petri dish in which to dip the cuttings, and the clean working surface. (Reproduced by permission of East Malling Research Station, Maidstone, Kent, U.K.©)

Figure 10-7. The effect of a quick dip, high concentration liquid hormone application to "burn" the tissues at the base of the cutting. Note the death of the basal tissues of the cutting and the development of callus tissue close to the region of optimal hormone strength for rooting. (Reproduced by courtesy of B. E. Humphrey, Hillier Nurseries (Winchester) Ltd., Romsey, Hampshire, U.K.)

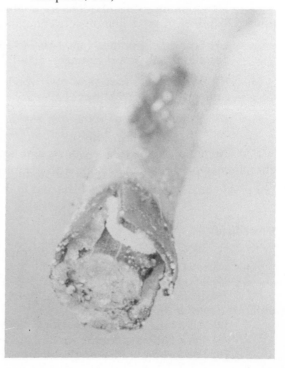

the solvents are very flammable. The procedure of using high concentrations requires considerable precision by the propagator.

An additional feature of this technique is that it promotes root emergence around the stem, thus removing the need for double wounding.

(iii) Conifers—It is important that only the ripened yellow-brown or brown wood at the stem base is dipped into the solution when propagating some conifers in the fall. The hormone concentration should be reduced by approximately 30–50% if the cuttings contain only unripened green wood of the current season's growth. I have noticed that × *Cupressocyparis leylandii* (Leyland Cypress) is particularly sensitive at 2,000–2,500 ppm—the green tissue turns brown and then black about 6 weeks after sticking if the normal optimum concentration has been in direct contact with the unripened tissue. *Juniperus* (Juniper) and *Taxus* (Yew) do not appear to be as sensitive and fewer problems should result.

Storage Procedures

The crystals received from the commercial chemical supplier must be kept in a refrigerator. Similarly, stock and unused dilute solutions should be refrigerated in labelled brown bottles. Sunlight degrades the solution, rendering it inactive—IAA is particularly sensitive. Solutions that become discolored through sunlight or that are contaminated with plant tissues must be discarded. Note that some of the commercial preparations are claimed to be stable in sunlight. The date of purchase or formulation should be recorded on the bottle label or kept in a notebook.

Soak Method

This low-concentration solution method involves soaking the cuttings for 12–24 hours in a weak solution of rooting hormone. In some instances, periods as low as 4 hours are used. The concentration of the rooting hormone is in the region of 20–250 ppm (0.002–0.025%). The final solution should contain from 0–5% concentration of the organic solvent.

This technique is favored by a number of European nursery operators, particularly in Holland. It is useful for many evergreen and deciduous shrubs, conifers such as *Sciadopitys verticillata* (Japanese Umbrella Pine) and some deciduous trees such as *Platanus* × *acerifolia* (London Plane). One reason for its success in rooting *Platanus* × *acerifolia* is thought to be that rooting inhibitors dissolve out during the soaking process. The uptake of the solution is influenced by temperature, but a major advantage is that there is plenty of opportunity for the cutting to readily absorb the rooting hormone. Forward planning is very necessary because the cuttings have to be removed from the solution as soon as the specified dipping period is completed.

Formulation of Stock Solution

There are two methods by which dilute solutions can be formulated.

(i) Preparation on the nursery, using laboratory crystalline products and proceeding in a manner similar to a quick dip stock solution.

Example:—To obtain 1000 ml (1 litre) of 100 ppm IBA

Accurately weigh out 0.1 g IBA and dissolve in 10–25 ml of 100% acetone or ethyl alcohol. The solution is made up to 1000 ml using pure distilled water. A few drops of ammonium hydroxide can be used to dispel any cloudiness or any crystals that form.

(ii) Purchase of a commercial product in tablet form. The Dutch product Rhizopon® comes in plastic tubes containing 20 tablets and in three formulations:—

> Rhizopon A—IAA 50 mg tablet
> Rhizopon AA—IBA 50 mg tablet
> Rhizopon B—NAA 25 mg tablet

The tablets are water-soluble (similar in principle to soluble aspirin) and are dissolved by shaking vigorously in a flask containing 1000 ml (1 litre) of distilled water. The strength of the solution is raised by increasing the number of tablets dissolved. The solution can be used immediately or stored temporarily in a labelled brown bottle in a refrigerator. The manufacturers of Rhizopon® (see Appendix 10-2) have produced two useful publications, *Growth Substances to Promote Root Formation in Cuttings* and *Rooting Guide,* which recommend powder concentrations for different plants and also suggest concentrations and periods of soaking.

Procedure

(1) Pour the solution into a solid plastic tray that is sufficiently deep to allow volume displacement of the solution by the cuttings. Flats or trays that have drainage holes or are difficult to clean should be lined with polyethylene film.

(2) Tie the cuttings in convenient size bundles and place them into the solution to a depth of 2.0–2.5 cm (¾–1″) for the recommended time period, keeping at a room temperature of around 18°C (65°F).

(3) Allow the solvent to evaporate from the stem base by placing the cuttings on a clean bench for about 15 minutes.

(4) Stick cuttings in the rooting medium.

(5) Discard the solution as it will be discolored by plant material and degraded.

Figure 10-8. Preparation of a flat with a polyethylene film lining for use in soaking cuttings in a low concentration of liquid rooting hormone. (Boskoop, Holland)

APPENDIX 10-1

Results of a Trial by Efford Experimental Horticulture Station to Compare the Effects of Liquid Quick Dips and Powder Hormone on Rooting of Rhododendron (1982)

VARIETIES	SERADIX 3 (0.8% IBA powder)	ACETONE + SERADIX 3	IBA (ppm)				SYNERGOL* (ppm)			
			2500	5000	7500	10000	2500	5000	7500	10000
			(5-second dip to 5 mm depth)				(5-second dip to 5 mm depth)			
Alice	17%	58%	50%	92%	67%	83%	58%	58%	75%	50%
Cunningham's White	67%	50%	63%	63%	75%	71%	75%	58%	38%	58%
Doncaster	0	0	0	14%	14%	14%	86%	71%	29%	0
Hugh Koster	82%	46%	73%	73%	46%	73%	63%	55%	91%	82%
Lady Clem. Mitford	58%	92%	92%	83%	100%	92%	75%	83%	50%	42%
Loder's White	43%	57%	43%	29%	71%	29%	43%	57%	29%	86%
Pink Pearl	71%	63%	42%	58%	54%	79%	79%	79%	83%	96%
Cilpinense	69%	75%	69%	63%	63%	75%	81%	75%	25%	69%
Mean	51%	55%	54%	59%	61%	64%	70%	67%	53%	60%

*Synergol—50% K-IBA, 50% Na-IBA

Summary

Response varied with ease with which varieties rooted.
A. *Easier rooting varieties* (Cilipinense, Cunningham's White, Hugh Koster, Pink Pearl)—Similar results were obtained from quick dips and Seradix and no advantage was seen as a result of dipping in acetone. Overall, a dip of 2500 ppm appeared suitable, with Synergol giving slightly better results than IBA.
B. *Moderate rooting varieties* (Lady Clementine Mitford, Loder's White)—The acetone dip gave a small improvement to performance in Seradix, and IBA dips between 5000–7500 ppm produced the best results, closely followed by Synergol at 2500–5000 ppm.
C. *Poorer rooting varieties* (Alice)—There was marked improvement where using acetone before using Seradix, but the best results were achieved with quick dips, 5000 ppm IBA or 7500 ppm Synergol.
D. *Difficult rooting varieties* (Doncaster)—This was the only variety to give a marked increase in rooting in response to the Synergol quick dip similar to that seen in 1981.

While results were somewhat variable, IBA in the range of 5000–7500 ppm or Synergol in the range of 2500–5000 ppm appear to be reasonable rates for rhododendrons, and there were indications that Synergol might be more suitable for some varieties, particularly the more difficult rooting ones. However, these results need confirming over another season.

(Reproduced by permission of Efford Experimental Horticulture Station, Lymington, Hampshire, U.K.)

APPENDIX 10-2

Some Commercial Preparations of Powder Rooting Hormones—Sources and Active Ingredients

Hormodin®

Merck Co., Inc.
Rahway, NJ 07065
U.S.A.

Hormodin #1—0.1% IBA
Hormodin #2—0.3% IBA
Hormodin #3—0.8% IBA

Hormoroot®

Hortus Products Co.
P.O. Box 275
Newfoundland, NJ 07435
U.S.A.

Hormoroot A—0.1% IBA + 15% Thiram
Hormoroot B—0.4% IBA + 15% Thiram
Hormoroot C—0.8% IBA + 15% Thiram

Rootone®

Amchem Products Inc.
Windsor, ON
N8W 3P6 Canada

Amchem Products, Inc.
Ambler, PA 19002
U.S.A.

Rootone® F—0.067% Naphthaleneacetamide
0.033% 2-methyl-1-naphtheneacetic acid
0.013% 2-methyl-1-naphthaleneacetamide
0.057% IBA
4.000% Thiram

Other Rootone® products include Improved Rootone® and Rootone® 10.

Stim-Root®

Plant Products Co. Ltd.
314 Orenda Road
Bramalea, ON
L6T 1G1 Canada

Stim-Root No. 1—0.1% IBA
Stim-Root No. 2—0.4% IBA
Stim-Root No. 3—0.8% IBA

Seradix®

May & Baker Ltd.
Dagenham, Essex RM10 7XS
England

Seradix No. 1—0.1% IBA in talc
Seradix No. 2—0.3% IBA in talc
Seradix No. 3—0.8% IBA in talc
Seradix L15 —1.5% IBA in talc

Murphy Hormone Rooting Powder®

Murphy Chemical Co. Ltd.
Wheathampstead
St. Albans, Hertfordshire
England

Murphy Hormone Rooting Powder—0.25% NAA + 3% Captan

Hormex®

Brooker Chemical Corp.
P.O. Box 9335
North Hollywood, CA 91605
U.S.A.

Hormex No. 1 —0.1% IBA
Hormex No. 3 —0.3% IBA
Hormex No. 8 —0.8% IBA
Hormex No. 16—1.6% IBA
Hormex No. 30—3.0% IBA
Hormex No. 45—4.5% IBA

Rhizopon®

A.C.F. Chemiefarma N.V.
Amsterdam
Maarissen
Netherlands

Rhizopon A —0.5% IAA in talc/carbon base
—0.7% IAA in talc/carbon base
—1.0% IAA in talc/carbon base
—50 mg IAA per tablet (long dip/soak application)
Rhizopon B —0.1% NAA in talc/carbon base
—0.2% NAA in talc/carbon base
—25 mg NAA per tablet (long dip/soak application)
Rhizopon AA—0.1% IBA in talc/carbon base
—0.5% IBA in talc/carbon base
—1.0% IBA in talc/carbon base
—2.0% IBA in talc/carbon base
—4.0% IBA in talc/carbon base
—8.0% IBA in talc/carbon base
—50 mg IBA per tablet (long dip/soak application)

Boots Rooting Powder®

Boots Farm Sales
Nottingham
England

NAA, IBA and Thiram

APPENDIX 10-3

Some Commercial Preparations of Liquid Rooting Hormones—Sources and Active Ingredients

Dip'N Grow®

> Alpkem Corporation
> P.O. Box 1260
> Clackamas, OR 97015
> U.S.A.

Clyde Jackson, a chemist with C & R Product Development, Oregon, worked with Edsal Wood some years ago to develop a liquid rooting hormone called Speedy Dip #2. This was not really available commercially but was later re-formulated as Jiffy Grow®, and C. Jackson then sold the manufacturing and licensing rights. Jiffy Grow® was later re-formulated again, leading to the development of Dip'N Grow®.

Dip'N Grow® originally contained dimethyl sulfoxide (DMSO) to encourage the penetration of the rooting hormone into the cutting, but Environmental Protection Agency (EPA) regulations made it necessary to omit DMSO from the formulation.

The product currently available contains 10,000 ppm (1.0%) IBA, 5,000 ppm (0.5%) NAA and a fungicide/bactericide. Dip'N Grow® (and other proprietary liquid formulations) provides instructions for dilution of the purchased stock solution with water (e.g., 1 in 5 to 1 in 20) for different species at various stages of growth. The base of the cutting is dipped for 3–5 seconds.

Dip'N Grow® should be used within 10 hours of dilution, otherwise its activity is reduced.

Woods Rooting Compound®

> Bonsai Village
> Wilsonville, OR 97070
> U.S.A.

This compound was developed by nurseryman and chemist Edsal Wood after Dip'N Grow® was already commercially available. He researched other organic compounds with penetration properties that could be safely used as an alternative to DMSO. This resulted in the use of dimethylformamide (DMF) in the formulation of his product.

Woods Rooting Compound® contains 10,000 ppm (1.0%) IBA and 5,000 ppm (0.5%) NAA, with 20% DMF as an additive to assist in the penetration of the hormones into the cutting. The product is diluted for use according to the manufacturer's instructions.

Both Dip'N Grow® and Woods Rooting Compound® have been gaining considerable popularity across the United States.

Synergol Rooting Hormone®

> Silvaperl Products Ltd.
> P.O. Box 8
> Harrogate, North Yorkshire HG2 8JW
> England

This is a water-based compound containing equal parts of the more soluble potassium salts of the hormones. It contains 5,000 ppm (0.5%) K-IBA, 5,000 ppm (0.5%) K-NAA, and boron.

Synergol Rooting Hormone® has been gaining popularity in the United Kingdom as a very useful and convenient alternative to powders.

Roots®

> Wilson Laboratories, Inc.
> Dundas, ON
> L9H 3H3 Canada

Roots® is a blue "liquid gel" rather than a solution. It contains a combination of 0.4% IBA and 0.01% etridiazole (Truban®), a fungicide.

REFERENCES AND SUGGESTED SOURCES FOR FURTHER READING

Blazich, F. A. 1980. Auxins other than indolebutyric acid which can effectively be used to stimulate rooting. *Comb. Proc. Inter. Pl. Prop. Soc.* **30**: 520–525.

Dirr, M. A. 1981. Rooting compounds and their use in plant propagation. *Comb. Proc. Inter. Pl. Prop. Soc.* **31**: 472–479.

————. 1982. What makes a good rooting compound? *Amer. Nurseryman* **155** (8): 33–34, 36, 38, 40 (April 15, 1982).

Ellyard, R. K. 1981. Rooting hormones—their effect on the rooting of some Australian species. *Australian Plants* **11** (No. 88), pp. 161–165 (Sept. 1981).

Gray, H. 1959. The quick dip alcoholic solution as an aid to rooting cuttings. *Proc. Pl. Prop. Soc.* **9**: 47–48.

Hartmann, H. T. & D. E. Kester. 1983. 4th ed. *Plant Propagation—Principles and Practices.* Prentice-Hall, Inc., Englewood Cliffs, N.J. Pp. 246–257, 318–323.

Howard, B. H. 1970. Solvents for the application of indolebutyric acid to hardwood cuttings. *Rep. East Malling Res. Stat. for 1969*, pp. 95–97.

————. 1974. Factors which affect the response of cuttings to hormone treatments. *Comb. Proc. Inter. Pl. Prop. Soc.* **24**: 142–143.

Macdonald, A. B. 1981. Developments for the use in rooting hormones. *Dig This* (B.C. Nursery Trades Association) **6** (3): 16–17 (May-June 1981).

Machen, J. 1977. Mixing rooting hormones. *Comb. Proc. Inter. Pl. Prop. Soc.* **27**: 259–263.

Nahlawi, N. & B. H. Howard. 1971. Effect of position of I.B.A. application on the rooting of plum hardwood cuttings. *Jour. Hort. Sci.* **46**: 535–543.

Roberts, A. N. & C. A. Boller. 1948. *Holly Production in Oregon.* Agric. Expt. St., Oregon State Univ., Bulletin 455.

Scott, M. A. 1982. *Nursery Stock Propagation—1982 Program.* Efford Experimental Horticulture Station, Lymington, Hampshire, U.K.

Snyder, W. E. 1966. Hormone-fungicide combinations in rooting. *Comb. Proc. Inter. Pl. Prop. Soc.* **16**: 267–272.

Ticknor, R. L. 1981. A comparison of several hormone formulations for rooting cuttings. *Comb. Proc. Inter. Pl. Prop. Soc.* **31**: 109–112.

————. 1982. Techniques for improving rooting during propagation. *Amer. Nurseryman* **155**(1): 67–69 (Jan. 1, 1982).

Vanderbilt, R. T. 1965. Rooting of broadleaved evergreens, especially hybrid Rhododendrons and species. *Comb. Proc. Inter. Pl. Prop. Soc.* **15**: 177–180.

Wain, R. L. 1974. Plant growth substances. *Comb. Proc. Inter. Pl. Prop. Soc.* **24**: 138–141.

Weiser, C. J. & L. T. Blaney. 1960. The effects of Boron on the rooting of English holly cuttings. *Amer. Soc. Hort. Sci.* **75**: 704–710.

Wells, J. S. 1963. The use of Captan in the rooting of rhododendrons. *Comb. Proc. Inter. Pl. Prop. Soc.* **13**: 132–135.

Williams, D. 1980. Chemical notebook: Rooting hormones—selection and use. *Grounds Maintenance* **15**(6): 10, 14, 16 (June, 1980).

Wood, E. A. 1981. New horizons in rooting hormones. *Comb. Proc. Inter. Pl. Prop. Soc.* **31**: 116–118.

Chapter 11

ROOTING MEDIA
(Rooting Composts)

One of the most important criteria for the successful rooting of cuttings is a reliable rooting medium. The influence of the medium is felt even before rooting occurs because of its water retention and aeration properties. The percentage of rooting and the quality of roots can, in many instances, be directly linked to the medium itself. Variation in root development increases costs as more grading is required to discard unrooted and poorly rooted cuttings so that a quality liner can be obtained.

It is surprising to note the different materials that have been used, either alone or incorporated with one or more alternative products. The components used to form rooting media are normally naturally occurring, but there has been increasing interest over the last decade in various artificial or manufactured substances. In many areas, advantages are obtained by using waste or surplus products from other industries—for example, sawdust and bark. More recently, there has been a renewed interest in using mycorrhizal fungi to increase both rooting percentages and actual root development, and in the incorporation of controlled-release fertilizers into the medium prior to sticking.

It is important to briefly discuss the criteria used in selecting an appropriate mix before documenting the characteristics of the different constituents used in rooting media.

CRITERIA TO CONSIDER WHEN SELECTING A ROOTING MEDIUM

(1) Cost

Transportation of the basic materials to the nursery is a major factor in the cost. Materials like sand are heavy while others like peat moss are bulky unless compressed into bales. Hence, there is a major advantage in utilizing local products to lower the cost, even though they may not be the ideal one for the purpose.

It is advisable to obtain a quotation if there is more than one supplier of the same product. Also, check their reliability for quality and delivery dates with local nursery operators. Contact other nurseries close to your own to see about the possibility of combining to bulk-order materials and then sharing the cost. Large orders often receive reduced per unit prices, and combining to bulk-order is therefore particularly helpful for smaller nurseries.

(2) Quality

Try to obtain a sample of a product intended for use in a rooting medium before ordering. Checks can then be made on grade or particle size, freedom from impurities such as silt and harmful salts, and to help clarify that it contains a minimum of weed seeds and diseases. The local extension officer in your area will be helpful in the procedures used to determine these criteria.

The pH of the components should be checked, particularly when it is known that they may have arisen naturally under high pH water conditions or where the nursery's own water supply is alkaline. An optimum pH for the rooting medium should be 5.5–6.5, with a pH range of 4.0–5.0 advised for ericaceous subjects. Consideration should be given to using rain water or de-ionizing equipment (see p. 113) if there is a possibility that the nursery water supply will raise the pH excessively.

(3) Physical Structure

This is really a continuation of quality but is separated because the physical structure can directly or indirectly determine the following:—

(a) Ability of the rooting medium to support the cutting. This is particularly important with larger-leaved evergreen and deciduous cuttings when the weight can easily cause the cutting to be dislodged—particularly under mist propagation.

(b) Easy sticking of the cuttings. There is nothing more frustrating than having difficulty in sticking the cuttings through unevenly graded or mixed components. A light firming using a template, or slightly increasing the moisture content, can often help to improve sticking. Excess firming will significantly lower the air/water ratio.

(c) Adequate aeration and free draining of the medium. Where possible, the optimum air-filled porosity range of the rooting medium should be around 30%, unless the water status of the cuttings is the over-riding consideration. The respiration rate is high during the process of rooting because the cutting is utilizing food products and forming new tissue. Oxygen is a primary element required for aerobic respiration so that the process can be carried out efficiently. The medium must provide adequate oxygen to the base of the cutting.

A common cause for the loss of cuttings is poor drainage of the rooting medium, particularly where intermittent mist propagation is used. This will reduce the oxygen and cause the cuttings to deteriorate. Early signs of poor drainage should be noted and immediately rectified, not left until the cuttings begin to rot. Signs of poor drainage include:—

(i) Water rapidly percolating between the fingers when a portion of the mix is squeezed in a clenched hand. Ideally, there should be sufficient moisture just to hold the mix together after it has been clenched in the hand, but without water seepage.

(ii) Rooting of the cuttings occurring near the surface of the medium. Closer examination will normally show that the middle and lower portion of the cutting below the surface will have decayed, resulting in root development near the surface where there is less moisture and more oxygen. The winter-flowering evergreen *Garrya elliptica* (Coast Silk-tassel) is particularly good at showing this symptom under poor drainage conditions. However, there will be no root development at all if these conditions persist.

Figure 11-1. Basal Stem Rot of Garrya elliptica (Coast Silk-tassel) cutting due to waterlogging of the rooting medium. Note the development of the root system further up the stem where improved aeration occurred near the surface of the medium.

Excess aeration problems can occur if the medium is too open, which also causes lack of cutting stability and insufficient moisture retention. The problem with some evergreens, particularly conifers, is that the drying out of the medium may not be visually shown in the foliage until some days or even weeks later, by which time it is often too late to correct the situation. A further symptom of excess aeration shown by a number of evergreens, particularly *Camellia*, *Ilex* (Holly), *Taxus* (Yew) and × *Cupressocyparis leylandii* (Leyland Cypress), is the formation of an excess amount of callus at the base of the cuttings. If this occurs under alkaline conditions, the problem is further accentuated by the hardening of the cell walls of the outer region of this undifferentiated parenchyma tissue, thus making it extremely difficult for roots to penetrate through from the stem tissue. Remember, it is wrong to think that the greater the amount of callus formed, the better will be the rooting. Callus forms to heal the cut surfaces and there is something wrong during the rooting process if it is excessive. Other causes of excess callusing, besides excess aeration in the rooting medium, are attributed to:—

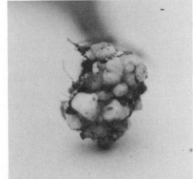

(i) Rooting cuttings at the wrong stage of growth

(ii) Incorrect selection of cuttings.

(iii) Too low a concentration of rooting hormone.

(iv) Too high rooting temperatures.

Figure 11-2. Excess callus development at the base of × *Cupressocyparis leylandii* (Leyland Cypress) cutting due to an excessively open rooting medium.

In conclusion, there are essentially three criteria that must be checked to help ensure good drainage of a medium:—

(i) That the product is well graded.

(ii) That its structure is retained during rooting—particularly where mist propagation and fogging (humidifying) units are used.

(iii) That there is alteration to the ratio of the rooting medium components to allow for changes in climate, propagation facility and, sometimes, the plant species.

(d) Development of a fibrous root system. This allows the smaller roots to retain a quantity of the individual particles when the cutting is removed from the medium and helps establishment following potting-up. A medium containing a very high ratio of fine or coarse sand tends to encourage a lack of secondary roots and those that do form are rather brittle.

(4) Mixing

Ideally, select a medium which does not require any mixing, e.g., pure Pine bark. If this is not possible, then the individual components should have the ability to be easily mixed by hand or machine so that they are equally dispersed in the medium. A component containing pieces of twigs, leaves, roots, etc. should be shredded and sifted before mixing.

It can be advantageous for a smaller nursery to prepare a large mix and store the unused material in large polyethylene bags or plastic boxes. The mix will, however, have to be checked for moisture content before using in case it has dried out.

(5) Standardization

There used to be, and in a few cases still is, a tendency for a nursery to have many different media with varying components and ratios. Every attempt should be made to standardize the mix for as wide a range of plants as possible. The number of necessary variations should be kept to a minimum.

Major Constituents For Rooting Media

A considerable amount of information is available on the characteristics and ratios for mixing rooting media, based both on research and on the observations of nursery operators. However, some of the literature is unfortunately conflicting. The aim of this section is to attempt to summarize the information and to make recommendations in the light of current propagation procedures. Two excellent references on the characteristics of individual components used in both rooting media and growing media are, firstly, chapter 2 of *Modern Potting Composts* by A. C. Bunt (George Allen and Unwin, 1976) and secondly, pp. 29–33 of *Plant Propagation: Principles and Practices* by H. T. Hartmann and D. E. Kester (Prentice-Hall, 4th. ed., 1983). A. C. Bunt, of the Glasshouse Crops Research Institute, Littlehampton, England, carried out important fundamental research on growing media for many years, and this has subsequently been of considerable benefit to the horticultural industry.

PEAT

Peat is the material most commonly used, and forms the basis of many different propagation media when mixed with other components. It is normally mixed with either fine or coarse sand particles, perlite, vermiculite or pumice, with bark, sawdust or loam being incorporated as a third component. Peat is formed by the partial decomposition of plants in areas of high rainfall, and the types of peat can vary considerably in color and structure. These differences are largely dependent on the species of plant from which they have been derived, on the degree of decomposition and on the geographical origin. The major sources of peat in the Northern Hemisphere are Russia, Canada, Scandinavia, Germany, Ireland and the United Kingdom.

The two main types of peat used in horticulture are sphagnum peat (peat moss) and sedge peat. Peat moss is the name often given to sphagnum peat after it has been harvested and dried.

(a) Sphagnum Peat (Peat Moss)

A. C. Bunt classifies sphagnum peat into two groups based on the cellular structure of the *Sphagnum* species largely forming the basis of the peat:—

(i) The *cymbifolia* group consisting of species such as *S. papillosum* and *S. imbricatum*. Peats within this group are looser with excellent water absorption and retention properties.

(ii) The *acutifolia* group consisting of species such as *S. rubellum* and *S. plumulosum*. Peats within this group have a closer texture but are not as good in retaining water.

Both groups are very acidic with a pH range of around 3.2–4.5, allow movement of water within them, and contain a very low level of available nitrogen. Younger sphagnum peat moss tends to hold more water, but its structure also gives more aeration.

(b) Sedge Peat

Sedge peat is largely derived from different sedges, reeds and grasses—for example *Carex* sp. (Sedge) and *Phragmites* (Reed Grass). These peats are darker in color and more decomposed than sphagnum peats. They have a higher nutrient content because drainage water from mineral soils percolates into the peat bog. They can be either acid or alkaline with a pH range of 4.0–7.5, depending on their origin.

Sedge peats are not generally suitable as a component for a rooting medium because they have poor aeration. They are more suitable for compressing into the peat blocks used in the propagation of some horticultural crops (see p. 209).

Purchasing Peat

Peat can be considered to be a more standardized material than mineral soils, but there are large differences between peat types in both physical and chemical properties. The grade and quality are also affected by the subsequent processing. Today, both harvesting and processing are very mechanical operations, therefore it is important that you evaluate samples and discuss the product with the supplier. Peat can be purchased either as compressed bales or as a loose bulk product. A medium grade sphagnum peat is generally recommended. Try to avoid peat moss harvested by systems using a milling process.

You should be particularly wary of some fine peats that will become compressed when used with mist propagation and thus not allow water movement. I saw this problem being created while writing this text when a nurseryman had been supplied with a low-quality fine grade peat. The rooting medium became saturated with water even when mixed with perlite, causing rapid deterioration of the cuttings.

One problem in some countries is that there tends to be a monopoly because few producers are able to supply large quantities to the horticultural industry. Thus, supplies may be difficult to obtain if the chain is broken due to industrial disputes. This was one reason why some nursery operators in Europe started to look for alternatives such as bark products some years ago.

Weed Seeds, Diseases and Pests

There can be other vegetation in the vicinity of peat harvesting areas and therefore weed seeds can be a problem. Depending on the location of the area, problem weed seeds can be *Rumex acetosella* (Sheep Sorrel), *Poa annua* (Annual Bluegrass), *Stellaria media* (Chickweed) and *Salix* sp. (Willow).

It has been claimed that some diseases have been introduced into the propagation unit by peat (see p. 209). Peat should be partially sterilized before use if it is found that a particular weed or disease problem does arise through its source. Peat is not normally partially sterilized (pasteurized) in Western Europe since the incidence of plant pathogens in the peat is low.

Pests should not be a problem, although it is thought that some parasitic nematodes may be introduced through the peat. It is an indirect pest, commonly referred to as fungus gnats, that is likely to be the problem. The life cycle flourishes in high organic matter under warm humid conditions, with the fungus gnat larvae feeding on the young developing roots of the cuttings.

Mixing Peat

Those who have handled bales of peat will appreciate that the weight can vary considerably from one shipment to another, due to variations in amounts of water content. Peat that is too dry will require moistening prior to mixing with other constituents, because dry peat may never become sufficiently moistened after the cuttings have been stuck. Applying a wetting agent such as Aqua-GRO® to peat during mixing has been found helpful. Larger operations sometimes have an automatic overhead spray line with coarse nozzles to pre-wet the peat either before or while mixing. If mixing with a rotavator on the floor, a useful way to pre-moisten smaller quantities of dry peat bales covered in polyethylene is to first insert a 45 cm (18″) long, rigid metal tube into the end of a hosepipe attached to a water tap. The metal tube is then thrust through the plastic and well into the peat bale, and the water turned on for about 5–6 minutes. The polyethylene will expand and contain the water, shrinking again as the peat moss absorbs the water. It may be necessary to insert the metal tube in two different areas of larger bales. Finally, the bale is broken open and the peat moss mixed. It does save the annoyance of spreading peat onto a concrete floor and adding water so that the dry peat floats for a period, causing the mixing operation to become messy.

BARK

There has been increasing interest in recent years in the use of shredded or pulverized bark in the horticultural industry, both as a growing medium and a mulching material. The reasons for this include:—

(i) Increasing price of peat moss.

(ii) Unreliability of peat supplies in some areas.

(iii) Subsequent weed problems arising from local sources of peat.

(iv) The need to "condition" the fine-grade peats now marketed in order to prevent compaction and waterlogging.

(v) The ready availability of crushed bark as a by-product from the forestry industry as a result of the de-barking of logs during the processing stage of the timber.

There is limited published research relating to the use of bark as a rooting medium, unlike many other rooting medium components.

The sources of barks can be categorized into two groups—hardwood barks (e.g., *Quercus*, Oak; *Fagus*, Beech) and softwood barks (e.g., *Abies*, Fir; *Picea*, Spruce; *Pinus*, Pine). A well-graded bark that has been allowed to compost and decompose has a satisfactory water-holding capacity while also allowing the movement of water. Nitrogen, usually in the form of ammonium nitrate, is normally added to the bark during the composting process to reduce the risk of crops suffering a setback due to nitrogen deficiency. The amount of supplementary nitrogen is dependent on the tree species from which the bark is derived. Composting the bark with added nitrogen is very likely to increase the pH of the pile.

The following notes should prove helpful if you are contemplating using bark:—

1. Check the tree species from which the bark has been obtained. Problems have arisen due to toxic compounds (mostly phenols and monoterpenes) with bark used as a growing medium. It is reasonable, therefore, to assume that a similar effect would arise when rooting cuttings. Barks that have caused problems include those from *Calocedrus decurrens* (Incense Cedar), *Juglans nigra* (Black Walnut), *Acer saccharinum* (Silver Maple), *Liriodendron tulipifera* (Tulip Tree), *Thuja plicata* (Western Red Cedar), *Pinus ponderosa* (Ponderosa Pine) and *Picea sitchensis* (Sitka Spruce). Bark from *Pinus nigra* (Austrian or Black Pine) and *P. sylvestris* (Scots Pine) does not seem to have the same problems.

In general, however, the pine barks have given the most reliable results and provide excellent properties for both rooting and growing media.

2. Bark should not be used from trees that have been infected with disease, e.g., *Phytophthora* and *Rhizoctonia*.

3. Bark should not be used from logs that have been floated in salt water prior to processing by the sawmill. These logs absorb chlorine and sodium from the seawater and these elements will cause problems. It is advisable to obtain a salt reading prior to delivery to avoid salt problems.

4. Softwood barks are more acidic than hardwood barks. The pH of the bark should be in the 5.0–5.5 range following processing, except when urea and/or phosphates have been added. The pH can rise to as high as 8 in such cases. Excessive pH of hardwood barks has been reduced by adding sulfur. Sulfur-treated barks have been used for growing media but there seems to be little information on their use in rooting media and any possible harmful effects on the cuttings.

5. Hardwood barks should be composted for a minimum of 10 weeks prior to use, and softwood barks for a minimum of 6 weeks. This decomposition of the bark causes it to become darker in color, increases the water-holding capacity, helps to remove harmful substances, lowers manganese toxicity levels and usually raises the pH if not properly controlled. The pile should be turned at least every two weeks. Processing is best done by a reputable company that specializes in preparing high-quality horticultural bark, rather than in the nursery.

6. It is generally recommended that the grade used for propagation be finer (below 7 mm particle size) than that used as a growing medium, e.g., Cambark® fine grade. The bark should contain little or no attached wood.

7. When purchasing a proprietary, ready-made product, it is advisable to check whether additional nitrogen has been added to the bark during the composting process—for example, the British product Forest Bark® (derived from spruce) has additional nitrogen added during composting, while Cambark® (derived from pine) does not.

8. There is some evidence that bark has anti-fungal properties and that it shows signs of suppressing nematodes. Further investigations are required into these aspects.

Hillier Nurseries (Winchester) Ltd., England, have traditionally based their rooting medium on a low peat to high sand ratio of 1:3. However, they have carried out trials to compare Cambark® (100% pine bark mix) used on its own and in combination with peat moss and/or sand. Initial observations showed that *Acer negundo* 'Aureo-marginatum' (Box Elder cv.) and *Chaenomeles speciosa* 'Nivalis' (Common Flowering Quince cv.) improved their root system development, while *Syringa vulgaris* 'Charles Joly' (Common or French Lilac cv.), *Abelia* × *grandiflora* (White Abelia) and *Potentilla davurica* 'Manchu' (Dahurian Cinquefoil cv.) had improved root systems and rooted more quickly in this bark rooting medium. Conversely, rooting performance of *Berberis thunbergii* 'Rose Glow' (Japanese Barberry cv.) and *Parthenocissus tricuspidata* 'Veitchii' (Veitch's Boston Ivy) was inferior, but not markedly or unacceptably so, to the standard 1:3 ratio of peat moss to sand used on this nursery. For ericaceous plants, a rooting medium containing a 1:1 ratio of peat moss and bark was marginally superior to a 100% bark medium. This nursery in 1985 was using 100% bark with the addition of Osmocote® (12–14 month) at a rate of 1.75 kg per m³ (3 lb/cu. yd.) for most of their propagation work.

Trials using Cambark® at Efford Experimental Horticulture Station, Hampshire, England, have demonstrated that:—

(i) A rooting medium containing 100% bark is more prone to drying out rapidly, compared to a 1:1 ratio of peat moss to bark and a 2:1 peat moss to coarse sand. (Investigations are underway on a medium containing 100% bark plus polymers that may help to solve this problem.)

(ii) A rooting medium containing a significant amount of bark must have a controlled-release fertilizer incorporated at mixing time to ensure cutting quality and good establishment following potting.

Bark is capable of locking-up nitrogen so that there is less risk of damage to the root system of the cutting compared to peat moss and sand mixes. A recommended rate in England for summer cuttings being rooted in a 1:1 ratio of peat moss and bark under mist propagation is to add 1.0 kg/m^3 (27 oz/cu. yd.) of either 8–9 or 12–14 month Osmocote® or Ficote® when leaching is at its maximum, while the rate is reduced to 0.75 kg/m^3 (20 oz/cu. yd.) of 12–14 month Osmocote® (17-10-10) or Ficote® (16-10-10) for winter cuttings under polyethylene film cover when leaching is at its minimum. The latter controlled-release fertilizer specifications retained the quality of the cuttings up to the time of potting.

Figure 11-3. A comparison of the root system development of *Camellia* cuttings grown in two "standard" rooting media. Left— 3:1 peat moss and coarse sand (grit). Right — 1:1 peat moss and pine bark plus incorporation of a 12-14 month controlled-release fertilizer at 1 kg/m^3 (27 oz/1 cu. yd.). (Reproduced by courtesy of Efford Experimental Horticulture Station, Lymington, Hampshire, U.K.)

Figure 11-4. A comparison of root development in the flat of cuttings rooted in two "standard" rooting media. Left — 1:1 peat moss and pine bark plus incorporation of a 12-14 month controlled-release fertilizer at 1 kg/m^3 (27 oz/1 cu. yd.) Right — 3:1 peat moss and coarse sand (grit). (Reproduced by courtesy of Efford Experimental Horticulture Station, Lymington, Hampshire, U.K.)

Experiments into the use of bark for rooting cuttings have suggested that it gives better results in winter than peat moss because it becomes less waterlogged, but that it is not so good for softwood summer cuttings where water supply to the cutting is a more important consideration.

In conclusion, both experimental work and commercial experience generally conclude that bark is best used in conjunction with peat moss rather than as a complete alternative. There is then better support of the cuttings and improved water-holding capacity without waterlogging. A mix containing equal proportions of sphagnum peat moss and Cambark® fine grade gives a marked improvement in root activity compared to a peat moss and coarse sand mix, as long as controlled-release fertilizers are added. The controlled-release fertilizer in the rooting medium is safer when bark is present as the nitrogen lock-up by the bark provides a safety factor against damage to the cuttings due to excessive nutrient release. The incorporation of a high-quality bark allows the formation of many fibrous roots that cling to the medium so that damage and root disturbance is reduced when potting-on. This, coupled with the improved quality of the cuttings that is maintained right up to potting, encourages faster establishment and uniform growth.

SAWDUST

This is another by-product formed during the processing of forestry products and is popular in North America. Many of the fundamental principles mentioned under bark also apply to sawdust—harmful substances, freedom from salts, nitrogen deficiency and avoiding possible disease sources.

Drainage problems in the mix are likely to arise if the sawdust is excessively composted. Excellent results are obtained in British Columbia using salt-free *Abies* (Fir) or *Tsuga* (Hemlock) sawdust as a growing medium. There should be no reason why it should not be used to substitute for a percentage of the peat moss in a rooting medium, bearing in mind that some liquid feeding of the cuttings may be necessary to avoid a nitrogen check prior to potting-up. A controlled-release fertilizer such as Osmocote® or Nutricote® can be used with sawdust.

FINE AND COARSE SANDS (GRITS)

Fine and coarse sands seem to be more popular in many European areas, where local sources exist, than in North America. NOTE:—Grits have been included in the category of coarse sand for the purposes of this text. The sands are normally mixed with peat moss either in an equal ratio or in a ratio of 2 parts peat moss to 1 part sand. Pure "sharp" sand has been used successfully alone to root *Hydrangea anomala* subsp. *petiolaris* (Climbing Hydrangea) and *Ilex crenata* cvs. (Japanese Holly), while media with a high ratio of sand to peat moss are particularly good for *Magnolia*. The best sources are generally those formed by the weathering of quartz rocks and sandstones. Some nurseries have moved away from sands to alternative materials such as perlite and crushed pumice because of rising costs, variability in quality and the weight factor. Remember that sand is heavy, particularly when wet. I have seen some disasters with overhead mist propagation when insufficient structural support was given to the propagation benches! There is also a greater risk of damage to the roots when removing the cuttings because of the increased weight of the rooting medium. The grade of sand (and grit), although similar from the chemical viewpoint, can give very different physical properties to media.

Mixes with low peat moss and high sand ratios have been used for many years at Hilliers Nurseries (Winchester) Ltd., England, and they have found that the concentration of rooting hormones could be successfully increased in such a mix to improve the rooting of certain difficult-to-root plants. The extra overhead misting required for these mixes means that the pH of the medium can increase rapidly, and there is a marked tendency for certain plants to develop more brittle roots and fewer secondary roots.

Purchasing Sands

The following notes will prove helpful when evaluating a potential source for fine and coarse sands:—

1. It is essential to obtain samples to check for grade, and for freedom from weed seeds, silt, harmful salts and organic matter. Sands should be washed to ensure that they are clean.

2. The pH in particular should be checked. Alkaline sands should be avoided, particularly if the local water supply is also alkaline.

3. A major cost will be that of transportation.

4. Try to personally visit the sand pit, particularly if there are several pits in one area, so that you can explain to the supplier the grade and quality expected. There can be local variations even within one pit.

5. Keep a quality check on the sands following each delivery and notify the supplier immediately of any problems.

6. Sands essentially vary according to location, origin, particle size and surface contour. This will, in turn, have a direct effect on their aeration, drainage and water-holding capacities. Fine sands are more suitable for rooting cuttings under polyethylene film while the coarser sands are more appropriate for use in a mist propagation facility where there is a greater need for adequate aeration and drainage.

7. A particle size specification ranging from 1–4 mm (1/16–1/6") has been recommended for sands to be mixed with peat moss. I find that a 3 mm (⅛") washed, lime-free, crushed, coarse sand gives good results. Aeration of the medium can be lowered if too fine a sand is used because it fills the pore spaces between the peat granules.

8. Sands must be uniformly graded. Non-uniform grading can lead to "packing" of fine particles between the coarser ones. [Some suppliers will grade sand only for very large orders.]

Types of Sands

At this stage I can only relate some experiences from Britain regarding the types of sands to select. Washed Cornish coarse sands, Windermere coarse sands and Bedfordshire sands are good, while many of the pits in the Thames Valley area around Staines and Datchet in south east England and the New Forest and Midhurst area in southern England should prove satisfactory, providing a good seam is selected.

Builder's sand should be avoided because drainage is variable, and it often contains silt, organic matter, weed seeds and harmful salts. It also "cakes" when it dries out, thus causing root disturbance.

Another type of material that has been used is processed from river flints. These are heated to a high temperature and then plunged in cold water where they shatter. The product is normally used in road-surfacing and is considerably more expensive for a nursery to purchase compared to normal sands. The grade for rooting cuttings does not seem to give as good drainage as a regular washed sand. "Cracker-grit" is a name sometimes given to a coarse sand that results from crushing stones in a cracking machine.

PERLITE

Perlite is a naturally-occurring volcanic material found largely in the United States and New Zealand. Chemically, it is made up of alumino-silicates. It is particularly popular in North America, but has become more widely used in Europe in recent years as an alternative to fine and coarse sands. The material available for horticulture is formed by heating the mined material to around 1000°C (1830°F). It is the resulting cellular structure that is largely responsible for making perlite an excellent material for rooting cuttings. It is light, sterile, contains no nutrients and has no buffer or cation exchange properties, but it gives very good drainage and aeration properties to the medium (the particles contain around 98% volume of air). However, these particles are largely "sealed", hence the air within them is not available to the cuttings. The pH falls in the 6.0–7.5 range.

The following notes should prove helpful regarding the use of perlite in rooting media:—

1. It may be used alone, but is best used with peat moss for woody ornamentals. This will increase the water-holding capacity and give the cuttings greater stability. Ratios of equal proportions are popular, or a ratio of 2 parts moss:1 part perlite can be used.

2. It is very light in weight and therefore is particularly useful for mist propagation benches because there is little chance of damage to the structure from weight stress.

3. Perlite should be considered as an alternative if problems arise because of unreliability in the quality of fine and coarse sands.

4. It is particularly useful as an alternative when problems have arisen with previous media because of inadequate drainage—for example, propagation of evergreens under mist propagation in the late fall and winter.

5. The "horticultural grade" perlite is used for propagation. This may be either a medium or coarse specification. Avoid products with a lot of fine and/or dust particles.

6. One problem with its use is the dust particles that arise when the manufacturer's bags are emptied. Personnel should always wear a dust mask over the nose and mouth when emptying bags and when mixing media containing perlite. The amount of dust can be reduced by directing a fine spray of water into the bag and over the perlite before mixing. Suppliers' products can vary in the degree of content of fine particles, although some are now providing perlite that has been decomposed to eliminate air-borne particles.

Figure 11-5. A well-rooted *Ilex aquifolium* cv. (English Holly) cutting just removed from a peat moss/perlite rooting mix. Note the adherence of the medium components to the root system. This will assist establishment of the cutting after potting.

7. It is light in weight and structure and therefore perlite mixes do retain some of the rooting media around the root system. This helps subsequent establishment following potting-up.

8. It is sterile and light in weight and therefore it is a useful material for rooting and shipping cuttings when there are specific plant quarantine regulations. Always contact the local plant quarantine office in advance to check the regulations for countries to which you intend to export.

VERMICULITE

Vermiculite is a material that has been used for many years in plant propagation. It is found as a natural deposit in the United States and South Africa, and is described as a hydrated silicate containing aluminum, iron and magnesium. The mined product is heated to around 1000°C (1830°F) for a short period and an expanding plate-like structure is formed as the contained water is converted into steam.

The final product is lightweight, normally has a pH range between 6.0–6.5, has a buffering action, and can take up a considerable amount of water. Vermiculite will not re-expand if excessively firmed or compressed.

It has been found to be good for rooting *Magnolia*, but it is normally incorporated with peat moss because support to the cuttings is not as good when it is used alone. Like perlite, it is a useful material for rooting cuttings intended for export to overcome specific plant quarantine regulations.

PUMICE

Pumice is another volcanic material and is found in western North America. It is made up of aluminum silicate and also contains small quantities of potassium and sodium. The porous nature created when water and gases were emitted as the volcanic material cooled means that pumice is very porous. Its good aeration, drainage and sterile qualities have made it popular with nursery operators when it is economical to transport from the source of supply. A grade containing aggregates between 3–6 mm (⅛–¼″) is recommended for propagation. However, problems have been experienced in obtaining a consistent grade from suppliers.

I have noted some excellent results in British Columbia when using pure pumice on *Juniperus* (Juniper), *Photinia* and dwarf *Pinus* (Pine), particularly during late fall and winter when drainage is a problem. What is interesting is that some nursery operators have rooted plants in pure pumice when other mixes have failed. It is best to use deep-sided flats so that there is a good depth of pumice into which to stick the cuttings. The fine particles amongst the larger aggregates help to produce a good fibrous root system, and these particles also adhere to some of the root system after the cutting is removed from the mix. It also produces a good medium when mixed with peat moss in 1:1 and 2:1 ratios, although it will be heavier in weight than a peat/perlite mix. It has also been useful to add as a 10–20% proportion to other mixes containing peat moss, sawdust, bark or sand constituents to improve aeration and drainage for cuttings being rooted in mist propagation facilities.

Plants successfully rooted in a pumice/peat moss medium include *Rhododendron*, *Juniperus horizontalis* 'Wiltonii' (Wilton Carpet or Blue Rug Juniper), *Cotoneaster apiculatus* (Cranberry Cotoneaster) and *Taxus* × *media* 'Hicksii' (Hicks' Yew).

EXPANDED POLYSTYRENE CHIPS OR BEADS

This material is a manufactured plastic product. It is inert, has no buffer action and is extremely stable to the extent that it does not deteriorate. Unlike vermiculite and pumice, it does not absorb water. Its main purpose is to increase aeration in the rooting mix. I have noted that polystyrene chips are not as effective as a peat/perlite mix because the overall drainage is not as good and a less fibrous root system is produced. It is not suitable for use alone for rooting cuttings, but is best mixed with peat moss.

LOAM

Loam is used as a rooting medium for rooting open-ground deciduous hardwood cuttings, and for cold frame and greenhouse propagation. It does not normally have the drainage capacity of many other media, therefore additional materials have to be incorporated. It provides cation exchange and buffer action, and thus a source of nutrients to the cuttings after rooting. Its major problem is as a source of weed seeds, pests and diseases unless it is partially sterilized (pasteurized) or fumigated.

1. Open Ground Facility

Deciduous hardwood cuttings are lined out in the open ground into a well-drained, weed-free, sandy loam, either in the fall or prior to bud burst the following year. It may be necessary to incorporate organic matter into the loam prior to lining out to improve the soil structure and water-holding capacity (see also p. 314).

2. Cold Frame Facility

A good-quality sandy loam can be successfully used as the major component for rooting many deciduous hardwood and conifer cuttings in the fall. Peat moss and, often, sand should be incorporated with the loam. A useful optimum mix is 2 parts sandy loam, 1 part peat moss and 1 part sand. This mix should be fumigated against soil-borne pests and diseases with methyl bromide or Basamid® prior to use. Fumigation will also eliminate most weed seeds, thus preventing weed competition with the cuttings. Avoid adding a heavy grade of crushed coarse sand if there is a high silt content in the loam, otherwise the surface becomes hard and "cakes"—particularly when overhead irrigation is installed.

3. Greenhouse Facility

The addition of loam into the rooting medium essentially provides a growing medium for the rooted cuttings. The incorporation of loam helps to provide a source of nutrients, reduces drying out of the medium, and the buffer action lessens the risk of root damage from over-feeding with liquid fertilizer. It will reduce drainage, therefore particular care needs to be taken to prevent waterlogging when rooting under a mist propagation unit. It is essential to partially sterilize (pasteurize) the loam using steam or to treat with a soil fumigant.

The incorporation of loam into the rooting medium is useful when cuttings are rooted during the summer and need to be held until the following year before potting-up. For example, Treasures Nurseries, Tenbury Wells, England, found that they obtained a superior rooted cutting of *Clematis* with improved establishment following potting-up. In addition, there were fewer losses over the winter because a stronger root and shoot system developed prior to the fall. It also helped management of the crop because the majority of the potting could be held for a pre-determined period.

There are two ways in which propagators incorporate the loam into a rooting medium:—

(i) Incorporation of the loam in a peat/sand or peat/perlite mix. The optimum ratio is 3 parts peat moss, 2 parts sand and 1 part loam.

(ii) "Layering" the medium. Use a flat with a minimum depth of 10 cm (4"), and place a layer of a loam-based growing medium over the bottom following with a layer of a peat/sand (or peat/perlite) rooting medium and then a thin layer of pure sand on the surface. The principle here is that the cuttings root in a well-drained rooting medium, then the roots go down into a loam-based growing medium so that more growth is obtained prior to potting-up.

Additional Constituents Incorporated Into Rooting Media

FUNGICIDES

These are used mainly as a preventative against soil-borne pathogens (see p. 314).

FERTILIZERS

These are mainly the controlled-release fertilizers to promote root and shoot development after rooting of the cuttings (see p. 314). Controlled-release fertilizers are normally mixed into the rooting medium. Placing a layer of Osmocote® over the base of the flat underneath the rooting medium has been found to be effective for rooting cuttings in pure pine bark. A 12–14 month controlled-release fertilizer is preferred in the summer, while a 16–18 month release product can be used in the fall.

MYCORRHIZAL FUNGI

A renewed interest has developed in the use of mycorrhizal fungi to assist the rooting of cuttings. Considerable research has been carried out on how mycorrhizal fungi can be used to assist the establishment of coniferous seedlings—particularly for land reclamations where many of the soils are thin and contain a low level of nutrients.

The word mycorrhiza is derived from *myco* = fungus and *rhiza* = root. Over 85% of trees (and many other plants) contain mycorrhiza in and around their root systems. Scientists have classified mycorrhizal fungi into three groups. Ectomycorrhizae virtually exist as a sheath around the root system, just penetrating into the outer cells of the root. Endomycorrhizae penetrate deeper into the root but are sparse around the outside. Ectendomycorrhizae are an intermediate group that are little known.

They are beneficial to the plant because they assist in nutrient and water uptake, help it to resist some diseases, and assist in counteracting stress due to temperature and moisture changes. The mycorrhizal fungus, on the other hand, benefits by receiving needed organic compounds from its association with the plant.

This successful close beneficial relationship of two dissimilar organisms is referred to as a symbiotic association—both organisms are benefiting from each other. The term "mycorrhizal association" is sometimes used. The application of mycorrhiza to rooting cuttings can now be explained.

A region in Belgium that I have always found fascinating is the Lochristi area, which specializes in the production of azaleas and rhododendrons. The immaculate intensive nurseries in this area grow their crops in frames and open ground in a medium made primarily from decayed spruce and pine needles with other leaf litter added. One major reason cited for the healthy root and shoot growth of the plants is the naturally-occurring mycorrhizae contained in this medium.

More recently, research has been carried out by R. G. Linderman at Oregon State University, Corvallis, Oregon, to evaluate why and how mycorrhizae can be beneficial for rooting cuttings. He used selections of the ericaceous ground cover *Arctostaphylos uva-ursi* (Kinnikinnick) as part of his project. A mycorrhizal inoculation was cultivated in the laboratory and then added to the rooting medium. Cuttings grown in treated and untreated media were compared after about eight weeks. Most of the treatments showed a very positive effect, not only in increased root development but also on actual rooting percentages. It was thought that this may be due to a compound actually produced by the mycorrhizae. There was also found to be a beneficial carry-over effect to the treated rooted cuttings following potting-up.

Verl Holden, Holden Wholesale Growers Inc., Silverton, Oregon, is a nurseryman who has always been willing to try new developments in technology. He improved the rooting percentage of *Arctostaphylos uva-ursi* 'Massachusetts' (Kinnickinnik cv.) from 75% to over 95% by inoculating the rooting medium with a solution made from water and mycorrhizal roots. The procedure he used was to remove from the growing-on stock sufficient mycorrhizal roots to quarter-fill a

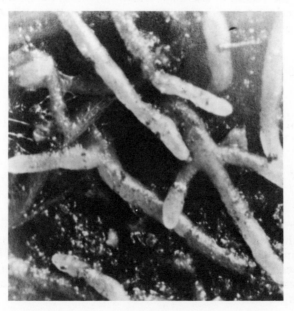

Figure 11-6. Mycorrhizal roots of *Arctostaphylos uva-ursi* (Kinnickinnik), x180. The medium was inoculated with the Mycorrhizal fungi which subsequently grew around and within the *Arctostaphylos* roots. (Reproduced by courtesy of William Snyder and Verl Holden, Holden Wholesale Growers, Inc., Silverton, OR, U.S.A., and by permission of the International Plant Propagators' Society.)

domestic cup, also adding some water. The roots and water were liquified using a kitchen blender, filtered through a screen and the filtrate then thoroughly mixed in a 95 l (25 gal) tank of water. The cuttings were stuck and the tank contents sprayed under pressure to thoroughly drench the rooting medium. This amount of spray will treat approximately 50,000 cuttings direct-stuck at 1.3 cm (½″) spacing into a rooting medium in a bench.

The cuttings were examined 6–8 weeks later and showed a definite improvement in root system development and overall health. Losses in establishment following potting-up of the cuttings were also significantly reduced. This is another example of how fundamental research can be adapted and used as a potential aid by the plant propagator.

There are many facts yet to be known, such as which particular mycorrhizal fungus is best for a specific plant, and the most economic and effective way for the propagator to culture and apply the treatment. There seems little benefit in providing inocula for plants that are easy to root, but there is plenty of scope for less predictable plants—such as conifers and those in the Ericaceae (Heath family).

APPENDIX
Recommended Rooting Media—Components and Ratios

The media below all have peat moss as the basic component. The following points will prove helpful when initially selecting a medium to use:—

1. Check source, grade, quality and price.

2. For general use, first try equal parts of peat moss with either coarse sand, perlite or pumice.

3. For bark, sawdust, loam or expanded polystyrene, first try a ratio of not more than one-third. Commercial experience has also shown that a pure bark rooting medium is successful (p. 358).

4. The ratios may well require altering depending on:—

(a) The plant being rooted—many ericaceous plants respond to a higher peat moss ratio.

(b) The propagation facility being used—more attention to drainage will be required for mist propagation. Media containing a high ratio of peat moss are more suitable for cuttings being rooted under polyethylene film than in a mist propagation facility.

(c) The season of the year. A medium containing 2 parts peat moss to 1 part perlite is used for summer propagation of softwood cuttings under polyethylene film, while a ratio of 1 part peat moss to 1 or 2 parts perlite is used for fall and winter propagation when more drainage is required.

5. Be prepared to undertake a number of trials on the nursery and to adapt according to the conclusions reached.

6. Carry out extensive trials when incorporating a new local product resulting from the processing of manufactured or natural plant products.

Tabulated below are a range of rooting media that have been found to be successful in commercial practice in either North America or Europe. It is hoped that this will serve as a basis onto which the newly-established propagator can build. The variation of components and ratios will be largely due to product availability and cost, geographical location, propagation facility, and the species of plants being rooted.

NOTE:—

(i) Unless otherwise stated, peat moss serves as the basic component in each medium.

(ii) Media marked * are particularly suitable for a mist propagation unit where greater aeration and drainage are required.

COMPONENT	RATIOS	
Sands	*(a) 1 pt peat moss 1 pt sand	(b) 2 pts peat moss 1 pt sand
	(c) 3 pts peat moss 1 pt sand	(d) 4 pts peat moss 1 pt sand
	*(e) 1 pt peat moss 1 pt fine sand 1 pt crushed coarse sand	
Perlite	*(a) 1 pt peat moss 1 pt perlite	(b) 2 pts peat moss 1 pt perlite
	(c) 3 pts peat moss 1 pt perlite	*(d) 1 pt peat moss 2 pts perlite
Vermiculite	(a) 1 pt peat moss 1 pt vermiculite	(b) 1 pt peat moss 1 pt sand 1 pt vermiculite
Pumice	*(a) Pure pumice	*(b) 1 pt peat moss 1 pt pumice
	(c) 2 pts peat moss 1 pt pumice	*(d) 1 pt peat moss 2 pts pumice
Bark	*(a) Pure bark	(c) 1 pt peat moss 1 pt perlite 1 pt bark
	(b) 1 pt peat moss 1 pt sand 1 pt bark	*(d) 1 pt peat moss 1 pt bark
Sawdust	(a) 1 pt peat moss 1 pt sand 1 pt sawdust	(b) 1 pt peat moss 1 pt perlite 1 pt sawdust
Expanded Polystyrene	*(a) 1 pt peat moss 1 pt pumice 1 pt polystyrene	*(b) 1 pt peat moss 1 pt sand 1 pt polystyrene
Loam	(a) 1 pt peat moss 1 pt perlite 1 pt loam	(b) 3 pts peat 2 pts sand 1 pt loam

REFERENCES AND SUGGESTED SOURCES FOR FURTHER READING

Bergstrom, D. 1976. An underground boost for seedlings. *Forest Research*, USDA Forest Service, October 1976.

Bluhm, W. L. 1978. Peat, pests, and propagation. *Comb. Proc. Inter. Pl. Prop. Soc.* **28**: 66–70.

Brighton, C. A. 1973. E.P.S. improves the aeration, drainage and temperature of composts. *Nurseryman & Garden Centre,* September 27, 1973, pp. 392–395.

Bunt, A. C. 1976. *Modern Potting Composts. A Manual on the Preparation and Use of Growing Media for Pot Plants.* George Allen & Unwin Ltd., London.

Cook, C. D. & B. L. Dunsby. 1978. Perlite for propagation. *Comb. Proc. Inter. Pl. Prop. Soc.* **28**: 224–228.

Deen, J. L. W. 1979. Friendly fungi. *GC & HTJ* **185**(28): 21–22 (July 13, 1979).

Ferguson, J. J. & J. A. Menge. 1982. How and why to add mycorrhizal fungi to plants in the field. *Amer. Nurseryman* **156**(6): 67–71 (September 15, 1982).

Gartner, J. B. 1981. Amendments can improve container growing media. *Amer. Nurseryman* **153**(3): 13, 70–73, 76–78 (February 1, 1981).

———, S. M. Still & J. E. Klett. 1973. The use of hardwood bark as a growth medium. *Comb. Proc. Inter. Pl. Prop. Soc.* **23**: 222–231.

Hartmann, H. T. & D. E. Kester. 1983. 4th ed. *Plant Propagation: Principles and Practices.* Prentice-Hall, Inc., Englewood Cliffs, N.J.

Holden, V. L. 1978. The use of mycorrhizae in the propagation of *Arctostaphylos uva-ursi. Comb. Proc. Inter. Pl. Prop. Soc.* **28**: 132–133.

Inose, K. 1971. Pumice as a rooting medium. *Comb. Proc. Inter. Pl. Prop. Soc.* **21**: 82–83.

Johnson, C. R. & J. A. Menge. 1982. Mycorrhizae may save fertilizer dollars. *Amer. Nurseryman* **155**(2): 79–87 (January 15, 1982).

Linderman, R. G. 1978. Mycorrhizae in relation to rooting cuttings. *Comb. Proc. Inter. Pl. Prop. Soc.* **28**: 128–132.

Loach, K. 1981. Propagation under mist and polyethylene—history, principles and development. *Proc. 21st Askham Bryan Horticultural Technical Course (U.K.),* pp. 23–31.

———. 1983. Rooting mixes for leafy cuttings. *New Zealand Gardener,* April 1983, pp. 3–4.

Molina, R. 1980. Ectomycorrhizal inoculation of containerized western conifer seedlings. USDA Forest Service, Research Note. P.N.W.—357, April 1980.

Noland, D. A., and D. J. Williams. 1980. The use of pumice and pumice:peat mixtures for propagation media. *The Plant Propagator* **26**: 4, 6–7

Reisch, K. W. 1967. Rooting mediums. *Comb. Proc. Inter. Pl. Prop. Soc.* **17**: 356–363.

Self, R. L. 1978. Pine bark in potting mixes, grades and age, disease and fertility problems. *Comb. Proc. Inter. Pl. Prop. Soc.* **28**: 363–368.

Vermeulen, J. P. 1965. Rooting-growing media. *Comb. Proc. Inter. Pl. Prop. Soc.* **15**: 97–104.

Chapter 12

DISEASE PREVENTION AND CONTROL FOR CUTTINGS

The successful control of plant diseases caused by fungi is of major importance in the production of quality crops.

Modern intensive systems of crop production have frequently aggravated or provoked disease problems because more crops are being grown in containers (usually closely spaced on beds) which require frequent irrigation during the summer. Crops may also be grown in "protected" environments, e.g., plastic-covered structures, which can create a warm and humid atmosphere conducive to the establishment and spread of a number of diseases. The encouragement given to the export of plant material and the more efficient shipping of plants means that there is also a greater possibility of disease spread if quality control is not maintained and/or plant quarantine regulations ignored.

The introduction of new fungicides to control diseases has not meant that the problem has been solved because some pathogens can build up resistance to the active ingredient, thus making it necessary to use a rotation of different chemicals as part of the pesticide program. Successful disease control in the nursery starts in the propagation department, and any pesticide program must be integrated with the method of propagation and the system of crop production. This chapter will outline the role that the plant propagator can play in reducing disease incidence.

The following terms are used in the text for fungal structures and diseases:—

acervulus (pl. acervuli)	fruiting body composed of an exposed disc-shaped mass of conidiophore tissues producing conidia in humid conditions
conidiophore	erect asexual hypha bearing conidia as reproductive structure
conidium (pl. conidia)	asexual spore abscisced (released) from conidiophore
hypha (pl. hyphae)	fungal thread
mycelium (pl. mycelia)	mass of interwoven hyphae forming the vegetative portion of the fungus
pathogen	organism causing disease in a particular host or range of hosts
pycnidium (pl. pycnidia)	sporing body, usually flask-shaped or globose
sclerotium (pl. sclerotia)	hard compact mass of hyphae that can survive adverse conditions
spore	minute reproductive structure, may be unicellular or multi-celled

Figure 12-1. The efficient implementation of an effective disease prevention and control program at all stages from the care of stock plants to cutting propagation and through to shipping is necessary to produce a quality crop. The photograph shows an excellent crop of heathers intended for retail sale. Heathers are particularly prone to soil-borne diseases, so nursery hygiene, good observation and quick response to any potential problem(s) are all vital. (Windlesham Court Nurseries, Sunningdale, Surrey, U.K.)

DISEASES OCCURRING DURING PROPAGATION

The following are the major pathogens which usually cause losses during propagation. Damage can sometimes be due to a complex of diseases.

(1) *Pythium* (Collar Rot, Root Rot)

A number of different species of *Pythium* may attack cuttings of woody ornamentals. It is the young, soft tissues that are prone to infection, and softwood cuttings and germinating seedlings are particularly susceptible when the rooting medium is over-wet. The stem area (hypocotyl) just above and the roots just below the surface of the rooting medium are most vulnerable to attack. The fungus penetrates the host cells causing a progressive rot of the tissues. *Pythium* has the ability to survive in soils in the absence of a host and therefore may re-infect subsequent crops.

(2) *Rhizoctonia* (Damping-off)

Rhizoctonia is a soil-borne fungus that can be carried on cuttings and seeds. It has a wide host range and survives as sclerotia in the soil or on weeds and crop debris. It is particularly damaging under warm humid conditions, which occur particularly in poorly ventilated propagation units during the summer months.

Young roots are particularly prone to attack. Two visual features of attack are that the infected tissue is often reddish-brown, and the mycelium forms a mass of threads or webs which can be seen on the surface of the rooting medium and lower leaves in serious attacks.

(3) *Phytophthora* (Root Rot, Foot Rot, Collar Rot)

Species of *Phytophthora* cause major disease problems in the nursery. They are soil- and water-borne fungi which attack a very wide range of hosts—*Phytophthora cinnamomi* has a host list of more than 800 species, including conifers and ericaceous plants. Species that are particularly troublesome in the propagation stages of woody plants are *Phytophthora cactorum*, *P. cinnamomi*, *P. citricola* and *P. cryptogea*. High temperatures and an over-wet rooting medium will encourage disease spread because these fungi grow rapidly between 20–30°C (68–86°F) and produce motile spores in water. The root systems and stem bases of cuttings are prone to attack. Infected roots rot and turn brownish-black in color, and lesions (discolored areas that can be seen when the bark is removed) may develop at the base of the stem.

Depending on the host and environmental conditions, *Phytophthora* root rot may progress quickly, causing obvious foliar wilt, die-back and death. Foliar damage may not develop if the root infection spreads slowly and these infected but "symptom-less" plants can be a means of disease spread. Stock plants should be carefully watched for signs of infection. The leaves of rhododendrons become smaller, turn pale green and wilt; dead necrotic areas occur later within the leaf tissue. Under extreme cases, the leaves fall to the ground. In heathers, the foliage turns brown, with subsequent leaf drop and the plant can be quickly killed. In conifers, the foliage color fades, becoming grayish as the plants wilt, and later turning a light or rusty brown as the foliage becomes desiccated and the plant dies.

These fungi produce "resting spores" that can survive in soil under drought conditions and/or in the absence of a living host. Fungal spores can be splashed from infected soil onto foliage and thus be transferred on cutting material. Spores can also be spread in "untreated" non-mains water supplies.

Figure 12-2. Stock plants of many ericaceous species are particularly susceptible to infection by the soil-borne disease *Phytophthora cinnamomi* (Root Rot). The photograph shows severely infected *Rhododendron* plants.

(4) *Ascochyta clematidina* (Clematis Wilt)

This is a disease specific to *Clematis* that has been known to cause widespread losses in the nursery. It is characterized by stem lesions, particularly at the stem base, and necrotic patches on the leaves.

It is the leaf infection that can give rise to problems in the propagation house because the over-wintering stage (pycnidia) can persist on fallen leaves to re-infect stock plants or liners used as a source of softwood cuttings.

(5) *Sclerotium rolfsii* (Southern Root Rot, Southern Stem Rot)

This is a propagation disease that is common in areas such as Florida and other southern U.S. states where high temperature and excessive moisture conditions prevail. A pH range of 3.0–5.0 is also known to encourage infection. It infects a wide host range, causing a basal stem rot. Closer examination will show that these stem lesions are covered by a white mycelium. The cuttings later wilt due to girdling of the stem base.

This is a highly persistent pathogen, liable to re-infect subsequent crops if a high standard of hygiene is not maintained on the nursery.

(6) *Cylindrocladium* [Root Rot (Damping-off)]

Azalea, *Magnolia* and *Ilex vomitoria* (Yaupon or Cassine) have suffered from attack by this soil-borne pathogen during the propagation stage. Two prevalent species attacking ornamentals are *C. scoparium* and *C. floridanum*. Once again, spread is encouraged by high humidity conditions. The symptoms on cuttings can be three-fold—reduced root development, uneven reddish-brown spots on the leaf margins, and wilting due to formation of stem cankers. It is recommended that cuttings should be treated with fungicide and particular attention be given to the stock plants to ensure that they are disease-free to avoid introducing the disease into the propagation house.

(7) *Pestalotiopsis (Pestalotia), Monochaetia* **(both Leaf Blotch, Needle Blight, Stem and Twig Die-back) and** *Glomerella cingulata* **(Glomerella Blight)**

Research on diseases during propagation during the last seven years by Pauline M. Smith at the Glasshouse Crops Research Institute, Littlehampton, England, has explained why nursery operators have experienced increasing losses due to species of *Pestalotiopsis (Pestalotia)* and *Monochaetia* (two closely related genera), particularly in *Camellia, Rhododendron,* heathers and conifers. These are good examples of foliar diseases that have developed due to high humidity environments when crops used as stock plants are grown densely on container beds and irrigated by overhead spray lines. Water plays a major role in the life cycle of these diseases as it is necessary for the production, germination and dispersal of spores in water splash. These diseases are also more serious when the plants are under stress or wounded by pruning and physical damage. Leaf symptoms can develop on crops of any age, but stem infection and die-back is particularly damaging during propagation and in young plants. It is important to include these diseases in this section because losses during rooting and in the early stages of production can be reduced by correct management of stock plants and care in preparation of cuttings.

Pestalotiopsis guepini and *Monochaetia karstenii* infect *Camellia*. Cultivars that are particularly prone to infection are the *C.* × *williamsii* forms 'Debbie' and 'Donation'. Visual symptoms are characterized by irregular brown blotches arising at the leaf edges and then spreading over the surface. Defoliation and die-back of stems can also occur. Small pinpoint black sporing structures (acervuli) develop on the infected leaf tissue, thus providing a source of re-infection. The bud scales can also be infected.

Pestalotiopsis sydowiana attacks *Rhododendron,* resulting in silver-grey blotches surrounded by a brown margin. Defoliation and shoot die-back can later result. Spores of the fungus transferred on cuttings can cause rotting during propagation.

Pestalotiopsis funerea causes needle blight on many conifers, with the foliage turning brown and possible twig die-back. *Cedrus* (Cedar), *Chamaecyparis* (False Cypress), × *Cupressocyparis* (Hybrid Cypress), *Pinus* (Pine), *Pseudotsuga* (Douglas Fir) and *Thuja* (Arborvitae) are among those known to be infected. *Juniperus* (Juniper) are particularly prone to show serious symptoms of attack.

A virulent strain of *Glomerella cingulata* (Glomerella Blight) has recently become a problem, particularly on *Camellia,* and whole crops have had to be discarded. The symptoms are similar to *Monochaetia,* but more aggressive. The lesions form on stems and leaves and then develop into a severe twig blight, making it devastating on young stock.

(8) *Botrytis cinerea* **(Gray Mold)**

This is a fungus which infects a very wide range of hosts, giving a characteristic covering of gray mold (actually a dense covering of conidiophores) to infected tissue. It often arises as a secondary infection after primary damping-off diseases have damaged tissue, or on senescing foliage or dropped flowers, and then infects healthy tissue. Plant debris in the propagation house has been shown to carry the fungal infection. Poor ventilation and warm humid conditions encourage infection and spread. Over-crowding of plants also encourages infection.

(9) *Verticillium dahliae* **(Vascular or Verticillium Wilt)**

Verticillium dahliae is often transferred from infected stock plants on the cuttings and great care should be taken in selecting material for propagation. *Acer* spp. (Maple) are particularly prone to Verticillium Wilt.

(10) *Fusarium* **spp. (Root Rot, Wilt)**

Fusarium species attack the roots of many woody plants and cause rotting of cuttings during propagation.

Other diseases that occur during propagation include:—*Thielaviopsis* (Root Rot), *Oidium* (Powdery Mildew), *Peronospora* (Downy Mildew), *Phomopsis* (Canker and Die-back), *Botryosphaeria* (Die-back), *Alternaria* (Leaf Spot) and *Cercospora* (Leaf Spot).

Figure 12-3. Different stages of *Monochaetia karstenii* infection on *Camellia*. Left — sporadic leaf infection. Center — severe infection in which the pathogen entered through the trimmed leaves. Right — defoliation and stem die-back. (Reproduced by permission of the Glasshouse Crops Research Institute, Littlehampton, Sussex, U.K.)

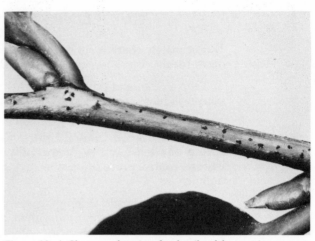

Figure 12-4. Close-up showing the details of the sporing structure (acervuli) of *Monochaetia karstenii* on a *Camellia* stem. (Reproduced by permission of the Glasshouse Crops Research Institute, Littlehampton, Sussex, U.K.)

Figure 12-5. *Pestalotiopsis (Pestalotia) sydowiana* infection on trimmed leaves of *Rhododendron* cutting. Note the concentric rings of sporing structures (acervuli). (Reproduced by permission of the Glasshouse Crops Research Institute, Littlehampton, Sussex, U.K.)

Figure 12-6. *Pestalotiopsis (Pestalotia) funerea* infection on *Juniperus* (Juniper). Note the black spore exudate. (Reproduced by permission of the Glasshouse Crops Research Institute, Littlehampton, Sussex, U.K.)

Figure 12-7. Sclerotia of *Botrytis cinerea* (Gray Mold) on *Vitis* (Grape) cuttings. (Reproduced by permission of the Glasshouse Crops Research Institute, Littlehampton, Sussex, U.K.)

GUIDELINES FOR DISEASE CONTROL

Unfortunately there is no one solution to disease control, but there are some important basic procedures that can go a long way to reduce disease incidence. These are as follows:—

1. Keep a clean and tidy nursery. This is not wasted money as staff working for the company will have greater respect and be more conscious of maintaining a high standard of cleanliness. Untidiness leads to sloppy work habits and lost revenue.

2. Encourage good cultural control techniques, not a reliance only on chemicals. The spread of disease can be dramatically reduced by commonsense and well-implemented cultural control procedures, thus saving money in the costs of chemicals and their application.

3. Formulate a pesticide program for each section of the nursery—including the disease control program for the propagation department. This is best written up in a tabulated form that contains the following information:—

(a) Name of active ingredient and appropriate commercial product

(b) Time and frequency of application

(c) Rate and method of application

(d) Safety procedures

(e) Additional specific comments (e.g., sensitivity to damage of a particular species or cultivar).

Review the program at regular intervals and make necessary amendments in the light of past effectiveness and the type of crop being grown.

4. Understand the spectrum of diseases controlled by individual chemicals and that certain diseases are able to build up resistance to certain chemicals.

5. Ensure that the implementation of the pesticide program is properly supervised, correct safety clothing and equipment used, and that the reasons for this are explained to the staff.

6. Understand that a number of chemicals do not actually eradicate a disease but rather act as a "preventative" from infection.

7. Keep in touch with your local specialist extension officer/advisor and horticultural chemical supplier for up-to-date information on research, recommendations and new products. It is much better to attend a demonstration day at a research station or nursery to obtain information than to just rely on reading the literature.

There are essentially 5 phases during the propagation cycle at which disease control should be implemented:—

(1) Establishment and maintenance of stock plants

(2) Collection of cuttings

(3) Cutting preparation facility

(4) Cutting preparation and sticking techniques and methods

(5) Aftercare facility and care of cuttings.

Some guidelines for each of these stages are proposed, and these will also help to consolidate some of the information just presented.

(1) Establishment and Maintenance of Stock Plants (see also p. 246).

Correct nursery practices for the care of stock plants, whether grown for the purpose or as part of the production crop, is a topic that can be overlooked by the propagator. It is at this phase that many diseases can originate and are then transferred with the propagation material to the rooting bench and subsequently to the young rooted plants. Particular care has to be taken with the soil-borne pathogens which are more liable to pass undetected in the early stages of attack and are often more difficult to control than those infecting leaves and stems.

Figure 12-8. One method that has been investigated as a means of lessening the risk of soil-borne disease infection to cutting material is to cover heather stock plant beds with woven polypropylene fabrix (MyPex® or Propex®). The stock plants are then planted through the fabric into the well-drained, raised beds. The material allows rain and irrigation water to seep through into the beds and also acts as a mulch.

(a) Cultural Control

(i) Obtain or purchase high quality disease-free stocks—they should be personally inspected whenever possible and it is advisable to request a test to identify potential pathogens if there is a risk of soil-borne diseases. The local extension service will usually carry out such a test.

(ii) Grow stock plants on disease-free, well-drained land. Raising the bed level above the normal height can be useful to assist surface drainage.

(iii) Grow plants in isolated containers if the open-ground land is infected with disease organisms.

(iv) Designate a set of cultivation and irrigation equipment for use only in the stock bed area if there is a risk of disease spreading from and into other areas of the nursery. However, this may not always be practical because of cost and nursery management.

(v) Discard and burn stock plants and growing stock infected with soil-borne, viral or bacterial diseases for which there is no effective cultural or chemical control.

(vi) Remove flower buds that may harbor disease, e.g., *Monochaetia karstenii* and *Pestalotiopsis guepini* on Camellias.

(b) Chemical Control

(i) Fumigate the soil before planting stock plants. This is particularly effective for crops that are to be intensively planted and which are susceptible to soil-borne diseases (see p. 56 and p. 243).

(ii) Institute a regular program of foliar sprays and/or soil drenches. It is vital to know what disease you are trying to control. For example, it is a waste of time to carry out a program of foliar sprays on unhealthy foliage when the actual cause is a soil-borne disease that is more effectively controlled by soil fumigation and soil drenches.

Pauline M. Smith at the Glasshouse Crops Research Institute, England, has carried out research on *Pestalotiopsis* and *Monochaetia* species affecting camellias, rhododendrons and conifers and has found that prochloraz/manganese complex (a fungicide that was initially sold for use on mushrooms) shows very promising results in controlling these and related diseases on broadleaved evergreens when applied to stock plants, to prepared cuttings and to the rooting medium. Sportak® 40 or 45% a.i. formulations of prochloraz are sold for use on cereals and carry no label recommendations for use on ornamentals. However, some growers (at "their own risk") are using it at 250 ppm on stock plants and appear to be satisfied. [The rate may have to be reduced for cuttings as this formulation of prochloraz can retard rooting in shy-rooting species.] Furalaxyl, a related compound that is sold in the United Kingdom as Fongarid®, is very useful for treating cuttings as it is less likely to cause phytotoxicity or to retard rooting.

More recently, another prochloraz/manganese complex has been developed and marketed as Octave® and is to be recommended for ornamentals. Octave® is not widely registered as yet, but growers should certainly be aware of its potential uses for nursery stock propagation.

It is helpful to apply fungicide to stock plants prior to or just after cutting removal or other necessary pruning. In addition to the prochloraz/manganese and related compounds, carbendazin/maneb (Delsene M®) and benomyl (Benlate®) may be used at the recommended rates for specific diseases of ornamentals.

A fungicide that is being used effectively in the United States is metalaxyl (Subdue 2E®). It has been claimed to be particularly effective against *Phytophthora* and *Pythium* (Collar and Root Rots). It is applied at label specifications as a drench to cuttings, and is a systemic fungicide so that it checks the pathogen within the plant tissues. It should not be used on *Euonymus* as damage can occur.

(2) Collection of Cuttings

(a) Cultural Control

(i) Use new polyethylene bags for collection. Bags or other utensils that are to be re-used should be first washed out with chlorinated water (30 ppm chlorine) and then thoroughly rinsed with clean water as a precaution.

(ii) Where possible, avoid using shoots likely to be covered with soil particles because of water splash from heavy rain or overhead irrigation. This applies particularly to plants such as conifers and heathers, and will reduce the risk of spreading soil-borne diseases into the propagation unit.

(iii) Ensure that the bags or collection utensils do not come into contact with soil or diseased foliage and stems during collection.

(b) Chemical Control

Soak and dip hand tools in sterilizing solutions if there is a possibility of transferring disease by this means. One procedure to use is to dip the cutting blades of pruners or knives into alcohol (ethyl, methyl or isopropyl) or, alternatively, in a solution of Physan® at 200 ppm. Naked flames or cigarettes must be kept away from the alcohol solutions.

(3) Cutting Preparation Facility.

A clean facility need not necessarily be expensive in terms of costs. The prime aim is to instill tidy work habits into staff and have a regular procedure for starting the day's work and for cleaning up at the end of the day.

(a) Cultural Control

(i) Remove all plant debris from refrigerators, benches, flats, utensils and floor area.
(ii) Ensure that mixed, sterilized rooting medium is not re-contaminated during storage.

(b) Chemical Control

Chemical control can provide a useful routine back-up to cultural techniques. These include:—

(i) Disinfect (sanitize) working surfaces, used flats or pots, and knives and pruners with Physan®. Physan® (a highly refined mixture of organic ammonium chloride compounds) has proved to be very satisfactory in the United States for this purpose and is more persistent than chlorine water. It can be applied as a spray, with a sponge or as a drench or dip—whichever is most appropriate. It has also been used for mildew and damping-off disease control, as well as for algae. Physan® has been helpful in preventing spread of diseases at Monrovia Nursery, Azusa, California, where stock plants of *Euonymus* and *Pyracantha* (Fire Thorn) are sprayed with a solution containing 200 ppm Physan® 24 hours before cuttings are collected.

(ii) Alternative disinfectants that have been found to be useful are quaternary ammonium compounds at 1 part in 80 parts of water; 50% phenol-based lysol at 1 part in 10 parts of water; and ordinary household bleach at 1 part in 10 parts of water. These are not effective against the resistant stages of the fungal life cycle.

(iii) Formaldehyde is an alternative when used in the form of commercial Formalin®, but extreme care is needed during handling and during the post-application period. Used pots or flats can be effectively cleaned by dipping them into a solution of 1 part Formalin® to 40 parts water. Hand tools can be dipped into a solution of 1 part Formalin® to 20 parts of water, and then immediately rinsed in running water.

An alternative is to soak flats and pots for 24 hours in a tank containing a 2% solution of commercial Formalin®. The tank must be covered at all times. The items are rinsed with water on removal and placed outdoors until all traces of fumes have disappeared.

CAUTION:— It is essential that full face mask, rubber gloves, rubber boots and specified safety clothing be used during and after the application of Formalin® (confirm the regulations with the local health and safety authority before use). Therefore, I would recommend using the chemicals listed under (i) and (ii), only resorting to Formalin® if necessary.

(4) Cutting Preparation and Sticking

The cuttings are most vulnerable to initial infection at this stage, because of the physical handling and also because the cut tissues provide a site for infection.

(a) Cultural Control

(i) Discard frosted, damaged and sun-scalded shoots.

(ii) Prevent shoots from being bruised and placed under stress during handling. Wilted cuttings are more prone to subsequent fungal attack.

(iii) Use knives and pruners with sharp cutting edges so that clean cuts are made to correctly prepared cuttings.

(iv) Where feasible, do not reduce the size of the leaf lamina on cuttings where the cut leaf surface will readily invite fungal infection—for example, *Monochaetia*, *Pestalotiopsis* and *Glomerella* on *Camellia* and *Rhododendron*. [This should be regarded as a positive recommendation for *Camellia*, where cut laminas are a primary point of entry for infection.]

(v) Check the source of peat moss to ensure that it is not bringing in disease. There have been a few problems when *Penicillium* and *Pythium* spp. carried in the peat moss have resulted in Basal Stem Rot to *Rhododendron* cuttings. However, there may not be any problems if the level of pathogens in the peat moss is low. Partial sterilization (pasteurization) of the peat moss can overcome this problem.

(vi) Shredded sphagnum moss has been used in rooting and seed sowing media as it is claimed to have a natural inhibiting effect on damping-off diseases. There have also been reports from Australia that *Eucalyptus marginata* (Jarrah) sawdust inhibits root disease development for container plants, and so this product could have a possible use for propagation media.

(b) Chemical Control

It is usual to carry out chemical control in two stages. Firstly, the cuttings are immersed in a solution of a fungicide after preparation but before the rooting hormone is applied. Secondly, an overall drench should be applied to the cuttings after sticking. This not only gives a further covering of fungicide to stem, buds and leaves, but also percolates into the rooting medium to increase the overall effectiveness. The pathogen is either killed or its development inhibited, depending on the active ingredient of the fungicide.

Two fungicides are sometimes mixed together to overcome the problem of pathogens building up resistance to certain fungicides and to widen the control spectrum. *Note:* It is important to check prior to application that it is safe to mix fungicides or pesticides.

(i) Immerse the prepared cuttings in a solution containing benomyl (Benlate®) at 1 g per litre (0.3 oz/288 fl. oz.) and/or captan (Orthocide®) at 1.3 g/l (0.4 oz/295 fl. oz.). This can be conveniently done by taking the cuttings in a gloved hand and then immersing and slightly swirling them in the solution. If there is risk of damage to the tissue, place the cuttings in a wire-mesh cage before immersing. The cuttings are allowed to partially dry to remove any excess water droplets before applying the rooting hormone.

[Note: There have been cases of skin irritations caused by reactions to fungicides when prepared cuttings are immersed prior to sticking. The cuttings have to be handled at the time of sticking and these staff may also be affected. In these circumstances, it is recommended that the immersion procedure be omitted and a fungicidal drench after sticking be relied on for disease prevention.]

Monrovia Nurseries, California, have used Physan® solution at a strength of 200 ppm for treating cuttings prior to rooting, except on azaleas where there are phytotoxicity problems. The strength is raised to 600 ppm for *Euonymus* and *Pyracantha* (Fire Thorn) which are prone to disease infection in that area of the country.

(ii) A fungicide may be mixed with the rooting hormone powder to give protection to tissue at the cutting base, e.g., benlate (Benomyl®), thiram (Thiram®) or captan.

(iii) A watering can or sprayer with a coarse nozzle is used to drench the cuttings with a fungicidal solution, ensuring that a sufficient quantity percolates all the rooting medium in the flat. Fungicides for this purpose include benomyl, captan, etridiazol, furalaxyl, prochloraz/manganese complex and thiram. (The concentration of etridiazol may be critical with some species if root retardation is to be avoided.)

(iv) The fungicide can be incorporated into the rooting medium prior to sticking the cuttings. This will entail a thorough mixing as only a small quantity of fungicide is needed for a large volume of rooting medium.

(5) Aftercare Facility and Care of Cuttings

This entails having a clean facility before the cuttings are placed within the propagation unit and their subsequent care afterwards. I am convinced that it is in the aftercare of the cuttings where some nurseries fail to maintain the necessary standard of hygiene. This is perhaps mainly due to the propagator not being sufficiently observant, to poor supervision, and often to plain laziness. Cuttings that die or leaves that drop off must be removed immediately, not left until the next day. (It is like teaching people how to water plants correctly—the nursery suffers if fundamental operations are not carried out systematically and if the staff do not have a "feel" for their responsibilities.) Damaged and diseased cuttings under high temperatures and humidity conditions are a primary source for spreading infection.

(a) Cultural Control

(i) All benches, floor beds, pathways and sides of the greenhouse must be thoroughly clean. The problem confronting the propagator is finding the best time to do this as it is probable that propagation is carried out during most months of the year. It is relatively simple to organize houses that are mono-cropped, for example, direct sticking and bench grafting. The mixed nursery using a variety of techniques may find that a useful period is (1) just after softwood summer propagation and prior to evergreen hardwood cuttings, or (2) after hardwood evergreen cuttings and bench grafting but before the summer softwood propagation period.

(ii) Regularly inspect and pick over the cuttings to remove diseased and dead tissue.

Figure 12-9. Regular inspection of the cuttings and the removal of diseased and dead material will assist in reducing losses from infection.

(iii) It is essential to have a clean water supply, particularly where intermittent misting and humidifiers are used. *Pythium* and *Phytophthora* are two pathogens that can be harbored in water from rivers, streams and water storage tanks. Mains and borehole water should not present these problems unless stored before use in an uncovered tank or reservoir that has been contaminated by plant debris, etc.

(iv) Improve ventilation within the greenhouse. The design of some propagation facilities may mean that this cannot be done effectively without causing cultural problems in the aftercare of cuttings.

(v) Absorbent foot pads containing a disinfectant and placed in a metal tray at the entrance to the propagating house can prove helpful where where is a risk of transferring soil-borne diseases from adjacent infected land. It is important to police this properly, otherwise staff will forget its importance after the first few weeks. This procedure can be particularly useful when the propagation facility is at floor level.

(b) Chemical Control

(i) Chemicals such as chlorinated water (bleach), Physan® and copper-based compounds (cuprous oxide and cupric oxide) applied as pressure sprays have been used successfully as an alternative to pressure steam cleaning. A 2% solution of Formalin® is a traditional material, but extreme care needs to be maintained during and after its application. Methyl bromide canister smokes are successfully used in houses that can be effectively sealed, for example, polyethylene-clad houses, but once again extreme care is needed as it is a very poisonous compound if not used correctly. (Some countries have regulations stating that methyl bromide fumigation must be carried out by licensed contractors.)

The problem with many chemicals is that the fumes that arise after the treatment are phytotoxic to any other plant material within the greenhouse. Therefore, material either has to be moved out or one has to wait until the house is completely empty. Ensure that the house is kept well ventilated after it is opened up following the treatment to avoid any fumes from subsequently harming the plant material and that hazard notices are posted to warn staff.

(ii) Follow-up sprays, or sometimes dusts, can be applied to the cuttings at 14–21 day intervals until they are well rooted. Again, it is advantageous to alternate the chemicals used:—for example, alternating benomyl (Benlate®) and/or captan (Orthocide®) with a prochloraz/manganese complex. A recommended sequence in Britain is a routine fungicide application every 14 days using benomyl (Benlate®), iprodione (Rovral®) and captan in rotation, and backed up by the removal of diseased and dead tissue.

The method of propagation will determine the frequency of application. For example, one initial application at sticking followed by another 14 days later may be sufficient when rooting under contact polyethylene film in winter. However, fungicides should be applied on a regular basis to replenish residues lost by leaching when mist spraying is used.

Figure 12-10.
Poor aftercare procedures encourage disease infection of *Clematis* cuttings.

Figure 12-11.
A healthy flat of rooted softwood cuttings of *Clematis* resulting from good aftercare procedures.

APPENDIX

Different states, provinces and countries can have different regulations concerning official approval for product use and its method of application. The manufacturers' product names in relation to the active ingredient may also differ, for example, in North America compared to Europe. It is therefore important when using any compound to adhere to the following guidelines:—

(i) Check the manufacturers' product name against the active ingredient contained in the compound.

(ii) Ensure that the chemical is registered in your area for the crop and use intended before application. Also, confirm any necessary protective equipment and clothing required for the selected chemical.

(iii) Check the manufacturers' label for crop use, method and rate of application. Consult the local extension officer when using a compound for the first time or on a different crop. Try also to contact other nursery operators to obtain information on their experience—particularly with relation to phytotoxicity effects for different genera, species and cultivars.

(iv) Check to ensure that chemicals are compatible for safety and effectiveness before mixing two together. Some pesticide combinations can precipitate out, thus making them ineffective.

(v) Treat a small area first on a trial basis to test for any phytotoxicity before using a new chemical or a higher rate of application on the crop as a whole.

(vi) Ensure that a record is kept for cuttings that show phytotoxicity so that they can be treated with an alternative chemical in future.

REFERENCES AND SUGGESTED SOURCES FOR FURTHER READING

Anon. 1978. Control of phytophthora in hardy nursery stock. *GC & HTJ* **184**(22): 20–21 (December 1, 1978).

B.C. Ministry of Agriculture and Food. 1983. *1983 Nursery Production Guide.* Ministry of Agriculture and Food, Victoria, B.C.

Brooks, F. T. 1953. 2nd ed. *Plant Diseases.* Oxford University Press, London.

Connor, D. 1977. Propagation at Monrovia Nursery Company: sanitation. *Comb. Proc. Inter. Pl. Prop. Soc.* **27**: 102–106.

Coyier, D. L. 1978. Pathogens associated with peat moss used for propagation. *Comb. Proc. Inter. Pl. Prop. Soc.* **28**: 70–72.

Ebben, M. H. & F. T. Last. 1966. Clematis wilt. *Glasshouse Crops Research Inst. Ann. Rep. 1965,* pp. 128–131.

Farthing, J. 1978. Fongarid gives improved winter rooting of ornamentals. *Nurseryman & Garden Centre,* November 26, 1978, pp. 40–42.

Goss, O. M. 1978. Pathogens in plant propagation. *Comb. Proc. Inter. Pl. Prop. Soc.* **28**: 400–405.

Humphrey, W. A. & T. W. Mock. 1979. New fungicide evaluated for control of root rot fungi. *Comb. Proc. Inter. Pl. Prop. Soc.* **29**: 41–43, 47–49.

Hurford, N. 1979. Fungal pathogens of ornamentals. *GC & HTJ* **185**(6): 14–17 (February 9, 1979).

Lambe, R. C. & W. H. Wills. 1980. Soil-borne fungus diseases of ornamentals. *Comb. Proc. Inter. Pl. Prop. Soc.* **30**: 485–492.

Ministry of Agriculture, Fisheries & Food, U.K. 1979. *Phytophthora foot rot of hardy nursery stock.* Leaflet No. 625. Ministry of Agriculture, Fisheries and Food, London, U.K.

_____. 1982. *List of Approved Products and Their Uses for Farmers and Growers.* Agricultural Chemicals Approvals Scheme, Ministry of Agriculture, Fisheries and Food, Middlesex, U.K.

Ormrod, D. H. 1975. Fungicides and their spectra. *Comb. Proc. Inter. Pl. Prop. Soc.* **25**: 112–115.

Pirone, P. P. 1979. 5th ed. *Diseases and Pests of Ornamental Plants.* The Ronald Press, New York.

Scott, M. A. 1983. *Monochaetia karstenii*—a leaf disease of camellia. *Comb. Proc. Inter. Pl. Prop. Soc.* **33**: 222–225.

Smith, P. M. 1979. The increasing problem of Pestalotiopsis in nursery stock. *"Forward"* (A.D.A.S.), March 1979, pp. 45–46.

_____. 1982. Woody problems. *GC & HTJ* **191**(11): 21–23 (March 12, 1982).

_____. 1982. Diseases during propagation of woody ornamentals. *Proc. XXIst Inter. Hort. Congr.,* Hamburg. pp. 884–893.

_____, A. V. Brooks, E. J. Evans & A. Halstead. 1984. *Pest and Disease Control of Hardy Nursery Stock, Bedding Plants and Turf.* British Crop Protection Council Publications, Croydon, U.K.

Ware, G. W. 1982. *Fundamentals of Pesticides. A Self-Instruction Guide.* Thomson Publications, Fresno, CA.

Figure 13-1. A propagation greenhouse utilized for direct sticking of cuttings for sale as liners. Note the installation of metal hoops and mist lines which will be covered by polyethylene for summer softwood cuttings. (Bruce Morton, Hybrid Nurseries, Pitt Meadows, B.C., Canada)

Chapter 13

DIRECT STICKING

Direct sticking is essentially the sticking of cuttings into a container (usually ranging in size from 6 cm/2¼" to 21 cm/8" diameter) to eliminate both the need to stick cuttings into flats, beds or benches filled with rooting medium and to subsequently transfer the cuttings into liner pots.

The principles and use of unit containers for direct sticking are explained in the text largely by describing the system used at two recently established nurseries in Pitt Meadows, British Columbia—Christie Nurseries and Hybrid Nurseries. Both of these nurseries were established to fill a local need by providing quality liners to larger growers. They developed a simple but very effective system of direct sticking into liner pots to provide the market with quality ground covers, broad-leaved evergreen shrubs and conifers for container growing, open-ground production and for direct planting (ground covers) on landscaped sites.

There are two main advantages to the direct sticking production program:—

(i) Faster turnover of crops, saving up to 60% in time compared to the traditional production of liners from cuttings rooted in flats. This is because larger or multiple cuttings can be used, thus reducing handling costs. However, more space is required compared to conventional propagation in flats.

(ii) A more uniform product can be produced, with improved shoot and root growth. This, in turn, results in minimal losses following potting of the liners at the customer nurseries.

PLANNING

It is essential to carefully plan all steps in the production system, including the available and/or potential market for the product. The timing of sticking is very important as production must be scheduled so that the product is ready at the peak period(s) of market demand. It is necessary to calculate the annual crop throughput, to group plants with similar rooting and growing-on periods for each greenhouse in the nursery, and set up a quality control program from cutting collection until delivery to the customer.

The stage at which the crop is marketed is critical as an insufficiently developed root system results in poor subsequent establishment at the customer nursery, while a crop will begin to deteriorate if it is left too long in the propagation greenhouse. For example, the optimum production schedule for ground covers is between 10–12 weeks. Many species stuck during February through to July are barely acceptable 6 weeks after sticking and can deteriorate rapidly after 16 weeks, becoming over-grown and difficult to manage. This deterioration has been successfully reduced in some ground cover crops by spraying with a growth regulator when the crop is at its peak. For example, dikegulac sodium (Atrinal®) has been used successfully at 500 ppm for *Hedera helix* (English Ivy).

EXPLANATION OF THE SYSTEM

A direct sticking system can be divided into four phases, as indicated on the chart below.

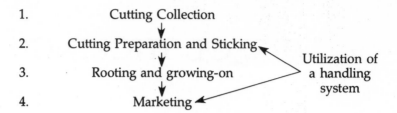

Cutting Collection

To ensure that there is sufficient propagation material, it may be that much of the collecting time initially will be spent away from the nursery taking cuttings from other nurseries, parks and, for some native plants, in the wild. For long-term success, it is essential to establish nursery stock beds that will provide sufficient quantities of cuttings. The production crop will also provide cutting material of vigorous growing species.

Cutting Preparation, Sticking, Rooting Medium and Utilization of a Handling System

This is the phase that provides the key to producing a uniform liner. Rooting should take place over as short a period as possible, and the end result must be a low percentage of unrooted cuttings. Uniform cutting preparation and sticking more than one cutting per pot are factors that help to achieve uniformity.

The cuttings are often longer than usual, but the standard techniques for preparing stem cuttings are employed (Chapter 8), and rooting hormones are used in the form of both powders and liquids. Powders ranging from 0.1–0.3% IBA are used for softwoods, while the concentration ranges from 0.8–1.6% IBA for evergreen hardwood cuttings, depending on the ease of rooting. One liquid hormone sometimes used is Woods Rooting Hormone® (Appendix 10-3) diluted with water to produce a 1:20 ratio for softwood cuttings, 1:10 for broad-leaf evergreens, and 1:7 for evergreen hardwood cuttings of conifers.

Two convenient sizes of pots used for direct sticking are 6 cm (2¼″) and 10 cm (4″) in diameter. The chart below shows the size of container into which these liners are usually subsequently potted.

6 cm (2¼″) Containerize into a 15 cm (6″) diameter container.
10 cm (4″) Containerize into a 15 cm (6″) diameter container, or a 21 cm (8″) diameter container if the liner is of sufficient size. (The 10 cm/4″ pot is also used for customers wishing to plant ground covers directly into the landscape site without further growing-on.)

The rooting medium should have good aeration and drainage properties and should contain some nutrients to encourage root and shoot growth after rooting. The trick is to obtain the correct nutrition level without salt build-up, which causes root damage. Controlled-release fertilizers mixed with the medium have proved to be the most convenient and satisfactory method, providing that there are both routine checks made for salt levels and regular leaching with water. The amount of fertilizer and the frequency of leaching have to be adjusted according to the time of year and location of the nursery. For example, the amount of the controlled-release fertilizer is reduced by half, and omitted entirely in some cases, during the fall and winter. The medium is leached out once a month. When the controlled-release fertilizer is omitted, liquid feeding commences when the roots can be seen at the side or base of the rootball and subsequently continues on a regular basis.

The following components for a rooting medium have been used as a guideline for direct sticking in southwestern British Columbia.

Figure 13-2. Direct stuck single nodal (leaf bud) cuttings of *Magnolia* × *soulangiana* (Saucer Magnolia). Note the use of a flat to retain the pots to make handling easier. The leaf laminas should be reduced only if necessary as the cut surfaces can act as entry points for disease.

Figure 13-3. The effect of incorporating a controlled-release fertilizer into the rooting medium for *Hydrangea* cv. cuttings direct stuck in July under mist. Left—no fertilizer added. Right—12–14 month controlled-release fertilizer incorporated at 1 kg/m³ (27 oz/1 cu. yd.).

Basic Components

2 pts—Sphagnum Peat Moss
1 pt —Pumice
1 pt —Perlite (coarse grade)

Additional Components

To each cubic meter (cubic yard) of mix is added:—

(i) Controlled-release Fertilizer

Osmocote® 18-6-12 (6–9 month)
(a) Early Spring and Summer—2.4–3.5 kg (4–6 lb)
(b) Fall—Broad-leaved Evergreens—1.5–2.4 kg (2½–4 lb)
(c) Winter (Jan/Feb)—Conifers—Zero

[*NOTE:*—Lower levels of Osmocote® are generally used in Europe.]

(ii) Trace Elements and Lime

Micromax®—890 gm (1½ lb)
Dolomite Limestone—3 kg (5 lb)
Gypsum—1.2 kg (2 lb)

A robust tray is necessary to support the pots for handling, including shipping to the customers' nurseries. Square pots are preferable as they will help to ensure that the space available in the tray is fully utilized. No matter which type of pots are used, they should pack tightly in the tray to avoid lateral movement and thus minimize damage to the plants. Various makes of trays should be evaluated for design and price. The trays can be returnable or non-returnable, and it is necessary to include their costs in the overall production costs.

A machine may be used to fill the pots with rooting medium, after which they are placed in the trays and set on the floor of the greenhouse where basal heat of 18–21°C (65–70°F) is maintained by circulated hot water or electric cables. The prepared cuttings are immersed in a mixture of benomyl (Benlate®) and/or captan, then dipped into the rooting hormone and stuck directly into the pots. The rooting medium may then be drenched with fungicide, e.g., benomyl (Benlate®) for soft leafy cuttings and prochloraz for broad-leaved evergreens (p. 377).

Mist or foggers are effective for propagation in the spring and summer. Fall and winter cuttings are normally covered over with polyethylene film.

Figure 13-4. An expanded polystyrene tray with cavities for retaining the pots during rooting and for marketing. This tray design requires additional propagation space compared to flats in which the pots are packed rim to rim.

Figure 13-5. A young liner of *Arctostaphylos uva-ursi* 'Vancouver Jade' 10 weeks after direct sticking. Two cuttings were stuck in the center of the pot.

Rooting and Growing-On

The rooting medium must not contain excess water during rooting, particularly after leaching. This again emphasizes the need to use a well-drained rooting medium. Watering is increased once rooting has occurred to provide the needs for growth and development according to the prevailing weather conditions.

Liverworts and mosses are likely to build up in the presence of overhead misting and in the fall when the rooted cuttings do not fill in over the surface of the rooting medium. [The liverworts and mosses cover the surface of the rooting medium when there is little overall cover of leaves over the pot, e.g., *Arctostaphylos* (Manzanita), *Genista* (Broom) and *Vinca* (Periwinkle).] Dodine acetate (Cyprex®), dichlorophen (Algofen®) and Algimine® are among the chemicals used as a preventative, reducing the risk of damage to the cuttings. This is far easier than removing established liverworts and mosses from the surface of the rooting medium.

It is probable that leaf and other plant debris will build up over the surface of the pots after late summer/fall propagation. This debris must be removed to reduce potential sources of fungal infection and/or places for adult vine weevils to hibernate. A simple method of cleaning up is to use a commercial vacuum machine (similar to those used by gas stations to clean the inside of cars) to suck up all this loose debris.

Liners that are to stay for more than 12–14 weeks in the greenhouse can sometimes benefit from a top dressing using a controlled-release fertilizer or, alternatively, a liquid feed with a compound fertilizer (20:20:20) at the recommended dilution rate. There should be regular checks for pest and disease build-up, particularly for mites, aphids, mildew and *Phytophthora* (Root Rots). Diseases that have been found difficult to control are *Phoma exigua* var. *exigua* (Black Stem) on *Vinca* (Periwinkle), *Amerosporium trichellum* (Leaf Spot) and *Xanthomonas hederae* (Bacterial Leaf Spot) on *Hedera* (Ivy), and *Pseudomonas* and *Coryneum* giving "Shot Hole" symptoms on *Prunus laurocerasus* cvs. (Cherry Laurel).

One difficult decision that will have to be made at some point in time is whether or not the crop should be discarded due to variable rooting or to a check in growth that will affect the quality of the saleable product. Questions to consider when making this decision include:—

(i) The percentage of rooting in relation to the ease in obtaining cuttings, the additional production time required and the final selling price. A rooting percentage below 70% for easy-to-root ground covers and shrubs means that it may well be more economical to completely re-stick than to spend time grading through the crop and throwing out rejects. A figure of 60% is perhaps more realistic for slower rooting and higher priced broad-leaved evergreens.

(ii) The ability of the cuttings to develop a new root system if root damage has occurred after rooting. The crop should be discarded if the root systems are badly damaged by cold temperatures. Crops infected with soil-borne diseases, e.g., *Phytophthora cinnamomi* (Root

Rot), should be discarded.

(iii) The ability of the crop to develop a new shoot system after pruning back if scorch, foliar disease and/or lack of maintenance has caused major damage to the shoots.

(iv) The restraints that positive answers to the previous three questions will place on the remaining production schedule with regard to space and projected numbers for sale.

Marketing

As previously stressed, the time of marketing is critical to prevent deterioration of the crop and to ensure that there is adequate space for the succeeding crop. It is useful to have an area available that can be used for, firstly, any necessary hardening-off, and secondly, to act as a temporary holding area if the crop needs to be held before shipping. It is at this stage that holding trays are particularly useful for moving the plants from the growing houses and stacking onto trucks. The method, type and number of labels required for the plants will depend on the customers' requirements.

Figure 13-6.
A quality crop of *Arctostaphylos uva-ursi* 'Vancouver Jade' ready for shipping. Note the sturdy flats for handling the liners. (Brian Christie, Christie Nurseries, Pitt Meadows, B.C., Canada)

Figure 13-7. A (left). December-stuck liners of *Thuja occidentalis* 'Brandon' (Eastern Arborvitae cv.) photographed in late April. Note the well-developed root system. **B (right).** October-stuck liners of *Pieris* 'Forest Flame' photographed in late April. Note the consistency of shoot development.

OTHER DIRECT STICKING PRODUCTION SYSTEMS

Summarized below are two other direct sticking production systems that have been successfully utilized by the nurseries involved.

A. Hillier Nurseries (Winchester) Ltd., Ampfield, Romsey, Hampshire, U.K.

This nursery has found that the modern rooting media have made the direct sticking concept feasible. The traditional media that were loam-based or used only peat/sand were not porous enough to permit misting or fogging without the medium becoming waterlogged. The rooting medium used contains 60% peat moss, 40% pine bark (Cambark® fine grade) and 12% coarse sand (grit) into which is incorporated 1.5–2.0 kg (3.3–4.4 lb) of 16–18 month Osmocote® (16-9-9) plus trace elements.

Figure 13-8.
A crew direct sticking softwood cuttings in a low polyethylene tunnel (sun tunnel) facility. The pots were filled with the rooting medium just prior to sticking. (Hillier Nurseries (Winchester) Ltd., Romsey, Hampshire, U.K.)

The softwood summer cuttings, e.g., *Potentilla* (Cinquefoil), *Spiraea* (Spirea) and *Weigela*, are stuck into 7.5 × 7.5 cm (3 × 3") and 10 × 10 cm (4 × 4") liner pots, 11 cm (4½") diameter intermediate pots, and 13 cm (5") and 15 cm (6") diameter final pots. The propagation facility used consists of either low polyethylene tunnels (sun tunnels) or mobile, "walk-in" polyethylene tunnels over pre-made beds in which are placed down the empty pots. The filling of the pots with rooting medium is mechanized by using a tractor straddling the bed and hauling a sanding box (as used in open-ground seed beds to cover the seeds). The mobile walk-in polyethylene tunnels are then pulled over the beds of filled pots. Two to four cuttings are stuck per pot, depending on the container size. The plants are hardened-off after they have rooted, and the process is then repeated on adjacent beds, with the mobile tunnels being re-positioned as necessary. Saleable plants are obtained within 8 months from sticking the cuttings.

B. Briggs Nursery, Olympia, Washington, USA

Briggs Nursery has designed their direct sticking system to dovetail into the nursery potting system (e.g., materials handling, pot size and growing medium). The amount of direct sticking is also very largely dependent on available space on the nursery as multiple cuttings are stuck into gallon containers. The cuttings are rooted in walk-in polyethylene tunnels equipped with overhead misting lines.

Four examples of direct sticking systems used at this nursery are:—

(i) *Pieris japonica* 'Mountain Fire' (Lily-of-the-Valley Bush cv.)

Some 3–4 cuttings are stuck in August in 15 cm (6") diameter pots. The following spring, the root ball is removed and divided to give individual rooted cuttings. They are individually potted into 15 cm (6") diameter containers and grown-on for a full growing season as saleable stock.

(ii) *Rhododendron impeditum*

Nine cuttings are direct stuck in May in 15 cm (6″) pots. The root ball is divided in the following spring and each rooted cutting is potted into a 15 cm (6″) diameter container. They are then grown-on for two full growing seasons as saleable stock.

(iii) *Potentilla fruticosa* cvs. (Shrubby Cinquefoil)

Three cuttings are direct stuck in May into 15 cm (6″) diameter containers. The cuttings are not re-potted but are grown-on in the same container for sale in the fall of the same year.

(iv) *Pyracantha* cvs. (Fire Thorn)

Single, 45–60 cm (18–24″) long cuttings are direct stuck in July into 21 cm (8″) diameter containers. They are available as saleable stock by the following spring.

Figure 13-9. A (Left). A quality crop of *Leucothoe catesbaei* 'Rainbow' in early fall, 6 months after direct sticking 2–3 cuttings into 15 cm (6″) diameter pots. B (Right). *Cotoneaster* × *watereri* 'Pendulus' (*C.* 'Hybridus Pendulus') in early fall after direct sticking a single 45–60 cm (18–24″) long cutting in a 21 cm (8″) diameter container in the previous July. (Bruce Briggs, Briggs Nursery, Olympia, WA, U.S.A.)

REFERENCES AND SUGGESTED SOURCES FOR FURTHER READING

Baldwin, I. & J. Stanley. 1982. Tips on handling plants efficiently. *Amer. Nurseryman* **155**(10): 19–21 (May 15, 1982).

Meadows, S. B. 1981. Developments in direct rooting. *Comb. Proc. Inter. Pl. Prop. Soc.* **31**: 655–658.

Parkerson, C. H. 1983. Direct rooting of dormant cuttings. *Comb. Proc. Inter. Pl. Prop. Soc.* **33**: 274–276.

Pinney, T. S., Jr. 1982. Direct sticking of cuttings in Gro-Plugs®. *Comb. Proc. Inter. Pl. Prop. Soc.* **32**: 612–615.

Chapter 14

ROOT CUTTINGS AND DIVISION

ROOT CUTTINGS

Propagation by root cuttings is an under-utilized technique that should be given greater attention by plant propagators as a useful method under certain situations. There has been only a limited amount of research into the method, and that has been orientated to fruit production rather than ornamental woody plants. It does not have the "glamor" of other techniques, such as grafting, which usually require greater skills and more sophisticated facilities. This is, perhaps, one reason why it has been neglected. However, the increasing costs of production make it wise for nursery operators to evaluate root cutting propagation for possible use in their particular circumstances. The aim of this chapter is to provide a balanced account, based on both recorded and observed information, of the principles involved in and the application of root cutting propagation so that its function on the nursery can be evaluated.

Propagation by root cutting is the technique in which plant roots are severed into individual pieces, each of which is capable of developing adventitious buds and roots and, therefore, of regenerating into complete plants. The technique has been known since the seventeenth century, but its only use in nurseries today is as a reliable method for the propagation of some herbaceous perennials and alpines. It is, however, a dependable method for some woody plants, such as *Rhus typhina* 'Laciniata' (Staghorn Sumac cv.), *Ailanthus altissima* (Tree-of-Heaven) and *Aesculus parviflora* (Dwarf Horse-chestnut). Many plants successfully propagated from root cuttings belong to the plant families Bignoniaceae, Fabaceae (Leguminosae) and Rosaceae.

Nursery Uses for Root Cutting Propagation

The uses and advantages of root cutting propagation on a nursery may be summarized as follows:—

(i) Can be carried out using relatively unskilled labor.

(ii) Requires limited propagation facilities.

(iii) Can be carried out during mid to late winter when weather conditions are unsuitable for outdoor work.

(iv) May supplement other propagation techniques. For example, when seed is in short supply or unavailable for such plants as *Rhus glabra* (Smooth Sumac), *Clerodendrum trichotomum* (Harlequin Glory-bower), *Maclura pomifera* (Osage Orange) and *Maackia chinensis* (Chinese Maackia).

(v) Provides a relatively fast way to multiply clonal material.

(vi) Is a useful technique for some plants where other methods have not been found satisfactory. For example, *Elliottia racemosa* (Georgia Plume), a tree native to the southern United States in which both seed and stem cutting propagation have proved difficult.

(vii) Is useful when one sex of a dioecious plant is required. For example, female trees of *Ailanthus altissima* (Tree-of-Heaven) bear flowers that are free of the unpleasant odor associated with male flowers. The female trees bear reddish-brown clusters of winged fruits.

Figure 14-1. Four examples of woody plants propagated successfully by root cuttings are the following. A (top left). *Aesculus parviflora* (Dwarf Horse-Chestnut). B (top right). *Catalpa coreana*. C (below left). *Rubus biflorus*. D (below right). *Zanthoxylum ailanthoides*.

(viii) Can be used to induce vigor back into neglected stool beds that have not been heavily pruned, by taking root cuttings from the existing plants. Today, however, the availability of virus-free material means that it would be far wiser to start a new stool bed by purchasing new layers from a certified source.

(ix) It lends itself to direct rooting (see Chapter 13) in that 2.5–10 cm (1–4″) cuttings may be made and stuck vertically in a liner container. Liners will be available for either planting out or sale 12–20 weeks later.

Limitations of Root Cutting Propagation

The limitations of root cutting propagation may be summarized as follows:—

(i) Results for some species can be variable from year to year for no apparent reason. For example, species of *Paulownia*.

(ii) Handling of roots from outside stock plants is messy if they are not sufficiently washed beforehand.

(iii) There is little published information on the number of potential plants that can be obtained from stock plants, which, in turn, makes it difficult to determine whether the method is an improvement on alternative standard propagating techniques. Therefore, each propagator must rely on his/her own observations which, in turn, are likely to prove to be the deciding factor.

(iv) Severed roots, either in an outdoor stock plant area or from a crop of liners stuck directly into the bed, may cause a weed problem with the next crop grown or in an adjacent bed.

(v) Some plant chimeras, such as the variegated *Aralia chinensis* 'Variegata' (Variegated Chinese Aralia), will not regenerate true-to-type from root cuttings. In these plants, the inner and outer tissues of the root are of different genetic structure and will give rise to plants typical of the type species.

Research and Development

As indicated earlier, research on root cutting propagation has been limited. One noteworthy research project was undertaken by J. P. Hudson of the School of Agriculture, University School of Nottingham in England. This fundamental work on raspberry propagation in the 1950s and early 1960s established many of the factors important in root cutting propagation. He divided the factors affecting the propagation phase into two types—firstly, those factors that determine regeneration success *prior* to removal of the cutting from a stock plant, which he called "Plant Capacity", and secondly, those factors that determine regeneration success *after* removal of the cutting from the stock plant, or "Plant Performance". The time of year for taking cuttings was one of the "Plant Capacity" factors, and J. P. Hudson used the expression "on-season" for the period of successful ability to root and "off-season" for poor ability to root.

One exponent of this thinking has been P. D. A. McMillan Browse who has written and taught on the application of J. P. Hudson's work to woody ornamentals. Further information may be obtained from the references listed under his name at the end of the chapter.

Alfred J. Fordham, former propagator at the Arnold Arboretum, carried out some interesting experiments in relation to the juvenility factor of material from root cuttings, using *Albizia julibrissin* (Silk Tree) and *Elliottia racemosa* (Georgia Plume). He demonstrated that the shoots arising from root cuttings showed "juvenile characteristics", which can be used to advantage by the plant propagator. The foliage of the new shoots showed no visual sign of juvenile characteristics, but A. J. Fordham's results showed that cuttings taken of these shoots rooted much faster than cuttings taken from stem shoots. Little success was achieved with stem cuttings.

Research has shown that certain growth regulators such as IAA, IBA and NAA, which are used to encourage root formation in stem cuttings, can inhibit shoot development in root cuttings. Cytokinins have been successful in promoting shoot formation on root cuttings, but inhibit root development when applied to the outer upper areas of the cuttings.

PROCEDURE FOR ROOT CUTTING PROPAGATION

There are a number of procedures involved in stock plant management, preparation of cuttings, facilities and aftercare of root cuttings.

Stock Plants

Siting and management of the stock plants should be carefully planned because of the advantages of vigor and freedom from disease. The goal is to obtain disease-free vigorous roots of about pencil thickness (ca. 6 mm/¼") in diameter—the actual thickness will depend on the genus and species involved. As with many woody plant stems, pruning will induce vigor and the aim should be to use one- (or, if necessary, two-) year-old roots.

Essentially, there are four ways to manage the stock plants based on their location.

(1) Sited in the Open Ground

Plants growing in a specific area outside are normally lifted annually, roots suitable for propagation removed, and the plants then replanted either into the original or into an adjacent site. The soil needs to be well prepared (see p. 243) so that maximum root development will occur and to allow easy lifting and subsequent handling during propagation. The quantity of roots removed annually will depend largely on the individual species and its ability to successfully re-establish after replanting. Suitable modifications will have to be made to accommodate this factor. For example, it may be beneficial to lift in alternate years and to provide some form of trickle irrigation to the plants. The plants should be replaced with new stock every 3–4 years.

Stock plants grown in the open ground do present problems and should be treated carefully. Firstly, unlimited root development can cause problems of identification if the root systems of adjacent species grow into each other. This occurs, for example, in *Rhus* species (Sumac). Some form of physical barrier can help to reduce this outcome. Secondly, there may be a build up of a serious "weed problem" because the root sections remaining in the soil will re-grow. I have seen this problem with ornamental *Rubus* where the area became a complete thicket after only three years. This characteristic can be turned to your advantage in some cases. The original stock plants are lined out in the open ground and left to establish for two years. During the next dormant period, a cultivator is taken down the row to sever the roots, and the ground firmed by lightly rolling. The root pieces grow to produce liners by the following fall or winter, and can then be lifted for growing-on or selling—the latter has been used for the mail order trade. Trees raised by this technique include *Ailanthus altissima* (Tree-of-Heaven) and *Rhus typhina* (Staghorn Sumac).

(2) Using Bare-Root Saleable Plants

A proportion of roots can sometimes be removed from plants to be sold, provided there is sufficient root development. Care must be taken, however, not to reduce the quality of the plant supplied to the customer.

(3) Sited in Containers

The advantages of growing stock plants in containers include much less risk of subsequent misnaming as the root system is restricted, cleaner handling of the roots as they are grown in a prepared growing medium, potential weed problems are eliminated, and closer attention can be given to establishment following re-potting of the stock plants. The containers should be large enough to ensure adequate root system development. Root-curl problems may arise if the container is too small, thus reducing the number of potential cuttings, and making vertical sticking difficult because they are coiled.

(4) Established Mature Plants

The removal of a few roots from an established plant is feasible if a small quantity of cuttings are required to provide some initial stock. Subsequent regeneration may be slower, but it does provide an initial source—particularly if the plant is scarce in cultivation. I have carried this out successfully with *Campsis* (Trumpet Creeper), cultivars of *Chaenomeles* (Flowering Quince) and some *Daphne* species. One word of caution—do check that the plant has not been grafted, otherwise time is wasted by propagating the rootstock.

Preparation of Cuttings

Although the basic principles are the same, there are variations in procedure depending mainly on the species being propagated and on the facility to be used for their aftercare.

(1) Time of Year

The optimum period for taking root cuttings is December to February, although this period can be extended into early spring for some species, particularly when they are to be placed into a greenhouse. However, October to November may be preferable if the cuttings are to be stuck directly into the open ground after preparation, for example, as in *Ailanthus altissima* (Tree-of-Heaven). This is due to the better soil conditions at this time. However, there can be considerable losses in cold and high rainfall areas due to decay of the cuttings.

(2) Selection of Material

The four important factors to consider are:—
(a) That vigorous, one-year-old roots are selected as they have greater potential to successfully regenerate.
(b) That the roots are fleshy and, depending on the plant being propagated, about pencil thickness in diameter. Sufficient food reserve is important to support the developing cutting.
(c) That roots as close as possible to the crown of the plant are taken, as these have a greater potential for success. These roots are not only thicker with greater food reserves, but also there is a greater likelihood of increased adventitious bud initiation and development. An interesting fact related by P. D. A. McMillan Browse states—". . . . although it has been shown that thicker cuttings produce shoots more effectively, those produced from thinner roots establish better."
(d) That weak, damaged or diseased roots are discarded.

(3) Preparation of Cuttings

Roots should first be washed so they are clean to handle and do not inhibit the use of hand pruners or knives. Knives should be used with caution because while a root may look fleshy and easy to cut, core tissues can be quite hard—a number of cut thumbs have been observed!

P. D. A. McMillan Browse has provided useful guidelines for the length of cutting required, based mainly on the propagation facility. They can be summarized in the following table.

TABLE 14-1. Facility, Length of Cutting and Time for Regeneration in a Northern Temperate Climate

FACILITY	CUTTING LENGTH	PERIOD OF REGENERATION
Warm Greenhouse 12°C (54°F)	2.5 cm (1″)	4 weeks
Cold Frame	5.0 cm (2″)	8 weeks
Open Ground	10.0 cm (4″)	16 weeks

[The above guidelines are likely to vary according to the species propagated and to the geographical location of the nursery.]

The correct polarity is necessary when cuttings are stuck vertically. To assist the propagator in the visual determination of this, the upper part of the cutting is cut horizontally while a sloping cut is made on the basal end. Two terms that are sometimes used here require explanation. The upper part of the cutting is referred to as the *proximal* end as it is the part nearest to the crown or center of the plant, while the basal part is called the *distal* end or the part furthest away from the crown.

Diagram 14-1. Sequence for Preparing Root Cuttings

A. The root system of the stock plant is trimmed, washed and surface-dried.

proximal end

distal end

(ii)

(i)

B. The fleshy vigorous roots suitable for cuttings are severed and individual root cuttings are prepared as indicated. (i) A horizontal cut is made at the apex of the cutting. (ii) A slanting cut is made at the base of the cutting.

C. The prepared cutting.

D. The root cuttings are placed in a polyethylene bag and shaken with a fungicide before sticking.

(4) Application of Fungicide

The prepared cuttings are placed into a polyethylene bag and then shaken with a small amount (approximately 5 g (1 teaspoon) to 100–150 cuttings) of fungicide, such as Thiram®, Benlate® or captan, so that they are well-coated for protection against infection—particularly at the cut surfaces.

(5) Facility and Aftercare

The type of facility required is essentially determined by the geographical location of the nursery and by the plant being propagated. Aftercare procedures will obviously depend partly on the type of facility, but it is essential to pay careful attention to the provision and maintenance of good growing conditions. The correct environment, i.e., aeration, temperature and moisture, is important. Lack of oxygen and low temperatures, particularly in combination with excessively moist conditions, will quickly result in loss of the cuttings. Three types of facility are commonly used—open ground, cold frame and heated greenhouse.

Figure 14-2. Root cuttings will readily regenerate providing the correct environment is provided during the aftercare procedure. A (left). Regeneration from a vertical-stuck root cutting of *Rhus typhina* (Staghorn Sumac). B (right). Regeneration from a horizontal-stuck root cutting of *Populus canescens* 'Tower' (Tower Poplar).

(a) Open Ground—The basic requirements for open-ground propagation are a sheltered site with soil that is easily worked and free from perennial weeds. Soil fumigation with methyl bromide or Basamid® should be considered as this will reduce the incidence of soil-borne pests and diseases, as well as reducing the annual weed population in the subsequent growing season. Irrigation must be available to support the growing plants, particularly in the late spring and early summer. The incorporation of peat moss or well-rotted organic matter should be considered, as well as adjustment of the pH to about 5.5—the upper end of the scale is preferred for such plants as *Syringa vulgaris* (Common or French Lilac). Nutritional requirements are not high, so a base dressing of a 6-8-6 balanced fertilizer at 34 g/m² (1 oz/sq. yd.) should be sufficient.

Species that have been successfully raised outdoors include *Ailanthus altissima* (Tree-of-Heaven), *Rhus typhina* (Staghorn Sumac), *Chaenomeles* species (Flowering Quince) and *Syringa* (Lilac). The number of species will increase in warmer southern latitudes.

There are two ways in which to handle cuttings for open-ground propagation—callus in boxes or flats and then plant out, or "direct sown".

(i) Callus in Boxes or Flats—The prepared cuttings are tied into bundles of 15–25 for ease of handling, and placed vertically, providing correct polarity, into boxes or flats sufficiently deep to allow the cuttings to be just covered by the medium. The medium can be a mixture of equal proportions of either peat moss and sand or peat moss and perlite, and should be just moist but not excessively wet. I have used pure sand successfully, but there is a weight problem and a greater chance of drying out. The boxes or flats are then placed in a frost-free shed to allow callusing of the cut surfaces. The rate of callusing can be increased by holding the cuttings at a constant temperature of about 5°C (41°F), which should result in sufficient callusing in 5–6 weeks.

The callused cuttings are lined out in the open ground in early spring when soil temperatures have risen and soil conditions have improved. They should be stuck vertically into the soil with the upper surface just below soil level, and spaced 5–10 cm (2–4″) apart, depending on the habit of later growth. It is sometimes recommended that the

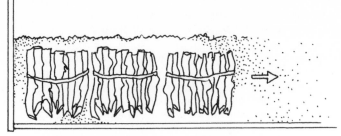

Diagram 14-2. Bundles of cuttings being callused in boxes.

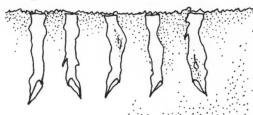

Diagram 14-3. Vertically stuck root cuttings at 5–10 cm (2–4″) spacing in the open ground.

upper 1.3 cm (½″) should remain above the soil surface, but this is inadvisable as the exposed area acts as a "wick" to the atmosphere, thus dehydrating and resulting in the loss of the cutting. The cuttings may have to be re-firmed if lifted up by ground frosts. Irrigation should be available in case of dry weather. The site should be kept weed-free during the growing season—there seems to be little published work on the use of herbicides and therefore recommendations cannot be given. The liners are lifted in the following fall or winter for growing-on in the open ground or in containers.

(ii) **"Direct Sown"**—This technique involves "sowing" or scattering the prepared cuttings in a pre-made drill which is then covered over as for seeds. This is a method that has been used in eastern U.S.A. and is described by William Flemer III of Princeton Nurseries, New Jersey. The root cuttings should be 5.0–7.5 cm (2–3″) long, while the diameter may vary. For example, cuttings of *Populus* (Poplar), *Rhus* (Sumac), *Ailanthus* (Tree-of-Heaven) and *Sassafras* should be 1.3–2.5 cm (½–1″) in diameter, while *Clerodendrum* (Glory-bower), *Comptonia* (Sweet Fern) and *Rosa nitida* (Shining Rose) cuttings should be 2.5 cm (1″) in diameter. The cuttings are placed into boxes containing slightly moist sand for 3 weeks to induce pre-callusing. They are then "sown" into 5.0 cm (2″) deep drills on a well-prepared site and covered with soil. In this method, the cuttings are not stuck vertically.

The well-known East Coast United States propagator, James S. Wells, described in the early 1960s a technique used in Holland to propagate *Chaenomeles* (Flowering Quince) by "direct sown" root cuttings. In this variation, the roots are cut in early spring into 2.0–2.5 cm (¾–1″) portions without determining correct polarity. They are sown in drills and covered with a mixture of peat and sand in equal proportions. The major factor considered essential for success is to avoid drying out of the roots during handling and after "sowing" in the drills.

(b) Cold Frame—Cold frame propagation of root cuttings offers a low-cost intensive technique with advantages over open-ground propagation because of the greater protection. Many hundreds of liners were once obtained each year at Hadlow College of Agriculture & Horticulture, Kent, England, using this technique. It is very suitable for species such as *Clerodendrum trichotomum* (Harlequin Glory-bower), *Rhus glabra* (Smooth or Scarlet Sumac), *R. copallina* (Shining Sumac), *R. typhina* 'Laciniata' (Staghorn Sumac cv.) and *Rubus thibetanus*. This list can be extended to include *Aesculus parviflora* (Dwarf Horse-chestnut), *Aralia chinensis* (Chinese Aralia), *Chaenomeles* (Flowering Quince) and *Populus tremula* (European Aspen). The traditional practice is to root directly into the prepared beds, but this has the major disadvantage of root disturbance on lifting, leaving many severed roots which may cause a weed problem later. One solution to this problem, and also to make handling easier, is to stick into deep flats or containers which are then placed into the cold frame. However, they will require handling sooner than when direct stuck into the frame bed.

The construction of cold frames and their preparation for rooting cuttings are described in Chapter 3 and Chapter 9. The site should be sheltered and well-drained, with the frame bed soil amended as necessary by the addition of peat moss and sand or perlite so that there will be sufficient aeration and root development. The pH should be in the region of 5.5–6.5. A base dressing of a 6-8-6 ratio compound fertilizer at 34 g/m² (1 oz/sq. yd.) is beneficial.

Aeration and soil moisture are important factors for success, therefore it is better to begin preparation of the frame during the fall or early winter, rather than leaving it until mid- to late-winter when root cutting propagation takes place. Once the soil is prepared, the lights should be put back onto the frame and tied down. Any additional moisture requirements can be rectified when the cuttings are stuck. Fumigation of the frames should be considered to reduce the incidence of soil pests and diseases, and weeds.

At planting time, the soil in the frame beds is raked down, lightly firmed, and a planting board used to stick the root cuttings. The cuttings should be stuck vertically in rows, using 5.0 cm (2") square spacing, with the upper horizontal cut at soil level. The cuttings are then covered with a 1.3 cm (½") layer of clean lime-free coarse sand (grit) or perlite. This assists in adequate aeration and deters slugs. However, it should be stressed that good results have also been obtained by using a covering of soil.

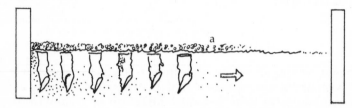

Diagram 14-4. Vertical stuck root cuttings spaced at 5 cm (2") in a cold frame. a—covering of coarse sand (grit) to a depth of 1.3 cm (½").

The lights are placed back over the frame and secured. A thermal blanket or burlap (hessian) matting should be used during severe cold conditions. Ventilation should be increased as the air temperature rises, and the lights may be removed completely by April. Shading of the glass lights to reduce the likelihood of scorch will be necessary as the shoots develop. Irrigation and hand weeding are important, particularly during the early stages of development. The rooted cuttings remain in the frame until the following fall and winter, after which they are removed for re-lining out or containerizing.

The principles are the same when cuttings are rooted in flats or containers within the cold frame. The recommended container medium is one part peat moss to one part coarse sand (grit), but I find it beneficial to also add one part of sterilized loam. The cuttings are stuck vertically, and covered with the medium or with coarse sand (grit) or perlite.

The cuttings are removed from the flats and potted when the root system is well developed. If the containers are large enough, the cuttings may remain in them throughout the first growing season but will require liquid feeding. The cuttings must not be potted-up too early, with insufficient root system development, otherwise losses will occur during establishment.

(c) Greenhouse—A greenhouse facility provides more flexibility on the time of taking cuttings and in the range of plants grown. Thus, plants grown in temperate regions may include *Campsis* spp. (Trumpet Creeper), *Koelreuteria paniculata* (Golden Rain Tree), *Paulownia* spp., *Zanthoxylum simulans* (Flatspine Prickly Ash) and *Albizia julibrissin* (Silk Tree).

Figure 14-3. Prepared and graded root cuttings of *Campsis radicans* (Common Trumpet Creeper).

The basic procedure is described on p. 394, but one can use root cuttings as small as 2.5 cm (1") long. The cuttings are stuck vertically into flats with the upper cut surface at soil level, using a mix of equal parts of either peat and coarse sand (grit) or peat, coarse sand (grit) and sterilized loam. I have no experience in adding a controlled-release fertilizer to the medium for root cuttings, but it would certainly be worth evaluating. The cuttings are covered either with the mix or with

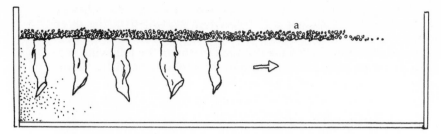
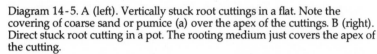

Diagram 14-5. A (left). Vertically stuck root cuttings in a flat. Note the covering of coarse sand or pumice (a) over the apex of the cuttings. B (right). Direct stuck root cutting in a pot. The rooting medium just covers the apex of the cutting.

coarse sand (grit) or perlite. The air temperature can range from 2–7°C (36–45°F), but it must be remembered that daytime temperatures will increase as the weeks progress. Excessively warm temperatures cause too much shoot growth and too little root growth, resulting in the potential loss of cuttings. Therefore, attention needs to be given to shading and irrigation. The cuttings should be potted-up after a sufficient root system has developed. An alternative method would be to direct root into containers, but the growth rate will be faster than in a cold frame and it is therefore probable that they will need re-potting into a larger container during the same year.

Kalmia Farm Nurseries in Maryland reported that a greenhouse provided a satisfactory low-cost method for rooting both *Chaenomeles* (Flowering Quince) and *Syringa* (Lilac) cuttings. They used cuttings that were 10 cm (4″) long, inserting them vertically into containers that were 7.5 cm (3″) deep. The top 1.3 cm (½″) of the roots projected above the soil surface and was covered with perlite. The air temperature was maintained around 0.5–2°C (33–36°F) from December to March, and was then increased to 7–10°C (45–50°F) during March and April. The plants were watered about once a month during the first period, increasing to 2–3 times a month in the second regime. Liquid fertilizer was applied in April when the plants were about 15–20 cm (6–8″) tall. The growth had reached 30–60 cm (12–24″) by July, when the plants were ready for open-ground planting.

The appendices indicate the range of plants that may be propagated by root cuttings, including some well-known and some rare to the nursery trade. Some references identify a substantial number of plants propagated by root cuttings, but it is sometimes difficult to ascertain whether they are actually feasible in a nursery situation. Therefore, the species included in the appendices are those that I have observed as being successful, that are specifically documented as suitable for commercial application in nurseries, or that have been mentioned in personal communications with practising propagators. You will have to evaluate the success of root cutting propagation in relation to your own situation and to compare its viability with alternative techniques.

DIVISION

Propagation by division was a traditional method used on nurseries that served as a reliable technique for producing a small quantity of woody plants. It has only a limited use today as there are far more efficient methods for propagating woody plants. However, division is still very much a standard method used to propagate herbaceous perennials. Propagation of woody plants by cuttings will generally produce a more standard plant for sale compared to a plant raised by division.

Plants that lend themselves to division are those with a thicket-like habit in which dense multiple stems arise from buds below soil level, e.g., *Aronia* spp. (Chokeberry). Some plants are capable of producing more isolated shoots from below soil level. These are termed suckers, and often arise away from the crown of the plant. A good example is *Amelanchier alnifolia* (Common or Western Saskatoon) where the removal of suckers with a sharp spade is used in the Canadian prairies to propagate the clonal forms grown for their fruits, such as *A. alnifolia* 'Honeywood' and 'Smokey'. Other vegetative techniques are unreliable, except for micropropagation.

Division is best carried out in early spring before the dormant buds begin to swell. The plants are lifted or suckers cut off, and excess soil is removed by washing or shaking the root system. Individual divisions are made using a knife, a narrow sharpened spade, pruners or, in some cases, simply by pulling the shoots apart from each other. The stems are reduced in height, the root system trimmed, and the divisions containerized, bedded or replanted in the open ground. Ample irrigation is necessary to prevent the old roots and developing root systems from drying out. The plant can be heavily pruned back during the dormant season of the following year to improve the quality of the saleable plants and to increase the number of shoots arising below soil level.

APPENDIX 14-1.
Selected List of Plants Appropriate for Open-Ground Root Cutting Propagation

Ailanthus altissima (Tree-of-Heaven)
Chaenomeles spp. (Flowering Quince)
Rhus copallina (Shining Sumac)
Rhus glabra (Smooth or Scarlet Sumac)
Rhus typhina (Staghorn Sumac)
Robinia kelseyi (Kelsey or Alleghany Moss Locust)
Robinia pseudoacacia (Black Locust)
Rosa nitida (Shining Rose)
Syringa vulgaris (Common or French Lilac)

APPENDIX 14-2.
Selected List of Plants Appropriate for Cold Frame Root Cutting Propagation

Aesculus parviflora (Dwarf Horse-chestnut)
Amelanchier alnifolia (Common or Western Saskatoon)
Aralia chinensis (Chinese Aralia)
Catalpa bignonioides (Indian Bean)
Catalpa bungei (Manchurian Catalpa)
Catalpa ovata (Chinese Catalpa)
Chaenomeles speciosa cvs. (Common Flowering Quince)
Clerodendrum bungei (Kashmir Bouquet)
Clerodendrum trichotomum (Harlequin Glory-bower)
Paulownia tomentosa (Royal Paulownia or Empress Tree)
Populus tremula (European Aspen)
Populus tremuloides (Quaking Aspen)
Rhus copallina (Shining Sumac)
Rhus glabra (Smooth or Scarlet Sumac)
Rhus typhina (Staghorn Sumac)
Rosa nitida (Shining Rose)
Rubus biflorus
Rubus thibetanus
Sambucus canadensis (American Elder)
Sassafras albidum (Common Sassafras)
Syringa vulgaris (Common or French Lilac)

APPENDIX 14-3.
Selected List of Plants Appropriate for Greenhouse Root Cutting Propagation

Aesculus parviflora (Dwarf Horse-chestnut)
Albizia julibrissin (Silk Tree)
Amelanchier lamarckii
Aralia chinensis (Chinese Aralia)

Bignonia capreolata (Cross Vine)
Broussonetia kazinoki (Kazinoki Paper Mulberry)
Campsis radicans (Common Trumpet Creeper)
Catalpa bungei (Manchurian Catalpa)
Cedrela sinensis (Chinese Cedar)
Cladrastis sinensis (Chinese Yellowwood)
Clerodendrum trichotomum (Harlequin Glory-bower)
Comptonia peregrina var. *asplenifolia* (syn. *C. asplenifolia*)
    (Littleleaf Common Sweet Fern)
Daphne genkwa (Lilac Daphne)
Daphne mezereum (February Daphne)
Decaisnea fargesii
Dendromecon rigida (Tree or Bush Poppy)
Embothrium coccineum (Chilean Fire Tree)
Gymnocladus dioica (Kentucky Coffee Tree)
Indigofera incarnata (syn. *I. decora*) (Chinese Indigo)
Kalopanax pictus (Castor-aralia)
Koelreuteria paniculata (Golden Rain Tree)
Lagerstroemia indica (Common Crape Myrtle)
Maclura pomifera (Osage Orange)
Meliosma cuneifolia
Orixa japonica (Japanese Orixa)
Paulownia tomentosa (Royal Paulownia or Empress Tree)
Phellodendron amurense (Amur Cork Tree)
Picrasma quassioides (Korean Bitter Tree or India Quassiawood)
Romneya coulteri (Matilja Poppy or California Tree Poppy)
Xanthoceras sorbifolium (Hyacinth Shrub or Yellow Horn)
Zanthoxylum piperitum (Japan Pepper)

APPENDIX 14-4.
Plants Successfully Propagated by Division and/or Suckers

Amelanchier alnifolia cvs. (Common or Western Saskatoon)
Amorpha fruticosa (False Indigo)
Andromeda polifolia (Bog Rosemary)
Aronia (Chokeberry)
Berberis buxifolia 'Nana' (Dwarf Magellan Barberry)
Buxus sempervirens 'Suffruticosa' (Dwarf Boxwood)
Danae racemosa (Alexandrian Laurel)
Desmodium tiliifolium (Linden-leaf Tick Clover)
Erica spp. (Heather)
Gaultheria spp. (Wintergreen)
Hypericum spp. (St. John's-wort)
Mahonia aquifolium (Tall Oregon-grape)
Menziesia ciliicalyx
Pernettya mucronata (Chilean Pernettya)
Polygala chamaebuxus (Ground-box Polygala)
Rubus spp. (Bramble)
Ruscus aculeatus (Butcher's Broom)
Sarcococca hookerana var. *humilis* (Himalayan Sarcococca var.)
Sorbaria tomentosa (Lindley False Spiraea)
Spiraea spp. (Spirea)
Syringa spp. (Lilac)
Vaccinium macrocarpon (American Cranberry).

REFERENCES AND SUGGESTED SOURCES FOR FURTHER READING

Fordham, A. J. 1969. Production of juvenile shoots from root pieces. *Comb. Proc. Inter. Pl. Prop. Soc.* **19:** 284–287.

Flemer, W., III. 1961. Propagating woody plants by root cuttings. *Comb. Proc. Pl. Prop. Soc.* **11:** 42–47.

Hartmann, H. T. & D. E. Kester. 1983. 4th ed. *Plant Propagation: Principles and Practices.* Prentice-Hall, Inc., Englewood Cliffs, N.J.

Heuser, C. W. 1977. Factors controlling regeneration from root cuttings. *Comb. Proc. Inter. Pl. Prop. Soc.* **27:** 398–402.

Hudson, J. P. 1953. Propagation by Root Cuttings. *Misc. Publ. No. 5.* Univ. of Nottingham School of Agriculture, Sutton Bonington, England.

———. 1955. The regeneration of plants from roots. *Rep. XIVth Inter. Hort. Congr.,* pp. 1165–1172.

———. 1956. Increasing plants from roots. *Gardeners Chronicle and Illustrated,* May 12, 1956, pp. 528–529.

McMillan Browse, P. D. A. 1980. The propagation of plants from root cuttings. *R.H.S. The Plantsman* **2:** 54–62.

Orndorff, C. 1977. Propagation of woody plants by root cuttings. *Comb. Proc. Inter. Pl. Prop. Soc.* **27:** 402–406.

Sheat, W. G. 1948. *Propagation of Trees, Shrubs and Conifers.* Macmillan & Co. Ltd., London.

Stoutemeyer, V. T. 1968. Root cuttings. *The Plant Propagator,* **14**(4):4–6.

Wells, J. S. 1961. Chaenomeles. *Comb. Proc. Pl. Prop. Soc.* **11:** 119–123.

SECTION E

SECTION F

Chapter 15

LAYERING

Layering represents a group of techniques for clonally propagating plants that has been referred to in books for both the professional and the amateur for many years. I regard two publications by Philip D. A. McMillan Browse as foremost in describing the various methods used—firstly, *Stooling Nursery Stock,* and, secondly, a series of articles included in his publication *Propagation for the Nursery Trade.* These publications have been used as the basis on which to build some personal observations, and to relate a number of contrasting procedures used in both Europe and North America.

Propagation by layering differs from other techniques in that it involves the development of adventitious roots on a stem while the latter is still attached to the parent plant. In practice, this shoot is severed from the parent plant at a time when sufficient roots have formed for it to successfully establish and grow away when planted out in the open ground or potted into a container. Despite being one of the most reliable techniques for the propagator to use in regenerating clonal material, the ability of the different genera and species of woody plants to propagate by this technique may vary considerably—for example, some plants, such as *Malus* (Apple, Crab Apple) and *Tilia* (Linden), have the ability to form adventitious buds adjacent to the cut stem and are thus able to produce a high quantity of layers over a given area.

Some plants are able to layer themselves naturally, for example, the tips of the growing shoots of the wild Bramble or European Blackberry (*Rubus fruticosus*) can layer themselves during the summer. Natural layering is a major reason for the success of quick coverage by some ground cover plants—three good examples being *Hedera helix* 'Goldheart' (English Ivy cv.), *Rubus calycinoides* (Taiwan Creeping Rubus) and *Epigaea repens* (Trailing Arbutus). In all three examples, adventitious roots develop along the stems lying directly on the soil surface.

Historically, the practice of layering has been recorded for many centuries in both Asia and Europe and some of the same principles, with obvious modifications, are used today by professional propagators. An interesting print dated 1608 is in existence that shows the practice of circumposition, best described as air layering, in which damp moss was used to cover an area around the stem from which a strip of bark had been cut and removed. The moss was kept continuously damp until sufficient roots had formed for establishment, at which time the piece could be severed from the parent plant. About three centuries ago a technique was developed in which soil was mounded around the base of a shoot arising at the base of an established Quince tree (*Cydonia oblonga*) that had been cut back. This technique is now modified and seen today in the open-ground scale production of rootstocks by stooling (mound layering). Private gardens have carried out layering when a few plants are needed or to cover up a bare area at the lower part of a tree. This may be done with camellias when a supple lower branch is anchored by a peg or stone and simply layered into the surrounding soil, thus improving the overall visual effect of that particular specimen.

Nurseries in Europe during the 18th, 19th and early 20th centuries relied heavily on layering for vegetative propagation of plants. It also proved a valuable technique to increase woody plant material collected by plant explorers after the initial plants had established themselves. As technology developed and changed with the introduction of mist propagation, fogging, hardwood cutting bins and micropropagation, the need for layering as a standard technique has been very much reduced. Nevertheless, layering is not a technique that should be overlooked as some nursery operators are very dependent on it, and thus it warrants an important chapter in this book.

Figure 15-1.
The use of rocks to retain stems of rhododendrons in the soil for simple layering was one of the early methods of propagation used in nurseries.

One can still see it effectively used in nurseries in Belgium, Holland and France. For example, it is the basis in the Wetteren area of Belgium for the propagation of clonal forms of *Corylus maxima* (Giant Filbert) and *Corylus avellana* (European Filbert or Hazelnut), while in Boskoop, Holland, I have seen a specimen of *Magnolia* × *soulangiana* (Chinese or Saucer Magnolia) that, it was claimed, was capable of producing some 500 layers annually by simple layering. Stooling or mound layering is a standard technique used for the production of *Malus* rootstocks in Europe and North America. Research and development has recently been undertaken in Britain and North America with this technique to mechanize the operations and to increase the number of graded saleable products from the layer beds.

Merits and Limitations of Layering

Before contemplating the establishment of layer beds, it is important to consider the merits and limitations of the technique.

The merits may be listed as follows:—

(1) When there are limited facilities for alternative methods of vegetative propagation other than open-ground propagation, such as budding and hardwood cuttings. In some situations it may not be possible to construct structures or install services to provide the necessary facilities for mist propagation, heated bins, etc.

(2) To produce a larger plant over a shorter time scale as compared with cutting propagation. For example, plants such as rhododendrons in the Falconeri series, *Corylus maxima* 'Purpurea' (Purple Giant Filbert), and *Prunus tenella* 'Firehill' (Dwarf Russian Almond cv.) can be produced for sale quickly through layering.

(3) To obtain plants on their own roots that otherwise could present difficulties if raised from root or stem cuttings or when grafted. For example, *Hamamelis* cvs. (Witch Hazel) worked onto *H. virginiana* (Common Witch Hazel) and cultivars of *Syringa vulgaris* (Common or French Lilac) worked onto *S. vulgaris* can result in specimens whose growth and habit is hampered by excessive suckering of the rootstock. Layering can provide an alternative for the production of a small number of plants if propagation by cuttings is not possible. It ensures that the resulting plant remains on its own roots and is true-to-name. *Syringa vulgaris* cvs. lend themselves to layering as they naturally produce suckers.

(4) A reliable technique for the large-scale open-ground production of clonal rootstocks such as the *Prunus avium* (Mazzard) selection Mazzard F12/1 and the *Malus* rootstock

Malling 9 where propagation by cuttings is not economically viable. A consistent quantity of layers can normally be guaranteed once the layer beds are well established.

(5) It offers the opportunity for a specialist nursery to propagate a small number of plants on site from a stock plant that may be on the decline and for a botanical garden to reproduce a limited number of potential specimens for display.

The limitations of layering may be listed as follows:—

(1) It is generally a more expensive technique than other methods. The small number of plants produced by most methods of layering and the high cost of land and labor means that other methods of propagation are usually cheaper. However, layering by stooling is said to be as economical as hardwood cuttings for some easy-to-root fruit tree rootstocks, even without mechanization.

(2) Extensive areas of land are usually required.

(3) Some of the techniques are straightforward but others require in-built knowledge gained by experience and skill—particularly in relation to the timing of cultural procedures.

(4) It is not easy to mechanize due to the layout of plants and the risk of damaging or dislodging shoots, particularly those laid upon or placed into the soil in a circumference around the stock plant such as with simple or French layering. Stooling (mound layering) lends itself best to mechanization as soil can be more easily mounded or removed from the base of the shoots within straight rows.

(5) The build-up of soil-borne diseases and their subsequent infection of the developing layers. This, in turn, means that one introduces the disease to the site to which the layers are transplanted or shoots re-layered. A good example of this is the high incidence of both Crown or Root Gall (*Agrobacterium tumefaciens*) and Specific Cherry Replant Disease (*Thielaviopsis basicola*) in the Mazzard F12/1 layer beds, which, in turn, was subsequently a significant factor in their decline. Similarly, *Verticillium* build-up in layer beds of *Acer* (Maple) and *Cotinus* (Smoke Tree) will lead to a rapid decline of parent plants and infection of saleable layers. *Phytophthora* spp. build-up has made it necessary to fumigate the soil before planting mother plants for apple rootstock production in the Pacific Northwest area of the United States. Soil pests will also significantly reduce yields, particularly when there is a build-up of nematodes.

(6) It is difficult to implement a chemical weed control program due to possible damage to the newly-developing shoots and the inhibition of the formation of roots on the stems.

Physiological Basis of Layering

There are essentially two basic principles involved in successful layering. Firstly, the induction of a constriction in the stem by bending, cutting or twisting. This is believed to restrict the flow of natural auxins and carbohydrates at the point of constriction, thus promoting the initiation and subsequent development of roots. Secondly, the principle of excluding light from the stem. This may be carried out by blanching, which is the exclusion of light from a stem that has been exposed to light, or by etiolating, where the stem has not previously been exposed to light. Exclusion of light is thought to decrease the amount of material deposited in the cell wall and to increase the number of parenchyma cells in the treated areas of the stem, thus assisting in the initiation and development of roots. Some techniques may be a combination of both principles, for example, the modified French layering of the soft-growing shoots of *Syringa vulgaris* (Common or French Lilac) cultivars.

ESTABLISHMENT OF A LAYER BED

Layering demands a long-term investment in land, labor and plant material. Therefore, three fundamental factors must be considered before adopting this technique on a significant scale. These are, firstly, to ensure that the layering technique chosen is the most efficient one for the plant being grown; secondly, whether an alternative propagation technique might not better suit the grower's circumstances; and, thirdly, that there is a market outlet for the layers produced.

There are two basic systems of managing the mother plants. The first system is to have the mother plants permanently sited where they can remain *in-situ* for up to 15–20 years or more, while the second system is to lift the mother plants from an area in the nursery, layer them and then discard or replant into another site. The choice will be largely determined by the species to be layered.

In addition to a suitable site for layering the mother plants, the success of any layering production system demands that these plants are kept in prime condition so as to furnish the maximum potential number of layers in each successive year. Unfortunately, inadequate maintenance has been a major contributing factor to the run-down of layer beds. It is essential that ample time be allowed for preparation of both the site and the soil of a layer bed as it is difficult to carry out modifications once the mother plants are established. This is especially true with perennial weeds such as *Convolvulus arvensis* (Perennial or Field Bindweed).

Once the decision has been made on the system for managing the mother plants and the technique chosen, the following list will provide some guidelines on factors to consider in establishing a layer bed.

(1) Location

The site should be sheltered from the wind and away from frost pockets. Specialized fencing should be provided where necessary against rodent damage—I have seen devastating damage to both mother plants and layers by rabbits and other rodents where adequate fencing was not installed. The provision of shading, either by deep-rooted, large, deciduous trees or by a structure clad with wooden laths or a heavy-duty plastic material (e.g., Paraweb® or Tensar® snow fence), should be considered for such genera as *Rhododendron* and *Camellia*.

(2) Soil Type

The soil ideally should be a sand-based loam that can be easily worked, warms up quickly in the spring, drains well and provides the necessities to build up a fibrous root system to the layers, besides ensuring adequate vegetative growth. The pH should be just below neutral for most species and if not, must be adjusted accordingly. It is more likely that Specific Apple Replant Disease (S.A.R.D.) could reduce the life of apple rootstock stool beds if they are established on light soils.

The organic matter content should be around 3% and the use of bulky organics or green manuring should be considered where necessary. (Remember that weeds may be introduced with the use of bulky organics—particularly farmyard (steer) manure.) The nutrient status should be analyzed and adjusted with a base dressing prior to planting, with an emphasis on phosphates rather than nitrogen to encourage root development rather than excessive vegetative growth.

(3) Drainage

The site needs to be assessed for efficient drainage over the long term. Where necessary, a drainage system should be installed, using correct materials and drain pattern to allow sufficient movement of water away from the layer bed itself.

Subsoiling should be considered and ideally carried out during the summer months when the soil is dry, so that maximum shattering effect is achieved.

(4) Soil-Borne Pests and Diseases

There is an increasing problem of soil-borne pests and diseases in growing nursery stock, and layer beds are no exception. The decline of layer beds due to soil-borne disease has been highlighted in recent years by the research work at East Malling Research Station, England, on the effects of Root Gall (*Agrobacterium tumefaciens*) and Specific Cherry Replant Disease (*Thielaviopsis basicola*) on Cherry, *Prunus avium* Mazzard F12/1. Other diseases transmitted through the soil are *Verticillium* spp. affecting, in particular, *Acer* (Maple) and *Cotinus* (Smoke Tree), and *Phytophthora cinnamomi* affecting ericaceous plants such as *Rhododendron*, particularly under wet conditions. Nematodes are a problem in some locations and must be eliminated before planting. Cutworms can be a problem during continual dry weather when they can ring the stems of the layers in the mound. Woolly aphids can be a problem at the base of the shoots in some apple stool beds.

As indicated earlier, the grower should be particularly careful when using ground that has been previously used for nursery stock—especially when rotational practices have not been followed. Nematodes have a wide host range and cause problems relating to plant quarantine regulations on the movement of nursery stock, therefore analyses for identification and degree of population need to be made. This is particularly so with the Potato Cyst Nematode (P.C.N.)— many countries insist that soil be tested to confirm that it is eelworm-free in order to comply with strict regulations on shipping plants.

Figure 15-2.
Some specialist growers of fruit tree rootstocks fumigate the layer beds with methyl bromide to control soil-borne pests, diseases and weed seeds before planting the mother plants. Note the use of polyethylene film to seal in the chemical following injection into the soil. (Reproduced by courtesy of Oregon Rootstocks, Inc., Woodburn, OR, U.S.A.)

Should soil-borne pest and disease problems exist, soil fumigation must be carried out using materials such as methyl bromide, methyl isothiocyanate and chloropicrin (see Chapter 1 on Seed Propagation for characteristics and method of application).

(5) Irrigation

The value of irrigation for layering plants is four-fold:—

(a) To ensure adequate water for vegetative growth and root development—lack of water can have a dramatic result on growth, particularly on soils prone to surface capping. [However, F. P. Matthews Ltd., Tenbury Wells, England, have experienced some of the best yields of apple rootstocks from stool beds during dry seasons. They have found that rooting depends more on the vigor of the mother plants.]

(b) To aid establishment of mother plants.

(c) To assist in lifting of the layers during dry conditions, and the retention of soil by the roots.

(d) To make residual herbicides more effective.

Overhead irrigation using spray lines or rotating sprinklers is successful, while trickle irrigation can be effective for the establishment of the mother plants.

(6) Mechanization

As indicated earlier in the chapter, one disadvantage of layering is the limited degree to which the operation may be mechanized. Factors that will determine this are access and slope of land, soil type, plant material, and the layering method used. Machinery is used mainly for initial planting and routine cultivations, but efficient specialized machinery is available for mounding-up soil, harvesting, and bundling layers and will be described under stooling (mound layering).

SELECTION OF MOTHER PLANT MATERIAL

It is important to recognize that the source and quality of the initial mother material is an essential factor for success. Items to check are trueness-to-name and, where applicable, that it is free from all known viruses. Unfortunately, virus-free material is currently limited to only a few genera, such as *Malus* and *Prunus*. Although some ornamental plants may not fulfill the grade and specifications for normal selling, they can be useful for layering as long as the root system is sufficient for good establishment—an example being a tree of *Acer cappadocicum* 'Rubrum' (Red Coliseum Maple) with numerous shoots arising from the bed. One word of caution: one must check whether a tree has been grafted or budded. Whenever possible, use unworked material as problems will occur with suckering—for example, *Hamamelis* grafted onto *H. virginiana* (Common Witch Hazel) rootstock, *Syringa* cvs. on *S. vulgaris* (Common or French Lilac) and *Tilia mongolica*

Figure 15-3.
A micropropagated virus-free liner of a *Malus* (Apple) rootstock to be planted in a stool bed as a mother plant. (Microplant Nurseries, Inc., Woodburn, OR, U.S.A.)

(Mongolian Linden) on *T.* × *europaea* (syn. *T.* × *vulgaris*) (European Linden). This excess suckering quickly leads to a decline in layer production from the original plants and causes problems in identification.

LABELLING AND DOCUMENTATION

Permanent display labels are required, particularly where there are numerous plants from the same genus. Documentation should include: details of the source, date of planting, and subsequent yields over a given area. A master plan of the layer bed for overall reference should be formulated.

RENEWAL OF LAYER BEDS

The time for renewal of plant material will largely depend on the yield and quality being maintained, the method of layering and the plant material being grown. Other associated factors affecting this will be soil conditions, and the build-up of perennial weeds and soil-borne diseases.

As with other propagating techniques, perseverance with observational records is invaluable for future use, particularly when confronted with a decision to renew a layer bed. A replacement stool bed should be allowed to establish for at least three years before removing the old stool bed. The optimum period for a productive stool bed of apple rootstocks in heavier soils is considered to be 15–20 years. This is often reduced to 8–12 years for M.M.106 rootstocks as it is difficult to retain sufficient vigor after this time.

TECHNIQUES OF LAYERING

Philip McMillan Browse developed an effective method of classifying the different layering techniques based essentially on the stem and soil relationship used. The three classes developed are as follows:—

(a) Where soil is mounded up to the stem. Examples include stooling (mound layering), trench (etiolation) layering, and French (continuous) layering.

(b) Where the stems are lowered and placed into the soil. For example, simple layering, compound or serpentine layering, and tip layering.

(c) Where stems are not covered by soil. For example, air layering.

STOOLING OR MOUND LAYERING

Stooling or mound layering involves the induction of adventitious roots at the base of stems by mounding-up soil so as to exclude light by blanching. There are no published statistics, but it is probable that this technique is the most widely used layering method today. It is the main technique used in both Europe and North America to clonally propagate *Malus* rootstocks such as Malling 9, Malling 26 and Malling Merton 106, despite advances made over the last decade in hardwood cutting propagation. It has been used to a much lesser extent on ornamentals, including *Tilia* × *euchlora* (Crimean Linden) and *Prunus cerasifera* 'Nigra' (Black Myrobalan Plum). Stooling today is an efficient, mechanized, economical propagation system.

The plants suited to this technique must produce numerous new crown shoots to withstand the cutting back of stem growth each year so that vigorous shoots will be available annually. Stooling is best suited to material with an upright growth habit that otherwise could be damaged if brought down horizontally into the soil.

The procedures described are largely based on cultural practices used in Great Britain.

Procedure

Stage 1

The mother plants are planted when soil and weather conditions permit, spaced 23–30 cm (9–12″) apart in the row. The rows are best orientated north-south in order to efficiently utilize sunlight and to prevent the beds from becoming excessively dry on the south side. The distance between the rows depends on whether mounding and harvesting will be carried out by hand or mechanically. The distance for hand labor varies from 1.0–1.2 m (3½–4′), while it is 1.8–2.4 m (6–8′) if mechanization is intended. The row width will depend on the width of the tractor or cultivation machinery, but machinery designed to straddle multiple rows can save space, e.g., the French-designed Polybob® tractor.

The height of the rootstock is reduced to 45–60 cm (18–24″) either immediately prior to or after planting to reduce the chance of wind damage affecting root development.

Stage 2

The plants are encouraged to grow on for one full growing season to encourage a well-developed root system before layering commences.

Stage 3

During the following February, the main stem is cut back cleanly 2.5 cm (1″) above the soil surface, using a knife or hand pruners. Hasty upward movements while cutting must be avoided, otherwise the roots may be dislodged. This cutting back encourages adventitious buds to break low during the spring.

An alternative technique in Oregon for the establishment phases of a stool bed is to employ the procedure used for etiolation (trench) layering (p. 420). The rootstock is planted at a 30–45° angle and allowed to establish for one year. Early the following year, the main stem is bent down and held onto the surface of the soil by twine which is laced and fixed into position with hop clips. The advantage of this method is that it has been found to produce a heavier crop of layers during the earlier years of the stool bed. Recent commercial nursery experience in England has shown that this method has no benefit in the first cropping year of the stool bed, in year two there is a 100% improvement although many of these layers are not rooted, while in year three there is an 80% improvement of rooted layers compared to the traditional stooling planting and establishment procedure.

Stage 4

Each stool should form an optimum number of 2–5 stems during the first season. When these stems reach a height of about 15–20 cm (6–8″), soil is carefully mounded-up to a height of about 5.0–7.5 cm (2–3″) at the stem base. The soil needs to be moist and friable, so the operation may be made easier by running a cultivator down the rows beforehand. Complete contact between the soil and the stem must be assured when placing the earth around the developing shoots so that

Figure 15-4.
One manual method to mound the soil in and around the developing shoots in a layer bed is to use a draw hoe. (Nick Dunn, F. P. Matthews Ltd., Tenbury Wells, Worcestershire, U.K.)

adequate darkness and moisture is ensured. Thus, the mounding soil must be free of clods, stones, etc. It may be uneconomical to mound-up during the first production year. The shoots may instead be left to develop and then used as dormant hardwood cuttings rooted in a heated bin (p. 321).

Timing is important because shoot damage can occur if mounding is carried out too early, particularly for heavier soils. On the other hand, inadequate root development will occur if mounding is done after the stems become too hardened. Shy rooters such as Malling 9 have been mounded-up when only 7.5 cm (3″) in height. The operation may have to be repeated if erosion of the mound occurs during periods of high rainfall. Alternative materials used for mounding-up include peat moss, sawdust, and a mixture of the two mixed with the soil.

The mounding-up process must be repeated during early July, this time up to half the height of the shoot. Mounding-up more than half the stem height at any one time can be detrimental to growth. Some nurseries undertake a third mounding-up during early August. The final mounding-up should result in a soil depth of 15–20 cm (6–8″) at the base of the stem.

The traditional method used to mound-up the stems is to use a shovel to move the loose soil from between the rows to in and around the stems, but some interesting ideas for mechanizing this operation have developed during recent years. The more conventional approach is to plough a ridge as close as practicable to each side of each row and then hoe or rake some of the soil crumbs into the middle of the stool. However, other interesting innovations have been devised recently by Frank P. Matthews Ltd. of Tenbury Wells, England, who stool an area up to 8 ha (20 acres). Their ideas are as follows:—

(a) A machine that combines the effect of a land-driven rolling tined cultivator with that of compressed air from an air blast spray. The compressed air keeps the shoots vertical, while soil is pushed into and around the shoots within the stool bed by having the cultivator at different settings. This machine can cover 8 ha (20 acres) in 11 hours. The work begins from the first week of June and continues at two-week intervals until late July. This "little and often" procedure ensures a good mound of soil and excellent weed control.

(b) Long Ashton Research Station, University of Bristol, Bristol, U.K., developed a machine in the early 1970s that could mound-up one side of the stool bed by throwing up previously cultivated soil with a power-take-off driven ride spinner. There was a steel plate that both directed the soil to a ridge and deflected the shoots. Frank P. Matthews Ltd. have taken this machine a stage further by adapting it to a two-way machine so that two rows can be ridged up simultaneously using a combination of steel and rubber deflectors. A land-driven hay turner head has been added at the rear to lift up wrongly positioned shoots. This machine is used for the final mounding-up stage in the first week of August.

Figure 15-5. A custom-made machine to mound-up stool beds using a combination of steel and rubber deflectors. Note the hay turner heads installed at the rear of the machine to lift up wrongly-positioned shoots. (F. P. Matthews Ltd., Tenbury Wells, Worcestershire, U.K.)

Figure 15-6. Sawdust is transported to the layer beds and then mounded in and around the developing shoots of *Malus* (Apple) rootstocks. (Reproduced by courtesy of Oregon Rootstock, Inc., Woodburn, OR, U.S.A.)

The Oregon Rootstock Inc., Woodburn, Oregon, use fresh *Abies* (Fir) sawdust instead of soil for mounding-up the stool beds. Sawdust is carted out to the layer beds and distributed between the rows during late May to early June. Either hand labor or a machine is used to place and firm the sawdust amongst the growing shoots 3–4 times during the growing season. Irrigation is applied to thoroughly moisten the sawdust which is also kept irrigated during the growing season. It is necessary to cart in approximately 20% of the original amount in subsequent years. The sawdust is not physically incorporated into the soil beneath it and therefore nitrogen deficiency is not a major problem. A top dressing is applied three times during the growing season beginning in early March to give a total of 150–175 units of N.

Summer Maintenance

This is the relatively routine work associated with pest, disease and weed control. Likely problems that can arise include leaf rollers, leaf hoppers, aphids, mites, mildew and scab. These can be kept in check using systemic materials such as diazinon and malathion for pests and benomyl for diseases. Woolly aphids can cause considerable shoot damage and particularly like the environment created by mounding with soil or sawdust, which can lead to problems in their control.

Annual weeds may be a problem after the final mounding-up, including Black Nightshade (*Solanum nigrum*). These may be controlled by the careful application of contact herbicides such as paraquat, or by the use of some residual herbicides, including lenacil (Venzar®) chloroxuron (Tenoran®), napropamide (Devrinal®) and simazine. The latter should be used at a quarter or half rate to reduce the risk of damage to susceptible plants and to avoid inhibiting root development.

Harvesting and Grading

Depending on location, the harvesting of the layers commences in November or December. The grower should not be tempted to harvest too early to avoid excessive damage to the growing roots, particularly during a moist fall following a dry summer in which irrigation has not been available. Timing also depends on the plant type being lifted. The laying down of straw between the rows should be considered to make the operation cleaner and to prevent damage to soil structure. The framework of the stool must first be exposed in order to easily remove the rooted shoots. This can be done manually or mechanically, using a ridge plough to remove the soil from the center of the bed to the inter-row. The correct depth is critical and a hydraulically-controlled depth skid can be used to maintain this satisfactorily. The traditional method of using a good horse plough can also do this work very accurately.

Figure 15-7. Pesticide application is an important routine operation in the production of a quality crop of rootstocks. Note irrigation in progress in the background to ensure maintenance of the optimum moisture levels of the sawdust and soil. (Reproduced by courtesy of Oregon Rootstock, Inc., Woodburn, OR, U.S.A.)

Figure 15-8. Inspection of a well-maintained *Malus* (Apple) rootstock stool bed during August. (F. P. Matthews Ltd., Tenbury Wells, Worcestershire, U.K.)

Figure 15-10. Subsequent handling of the layers after lifting can be eased by using a machine which severs the stems with a cutter bar and then ejects the pulverized material over the soil. (Oregon Rootstock, Inc. Woodburn, OR, U.S.A.)

Figure 15-9. Assessing root development at the base of a shoot in October on a Danish stool bed enterprize. Note the root development that has occurred at the stem node.

Figure 15-11. "Splitting-back" the layer beds to facilitate mechanical harvesting of the layers. This machine can be fitted with a flail attachment to remove leaves if necessary. (Reproduced by courtesy of F. P. Matthews Ltd., Tenbury Wells, Worcestershire, U.K.)

Figure 15-12. Close-up of the machine used to "split-back" the layer beds (Figure 15-11) showing the depth control. (Reproduced by courtesy of F. P. Matthews Ltd., Tenbury Wells, Worcestershire, U.K.)

Figure 15-13. A rear-mounted unit severs the stems of the layers with a sawblade. (Reproduced by courtesy of F. P. Matthews Ltd., Tenbury Wells, Worcestershire, U.K.)

Figure 15-14. Close-up of the rear-mounted unit in Figure 15-13 showing the sawblade and its replaceable teeth. (Reproduced by courtesy of F. P. Matthews Ltd., Tenbury Wells, Worcestershire, U.K.)

Figure 15-15. A cradle can be used to transport the severed rootstocks from the layer beds to the cold store facility for subsequent trimming, grading and shipping. (Reproduced by courtesy of F. P. Matthews Ltd., Tenbury Wells, Worcestershire, U.K.)

Figure 15-16. The layers are placed on a conveyor belt and then removed according to grade. (Reproduced by courtesy of F. P. Matthews Ltd., Tenbury Wells, Worcestershire, U.K.)

The Oregon Rootstock Inc. uses a tractor-powered machine that is pulled down the rows in late October to early November to reduce the height of the shoots to 60 cm (24") prior to harvesting. The shoots are severed with a cutter bar, the material pulverized and then ejected over the layer bed. This procedure makes it easier to handle the layers following harvesting as they are of a uniform height and unwanted leaves and stem lengths are not brought into the grading shed.

The layers are removed from the stool bed as low down as possible to avoid "upward build-up" of the mother plant's framework. Careless harvesting can reduce the subsequent year's production by about 15%. The layers can be removed in one of four ways:—

(a) Manually, using hand pruners.

(b) Manually, pulling and tearing off the layers. Some plants do not break away easily so they must be cut. There is a definite knack needed to undertake this method satisfactorily.

(c) Mechanically, using a mounted power-driven rotating circular sawblade controlled by a hydraulic depth control. As experience grows, the depth can be judged by the noise the sawblade makes in the soil. Damage to the stool bed will occur if the cutter is set too low, and an uneven stool bed will result if it is too high. The length of life of the blade depends on its formulation—a Newman cutter type will last up to 0.8 ha (2 acres) and then require re-sharpening while other types are used for one hour and then discarded. The soil components also determine the length of use for the blade—sandy soils are especially abrasive.

Before mechanically harvesting layers, it is important to ensure that the mother plants are well-established in the soil so that they will offer resistance to the sawblade— commercial experience has shown that M.9 layers may have to be manually removed until the third or fourth crop.

(d) Mechanically, using a tractor-mounted cutter bar to cut through the bed when sawdust is used for mounding the shoots. The sawdust is left to protect the stools from winter injury after the rootstocks have been removed, and is then removed with a power-driven brushing machine in the following spring.

After harvesting, the layers are taken to the grading shed where the gradeable material is selected and the remainder is discarded. A successful procedure is then to place the layers onto a conveyor belt which drops them onto a large turntable. Staff remove them from the turntable and place them on benches in their respective grades. The turntable is useful as it allows flexibility by avoiding "bottle necks" because any excess layers continue on the turntable for one or more circuits. This evens out the erratic supply from the conveyor belt.

The layers are graded on stem caliper taken just above the root system. A typical grade sequence is 3–5 mm (1/8"), 5–7 mm (3/16"), 7–9 mm (5/16") and 9–12 mm (3/8"). Some nurseries offer transplanted layers of the middle grades, thus offering customers rootstocks with a greater number of roots. Any side shoots arising from the main stem are removed with pruners and the root system is reduced to around 1.3 cm (1/2") as the employees handle the layers. The layers are bundled, labelled and, if necessary, cold stored or heeled-in in a sheltered rodent-free location until shipping.

Figure 15-17.
A simple hand-held grader to measure the stem caliper.

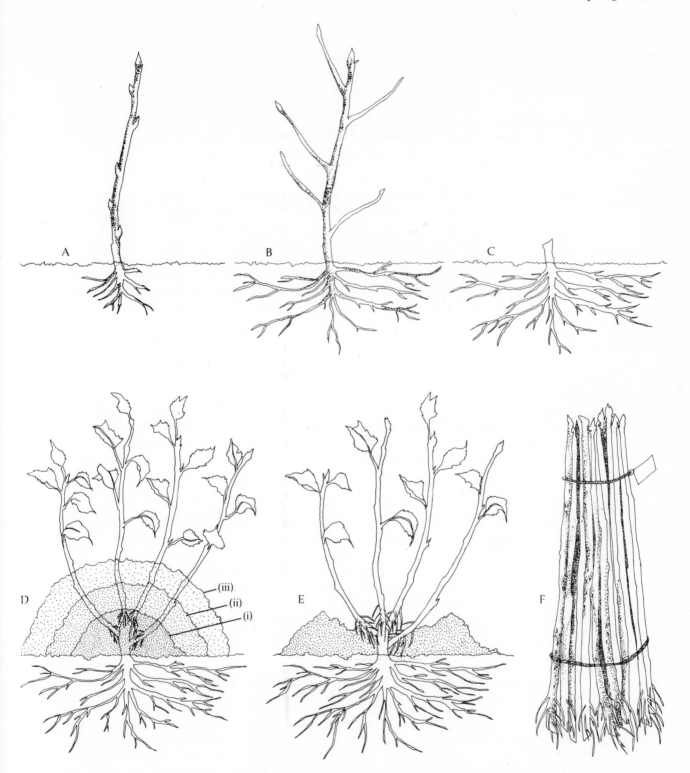

Diagram 15-1. Stooling or mound layering. A. The mother plant is planted during the dormant season and allowed to establish for one growing season. B. A substantial root system has developed by the end of the first year after planting. C. The stem is cut back to 2.5 cm (1″) above soil level in the following February to encourage shoots to develop from the base of the mother plant. D. Mounding-up is normally carried out in two or three stages—(i) when the shoots are 15–20 cm (6–8″) tall; (ii) in early July; (iii) in early August (optional). *NOTE:* Some nurseries now prefer to mound soil mechanically at 2-week intervals, using a "little and often" procedure. E. The first crop of layers are harvested two years after planting the mother plant. The mounds are opened up during late fall and winter to expose the roots at the bases of the shoots. F. The layers are removed, graded, bundled and labelled, and cold stored until shipping.

Figure 15-18.
A bed of transplanted layers being grown-on for a further season to encourage increased numbers of roots. (F. P. Matthews Ltd., Tenbury Wells, Worcestershire, U.K.)

Defoliation

Some rootstocks are characterized by late leaf drop during a mild fall and early winter. The apple rootstock M.M.11 sheds its leaves early, M.7 and M.M.106 are intermediate, and M.26 is late. This makes the timing of harvesting the latter more difficult. Removal of leaves is beneficial, allowing easier harvesting and grading out, and reducing the risk of leaf-borne disease during cold storage. The grower may wish to remove the leaves either mechanically or chemically.

Power-driven machines using a tractor with leather flails driven by a rotating drum can force off many of the leaves, but stem and bud damage may result, especially if the wood is not well ripened. Damage can be visually latent in that it may not be observed until growth commences the following spring. Successful chemical removal involves the activation of the natural process leading to the breaking of the abscission zone of the leaf between the petiole and the stem but without causing subsequent stem and bud damage. Chemicals used have included Ethrel® to stimulate ethylene production within the leaf and copper-based materials such as copper oxychloride mixed with ammonium sulfate (see p. 328), with some good results being achieved. Present research into newer chemicals, such as N.252 and the Fisons Ltd. compound N.C.9634, has shown encouraging results. Generally, the effect of defoliants has not always been consistent due partially to weather conditions and also to the state of growth of the rootstock. Chemical defoliants are normally applied 2–3 weeks prior to lifting. Complete defoliation before lifting is not strictly required when chemicals are used, because many leaves will drop off at the weakened abscission zone when the shoots are handled during the harvesting process.

Winter Maintenance

The stools are sometimes left exposed during the winter to give light to the remaining stubs and so encourage bud development, except in very cold areas where some soil is returned for protection. In Oregon, sawdust is retained over the stool beds after harvesting until March to provide winter protection. Dead wood is removed and any perennial weeds taken out. Organic matter should be added to the soil at this time. The use of residual herbicides after the soil disturbing conditions are concluded should be considered if the climate is such that winter-germinated weeds can build up. [The build-up of most residual herbicides can be prevented by applying at half-strength as a "strip row", stool width application in February, followed by a half-strength application over the whole area after the final mounding in August.]

Yield of Stool Beds

Published figures on yields are difficult to locate, especially for ornamentals. Yields will vary according to rootstock type, age of stool bed and climatic conditions. The following figures give optimum yields from a productive stool bed area planted at 0.3 m × 1.8 m (1 × 6′) spacing and may be used as a guideline.

ROOTSTOCK	YIELD PER METER	YIELD PER ACRE	% OF LAYERS ROOTED
M.M.106	25	40,000	100
M.9	18	30,000	70
M.26	15	25,000	90
Quince A	30	50,000	100

(Source: F. P. Matthews Ltd., Tenbury Wells, Worcestershire, England.)

Yield and Grade-Out Improvement from Stool Beds

The improvement of yield from stool beds involves, firstly, a critical examination of one's own husbandry techniques, and then, secondly, appraising the timing and methods used for fertilization, mounding-up, irrigation, etc. The improvement of soil fertility and structure is a long-term objective that has a manifold effect on yield and to which the grower must pay continuing attention.

Research and development on stool bed yields and grade-out improvement has been limited, but East Malling Research Station personnel have carried out some pioneer work, especially since 1979, using three approaches.

(i) Clonal Selection

Clones of the important apple rootstock Malling 9 have been collected and compared at a number of centers in Europe. Twenty or so clones compared in stool bed trials at East Malling differed in the numbers and sizes of shoots produced, rooting ability and quality of root systems, leaf shape, and tendency to produce spines. No single clone combined all the advantageous characters—high shoot production in some strong-growing clones being offset by excessive frequency of spines. A number of clones selected for high shoot production and rooting coupled with acceptable levels of spine production have gone forward for nursery trials.

(ii) Growth Control Chemicals

The sucker-control agent Tip-off®, a mixture of naphthaleneacetic acid (NAA), decanol and emulsifiers, was successfully sprayed at a concentration of 4% product on stool beds of M.M.106 in early spring when the first growth was 5 cm (2″) tall to remove weak unsaleable shoots, but leave marketable shoots to grow longer than normal (given adequate moisture and soil fertility). The timing of application is critical because potentially weak shoots start to grow before ones that are more dormant but arise on thicker stems. Delaying the application of Tip-off® will kill potentially valuable shoots.

(iii) Selective or Biennial Harvesting

An alternative to removing weak shoots by chemical treatment is to allow these shoots to grow for two seasons. This can be achieved either by selectively harvesting only large shoots each year or by harvesting all shoots on a biennial cycle. Trials with both techniques at East Malling increased the numbers of high-grade shoots in both M.M.106 and M.27 when compared to the accumulated annual harvests over a two-year period. Rooting in the less ready-rooting M.27 was enhanced by biennial harvesting, and the stool beds showed increased vigor up to three years later.

ETIOLATION OR TRENCH LAYERING

This technique serves as the basis for the vegetative propagation of *Prunus avium* (Mazzard) Mazzard F12/1 rootstocks, although it has been used also on such crops as Quince, Mulberry, Apple and Walnut. It involves the initiation and development of roots at the base of a stem by virtually excluding light during the early part of shoot development from a mother plant trained to grow horizontally in a shallow trench. It differs from stooling or mound layering in that the developing shoots are covered with soil in the early growth phase while still leafless and thus are etiolated (not previously exposed to light), whereas shoot growth in stooling has occurred and chlorophyll is present prior to mounding-up the soil. Thus, the stems are blanched after development in stooling.

The major advantages of etiolation layering are:—

(i) It may be used for plants that do not respond to other layering techniques as it relies on etiolation to initiate and develop roots.

(ii) It is possible to increase the yield and obtain a more even grade of crops such as apple rootstocks than by stooling. Not all authorities would agree with this statement. However, Traas Nurseries, a well-known Canadian producer in Langley, British Columbia, have increased their yield substantially per meter- or foot-run of bed compared with stooling, particularly during the early years after planting the mother plants. It was found that this method gave maximum production in the shortest time (see also p. 411).

Etiolation layering does have disadvantages, one of which has been a major contributing factor to its virtual disappearance as a viable technique in Britain. The disadvantages include:—

(i) It is more precise and therefore costly in labor—particularly in relation to the number of times that the bases of the stems are covered.

(ii) The reduction in yield due to the build-up of soil-borne diseases in established beds.

Procedure

The principles and methods for establishment of a layer bed using etiolation layering is as for stooling, the cultural differences begin from the time of planting. Assuming one is to grow Mazzard F12/1 layers, the procedure may be summarized as follows.

Stage 1

The planting distances for the mother plants are 0.6–0.8 m (2–2½') between the plants and 1.4–1.5 m (4½–5') between the rows. The distance between the rows may be increased up to 2.5–3.0 m (8–10') if mechanical cultivation is used. Double rows may be used with 0.6 m (2') spacing normally advised between the two single rows. The mother plants are planted at a 30–45° angle, not vertically, thus making the subsequent horizontal layering easier.

Stage 2

The plants are usually allowed to grow on for one full growing season to encourage a well-developed root system prior to the first layering.

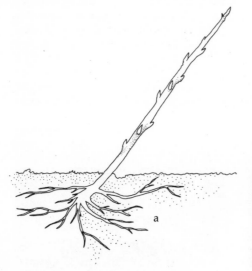

Diagram 15-2. Etiolation or trench layering. The mother plants are planted at a 30–45° angle and normally allowed to establish for one complete growing season before laying down. a—note the development of the root system by the end of the first growing season.

Figure 15-19. Newly established *Malus* (Apple) rootstocks intensively planted for etiolation layering. The intensive planting will increase production during the early life of the bed. Note that the rootstocks are planted at a 45° angle. (F. P. Matthews Ltd., Tenbury Wells, Worcestershire, U.K.)

Stage 3

A shallow trench about 5.0 cm (2″) deep and 23 cm (9″) wide is made during the late summer to early fall of the first year or the latter part of the winter of the following year. The mother plants will be laid down in this trench. Some soil needs to be removed from the base of the plants to facilitate the initial bending of the main stem to a horizontal position and to prevent an upward bow of the stem. Lateral shoots are tipped and weak ones severely reduced so that they can be accommodated within the width of the trench. When laying the plant horizontally, it is important that all the shoots are level so that subsequent bud break is even along the stems.

The tension placed on the stems means that thorough attention has to be given to pegging down. Robert J. Garner, a well-known exponent of etiolation layering, suggests in his book *The Grafters Handbook* that the main peg should be placed towards the base of the stem and should be made by sharpening the end of a dry piece of wood (for example, *Castanea sativa*, Spanish Chestnut) that is 30 cm (12″) long with a 5 cm (2″) nail firmly inserted horizontally about 2.5 cm (1″) from the top. The lateral shoots may be pegged down with 10-gauge wire, using 38 cm (15″) lengths formed into "U" shapes. The laying down of the mother plants in late winter reduces the risk of the pegs being lifted by frost, which is a problem if the procedure is carried out in the fall or early winter. A more modern method is to use twine, which is laced down the row and fixed into position with hop clips, to hold the main stem in a horizontal position.

Figure 15-20. A jig has been designed to ease the use of twine and hop clips in laying the stems of the mother plants onto the soil. A. The jig in use. B. Placing the hop clip into the base of the jig. C. Feeding in the twine. D. Pressing the clip and twine into the soil alongside the plant stem. E. The twine laced over the stems after removal of the jig. (F. P. Matthews Ltd., Tenbury Wells, Worcestershire, U.K.)

Stage 4

The mother plant, now pegged down in the trench, is covered before the buds swell with a 2.5 cm (1″) layer of friable soil. The young shoots start to emerge through the soil during April and are again covered with friable soil when they are at the "crook stage" before leaf development (similar to the emergence of the garden pea). This operation is repeated up to three times. It is important not to cover areas where shoots have not emerged—hence the importance stressed earlier of initial level pegging of the stems to ensure even bud break. It may be better to use peat moss or sawdust as a covering instead of soil. This stage of the production procedure must be carried out methodically in order to take advantage of the benefits of rooting the stem bases.

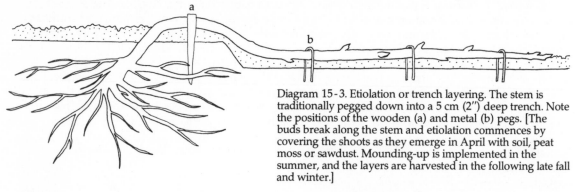

Diagram 15-3. Etiolation or trench layering. The stem is traditionally pegged down into a 5 cm (2″) deep trench. Note the positions of the wooden (a) and metal (b) pegs. [The buds break along the stem and etiolation commences by covering the shoots as they emerge in April with soil, peat moss or sawdust. Mounding-up is implemented in the summer, and the layers are harvested in the following late fall and winter.]

Stage 5

The shoots are allowed to grow to 7.5–10.0 cm (3–4″) high and are then mounded-up to half their height. Mounding-up higher than this can inhibit growth. This procedure is repeated in July as for stooling or mound layering. The procedures for summer maintenance are as for stooling.

Stage 6—Harvesting and Grading

The soil may be removed from the stems from November onwards and the techniques of harvesting by hand and machine are similar to those previously described under stooling. An unrooted or rooted shoot must be left every 30 cm (12″) along the bed and pegged down to ensure a continuation of cropping for the following year. The pegs should be checked for firmness well before the buds begin to grow the following year. Grading procedures and specifications are normally similar to those used for stooling.

Figure 15-21. Manual removal of the soil and severing of the stems at the crown of the plants while harvesting *Prunus avium* Mazzard F12/1 layers.

Figure 15-22. The extensive root systems at the crown of a layer bed.

Replant Diseases of *Prunus* and *Malus*

It is appropriate to outline some details of replant diseases at this point as the two layering methods described so far are those used for *Prunus* and *Malus*.

Work carried out by research workers at East Malling Research Station has shown the importance played by soil-borne diseases in the decline of yields in *Prunus* and *Malus* orchard cropping. They are referred to as Specific Cherry Replant Disease (S.C.R.D.) and Specific Apple Replant Disease (S.A.R.D.). The disease only occurs on plant species planted on land where the same or closely-related species have been grown, hence the prefix "specific".

The pathogen affecting *Prunus* Mazzard F12/1 layer beds has been identified as *Thielaviopsis basicola,* which is parasitic on the root surfaces. The growth of the root tip exceeds that of the pathogen at low soil infection levels, with little resultant damage. However, a build-up of *Thielaviopsis basicola* in the soil leads to infection of the root tips, causing reduced growth. The problem occurs in Mazzard F12/1 layer beds when soil in proximity to the shoots is continually re-used for the annual mounding-up operation, so that the pathogens build up in the soil. The developing roots can easily pick up infection, reducing growth and lowering the yield. Similarly F12/1 beds have been infected by Crown Gall (*Agrobacterium tumefaciens*), which has become an increasing problem in the United Kingdom in ornamental cherry production using these rootstocks. The galls have a tendency to arise at the point where the shoot was removed the previous year and at the bend of the layer that may be formed when pegging down during the winter. These two diseases, combined with the introduction of the easy-to-root cherry rootstock *Prunus* 'Colt', have been responsible for the decline in etiolation layer beds in the United Kingdom. In addition, infected layers re-lined out in nurseries for budding have transferred the infection to other sites, resulting in problems building up in the soil there.

Research has shown that good levels of control in infected F12/1 layer beds can be achieved with benomyl (Benlate®) applied in one of three ways. An application in early May is most significant because it is the time when new growth emerges through the soil cover. The second option is in late July when the roots begin to form, and the final option is a two-stage application in early May and in July. The rate of application used in the tests was 146.5 g benomyl in 71.6–143.2 l water (dependent on soil moisture) per 30 m of row (5.25 oz. in 16–32 Imp. gal per 100'). Chloropicrin effectively controls the disease when used as a soil fumigant injected at the rate of 281 l/ha (25 Imp. gal/acre) on infected land intended for use as a new layer bed. The addition of organic matter to the layer bed will mask the disease but not control it.

The picture is much less clear for apple rootstock layer beds. However, it is known that *Pythium sylvaticum* and another *Pythium* species are the pathogens responsible for Specific Apple Replant Disease (S.A.R.D.) in fruiting apple orchards. At the time of writing, there appears to be limited work on this disease in relation to apple stool beds. Nevertheless, it would be prudent to fumigate a new *Malus* layer bed prior to planting with chloropicrin or methyl bromide or alternatively, to consider drenching with a Formalin® solution. East Malling Research Station have demonstrated that a dilute solution of Formalin® is effective when applied as a drench on newly raked soil. The treated area is then flooded with water one day later and covered with polyethylene sheeting for 24 hours to retain the gases. Nursery operators have found that covering with polyethylene sheeting can be omitted and have obtained good results with irrigation or flooding to cap the soil surface. However, the success of this method does depend on the soil type. The soil is opened up and left for 3–6 weeks, depending on the soil type. The area must be tested for absence of residues by carrying out a seed test using lettuce or cress prior to planting.

There are a number of nurseries in Europe and North America where layer beds are currently successful with few problems caused by soil-borne diseases. However, the experiences of research workers and growers in the United Kingdom need to be understood so that propagators in unaffected areas are aware of the problems that could arise on their nurseries.

CONTINUOUS OR FRENCH LAYERING

This intensive technique, plus its variations, has been very important in the European nursery stock industry although it is now losing favor, mainly due to the introduction of the modern techniques of cutting propagation and the labor costs involved. I have seen some excellent, productive layer beds in Holland and Belgium based on French layering.

This technique involves the mounding-up of vigorous one-year-old stems previously pegged down horizontally in a circular fashion around the mother plant. It is a modification of stooling, but has some similarity to etiolation layering in that one mounds-up the growth arising from horizontal vegetative stems. However, this is blanching and not true etiolation. Continuous layering is used to propagate ornamentals such as *Alnus* × *spaethii*, *Cotinus coggygria* 'Royal Purple' (Purple Smoke Tree), *Prunus tenella* 'Firehill' (Dwarf Russian Almond cv.), *Cornus alba* 'Westonbirt' (Westonbirt Dogwood) and *Cercidiphyllum japonicum* (Katsura Tree).

The length of life of the layer beds is less consistent than in stooling or etiolation layering. For example, some *Acer* (Maple) seem to resent the heavy pruning and are susceptible to attack by Coral Spot (*Nectria cinnabarina*) where the pathogen infects dead wood around the cut surfaces and then proceeds to infect living tissue during the summer.

Procedure

Once the layer bed facility has been prepared, the procedure is as follows:—

Stage 1—Planting and Establishment

The plants are set 1.8–3 m (6–10′) apart, depending on genus, species and cultivar used. The spacing is directly dependent upon the space needed to lay the new shoots out in a circle around each mother plant. The mother plants are allowed to grow-on for one year to aid establishment of the root system.

Stage 2—Heading Back

All vegetative growth is cut back to a height of 2.5 cm (1″) in the following winter.

Stage 3—Growing-On

One difference between this method and stooling or etiolation layering is that the new pruned shoots are not mounded-up at this stage but are allowed to grow naturally for another full growing season to provide the basic framework for the third year.

Stage 4—Pegging Down

The shoots are pegged radiating from the mother plant during the late winter of the next year (the commencement of the third year after planting). They are held down horizontally onto the surface of the soil with U-shaped wire pegs, ensuring that they are all level. It is important to achieve even bud break along the stems, and they should therefore be pegged down well before the buds swell. *Cotinus coggygria* (Smoke Tree) is particularly prone to uneven bud break if these conditions are not met.

Stage 5—Formation of Shallow Trench and Mounding-Up

The new shoots from the horizontal stems are allowed to reach 10 cm (4″) in height and the pegs are then removed. A shallow trench is then made adjacent to each stem. This trench must be deep enough to just expose the growing shoots above the surface of the soil when it is filled in. The horizontal stem is now re-pegged into the trench, particularly towards the base to prevent it from springing up later, and the trench filled in. Care must be taken at this stage not to bruise the soft growth, especially with *Cotinus coggygria* (Smoke Tree) and *Cercidiphyllum japonicum* (Katsura Tree).

Figure 15-23. French layering of *Cotinus coggygria* 'Royal Purple' (Purple Smoke Tree). Numerous young shoots are developing shortly after the mother plant has been laid into a shallow trench.

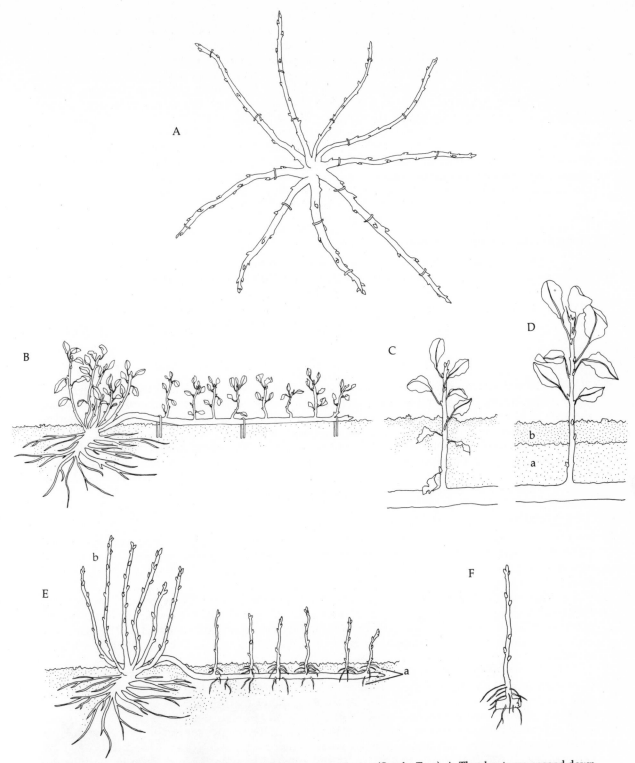

Diagram 15-4. French or continuous layering of *Cotinus coggygria* cvs. (Smoke Tree). A. The shoots are pegged down onto the soil surface during the late winter following the second year from planting the mother plant. B. The new growth from the layered stem should develop evenly along the stem. C. The pegs are removed when the soft shoot growth reaches 10 cm (4″) and each shoot is laid down into an adjacent trench so that the shoot tip is just above the soil surface, re-pegging as necessary. (The diagram shows the shoot development about 2–3 weeks later.) D. The developing shoots are again mounded-up in June (a) and the procedure is sometimes repeated in July (b). E. A substantial new root system has developed along the layered stem and at the bases of the one-year worked shoots by leaf fall (a). Vigorous shoots have also developed on the mother plant (b) for laying down the following year. F. The horizontal stem is severed from the mother plant, removed from the soil and then cut into individual layers for subsequent potting-up or open-ground planting.

Sufficient growth should have occurred by early June that the shoots should require mounding with soil to a height of about 10 cm (4"). This operation sometimes is repeated in July. This work is time-consuming and does not lend itself to mechanization, although it may be simplified for some plants. For example, good results have been achieved for *Cornus alba* cultivars (Red-bark or Tatarian Dogwood) by just covering the pegged dormant stems with soil, without unpegging and lowering into a trench. The Climbing Hydrangea, *Hydrangea anomala* subsp. *petiolaris* (syn. *H. petiolaris*), will form a sufficient root system when the stems are simply pegged down onto sandy soil, without any trenching or mounding-up.

Wilfrid G. Sheat in his book *Propagation of Trees, Shrubs and Conifers* shows an interesting plate of how *Cotinus coggygria* (Smoke Tree) was layered. The stems were held horizontally level about 7.5 cm (3") above ground level and the soil was then mounded over this structure when the shoots had developed along the stem. To encourage even root development, the stem adjacent to the crown of the mother plant was cut vertically part of the way through the stem and then horizontally in two opposing directions (thus forming a "T"-shape) in the early fall and bound with tape. The rooted shoots were lifted the following spring.

Stage 6—Harvesting and Grading.

The layers are cut through as close as possible to the mother plant at leaf-fall time and left for about 4–6 weeks. The layered stems are then carefully eased up from the soil with a fork and cut into individual layers with hand pruners. These layers are graded, the roots protected from drying out, and subsequently either sold or grown-on in the open ground or containers for a further 1–2 years. One-year-old ripened shoots arising from the center of the mother plant are used to continue the cycle the following year.

Maintenance

Once the layers have been lifted, all other broken, weak, dead and unrooted stems are removed by cutting back to the mother plant. All prunings should be removed and burnt to lessen the risk of Coral Spot infection. Organic matter should be incorporated into the layer bed to improve the soil structure and water holding capacity, and the mother plants mulched. A useful alternative to manure is spent hops or other processed organic material. Soil analysis may indicate that a top dressing of a compound balanced fertilizer will be needed for the next year's growth.

Summer maintenance consists mainly of weed control, irrigation and spraying against pests and diseases such as aphids, capsids, spider mites and mildew.

SIMPLE LAYERING

Simple layering is probably the best known layering technique to most professional and amateur growers. An extremely wide diversity of woody plants have been successfully propagated by this method, ranging from some of the small alpine shrubs to conifers and large broad-leaved trees.

Simple layering involves the constriction of the stem, normally by bending or twisting, followed by siting and pegging a length of stem below soil level while still attached to the parent plant. Root initiation and development is promoted by the constriction assisted by the blanching caused by covering with soil, especially in those stems laid down during the summer while in growth.

The final yield is not as large as in continuous layering because only one layer is produced from each stem. Thus, the grower is well advised to determine whether a plant may be successfully propagated by continuous layering or stooling rather than by simple layering. (See list of plants suitable for layering in Appendix 15-4).

Simple layering was one of the basic propagation techniques for nurseries during the first quarter of the twentieth century, as it was a reliable method for both common and choice woody ornamentals. It was particularly important for the genera *Rhododendron* and *Magnolia*, and for the family Hamamelidaceae. Conifers were also simple layered, including *Juniperus sabina* 'Tamariscifolia' (Spanish or Tamarix Juniper) and forms of *J. squamata* (Single-seed or Scaly-leaved Nepal Juniper). Old over-grown stock plants of *Thuja occidentalis* (Eastern Arborvitae) and *Chamaecyparis lawsoniana* (Lawson Cypress) were "wrenched", then removed and layered down in the following fall in order to continue the clonal material. The layers were lifted about eighteen months later and the mother plant was then destroyed. The book *Propagation of Trees, Shrubs and Conifers* by Wilfrid G. Sheat gives a fascinating account of the different layering techniques used in past years for a wide variety of woody ornamentals. The development of the more sophisticated cutting propagation techniques has led most nursery operators to abandon simple layering.

Currently, there are excellent layer beds in production at nurseries in some European countries, including Britain, Holland and Belgium, and it is therefore worth describing the procedures used.

Figure 15-24. A highly productive mother plant of *Magnolia* × *soulangiana* (Chinese or Saucer Magnolia) in late May. Note the layered shoots around the perimeter and the vigorous shoots to the center of the mother plant. These latter will be used for simple layering in the following winter. (Odemez, France)

Figure 15-25. A newly-established mother plant of a cultivar of *Corylus avellana* (European Filbert) will be used for simple layering.

Figure 15-26. An established young mother plant of *Acer cappadocicum* 'Rubrum' (Red Coliseum Maple) produces strong vigorous growth for simple layering in the next winter.

Procedure

Stage 1—Planting and Establishment

The following points should be considered when planning a layer bed for simple layering that will contain a range of woody plants:—

(i) Planting distances should be varied according to habit and vigor.

(ii) Specific soil requirements—for example, low pH (acidic) conditions for *Rhododendron* versus the more alkaline situations required for the French hybrids of *Syringa* (Lilac).

(iii) Differing time periods from pegging down the layers until lifting. The time to development of good roots may be as little as 5 months for *Cornus alba* (Red-bark Dogwood) cultivars, or as long as 2 years for some *Rhododendron* forms. This means that some plants can only be layered in alternate years, so that double the number of mother plants may have to be planted in order to produce the requisite annual number of layers.

(iv) Some plants do not produce sufficient annual growth to allow layering each year while other plants, for example, *Halesia* (Silver-bell), need periodic resting otherwise they are short-lived and non-productive. It may be necessary to increase the number of mother plants in this case.

(v) Incidence of soil-borne disease—for example, *Phytophthora cinnamomi* (Root Rot) affecting *Rhododendron* and other members of the Ericaceae.

Details on site preparation up to planting are as referred to in the section on pp. 407–409. The planting distances will depend on the plant being layered and also on the mechanization available for limited inter-row cultivation. The distances will vary between 1.8–3.0 m (6–10′) square, and one to two years should be allowed for the development of an established root system.

Stage 2—Heading Back

Most subjects for simple layering may be cut back to 2.5 cm (1″) above soil level to encourage vigorous one-year stems for subsequent laying down. Plants such as rhododendrons will not readily respond to this; therefore, the technique is modified by bringing in rhododendron plants that are already branched, re-planting the mother plant at an angle and laying the stems down for subsequent pegging.

Stage 3—Layering of Stems

There are three periods when simple layering may be employed—fall, late winter/early spring, and summer. Summer is sometimes used when dormant stems are brittle and to encourage early rooting as the stems are in growth. Observations have been made as to the preferred time for certain plants. For example, Wilfrid G. Sheat in his book *Propagation of Trees, Shrubs and Conifers* states that *Disanthus cercidifolius* should be layered in May when the new shoots are about 10 cm (4″) long, while dogwoods such as *Cornus alba* (Red-bark Dogwood), *C. florida* (Eastern Flowering Dogwood), *C. kousa* (Kousa Dogwood), *C. nuttallii* (Western Flowering Dogwood), and *C. stolonifera* (Red-osier Dogwood) are best in mid-summer when growth is flexible but not soft enough to easily bruise. July and August are mentioned for *Chimonanthus* (Wintersweet), *Eucryphia* and *Fothergilla*; fall is suggested for *Corylus* (Filbert); and early spring for *Corylopsis* (Winter Hazel).

The process begins by layering the shorter stems first, gradually working out in a circular fashion from the stool so that the longest stems are used last.

Both hands are used to form a constriction in the part of the stem to be covered by soil. The distance of this constriction from the tip depends on the plant—for example, 15 cm (6″) in *Corylus* (Filbert) but 30 cm (12″) in *Cercidiphyllum* (Katsura Tree). A number of different ways are used to achieve the constriction:—

(i) Bending the stem upwards.

(ii) Twisting the stem to rupture the tissues.

(iii) Creating a tongue on the shoot by making a 2.5–5.0 cm (1–2″) sliver and then bending the stem. This technique is useful when the stem is brittle.

(iv) Girdling the stem by removing a narrow strip of bark all around it.

(v) Constricting the stem by twisting copper wire into the stem tissues.

In practice, methods (i), (ii) and (iii) have been more widely practiced than the others, but the choice is influenced by the specific plant, the time of year and the experience of the propagator. It has been recommended by individual propagators that *Chionanthus virginicus* (White Fringe Tree) should have the stems bent upwards, *Clethra* stems should be twisted, and *Magnolia* stems tongued.

The stems are then firmly pegged down and covered with soil to a depth of 7.5–10 cm (3–4″). The procedure for soil cover can be achieved in three ways:—

(i) By using friable soil from the surrounding area.

(ii) By in-filling with prepared soil, to which sand or peat moss may be added.

(iii) By pegging down onto the soil surface and then mounding over the constricted area with either friable surrounding soil or a specially-prepared medium. I saw an adaptation of this method being used by the enterprising Derek Thursfield of Kerry Hill Nurseries,

Figure 15-27. Simple layering of *Platanus* × *acerifolia* (London Plane). Note the vertical orientation of the shoot tip that develops after constriction of the stem. (Notcutts Nurseries, Woodbridge, Suffolk, U.K.)

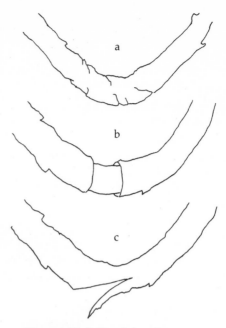

Diagram 15-5. Simple layering. Methods of stem constriction include a—twisting; b—girdling; c—creating a tongue.

Figure 15-28. Modified simple layering of *Rhododendron* 'Cunningham's Blush'. Note that only one side of the mother plant has been layered—the other side will be layered in the following winter. (Kerry Hill Nurseries, Bucknell, Staffordshire, U.K.)

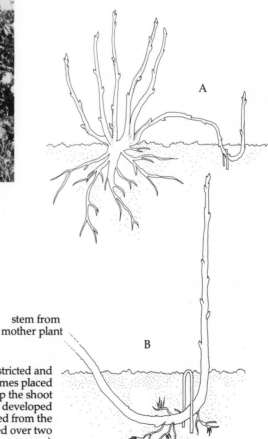

stem from mother plant

Diagram 15-6. Simple layering. A. The stem is constricted and pegged down during late winter. A cane is sometimes placed adjacent to the shoot and the stem tied to it to keep the shoot vertical. B. Sufficient root development has normally developed by the following fall to allow the stem to be severed from the mother plant. (Some species are sometimes layered over two years.)

Figure 15-29.
A well-branched liner of *Rhododendron* that has been lined-out for one year after harvesting from the layer bed. (Kerry Hill Nurseries, Bucknell, Staffordshire, U.K.)

Bucknell, England. Well-established mother plants of *Rhododendron* 'Cunningham's Blush' were planted in rows as for stooling. Stems from one side of the row were layered one year and those from the other side in the following year. This alternate year procedure allowed the stems to gain sufficient length for the simple layering technique.

Bent stems may form on the layers, in which case the newly-layered shoots may be staked and tied in at the time of pegging down.

Stage 4—Harvesting and Grading

The period between layering and lifting varies from 5 months to 2 years, depending on the subject. The layered shoots should be severed in the fall, as close as possible to the mother plant stool, and may be lifted about 4–6 weeks later. Root growth on many plants continues well into the latter part of the year and premature removal should be avoided for that reason. The layers are graded, the roots protected from drying out, and then planted out for growing-on either in open ground or in containers.

Maintenance

After lifting is completed, all broken, dead, weak and unrooted shoots are removed and burnt. As described in continuous layering, consideration should be given to the improvement of soil structure with the addition of organic matter, top dressing with a compound balanced fertilizer (6-8-6 ratio), and spraying against pests and diseases such as aphids, capsids, spider mites, vine weevils and mildew. Irrigation, particularly during the early stages of root development, may be required and weed control will be necessary.

SERPENTINE OR COMPOUND LAYERING

Serpentine or compound layering is a traditional technique used for plants with long flexible stems, such as the climbing vines *Clematis, Vitis,* and *Wisteria.* It may be defined as a modification of simple layering in which the stems are multiple-layered by being placed below soil level at a number of locations along their length.

Today this technique has little application in the nursery, although I have seen it being used with *Wisteria* in Holland. The procedure is carried out during early spring or fall. The stems are twisted, girdled or tongued before bending, and are usually placed down in a circular pattern to

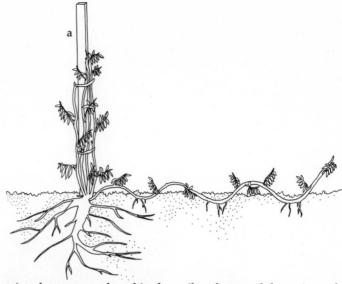

Diagram 15-7. Serpentine or compound layering of *Wisteria*. Sufficient roots have developed along the stem by late summer to allow severing from the mother plant and lifting in the subsequent fall or winter. Shoots to be used for layering in the following year have been tied onto a pole (a).

utilize space more efficiently. The constricted areas are placed in the soil and pegged down in such a way that vegetative buds on the stem are above soil level. The stems are severed from the mother plant after one growing season (although some *Vitis* may need two) and then cut into the individual layers for growing-on. The layers for the next year are provided by new shoots, sometimes tied to a post, arising from the center of the mother plant.

TIP LAYERING

This technique is a modification of simple layering that is traditionally used for the fruiting *Rubus* such as Loganberry and Blackberry, and occasionally for ornamental *Rubus* such as *R. thibetanus*. Tip layering depends on the acute bending of the soft growing tip during the summer to place it beneath the soil level. This encourages rapid root development with a minimum of stem growth. It does represent perhaps the quickest turn around period from the time of layering to lifting. The intensive method using single leaf bud cuttings has reduced tip layering to minor significance in today's modern nursery. Another alternative technique is the use of root cuttings (see Chapter 14) which, although intensive, can have the disadvantage of clonal variation in the subsequent progeny. This variation is likely to extend to the production of plants with thorny stems from the thornless fruiting periclinal chimaera cultivars of Blackberry.

Procedure

The mother plants are planted on a weed-free site with light friable soil, 2.5–3.8 m (8–12') apart, and are then cut back to 15–23 cm (6–9") in height. They should be allowed to establish for one year if planting is carried out late into the growing season.

Each year after establishment, the number of lateral shoots should be increased by tipping the new shoots when they are about 45–60 cm (18–24") long. This produces a larger number of potential layers by July, when the shoots should be up to 0.9–1.3 m (3–4') long. To tip layer, use a trowel to make a hole about 10–15 cm (4–6") deep, with a vertical side away from the mother plant and a sloping side towards it. The tip of the shoot is placed down along the sloping side into the bottom of the hole. This procedure forces many more breaks along the shoot, thus increasing the number of potential layers. The incentive to root is reduced if the shoot is bent upwards. It is then covered over with soil and firmed. The layers should have well-developed fibrous root systems and a dominant terminal shoot bud with some accompanying axillary buds by the following November, when they may be lifted.

DROP LAYERING

This technique is actually a form of division but is sometimes included as a layering technique because it relies on the principle of blanching to encourage rooting of the stems. It helps to ensure that more roots develop along the stem of some plants compared to those that form on shoots removed by conventional division (p. 399). Drop layering is defined as the placing of a complete plant into a prepared hole or furrow and then covering all but the shoot tips with soil to encourage roots to form on the stems. The whole mother plant is lifted at the end of one or two growing seasons and is divided into the individual layers. The process is repeated the following year using a new mother plant. This contrasts with stooling, in which the soil is mounded-up to the stems and the mother plants remain *in-situ* from year to year.

Drop layering has limited use and is normally orientated to dwarf ericaceous plants such as *Leiophyllum buxifolium* (Box Sand Myrtle), *Cassiope,* a range of dwarf rhododendrons and, very occasionally, conifers. I have seen it used effectively under commercial conditions to provide a large number of *Berberis buxifolia* 'Nana' (Dwarf Magellan Barberry)—the furrow into which the mother plants were placed was made by a plough. Drop layering is also effective for *Buxus sempervirens* 'Suffruticosa' (Dwarf Boxwood).

A variation of this technique used in Denmark for ornamental shrubs is to place a hollow plastic tube, 30 cm (12″) in diameter and 30 cm (12″) long, over the plants. The tube is filled with a loam and peat moss mix, and is easy to irrigate. The plants are lifted and divided at the end of the season.

Figure 15-30. Modified drop layering of *Chamaecyparis lawsoniana* cvs. (Lawson Cypress). Note that the foliage has been stripped from the base of the mother plants but that there is a considerable amount of stem and foliage above soil level. (Kerry Hill Nurseries, Bucknell, Staffordshire, U.K.)

Figure 15-31. Mother plants of *Chamaecyparis lawsoniana* 'Ellwoodii' (Ellwood Cypress) are lifted after one season and individual shoots with roots at the base are removed and grown-on.

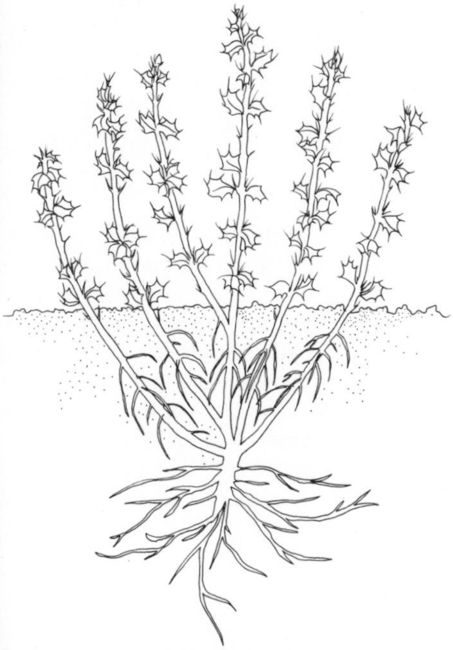

Diagram 15-8. Drop layering of *Berberis buxifolia* 'Nana' (Dwarf Magellan Barberry). The mother plant in the fall following layering, showing the roots developed at the stem bases. The plant is lifted and severed into the individual layers.

Procedure

The chosen mother plant should have a well-branched framework of axillary shoots and a well-developed root system. The leaves are normally removed from the part of the stem that will be below soil level. The plant or plants are placed in prepared holes or furrows in early spring, ensuring that the shoots are splayed out and that the growing tips are just above the surface of the soil. Subsequent root development may be inhibited, stems may die back and lifting could be difficult if the hole or furrow is excessively deep. The soil is filled in around the roots and shoots, firmed and irrigated if necessary.

During November of either the current or the following year, depending on the genus, the mother plant is lifted and divided into individual layers, each with a sufficient root system for subsequent establishment in containers or open ground.

AIR LAYERING

Air layering, sometimes referred to as circumposition, marcottage or Chinese layering, is one of the oldest methods of vegetative propagation techniques and was used by the Chinese about 4,000–5,000 years ago. An aerial stem is constricted and materials that will provide the necessary environment for inducing the formation of roots are secured around this constriction. The aerial stem is severed from the mother plant when the root system has developed sufficiently to permit establishment. This reliable technique is used only for very specific needs of hardy woody plants in commercial nurseries today, so is really more applicable to the amateur gardener. It has been used in nurseries to produce a single plant in cases where stems are so positioned that they cannot be layered below soil level.

Procedure

Air layering should be carried out between April and August. A constriction is made 12.5–30.5 cm (5–12″) from the tip of the aerial shoot, either by girdling or making a tongue about 2–2.5 cm (¾–1″) long. The application of a rooting hormone, such as 1–2% IBA in talc or 2,500 ppm IBA in solution, to the cut surfaces may be beneficial. A handful of slightly moistened sphagnum moss forming a ball about 15–25 cm (6–10″) in diameter is placed over the constricted area. This ball is covered with a piece of polyethylene about 20–25 cm (8–10″) square, the four ends are folded over and firmly secured to the shoot with self-adhesive waterproof tape to ensure humidity levels are retained around the cut surfaces. Sufficient roots should have formed after two years to allow establishment and the aerial stem is then severed from the mother plant.

Further details of this technique may be found in *The Grafter's Handbook* by R. J. Garner or *Plant Propagation: Principles and Practices* by H. T. Hartmann and D. E. Kester.

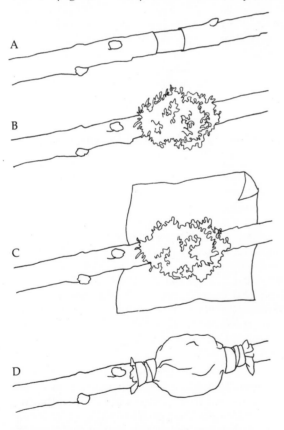

Diagram15-9. Air layering. A. The stem is girdled (or tongued). B. A rooting hormone is applied to the cut surfaces and the area is then covered by a handful of moist sphagnum moss. C. A square of polyethylene is wrapped around the moist sphagnum moss. D. The polyethylene is tied onto the stem on either side of the area.

Figure 15-32. Air layering of *Mahonia aquifolium* 'Compactum' (Tall Oregon-grape cv.) has been undertaken commercially because of the unreliability in rooting from cuttings of this cultivar. A (top). The root system within the moist sphagnum moss. (A small amount of sphagnum moss was soaked initially in an IBA solution, placed into the cut along the stem, and this was then surrounded by moist sphagnum moss, covered and tied-in.) B (bottom). The rooted stem is severed from the mother plant, potted-up and grown-on for sale. (Monrovia Nurseries, Azusa, CA, U.S.A.)

OTHER SPECIALIZED LAYERING TECHNIQUES USED BY NURSERY OPERATORS

1. Stooling of *Magnolia*

An interesting technique for layering magnolias was reported in the Combined Proceedings of the International Plant Propagators' Society (Vol. 14, 1964) by the Chase Nursery Company in Alabama. The method is essentially a modification of stooling or mound layering in that sawdust is placed around the lower 45 cm (18″) of the stem during mid-summer. The company reported an annual production of 20,000 layers from a total of about 500 stools, which means that each stool produced about 40 layers.

Procedure

The annual growth is allowed to reach a height of 1.2 m (4′), when the basal leaves are removed up to a stem height of 45 cm (18″). A sharp knife is then used to make a sliver or tongue about halfway into the stem just underneath a bud, 0.8% IBA in talc is mixed with sphagnum moss and placed on the sliver and into the cut area of stem.

Bottomless containers are made from waterproofed paper held open by wire stakes and placed over each stool. Well-rotted sawdust is then placed into the container up to the level from which the leaves have been removed. Additional support is provided by mounding the soil around the base of each container. The wire stakes are removed because they are no longer necessary and are re-used to provide initial support for the next container. Irrigation from the top is provided to each container. The cuts should have callused within three weeks. The stems are reduced in height to 15–21 cm (6–8″) above the container in late summer, and an adequate root system will have formed for harvesting in the fall. The layers are harvested by removing the sawdust and severing them close to the stool. The cycle is repeated the following year.

Thus, this technique is based on the principle of blanching and stem wounding, and rooting is also encouraged by the moist medium surrounding the stems during the warm summer temperatures.

Modified French Layering of *Syringa, Corylus, Hydrangea* and *Tilia*

A. *SYRINGA* (LILAC)

The Henri Calle Nursery (Wetteren, Belgium) has always intrigued me because of its methods of layering. Henri Calle's father saw *Syringa vulgaris* cvs. (Common or French Lilac) being layered in Boskoop during 1925 and returned to Belgium to duplicate the technique, which was essentially a hybrid between French layering and stooling. Calle Nurseries significantly increased production after 1945 and today produces a specialist high-quality product. The major problem that developed was due to the fungal disease *Pythium,* which caused a deterioration in production and loss of some mother plants. Today, the application of fungicidal drenches using etradiazol (Aaterra®) and Bayer 5072 seems promising. Red and blue cultivars of Lilac are currently performing well, but the double white *S. vulgaris* 'Madame Lemoine' is considerably more difficult. The ideal soil is a fertile sandy loam in a region where the water table is below 10 m (33′) during the winter. The main reason that this technique is not used either in Boskoop, Holland, or in the Loire Valley in France is because of their high winter water tables.

Procedure

Stage I

The mother plants are planted at a density of 3–4 per meter (3′) row with 1.2 m (4′) between rows. They may be on their own roots or grafted on *Ligustrum vulgare* (English Privet)—this is a nurse graft and therefore the scion should later develop its own root system. The mother plants are lightly pruned and allowed to grow for one year to build up an established root system.

Stage 2

All shoots are cut back to soil level in the following February.

Stage 3

The new growth is allowed to reach a length of 10–15 cm (4–6"), and sand is then placed over the stem so that the growing tip is just above soil level. This causes the stem to be directed at an oblique angle while the shoot continues to grow upright. Roots develop during the summer on the parts covered by sand.

Stage 4

The following February, the previous year's shoots are cut back just above the area of stem where the roots have formed. In spring, the new shoots are covered by sand when they are 10–15 cm (4–6") long. This process is repeated for a further two years to form the foundation framework of the stool bed.

Stage 5

The first full crop of layers can be taken about 5 years after the initial planting of the mother plants, by which time there will be a multitude of shoots arising from below soil level. A handful of soil is placed on each stem when it is 10–15 cm (4–6") long, causing it to lie at an oblique angle. The shoots are laid down so that they are spaced virtually all around the mother plants.

Stage 6

The first weeds begin to germinate about three weeks later. Further soil is laid down onto the developing stems at this time. This process may be repeated 2 or 3 times during the early part of the season. Foliage from the layers covers the area, thus reducing the problem of annual weeds by smothering them.

Stage 7

The layers are ready to harvest by the next late fall or early winter. The shoots should be severed with pruners while the stool beds are young, later they are simply pulled and wrenched off. The layers must be severed as low down as possible as it is important to keep the basal framework of the mother plants low. This allows more roots to be retained on the layer, and, at the same time, keeps down the overall height of the stool bed framework.

The layers are held in cold storage until early April when they are planted in the field and grown-on for a further two years before selling.

Summer Maintenance

Irrigation during dry weather in spring and early summer will aid root development. The sides of the stool beds are kept clear of annual weeds by hand weeding or the use of paraquat (Gramoxone®).

Dried cow or chicken manure is applied over the soil surrounding the stool beds during February to help retain the organic matter levels in the soil.

Winter Maintenance

Stem and root debris is left over the stool bed until early April. This gives the stool bed some protection against frost. The debris is removed and a brush used to physically clean up the beds. Alternatively, a high-pressure water spray can be directed at the stool bed framework to assist in the cleaning up process.

B. SUMMARY OF OTHER CROPS LAYERED IN WETTEREN, BELGIUM

(i) *Corylus maxima* cvs. (Filbert)

Hazelnuts and filberts have been a specialist crop in the Wetteren area since the early 1900s, and received a new lease of life after the Second World War in 1945 when a number of improved cultivars were received via Holland. The cultivars mainly grown today are the ornamental purple-foliaged *Corylus maxima* 'Purpurea' (Purple Giant Filbert) and the fruiting forms of *C. maxima* such as 'Hales Giant' and 'Red Zeller Nut'.

Henri Calle plants the mother plants deeper than he would Common or French Lilac. After a year of establishment, the new growth is pruned back only to half its length, not to soil level. The stems are bent and tied down in April so that they are horizontal with the soil surface. The

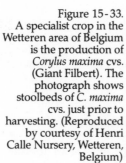

Figure 15-33.
A specialist crop in the
Wetteren area of Belgium
is the production of
Corylus maxima cvs.
(Giant Filbert). The
photograph shows
stoolbeds of *C. maxima*
cvs. just prior to
harvesting. (Reproduced
by courtesy of Henri
Calle Nursery, Wetteren,
Belgium)

Corylus stems are covered with soil during May, and again in June. This should provide a sufficient depth of soil for the emerging root system at the base of the stem. During July, a top dressing of sodium nitrate is applied to the beds at a time when the surface of the foliage is dry. A brush is taken over the stems to dislodge any remaining fertilizer to overcome possible leaf scorch. The remainder of the procedures are similar to those described for *Syringa vulgaris* cvs. (Common or French Lilac).

(ii) *Hydrangea paniculata* 'Grandiflora' (Peegee Hydrangea)

The procedure is the same as that used for *Syringa vulgaris* cvs. (Common or French Lilac) except that the growing tips of the soil-covered shoots are pinched back when they reach a height of 20 cm (8"). This results in a layer with three shoots arising from the base. Otherwise a single stem forms, which is terminated in late summer by a large flower head that causes the stem to bend. The tips of these shoots can be removed in July and used for softwood cutting propagation in low polyethylene tunnels (sun tunnels) (Chapter 3).

(iii) *Tilia* × *europaea* 'Pallida' (syn. *T.* × *vulgaris*) (European Linden cv.)

Modified French layering has been found to be a useful method for this *Tilia* (Linden), but root formation at the stem base is shy. This means that the layers have to be transplanted for a season after harvesting and prior to the final lining out in the open ground.

APPENDIX 15-1.
Plants Successfully Mound or Stool Layered

Apple Rootstocks: Malling 2
                               Malling 7
                               Malling 9
                               Malling 26
                               Malling 27
                               Malling Merton 104
                               Malling Merton 106
                               Malling Merton 111

Pear Rootstock: Quince A

Castanea sativa (Spanish Chestnut)
Chaenomeles japonica cvs. (Japanese Flowering Quince)
Daphne cneorum (Garland Flower)
Prunus cerasifera 'Nigra' (Black Myrobalan Plum)
Prunus glandulosa 'Alboplena' (White Dwarf Flowering Almond)
Prunus glandulosa 'Sinensis' (Double Pink Flowering Almond)
Prunus tenella 'Firehill' (Dwarf Russian Almond cv.)
Prunus triloba (Flowering Almond)
Pterocarya fraxinifolia (Caucasian Wingnut)
Rhododendron (Dwarf types, e.g., *R. impeditum*)
Syringa vulgaris cvs. (Common or French Lilac)
Tilia cordata (Little-leaf Linden)
Tilia × *euchlora* (Crimean Linden)
Tilia × *europaea* (European Linden) (syn. *T.* × *vulgaris*)

APPENDIX 15-2.
Plants Successfully Etiolated or Trench Layered

Juglans regia cvs. (English or Persian Walnut)
Malus rootstocks as listed under stooling
Morus (Mulberry)
Prunus 'Brompton'
Prunus 'St. Julien A'
Prunus Mazzard F12/1

APPENDIX 15-3.
Plants Successfully Continuous or French Layered

Acer cappadocicum 'Aureum' (Yellow Coliseum Maple)
Acer cappadocicum 'Rubrum' (Red Coliseum Maple)
Acer rubrum cvs. (Red Maple)
Acer saccharinum 'Weiri' (syn. 'Laciniatum') (Weir Cutleaf Maple)
Alnus × *spaethii*
Amelanchier alnifolia (Common or Western Saskatoon)
Amelanchier canadensis (Shadblow Serviceberry)
Cercidiphyllum japonicum (Katsura Tree)
Cornus alba cvs. (Red-bark or Tatarian Dogwood)
Corylus avellana 'Aurea' (Golden European Filbert)
Corylus maxima 'Purpurea' (Purple Giant Filbert)
Cotinus coggygria 'Royal Purple' (Purple Smoke Tree)
Hoheria glabrata (Lacebark or Mountain Ribbonwood)

Hydrangea aspera subsp. *aspera* (syn. *H. villosa*)
Hydrangea paniculata 'Grandiflora' (Peegee Hydrangea)
Hydrangea quercifolia (Oakleaf Hydrangea)
Prunus glandulosa cvs. (Dwarf Flowering Almond)
Prunus padus (European Bird Cherry)
Prunus pumila (Sand Cherry)
Prunus serotina (Wild Black Cherry)
Prunus tenella 'Firehill' (Dwarf Russian Almond cv.)
Stachyurus praecox
Syringa vulgaris cvs. (Common or French Lilac)
Viburnum × *bodnantense* (Bodnant Viburnum)
Viburnum farreri (Fragrant Viburnum)
Viburnum plicatum f. *tomentosum* (Double-file Viburnum)

APPENDIX 15-4.
Plants Successfully Simple Layered

Amelanchier alnifolia (Common or Western Saskatoon)
Amelanchier canadensis (Shadblow Serviceberry)
Arbutus menziesii (Pacific Madrone)
Arbutus unedo (Strawberry Tree)
Azara microphylla 'Variegata' (Variegated Boxleaf Azara)
Camellia japonica cvs. (Common or Japanese Camellia)
Camellia reticulata cvs. (Net-veined Camellia)
Carpenteria californica (Tree or Bush Anemone)
Chimonanthus praecox (Wintersweet) (syn. *C. fragrans*)
Corylopsis pauciflora (Buttercup Winter Hazel)
Corylopsis willmottiae (Willmott Winter Hazel)
Corylus avellana cvs. (European Filbert)
Corylus maxima 'Purpurea' (Purple Giant Filbert)
Daphne blagayana (Balkan Daphne)
Daphne cneorum (Garland Flower)
Davidia involucrata (Dove or Handkerchief Tree)
Dipteronia sinensis
Disanthus cercidifolius
Distylium racemosum (Isu Tree)
Drimys lanceolata (Pepper Tree) (syn. *D. aromatica*)
Enkianthus campanulatus (Red-veined Enkianthus)
Erica species (Heath)
Eucryphia glutinosa (Eucryphia)
Fothergilla monticola (Alabama Fothergilla)
Halesia carolina (Carolina Silver-bell)
Hamamelis mollis (Chinese Witch Hazel)
Ilex aquifolium cvs. (English Holly)
Kalmia latifolia (Mountain Laurel)
Laurus nobilis (Laurel, Sweet Bay)
Liquidambar formosana (Formosan Sweet Gum)
Magnolia × *soulangiana* cvs. (Chinese or Saucer Magnolia)
Nothofagus betuloides
Parrotia persica (Persian Parrotia)
Parrotiopsis jacquemontia (Jacquemont's Parrotia)
Photinia villosa (Oriental Photinia)
Pieris japonica cvs. (Lily-of-the-Valley Bush)
Platanus × *acerifolia* (London Plane)
Rhododendron species & cultivars
Schizophragma hydrangeoides (Japanese Hydrangea Vine)
Syringa vulgaris cvs. (Common or French Lilac)
Tilia × *euchlora* (Crimean Linden)

APPENDIX 15-5.
Plants Successfully Serpentine Layered

Celastrus scandens (American Bittersweet)
Clematis species and cultivars
Lapageria rosea (Chilean Bellflower)
Smilax species (Greenbrier)
Vitis species and cultivars
Wisteria floribunda (Japanese Wisteria)
Wisteria sinensis (Chinese Wisteria)

APPENDIX 15-6.
Plants Successfully Drop Layered

Berberis buxifolia 'Nana' (Dwarf Magellan Barberry)
Buxus sempervirens 'Suffruticosa' (Dwarf Boxwood)
Calluna species and cultivars (Heather)
Cassiope species and cultivars
Daphne cneorum (Garland Flower)
Erica species and cultivars (Heath)
Hebe hectorii
Kalmia angustifolia (Sheep Laurel)
Leiophyllum buxifolium (Box Sand Myrtle)
Rhododendron (Dwarf species/cultivars)

REFERENCES AND SUGGESTED SOURCES FOR FURTHER READING

Anderson, M. A. & A. E. Elliott. 1983. Stool bed production of clonal Apple rootstocks. *Comb. Proc. Inter. Pl. Prop. Soc.* **33**: 41–45.

Chase, H. H. 1964. Propagation of oriental Magnolias by layering. *Comb. Proc. Inter. Pl. Prop. Soc.* **14**: 67–69.

Garner, R. J. 1944. *Propagation by Cuttings and Layers. Recent Work and Its Application, With Special Reference to Pome and Stone Fruits.* Techn. Comm. No. 14. Imperial Bureau of Horticulture and Plantation Crops, East Malling, Kent, England.

_____. 1958. Rev. ed. *The Grafter's Handbook.* Faber & Faber Ltd., London. (pp. 65–71)

Hartmann, H. T. & D. E. Kester. 1983. 4th ed. *Plant Propagation: Principles and Practices.* Prentice-Hall, Inc., Englewood Cliffs, N.J.

Hills, L. D. 1959. Rev. ed. *The Propagation of Alpines.* Faber & Faber Ltd., London.

Howard, B. H. 1978. Plant propagation. *East Malling Research Station Annual Report for 1977*, pp. 69–71.

_____. 1979. Plant propagation. *East Malling Research Station Annual Report for 1978*, pp. 77–81.

_____. 1980. Plant propagation. *East Malling Research Station Annual Report for 1979*, p. 79.

_____. 1984. The effects of NAA-based Tipoff sprays on apple shoot production in MM.106 stoolbeds. *Jour. Hortic. Sci.* **59**: 303–311.

Lawson, G. 1982. Modifying tools for a specialist enterprise. *The Grower*, April 22, 1982, pp. 27–28.

Lovelidge, B. 1978. Tailor-made machinery a necessity for rootstocks. *The Grower*, May 11, 1978, pp. 1099–1100.

Marston, M. E. 1958. The history of vegetative propagation. *Rep. XIVth Inter. Hortic. Congr.*, pp. 1157–1164.

McMillan Browse, P.D.A. 1969. Propagation by layering. *Gardeners Chronicle/Horticultural Trade Journal* **166**(15): 18–20; **166**(16): 12–14; **166**(17): 33–35.

_____ . no date. *Propagation for the Nursery Trade.* A Gardeners Chronicle/Horticultural Trade Journal Handbook, London, U.K.

_____ . 1980. *Stooling Nursery Stock.* Grower Guide No. 19. Grower Books, London, U.K.

Ministry of Agriculture, Fisheries & Food, U.K. 1969. 5th ed. *Fruit Tree Raising. Rootstocks and Propagation.* Bull. No. 135. Her Majesty's Stationery Office, London, U.K.

Sheat, W. G. 1957. *Propagation of Trees, Shrubs and Conifers.* Macmillan Ltd., London, U.K.

Tukey, H. B. 1963. The historical background, the development, and propagation of clonal apple rootstocks in America. *Comb. Proc. Inter. Pl. Prop. Soc.* **13**: 244–261.

Wells, J. S. 1955. *Plant Propagation Practices.* The Macmillan Co., New York.

SECTION F

Figure 16-1.
It is important to give students and trainees thorough instruction in grafting, not only teaching them the correct care and use of materials but also the importance of compatible scion/rootstock combinations and the correct aftercare procedures. (Students bench grafting pines, Hadlow College of Agriculture & Horticulture, Tonbridge, Kent, U.K.)

Figure 16-2.
Robert J. Garner, the international authority on grafting, examines a clone of *Mespilus germanica* (Medlar) top-worked on a Quince A (Angers Quince) rootstock at his home in East Malling (Maidstone, Kent, U.K.). Mr. Garner won 1st prize on 3 occasions at Royal Horticultural Society shows in London with the very large fruits from this particular clone.

Chapter 16

PRINCIPLES OF GRAFTING

Grafting represents perhaps the most fascinating aspect of conventional propagating techniques. It forms a very important stage in the production of both open-ground and container-grown plants, and is one reason why so many choice and unusual plant forms can be offered on the retail market today.

Within a wider context, grafting has many varied horticultural applications besides nursery production, including, for example, fruit growing, greenhouse production and, occasionally—in the amenity field—repairing damaged trees. It may occur naturally—shoot or root systems of certain plants can join together if they are growing in an over-crowded situation and if the growth patterns of the outer tissues are in the same direction. Such natural grafting has been recorded with shoots of *Hedera* (Ivy), *Salix* (Willow), *Fagus* (Beech) and *Pinus* (Pine), and in the root systems of *Arbutus menziesii* (Pacific Madrone) and *Pseudotsuga menziesii* (Douglas Fir).

Successful grafting in the modern nursery requires that the propagator demonstrate considerable proficiency in the technique, with sound basic instruction followed by wide experience to attain a high degree of competence and speed. As will be seen later, it also requires knowledge of scion/rootstock compatibility and an in-built ability to care for the grafts until the union has formed, and a detailed knowledge of the requirements and growth patterns of individual plants.

The most renowned book on grafting is Robert J. Garner's *The Grafter's Handbook*. These chapters on grafting will deal with a topic not often covered in detail in textbooks—the techniques used for grafting of woody ornamentals in the nursery trade, emphasizing the various skills used in the process and in the aftercare of the plants.

Terminology

Grafting is a technique used to unite "parts" of different plants by bringing the cambium of each into contact and then creating a situation under which the cut surfaces can unite and grow away together. The technique involves two important stages—the knifework or carpentry used in the preparation of the grafting surfaces, and the procedures for aftercare. The propagator typically learns the grafting skill first, but requires extended experience to become familiar with the aftercare procedures. Many a fine crop of newly grafted stock has been lost due to poor aftercare.

Definitions of Terms Used in Grafting

Scion—The part of the graft that will provide the new shoot system. The scion may be united either at the apex or side of the rootstock. For example, *Hibiscus syriacus* 'Blue Bird' (Rose-of-Sharon cv.) wedge grafted on *H. syriacus* and *Picea pungens* 'Hoopsii' (Hoops Blue Spruce) side-veneer grafted on *P. abies* (Norway Spruce) respectively.

Rootstock/Understock—The lower part of the graft. It normally possesses a root system that will support the subsequent shoot development from the scion. For example, *Picea abies* (Norway Spruce) to receive the *P. pungens* 'Hoopsii' (Hoops Blue Spruce) scion.

Scion rooting—The development of roots from the scion after grafting.

Nurse Graft—The rootstock supports the scion growth only during the early stages of development, the scion eventually developing a sufficient root system to support itself.

For example, *Syringa vulgaris* 'Madame Lemoine' (Common or French Lilac cv.) grafted on *Ligustrum ovalifolium* (California Privet).

Open-ground (Field) Grafting—A multi-budded dormant scion is grafted onto an established open-ground rootstock. For example, *Prunus serrulata* 'Shirofugen' grafted onto *P.* 'Colt' in late winter.

Open-ground Budding/Bud Grafting—A method of grafting, normally done in summer, in which a single bud with rind (with or without a sliver of wood) is placed within the rootstock. For example, *Acer platanoides* 'Crimson King' (Crimson King Maple) budded onto *A. platanoides* (Norway Maple) in mid-July. Budding is sometimes used in bench grafting.

Dormant Bench Grafting—Grafting is carried out at the bench in a protected structure during the winter, normally using dormant deciduous hardwood, evergreen hardwood or sometimes softwood scion material.

Summer Bench Grafting—Grafting is carried out at the bench in a protected structure during the late summer, normally using semi-ripe wood scion material.

Bottom-working (Low-working)—The graft is sited near ground level, the optimum height being 10 cm (4") above the soil. For example, *Gleditsia triacanthos* var. *inermis* 'Sunburst' (Sunburst Honey Locust) grafted 10 cm (4") above soil level onto *G. triacanthos* (Honey Locust) rootstock.

Top-working—The graft is sited at an optimum height of 0.5–1.8 m (1½–6') above ground level. [*NOTE:* This must not be confused with the top-working by cleft grafting of mature fruit trees.] For example, (a) miniature roses budded 0.5 m (1½') above soil level on *Rosa canina* 'Pfänder' (Dog Rose cv.); (b) *Acer pseudoplatanus* 'Brilliantissimum' (Sycamore Maple cv.) grafted 1.5 m (5') above soil level on *A. pseudoplatanus* (Sycamore Maple) rootstock.

High-working—This is essentially a category of top-working in which the scion is placed high on the rootstock stem—sometimes as high as 2–2.5 m (6½–8'). It is commonly used to shorten the period between production and marketing for standard weeping trees. For example, *Prunus subhirtella* 'Pendula Rubra' (Red Weeping Cherry) on *P. avium* Mazzard F12/1 rootstock.

Reasons for Grafting Plants

Grafting is used to propagate nursery stock for the reasons outlined below.

(1) To obtain special forms of plants for both the home garden and public landscape. This can be seen in some trees with either a weeping or a dense rounded habit. The technique used varies—some weeping trees will grow as spreading shrubs if bottom-worked but will show the true weeping habit and form an attractive tree if top-worked on to a clear stem. For example, *Cotoneaster* 'Hybridus Pendulus' (= *C.* × *watereri* 'Pendulus') grafted onto the rootstock *C. bullatus* (Hollyberry Cotoneaster) and *Caragana arborescens* 'Lorbergii' (Lorberg's Siberian Pea Shrub) onto *C. arborescens* (Siberian Pea Shrub). Similarly, some compact trees will grow as large shrubs if bottom-worked, as the growth pattern makes it difficult for them to develop the terminal leader necessary to form a satisfactory stem. For example, *Acer pseudoplatanus* 'Brilliantissimum' grafted onto the rootstock *A. pseudoplatanus* (Sycamore Maple) and *A. platanoides* 'Globosum' (Globe Norway Maple) grafted onto the rootstock *A. platanoides* (Norway Maple).

(2) To propagate plants that are difficult or virtually impossible to raise by alternative vegetative techniques. Cuttings of some plants will root, but it is difficult to get them to establish and grow away at an economical rate. The deciduous broad-leaf tree *Liriodendron tulipifera* 'Aureomarginatum' (Tulip Tree cv.) and the conifer *Sequoiadendron giganteum* 'Pendulum' (Weeping Giant Sequoia) are two examples of this type.

(3) To perpetuate clonal material that has advantages over seed-raised stock, for example, the purple-leaved beeches. *Fagus sylvatica* 'Atropunicea' (formerly 'Purpurea') (Bronze or Purple Beech) raised from seed has a smaller leaf size and less intensity of color, particularly towards the end of the growing season, than does the clonal form *Fagus sylvatica* 'Riversii' (Rivers Purple Beech). The latter will command a higher price at the point-of-sale.

(4) To produce a crop of certain plants within a shorter space of time than when propagated by some other vegetative techniques. The majority of *Clematis* are raised from cuttings,

Figure 16-3. Three examples of conifers of differing growth habits that require grafting. A (left). *Sequoiadendron giganteum* 'Pendulum' (Weeping Giant Sequoia), photographed at VanDusen Botanical Garden, Vancouver, B.C. B (center). *Picea pungens* 'Glauca Prostrata' (Prostrate Blue Spruce). C (right). *Abies lasiocarpa* var. *arizonica* 'Compacta' (Dwarf Corkbark Fir).

but the large-flowered hybrid forms can be brought to the point-of-sale within an optimum period of 5–6 months when grafted, as against 18 months from softwood cuttings. This is one reason why plants such as *Elaeagnus pungens* 'Maculata' (Golden Elaeagnus), *Viburnum carlesii* (Korean Spice Viburnum) and *Syringa vulgaris* cultivars (Common or French Lilac) were grafted in European countries such as Holland. [It is a point of debate by some nursery operators as to whether it is ethical to supply material that is prone to give problems later due to excess suckering of the rootstock.]

(5) To obtain the benefits of individual characteristics of specific rootstocks. These benefits can be subdivided as follows:—

(a) Growth rates and eventual height—Some stocks may encourage dwarfing or induce vigor into the scion growth. For example, the clonal apple rootstocks raised at East Malling Research Station and known as the Malling (M) or Malling Merton (M.M.) range.

There is now increasing interest in the use of the very dwarfing Malling 27 rootstock to produce small Flowering Crab Apple Trees such as *Malus* 'Golden Hornet' (Golden Hornet Crab Apple) for use in small gardens. In contrast, the vigorous Malling 25 is a satisfactory stock to produce good quality stands of most *Malus* spp. and cvs. for conventional open-ground production. Undoubtedly, selections of rootstocks will be made available in the future that will give more totally clonal trees (this is already illustrated with Japanese Cherries on *Prunus* 'Colt' rootstocks) to overcome genetical variation of seedling rootstocks.

(b) Resistance to disease—Soil-borne disease is a major problem in open-ground nursery production, and breeding programs to overcome infection are intricate and long-term. Some of the significant advances have been made in the greenhouse production of salad crops such as cucumbers and tomatoes, but there has been some important work over the years with woody plants. A good example of this is in *Prunus*—the *Prunus avium* selection Mazzard F12/1 is resistant to *Pseudomonas mors-prunorum* (Bacterial Canker) while the newer dwarfing rootstock *Prunus* 'Colt' appears to be more resistant to *Thielaviopsis basicola* (Specific Replant Disease of Cherry) and *Agrobacterium tumefaciens* (Crown or Root Gall). The rootstock *Juglans nigra* (Black Walnut) should be used in areas where *Armillaria mellea* (Shoestring Root Rot) occurs, instead of *J. regia* (English or Persian Walnut).

Considerable benefits could be gained by having available rootstocks with a high degree of resistance to *Phytophthora cinnamomi* for *Rhododendron* and to *Verticillium* spp. (Verticillium Wilt) for specific maples grown in open ground.

(c) Resistance to pests—This is possibly more important in fruit production than in woody ornamentals. For example, the introduction of *Malus* rootstocks resistant to *Eriosoma lanigerum* (Woolly Aphid), originally developed jointly by East Malling Research Station and the John Innes Institute when it was based at Merton. Since 1952, a range of resistant *Malus* stocks has been available under the name Malling Merton (M.M.)—for example, M.M.111, which is a vigorous stock preferred by some ornamental tree producers.

(d) Tolerance to different soil types—Specific rootstocks have advantages in overcoming problems related to pH, soluble salt levels and moisture of the soil. The rose rootstock Laxa is widely accepted in Britain for the open-ground production of bush roses, particularly in more alkaline soils. However, it does not perform well in soils where the pH is below 5.5 and thus is not recommended for the major nursery area around Chobham, Woking and Bagshot in Surrey, England. *Rhododendron* 'Cunningham's White' is claimed to be more tolerant to higher pH levels than is the more widely used *R. ponticum* (Pontic Rhododendron).

In areas where drier conditions prevail because of sandy soil, the vigorous *Malus* rootstock M.M.111 is preferred over M.2 (Doucin) for the production of ornamental crab apples. However, M.M.111 is not compatible with all ornamental *Malus*, notably *M. tschonoskii* (Tschonoski Crab Apple). The deep-rooted *Rosa rubiginosa* (Eglantine or Sweet Brier) has been recommended for the production of roses in dry sandy soils.

(6) Grafting may be used to encourage flowering earlier in the life span of the plant. A disadvantage of some species raised from seed is that the time period between germination and flowering can be considerable. For instance, some species of *Magnolia* can take 15 or more years to flower, while *Wisteria* can take up to 5–7 years. The collection of scion wood from mature plants of *Wisteria sinensis* (Chinese Wisteria) is known to encourage earlier flowering.

One advantage of grafting over cuttings for *Clematis* has already been mentioned, but a further advantage claimed is that the plants come into flower earlier, particularly along the shoot area tied into the cane.

A related use is in breeding programs. The dominance of juvenility in seedling-raised plants means that it may be many years before a plant breeder observes the flowering and fruiting potential of the progeny of crosses made. Grafting on dwarf rootstocks is known to induce flowering in certain instances and may be used to speed up the process. When a promising selection has been made, the initial scion material may be quickly bulked-up by grafting or budding onto a compatible rootstock and grown-on under protection.

(7) Production of "Plus Trees" in forestry breeding programs. An important aspect in the production of superior seed of forest trees are "Plus Trees". These are selected forms that are grafted to provide a seed bank in the "seed orchard".

(8) Production of "Novelty Trees". This is difficult to define, but essentially they are trees intended mainly for retail sales that constitute an "unusual" scion/rootstock combination providing either more than one cultivar on a plant ("Family Trees") or a plant providing an unusual visual effect. Three examples of "Novelty Trees" are:—

(a) Three apple cultivars can be grafted onto a two-year-old tree, thus giving the customer a sequence of cropping. The varieties have to be chosen carefully to obtain similar growth habits and avoid problems in pollination. One example of a "Family Apple Tree" combination involves the cultivars 'Discovery', 'Fortune' and 'Sunset'. Alternatively, a *Malus* rootstock such as M.26 may be chip budded with 2 or 3 sets of opposite pairs of buds worked at a set distance apart up the stem. Each pair of buds can be a different cultivar, and subsequent training forms a 2- or 3-tier espalier tree. Very occasionally, tree (standard) roses have been produced with three different cultivars budded onto the rootstock.

(b) A range of ornamental Cherry trees known as "Sheraton Trees" in Britain have the attractive shiny reddish-brown bark of *Prunus serrula* (Birch-bark Cherry) on the stem and the showy flowers of cultivars like *P. serrulata* 'Kwanzan' (Kwanzan Cherry) to provide additional color. This is achieved by budding *P. serrula* on *P.* Mazzard F12/1 rootstock, allowing it to grow to about 1.5 m (5') tall, and then top-working the cultivar.

(c) In Holland, a full or half-standard "tree broom" is produced by grafting a cultivar of *Cytisus scoparius* (Scotch Broom) on a stem of *Laburnum anagyroides* (syn. *L. vulgare*) (Golden-chain Tree or Common Laburnum). Similarly, an unusual effect may be achieved by top-working *Cotoneaster horizontalis* (Rock Cotoneaster or Rockspray), with its herringbone-like growth, onto a *Cotoneaster bullatus* (Hollyberry Cotoneaster) stem.

Figure 16-4.
A 3-tiered espaliered
apple tree. One pair of
buds of each of three
different varieties were
chip budded on the
rootstock. (Westham
Island Nurseries, Delta,
B.C., Canada)

(9) For virus indexing in research programs. This is used as a means of detecting viruses during the cleaning of virus-infected stock to produce a virus-free clone. An example is the use of *Prunus serrulata* 'Shirofugen' as an indicator plant for Necrotic Ring Spot Virus.

(10) Repairing damaged trees or trees with delayed incompatibility. Essentially, this is not a nursery technique but could be used to repair a specimen tree that is important for providing stock material. Trees may be damaged by rodents, machinery, disease, or the graft union may slowly weaken due to incompatibility. A graft may be carried out to bridge or cover the damaged area or to re-strengthen the union between rootstock and scion.

(11) To change an existing cultivar on a tree. This is normally used in fruit growing where it may be desirable to replace one cultivar on a mature tree with another. It has also been done with ornamental *Prunus* when another flowering cultivar was grafted onto the tree. It is done by the process of framework or top-working. The reader should refer to Chapter 8 in R. J. Garner's *The Grafter's Handbook* for a comprehensive account.

(12) To produce inter-stem trees. An additional piece of scion 10–30 cm (4–12″) long is grafted between the normal rootstock and cultivar. This inter-stem can provide one or more particularly beneficial characteristics not given by the conventional rootstock, for example, hardiness or dwarfness.

It has been mainly used in fruit production, but has a possible application for ornamentals in cases where the rootstock is selected for good anchorage and soil type. In these cases, the inter-stem could provide a desired dwarfing effect to the scion. For example, the use of an inter-stem of rootstock M.27 between M.25 rootstock and the scion cultivar *Malus* 'King'.

Limitations of Grafting

As with other propagation methods, there are limitations to grafting. These include the ones outlined below.

(1) Methods of grafting that may require additional facilities to provide a controlled environment during the aftercare; for example, Japanese Maples propagated by bench grafting.

(2) The need for reliable and skilled personnel, who will require training and consequently higher remuneration.

(3) Additional costs that are involved in growing or purchasing rootstocks.

(4) Problems that may result from delayed incompatibility between rootstock and scion.

(5) Rootstocks that exhibit excess suckering, resulting in a deterioration in the quality of scion growth over the years. This can often be prevented by correct removal of suckers during the propagation stage, grafting lower on the rootstock, using an alternative rootstock, or removal of suckers soon after planting in the permanent site. Troublesome rootstocks include *Cotoneaster bullatus* (Hollyberry Cotoneaster), *Crataegus laevigata* (syn. *C. oxyacantha*) (English Hawthorn), *Elaeagnus angustifolia* (Oleaster), *Prunus padus* (European Bird Cherry), *Rosa canina* (Dog Rose), *Sorbus aucuparia* (European Mountain Ash), *Syringa vulgaris* (Common Lilac) and *Viburnum lantana* (Wayfaring Tree).

(6) Possible changes in the normal growth habit. This can be desirable in many cases, but in specialty items, such as dwarf conifers, the eventual height can be greater than originally anticipated with plants raised from cuttings. Two examples are the slow-growing *Chamaecyparis obtusa* 'Nana Gracilis' (Dwarf Hinoki Cypress) grafted onto *C. lawsoniana* (Lawson Cypress) and *Cryptomeria japonica* 'Bandai-Sugi' (Japanese Cedar cv.) grafted onto *C. japonica* 'Elegans' (Plume Cryptomeria).

Factors Contributing to a Successful Graft Union

Having explained the reasons for grafting, it will now be helpful to summarize the factors that can contribute to the overall success.

(1) The operator must be proficient in the grafting skill to be carried out. The importance of thorough training and subsequent practice cannot be over-emphasized.

(2) Correct and efficient equipment and materials are required, appropriate to the type of graft to be carried out. For example, the knife must be sharp, well-balanced, and the blade kept clean. The tying materials need to have the correct properties and to be stored correctly, for example, degradable budding ties stored in the light will deteriorate in strength and lasting quality.

(3) An operator doing bench grafting must be comfortable at the bench, with seating that is at the correct height and provides support. The work surface area should be clean, and the materials laid out so as to increase the efficiency of the grafting operation.

(4) The rootstock and scion should be true-to-name and compatible.

(5) The use of virus-free material should be encouraged, when available, to improve the percentage success rate and the subsequent quality of the plant.

(6) Intimate cambial contact between rootstock and scion is necessary so that they will unite to form a common vascular system. Therefore, good matching is vital—particularly when the scion and rootstock are of different diameters—together with firm tying-in that will not loosen during the aftercare.

(7) The correct time of year is important, relative to the plant to be grafted and the technique to be used. For example, in the summer budding of roses when the cambium of the rootstock must be active.

(8) The scion and rootstock must be at the correct stage of growth or condition. This may require special pre-care of the rootstock prior to grafting. For example, the rootstocks of *Juglans* (Walnut) should be thoroughly dried off when used for pot bench grafting of *Juglans* cultivars.

(9) The aftercare of the grafts is a significant factor for success and must include attention to:—

(a) Correct environmental factors such as temperature, humidity, and, where appropriate, shading and ventilation.

(b) Prevention of drying out of the cut surfaces. This may be achieved by the type and efficiency of the tying material used, and the ability of the operator to tie-in properly. Where appropriate, waxing of the union and scion apex will reduce drying out. The natural sap rise during summer budding is very helpful in preventing drying out of the cut surfaces.

(c) Prevention of pest and disease infections, such as *Thomasiniana oculiperda* (Red-bud Borer) larvae (see p. 475) on open-ground summer budded *Malus* and *Botrytis* infections on *Betula* (Birch) bench grafts.

(d) The time period between grafting and removal of the tying-in material. This is particularly important with polyethylene tape, which will bite into the plant tissues if retained too long and cause a constriction as stem girth increases.

Formation of the Graft Union

To appreciate some of the implications involved, it is necessary to consider the process leading to a successful compatible graft union.

The damaged surface cells brown and die soon after the knife cuts are made. Callus tissue made of thin-walled parenchyma cells will begin to form, provided that the cuts on the rootstock and scion are matched, tied in firmly and the aftercare procedure is conducive to the formation of a union. Parenchyma cells also form as a healing tissue over any exposed scion surface. A white band on the outside of the stem at the graft site can be seen as the parenchyma cells interlock.

Plants such as *Prunus* and *Hibiscus* are prone to produce a considerable amount of visible callus when bench grafted. These parenchyma cells are weak, and prone to desiccation and mechanical dislodgement.

Later, new cambial cells form within the callus tissue between scion and rootstock, and this is one reason why it is important initially to match the cambial regions. These newly-formed cambial cells then differentiate to produce new phloem to the outside and new xylem to the inside so that a complete and compatible union is formed. Deposits will be laid down in the cell walls to strengthen them. The end result is that the rootstock and scion will grow "as one" to carry out the normal functions of a plant stem.

GRAFT INCOMPATIBILITY

Graft incompatibility is defined as the partial or complete failure of the union between scion and rootstock. This is a complex subject that has created a considerable amount of fundamental research over the years on plant anatomy and physiology—particularly in relation to fruit tree propagation. Knowledge of compatible combinations for woody ornamentals has been gained largely through trial and error by nursery operators , the information recorded and subsequently communicated. It would not be appropriate in this book to discuss at length the theoretical principles involved in graft incompatibility, but instead I will examine the problem in relation to the nursery operation. Detailed accounts of the reasons and processes involved in graft incompatibility may be found in *Plant Propagation: Principles and Practices* by H. T. Hartmann and D. E. Kester (Chapter 11) and *The Grafters' Handbook* by R. J. Garner (Chapter 2).

The success of the union between the rootstock and scion is largely determined by the degree of botanical affinity between them. Some plant families present few problems, even to the extent that different genera can be grafted together. For instance, it was traditional practice in the family Hamamelidaceae to graft *Parrotia persica* (Persian Parrotia) onto *Hamamelis virginiana* (Common Witch Hazel). There is some heavy suckering of the rootstock in the early stages, but a compatible union forms and results in vigorous scion growth. Intergeneric grafting, however, is often restricted to nurse grafting, using sections of root as the understock. This is sometimes practiced in the family Oleaceae, where cultivars of *Syringa vulgaris* (Common or French Lilac) are grafted either onto *Fraxinus excelsior* (European Ash) roots or onto seedlings of *Ligustrum ovalifolium* (California Privet). A further example is seen in the family Bignoniaceae, which includes trees such as *Paulownia tomentosa* (Royal Paulownia or Empress Tree) as well as an interesting range of climbing vines, including *Bignonia capreolata* (Cross Vine) and *Campsis radicans* (Common Trumpet Creeper). The attractive salmon-red flowered *Campsis* × *tagliabuana* 'Madame Galen' (Madame Galen Trumpet Vine) is occasionally grafted onto 10 cm (4") pieces of *Catalpa bignonioides* (Indian Bean). Also, *Chamaecyparis nootkatensis* 'Pendula' (Weeping Yellow Cedar) can be grafted onto *Platycladus (Thuja) orientalis* (Oriental Arborvitae).

The family Fabaceae (Leguminosae) offers a limited range of intergeneric combinations, for example, the use of the rootstock *Laburnum anagyroides* (syn. *L. vulgaris*) (Golden-Chain Tree or Common Laburnum) in top-working a number of *Cytisus* forms.

Conversely, there is a much more complex relationship in families such as the Rosaceae and Aceraceae, and in the genus *Quercus* (Oak). The dividing line for success or failure between two genera within a family or two species within a genus can be very small, and the use of the incorrect rootstock brings about incompatibility. The Hungarian Oak, *Quercus frainetto,* must be grafted onto *Q. robur* (English Oak), as incompatibility will occur later if *Q. cerris* (Turkey Oak) or *Q. rubra* (Red Oak) rootstocks are used. Similarly, maples with a "milky" sap should not be grafted onto species with a "non-milky" sap, otherwise delayed incompatibility will occur in the great majority of cases.

The genera which have been reported to display slight to severe graft incompatibility problems include:—

Acer (Maple)	*Quercus* (Oak)
Cornus (Dogwood)	*Rhododendron*
Juglans (Walnut)	*Sorbus* (Mountain Ash)
Prunus (Cherry, etc.)	*Tilia* (Linden)
Pyrus (Pear)	*Pinus* (Pine)

Knowledge of the correct scion and rootstock relationship is vital in the production of many nursery crops—in particular, conifers and trees. The incorrect choice of rootstock can lead to crop failure, weak growth and poor quality, which, in turn, causes a substantial loss of revenue. A general rule for genera containing a large number of species is that few incompatibility problems occur if the scion and rootstock are selected from within the same section or series.

The propagator has two fundamental responsibilities. Firstly, to seek out and use the correct understock required to produce a high quality product, and secondly, to choose a rootstock that is compatible so that a lasting union is formed when the plant is placed in position by the home-owner or landscaper.

Classification of Graft Incompatibility

From the propagator's point of view, it is helpful to classify the types of incompatibility on the length of time a union remains relatively stable. However, the time periods mentioned should be treated as guidelines only as there are periods of overlap between the types.

(1) Immediate Graft Incompatibility

This condition arises when there is little or no attempt by the scion and rootstock to unite. If a union does occur, then it quickly deteriorates shortly after the bud breaks. Examples cited include *Gleditsia triacanthos* cvs. (Honey Locust) on *Robinia pseudoacacia* (Black Locust) and *Acer rubrum* cvs. (Red Maple) on *A. platanoides* (Norway Maple).

It is important to distinguish between poor grafting, mechanical injury, and immediate graft incompatibility. I recall seeing a nursery greenhouse where *Robinia pseudoacacia* 'Frisia' had been whip grafted onto *R. pseudoacacia* (Black Locust). The grafts had nearly all failed and the propagator felt that graft incompatibility was the cause, although this is normally a compatible union. Closer examination of the grafts showed that the reason for the failure was because either the matching was poor and/or the tying-in too loose. The only point of contact between rootstock and scion on those still alive was the area of exposed scion tissue above the union. This was all that was holding the scion and rootstock together, making the union very weak. The remaining cut surfaces had not healed together, leaving a visible gap.

Figure 16-5. An example of poor technique. *Robinia pseudoacacia* 'Frisia' (Black Locust cv.) whip grafted onto *R. pseudoacacia* after release of the tie. Note that callus formation between the scion and the rootstock has occurred only at the top of the graft. This is probably due to loose tying and/or very poor matching.

Scions can be dislodged as the union forms—*Betula* (Birch) bench grafts are particularly susceptible to this—or the new maiden growth of a tree may be dislodged at its base from the rootstock when carelessly tied to the cane or snag. This is a particular problem in trees where the maiden growth arises at a wide angle from a budded rootstock. For example, *Prunus sargentii* (Sargent Cherry) can completely or partially snap away from the rootstock. [The development of shoot guides (bud guards) has helped to overcome this problem, see p. 467]

The propagator should not necessarily assume that it is graft incompatibility when a scion and rootstock combination fails, but should check the cultural management to see if the problem can be attributed to other causes.

(2) Partially Delayed Graft Incompatibility

Essentially, this condition occurs when the union fails after a period of 4–6 months up to 3–5 years. As in immediate graft incompatibility, it normally occurs during the production stage in the nursery. It is thus up to the propagator to develop a keen eye and to methodically record all observations. One of the problems that sometimes occurs is that the growth habits of certain plants may not be consistent from one year to the next, so making detection more difficult.

To illustrate this type of graft incompatibility, three examples that I have seen in nurseries are described.

(a) *Sorbus aria* 'Lutescens' (White Beam cv.) budded onto *Crataegus laevigata* (syn. *C. oxyacantha*) (English Hawthorn). This combination has been widely used in Europe for the White Beam *Sorbus* but receives criticism from growers because of its inconsistency in performance. This scion/rootstock combination can also be one reason for failure of these trees to grow successfully in their final site. There was an overnight period of very strong winds one June, following which I saw an excellent stand of *S. aria* 'Lutescens' in which about 30% were broken away at the union, with 2 m (7′) of scion growth lying on the ground. Examination of the union showed that the tissues of both the central core and periphery were dead, this being a major contributor to union breakdown. The correct rootstock to use is either *Sorbus aria* (White Beam) or *S. intermedia* (Swedish White Beam).

Figure 16-6. A (Left). Partially delayed graft incompatibility of *Sorbus aria* 'Lutescens' (White Beam cv.) on *Crataegus laevigata* (syn. *C. oxyacantha*, English Hawthorn) is shown sometimes after a strong wind. B (Right). A close-up of the snapped union.

(b) *Pyrus calleryana* 'Chanticleer' (Callery Pear cv.) budded onto Quince A. The maiden growth grew away well in the spring following budding, but growth had stopped by early July, the foliage became pale, and intense fall color had set in by August. Close examination of the union showed that it took a minimum of hand pressure to break the scion from the rootstock. The correct rootstock is either *Pyrus calleryana* (Callery Pear) or *P. communis* (Common Pear).

(c) *Acer rufinerve* (Red-vein Maple) and other Snake Bark Maples budded onto *A. pseudoplatanus* (Sycamore Maple). The length of time that this combination is successful can vary; it perhaps fits more appropriately into the next classification, fully delayed incompatibility. I first noticed Snake Bark Maples budded onto *Acer pseudoplatanus* on some stock imported to Britain. The union formation did not look correct at first glance because, although the growth rate and caliper of the scion was excellent, a shoulder effect and excessive rootstock suckering were clearly evident. Subsequent discussion confirmed the view that this combination was undesirable as it could lead to partial incompatibility. The correct rootstock would be one of the other species in the Snake Bark Maple group.

Figure 16-7. Possible partially delayed incompatibility symptoms shown by *Acer rufinerve* (Red-vein Maple) worked on *A. pseudoplatanus* (Sycamore Maple). Note the "shoulder effect" developing and sucker growth from the rootstock. (*Acer rufinerve* should be grafted onto another species in the Snake Bark Maple group.)

(3) Fully Delayed Graft Incompatibility

This category provides us with some of the "text book" classic situations in fruit production when growth is not normally affected until 15–20 years after propagation. It was seen in pears when the early clone of Bartlett Pear was worked onto the standard clones of Quince.

One clue to the development of this condition is the formation of a shoulder (development of an over-growth of rootstock) or inverted shoulder (over-growth of scion) effect. Some rosaceous trees are prone to this, becoming top-heavy if the inverted shoulder effect occurs and, therefore, liable to break under strong windy conditions. However, it must be stressed that over-growth of rootstock and/or scion does not necessarily mean that the union is always incompatible.

Visual Symptoms of Graft Incompatibility

A number of visual symptoms have already been identified in the text, but it will be useful to summarize those of which the propagator should be warned.

(1) Development of over-growths by rootstock or scion, resulting in the shoulder or inverted shoulder effect.

(2) Low success rate in the percentage of scions that grow away.

(3) Lack of overall vigor of the tree, dieback of shoots and, sometimes, pale leaf color.

(4) Premature fall color and leaf drop.

(5) Excessive suckering of the rootstock combined with poor growth or dieback of the scion.

(6) Mechanical weakness between scion and rootstock with little pressure required to break them apart. Inspection of the union itself will often confirm this—one may see the tissues growing away at different tangents from each other, or there may be actual death of areas of the vascular tissue itself, such as the phloem.

(7) A marked difference in the bark pattern and structure of the scion or rootstock may give an indication of incompatibility.

Suggested Reasons For Graft Incompatibility

Having discussed the importance of graft incompatibility in relation to the nursery operation, its classification and symptoms, it is appropriate to summarize reasons for its occurrence. The propagator needs to understand that the causes are often complex and that there are conflicting opinions as to why it should occur with certain plants.

It should be stressed that nutritional or disease problems can cause weak growth, dieback, premature leaf fall, and discoloration of tissue. Therefore, alternative reasons for the failure of grafted plants should also be considered, rather than immediately assuming graft incompatibility.

Some suggested reasons for graft incompatibility can be summarized as follows:—

(1) The use of genetically different plant material for scion and rootstock. It was mentioned earlier that the level of tolerable genetic differences depends very much on the family, genus and species of the plants being grafted.

(2) Plant viruses, especially the latent type, can reduce the overall percentage success quite dramatically, particularly when budding ornamental *Prunus* (Cherry). There has been major development in the production of virus-free material for both scion and rootstock by several associations, including the East Malling Long Ashton (E.M.L.A.) Scheme in Britain and the British Columbia Landscape Plant Improvement Association in Canada, with the aim of providing virus-free scion wood of *Prunus* and *Malus*.

[*Juglans regia* clones (English or Persian Walnut) worked onto *J. hindsii* (California Black Walnut) have shown reduced shoot growth and fruiting after 15–20 years. The union breakdown that occurred was thought to be due to graft incompatibility but recent studies have shown that this condition (often referred to as black-line) is due to a virus infection.]

(3) The use of an excessively vigorous rootstock with a very weak growing cultivar.

(4) The formation of layers of cork tissue extending between scion and rootstock. This effectively acts as a barrier to the transport of water and nutrients, as well as causing mechanical weakness.

(5) The failure of the fibers of the scion and rootstock to interlock effectively.

(6) The death of cambium and phloem tissues at the graft union can cause delayed graft incompatibility.

(7) The abnormal distribution of starch at the actual graft union and differences in biochemical compounds or reactions between stock and scion.

Overcoming Graft Incompatibility Problems

The most important point is to ensure the use of the correct rootstock. As previously indicated, there is considerable published information available but plant propagators may have to rely on their own knowledge, based on their records and past experience. If scion wood is received and the appropriate rootstock is not known, then the propagator should be prepared to undertake a few simple trials using alternative rootstocks, beginning with scion/rootstock combinations of similar genetical affinity.

Virus-free material of scion and rootstock should be used whenever available to improve both the percentage success in take and subsequent growth. The full benefits of virus-free scion material are obtained by also using virus-free rootstocks.

Double-working, using an intermediate stem piece that is compatible with both scion and rootstock (described on p. 489), may be successful. This is normally used in fruit tree production but the same principle can be applied to ornamental trees if desired.

The inarching or bridge-grafting of a stem can be used to repair and strengthen a specimen plant after graft incompatibility has set in, but the stem must be compatible with both rootstock and scion. An extreme case of graft incompatibility in a specimen plant may be overcome by approach grafting in which new young rootstocks are planted around the tree and then grafted into the scion above the previous union.

Further information on these specialized grafts may be obtained from *The Grafters' Handbook* by R. J. Garner (Chapter 8) and *Plant Propagation: Principles and Practices* by H. T. Hartmann and D. E. Kester (4th ed., Chapter 12).

PROGRAMS TO OBTAIN VIRUS-FREE SCION WOOD AND ROOTSTOCKS

Reference has already been made to the principles of clonal selection in Principles of Vegetative Propagation (Chapter 6), but it is important to deal more fully with the topic in relation to the production and availability of virus-free budwood.

It was not so long ago that the mechanisms by which plant viruses multiply, are transmitted, and affect plant growth were largely unknown. The words "losses due to virus infection" have been used as a rationalization for the unhealthy appearance of a crop of trees when this was, in fact, sometimes due to nutritional disorders, to herbicide applications, or to an imbalance of the correct water requirements. However, the issue has become focused, and its importance more fully understood, over the last decade because of the increased importation of nursery crops—for example, *Rosa rugosa* (Rugosa Rose) stems for standard rose production and Plum rootstocks imported into Britain from some continental European countries. The practice of obtaining bicolored patterns in *Camellia* flowers by purposely grafting onto virus-infected rootstocks is still done occasionally and can only help in perpetuating virus problems. Propagators have known for a considerable time that factors beyond their immediate control led to low percentage success in the budding operation, to plant losses, and to reduction in overall quality. The causes were largely due to virus infection. Unfortunately, there was little they could do to rectify the problem.

Some excellent fundamental research has been carried out over the last two decades in Europe, North America and Australasia and has provided many of the answers. Most of this work has been related to fruit production, but recently greater resources have been given to woody ornamentals. The benefits of this work are now being rewarded in many different countries by the initiation of carefully monitored schemes to supply virus-free material to the nursery trade.

Virus particles are extremely small (submicroscopic). They are translocated within the plant through the cell protoplasm, sieve tubes of the phloem tissue, and, sometimes, xylem tissue. Virus infection can be spread between plants by a number of agents, including sap-sucking insects, nematodes, the natural grafting of roots, and vegetative propagation techniques such as grafting and cuttings. In tree production, virus infection is often transmitted to the scion by grafting onto virus-infected rootstocks.

The visual symptoms of viral infections are varied, but include mosaics, ringspots, leaf distortions, vein banding and shoot necrosis. There is also a group of viruses that have virtually no visual symptoms and can be detected only by laboratory tests—these are referred to as latent viruses. Latent viruses have caused problems in both identification and subsequent elimination from some plants. It is known that different species within the same genus can be sensitive to different plant viruses. Thus, a particular virus may be detected visually in one species but will be latent and masked in another. The virus-sensitive plants are used as virus indicators or detectors. Some fundamental research on this subject, using both fruiting and ornamental *Malus,* was carried out by A. I. Campbell at Long Ashton Research Station, Bristol, England. This research confirmed that ornamental *Malus* cultivars vary considerably in their degree of susceptibility to different viruses.

The development of virus-free ornamental material has essentially been restricted to *Prunus* and *Malus,* but many of the cultivars of even these two genera are not virus-free as the cleaning-up process takes a long time.

Roses are another important economic crop in which viral infection is important. The problems have been caused largely by vegetatively-raised rootstocks, such as the *Rosa rugosa* (Rugosa Rose) stems used for standard (tree) roses in Europe and the *R. multiflora* (Baby or Japanese Rose) selections used in the United States and New Zealand, which are able to perpetuate the disease from crop to crop. The virus problems with *R. rugosa* stems in Europe include Arabis Mosaic Virus, Rose Wilt and Strawberry Latent Ringspot—the latter being transmitted by nematodes. Research is being carried out, notably at the Virology Department of the Glasshouse Crops Research Institute, Littlehampton, U.K., with the aim of making available virus-free clones of roses.

As already indicated, there are currently numerous schemes in operation for the provision of virus-free material—particularly in Canada, America, Britain, Holland, New Zealand and France. The British E.M.L.A. Scheme is explained in order to outline the principles and procedures used in a virus-tested program for woody plants.

The name E.M.L.A. is derived from the first letters of East Malling Research Station and Long Ashton Research Station which collaborated in 1965 to make available to the trade a wide range of virus-tested clones of fruit tree rootstocks and cultivars as well as ornamental *Prunus* and *Malus.* The E.M.L.A. rootstocks and mother trees for scion wood are stated to be true-to-name and free from all known viruses. This ensures the purchase of a known entity. There are government-specified regulations under which the virus-free mother material is checked to ensure that it is up to standard. The virus-free clone receives the prefix E.M.L.A. on a special label when distributed to the trade—for example, the rootstock Malling 9 - E.M.L.A.

The material is distributed through membership in the Associations of the two research stations and through an organization called the Nuclear Stock Association (Tree Fruits) Ltd. (usually referred to as N.S.A. (Tree Fruits) Ltd. or N.S.A.). The N.S.A. is essentially a non-profit organization with its own Board of Directors and is open to parties interested in propagating E.M.L.A. plant material. Members who wish to produce and distribute E.M.L.A. material can apply for a Ministry of Agriculture Special Stock (S.S.) Certificate providing they conform to the requirements and regulations governing site, soil and freedom from pests and diseases.

Figure 16-8.
A mother tree orchard of ornamental and fruiting *Malus* and *Prunus* established to provide virus-free (E.M.L.A.) scion wood. (F. P. Matthews, Tenbury Wells, Worcestershire, U.K.)

A mother tree orchard to provide scion material can be established once the virus-free material has been purchased. Similarly, a rootstock grower can purchase E.M.L.A. layers to provide the material for planting up layer beds. Further E.M.L.A. material can be purchased when necessary for replacement or expansion.

One research station's procedure for producing virus-free material of *Malus* can be broken down into the following stages:—

(1) Initial testing using two buds of sensitive indicator plants, for example, the apple *Malus* 'Lord Lambourne' for detection of Mosaic Virus, Rubbery Wood Virus and Chat Fruit or *M.* × *platycarpa* (Big-fruit Crab Apple) for Scaly Bark and Chlorotic Leaf Spot.

(2) The plant to be made virus-free is placed in a heat chamber at a temperature of 37°C (98.6°F) for 4 weeks of 16-hour days. This inactivates the development of the virus while allowing increased growth of the terminal shoot. The shoot tip is removed after being in the heat chamber for the required period in the expectation that it is free of virus particles.

(3) The tip, 1.0 cm (⅜″) long, is carefully grafted onto a compatible virus-free rootstock.

(4) The new plant is then thoroughly re-tested using sensitive indicator plants in case virus infection has survived the heat chamber treatment.

(5) The virus-tested clone is numbered and fully documented.

(6) This clone is budded and grafted on young virus-free rootstocks to provide plants or scion material for release.

(7) The plant material is multiplied and then released to nurseries.

Contact your local extension officer to locate the nearest source in your area for virus-free material.

REFERENCES AND SUGGESTED SOURCES FOR FURTHER READING

Adcock, G. 1969. Propagation of Picea breweriana. *Gardeners Chronicle & New Horticulturist*, February 7, 1969, pp. 29–30.

Dummer, P. 1970. Propagation of Daphnes. *Gardeners Chronicle*, June 5, 1970, pp. 21–23.

Garner, R. J. 1950. Grafting. *Research* **3**: 248–253.

———— . 1979. 4th ed. rev. *The Grafter's Handbook*. Faber & Faber Ltd., London, U.K.

Gudziak, A. 1981. *Illustrated Techniques in Budding and Grafting*. Department of Plant Science and Faculty of Forestry, University of Manitoba, Winnipeg, Manitoba.

Hartmann, H. T. & D. E. Kester. 1983. 4th ed. *Plant Propagation: Principles and Practices.* Prentice-Hall, Inc., Englewood Cliffs, N.J.

Herrero, J. 1951. Studies of compatible and incompatible graft combinations with special reference to hardy fruit trees. *Jour. Hortic. Sci.* **26:** 186–237.

McMillan Browse, P. D. A. 1971. The propagation of Rowans and Whitebeams. *Gardeners Chronicle & H.T.J.* **170**(27): 24–25 (December 21, 1971).

_____ . 1972. Propagation of flowering and fruiting crabapples. *Gardeners Chronicle & H.T.J.* **172**(4): 20–22 (July 21, 1972).

_____ . 1973. The propagation of Ash. *G.C. & H.T.J.* **174**(24): 20–21 (December 21, 1973).

Ministry of Agriculture, Fisheries & Food, U.K. 1969. 5th ed. *Fruit Tree Raising. Rootstocks and Propagation.* Bull. No. 135. Her Majesty's Stationery Office, London, U.K.

_____ . 1978. Notes on New Fruit Varieties. Colt, A New Rootstock for Cherries. *N.F.T. Leafl. No. 9.* Ministry of Agriculture, Fisheries and Food, London, U.K.

_____ . 1981. *Ornamental Nursery Stock Reports.* Luddington Exper. Stat., Ministry of Agriculture, Fisheries and Food, London, U.K.

N.A.K.B., Netherlands. no date. *Certification of Fruit-trees and Rootstocks in the Netherlands.* Nederlandse Algemene Keuringsdienst voor Boomkwekerijgewassen—N.A.K.B., The Hague, Netherlands.

Nelson, S. H. 1968. Incompatibility survey among horticultural plants. *Comb. Proc. Inter. Pl. Prop. Soc.* **18:** 343–407.

Rogers, W. S. & A. B. Beakbane. 1957. Stock and scion relations. *Ann. Rev. Pl. Physiol.* **8:** 217–236.

Traas, J. 1967. Types of rootstocks used in fruit tree production. *Comb. Proc. Inter. Pl. Prop. Soc.* **17:** 50–55.

Webster, A. D. 1976. New and dwarfing rootstocks for cherries and plums. *Proc. 12th Refresher Course for Nurserymen,* Pershore College of Horticulture, Worcs., U.K., pp. 9–13.

Chapter 17

OPEN-GROUND BUDDING

Budding, which is really bud grafting, is a standard technique for propagating a number of woody ornamentals in the open ground during the summer months. It is a more economical technique than grafting as only one bud is used in budding, compared with an optimum of 3–5 for grafting. It is also normally carried out when the rootstock is in active growth with rapidly dividing cambial cells. The role of budding has widened with developments in propagation facilities, production systems, tying-in materials, and the refinement and adaptation of the actual technique. These roles include uses in bench grafting, budding *in-situ* on container-grown rootstocks, and, in certain instances, as an alternative to late winter/spring whip and tongue grafting.

Budding is essentially the use of a single bud (the scion) plus a portion of rind with or without a sliver of wood that is sited on the rootstock between two flaps of rind (e.g., T-budding), replaces a section of rind (patch budding), or replaces a pre-cut veneer of rind and woody tissue (chip budding).

Specific Uses of Budding

The best known role is probably in the production of bush and tree (standard) roses, offering the opportunity in many countries for the employment of contract budders. It is the major technique for the production of ornamental standard (shade) trees, either bottom- or top-worked (p. 473). Budding is the primary method used in the propagation of many fruit trees, such as apples, pears, plums, cherries and peaches, as well as nut-bearing trees such as pecan and walnut. On a more specialized basis, it has been used for a number of flowering shrubs, such as some *Hamamelis* (Witch Hazel), *Magnolia* and *Syringa* (Lilac), both in the open ground and as a form of bench grafting.

Figure17-1. Summer budding is the primary method used to vegetatively propagate both ornamental and fruit trees. The operation is normally carried with two operators—one budding and the other tying-in. (F. P. Matthews Ltd., Tenbury Wells, Worcestershire, U.K.)

Figure 17-2. A plastic tie is used to support the maiden growth of a *Syringa vulgaris* cv. (Common or French Lilac) that was open-ground budded in the previous summer.

Fundamental Considerations When Open-Ground Budding (and Dormant Season Grafting)

A number of issues should be carefully considered before embarking on a program of propagating a nursery crop by budding in the open ground. These may be summarized as follows.

(1) The Market

As much planning as possible is needed to secure a ready market for the crop. It is sometimes easier to predict the demand for a shorter term crop, such as roses which occupy the land for two years, than for the traditional standard or shade trees which occupy the land for three to four years. A smaller nursery with good soil may obtain a good return by growing one-year maiden budded trees. The crop occupies the land for two years, with budding carried out in the first summer and then allowed to grow-on for one year. This provides an excellent product for sale either for growing-on in containers or for lining out in the open ground.

(2) Site and Soil Type

The location of the site is important. The area must be relatively level and protected from damaging winds, so the provision of windbreaks of either living plants or artificial material should be considered. Excessive wind can be detrimental for four reasons. Firstly, a reduction in the development of scion growth, particularly height. Secondly, problems in staking and tying—for example, loose canes. Thirdly, "blow-out" (removal) of the new maiden growth shortly after it starts to grow in the spring after budding. Fourthly, physical damage to stems and leaves, particularly those with a thin leaf lamina such as *Acer platanoides* (Norway Maple) cultivars.

Protection against vermin is vital, therefore proper fencing should be installed. I have seen incalculable damage to rootstocks both before and after budding on *Fraxinus* (Ash) and *Robinla* (Locust), especially when the bark was gnawed and stripped by rabbits.

The correct soil type is important. It should be a sandy loam with plenty of organic matter, which is easily worked and retains water and nutrients so that a fibrous root system will develop. The soil should be well prepared beforehand, ensuring that it is free from perennial weeds, subsoiled if necessary, and has the correct pH and nutrient levels for the species to be grown.

The geographical location of the site will very largely determine the range of trees that can be grown, and the time taken from budding until the crop is sold.

(3) Skills

Nursery owners must be aware of their own skills in budding, as well as those of their employees. Consideration must be given to re-training, if necessary. Training organizations, e.g., the Agricultural Training Board in Britain, have been very important in the development of skills of nursery workers with the introduction of training groups and training days.

Chip budding trees has many benefits over the conventional T- or shield budding. However, some employees, particularly those on contract or piece rates, have shown considerable resistance to learning a newer and improved technique. Thorough re-training is required under these circumstances, not only to teach a new skill, but also to convince the employees that the technique is better for them, the employer, and the crop being grown. [Studies at East Malling Research Station, Kent, England, have shown that chip budding is easier to learn than T-budding and that the speed of chip budding most tree crops is at least equal to T-budding.]

(4) Source of Scion Wood (Budwood)

As with open-ground grafting, the decision must be made as to whether to rely for a source of scion wood on permanent mother trees, the growing crop, or to buy in from elsewhere. In practice, it is sometimes a combination of all three that is used.

(5) Disease Prevention

This wide and often complex topic can be briefly summarized and subdivided as follows:—

(a) The rootstock itself should not be infected by soil-borne diseases such as Verticillium Wilt (*Verticillium albo-atrum* or *V. dahliae*) on *Acer* (Maple), and Crown Gall (*Agrobacterium tumefaciens*) and Specific Cherry Replant Disease (*Thielaviopsis basicola*) on *Prunus*. These will both directly and indirectly affect rootstock development, bud-take, and subsequent maiden growth. The source of the rootstock needs to be carefully checked for reliability, and, where necessary, consideration should be given to fumigation of the soil before planting the rootstocks, using chemicals such as chloropicrin for Crown Gall, Specific Cherry Replant Disease and Verticillium Wilt.

Verticillium is one of the first pathogens to re-invade from untreated soil below or adjacent to the treated area.

There have been reports of considerable success in New Zealand with the use of a material called Dygall® for preventing Crown Gall (*Agrobacterium tumefaciens*) infection in newly planted seedling rootstocks or callused cuttings of fruit trees and rose rootstocks. Dygall® (marketed by Mintech (N.Z.) Ltd., T.N.L. House, P.O. Box 440, Nelson, New Zealand) is a non-pathogenic culture of the closely related *A. radiobacter*. The roots, callused cuttings or, in some instances, peach seeds are dipped into the culture prior to planting. Dygall® will not control existing soil infections but is recommended as a simple and economical biological control for preventing susceptible crops from being infected with Crown Gall.

(b) Both virus-free scion wood and rootstocks should be used where available—a particularly damaging virus being Necrotic Ring Spot Virus on *Prunus.* It is important to appreciate that one virus-infected scion can quickly result in infection of a row of rootstocks as a single bud is normally budded onto each rootstock.

(c) An efficient overall pest and disease spray program is necessary if there is to be healthy growth on wood intended for use as scions. Reduction in the amount of extension growth and weakened growth can be caused by a number of pests and diseases, resulting in poor quality of buds intended for use as scion material. Examples of this include aphid attack (particularly on *Prunus*), eriophid mite on *Fraxinus* (Ash), and scab on *Malus.*

Bacterial diseases present a more difficult problem as chemical control is largely ineffective. For example, Fireblight (*Erwinia amylovora*) affects many Rosaceous trees, especially *Crataegus* (Hawthorn), *Cotoneaster, Pyrus* (Pear), and *Sorbus* (Mountain Ash). Attacks by this disease can vary from year to year, largely depending on weather conditions and a nearby source of inoculum. I recollect seeing severe losses some years ago in a range of two-year-old trees that were being relied upon to supply scion wood for budding, thus making it necessary to obtain budwood from an outside source in an unaffected area.

(6) Planning the Budding Operation

The larger the nursery and the wider the range of cultivars of roses or trees that are to be budded, the more important it is to have a reliable person to organize both the cutting and distribution of the scion wood (budwood). It is advisable to delegate this responsibility to at least two persons, rather than simply running it on a day-to-day basis using whoever may be available.

Inefficient organization loses both time and money, so the person(s) responsible must be able to identify plant material correctly, collect sufficient scion wood (budwood) to allow the budders to operate at maximum efficiency, carry out correct handling and storage procedures to keep it fresh (remembering that such material is very prone to deteriorate through water loss), and either knows personally or is correctly informed when the rootstocks are at the right stage for budding.

(7) Rootstock Compatibility

This has been discussed more fully (see Chapter 16), but its importance is stressed again because selection of the correct rootstock is vital, particularly for shade trees. Guidance on this can be obtained from the tabulated guide in the Appendix, and by seeking advice from both extension officers and other local nursery operators. However, there are always cases in which it is difficult to obtain information, so the propagator must build on personal experience. Genera likely to cause problems in immediate or delayed incompatibility include *Acer* (Maple), *Prunus, Sorbus* (Mountain Ash or Rowan) and *Tilia* (Linden).

(8) Source of Rootstocks

Regrettably, this important aspect is too often overlooked, not only by the purchaser but also by the supplier. Experimental work on seedling rootstocks has shown that good quality seedling rootstocks survive transplanting better but do not necessarily appear to always influence maiden tree size. The latter can be influenced by the variation in compatibility between scion and rootstock due to genetical variation in the seed source. However, if there is one statement by experienced tree-growers that has made an impression on me, it is: "A poor quality stock will not produce a quality tree". It sounds obvious, but in practice it is sometimes not easy to know what to look for unless one is relatively experienced. The following points will assist the nursery operator proposing to purchase rootstocks for open-ground budding:—

(i) Ensure that the grade specified and ordered from the catalogue is delivered to the nursery. A number of the bundles should be opened and checked for overall quality—particularly to size (e.g., diameter of hypocotyl), consistency of grade, root system development, straightness of stem (particularly at the point where budding and grafting is to be carried out), and whether the rootstocks are dried out. The latter problem is commonly discovered towards the center of the bundle. Drying out of the bundles is more common if the delivery has been delayed or in-transit time is lengthy. Sometimes the supplier has been awaiting delivery of a particular item to complete the order, resulting in an extended storage period for the remainder. Bare-root material being transported from one cold storage facility to another easily dries out if not carried or stored correctly.

(ii) In many cases, it is preferable to obtain one-year transplanted seedling stock (i.e, one year in the seed bed and one year transplanted) for the majority of stocks, especially *Acer* (Maple), *Carpinus* (Hornbeam), *Fraxinus* (Ash), *Tilia* (Linden), and *Sorbus* (Mountain Ash). The cost is greater but root system development, is usually better, which will help establishment and subsequent growth. Alternatively, a good seedling grower should be able to supply good quality one-year undercut seedlings (two years in the seed bed but undercut after the first growing season). One practice sometimes carried out is to buy smaller grade one-year rootstocks and line them out intensively in beds for a further year before planting out for budding.

Figure 17-3. *Carpinus betulus* (European Hornbeam) lifted after two seasons of growth. Left—one-year transplants. Note the increased fibrous root system. Right—one-year undercut seedling. Note the less fibrous root system but extended shoot growth.

Some rootstocks are sold as one-year seedlings because they are likely to be excessively large for planting and subsequent budding if left to grow on. These include trees such as *Prunus avium* (Mazzard) *Prunus padus* (European Bird Cherry), *Malus sylvestris* (Crab Apple), *Gleditsia triacanthos* (Honey Locust), *Cotoneaster bullatus* (Hollyberry Cotoneaster) and *Robinia pseudoacacia* (Black Locust). These more rapidly growing rootstocks are sometimes undercut in the summer to increase the amount of fibrous roots and to check growth, but irrigation must be available to follow undercutting.

Clonal rootstocks are purchased as layers or as callused or transplanted hardwood cuttings. Layers (e.g., Malling 9) may be harvested after one season of growth and are termed one-year layers. These are normally sold in three grades—Grade 1 (9–10 mm), Grade 2 (7–8 mm) and Grade 3 (5–6 mm). The bracketed figure is based on the caliper of the stem just above soil level. Some growers prefer to purchase two-year transplanted layers—the smaller grades or shy-rooting clones are grown-on for a further year to allow more root system development. Hardwood cuttings (e.g., St. Julien A and Quince A) and smaller-caliper *Prunus* 'Colt' rootstocks are normally produced as two-year hardwood cuttings. These are rootstocks rooted from hardwood cuttings callused in a heated bin and then transplanted to grow-on for a season in order to build-up the root system.

(iii) Ensure that the supplier delivers the rootstocks at the agreed time. Late delivery results in financial loss for the buyer because late planting often entails more irrigation, increases losses during establishment, results in a poorly developed rootstock at the time of budding, and has an indirect effect on maiden growth the following year. [This latter problem is accentuated if the rootstocks have not previously been cold stored by the supplier.]

(iv) Records should be kept of the performance of rootstocks from every source. Particular attention should be given to performance in establishment, subsequent growth, bud take, compatibility, and quality of the final crop. Subsequent disease incidence of trees should be recorded—for example, the soil-borne diseases such as Verticillium Wilt (*Verticillium* spp.) and Crown or Root Gall (*Agrobacterium tumefaciens*).

(v) Where practical, it is wise to view the rootstocks in the field with the supplier, so that each other's requirements can be appreciated. More than one source should be tried initially, but once a satisfactory source is found, keep to it—both supplier and buyer will benefit in the long term. The rootstocks should be obtained within one's own country whenever possible, in order to encourage self-sufficiency of the nursery industry. However, the limiting factors are often availability, quality and price.

Some suppliers of vegetatively raised rootstocks, for example, *Prunus avium* F12/1 and the Malling apple rootstocks, prefer to build up a number of regular customers, developing a relationship in which they know the buyer's likely requirements 2–3 years ahead of time. Changes in production numbers from layer beds requires long-term planning by the supplier.

It is sometimes tempting to consider raising one's own rootstocks in the nursery. In the great majority of cases, this is best left to the specialist supplier who has both the expertise and the equipment. It is not worth trying to save a few cents and then produce an inferior product. However, there are specific cases where it may be justified—for example, a large tree nursery may buy-in large quantities of rootstocks and have the land, labor and capital to set up their own seedling stock enterprise. Also, where patent laws allow, a nursery can consider setting up mother hedges of rootstocks that can be readily rooted from hardwood cuttings, for example, Quince A, and *Prunus* 'Colt' and 'Myrobalan B'.

(9) Establishment of Rootstocks

Correct soil preparation and early establishment of rootstocks are of prime importance for the production of a well-developed rootstock at the time of budding and thus for a high quality product.

Factors such as soil type, quality rootstocks, correct planting and good aftercare all contribute to good establishment. The root system must be allowed to build up to provide a "power house" for obtaining maximum growth in the following season. Many poor crops of roses and trees can be attributed to poor rootstock establishment. It also affects the overall success of bud take. Research at East Malling Research Station has shown that for every 1% loss of growth (measured by stem diameter) due to herbicide damage there is an average loss of approximately 1.5% of bud take in a range of ornamental trees.

(10) Tying-In Buds

The correct choice of material to tie-in the buds must be made. A material degradable in light should have sufficient tension and longevity to hold the bud into the rootstock until a satisfactory union is made. The merits and limitations of the different types of available tying-in materials are detailed in Chapter 4.

Collection, Handling and Storage of Budwood

As with grafting, it is imperative that the operator carefully plans and implements the correct collection procedures. The four main criteria are a responsible supervisor; the correct timing for collection of budwood in relation to rootstock development; quantities to be budded and number of available budding crews; and, finally, correct handling and storage procedures.

Essentially, cold storage of budwood has two uses. Firstly, to give the budding operator more flexibility with labor availability and weather conditions after the budwood has been collected. This can be described as short-term storage. Secondly, the collection of ripened wood for spring chip budding the next season (see p. 486). This is described as long-term cold storage.

Firstly, it must be appreciated that the budwood is taken from growing shoots during the summer and therefore it is quickly prone to deterioration caused by bruising during handling, water loss and heat build-up, which, in turn, encourages infection by diseases such as *Botrytis*. Short-term cold storage may be done simply by wrapping the budsticks in moist sacking and placing in a cool shady place or a refrigerator. However, a better procedure for summer cold storage of budwood is to wrap the surface-dry budsticks in polyethylene film and place in a refrigerator at 3°C (38°F). This should keep the budwood in good condition for at least five days and, in some cases, for ten days.

Experimental work and commercial experience in Europe and North America has shown that rose and tree budwood can be successfully stored from late summer or early fall through to the next spring and summer. The initial criterion for success is to ensure that the budsticks are prepared from shoots that are of high quality, well-ripened and disease-free. This means that the wood is collected late in the season. Avoid shoots that have broken late as they have not had the opportunity to become sufficiently hardened.

The procedure for storage of budwood for spring chip budding is to collect healthy ripened shoots late in the season, place the bundles in a sealed polyethylene bag with a few drops of water adhering to the inner surface, and then place into a cold storage facility at 1°C (34°F). If a jacketed (indirect) cold store facility with very high relative humidity is available, the budwood is left unwrapped and placed on an open shelf in the store at −1 to 0°C (30–32°F). Above these temperatures, there is a likelihood that the buds will swell and break while in storage, especially after six months. Also, higher temperatures mean that there is more danger of losses from disease infection.

A more elaborate, traditional procedure that has been used successfully is as follows. A box is lined with a sheet of polyethylene to contain the sand and also to reduce the risk of excessive drying out. A layer of moist sand is next placed on the bottom of the box. The budsticks are dusted with thiram or captan and placed on the moist sand in a single layer. Further moist sand is placed over the budsticks, followed by another layer of budsticks. This procedure of alternate layers is continued until the box is full. It is then labelled, dated, the lid fastened down, and cold stored.

The signs of budwood deterioration are shrivelling of the stem and blackening of the tissue, particularly around the bud. This is especially so for *Acer* and *Prunus*. The wide variation in genus and species of trees means that there will be more variables in the degree of performance of successful storage.

Planting of Rootstocks

Rootstocks need to be planted early enough to allow sufficient time for establishment and root development before budding takes place. If the soil has been prepared, they may be planted out in the fall, which has the benefit of easing the planting workload in the spring and also enables root development to begin prior to the winter. However, the normal time for planting, depending on prevailing weather conditions and locality, is late winter and early spring—the latter capable of being extended with the provision of cold storage facilities and irrigation.

(a) Shade Tree Rootstocks

The bundles should be untied, the centers checked for dryness, disease or rodent damage, and the rootstocks prepared for planting. If necessary, the roots should first be pruned back to aid planting and subsequent root development. Secondly, the height is reduced to around 0.6 m (2') to facilitate planting and to minimize dislodgment due to wind. Thirdly, the bases of the rootstocks are cleaned up by removing all growth flush to the single remaining stem to about 15 cm (6") above the height at which the scion is to be budded. This reduces suckering and also reduces the workload involved in rootstock preparation at the time of budding.

The spacing of the rootstocks largely depends on the size of tree required at marketing, mechanization and on local traditions. For example, two relatively widely used planting systems are:—

(1) One method used in Europe to produce a three-year-old tree of specification 6–10 cm (2½–4") or 8–10 cm (3¼–4") (circumference at 1 m (3') above soil level) is a spacing of 38–45 cm (15–18") between the rootstocks and 1.0 m (3') between the rows, with a 2.0 m (6') spacing every eight rows to allow tractor access.

(2) A successful spacing used in the northwestern United States for one- to two-year

budded trees is 30 cm (12″) between the rootstocks and 1.2–1.5 m (4–5′) between the rows.

Planting may be done by hand, slitter ('nickingbar) or by machine. The roots should not all be placed to one side only as this will serve to restrict root development. This is particularly important when using a slitter to form the furrows—if a furrow "smears" due to wet silt or clay, the result will be a poor quality one-sided root system on the tree at the time of lifting. Hand planting allows earlier planting in soils prone to smearing, and is still used in a few major tree nurseries to overcome one-sided root development.

[An alternative technique that is occasionally used to provide established rootstocks at the time of budding is to directly drill seed previously treated to overcome pre-germination problems, thin to the appropriate distance in the row, and then bud that same year. The stocks are undercut the following fall to induce a fibrous root system. This method has been used in the southwestern United States for budding various *Cornus* (Dogwood) onto *Cornus florida* (Eastern Flowering Dogwood) rootstocks. The opportunity to carry this out in most areas is limited as it requires a long growing season, a rootstock that will grow large enough to accept a bud in the same year as germination, and scion growth that is not noticeably restricted the year following undercutting of the established rootstock. This system has been preferred in some instances to the use of transplanted rootstocks because subsequent staking could be omitted and a union with great strength resulted.]

After planting, the land is lightly cultivated, irrigated if necessary, and a residual herbicide is usually applied.

(b) Rose Bush Rootstocks

Rose rootstocks are normally well graded with the root and shoot systems cut back ready for planting. The specification normally used in Europe for seedling rootstocks is 5–8 mm (diameter at the hypocotyl) but the 4–8 mm grade may be used for fall planting or in areas with excellent growing conditions. In North America, where cuttings are used, the normal guideline for caliper size is "pencil thickness". Planting with a slitter or by machine is the accepted method for the majority of roses now produced on a medium to large scale. The planting distance can vary, but two optimum systems used are:—

(i) 15 cm (6″) between the rootstocks and 80 cm (2′8″) between the rows.

(ii) 17.5 cm (7″) between the rootstocks and 1.0 m (3′) between the rows.

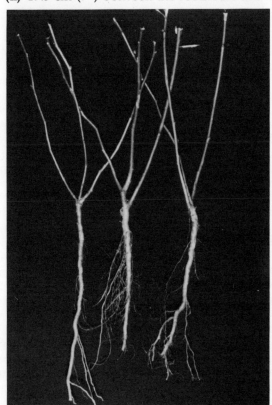

Figure 17-4. 5–8 mm grade seedling rootstocks of *Rosa multiflora* (Baby or Japanese Rose). Note the roots and stems have been pruned to facilitate storage, handling and planting.

The seedling rootstocks are planted so that the hypocotyl (the area of stem just above the root system into which the scion bud is placed) is just above soil level. The normal practice is then to mechanically mound-up (earth-up) soil over the hypocotyl to reduce drying out of the rootstock and to keep the rind of the hypocotyl soft so that it lifts readily at the time of budding. Rootstocks from cuttings do not have a defined hypocotyl and are normally lined out as pre-callused material. This operation is now largely mechanized, so that some 40,000 rootstocks may be planted in an 8-hour day using a two-row, tractor-drawn planting machine manned by four people. Following planting, the pathways may be lightly cultivated, a residual herbicidal application of simazine applied at 1.12–2.24 kg active ingredient/hectare (16–32 oz a.i./acre), and irrigated if necessary.

Rootstocks in North America are normally raised from hardwood cuttings. For example, the planting procedure at Aldergrove Nurseries, Aldergrove, British Columbia, is to stick 25 cm (10″) long, callused cuttings of thornless *Rosa multiflora* (Baby or Japanese Rose) to half their length in early spring. The spacing used is 19 cm (7½″) between the cuttings and 1.1 m (3½′) between the rows. Two cultural operations are carried out just prior to sticking:—

(i) A mechanically-made mound, 5 cm (2″) high, is formed down the rows and the cuttings are stuck into this. This assists in cutting establishment.

(ii) A mixture of Devrinol® and simazine is applied over the soil. Experience has shown that there is considerably less damage to the cuttings in this case than when there is post-sticking application.

The soil is removed from the bases of the rootstocks by pressurized air a few days before budding to allow the stem bases to "green-up". This nursery has found that budding is made easier by allowing "greening-up" rather than budding onto blanched stems.

Source of Scion Wood for Shade Trees

When planning the annual budding program, thought must be given to the source of the scion material. It is probable that an established nursery will be able to fulfill its requirements within the nursery itself, but an alternative source may be necessary in case of failure of the previous year's crops or death of the mother trees. A nursery planning to add additional species and cultivars to its current catalogue will need to obtain budwood initially from a reliable source.

There are four sources of scion wood as outlined below.

(i) Mother Tree Scion Orchard (for summer budding and dormant season grafting)

An area within or closely adjacent to the tree nursery should be designated for the planting of mother trees to provide scion wood. Virus-free trees bought in for mother stock will usually arrive as mother trees, although this does depend on the source.

Extra ground is required, but the orchard system has the advantage that one is dealing with a "known quantity" each year. The E.M.L.A. *Prunus* cultivars were originally planted as a small mother tree orchard at Hadlow College of Agriculture & Horticulture, England, and it proved very advantageous so that the concept was expanded into other areas for a range of ornamental trees, particularly those to be used for bench grafting. Another advantage is that the mother tree can be maintained even if the nursery decides to delete that particular cultivar from its catalogue. The mother tree is then available if it is decided to re-introduce the cultivar in the tree production program. This is not so easy if one is relying on young trees in the nursery rows for scion wood.

Careful attention should be paid to location of the site, rodent and wind protection, and soil preparation (see preparation of stock beds for cuttings, p. 242). Soil fumigation should be considered if there is any possibility of problems resulting from soil-borne pests and diseases such as nematodes and *Agrobacterium* (Crown or Root Galls).

Accurate records must be kept to provide information on the original source, date received, and location on the nursery. Labelling must be clear and accurate.

The space available and the number of trees to be grown will determine whether they are planted closely within the row to form a hedge (for example, 1 x 2 m/3½ x 7′ spacing) or in a 2 m (7′) square pattern. Variations on these spacings may be formulated, but sufficient space must be left between each plant to ensure that scion wood is not mixed when collecting.

The mother trees should be allowed to establish for one year after planting to allow for development of the root system, and to promote vigorous growth of the scion wood the following year. First year growth is cut back hard into the older wood in the winter after establishment to form a basic framework. This will result in vigorous shoots growing away to provide scion wood material for summer budding and also for grafting during the following February/March, i.e., the

Figure 17-5. A well-established "orchard" tree of E.M.L.A. ornamental *Prunus* (Cherry) to provide scion wood for summer budding and/or dormant season grafting. Note that vigorous one-year-old shoots have been induced by pruning hard into the inner framework of the tree. (Reproduced by permission of East Malling Research Station, Maidstone, Kent, U.K.©)

Figure 17-6. A mother tree hedge is a reliable method to provide vigorous healthy scion wood of ornamental trees. (Keith Warren, J. Frank Schmidt & Son Co., Boring, OR, U.S.A.)

Figure 17-7. Close-up of two *Acer platanoides* cvs. (Norway Maple) from the hedge shown in Figure 17-6. These demonstrate how the height was retained at 1.8 m (6') the previous winter in order to facilitate bud wood collection and how the lower branches up to a height of 60 cm (2') were removed to assist open-ground cultivation. (J. Frank Schmidt & Son Co., Boring, OR, U.S.A.)

second year after planting. The shoots remaining after the scion wood has been collected are pruned back the following winter, any snags are headed back, and diseased or very old wood removed.

The mother plants should not be pruned annually to almost ground level unless they are on their own roots, otherwise there is a strong possibility that sucker growth will develop from the rootstock. Such sucker growth is likely to become mixed with the scion wood when collecting. It is also probable that the shoots will be too vigorous to provide suitable budsticks and will make it difficult to match up the scion and rootstock.

A successful method used at J. Frank Schmidt & Son Co., Boring, Oregon, is to develop a 1.8 m (6') high mother tree hedge over a three-year period to provide scion wood. The maiden growth is stopped at 1.4 m (4½') during the first year following planting the hedge, at 1.6 m (5¼') the second year and at 1.8 m (6') in the third year. It is pruned back to 1.8 m (6') in subsequent years to make scion wood collection easier. The lowest branches arise at 60 cm (2') above ground level to facilitate cultivation. More light is encouraged to reach the lower branches and thus produce healthy scion wood development by having the branch framework at the base of the tree longer than the middle and upper areas. The lowest branches are cut back to 30–45 cm (12–18") and the middle and upper branches to around 15 cm (6") during the annual pruning in February. This procedure has provided a considerable quantity of high-quality budwood of the correct caliper for the summer budding program.

Trees with thin and small buds on slender stems, e.g., *Betula* (Birch) and *Alnus* (Alder), can cause difficulties at budding time. A systematic pruning program of the mother trees will greatly improve the situation because the subsequent budsticks will be more vigorous, longer, of wider caliper, and have more and larger buds. The development of plump buds on vigorous stems of the current season's growth is important for successful open-ground budding of *Quercus* (Oak) and *Cercis canadensis* cvs. (Eastern Redbud). Trials at Hillier Nurseries (Winchester) Ltd., England, indicate that small buds on two-year-old wood are best for *Quercus* (Oak) budsticks. The rootstocks are planted during the spring and cut back early in the following year. The scion is then chip budded onto the current season's vigorous growth.

If a nursery has decided to specialize solely in one-year whip or maiden tree production, then it is essential to plan and locate a mother tree orchard for the scion wood. The maiden trees in this instance would normally be lifted and dispatched after one season of scion growth from budding the previous year. This means that there is little or no suitable budwood available because the previous year's crop is unlikely to have sufficient quantity or quality of wood. However, this problem may be largely overcome if there are sufficient 2- to 3-year-old worked trees on the property.

(ii) Trees in Nursery Rows

This provides the major source of scion wood on many tree nurseries (see also p. 498). The shoots are collected from 2- to 3-year-old trees, either from the axillary side shoots arising from the main stem or by reducing the number of shoots forming the head of the tree in instances where the axillary side shoots are not of suitable vigor. The axillary side shoots are excellent for use in budding maples. The potential scion wood is in active growth, therefore it is vital that a systematic pest and disease program is implemented. The nursery rows must be clearly labelled in order to avoid possible mixing of scion wood at the time of collection.

Figure 17-8. The usual source of budwood is from the current season's growth on 2- to 3-year-old trees in nursery rows. Left, a quality drift of *Sorbus aria* 'Lutescens' (White Beam cv.) budded onto *S. aria.* James Coles & Sons (Thurnby) Ltd., Leicester, U.K.)

(iii) Purchase or Outside Collection

Purchasing or collecting outside the nursery is necessary when previous crops have failed or the nursery wishes to increase the range of trees grown. In addition to confirming costs and any patent regulations, the method of shipping the budwood must be checked. This is because the main disadvantage of using outside sources is that budwood is very prone to deterioration caused by water loss and heat build-up when shipped incorrectly. If the time period for getting the particular tree into production is not a limiting factor, consideration could be given to purchasing maidens for planting up, establishing and pruning back the following winter to obtain fresh scion wood for the summer.

(iv) Mother Trees under Protection

The trees may be grown in containers or in a soil border within a protected structure of glass, polyethylene or shade cloth. This method provides an advantage in obtaining early scion wood, or alternatively in encouraging extra growth early in the season, thus providing a greater number of buds at the normal time. Problems that may arise include limited shoot growth because the terminal bud becomes dormant during early summer, probably due to excessively high temperatures, and that the soft growth is prone to pest and disease attack. I noticed that the dormancy problem is particularly apparent when growing *Sorbus aria* cvs. (White Beam) under a glass or polyethylene structure.

Shoot Guides

Shoot guides were used in nurseries in the 1940s for raising fruit trees for orchard planting, and there has recently been increasing interest in these guides to direct the early stages of scion growth. Essentially, it encourages the stem to grow as vertically as possible shortly after it emerges from the rootstock, thus overcoming the problems caused by a "dogleg" forming when the scion breaks at a wide angle. The guides also protect the buds from rabbits and reduce the necessity for staking.

In North America, this development was largely pioneered by J. Frank Schmidt and Son Co., Boring, Oregon, under the trademark "Grow-Straights®". The support consists of a piece of right-angled metal, pointed at one end so that it may be easily pushed into the soil. It is available in 15 cm (6"), 23 cm (9"), 30 cm (12"), and 45 cm (18") lengths, with the top of the latter three sizes being flared to reduce the possibility of abrasion to the soft scion growth. The Grow-Straights® are pushed into the soil about 0.5 cm (¼") to 1.0 cm (⅜") in front of the dormant bud.

Benefits claimed for the use of Grow-Straights®, besides the elimination of dogleg stems at the base of the scion growth, are: more protection against wind damage; overcoming the need for staking some cultivars, or delaying the time at which it is necessary to tie the shoot to the cane; less risk of damaging the scion when the tree is staked; and, increasing the overall percentage of first-quality trees.

In Europe, a product made of either aluminum alloy or plastic is available through Brinkman Wholesale and Tree Growers, Chichester, Sussex. This product is called a "Bud Clip" and the two ends are folded around the union with the concave upper section over the bud. The objective of these bud clips is again to support the early scion growth and to avoid doglegs. This design is usually preferred in Europe over the North American design described above.

Figure 17-9. A series of three photographs demonstrating the use of the metal "Grow-Straight®" shoot guide on *Acer platanoides* 'Crimson King' (Crimson King Maple). A (left). Note the position of the bud in relation to the shoot guide. B (center) and C (right). Note the protection and support that the shoot guide provides to the young shoot. (Reproduced by courtesy of J. Frank Schmidt & Son, Co., Boring, OR, U.S.A.)

T-BUDDING OR SHIELD BUDDING

The technique of T- or shield budding is the predominant method for propagating open-ground roses, ornamental trees, and fruit trees. The rose-growing industry is perhaps still the leader in mechanization for open-ground nursery stock, but budding is one of the few operations still carried out by hand. The name T-budding is derived from the shape made by the cuts on the rootstock, while the alternative name, shield budding, is based on the shape of the piece of stem that carries the scion bud.

This technique involves the placement of a scion bud shield, with or without a small sliver of woody tissue, between two flaps of rind on the rootstock. Callus tissue develops during the first two weeks, mainly from the cellular tissue of the rootstock rather than from the budshield. The spaces between scion and rootstock begin to fill and a "bridge" forms between them. The scion is susceptible to desiccation during these early stages of development, so the temptation to remove the ties too early must be resisted. Early tie removal also allows the flaps to lift and break the callus. Cambium between the scion bud and rootstock begins to develop within the callus tissue starting at the cut edge of the existing cambium. In roses, it is believed that this occurs within 10–14 days after budding, but the cambium-forming time period is more variable in trees. Phloem and xylem vascular elements begin to be formed once a complete cylinder of cambium has been developed by the link between the rootstock and scion. The process is concluded by the development of a joint vascular system between scion and rootstock. It is known that this latter process is not necessarily fully completed in trees prior to the onset of the winter.

Considerable dexterity of the wrists and the fingers is required, but extremely high work rates are achieved by experienced budders. For example, the optimal rate in roses is 1,500–2,000 buds inserted into the rootstocks in an 8-hour day, while figures of 3,000 and over are reached by many contract budders. An onlooker never ceases to be amazed at the work rates achieved by experienced rose budders. The scion and rootstock need to be handled carefully and quickly so that there is the minimum of bruising and water loss of the actively growing tissue. The knife blade, scion and rootstock must be free from soil, grease and dirt. The success rate in bud take normally achieved by contract budders is at least 80–90%.

The technique is basically the same for ornamental shade trees but sometimes there are one or two slight modifications. The work rates are generally slower, partly because tree rootstocks are planted further apart than rose stocks, and it is also more important to achieve a high percentage bud take because each plant will ultimately have a higher financial value. *Prunus cerasifera* cvs. (Myrobalan Plum), *Sorbus aucuparia* (European Mountain Ash), *Crataegus laevigata* (syn. *C. oxyacantha*) (English Hawthorn) and the *Cotoneaster* × *watereri* group (Waterer Cotoneaster) are quick to bud, while *Acer* (Maple) requires considerably more care and therefore a slower work rate.

Timing is important when budding as it is vital that the rind of the rootstock lifts with ease to accommodate the scion bud. The rind often tears, the budding process is considerably slower, and the chances of success are much reduced if the rind has to be forced away from the wood. Thus, factors such as genus, species, time of year, prevailing weather conditions, and root development are all factors that will determine the correct period for budding. Irrigation is beneficial during dry weather periods to ensure that the rind will lift satisfactorily.

1. T- OR SHIELD BUDDING OPEN-GROUND ROSES

The dexterity required in the operation has resulted in some variations on the traditional budding knife (see Chapter 4). It is important to have a well-balanced knife that will allow precise and quick movements. Technology has led to the evolution of prototype mechanical aids, for example, the "Budding Gun" (see p. 202), to overcome the necessity to use a knife, thus enabling the budding process to be carried out by unskilled labor. Initial field trials of this aid did not achieve the results expected from the first experiments, therefore the "Budding Gun" is currently not recommended for commercial use.

Efficient, large-scale open-ground rose production is highly dependent on mechanization. The initial preparation of the rootstock is assisted by machines that remove the soil around the base of the hypocotyl. The standard equipment in Europe is a tractor-drawn machine that directs a strong blast of air to the base of the rootstock, thus forcing the soil away and exposing the hypocotyl. "Nursery ingenuity" has developed another mechanical aid in a tractor-drawn machine that achieves a similar result using a series of rotating polypropylene brushes, driven by the power-take-off-unit of the tractor, to physically remove the soil. In sunny and warm locations, it is important that the removal of soil from the hypocotyl is carried out shortly before budding, otherwise the hypocotyl tissue will harden and make it more difficult to lift the rind.

Figure 17-10. A (left). The tractor-powered MJF rose rootstock brushing machine with rotating polypropylene brushes to physically remove the soil at the base of the rootstock and expose the hypocotyl. B (right). Close-up of the polypropylene brush. (Reproduced by permission of Horticulture Weekly, GC/HTJ, Haymarket Publishing, Twickenham Middlesex, U.K.)

Figure 17-11. A (left). The Delves budding trolley. A long metal gantry can be placed down over seedling rose rootstocks and then a seat with roller wheels in placed onto the gantry. B (right). Two budders and a tyer can sit comfortably on the seat and move easily down the row. Note the box for materials attached to the seat by the left of the person tying, and the good vision and access to the hypocotyl. (Reproduced by permission of Horticulture Weekly, GC/HTJ, Haymarket Publishing, Twickenham, Middlesex, U.K.)

Figure 17-12. A (left). The normal posture of the budder when budding bush roses. B (right). A heavy metal rod or pole laid over the rootstocks is a simple method to provide better vision and access to the hypocotyl.

A further example of mechanization in open-ground budding is the use of manual or battery-operated trolleys and lightweight carts (often fitted with bicycle wheels). The budder is able to have a better view of the base of the rootstock and the necessary tools and equipment are near at hand. The budder sits, kneels or lies on a basal platform (usually padded) and is able to carry out the knife-work quickly and with a significant reduction in the discomfort caused by continual bending and stooping.

A simple way to make budding easier, particularly for thorny seedling stocks, is to use a metal rod that is placed over a small section of about 20–30 rootstocks as the budder moves down the row. The rod is sited a little distance above the hypocotyl so that its weight compresses and draws the stems and foliage towards the budder. This gives the budder more freedom of movement at the hypocotyl, a better view, and reduces the risk of scratches on the wrists and arms by thorns on the rootstock stems.

Traditionally, a nursery employee begins as a tyer, working for a number of years before being allowed to become a budder. Today, it is important that staff are involved with budding early in their career, not only to give them confidence but also to act as a back-up where necessary to the normal crew of budders.

Sources of Scion-Wood (Budwood)

The budwood is normally collected from the current season's growth of maiden bushes budded the previous year. Circumstances may result in insufficient budwood being available or the maiden plants may not have reached the correct stage of development and budwood from the previous year's growth may be used in this case, providing that it has been cold stored satisfactorily over the winter and spring. Alternatively, the bushes may be planted in a greenhouse and pruned to produce scion wood early in the season.

Collection and Preparation of Scion Wood (Budwood)

There are differing opinions regarding the stage at which maiden growth for scion wood is collected. The optimum stage is considered to be when the flowers are fully open, but growers in more northerly climates may wait until petal drop. This later stage makes it easier to remove the thorns but more difficult to cut out the buds. Some nurseries collect the budwood early, just as the calyx splits to show petal color—the wood is easier to cut but removal of the thorns can be a problem. Care is needed when removing the thorns to prevent damage to the cut shoots (budsticks). The location of the nursery, the work schedule and personal preferences largely determine the stage at which the scion wood is collected for preparation as budsticks.

Tying-In

The removal of ties by hand has been eliminated with the introduction of degradable rubber ties which deteriorate in sunlight and become weakened as the hypocotyl expands. There are two basic designs of degradable ties available. Firstly, a square patch with a wire staple at one end which was initially marketed by Fleischhauer of West Germany—the tyer places the patch over the bud, pulls it behind the rootstock to create pressure over the bud, and then holds it firm by pushing the staple through the opposite end. Secondly, a tie with an enlarged central area to cover the bud is made by Rapidex Products (No. 1), Knutsford, England. The central section is placed over the bud, pulled from behind to exert pressure, the two ends crossed and brought to the bud side, looped and secured by looping again behind the bud. In North America, rubber strips that are spiralled around and over the cut surfaces are sometimes used.

Budding Procedure

[Note that the term "budwood" is usually substituted for scion wood in the descriptions of the actual budding operation. Both terms are used elsewhere in the text.]

Initial Rootstock Preparation

Remove the soil from the base of the rootstock by hoe or machine to expose the hypocotyl. This procedure is carried out as a separate operation before budding commences.

Budwood Collection

(1) Confirm the correct identification of the scion wood to avoid subsequent problems with misnaming.

(2) Use hand pruners to remove semi-ripened shoots when the flower is fully open (see above), ensuring that there is an optimum of 5–6 buds.

Figure 17-13. The current season's growth of maiden rose bushes budded the previous summer is the primary source of scion wood.

Figure 17-14. A small draw hoe is a convenient method to manually remove the soil at the base of the rootstock in order to expose the hypocotyl.

(3) Loosely bundle and label the shoots and place temporarily in damp sacking.

Preparation of Budstick (Prepared Scion Wood Shoot)

(1) Remove the leaf lamina, working from the base of the budstick, but retaining 5 mm (1/5″) of petiole.

(2) Remove the unripened tip of the shoot.

(3) Remove the thorns by either breaking them off with a lateral movement of the finger and thumb or slicing them off with a knife (*not* the budding knife).

(4) Tie the budsticks in bundles and label.

(5) Place the budsticks in damp sacking or a bucket containing 5 cm (2″) of water and put in the shade. Damp sacking should be placed over the bucket and budsticks. They may be temporarily cold stored at 3°C (38°F).

NOTE:—It is helpful to ensure at this stage that each budstick has suitable buds as this will prevent the budders wasting time selecting appropriate ones.

Preparation of Scion

(1) Hold the tip of the budstick towards you and make a cut 1.0 cm (3/8″) below the scion bud.

(2) Draw the knife through to just beyond the scion bud and then pull it away from the budstick, leaving a "tail" of rind. With experience, a shallow scion bud may be cut without a "tail" of rind.

(3) To provide a close fit to the curve of the rootstock, the "wood" is normally removed from the back of the scion bud, leaving the "eye" intact. This is achieved by easing back the "tail" to expose the wood to be removed. Hold the scion between the finger and thumb of one hand, ensuring that the cut surface is not touched, and make a sharp upward movement with the thumb and finger of the other hand to remove the wood. The inexperienced operator should always check that the bud "eye" has not been removed as well. Always ask an experienced person to demonstrate this procedure to you as there is a definite knack to doing it successfully.

[Some budders prefer to make the cut very shallow and retain the wood, particularly when the buds are more fully ripened. Some nurseries have also increased their overall "take" by leaving the wood in during the entire budding season. It would be advisable to try both methods initially to see which one best suits your locality and budders.]

Preparation of Rootstock

[A metal bar may be placed above the hypocotyl so that the foliage and stems of a section within the row are directed towards the operator (see p. 470). This can improve access to the hypocotyl.]

(1) Remove loose debris from the cutting surface of the hypocotyl, using either the spatula of the budding knife or coarse sacking.

(2) Make a horizontal cut, about 1.0–1.5 cm (⅜–⅝″) long, on the windward side of the hypocotyl. Some budders prefer to slightly angle this cut so that it will be on a slant to the subsequent vertical cut.

(3) Make a vertical cut about 3.5 cm (1⅜″) long, drawing the knife up to the horizontal cut.

(4) Ease the rind of the hypocotyl away from the woody tissue, using either the clean spatula of the budding knife or the cutting edge of the knife blade. If the knife blade is used, the hand should be turned slightly so as to lift the rind.

Bud Insertion

(1) Hold the scion bud by the base of the petiole or the lower part of the "tail" and carefully insert into the rootstock, ensuring that it is held beneath the two flaps of rind. The bud should be finally sited about half-way down the vertical cut and held snugly between the two flaps of rind. [Some budders prefer to use the blunt end of their budding knife to ease in the bud.]

(2) Remove the "tail" by placing the knife blade under slight pressure along the horizontal cuts.

(3) Finally secure the scion bud by tying-in with:—

(a) A degradable rubber patch over the bud and secured by a wire staple.

(b) A degradable rubber tie with enlarged central area to cover the bud. The tie is secured by overlapping and tying in the ends.

(c) Spiralling a rubber strip over the cut surfaces in a similar fashion to the method used for shade trees (see p. 476).

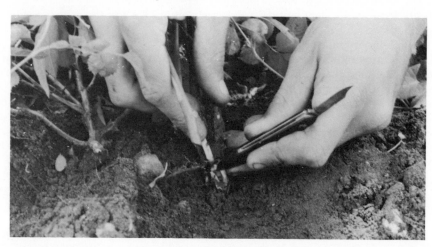

Figure 17-15. The spatula of a budding knife can be used to ease in the bud shield so that it fits snugly between the two flaps of rind on the hypocotyl.

2. T- OR SHIELD BUDDING TREES

Compared to roses, the open-ground budding of trees is a greater challenge to the nursery operator. The wide range of genera, species and cultivars means that the condition of the scion and rootstock, the timing, and the type of tying material all have a strong influence on the ultimate success. The dominant technique in North America and some European countries is T-budding, while chip budding has become the more popular technique in Britain.

The technique used for T-budding trees is fundamentally similar to that used on roses, although there are some refinements in some instances. The correct timing for budding can be critical, and there are essentially two schools of thought on this. Some nursery operators prefer to bud during early to mid-summer, while others prefer mid- to late summer and into early fall. The factors that have influenced this, besides personal preference, include geographical location, the genus or species being budded, the condition of the rootstock, and the condition and availability of scion wood.

It is claimed that budding late into the season will result in a more even bud break the following spring. One theory for this is that there is a shorter period during which the scion bud is influenced by rootstock growth above the union compared with budding earlier in the season.

A typical budding sequence for a range of species and cultivars in the Midlands and southern England would commence with *Acer platanoides* (Norway Maple), followed by *A. negundo*(Box Elder) and *A. pseudoplatanus* cvs. (Sycamore Maple) in late June to early July. The sequence could then move onto *Prunus* (Cherry), followed by *Malus* (Crab Apple) and *Pyrus* (Pear). Budding of *Sorbus* (Mountain Ash), *Crataegus* (Hawthorn) and *Fraxinus* (Ash) would take place in August, with the program ending with *Cotoneaster* in early to mid-September.

A different sequence is generally used in southwestern British Columbia. *Gleditsia* (Honey Locust), *Sorbus* (Mountain Ash) and *Fraxinus* (Ash) are budded in the latter part of July, followed by *Malus* (Crab Apple) in early August. *Acer* (Maple) is budded in mid-August followed by the ornamental *Prunus* (Cherry). The budding program concludes with *Betula* (Birch) and *Cornus* (Dogwood), which are budded during late August and early September respectively.

Budding technique affects the timing. The faster establishment of chip budding (p. 478) allows the budder to take advantage of the better survival capacity shown by riper budwood, which contains more carbohydrates, when budding later in the season. The chip budding season can start some 4 weeks later than T-budding. The optimum temperature of 15.5–18°C (60–65°F) is not reached for sufficiently long periods in temperate climates for the successful budding of some species. *Betula* (Birch) responds very well to warm temperatures after budding.

The site of the bud placement on the rootstock is important. In the Pacific Northwest region of North America, the tendency is to bud about 5 cm (2″) above soil level, while in Europe the optimum is about 10 cm (4″) for the average shade tree. In fruit production, the trees may sometimes be budded about 45 cm (18″) above soil level. This can assist in increasing the height of axillary shoots arising at the base of the maiden plant, and in reducing the risk of *Phytophthora cactorum* (Collar Rot) infection. Trees to be top-worked as standards and half-standards would normally be budded at 1.1–1.4 m (3½–4½′) and 1.7–1.8 m (5½–6′) respectively.

There are three schools of thought regarding the site of the bud in relation to the prevailing wind or sun. The first group prefers to bud into the prevailing wind (windward side), believing that there is less risk of the scion breaking away from the rootstock shortly after growth begins the following spring. The second group holds the view that the bud should be sited on the shaded side of the rootstock (normally the north) so that the bud is protected from the sun and to cause the scion to grow straight as it grows over the stock towards the sun. The third group believes that the primary objective should be to place the bud so that the new growth is not damaged by subsequent cultural operations—this normally means budding within the row.

There is less consensus on whether or not to remove the wood from the bud shield when budding shade trees. The decision will often depend on the condition of the scion wood. *Acer* (Maple) and *Cornus* (Dogwood) are two genera in which some propagators prefer to leave in the wood, while the wood is removed in *Tilia* (Linden). The wood should be left in if budding in the spring or if the scion wood has considerably hardened up in the summer and fall.

The following section details some specific variations in technique and problems that may confront the tree grower.

(1) "Sleepy Bud"

"Sleepy bud" is a term that is sometimes used by tree growers. The term is used when there is delayed, little or no scion growth in the spring following budding. The major causes of "sleepy bud" are:—

(i) Incomplete union formation in T-budding. The incomplete cambial link between scion and rootstock in the fall means that the union cannot support vigorous scion growth the following spring. The scion begins growth and then rests as a rosette until union formation is complete.

(ii) Overgrowth of rootstock callus tissue over the scion bud.

(iii) Damage to the scion bud caused by excessive physical pressure by the tie. This may be due to the rootstock swelling inside a plastic tie or to a rubber tie under tension.

(iv) An overdose of a "dormancy factor" from the rootstock top in the summer after budding. A vigorous rootstock top and early budding can cause "sleepy buds", and even total failure of the scion buds to grow away, in cherries and plums in particular.

Figure 17-16.
An overgrowth of callus
tissue that partially covers
the bud can give rise to
"sleepy bud".

(v) Small latent buds at the base of the budstick, e.g., in *Aesculus* (Buckeye or Horse-chestnut).

The first two causes of "sleepy bud" can be largely overcome by using chip budding instead of T-budding. The last three causes can result from any open-ground budding techniques and are not necessarily restricted to T-budding.

(2) *Acer platanoides* (Norway Maple)

The maples represent one of the most variable groups of trees for consistency in result of budding, particularly *Acer platanoides* (Norway Maple). S. J. Haines of James Coles and Son (Thurnby) Ltd., Leicester, England, is a foremost British nurseryman who has always been a leader in improving and modifying open-ground budding techniques. His thoughts relative to T-budding *Acer platanoides* cvs. may be summarized as follows:—

(i) Plant 2-year, 8–10 mm (1/3–2/5"), transplanted seedling rootstocks, reducing the height to 45 cm (18").

(ii) Avoid selecting soft and sappy budwood.

(iii) Select the budsticks from axillary shoots that have begun to harden up.

(iv) Reduce the influence of the rootstock by radically reducing its height shortly after budding.

The height of the rootstock above the union is reduced by 50% about 2–3 weeks after budding. This will assist in reducing the possibility of callus tissue covering and smothering the bud, which will result in partial or complete failure of the bud to grow away the following spring. This phenomenon has been recorded in the eastern United States when budding *Tilia* (Linden) onto vigorously growing rootstocks in mid-August. The reduction of the rootstock can be taken a stage further by reducing the height to 15 cm (6") above the bud 2–3 weeks later. This will encourage the bud to break, producing about 3–15 cm (1¼–6") of growth prior to the following winter. These short shoots of scion growth seem to be no more susceptible than the buds to cold temperature damage. This technique was subsequently successfully adopted by P. R. Read, formerly foreman of the tree department at Hadlow College of Agriculture & Horticulture, Kent. However, the development of chip budding has virtually eliminated the likelihood of this type of bud failure.

The performance of budding *Acer platanoides* (Norway Maple) is also improved by using a selected clone known for its high bud take success. The purple-leaved form of the popular *A. platanoides* 'Crimson King' (Crimson King Maple) is known in Britain to have a low success rate when budded, and nurseries will accept a take of between 20–30%. Studies by B. H. Howard of East Malling Research Station have confirmed that clones from different sources have considerable variation in success rates, with a range of 22–88%. One of the "high-take" clones was a selection from Hadlow College of Agriculture & Horticulture, and this clone has since been distributed to some nurseries, resulting in a significantly improved bud take.

(3) *Prunus* spp. and cvs. (Cherry)

I have noted one problem when T-budding some *Prunus* (Cherry), particularly when using small bud shields (e.g., *P. subhirtella* 'Rosea', Pink Spring Cherry, onto the vigorous *P.* Mazzard F12/1 rootstock). This problem occurs when dry soil conditions precede a return of moist weather shortly after budding. This combination of conditions causes the rootstock to go into rapid growth and thus increases the caliper of the stem. When this happens, the two flaps are pulled away from the vertical cut, leaving the scion fixed only at the top and bottom of the bud shield. The scion then begins to dry and die.

(4) *Gleditsia triacanthos* cvs. (Honey Locust)

The shape of the bud stick and the hardness of the wood means that it takes considerable skill to prepare the bud shield. The process can be made easier by collecting the scion wood when it is green, before any yellow or brown colorations appear due to the ripening of the wood.

(5) Red-bud Borer Attack on *Malus* (Crab Apple)

Thomasiniana oculiperda (Red-bud Borer) has presented a problem in budding *Malus* (Crab Apple) in some areas of Europe. It is thought that the adult is attracted by the aroma of sap arising from the cut surfaces. The female lays her eggs in the cut surfaces within a short period after budding and tying-in. The pink larvae bore into the newly-formed callus tissue, the cambium and, sometimes, into the bud itself. This problem can be prevented by smearing petroleum jelly over both the bud and tie shortly after tying-in. This is best carried out by having a third person on the budding team to follow behind the tyer. Infection can also be reduced by covering over the bud when polyethylene tape is used for tying-in, but care must be taken to ensure that the tension is not too tight or the bud itself will be damaged. Care must also be taken when removing the tie, as a nick caused by the knife blade will attract the insects. In this case, the larvae can work their way around the stem, ultimately damaging the original scion bud.

(6) Double Budding (Twin Budding)

This is a practice occasionally used to increase the overall percentage bud take in plants that are unreliable. I have seen this used effectively in T-budding for some *Prunus* (Cherry), *Betula* (Birch) and *Hamamelis* (Witch Hazel). Essentially, it involves budding two buds either on opposite sides of the rootstock or on the same side about 10 cm (4") apart up the stem. It is hoped that one of the two buds will successfully take. The disadvantages include:—the overall budding program will take longer; a scar may be left where one bud failed to take; and there may also be subsequent problems in tree training. Double budding can also be used to provide a more fully branched tree, e.g., *Prunus serrulata* 'Amanogawa' (Amanogawa Cherry).

(7) *Quercus palustris* (Pin Oak) for budding some *Quercus* (Oak)

Hopperton Nurseries, Inc., Kentucky, have reported a technique for open-ground budding some of the appropriate compatible cultivars onto this rootstock, based on the practice of first heading back an established rootstock and then using pruned mother trees to supply vigorous wood with a high quality bud.

The procedure is to plant a two-year seedling, allow one season's growth, and then to head back this established rootstock to soil level in the spring. Multiple shoots later appear and are allowed to reach about 12.5–15.0 cm (5–6") tall, when one is selected as a leader and the remainder removed. The rootstocks are budded in the following July-August.

(8) *Cercis canadensis* cvs. (Eastern Redbud)

Hopperton Nurseries have also had success with a similar technique for *Cercis canadensis* cvs. (Eastern Redbud), combining it with a top dressing of nitrogen as the rootstock begins growth and heading back the rootstock shortly after budding. Seedling *C. canadensis*, about 45–60 cm (18–24") tall, are planted in early spring and top-dressed with a nitrogenous fertilizer as growth begins. They are then pruned back to soil level and a single leader shoot selected from the multiple shoots that arise. Budding, using buds from mother trees, is done in the summer, and the rootstock is then headed back to just above the bud shield about 3 weeks later. This encourages about 30–38 cm (12–15") of scion growth in the same year thus preventing loss of buds over the winter. The post-budding pruning technique is similar in principle to that described for *Acer platanoides* cvs. (Norway Maple). A post-budding pruning technique is worth evaluating in the event of problems with "sleepy bud" or poor bud take with T-budding.

Budding Procedure

The T-budding procedure for shade trees is essentially the same as for bush roses (see p. 468). However, there are some variations in procedure, and the major ones are outlined below.

(1) Initial Rootstock Preparation

Use a knife (*not* a budding knife) to remove the lower leaves and shoots to approximately 17.5 cm (7″) above soil level to facilitate the budding process. The production of a clean "leg" (length) of rootstock stem to receive the scion bud is best done as a separate operation beforehand.

(2) Tying-In

The scion bud is secured by firmly tying-in with:—

(i) Rubber strips spiralled over the cut surfaces, ensuring that there are at least two turns below and three turns above the bud but that the bud itself is left exposed. The tying-in is completed with a half-hitch knot.

(ii) Polyethylene tape, either 1.3 cm (½″) or 2.5 cm (1″) wide and pre-cut into 15–20 cm (6–8″) lengths. Stretch the end of the tape over and beyond the basal cut and begin tying-in with it under tension. Overlap the edges of the tape on each turn—the bud itself is usually left exposed. Take the tape above the bud, covering all cuts, and finish with a half-hitch knot.

(iii) A degradable rubber tie with enlarged central area that covers the bud. The tie is secured by overlapping and tying-in the end.

(3) Release of Tie

The non-degradable plastic ties need to be removed within 4–6 weeks after budding to avoid stem constriction.

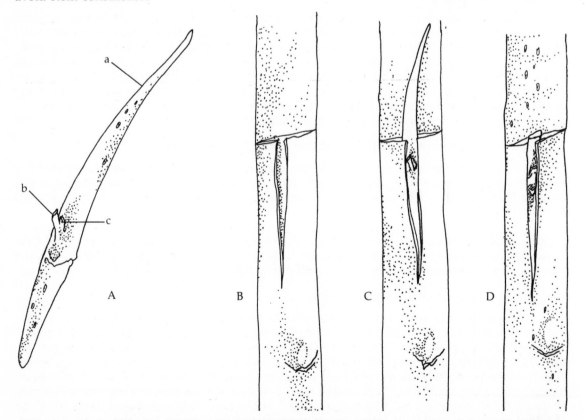

Digram 17-1. T- or shield budding of trees. A. The prepared scion showing (a) the rind, (b) the petiole, and (c) the bud. B. The prepared rootstock with horizontal and vertical cuts and lifted rind. C. Inserting the scion snugly between the two flaps of rind on the rootstock. D. The "tail" of the rind on the scion is removed flush with the horizontal cut. The bud is then tied-in.

Figure 17-17.
A rubber banding strip is used to tie-in the bud. Note the twist on the tie which helps to make the strip lie flat on the rootstock.

INVERTED T- OR INVERTED SHIELD BUDDING

Inverted T-budding is essentially the same as T-budding, except that the budstick is held at the base, the wood is left in the bud shield, and the horizontal cut is at the base of the vertical cuts. The technique is somewhat slower than T-budding because the bud is inserted upwards between the two flaps of rind.

It has traditionally been used under two circumstances. Firstly, for those trees that may have a heavy sap rise with the excess sap subsequently collecting around the bud after tying-in—for example, some *Acer* (Maple) and *Aesculus* (Horse-chestnut). Secondly, in areas of high rainfall where death of the bud shield could occur due to water collecting around it. The inverted T-cut assists in discouraging the collection of either excess sap or water around the bud.

There was a revival of inverted T-budding during the late 1960s and early 1970s in England because of research carried out at Long Ashton Research Station, Bristol. Fruit growers had been having problems with the semi-dwarfing rootstock M.26, experiencing lack of uniformity in the growth of maiden trees and problems of "sleepy bud" giving variable bud break in the

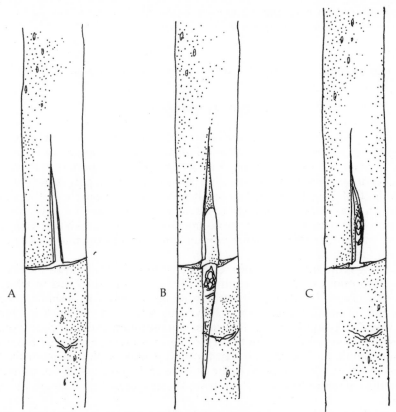

Diagram 17-2. Inverted T- or shield budding. A. The vertical and horizontal cuts to form the inverted "T" on the rootstock. B. Inserting the bud shield snugly up between the two flaps of rind on the rootstock. C. The "tail" of the rind of the scion is removed flush to the horizontal cut and tied-in.

spring following T-budding. Results with inverted T-budding showed an improvement in uniformity, reduced "sleepy buds", and increased laterals arising at a wider angle from the main stem. A number of nursery operators tried the technique with ornamental trees and results were encouraging. However, this work coincided with East Malling's work on chip budding and later seemed to lose its impetus in the nursery trade, because chip budding showed many of the advantages in growth that inverted T-budding claimed. Chip budding of ornamentals was easier to carry out for the majority of nursery workers and further experience has made it the more popular method.

Budding Procedure

As for T-budding trees but with the following modifications.

Preparation of Scion

(1) The *base* of the budstick is held towards the operator and a cut made 1.0 cm (⅜") *above* the scion bud.

(2) It is not necessary to remove the wood from behind the bud.

Preparation of Rootstock

(1) Make a horizontal cut at a height of 5–10 cm (2–4") above soil level.

(2) Make a vertical cut, 3.8 cm (1½") long, by drawing the knife blade up the stem away from the horizontal cut. The rind is lifted as in T-budding.

Bud Insertion

Insert the scion bud from below and ease it up the stem so that it is held in place between the two flaps of rind. Care should be taken not to allow loose debris from the rootstock or the thumb and fingers to touch the cut surface.

Tying-in

The bud is best tied by using 1.3 cm (½") polyethylene tape leaving the bud exposed, rather than with rubber strips or degradable rubber ties.

Removal of Ties

Ties should be removed within 4–6 weeks after budding to avoid constriction of the stem.

CHIP BUDDING

Chip budding has been recognized as a way of generally propagating open-ground trees since the 1930s, but it was not until the mid 1970s that nursery operators began to exploit its advantages. Its widespread use in Britain and its increasing importance in North America, particularly in Oregon and British Columbia, has been due very largely to the research work of B. H. Howard at East Malling Research Station. It serves as an example of the way in which a research worker can work with the industry to develop a technique. The development trials that were carried out on British nurseries with the co-operation of the Agricultural Training Board and the industry have meant that both research workers and nursery operators have benefited by a two-way flow of information.

Chip budding is the substitution of a scion, consisting of a bud, rind and sliver of wood, for a matching area of rootstock tissue. This contrasts with shield or T-budding in which the scion is eased in between two flaps of rind on the rootstock but does not replace a similar piece of tissue.

A faster rate of union formation is achieved by scion and rootstock in chip budding as compared with shield or T-budding. This is because the cambium of the stock and of the scion can be placed opposite and virtually adjacent to each other thus giving good "cambium to cambium" contact. One shortcoming of T-budding is that the rind is lifted at the secondary xylem position, thus moving the cut edge of the cambium to the outside of the bud shield. Callus needs to infill all spaces, and then the cambium has to develop from the existing edges through the callus to form the "cylinder".

The speed at which the union forms in T-budding increases in high temperatures, which may explain why some propagators have obtained as good results with T-budding as with chip budding.

Inverted T-budding has most of the problems of the T-bud, except that the edges of the

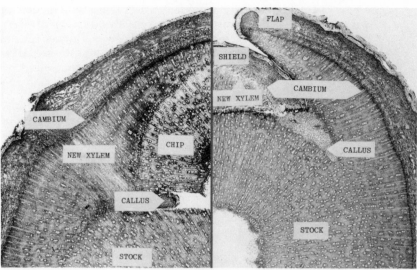

Figure 17-18. A well-defined, successful union between scion and rootstock that resulted from chip budding *Malus* (Apple). Note that the scion chip replaced a matching chip on the rootstock (versus the addition of a bud between two flaps of rind as in T-budding), and the evenness of the ring of callus tissue just above the perimeter of the chip bud. This indicates good matching by the budder. (Reproduced by permission of East Malling Research Station, Maidstone, Kent, U.K.©)

Figure 17-19. Transverse sections through part of the unions of chip (left) and T-buds (right) of *Acer platanoides* 'Crimson King' (Crimson King Maple) on *A. platanoides*. (Reproduced by permission of the Journal of Horticultural Science, U.K.)

cross cut result in good cambial contact between scion and rootstock. This contact is retained because it is below the bud, whereas in normal T-buds it is above the bud and often removed when heading back.

Comparisons of Chip Budding with T- or Shield Budding

(1) There is considerably less risk of bud failure caused by the pathogen *Nectria galligena* (Apple Canker) when budding *Malus*. The initial source of infection can result in further infections to the trees, resulting in stem cankers. Any spores present on scion wood used for T-budding will be inserted under the rind of the rootstock. This problem is reduced in chip budding because the spores are left on the surface as there is no flap of rind to cover them. Infection may be further reduced by spraying trees to be used for budwood with a Benlate® solution shortly before removal of scion wood. A range of similar fungicides are also suitable for use either as sprays or budstick dips.

(2) There is very often a higher overall percentage of success in bud take when using chip budding, particularly in trees that show low success rates with T-budding. Chip budding has improved results in such trees by 50 to over 100%.

Before taking up chip budding, nursery operators in Britain had been experiencing low bud takes with a number of *Prunus* specimens, such as *P.* × *hillieri* 'Spire', *P. sargentii* (Sargent Cherry), *P. subhirtella* 'Autumnalis' (Autumn Flowering Higan Cherry) and *P. serrulata* 'Kwanzan' (Kwanzan Cherry), 'Tai Haku' (Great White Cherry) and 'Ukon' (Ukon Cherry), even though virus-free E.M.L.A. budwood and rootstocks were available for some of them. *Acer platanoides* 'Crimson King' (Crimson King Maple) is another example in which chip budding improved the successful budding percentages. However, North American trials using chip budding on *A. platanoides* (Norway Maple) have not always confirmed the British results. The use of both chip budding and a clone known to improve bud take should give maximum success.

(3) The budding operation can be carried out over a longer period as chip budding is not dependent on the lifting of the rind as in T-budding. In practice, this means that budding can even be carried out in March using cold-stored scion wood from the previous year, and then re-commenced in June until late September using scion wood of the current season's growth.

(4) Chip budding provides greater resistance to cold temperature damage at the union. I have noticed this particularly with cultivars of *Acer platanoides* (Norway Maple), *A. pseudoplatanus* (Sycamore Maple), *Prunus padus* (European Bird Cherry) and *Fraxinus* (especially *F. oxycarpa* 'Raywood', Claret or Raywood Ash). This is because the vascular tissue of the rootstock and scion has largely united prior to the winter.

(5) Chip budding provides a greater uniformity and more vigor in the maiden growth, with the additional benefit of more and longer laterals. The latter is particularly useful for trees that may be shy in producing lateral shoots, and also provides a well-feathered product for growing-on in containers. The result is an excellent product for the garden center market. As the union is well developed prior to the winter, these benefits could be attributed to increased nutrient availability.

Figure 17-20. A (above). Excellent drifts of maiden chip budded E.M.L.A. *Malus.* note the evenness of height and side shoot development—both encouraged by chip budding. B (right). An individual maiden *Malus* propagated by chip budding and showing side shoot development. (F. P. Matthews Ltd., Tenbury Wells, Worcestershire, U.K.)

(6) Chip budding has enabled nursery operators in some geographical areas to widen the range of subjects that can be open-ground budded, providing an alternative to bench grafting. In southern Britain, *Betula* (Birch) and *Gleditsia* (Honey Locust) have been successfully budded, and I have had good results with *Quercus robur* 'Fastigiata' (Pyramidal English Oak) and *Robinia pseudoacacia* 'Frisia' (Black Locust cv.)—the latter by dormant spring chip budding. There are doubtless a number of areas in North America where both *Betula* and *Gleditsia* are successfully T-budded because of the warmer climate and a longer growing season with more sunlight.

(7) Chip budding may be adapted successfully for use as a method of bench grafting during the dormant months of January and February, particularly if there is a limited amount of scion wood (see p. 553). Subjects where this is successful include *Betula* (Birch), *Hamamelis* (Witch Hazel), *Fraxinus* (Ash) and *Magnolia*.

(8) Chip budding is not practical for open-ground bush rose production, but it does provide a useful alternative to top-working stem understocks for half- and full tree (standard) roses, especially when the rind is not lifting well. It has also been successfully used for bench grafting bare-root rose rootstocks for subsequent sale as rose bushes.

(9) Chip budding is claimed to be faster than T-budding as there are fewer movements involved. However, it would probably be much slower initially for an employee who has used T-budding for a number of years. Speed should not necessarily be the major criterion when budding trees—I feel that it is more important to ensure good carpentry, matching, and tying-in, especially as trees normally form a long-term crop.

The nursery at Hadlow College of Agriculture & Horticulture, Kent, was involved with the development work carried out by B. H. Howard, and I thus had the opportunity to follow the progress made. As a result, I am a strong supporter of chip budding as a reliable technique for open-ground budding of the majority of trees. Operators unfamiliar with the technique should use the method on a trial basis first—for example, by budding 50–100 rootstocks of each cultivar grown and then comparing the results with the standard budding method currently used. If the results are more successful, then the method can be introduced as a standard technique in the nursery. It is important to ensure that some sound practical instruction is provided beforehand. Sometimes there can be misleading results due, not to a poor technique, but to the materials used and the way in which the propagator is doing the operation. Some nursery operators found that poor results in early trials were due to the tying-in material and method of tying-in, rather than the technique itself.

Tying-in Materials

Research at East Malling Research Station and subsequent development work showed that the choice of tying-in material and method of tying-in were both critical. Early trials, some under the auspices of the Great Britain and Ireland Region of the International Plant Propagators' Society (I.P.P.S.), showed the value of using polyethylene tape compared with raffia, rubber strip, conventional degradable ties and P.V.C. strip. The standard tying-in material is either 2.5 cm (1″) or 1.3 cm (½″) wide clear or milky polyethylene tape. The width used depends largely on personal preference for handling and also on the size of the scion bud and diameter of rootstock. I find that the 1.3 cm (½″) tape is easier to manage and provides more flexibility in the tying movements.

The tape must be under tension while tying-in, and tied in tightly, especially just above and below the bud. As a general rule, the scion bud on the chip should be left exposed while ensuring that the cut surfaces are covered. This is particularly so for large and soft-budded subjects like *Betula* (Birch), *Prunus* (Cherry) and *Sorbus* (Mountain Ash) to prevent the pressure of the tie crushing the bud. Smaller harder buds like *Malus* (Apple, Crab Apple) can be covered but with somewhat reduced tension. It is advisable to cover the bud of *Malus* when budding in an area liable to attack by Red-bud Borer (*Thomasiniana oculiperda*).

Figure 17-21. The bud lifting away from one side of the rootstock is normally an indication of poor matching or loose tying-in (*Laburnum* × *watereri* 'Vossii').

Figure 17-22. A (right). The use of a degradable rubber strip for tying-in. Note that the tie covers the bud. B (far right). Natural degradation of the rubber strip normally begins 4–6 weeks after budding, depending on the climate.

Recently, East Malling Research Station and Rapidex Products Ltd., Cheshire, England, have worked together to formulate a suitable degradable rubber tie specifically for chip budding. This would reduce costs as the ties do not have to be physically removed. The criteria were that the tie must not be too thick or it would be difficult to handle, must be inexpensive, and able to sustain enough tension for a satisfactory union. There is less work with this type of tie as it does not have to be removed by hand.

Experiments so far have produced a tie that performs well in either width, providing that the chips can form a union quickly and the rootstocks make satisfactory growth. Initial results from samples given to some nursery operators in British Columbia and Oregon have also been good—even under the stronger sunlight conditions prevailing in these regions. The ties are unreliable if the rootstocks are of poor quality and have had a restriction in growth, for example, through lack of water or from herbicide damage—*Acer platanoides* 'Crimson King' (Crimson King Maple) is particularly sensitive to this. Light-degradable polyethylene tape has been found to be unsatisfactory as it does not deteriorate quickly enough.

Release of Ties

The optimum period for removal of the polyethylene tape is within 4–6 weeks after budding. This time period can be critical—if the ties are removed too early the bud chips will later peel away from the rootstock; if removed too late a stem constriction will occur as the tie bites into the stem.

I find that there is a temptation to remove the ties too early with some trees as the bud chips appear to be well united, particularly the cultivars of *Acer platanoides* (Norway Maple). This results in the upper and lower part of the chip beginning to peel away from the rootstock a few weeks later. The chip is then easily lifted away by early winter frosts. *Alnus* (Alder), *Fraxinus* (Ash) and *Prunus* (Cherry) are among the genera prone to forming a constriction should the tape be left on too long. This is even more liable to happen when a period of wet weather follows a very dry spell, conditions under which there is rapid stem caliper expansion of the rootstock. This causes distortion of the chip, and the weak point on the stem is prone to wind damage. I have noticed that such wind damage also splits the rootstock, making both chip and rootstock virtually useless.

The period during which the tie must be retained is increased if chip budding takes place later in the season. There is a case to be made for leaving the tie on until March if budding is done in early October—but in this instance it is best to cover the bud for protection and to prevent water accumulating in the folds of the tape.

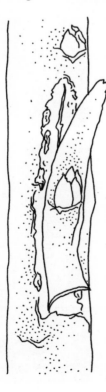

Diagram 17-3.
Removal of the ties too early means that the scion chip is likely to peel away from the rootstock at both the base and the apex.

Figure 17-23.
A severe constriction in the stem can develop as the rootstock caliper increases if polyethylene tape is not removed at the correct time (*Alnus glutinosa* cv.).

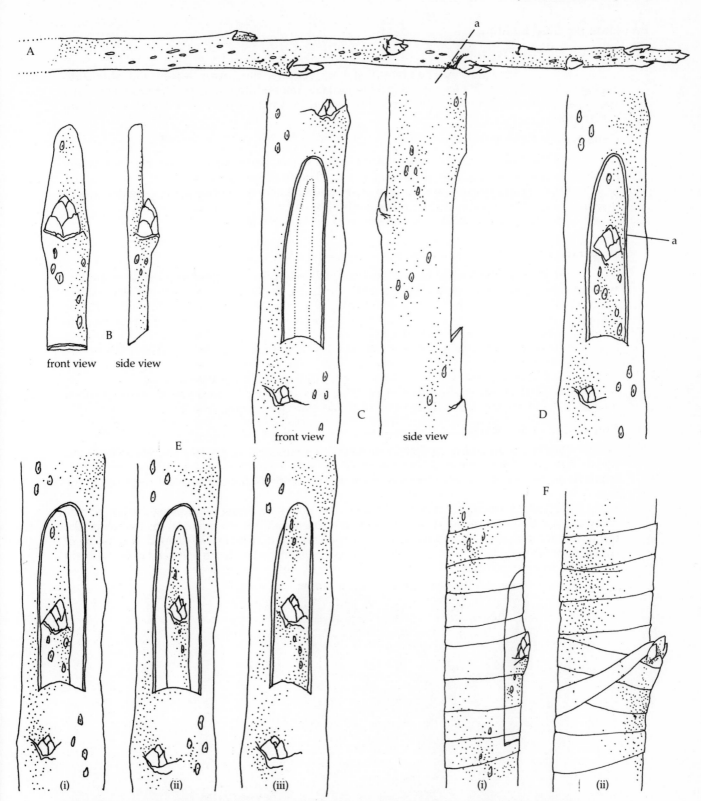

Diagram 17-4. Chip budding. A. The prepared bud stick ready for chip budding, showing (a) removal of the immature tip. B. Front and side views of the prepared scion (bud) chip. C. Front and side views of the prepared rootstock. D. Good matching-up of the scion (bud) chip and rootstock. Note (a) the ring of exposed rootstock tissue around the perimeter of the bud chip. E. Examples of correct and incorrect matching-up for scion of a different size from the rootstock. (i) Match the scion on one side of the cut only if the scion is smaller in width than the cut. (ii) Incorrect matching-up of a scion smaller in width than the cut. (iii) The scion was cut too long so that it extends above the apex of the cut on the rootstock. F. Examples of tying-in. (i) Small and hard buds are covered when tying-in with polyethylene tape. (ii) Soft and prominent buds are left exposed when tying-in with polyethylene tape.

Procedure for Chip Budding

Initial Rootstock Preparation

Use a knife (not the budding knife) to remove the lower leaves and shoots to approximately ·17.5 cm (7″) above soil level to facilitate the budding process. The production of a clean "leg" (length) of rootstock to receive the scion bud is best done as a separate operation beforehand.

Collection of Scion Wood (Budwood)

(1) Confirm the identification of the scion wood, particularly where there are many cultivars of one genus, e.g., *Sorbus* (Mountain Ash), *Prunus* (Cherry) or *Malus*.

(2) Use hand pruners or knife (not your budding knife) to remove semi-ripened shoots of the current year's wood containing an optimum of 8–15 buds.

(3) Wrap the shoots in damp sacking and place in the shade.

Preparation of Budsticks

(1) Remove the leaf lamina with a knife or hand pruners as close as possible to the bud without causing injury. There is a greater risk of injuring the buds if the leaves are removed by hand. However, good results have been achieved with trees such as *Sorbus* (Mountain Ash) by stripping off all the leaves by hand. The stripping should begin from the base of the budstick in order to reduce possible damage to the buds.

(2) Where applicable, remove the stipules, e.g., *Prunus avium* cvs. (Gean Cherry or Mazzard).

(3) Cut off and discard the unripened growth near the tip of the budstick.

(4) Tie the prepared budsticks in bundles, label and place in moist hessian in the shade or cool shed, or alternatively in polyethylene in a cold store for temporary storage.

Preparation of Rootstock

(1) Choose an area of smooth clean stem, approximately 10 cm (4″) above soil level, and make a cut 3 mm (⅛″) deep at an angle of 20–30° to form a small veneer. The site of this cut may either be on the side facing the inter-row pathway or on that facing the adjacent rootstock in the row.

(2) Make a second cut 3 mm (⅛″) deep and 4 cm (1½″) long by drawing the knife blade down to meet the basal veneer. This cut should match up with the one made on the bud chip. The top of this cut should be of an inverted "U"-shape and not narrow or "V"-shaped. It must be of sufficient depth to fully expose the woody tissue and adjustments in depth will need to be made on rootstocks with a thick rind.

Figure 17-24.
The wood on the rootstock is removed by holding the knife horizontally and drawing the blade down to the basal veneer formed by the first cut.

Preparation of Scion (Bud Chip)

(1) Hold the base of the budstick towards you, and make a 3 mm (⅛″) deep cut with an angle of 20–30° about 2 cm (¾″) below the scion bud.

(2) Make a second cut of similar length by cutting inwards for about 3 mm (⅛″) by drawing the knife down behind the bud to form a small veneer. Undue pressure when cutting beneath the bud can be relieved by removing the knife, returning the blade and then continuing to move the knife down to the veneer—however, this will slow down the operator's speed.

The ease with which the bud chips can be made varies considerably, depending very much on the diameter and shape of the budstick, and on the hardness of the wood. Bud chips of *Gleditsia triacanthos* cvs. (Honey Locust) are difficult to cut out, while *Sorbus* (Mountain Ash) cultivars present few difficulties. Some practice bud chips should be made prior to working on a particular scion in the nursery row.

(3) Hold the scion chip between the thumb and forefinger of the left hand, ensuring that the cut surface is not touched.

Figure 17-25.
The bud chip is prepared by drawing the knife down under the bud to the first cut. Note the central position of the bud on the chip and the index finger under the budstick to provide support.

Matching-up

The scion is placed so that a narrow margin of exposed cut surface of the rootstock tissue can be seen around the perimeter of the bud chip. The veneer on the rootstock holds the bud in place temporarily, thus freeing both hands for tying-in.

If the cut on the rootstock is not sufficiently long or wide enough, the tip of the blade may be carefully placed behind the bud chip and a sliver of wood removed, taking care not to dislodge the bud chip.

If the bud chip is much narrower than the rootstock, it should be matched up on one side only. A narrow cut on the rootstock to assist matching in small buds can normally be made by using only the tip of the knife blade.

Note that chip budding operators are expected to quickly develop the ability to cut rootstocks and scion chips·to exactly the right size.

Tying-in, Aftercare and Removal of Ties

(1) A 15–20 cm (6–8″) length of polyethylene tape, either 1.3 cm (½″) or 2.5 cm (1″) wide, is pre-cut or removed from the dispenser.

(2) Stretch the end of the tape over and beyond the basal cut, and begin tying-in under tension. Overlap the edges of the tape on each turn, applying pressure on the tape just above and below the bud chip. The bud itself is generally left exposed under most circumstances (see p. 481) but the cuts at the side are covered.

(3) Take the tape beyond the upper cut surface and complete the process with a half-hitch knot behind the upper part of the bud chip.

(4) The tie should be released 4–6 weeks later in most cases. This is usually done by pulling it away from the stem and cutting through the half-hitch knot.

Figure 17-26.
Union of a chip budded
Acer platanoides 'Crimson
King' (Crimson King
Maple) on *A. platanoides*
(Norway Maple)
rootstock after the first
season's (maiden)
growth. This was budded
in the previous summer.
(Reproduced by
permission of East
Malling Research Station,
Maidstone, Kent, U.K.)

Spring Chip Budding

Chip budding does not rely on the lifting of the rind and therefore spring chip budding offers an alternative to whip and tongue grafting. The procedure is essentially the same as for summer chip budding, but with the following modifications:—

(1) The scion chips are taken from one-year-old shoots of the previous year's growth. This normally means that the wood is collected in mid-winter and cold stored until the time of budding.

(2) The rootstock requires a full season's growth beforehand to ensure that it is well established to support the scion growth from the bud during the subsequent summer.

(3) The rootstock should be in growth, so the optimum period for spring chip budding is April/May.

(4) When tying-in, the bud of the chip should be left exposed to maximize maiden growth. The ties are removed 6–8 weeks after budding.

(5) Three weeks after the removal of the ties, the rootstocks are headed back either to a 10–15 cm (4–6") snag or just above the bud chip. This ensures that the scion bud breaks, otherwise the upper part of the rootstock will exert dominance, thus slowing down scion development and forcing the developing scion to grow out at a wide angle. It is important to ensure that the union has successfully united before heading back the rootstock.

Spring chip budding uses less scion material than conventional open-ground grafting and provides the opportunity to extend the budding season even further, thus taking some of the work load away from the summer. However, the vigor in growth is less than that obtained from a whip and tongue graft.

Two specific instances where spring chip budding could be used are as follows:—

(a) For cultivars of *Acer platanoides* (Norway Maple), which normally do not graft well in open ground.

(b) For *R. pseudoacacia* 'Frisia' (Black Locust cv.) where the soft scion wood in the summer renders it unsuitable for budding. I have seen 2.5 m (8') of growth after spring chip budding onto an established rootstock of *R. pseudoacacia* (Black Locust).

Spring chip budding should be done initially on a trial basis and the results carefully evaluated to see if it can be particularly useful for specific purposes.

STICK BUDDING (SHIELD GRAFTING)

The first time that I saw stick budding demonstrated was in Oregon, where it is being used as a specialist technique for open-ground budding and bench grafting of Japanese Maples. The technique could be described as a "hybrid" between whip grafting and T-budding in that a slanting cut is made at the base of a small scion with one, two or more pairs of buds which, in turn, is slipped between the two flaps of rind of a T-cut on the rootstock.

The technique is used in two situations. Firstly, as an alternative to normal T-budding onto 2- or 3-year-old seedling rootstocks in open ground. Secondly, in multiple or framework budding, using a relatively mature seedling about 5–6 years old. It is useful in cases where there are a number of unsold container plants, for example, of *Acer palmatum* 'Atropurpureum' (Red Japanese Maple). The nursery operator could framework stick bud *A. palmatum* 'Trompenburg' onto these unsold plants, thus changing the cultivar to one that may sell better at a future date. The rootstocks are container-grown and then brought into a shade structure, after which up to 15–35 scions may be budded onto each plant. Cultivars of *A. palmatum* such as 'Bloodgood', 'Irish Lace' and 'Osakazuki' may be propagated in this way.

Stick budding is carried out from mid-July to early September, by which time the scion wood will have hardened up. The scions need considerable care during preparation as difficulties can occur because the wood is hard, the stem is small and round, and a considerable amount of pith may be exposed. It is vital to use a sharp knife to obtain clean cuts.

Figure 17-27. Well-branched container-grown *Acer palmatum* (Japanese Maple) housed in a greenhouse for stick budding. (Iseli Nurseries, Boring, OR, U.S.A.)

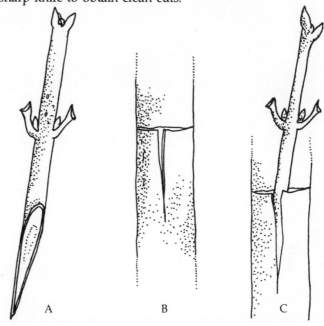

Diagram 17-5. Stick budding. A. The prepared scion with two pairs of buds and a sloping cut at the base. B. The prepared rootstock with horizontal and vertical cuts and lifted rind. C. The completed budding operation with the scion fitting snugly between the two flaps of rind on the rootstock. The cut surfaces of the scion and rootstock must be in direct contact with each other.

Budding Procedure

(1) Collect the scions using a small pair of pruners and cut off all the leaves, retaining a small length of petiole.

(2) Prepare small scions with one, two or more pairs of buds. Do not use either the apical or the basal pairs of buds on the budstick.

(3) Make a slanting cut, about 2 cm (¾") long, at the base of the scion.

(4) Make a T-cut in the normal manner on the rootstock, either 5 cm (2") above soil level for rootstocks grown in the open ground or as multiple cuts on the major framework of a more mature container-grown seedling.

(5) Tie in the bud with a rubber tie, ensuring that no gaps are left between each turn. Alternatively, 1.3 cm (½") polyethylene tape can be used. The bud should be left exposed in either case.

(6) Remove the tie after 4–6 weeks.

(7) Head back the rootstock in the following February to 15 cm (6″) above the bud, then to 5 cm (2″) above the bud one month later, with the final heading back being carried out two months later.

Figure 17-28. A (left). Stick budded *Acer palmatum* (Japanese Maple) after tying-in with a rubber strip. Note the half-hitch knot used to fasten off the strip. B (right). After removal of the tie. The short scion with two pairs of buds was slipped snugly between two flaps of rind, as in T-budding.

PATCH BUDDING

Patch budding is a specialized technique sometimes used for some tropical crops and for both pecans and walnuts in warm climates. A special two-bladed knife is used and may have either fixed or folding blades. A brief mention of the technique is made in case someone wishes to try it for ornamental walnuts—for example, *Juglans regia* 'Laciniata' (Cut-leaved Walnut).

The shield is much larger than in the techniques previously described. It is normally a square about 2.0–2.5 cm (¾–1″) wide with the scion bud in the center. Patch budding achieves matching of the cambium along all sides of the patch because it is a "substitution" method. The process is carried out in spring or late summer, but is dependent on the successful lifting of the rind from the woody tissue beneath. An appropriate cut is made on the rootstock to accommodate the scion. Full details on the application and procedure for the technique may be found in *Plant Propagation: Principles and Practice* (Chapter 13, 4th ed.) by H. T. Hartmann and D. E. Kester.

A modified technique, using a single-bladed knife, has been described by Ben Davis II (Ozark Nurseries, Oklahoma), who has had considerable success with *Diospyros kaki* (Japanese Persimmon), as well as with *Carya illinoinensis* (Pecan), and both *Juglans nigra* (Black Walnut) and *J. regia* (English or Persian Walnut). Experienced budders increased their work rate to 400–500 buds in an eight-hour day.

DOUBLE-WORKING BY BUDDING TO OVERCOME GRAFT INCOMPATIBILITY

These techniques have essentially been developed for fruit tree production, particularly pears where there are a number of cultivars that are incompatible with the Quince rootstocks. There are a few instances of double-working being successfully used in ornamental tree production, and it is useful if a specific incompatibility problem must be rectified by summer budding.

The principle of the technique is the placement of an intermediate sliver or shield of stem tissue between the scion and rootstock. This intermediate tissue is compatible with both scion and rootstock so that a union will form. Without the intermediate piece, the scion and rootstock would be unable to unite together to successfully form a permanent union. Additional information may be obtained by referring to pp. 149–150 and 233–236 in *The Grafter's Handbook* (4th ed.) by R. J. Garner.

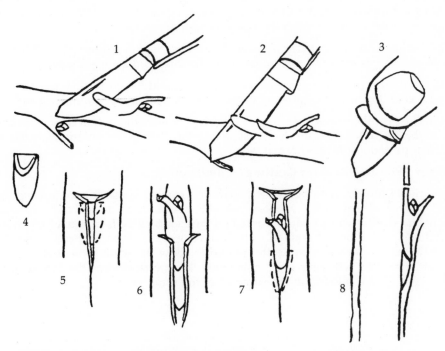

Diagram 17-6. Double-shield budding. 1. A shallow cut in a shoot of intermediate. 2. A second cut to procure the budless shield. 3. Shield held between knife and thumb. 4. Outer view of prepared shield. 5. Dotted line shows position of shield in the rootstock. 6. Bud shield on top of budless shield before sliding both down into place. 7. Shields home. 8. Diagrammatic side view. (Reproduced by permission of R. J. Garner from *The Grafter's Handbook,* 4th ed. rev., Faber & Faber Ltd., London.©)

(a) Double-Shield Budding

The double-shield budding technique was developed at the East Malling Research Station by R. J. Garner during the late 1940s and 1950s. There are three basic stages in the procedure.

(1) A small bud-less shield is cut and removed from the "intermediate budstick" in such a way that one side has a completely cut surface while the other is only partially cut, being made as a veneer from the first cut.

(2) The shield, with the small veneer cut at the top, is placed between the two flaps of rind near the top of the vertical cut in the rootstock.

(3) The normal bud shield is cut and slipped into the flaps of rind, ensuring that it is on the outside of the intermediate shield. It is then carefully pushed down, causing the intermediate shield to travel ahead until the intermediate shield reaches the bottom of the vertical cut. Tying-in is then carried out in the normal way.

(b) Nicolin Double-Shield Budding

The Nicolin method was developed after R. J. Garner developed the double-shield budding method. It is somewhat similar to the previous method in that the intermediate tissue is a bud-less sliver that has been pre-cut on both sides. The procedure is as follows:—

(i) The bud is sliced off the intermediate budstick. A second slicing cut is made to form a sliver of wood about 1.5 mm (1/16″) deep.

(ii) The intermediate sliver of wood is placed between the two flaps of rind of the normal T-cut on the rootstock, and the scion bud shield matched to the outer cut. Tying-in is then carried out in the normal way.

It is likely that a similar intermediate sliver of wood and the same principle could be used when chip budding.

(c) Laminate Budding

This method was described in 1959 by D. B. White at Iowa State University when it was found that the double-shield and the Nicolin techniques did not fulfill their expectations under their conditions. It differs from the previous techniques described in that it is carried out in two stages at approximately 3-week intervals. The procedure is as follows:—

(i) Multiple bud shields of the scion are budded in a spiral fashion, about 7.5 cm (3″) apart, onto a stem whose wood will be used for the intermediate stem piece.

(ii) About three weeks later, when the union should have callused, the scion bud shield and a very thin sliver of laminate of the intermediate tissue is removed with a knife.

(iii) This "Laminate Bud" of scion and attached intermediate stem tissue is then T-budded onto the desired rootstock, which will be compatible with the intermediate tissue. Tying-in is then carried out in the normal way.

(d) "Summer Budding/Dormant Grafting" Combination

Another technique described by R. J. Garner is carried out over two growing seasons, but has the disadvantage that a full growing season is lost. It is, however, very reliable. The intermediate bud shield (with a bud) is worked on the rootstock in the normal fashion and headed back the following year so that maiden growth develops. It is then reduced in height to a few centimeters (inches) in the next late winter period to allow the scion to be grafted onto it.

Another method is to whip and tongue graft the interstock onto the rootstock in the early spring. The scion is then budded in the summer of the same year.

APPENDIX

A Selected List of Scion/Rootstock Combinations for Shade Trees Propagated by Open-Ground Budding

SCION	ROOTSTOCK	COMMENTS
Acer negundo cvs. (Box Elder) [e.g., 'Aureo-marginatum']	*A. negundo* (Box Elder)	Variegated cvs. said to revert more following budding or grafting. Normally budded, but increasing emphasis on propagation by softwood cuttings.
A. palmatum cvs. (Japanese Maple) [e.g., 'Bloodgood']	*A. palmatum* (Japanese Maple)	Successfully open-ground budded in areas of N. America with reliable warm summers.
A. platanoides cvs. (Norway Maple) [e.g., 'Royal Red']	*A. platanoides* (Norway Maple)	*A. platanoides* rootstock used also for budding *A. amplum*, *A.* × *dieckii* (Dieck's Maple) and *A. lobelii*.
A. pseudoplatanus cvs. (Sycamore Maple) [e.g., 'Simon-Louis Frères']	*A. pseudoplatanus* (Sycamore Maple)	*A.* × *zoeschense* also successfully budded onto *A. pseudoplatanus* and *A. campestre* (Hedge Maple).
A. rubrum cvs. (Red Maple) [e.g., 'October Glory']	*A. rubrum* (Red Maple)	Increasing emphasis towards softwood cuttings partly because of delayed incompatibility of some cvs. on seedling rootstocks of *A. rubrum*. Layering still used.
A. saccharinum cvs. (Silver Maple) [e.g., 'Weirii', Weir Cutleaf Maple]	*A. saccharinum* (Silver Maple)	Often budded, but increasing emphasis towards softwood cutting propagation.
Aesculus × *carnea* 'Briotii' (Ruby Horse-chestnut)	*A. hippocastanum* (Common Horse-chestnut)	Some nurseries prefer to top-work *Aesculus*.
A. hippocastanum cvs. (Common Horse-chestnut) [e.g., 'Baumanii', Double-flowered Horse-chestnut]	*A. hippocastanum* (Common Horse-chestnut)	It is also recommended that the type species should be used as the rootstock (e.g., *A. indica* for *A. indica* cvs.) as *A. hippocastanum* is said to cause stem overgrowths at the union.
A. indica 'Sidney Pearce' (Indian Horse-chestnut cv.)	*A. hippocastanum* (Common Horse-chestnut)	
Betula pendula cvs. (Common Silver or European White Birch)	*B. pendula* (Common Silver or European White Birch)	Normally bench grafted but successfully budded in areas of N. America with reliable warm summers.
	B. pubescens (Downy Birch)	*B. pubescens* useful for wet soils.
B. spp. [e.g., *B. ermanii*; *B. utilis*, Himalayan Birch]	*B. pendula* (Common Silver or European White Birch)	Propagation by softwood cuttings is gaining popularity.
	B. pubescens (Downy Birch)	
Cornus 'Eddie's White wonder'	*C. florida* (Eastern Flowering Dogwood)	*C. florida* preferred to *C. nuttallii* (Western Flowering Dogwood) mainly because losses are less when transplanting.
C. florida cvs. (Eastern Flowering Dogwood) [e.g., 'Cherokee Chief', Red Flowering Dogwood]	*C. florida* (Eastern Flowering Dogwood)	Tests in British Columbia indicate that *C. kousa* may be a satisfactory rootstock.
C. kousa (Kousa Dogwood)	*C. florida* (Eastern Flowering Dogwood)	
Cotoneaster 'Hybridus Pendulus' (a.k.a. *C.* × *watereri* 'Pendulus')	*C. bullatus* (Hollyberry Cotoneaster) *C. frigidus* (Himalayan Cotoneaster)	*C. bullatus* mostly bottom-worked, *C. frigidus* mostly top-worked due to stronger stem. *C. bullatus* very prone to excess suckering.

SCION	ROOTSTOCK	COMMENTS
		The 'Watereri' group of Cotoneasters (e.g., *C.* 'St. Monica') are sometimes budded although most are propagated by cuttings. *C.* 'Hybridus Pendulus' successfully propagated by cuttings.
Crataegus spp. & cvs. e.g., *C. laevigata* 'Coccinea Flore Pleno' (Paul's Scarlet Hawthorn) *C.* × *mordenensis* 'Toba' (Toba Hawthorn) *C.* × *prunifolia* (Plum-leaf Hawthorn)	*C. monogyna* (Common Hawthorn) *C. pedicellata* (a.k.a. *C. coccinea*) (Scarlet Hawthorn)	*C. monogyna* can give unreliable anchorage to trees. *C. pedicellata* (*C. coccinea*) gives very coarse root system to trees and should be used only if absolutely necessary.
Fraxinus americana cvs. (White Ash) [e.g., 'Rose Hill']	*F. americana* (White Ash) *F. excelsior* (European Ash) *F. pennsylvanica* var. *lanceolata* (Green Ash)	
F. excelsior cvs. (European Ash) [e.g., 'Aurea']	*F. americana* (White Ash) *F. excelsior* (European Ash) *F. pennsylvanica* var. *lanceolata* (Green Ash)	
F. 'Moraine' (Moraine Ash)	*F. americana* (White Ash) *F. excelsior* (European Ash) *F. pennsylvanica* var. *lanceolata* (Green Ash)	
F. ornus cvs. (Flowering or Manna Ash) [e.g., 'Arie Peters']	*F. americana* (White Ash) *F. excelsior* (European Ash) *F. pennsylvanica* var. *lanceolata* (Green Ash)	*F. ornus* rootstocks sometimes used but *F. excelsior* gives greater vigor.
F. oxycarpa 'Raywood' (Claret or Raywood Ash)	*F. americana* (White Ash) *F. excelsior* (European Ash) *F. pennsylvanica* var. *lanceolata* (Green Ash)	If *F. oxycarpa* rootstocks are not available. *F. excelsior* preferable to *F. americana* and *F. pennsylvanica* var. *lanceolata* as an unsightly union is said to occur due to stem overgrowth.
F. pennsylvanica var. *lanceolata* 'Patmore'	*F. americana* (White Ash) *F. excelsior* (European Ash) *F. pennsylvanica* var. *lanceolata* (Green Ash)	In England, *F. pennsylvanica* var. *lanceolata* rootstocks are generally recommended for *F. pennsylvancia* var. *lanceolata* cvs.
F. 'Westhof's Glorie'	*F. americana* (White Ash) *F. excelsior* (European Ash) *F. pennsylvanica* var. *lanceolata* (Green Ash)	
Gleditsia triacanthos var. *inermis* cvs. (Thornless Honey Locust) [e.g., 'Ruby Lace', Ruby Lace Honey Locust]	*G. triacanthos* (Honey Locust)	Some propagators prefer *G. triacanthos* var. *inermis* (Thornless Honey Locust) as the percentage success rate is higher and there are no thorns.
× *Laburnocytisus adamii*	*L. anagyroides* (Common Laburnum)	
Laburnum anagyroides cvs. (Common Laburnum) [e.g., 'Aureum']	*L. anagyroides* (Common Laburnum)	*Cytisus battandieri* (Atlas or Moroccan Broom) and *Piptanthus nepalensis* (*P. laburnifolius*) (Evergreen Laburnum) are occasionally budded onto *L. anagyroides* rootstock.

SCION	ROOTSTOCK	COMMENTS
L. × *watereri* 'Vossii' (Voss' Long-cluster Golden-chain Tree)	*L. anagyroides* (Common Laburnum)	
Liquidambar stryaciflua cvs. (American Sweet Gum) [e.g., 'Worplesdon']	*L. styraciflua* (American Sweet Gum)	Increasing emphasis on propagation by softwood cuttings.
Malus spp. & cvs. e.g., *M. floribunda* (Japanese Flowering Crab Apple) *M.* 'John Downie' *M.* 'Royalty' *M. toringoides* (Cut-leaf Crab Apple)	M.M.106 M.M.111 M.25 *M.* 'Antonovka' *M. baccata* (Siberian Crab Apple) *M. sylvestris* (Crab Apple) (& selected strains, e.g., 'Bittenfelder')	*M.* 'Antonovka' or *M.* 'Columbia' are largely used in N. America because of ability to withstand very cold temperatures. *M.* 'Columbia' gives a coarse root system to trees. Occasionally incompatibility occurs, e.g., *M. tschonoskii* (Tschonoski Crab Apple) on M.25.
Prunus (a) Almonds *P. dulcis* cvs. [e.g., 'Roseoplena', Double Almond]	Brompton St. Julien A *P. dulcis* (Almond) *P. persica* (Peach)	
(b) Apricots *P. armeniaca* cvs. [e.g., 'Flore Pleno']	*P. armeniaca* (Apricot) Brompton St. Julien A *P. persica* (Peach)	The Japanese Flowering Apricots (e.g., *P. mume* 'Beni-shi-don') are successfully worked on *P. persica* and *P. cerasifera* (Myrobalan Plum). St. Julien A is said to produce a smaller tree.
(c) Bird Cherries *P. padus* cvs. [e.g., 'Watereri']	*P. padus* (European Bird Cherry)	Increasing emphasis towards cutting propagation but vigor is generally not as great. *P. padus* very prone to excess suckering.
(d) Cherries Includes many spp. & cvs., e.g., *P. sargentii* (Sargent Cherry) *P.* × *schmittii* *P.* × *yedoensis* (Japanese Cherry) *P.* × *hillieri* 'Spire' *P. subhirtella* 'Autumnalis' (Autumn Flowering Higan Cherry) *P. serrulata* 'Amanogawa' (Amanogawa Cherry) *P. serrulata* 'Kwanzan' (Kwanzan or Kanzan Cherry) *P.* 'Okame'	*P. avium* (Mazzard, Gean Cherry) *P. avium* Mazzard F12/1 *P.* 'Colt'	Some doubt regarding hardiness of *P.* 'Colt' in cold climates. Virus-tested seed should be used to produce *P. avium* seedlings.
(e) Choke Cherries *P. virginiana* cvs. [e.g., 'Shubert']	*P. padus* (European Bird Cherry) *P. virginiana* (Choke Cherry)	Increasing emphasis on softwood cutting propagation but vigor not generally as great. *P. padus* very prone to excess suckering.
(f) Peaches *P. persica* cvs. [e.g., 'Klara Mayer']	*P. persica* (Peach) Brompton St. Julien A	
(g) Plums (Cherry Plums) *P. cerasifera* 'Nigra' (Black Myrobalan Plum) *P.* × *blireiana* (Flowering or Blireiana Plum)	*P. cerasifera* (Myrobalan Plum) Myrobalan B St. Julien A	Many ornamental plums can be raised successfully from winter deciduous hardwood cuttings in heated bins.
(h) Others *P.* × *amygdalo-persica* 'Pollardii'	*P. persica* (Peach) St. Julien A	

SCION	ROOTSTOCK	COMMENTS
P. triloba (Flowering Almond)	Myrobalan B *P. cerasifera* (Myrobalan Plum) St. Julien A Brompton	

Pyrus calleryana cvs. (Callery Pear)
[e.g., 'Chanticleer']
	P. communis
	    (Common Pear)
	P. calleryana
	    (Callery Pear)
	P. ussuriensis
	    (Chinese or Sand Pear)
		Some populations of *P. communis* seedlings are known to give some incompatibility. *P. communis* is susceptible to Fireblight in N. America. *P. communis* 'Kirschensaller Moskbirne' is a recommended seedling selection used in Europe.

P. salicifolia 'Pendula'
    (Weeping Willow-leaved Pear)
	P. communis
	    (Common Pear)
	P. calleryana
	    (Callery Pear)
	P. ussuriensis
	    Chinese or Sand Pear)
		Cydonia oblonga (Common Quince) seedlings reported to be successful. Incompatibility arises with vegetatively-raised Quince rootstocks—overcome by using an interstock of *P. communis* 'Beaurré Hardy'.

Robinia hispida vars. & cvs.
    (Rose Acacia)
    [e.g., var. *macrophylla*, Smooth Rose Acacia]
	R. pseudocacia
	    (Black Locust)	

R. pseudocacia cvs.
    (Black Locust)
    [e.g., 'Frisia']
	R. pseudocacia
	    (Black Locust)
		Normally grafted, but respond well to spring chip budding.

Sorbus
 	
(a) Aucuparia Section
    (Pinnate, numerous leaves)
    e.g.,
    S. × *arnoldiana* cvs.
        [e.g., 'Apricot Queen']
    S. aucuparia 'Asplenifolia'
        (European Mountain Ash cv.)
    S. commixta
    S. hupehensis 'Rosea'
        (Red Hupeh Mountain Ash)
	S. aucuparia
	    (European Mountain Ash)
		S. americana (American Mountain Ash) and *S. intermedia* (Swedish White Beam) have been used successfully as rootstocks, but *S. aucuparia* must be used for *S. aucuparia* 'Rossica Major', *S. decora*, *S.* 'Joseph Rock' and *S. pohuashanensis*.

(b) Aria Section
    (Simple & compound leaves)
    e.g.,
    S. aria 'Lutescens'
    S. aria 'John Mitchell'
    S. hybrida 'Gibbsii'
	S. aria
	    (White Beam)
	S. intermedia
	    (Swedish White Beam)
		S. aria 'John Mitchell' and 'Wilfrid Fox' have caused incompatibility problems on *S. intermedia*.
		S. hybrida 'Gibbsii' is also compatible on *S. aucuparia*.
		
		S. latifolia (Fontainebleau Service Tree) has been used when shortage of usual rootstock occurs, but there are conflicting opinions on its suitability. *S. latifolia* said to be suitable for *S. torminalis* (Wild Service or Chequer Tree).
		Crataegus is inferior due to poor anchorage and unreliable compatibility.

Tilia spp.
 	
T. amurensis (Amur Linden)
	T. cordata
	    (Small-leaved European or Little-leaf Linden)
	T. × *europaea*
	    (European Linden)	

T. cordata cvs.
    (Small-leaved European or Little-leaf Linden)
    [e.g., 'Rancho', Rancho Linden)
	T. cordata
	    (Small-leaved European or Little-leaf Linden)
	T. platyphyllos
	    (Large-leaved Linden)
		Incompatibility problems have occurred when *T. cordata* and some small-leaved species have been worked on *T. platyphyllos*. Compatible clones of *T. cordata* and *T. platyphyllos* are now being developed.

SCION	ROOTSTOCK	COMMENTS
T. × *euchlora* (Crimean Linden)	*T. cordata* (Small-leaved European or Little-leaf Linden) *T. platyphyllos* (Large-leaved Linden)	
T. mongolica (Mongolian Linden)	*T. cordata* (Small-leaved European or Little-leaf Linden) *T.* × *europaea* (European Linden)	
T. americana cvs. (American Linden) [e.g., 'Redmond']	*T. americana* (American Linden) *T. platyphyllos* (Large-leaved Linden)	*T. platyphyllos* said to be generally more reliable for the larger-leaved species.
T. petiolaris (Pendent or (Weeping Silver Linden)	*T. americana* (American Linden) *T. platyphyllos* (Large-leaved Linden)	
T. platyphyllos cvs. (Large-leaved Linden) [e.g., 'Rubra', Red-twigged Linden]	*T. americana* (American Linden) *T. platyphyllos* (Large-leaved Linden)	
T. tomentosa (Silver Linden)	*T. americana* (American Linden) *T. platyphyllos* (Large-leaved Linden)	
Ulmus glabra cvs. (Scotch or Wych Elm) [e.g., 'Lutescens']	*U. glabra* (Scotch or Wych Elm) *U. pumila* (Siberian Elm)	*U. pumila* is well adapted for use in cold climates.
U. × *hollandica* cvs. (Dutch Elm) [e.g., 'Major', Dutch Elm]	*U. glabra* (Scotch or Wych Elm) *U. pumila* (Siberian Elm)	
Zelkova serrata cvs. (Japanese Zelkova) [e.g., 'Village Green']	*Z. serrata* (Japanese Zelkova)	There are opposing opinions on the suitability of *Ulmus* spp. as rootstocks for *Zelkova*.

NOTE: Most species are normally winter grafted if summer budding fails. However, some propagators have discovered that a number of species can give unreliable results when open-ground grafted. These species include *Acer, Betula, Cotoneaster, Laburnum* and *Fraxinus.*

REFERENCES AND SUGGESTED SOURCES FOR FURTHER READING

Agricultural Training Board, U.K. no date. *T-Budding.* Trainee Guide NSP.1.A.5. Agricultural Training Board, Beckenham, Kent, U.K.

———. no date. *Inverted T-Budding.* Trainee Guide NSP.1.A.6. Agricultural Training Board, Beckenham, Kent, U.K.

———. no date. *Chip Budding.* Trainee Guide NSP.1.A.7. Agricultural Training Board, Beckenham, Kent, U.K.

Agriculture Canada. 1968. *Fruit Tree Propagation.* Publication No. 1282. Agriculture Canada, Ottawa, Ontario.

Baldwin, I. & J. B. Stanley. 1982. Conserve body movement to work more effectively. *Amer. Nurseryman* **155**(7): 45–47 (April 1, 1982).

Davis, B., II. 1962. The modified patch bud. *Comb. Proc. Pl. Prop. Soc.* **12**: 136–139.

Flemer, W., III. 1980. Linden propagation—a review. *Comb. Proc. Inter. Pl. Prop. Soc.* **30**: 333–336.

Garner, R. J. 1979. 4th ed. rev. *The Grafter's Handbook.* Faber & Faber Ltd., London.

Gilbert, D. H. 1970. A guide to commercial rose bush production—Parts 1–3. *Garden. Chron.* (February, March and April, 1970).

Gudziak, A. 1981. *Illustrated Techniques in Budding and Grafting.* Department of Plant Science and Faculty of Forestry, University of Manitoba, Winnipeg, Manitoba.

Haines, S. 1969. Problems in Norway Maple and Sycamore-maple propagation. *Comb. Proc. Inter. Pl. Prop. Soc.* **19:** 206–207.

————. 1973. Standard trees by budding. *Area Meeting Proc., Inter. Pl. Prop. Soc., G. B. & I. Region,* pp. 1–6.

Hartmann, H. T. & D. E. Kester. 1983. 4th ed. *Plant Propagation: Principles and Practices.* Prentice-Hall, Inc., Englewood Cliffs, N.J.

Hopperton, H. W. 1971. New techniques in budding difficult trees. *Comb. Proc. Inter. Pl. Prop. Soc.* **21:** 360–361.

Howard, B. H. 1977. Chip budding fruit and ornamental trees. *Comb. Proc. Inter. Pl. Prop. Soc.* **27:** 357–365.

Mathies, J. 1975. Field budding practices. *Comb. Proc. Inter. Pl. Prop. Soc.* **25:** 31–32.

MacKay, I. 1962. The collection, storage and use of budwood. *Comb. Proc. Pl. Prop. Soc.* **12:** 142–144.

McMillan Browse, P. D. A. 1973. Standard trees by budding. *Area Meeting Proc., Inter. Pl. Prop. Soc., G. B. & I. Region,* pp. 1–14.

Ministry of Agriculture, Fisheries & Food, U.K. 1969. 5th ed. *Fruit Tree Raising. Rootstocks and Propagation.* Bull. No. 135. Her Majesty's Stationery Office, London, U.K.

Nicholson, H. 1959. Propagation of selected varieties of Honeylocust by budding. *Proc. Pl. Prop. Soc.* **9:** 58–61.

————. 1977. Field budding of Dogwood. *Comb. Proc. Inter. Pl. Prop. Soc.* **27:** 236–238.

Ross, D. M. 1980. Getting down to budding. *Comb. Proc. Inter. Pl. Prop. Soc.* **30:** 553–555.

White, D. B. 1959. "Laminate budding", a technique for budding incompatible woody plants. *Proc. Pl. Prop. Soc.* **9:** 194–197.

Widmoyer, F. B. 1962. Anatomical aspects of budding and grafting. *Comb. Proc. Pl. Prop. Soc.* **12:** 132–135.

Chapter 18

OPEN-GROUND GRAFTING

Grafting outdoors in the open ground is a major propagation technique in the commercial nursery. Its chief role is in the propagation of fruit and ornamental trees, and, in some instances, ornamental shrubs. The overall uses of open-ground grafting are summarized below.

(1) The production of shade tree cultivars in cases where the scion bud has died after budding during the previous summer. The term "grafting over" is used for the grafting of a rootstock in such a situation—it represents a "back-up" technique and provides a second chance to propagate trees in the open ground. Trees with which I have experienced problems from summer budding have been *Prunus sargentii* (Sargent Cherry), *Aesculus* × *carnea* 'Briotii' (Ruby Horse-chestnut) and *Malus* cultivars—the latter when Red-bud Borer (*Thomasiniana oculiperda*) killed the bud and bud shield shortly after budding (see p. 475). However, not all shade trees will success-fully graft in the open ground, particularly the cultivars of *Acer platanoides* (Norway Maple) such as *A. platanoides* 'Crimson King' (Crimson King Maple).

(2) The top-working (high-working) of trees, particularly those with a weeping habit—for example, *Fraxinus excelsior* 'Pendula' (Weeping European Ash), *Laburnum anagyroides* 'Pendulum' (syn. *L. vulgare* 'Pendula') (Weeping Golden-chain Tree) and *Prunus subhirtella* 'Pendula Rubra' (Red Weeping Cherry). Grafting is sometimes preferred to budding for such trees because a more substantial weeping effect can be obtained in the maiden year (see Chapter 19 on top-working).

(3) To propagate trees that are difficult to work with in conventional budding. For example, *Robinia pseudoacacia* 'Frisia' (Black Locust cv.) in which the bud is very small and the scion wood soft and easily bruised in the summer. The development of spring chip budding may re-duce the importance of this reason for grafting.

(4) Open-ground grafting sometimes enables the grower to produce multi-stemmed trees more easily early in the trees' life. The trees that fall into this category are generally fastigiate in habit, such as *Prunus serrulata* 'Amanogawa' (Amanogawa Cherry).

(5) It is used in the double-working of trees to overcome graft incompatibility (see p. 453 and p. 489).

Figure 18-1. Open-ground grafted ornamental weeping *Prunus* top-worked onto *P. avium* Mazzard F12/1. Note that both the top of the scion and the cut surfaces have been waxed over.

Source of Scion Wood

Scion wood may be obtained from three sources as indicated below.

(a) Mother Tree Scion Orchard (see p. 464)

(b) Trees in Nursery Rows—Trees already worked and intended for sale provide a ready source of scion wood when 2 or 3 seasons of scion growth have developed from the time of budding or grafting. Sufficient side shoots are normally available along the main stem or within the crown of the tree at this stage to allow some to be removed without reducing the overall quality of the tree. This widely used method is convenient and does not rely on the necessity to provide extra land on the nursery.

Again, one very important consideration in this method is to ensure that clear, methodical and concise instructions are given when collecting the scion wood, otherwise confusion may occur and result in mis-named scion wood. There are two reasons why such a mistake could happen. Firstly, if there is no clearly defined change between cultivars within a single row—the last tree of one cultivar may be confused with the first tree of the next. Secondly, confusion may occur if worked and un-worked trees are allowed to grow next to each other. The differences between dormant leafless wood of different cultivars of, for example, *Sorbus* (Mountain Ash) or *Malus* (Apple, Crab Apple) are not easily distinguished by an inexperienced person. The risk can be reduced either by tagging the un-worked trees with colored weatherproof tape or paint or by removing them from the row. It is advisable to delegate the task of organizing the collection, and the distribution of the scion wood whenever budding or grafting is in operation, to a reliable employee.

(c) Collection from Outside Sources—Material obtained this way gives the propagator more "unknowns" and means that more homework has to be done. One has to be sure that the source is reliable in providing healthy, true-to-name material. There should be few problems when obtaining virus-free material, but more care needs to be taken when scions are acquired from other establishments.

The scion wood may have to be shipped, in which case care has to be taken in packaging to avoid desiccation and heat build-up while in transit. Furthermore, it is advisable to try and check for the following one or two seasons that the purchased scion wood is true to type and that it compares favorably with the clone that already exists in the nursery. Any problem over naming will be much more difficult to rectify once such wood has been used for further propagation. It is important to ensure that a record is kept of the source and date on which it came to the nursery, so that there will be a reference available either for further purchase or should the material have to be discarded.

Collection of Dormant Scion Wood.

Incorrect collection of scion wood and its subsequent handling can be easily overlooked but can result in poor results after grafting. The secret is to be observant and methodical during this stage, as well as following the grafting success rate. If grafting results are not satisfactory, the procedure for collection of materials should be assessed as a possible cause, and amendments made the following year if necessary.

The time to collect scion wood can be gauged to some extent by an evaluation of the range of trees growing within one's own geographical area. In both Britain and southwestern British Columbia, I have noted that the Myrobalan Plums (e.g., *Prunus cerasifera* cvs.) very quickly flower and flush in late winter after a mild period of weather. These are quickly followed, in order of sequence, by the ornamental Peaches (e.g., *P. persica*), Almonds (e.g., *P. dulcis* cvs.) and Apricots (e.g., *P. mume* cvs., Japanese Flowering Apricot), and a number of the species such as *P. sargentii* (Sargent Cherry). Next in sequence come the Maples (e.g., *Acer platanoides* cvs., Norway Maple), Crab Apples (e.g., *Malus floribunda*, Japanese Flowering Crab Apple), Mountain Ashes (e.g., *Sorbus aucuparia*, European Mountain Ash), White Beams (*Sorbus aria* types), Hawthorns (*Crataegus laevigata* cvs.), and Horse-chestnuts (*Aesculus hippocastanum* cvs.). Finally, in the late spring come the Ashes (e.g., *Fraxinus excelsior* cvs., European Ash), Oaks (*Quercus* spp.), Black Locusts (*Robinia pseudoacacia* cvs.), and the Honey Locusts (*Gleditsia triacanthos* cvs.). This sequence of flowering and flushing of growth indicates the variable timing of sap rise in different species. A mild winter, or a long mild period following a very cold period, can quickly promote sap rise and swelling of the terminal and axillary buds. Scion wood ideally should be collected before sap flow occurs and certainly well before any swelling of the buds, otherwise the scions tend to prematurely flush and die-back after grafting. The exact timing for collection will depend on the geographical location—for instance, in southeastern England the wood was collected between mid-December and mid-January, weather conditions permitting.

A satisfactory procedure for the collection of scion wood is as follows:—

(1) Ensure that the scion wood to be collected is correctly named.

(2) Use hand pruners to cut healthy one-year-old vigorous but well-ripened scion wood (shoots) about 60–90 cm (2–3') long.

(3) Tie the scions into bundles of 25 or 50 with the base of the shoots in a uniform plane.

(4) Label each bundle, using weatherproof material.

(5) Store the scions in cold storage (see next section) or heel into a well-drained medium so that they are buried to a depth of 15–20 cm (6–8"), draw in the medium and firm to ensure good contact with the bundles and to lessen the risk of drying out. Ideally, the heeling-in site should be sheltered and north-facing to lessen the risk of temperature variations. It should also be rodent-proofed—I have seen severe damage to Apple, Cherry and Ash scion wood by mice when sufficient precautions were not taken.

In areas of extreme cold, such as eastern Canada and northeastern America, scion wood may be collected and cold stored in the late fall, thus avoiding possible cold temperature damage to the material. Also, milder but exposed areas can present problems when cold weather regularly damages the shoots. In this case, scion wood of cultivars such as *Fraxinus excelsior* 'Jaspidea' (Golden Ash), *Gleditsia triacanthos* cvs. (Honey Locust) and *Robinia pseudoacacia* cvs. (Black Locust) could also be collected in the late fall.

Cold Storage of Scion Wood

A temperature-controlled cold storage facility, such as a domestic refrigerator or a large direct or indirect (jacketed) cold store, is used for the storage of bare-root plant material. Advantage should be taken of such a facility for the storage of scion wood.

There are basically two different techniques for cold storing scion wood after it has been collected:—

(1) Boxes made of plastic or wood are partially filled with moist peat moss, sphagnum moss or sand, or a mixture of, for example, equal parts of peat moss and sand. The scion wood is surface-dried, laid in the box and covered with a thin layer of the medium or some form of sacking material. The boxes are then stored at an optimum temperature of 1–2°C (34–36°F). [This technique is an adaptation of a procedure once recommended by Agriculture Canada's Central Experimental Farm in Ottawa.]

(2) A more convenient method is to use polyethylene bags. A small quantity of water is placed in a bag of sufficient size and then shaken out, leaving a few droplets to provide some humidity. The scion wood is surface-dried and then placed into the bag, which is sealed, labelled and placed into the cold storage facility at 0–1°C (32–34°F). [It has recently been suggested in Holland that lower storage temperatures of −4 to −3°C (25–26°F) will give improved results.]

Little information has been recorded on the success rate for different genera at different lengths of time in cold storage, so the propagator's own observations should be noted. *Prunus sargentii* (Sargent Cherry) is one tree that has shown deterioration of the scion wood during storage. Factors that contribute in part to the final storage success include degree of ripeness of the wood, moisture, temperature levels, disease infection and length of time of storage.

R. J. Garner recommended a number of treatments to help ensure that scion wood is free from pests and diseases, and these are worthy of repeating here. A successful spray program in the nursery rows or mother plant area will do much to reduce losses. Aphids may be controlled by immersing the bundles in a nicotine and soap solution comprising 15 g (½ oz) 98% nicotine in 40–50 litres (8–10 Imp. gals) water. A greater threat is fungal attack, for example, *Botrytis*. R. J. Garner recommends that the scions be immersed in captan (Orthocide®), dodine (Cyprex®) or ferbam (Fermate®), using the optimum recommended spray concentration. Other compounds may also be used. It is important to ensure that the wood is surface dried before storage. Appropriate safety clothing and equipment *must* be used when necessary.

Dusting with fungicides is an alternative method to reduce disease infection. Desiccation of wood may be a problem during storage, and a spray or dip of an anti-desiccant compound made up of a polyvinyl-resin complex, such as Claritol®, S.600® or Wilt-Pruf® could be helpful.

Time of Year

The optimum period for whip and tongue grafting is late February to late March, but allowances should be made for geographical location. However, some propagators have found that the best results are obtained by grafting later in the season when the outdoor air temperature has risen to around 14–15.5°C (58–60°F). The grafting period can be extended well into April if:—

(i) A prolonged cold winter delays the natural bud break period of trees, especially on exposed sites.

(ii) Facilities exist for the cold storage of healthy scion wood. However, excessive rootstock growth and activity as a result of delaying the grafting period will reduce the percentage success rate, even when using cold-stored dormant scion wood.

(iii) Trees have a natural late bud break, for example, *Robinia pseudoacacia* cvs. (Black Locust).

Whip and tongue grafting has occasionally been carried out in the fall, and I have seen favorable results with some *Prunus* (Cherry) and *Aesculus* (Buckeye, Horse-chestnut) cultivars. The optimum period for fall grafting would be mid-September to early October. The two benefits of fall grafting are that it reduces the amount of late winter/spring grafting the following year, and that a considerable proportion of the tissues between stock and scion will unite prior to the onset of winter conditions. The latter assists in preventing losses over the winter period and helps in promoting early and more even scion growth the following year by allowing earlier water and nutrient uptake to the scion.

However, the propagator is best advised to rely on the late winter/spring grafting period. Fall grafting has a place in the specific circumstances outlined above, but there is little published information on its success for a range of genera and therefore it is not possible to recommend its use as an established practice.

WHIP AND TONGUE GRAFTING

The most common method used for open-ground grafting is the whip and tongue graft. This technique will be described in detail, but the principles involved are also important for the alternative methods of grafting.

Figure 18-2. Open-ground whip and tongue grafting of ornamental trees. Note the custom-made wooden boxes in which the grafter can conveniently store scion wood and materials.

Grafting Procedure

Initial Rootstock Preparation

(1) Any failures in rootstocks budded the previous summer should be left intact and not headed back, so that the grafter can easily see them.

(2) Use hand or long-handled pruners to head back the rootstocks to a height of 10–12.5 cm (4–5″) above soil level. If the rootstocks are continuous in the row, the grafting procedure may be speeded up by heading back sufficient stocks for 1–2 hours work.

(3) Use a knife to clean up the remainder of the rootstock by removing any shoots or snags. The grafting knife should not be used at this stage, otherwise the blade will lose its sharpened edge. A dry coarse rag is useful for removing material that may have adhered to the stem.

(4) Collect and dispose of all prunings from the working area to avoid subsequent infection by Coral Spot (*Nectria cinnabarina*). Nursery prunings are a prime source of infection and dispersal of this disease.

Scion Preparation

(1) Check to ensure the scion material is healthy and true-to-name.

(2) Use a grafting knife to remove the unripened scion tip and damaged wood. Cut the scion into pieces 10–12.5 cm (4–5″) long, with the uppermost cut sloping away from the bud. Each piece should have a minimum of 3 and a maximum of 5 buds. (However, this will depend on the species being grafted.)

(3) Place the semi-prepared scions into a box so the grafter can take them down the row.

(4) Make a sloping cut about 5 cm (2″) deep through the scion. The grafter should attempt to achieve three goals when making this cut:—

(a) The creation of a "stock bud" using the lowermost bud on the scion. This should be sited halfway down the cut surface but on the opposite side so that it has a chance of surviving should the scion be accidentally snapped at the top of the rootstock at a later date.

(b) The siting of the terminal bud of the scion towards the center of the rootstock after tying-in—this helps to achieve a straighter stem at the base of the tree.

(c) A straight level cut, both on the scion and the rootstock. One way to achieve this when preparing the scion is by keeping the elbows out in a level plane when making the cut. Rounded or uneven cuts are often caused when the grafter moves the elbows round to the back of the body and uses a hurried jerky motion.

(5) Make a downward cut about 1.0 cm (⅜″) long starting 1.0 cm (⅜″) from the top of the sloping cut, thus forming a tongue. This tongue needs to be sufficiently strong so that it will not weaken when interlocked with the rootstock. The depth and length may have to be varied according to the plant being grafted. The tongues on the scion and rootstock hold them together so that the grafter has both hands free for tying-in.

Rootstock Preparation

(1) Use the grafting knife to make a fresh cut across the top of the rootstock. If the rootstock is wider in diameter than the scion, some grafters make a shallow slanting cut on the side opposite to where the grafting cut will be made, thus removing the horizontal sharp edge. This will allow more efficient tying-in when using 2.5 cm (1″) wide polyethylene tape as a closer seal is obtained.

(2) Stand over the rootstock, select the straightest and "cleanest" area on one side of it, and make an upward movement with the knife to form a shallow sloping cut that is slightly shorter than the one on the scion. This cut is normally made right through the rootstock if it is of similar diameter to the scion.

(3) Make a tongue similar to that on the scion but beginning about 0.6 cm (¼″) down from the top of the sloping cut. The difference in the siting of the tongue on the rootstock helps to ensure that a small area of exposed scion about 0.3–0.5 cm (1/8–1/5″) long is left above the top of the rootstock. This is often referred to as the "church window". The advantage of the "church window" is that additional callus tissue develops between it and the top of the rootstock, thus making the top of the union stronger.

In North America, it is generally more common for a longer and deeper tongue to be made, compared to the method described. It is formed by making a downward cut beginning about one-third of the distance from the top of the sloping cut, with a matching cut to form the tongue on the rootstock. The "church window" of exposed scion is omitted with this technique.

Matching-up

(1) Carefully match the scion and rootstock so that maximum cambial contact is obtained. A useful guideline that is sometimes used is to aim for a very narrow ring of cut tissue to be visible between scion and rootstock. If the tongues are correctly sited, a 0.3–0.5 cm (1/8–1/5″) area of exposed scion tissue, the "church window", should remain above the top of the rootstock.

(2) If the cut surface of the rootstock is accidentally made much wider than that of the scion, the scion is placed to one side and matched only on that side. It is better to re-make the rootstock cut at a lower level, ensuring that the new cut is made more shallow.

Figure 18-3.
Matching-up the length of the cuts on the scion and rootstock for an ornamental *Prunus* graft.

Tying-in

(1) Remove a 25–30 cm (10–12″) length of either 2.5 cm (1″) or 1.3 cm (½″) wide polyethylene tape from the dispenser. The tapes can be pre-cut instead of preparing them for each graft, thus speeding up the process.

(2) Wrap the tape twice around the stem, beginning at the base of the graft, ensuring that it both covers and goes beyond the cuts. Wind the tape up the graft so that there is a slight overlap on each turn, keeping it flat and under tension. Complete the process by going just past the upper cut, and tie off with a half-hitch knot at the back of the stock. It is important to give a complete seal, especially over the top of the rootstock.

Faults specific to whip and tongue grafting that can contribute to failures are:—

(a) Insufficient tension on the tape. The initial two turns at the base must be tight otherwise the tape will subsequently slip and loosen.

(b) Allowing the tape to slip between the upper cut surfaces when it is brought over the top of the rootstock. Callus tissue that has formed will be dislodged when the tape is removed, thus loosening the union. This problem can be avoided when tying-in a smaller scion onto a larger rootstock by leaving a gap, which is then waxed over.

(c) If the tying-in is finished at the front of the scion, instead of on the rootstock, there is usually not sufficient strength to the tie and there is a strong likelihood that the scion will be damaged.

Waxing Over

A hot wax, cold wax or bitumen emulsion is used to seal the top of the scion and, if necessary, any exposed horizontal surface of the rootstock. For properties and use of different sealing materials, see Chapter 4.

Aftercare and Removal of Ties

(1) Wind can cause desiccation of the grafts on unprotected sites. A practice sometimes used is to cover the scion and union with a small polyethylene bag, securing it to the rootstock with string or raffia. Condensation will form in the bag so the tie should be sufficiently loose to allow the condensate to seep out, but not loose enough for the bag to blow off the graft. An alternative method is to tie securely and make one or two small slits at the base of the bag. The bag is slit from top to bottom when the scion growth is about 2.5 cm (1") long, then removed a few days later. This procedure is particularly useful for trees that break late in the season—for example, *Robinia pseudoacacia* 'Frisia' (Black Locust cv.) and *Gleditsia triacanthos* var. *inermis* 'Sunburst' (Sunburst Honey Locust)—and for nurseries located in exposed areas.

Figure 18-4. A (above). A small polyethylene bag secured at the base of the rootstock is a useful method of reducing desiccation of the scion on exposed sites. B (right). The polyethylene bag is slit after the buds have flushed and scion growth is 2.5 cm (1") long. The bag is removed entirely a few days later. (Notcutt Nurseries, Woodbridge, Suffolk, U.K.)

(2) Remove suckers on the rootstock when they are 2.5 cm (1") long, using a knife rather than rubbing them out with the thumb and finger. The knife will remove a greater proportion of the axillary buds immediately adjacent to the sucker (particularly with rosaceous subjects), thus reducing the amount of additional suckering. I find that an ideal knife for this purpose is a very sharp Tina 606, which has a pointed blade so that the operator can quickly work around the stem.

Some grafters like to encourage the development of suckers, within reason, as it is thought that they encourage the upward movement of sap to the scion. However, they compete with the scion if allowed to grow too long, and will also attract an early infestation of blackfly (aphid) to some trees, for example, *Prunus padus* (European Bird Cherry). This will form a source of infection to the scions of *Prunus padus* and other flowering cherries.

(3) The growth from the scion should be about 12.5–20 cm (5–8") long by early June and the polyethylene tape can be removed. The half-hitch knot is pulled away from the stem and the tape cut with a knife, collecting and disposing of all the removed ties. Care should be taken not to dislodge the scion when inspecting and untying the grafts.

(4) The upper shoot is normally selected to form the stem of the tree, the remainder being tipped back to 4 or 5 leaves. All the shoots are allowed to grow if a multi-stemmed tree is required, for example, *Prunus serrulata* 'Amanogawa' (Amanogawa Cherry), or if additional scion wood for budding is required in the summer. [The latter procedure is not a recommended practice as growth is directed away from the main stem of the maiden tree.]

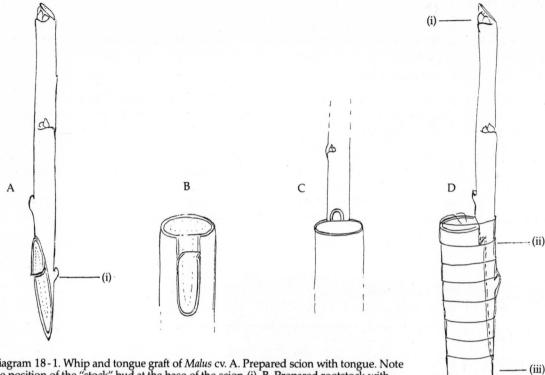

Diagram 18-1. Whip and tongue graft of *Malus* cv. A. Prepared scion with tongue. Note the position of the "stock" bud at the base of the scion (i). B. Prepared rootstock with tongue. C. Scion and rootstock matched to leave a small "church window", 3–5 mm (1/8–1/5") in length, of exposed scion tissue. D. The completed graft following tying-in. Note (i) the position of the terminal scion bud in relation to the apex of the rootstock; (ii) the interlocking of scion and rootstock; and (iii) that the tie is continued below the base of the scion to ensure a good seal. (The exposed cut surfaces of the scion and rootstock apex both will require waxing.)

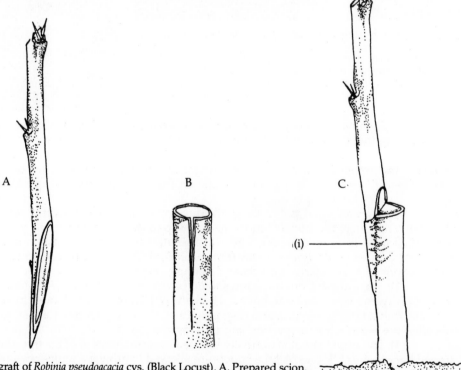

Diagram 18-2. Rind graft of *Robinia pseudoacacia* cvs. (Black Locust). A. Prepared scion. B. Prepared rootstock with the rind lifted to accommodate the scion. C. The completed graft prior to tying-in. Note that the scion is slipped between the two flaps of rind (i) on the rootstock, leaving a "church window" of exposed scion tissue.

ALTERNATIVE OPEN-GROUND GRAFTING METHODS

The whip and tongue graft is the most widely used method for open-ground grafting. However, other methods are occasionally used. This section outlines three methods that have been used in Europe.

RIND GRAFT

This grafting method is occasionally used for subjects with a thick rind or bark, such as *Robinia pseudoacacia* cvs. (Black Locust) and some *Tilia* (Linden) species and cultivars. It has been claimed that a union is more quickly formed, resulting in increased maiden growth of the scion.

The rind of the stock has to be lifted away from the wood, thus a reasonable amount of sap flow is required to prevent tearing of the tissues. This may mean that this method will have to be carried out slightly later in the growing season than whip and tongue grafting.

Grafting Procedure

Initial Rootstock Preparation

As for whip and tongue grafting.

Scion Preparation

As for whip and tongue grafting, except that no tongue is made on the scion.

Rootstock Preparation

(1) Make a fresh cut across the top of the rootstock with a knife.
(2) Insert the sharpened tip of the grafting knife into the rind about 5–6 cm (2–2¼″) below the top of the rootstock and draw it steadily up to the horizontal cut. Care should be taken to avoid cutting too deeply so that the blade enters the woody tissue.
(3) Slip the knife blade between the rind and wood, and carefully ease the rind away to give two opposite flaps. If this step is difficult to make and the rind tears, the probable cause is insufficient sap rise within the rootstock. The flattened part of a budding knife is a useful alternative to the knife blade as there is no risk of blunting the blade.

Matching-up

Slip the scion between the flaps of rind, starting at the top of the cut on the rootstock and leaving a 0.3–0.5 cm (1/8–1/5″) "church window" of exposed scion.

Tying-in, Waxing Over, Aftercare and Removal of Tie

As for whip and tongue grafting.

Figure 18-5. Open-ground rind graft of *Robinia pseudoacacia* 'Frisia' (Black Locust cv.) on *R. pseudoacacia*. Note how the rind is lifted to "envelop" the scion and the "church window" of exposed scion tissue above the rootstock.

Figure 18-6.
A successful union between *Prunus serrulata* 'Kwanzan' (Kwanzan or Kanzan Cherry) wedge grafted onto *P. avium* (Mazzard) rootstock. Note that the scion arises from near the center of the rootstock.

WEDGE GRAFT

This graft has been used in France for grafting cherries, but is generally little used in the nursery trade. The following description is an adaption of the technique.

Grafting Procedure

Scion Preparation

The procedure is as for whip and tongue grafting, except that two opposing slanting cuts are made so as to form a wedge. The thin base of the wedge should be rounded off to avoid damage during placement into the rootstock.

Rootstock Preparation

(1) Use a heavy duty knife or a sharpened metal cleft to make a vertical cut through the center of the rootstock. Sometimes a small mallet is used to hit the knife or cleft. This has to be relatively carefully controlled because there is a high risk of splitting the rootstock down the center.

(2) Place a small wooden or metal wedge into the cut, if necessary, to prevent it from closing, thus making it easier to match up the scion.

Matching-Up

Place the scion into the cut of the rootstock, leaving a "church window" of exposed scion tissue. It should be carefully matched with the cambium of the rootstock and, if necessary, moved over to one side.

Tying-In, Waxing Over, Aftercare and Removal of Ties

As for whip and tongue grafting.

SIDE WEDGE GRAFT

I have seen the side wedge graft effectively used outdoors in West Germany. It is used later in the growing season when the rootstock is already in active growth, particularly with trees that have a heavy sap rise early in the growing season. The rootstock is not de-headed at the point where the scion is to be placed, but retained. This lessens the risk of excessive sap flow "flooding" the union and causing possible losses, as the sap is encouraged to pass by the graft to the upper part of the rootstock. It is important to use fully dormant scion wood for this graft to be effective, therefore efficient collection and storage of the material is vital.

The carpentry used for this graft is based on that used for side wedge grafting pot-grown rootstocks at the bench (Chapter 19). Two opposite cuts are made on the scion to form a wedge. A flap consisting of bark and a sliver of wood is cut on the rootstock and the scion matched into this, tied in and waxed.

Figure 18-7.
A side wedge grafted *Tilia × euchlora* (Crimean Linden) on *T. platyphyllos* (Large-leaved Linden) rootstock is tied-in with raffia.

REFERENCES AND SUGGESTED SOURCES FOR FURTHER READING

Agricultural Training Board, U.K. no date. *Field Grafting—Whip and Tongue Method.* Trainee Guide NSP.1.A.4. Agricultural Training Board, Beckenham, Kent, U.K.

Agriculture Canada. 1968. *Fruit Tree Propagation.* Publication No. 1282. Agriculture Canada, Ottawa, Ontario.

Garner, R. J. 1979. 4th ed. rev. *The Grafter's Handbook.* Faber & Faber Ltd., London, U.K.

Gudziak, A. 1981. *Illustrated Techniques in Budding and Grafting.* Department of Plant Science and Faculty of Forestry, University of Manitoba, Winnipeg, Manitoba.

Hartmann, H. T. & D. E. Kester. 1983. 4th ed. *Plant Propagation: Principles and Practices.* Prentice-Hall, Inc., Englewood Cliffs, N.J.

Heuser, C. W. 1983. Graft incompatibility in woody plants. *Comb. Proc. Inter. Pl. Prop. Soc.* **33**: 407–412.

Ministry of Agriculture, Fisheries & Food, U.K. 1969. *Fruit Tree Raising.* Bulletin No. 135. Ministry of Agriculture, Fisheries and Food, London, U.K.

Widmoyer, F. B. 1962. Anatomical aspects of budding and grafting. *Comb. Proc. Pl. Prop. Soc.* **12**: 132–135.

Chapter 19

BENCH GRAFTING AND TOP-WORKING

BENCH GRAFTING

Bench grafting covers grafting and budding techniques carried out inside a covered structure, normally a shed or greenhouse. It is a standard method used to propagate a much wider range of plants than the other grafting and budding techniques previously described, including many of the rarer and high value woody ornamental plants that are not propagated satisfactorily by other means. One of many examples is seen in the Triflorum group of *Acer*—both *A. griseum* (Paperbark Maple) and *A. nikoense* (Nikko Maple) produce a low percentage of viable seed, making seed propagation erratic, while their ability to root as cuttings is unreliable. Conversely, the development of propagation technology in recent years has meant that some species and cultivars of important genera can be more economically propagated by cuttings. These genera include *Acer* (Maple), *Clematis*, *Magnolia* and *Rhododendron*.

Figure 19-1. Propagation by bench grafting is an integral phase of the production of many high-value nursery crops. A (left). Container production of trees for garden center sales. (W. R. Crowder & Sons, Horncastle, Lincolnshire, U.K.) B (right). Container production of top-worked and low-worked dissected-leaf cultivars of *Acer palmatum* (Japanese Maple). Note the shade cloth fabric for protection against the sun. (Monrovia, Nursery, Azusa, CA, U.S.A.)

The economics of bench grafting need to be carefully considered. The decision will largely depend on the species of plant to be propagated, the cost of rootstocks, expertise in grafting technique and aftercare, and the time period from grafting to the point-of-sale. Alternative methods should be considered before making the final decision.

Propagators specializing in bench grafting have to fully understand the plant material they are handling, so that they can quickly recognize the appropriate grafting technique and aftercare. They must be well acquainted with the correct scion/rootstock combinations.

The dividing line on choice of rootstock can be small, but critical. The genera *Acer* (Maple) and *Quercus* (Oak) represent examples of this when bench grafting some of the rarer species and selections. The size of plant material can vary considerably with the two extremes ranging from the placing of a scion into a seed for nurse seed grafting of *Quercus* (Oak), *Aesculus* (Horse-chestnut) or *Camellia* to the side grafting of the red-flowered *Aesculus* × *carnea* 'Briotii' (Ruby Horse-chestnut) on to a 1.8 m (6') stem of *A. hippocastanum* (Common Horse-chestnut).

The objective of this chapter is to introduce and explain the principles involved, and to describe the different grafting techniques using diagrams and named plant examples.

The three main systems of bench grafting can be initially categorized on the basis of the condition of the rootstock as follows:—

1. Bare-root rootstock
2. Pot-grown rootstock
3. Unrooted cutting

To these three main systems can be added the specialized techniques of nurse seed grafting and top-working.

The main phases of the bench grafting procedure are the same for all systems:—

1st phase   Source and production of rootstock

2nd phase   Preparation of rootstock for grafting

3rd phase   Carrying out the grafting techniques

4th phase   Transfer to aftercare facility and subsequent maintenance

5th phase   Hardening off and transfer to holding area

BARE-ROOT GRAFTING

Bare-root grafting is the attachment of the scion to a rootstock that has no growing medium and container surrounding it. Depending on the subject being grafted, the scion is worked onto a stem, hypocotyl or an actual piece of the root system. Woody ornamentals that are bare-root grafted are normally restricted to easier species. These include some deciduous trees, such as *Malus* (Apple, Crab Apple), *Sorbus* (Mountain Ash) and *Fraxinus* (Ash); flowering shrubs such as *Syringa vulgaris* cvs. (Common or French Lilac), *Hibiscus syriacus* cvs. (Rose-of-Sharon) and miniature roses; and climbing vines, such as *Clematis, Campsis* (Trumpet Creeper) and *Wisteria*.

Bare-root grafting is generally a simpler process than grafting onto pot-grown stocks, mainly because less time, space and lower costs are required for the production of rootstocks. Also, less complex grafting techniques are often used. Furthermore, there is more latitude in the aftercare requirements for the completed grafts to form a successful union. Two of the criteria for bare-root grafting to be successful are:—

(i) Deciduous scions must be fully dormant. Loss of grafts will occur if the scion buds flush prematurely, particularly before the union has formed in the aftercare facility or its final establishment in the growing-on production site.

(ii) The callused graft should both establish and grow away successfully in the final production site. It is important to remember that the root system has no surrounding soil until planted. Hence the advantage of pot-grown stocks or of using a compromise solution by potting-up the bare-root rootstock immediately after the grafting process.

It is tempting to over-emphasize the importance of speed when bare-root grafting and to neglect the importance of careful work. I have seen significant losses in open-ground bedded stock of deciduous trees and variable grade-out of those remaining. Inspection of the grafts showed that the carpentry and matching was poor, and that they had also been bedded out with an incomplete union formation.

Pot-grown rootstocks allow more attention to be given to the aftercare of the grafts, the ability to extend the period for bedding out or potting-on, and the opportunity for better establishment. Bare-root grafting should not be considered for many side-grafted ornamentals, e.g., *Acer palmatum* (Japanese Maple), *Alnus* (Alder), *Betula* (Birch), *Picea* (Spruce), *Cedrus* (Cedar) and *Pinus* (Pine).

Bare-Root Grafting Systems

Depending on the plant being grafted and the propagation facility available, the principal systems for handling bare-root grafts are outlined below:—

(A)   Graft

↓

Wax union and top of scion

↓

Plunge (and cover union as necessary) in peat moss contained in deep flats or bench.
Place in a frost-free greenhouse or shed for aftercare.

↓

Containerize or bed out in open ground

Examples:—
    Campsis (Trumpet Creeper)
    Fraxinus (Ash)
    Malus (Apple, Crab Apple)
    Robinia (Locust)
    Sorbus (Mountain Ash)
    Syringa (Lilac)
    Wisteria (Wisteria)

(B)   Graft

↓

No Waxing

↓

Plunge and cover union in peat moss contained in bench or deep flats.
Place in grafting case with base temperature at 18–21°C (64–70°F) for aftercare.

↓

Cold-store callused grafts at 1–4°C (34–39°F) until containerizing or lining out.

Examples:—
    Crataegus (Hawthorn)
    Malus (Apple, Crab Apple)
    Rosa (Rose)
    Syringa (Lilac)

(C)   Graft

↓

Wax top of scion

↓

Pot-up graft with union below surface of potting medium.
Place on open bench with air temperature *or* base temperature of 10°C (50°F) for aftercare.

↓

Harden-off and grow-on in containers for at least one year.

Examples:—
    Actinidia (Actinidia)
    Campsis (Trumpet Creeper)
    Hibiscus (Hibiscus)
    Parthenocissus (Woodbine)
    Wisteria (Wisteria)

(D)   Graft

↓

No waxing

↓

Pot-up graft with union below surface of potting medium.
Place in grafting case with base temperature at 18–21°C (64–70°F) for aftercare.

↓

Harden-off and grow-on in containers under protection.

Examples:—
    Clematis (Clematis)
    Miniature Roses

Time of Year

The bulk of bare-root grafting is carried out during January and February, using either fully dormant deciduous scion wood or forced vigorous softwood material. It can provide useful inside work for employees at a time when outdoor conditions are prohibitive for normal nursery operations.

The importance of timing in the collection, handling and storage of scion wood has been discussed on p. 498. It should be re-emphasized that dormant scion wood does mean *dormant,* particularly if the grafts are placed in an aftercare facility with air temperatures higher than they were exposed to when outside. Premature bud break of the scions before a union has properly formed will result in the loss of grafts—one has to be particularly careful with *Prunus* (Cherry, etc.) and *Pyrus* (Pear). Grafting can be extended into early March if the scion wood, and also perhaps the rootstocks, are cold stored. However, the later in the season that grafting is carried out, the more difficult it becomes to maintain the desired conditions during aftercare.

It may be necessary to force dormant mother plants into growth in order to obtain softwood material. A check should be made as to whether a cold temperature period is required before forcing so that vernalization (cold period) requirements are met. High temperature, high humidity and increasing the winter photoperiod (day length) with high or low intensity light sources can influence the amount and condition of the scion wood. The number of woody ornamentals that can be grafted using softwood scion wood is very limited, two examples being *Clematis* and miniature roses.

Rootstocks

Rootstocks may be raised in the nursery or purchased from an outside source. They can be raised from seed (*Hibiscus syriacus*, Rose-of-Sharon), hardwood cuttings (*Ligustrum ovalifolium,* California Privet), softwood cuttings (*Syringa tomentella*, Felty Lilac), layers (M.M.111), and pieces of root removed from either seed- or vegetatively-propagated plants (*Campsis radicans*, Common Trumpet Creeper).

It is important to obtain the correct grade and quality of rootstock. It should have a fibrous root system and a hypocotyl and stem that are both straight, free from side shoots and not excessively "woody". The caliper will depend on the plant being grafted, but "pencil thickness" (ca. 6 mm/¼") is a good guideline with which to begin. I have experienced frustrating situations with purchased stocks that are either too thin to successfully match the scion or too large with a coarse root system and poor quality stems, thus making them difficult to handle during grafting and aftercare. The causes of such poor rootstocks, besides inappropriate soils, are largely due to poor husbandry in rootstock production—particularly with relation to spacing of cuttings and sowing rates of seed, lack of irrigation producing irregular growth, omission of undercutting during the period between sowing and lifting, and, finally, poor grading out. It pays to carefully check out the source of rootstocks so that *both* the purchaser and supplier understand the requirements, otherwise loss of time and money and bad feeling can result.

The rootstocks, whether grown in the nursery or purchased, should be graded/re-graded for caliper and overall quality, and root pruned. This is also a convenient time to remove adventitious buds on the stem around and below the site of the graft union. This will significantly reduce the number of subsequent suckers in rootstocks such as *Syringa vulgaris* (Common or French Lilac). The rootstocks are then bundled (e.g., in 25s) or kept loose, labelled and stored prior to grafting. Methods of storage are as follows:—

(i) **Heeling-in in Open Ground**—The rootstocks should be heeled-in in a sheltered site away from prolonged sunlight. The site must be very well-drained. Coarse sand (grit) or bark can be added to the soil to improve the drainage. Artificial windbreaks of woven polypropylene are useful to surround the area, if the size of the heeling-in ground warrants it. Straw bales can be used but, although convenient, tend to attract mice which can cause considerable damage to the rootstocks. Checks should be made at regular intervals for vermin and moisture around the root systems. As with rootstocks for open-ground production, purchased bundles of rootstocks should be checked to ensure that the centers of the bundles have not dried out. It is preferable to untie the bundles and heel-in in rows to reduce the possibility of drying out.

The rootstocks should be removed from the heeling-in site about 3–5 days prior to grafting, and the root systems washed to remove soil and debris. The bundles should then be plunged into peat moss in boxes or in a specified floor area in a cool structure.

(ii) **Peat Moss or Sphagnum**—The rootstocks are graded, labelled and packed tightly in wood or rigid plastic boxes, ensuring that the root systems are well covered with slightly moistened peat moss or sphagnum moss. Lining the box with waterproof paper before adding the peat or sphagnum moss will help to retain moisture. The boxes are placed in a frost-free structure where there is little chance of temperature build-up. A specified floor area in a cool shed can be used as an alternative to boxes. The advantage of this system is that the rootstocks are directly on hand for grafting, whereas access to an outside site can be a problem during bad weather.

(iii) Controlled Cold Storage—Nurseries with controlled direct or indirect (jacketed) cold storage facilities can use these to effective advantage in the cold storage of rootstocks. There may be a problem of excessive drying out of roots in direct cold stores with movement of air. In this case, the bundles should be placed in loosely-tied polyethylene bags before storage. Covering the roots with moist peat moss normally provides sufficient protection.

The rootstocks should be dusted with a fungicide such as quintozene (Terrachlor®, PCNB®) prior to storage if *Botrytis* is likely to be a problem disease. *Botrytis* can be effectively controlled by keeping the temperature as close to freezing point as possible (0–1°C/32–34°F). The disease becomes aggressive when temperatures increase to 3–4.5°C (38–40°F).

The rootstocks have been stored in constant cold temperature and therefore initial rootstock activity may be stimulated by moving them, with the roots covered in moist peat moss, to a warm glasshouse at 15°C (59°F) about 10 days or more prior to grafting.

Scion Wood

The principles relating to the sources, mother plants, selection, handling and maintenance of deciduous dormant scion wood for grafting are discussed in Chapters 17 and 18. A hedgerow system can be used, but heavy annual pruning should be carried out to produce one-year-old vigorous vegetative scion wood. I find that growth of *Hibiscus* (Rose-of-Sharon) and *Syringa* (Lilac) will not be sufficient to produce the desired type of cutting scion unless they are heavily pruned annually. One-year-old dormant shoots from pruned mother trees are ideal, while the thicker feathered shoots from the two-year-old production crop of open-ground budded trees are a useful alternative.

Mother plants of climbing plants such as *Actinidia, Campsis* (Trumpet Creeper) and *Wisteria* can be grown outside and trained on a trellis or post. Propagators sometimes collect *Wisteria* scion wood from established garden plants. The use of mature wood helps to ensure flowering early in the production cycle. Dormant evergreen hardwood stems are used for *Clematis armandii* (Evergreen Clematis). The mother plants should be pruned back to about 45 cm (18″) high during late April/May to reduce the number of flower buds forming in the leaf axils on the subsequent growth.

Care must be used when handling softwood scion material to reduce both bruising and desiccation of tissue to a minimum.

Nurse Grafting

Nurse grafting is the use of a rootstock to support scion growth during the early stages of development until the scion eventually develops a root system of its own. Nurse grafting comes into its own with some of the bench grafting techniques, particularly when grafting onto a root piece or well down onto the hypocotyl. The following procedures should be adopted to encourage successful nurse grafting:—

(i) Root pieces or stem hypocotyl are used for the rootstock—root pieces are more effective.

(ii) An area of exposed cut surface ("church window") is retained on the scion after matching-up and tying-in to encourage scion rooting.

(iii) A rootstock that shows partially delayed incompatibility sometimes is used. Rootstocks of *Ligustrum ovalifolium* (California Privet) and root pieces of *Fraxinus pennsylvanica* var. *lanceolata* (Green Ash) have been used successfully for grafting *Syringa vulgaris* cvs. (Common or French Lilac). Root pieces of *Catalpa bignonioides* (Indian Bean) can act as a nurse rootstock for hybrids and cultivars of *Campsis radicans* (Common Trumpet Creeper).

(iv) Ensure that the graft union is well covered by peat moss or growing medium during the aftercare and that it is kept covered during the growing-on process in containers and open ground.

Aftercare

The types of facilities needed for aftercare of the grafts have been outlined under grafting systems (p. 511). The facilities are diverse, ranging from low-cost unheated to relatively expensive structures. In a frost-free structure, the completed grafts are waxed and packed tightly in boxes or placed on specified floor or bench areas, with the roots kept moist under dampened peat moss. Callusing can be speeded up by packing unwaxed grafts into moist peat moss with the unions covered and then placing in a grafting (closed) case with a basal temperature of 18–21°C (64–70°F). The grafts are hardened-off after 2–3 weeks and cold stored until subsequent containerizing or lining out in the open ground. In a facility with more bench or floor space, the rootstocks can be potted-up immediately after grafting and provided with an optimum air temperature of 10°C (50°F) but no basal heat. Softwood scion material must be enclosed in a heavily shaded grafting case with the base temperature set between 24–27°C (75–80°F), thus providing warmth and high humidity.

Some factors of particular importance in the aftercare of bare-root grafts are:—

(i) Avoid premature flushing of the scion buds before the union has adequately formed.

(ii) Ensure that there is sufficient shading to reduce the incidence of scorch and desiccation.

(iii) Ensure sufficient watering so that the medium around the roots does not dry out.

(iv) Inspect for fungal infection, particularly *Botrytis cinerea* (Gray Mold), as the buds swell and flush.

(v) Remove sucker growth from stem and roots. The warmer the environment the earlier the suckering will occur. However, it is normally done after the grafts have been hardened-off to avoid disturbing them. Some grafters will retain two or three suckers in order to encourage sap rise to the scion during the earlier stages.

Grafting Techniques

The grafts normally used are the whip or splice, whip and tongue, basal whip, wedge, rind, and one bud split scion. These grafts are not just specific to bare-root grafts but are also used on pot-grown rootstocks where appropriate.

WHIP (SPLICE) GRAFT

One reason for the increasing interest in bare-root grafting of ornamental trees is the increasing popularity of container trees for retail garden center sales. An excellent well-furnished product can be produced for sale with only one or two seasons growth after whip grafting, and trees suitable for the average house in a subdivision can be provided by using appropriate scions. Bare-root grafting is one of the three production systems available to achieve these objectives. Some of the cultivars of *Sorbus aucuparia* (European Mountain Ash) are excellent examples.

Shoots of the previous season's growth, about 60–90 cm (2–3′) long, are collected from

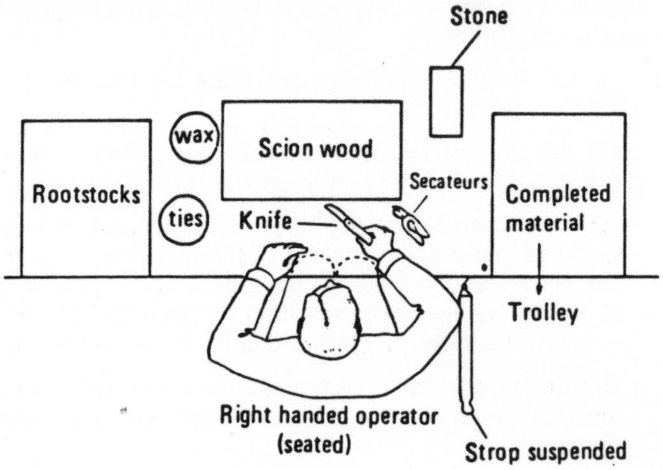

Diagram 19-1. The diagram suggests a convenient arrangement for the work bench. This may be altered to suit the individual, but try to ensure that you are comfortable and do not have to reach very far for any item. (Reproduced by permission of the Agricultural Training Board, Beckenham, Kent, U.K.)

either mother or nursery production trees, bundled, labelled and then heeled-in for ½–⅓ of their length in a cool, sheltered site away from direct sunlight. An alternative method, particularly if grafting late or during a period of continuous mild weather, is to wrap surface-dry scion wood in polyethylene film with a few drops of water adhering to the surface and then cold store between 0–1°C (32–34°F) (for further details see Chapter 18 under open-ground grafting).

The grafting is carried out during January and February. If a crew is being used, it is important to utilize the crew effectively by ensuring that the work procedures flow with no hold-ups.

Bitumastic emulsion seals should not be used to seal the graft. I have experienced considerable problems with seepage of the liquified emulsion into the cut surfaces when warm air temperatures after grafting hardened only the outside surface. Either hot or cold temperature waxes (Chapter 4) should be used where applicable to cover the union and tip of the scion. The complete scion and union may be immersed in a liquid hot wax, providing that the wax temperature is not excessive and that the buds on the scion are fully dormant and protected.

The grafts can be packed into moist peat moss retained in boxes after waxing, ensuring that the union is covered (covering the union is particularly important when it has not been waxed), and then stood down in a frost-free structure. If the union is excessively slow to form, it may help to set the air temperature at 10°C (50°F). Alternatively, the grafts can be potted into 10 cm (4″) deep pots ("long tom") and placed down on a bench with the basal heating set at 10–13°C (50–55°F) to gradually stimulate activity. Shading must be provided to reduce air temperatures and to prevent any subsequent scorch when the buds swell and flush.

I prefer the cold grafting technique for deciduous trees as I have noted that the vascular system is well united by the time of growing-on in the production areas. As indicated previously, the problem with high temperature callusing (18–21°C/64–70°F) of bare-root grafts just plunged in peat moss is that the union is held together largely by a lot of callus with insufficient interlocking between scion and rootstock. This then results in variable establishment.

Figure 19-2 (left). Graft union failure due to seepage of the liquid bitumastic emulsion between the cut surfaces of the scion and rootstock. Note the staining of the cambium and adjacent tissues.

Figure 19-3 (below). Whip grafted *Fraxinus oxycarpa* 'Raywood' (Claret or Raywood Ash) on *F. excelsior* (European Ash) rootstock after the scion and union were dipped into hot liquid paraffin wax.

Figure 19-4 (right). Successful whip graft of a *Syringa vulgaris* cv. (Common or French Lilac) on *S. vulgaris.* Note how the moist peat moss has adhered to the root system, thus helping establishment after containerization or planting out in open ground.

Grafting Procedure

Initial Rootstock Preparation

(1) Reduce the root system if necessary, using hand pruners. Dominant coarse roots should be removed.

(2) Head back the rootstocks with hand pruners or a knife (not a grafting knife) to leave an optimum 7.5 cm (3″) length of stem.

(3) Use a knife to remove the buds around and below the site of the graft union if subsequent suckering will be a problem.

(4) Clean up the base of the rootstock with a knife to remove side shoots and then with a dry rag to remove debris.

Scion Preparation

(1) Check the scion wood for health and trueness-to-name.

(2) Use a grafting knife to remove the unripened scion tip and any damaged wood. The scion is then cut into 10–12.5 cm (4–5") lengths, with the uppermost cut sloping down away from the bud. Each scion length should have a minimum of 3 and a maximum of 5 buds. The prepared scions are placed into a tray within easy access to the grafter.

(3) Make a slanting cut, 4–5 cm (1½–2") long, through the scion. The lower bud will form the stock bud and, if feasible, the uppermost bud should be facing towards the center of the rootstock after tying-in (see p. 501 for reasons).

Rootstock Preparation

(1) Use the grafting knife to make a fresh cut across the top of the rootstock.

(2) Make a slanting cut just slightly shorter than the length of the cut on the scion.

Matching-up

(1) Carefully match the cut surfaces of the scion and rootstock so that a small ring of cut tissue is visible between them and a 3–5 mm (1/8–1/5") area of exposed scion tissue, the "church window", remains above the top of the rootstock.

(2) If the cut surface of the rootstock is much wider than that of the scion, the scion is placed to one side so that the tissues are matched with the rootstock along one side only.

Tying-in

Use a rubber grafting strip (band) or fillis string to hold the scion and rootstock firmly together. Two turns are made at the top of the graft and the tie is then spiralled down, leaving a small gap of 3 mm (1/8") between each turn, and finished off with a half-hitch knot just below the union.

Polyethylene tape, 1.3 cm (½") wide, can be used as ties for cold grafting but difficulties may arise initially in making the tying-in firm enough. It is not necessary to wax over the union subsequently unless there are areas of exposed cut surface.

Waxing

(1) For cold grafting aftercare facilities, both the union and top of the scion should be sealed by painting over with a hot or cold liquid grafting wax. Alternatively, both the scion and graft may be immersed in a liquid hot wax (see p. 191).

(2) For a warm aftercare facility, waxing is not necessary if the graft union is below moistened peat moss. However, some propagators still wax the scion tip.

Aftercare

The grafts are placed in the selected aftercare facility (see p. 514). Rubber and string ties below moist peat moss are likely to deteriorate and break after the union has formed. Similarly, the ties of cold grafts should deteriorate when they are bedded out or potted-up, providing the union is below the level of the soil or growing medium. If, however, the union is to remain above the soil or growing medium following cold grafting, then it is probable that the tie will have to be removed when tissues expand after hardening-off or a stem constriction will result. Polyethylene tape must be removed under all circumstances.

BASAL WHIP GRAFT

The base of the scion is matched into a small veneer on the rootstock, which can make it easier for tying-in. The technique is somewhat similar to side veneer grafting (p. 544) except that the top of the rootstock is removed above the site of the graft union before the cuts on the rootstock are made. This graft has been used successfully on many deciduous trees that are whip grafted, e.g., *Aesculus* (Horse-chestnut), *Carpinus* (Hornbeam) and *Malus*. Some propagators prefer the basal whip graft to the whip and tongue graft for bench grafting in situations where staff have difficulty in cutting and interlocking the tongues.

Figure 19-5. Container-grown *Robinia pseudoaoacia* 'Frisia' (Black Locust cv.) whip grafted onto bare rootstocks of *R. pseudoacacia* make an attractive product for garden center sales. (W. R. Crowder & Sons, Horncastle, Lincolnshire, U.K.)

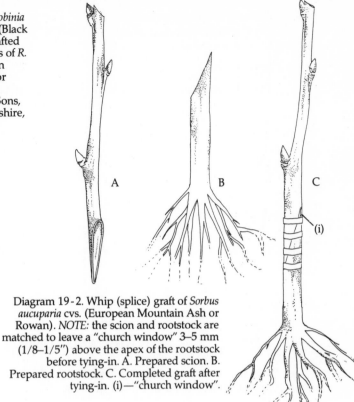

Diagram 19-2. Whip (splice) graft of *Sorbus aucuparia* cvs. (European Mountain Ash or Rowan). *NOTE:* the scion and rootstock are matched to leave a "church window" 3–5 mm (1/8–1/5") above the apex of the rootstock before tying-in. A. Prepared scion. B. Prepared rootstock. C. Completed graft after tying-in. (i)—"church window".

Grafting Procedure

Initial rootstock preparation, tying-in and aftercare are as for whip grafting.

Scion Preparation

As for whip grafting, except that the scion is reversed after making the slanting cut and a sloping cut 3 mm (⅛") long is made at its base.

Rootstock Preparation

(1) Hold the rootstock with the root system towards you.

(2) Make a cut, 4 mm (1/6") deep and angled at about 30°, 4 cm (1½") from the top of the already prepared rootstock. (The overall length of this cut should be slightly shorter than that on the scion to ensure a "church window" of exposed scion tissue above the top of the rootstock.)

(3) Make a straight cut down from the top of the rootstock to meet the first cut, thus forming a veneer at the base.

Matching-up

The scion and rootstock are matched as for the whip graft, except that the reverse cut of the scion is also matched up with the base of the veneer cut on the rootstock.

REVERSE BASAL WHIP GRAFT

This variation of the basal whip graft, sometimes called a reverse veneer graft, has been successfully used at Waterers Nurseries Ltd., Bagshot, England, for nurse root grafting *Wisteria* and *Hibiscus* (Rose-of-Sharon) onto root pieces.

The cuts on the scion and rootstock are essentially reversed. The veneer cut is made on the scion, with the base of the scion sloping towards the rootstock, and the appropriate slanting cut is made on the root piece. These are matched, tied and then callused in a grafting case at 18–21°C (64–70°F) with the graft unions covered by plunging in a moist medium of equal parts of sand and peat moss.

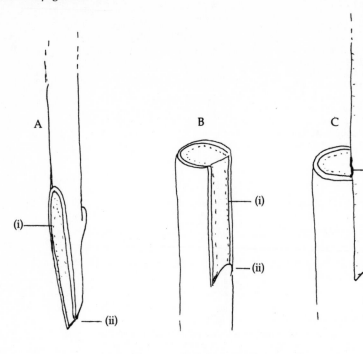

Diagram 19-3.
Diagrammatic
representation of a basal
whip graft.
A. Prepared cuts on
scion. (i)—slanting cut of
4–5 cm (1½–2"); (ii)—
reverse cut, 3 mm (⅛")
long.
B. Prepared cuts on
rootstock. (i)—sloping
cut slightly shorter than
on scion. (ii)—veneer cut,
4 mm (1/6") deep.
C. Matched scion and
rootstock indicating
"church window" (i) of
exposed scion tissue.

WHIP AND TONGUE GRAFT

This traditional open-ground graft, in which the scion is interlocked into the rootstock before tying-in, is also used in bench grafting.

Grafting Procedure

Initial rootstock preparation, tying-in and aftercare are as for whip grafting. Further details on the procedure are found in Chapter 18 on open-ground grafting.

APICAL WEDGE GRAFT

This traditional graft, sometimes referred to as a cleft graft, is used on a number of woody ornamentals with softer tissue that will not split at the base when the vertical cut is made. It is thus particularly appropriate for roots and hypocotyls. We found that it was an ideal technique to use as the first method for teaching grafting to students at Hadlow College of Agriculture & Horticulture. It demonstrates the principles of knife control and matching-up, and the end result on completion of the aftercare period was usually successful, even with the variable proficiency demonstrated in the carpentry.

The completed grafts may be either packed into moistened peat moss contained in flats or potted-up immediately after grafting and moved to a cold or warm aftercare facility. I have seen both *Wisteria* and *Campsis* (Trumpet Creeper) grafted on roots, then waxed and successfully callused in a shaded cold frame. *Hibiscus* (Rose-of-Sharon) can also be successfully cold stored until subsequent handling for growing-on, as long as they have had 2–3 weeks in a warm grafting case beforehand.

Examples of plants that can be wedge grafted:—

SCION	ROOTSTOCK
Hibiscus syriacus 'Blue Bird' (Rose-of-Sharon cv.)	*Hibiscus syriacus* (Rose-of-Sharon)
Wisteria floribunda 'Macrobotrys' (Japanese Wisteria cv.)	*Wisteria sinensis* (Chinese Wisteria)
Campsis × *tagliabuana* 'Madame Galen' (Madame Galen Trumpet Vine)	*Campsis radicans* (Common Trumpet Creeper)

SCION	ROOTSTOCK
Parthenocissus tricuspidata 'Veitchii' (Veitch's Boston Ivy)	*Parthenocissus quinquefolia* (Virginia Creeper)
Actinidia kolomikta (Kolomikta Actinidia)	*Actinidia arguta* (Bower Actinidia, Tara Vine)

Grafting Procedure

Initial Rootstock Preparation

(1) Reduce the root system if necessary, using pruners. Dominant coarse roots should be removed.

(2) Head back the main shoot into the softer tissue of the hypocotyl ("neck" or "root collar") of the seedling, using either hand pruners or a knife.

(3) If root pieces are being used instead of seedlings, the roots should be washed, dried, and cut into pieces 7.5–10 cm (3–4") long.

Scion Preparation

(1) Check the scion wood for health and trueness-to-name.

(2) Use a grafting knife to remove the unripened scion tip and any damaged wood. Cut scion into 10–12.5 cm (4–5") lengths, with the uppermost cut sloping down away from the bud.

(3) Make two slanting cuts, each about 3 cm (1¼") long, on opposite sides of the scion so that they meet at the base to form a wedge. (The cut on the scion should be slightly longer than the vertical cut on the rootstock to ensure a "church window" when matching.)

Rootstock Preparation

(1) Use a knife to make a fresh cut at the top of the rootstock.

(2) Make a vertical cut, 3 cm (1¼") long, down the center of the hypocotyl.

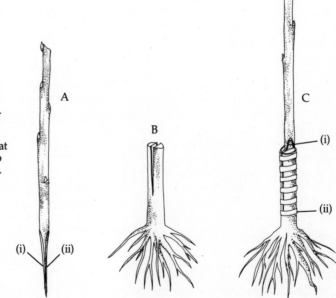

Diagram 19-4. Apical wedge graft of *Hibiscus syriacus* cvs. (Rose-of-Sharon). A. Prepared scion. (i) and (ii) are two opposing sloping cuts to make the wedge. B. Prepared rootstock. Note that the vertical cut is made well down into the hypocotyl (root "collar" or "neck"). C. The completed graft following matching and tying-in. (i)—"church window" of exposed scion tissue; (ii)—tying-in completed below the vertical cut on the scion.

Matching-up

(1) Carefully match the cut surfaces of the scion and rootstock on both sides of the two cuts, with a 3–5 mm (1/8–1/5) "church window" showing above the apex of the rootstock.

(2) If the cut surface of the rootstock is much wider than that of the scion, the scion is placed to one side so that the tissues are matched with the rootstock along one side only.

Tying-in and Aftercare

As for whip grafting (see p. 516).

INLAY GRAFT

The inlay graft may be used as an alternative to a wedge graft if the diameter of the rootstock is greater than that of the scion. The term "inverted inlay graft" is used when the scion is of greater diameter than the rootstock.

The technique is described in the section on pot-grown rootstocks (p. 558). The procedure used is similar to that for a wedge graft, except for the different carpentry involved.

ONE BUD SPLIT SCION

This traditional nurse graft was widely used in Europe for propagating *Clematis* but has now, with few exceptions, been superseded by softwood cutting propagation. Nevertheless, it is worthwhile outlining the technique here. As indicated earlier (p. 511), its main advantage is that a saleable plant is available within 5–6 months after grafting, compared with the average 18 months from cuttings. It is also useful for *Clematis armandii* (Evergreen Clematis) if there should be difficulty in rooting from cuttings, problems with establishment after potting-up, and/or failure of the axillary bud to break. In the past, there have been claims, largely unproven, that grafted plants are less liable to be infected by *Ascochyta clematidina* (Clematis Wilt).

The grades of rootstock used are one-year *Clematis vitalba* (Traveler's Joy) seedlings with a hypocotyl or root piece caliper of 3–4 mm (1/8–1/6"). The larger 5–8 mm (1/5–1/3") grade is normally preferred for *C. armandii* (Evergreen Clematis).

Grafting is carried out during late January to February using material with a single vegetative bud on each scion. In order to obtain sufficient material, the containerized mother plants can be brought in during mid-December from the outdoor standing-down area to a greenhouse with an air temperature of 10–15°C (50–60°F), and stimulated into growth. Particular attention must be

Figure 19-6.
Fillis string used to support stem growth of *Clematis* for subsequent use in grafting. (Angers, France)

Figure 19-7.
Young liner of a large-flowered *Clematis* cv. propagated by a one bud split scion graft. The rootstock was potted into a 6 cm (2½") pot immediately after grafting.

given to pest and disease control during this stage, the time of grafting and during aftercare—these include aphids, red spider mites, mildew, Clematis Wilt and Botrytis.

An effective method that I have seen used in France is to plant the mother plants in the soil border of a heated greenhouse, trailing them up fillis string attached to a wire 2.5 m (8′) above soil level. The fillis string is cut at each end when growth reaches the top wire and brought to the grafting bench with the scion growth twined to it.

Particular care is required when handling the scion wood to avoid bruising and desiccation. Short-term cold storage can be helpful.

One to two weeks before grafting, the rootstocks are brought in from outside, trimmed, washed and then packed into flats containing moist peat moss. The flats are stored at a temperature of about 8°C (45°F).

The aftercare procedure is more specific than for the previous techniques described. Thin strands of moist raffia or cotton twine are the best materials to use for tying-in. After tying-in, the grafts are immediately potted into either 6 or 7.5 cm (2½ or 3″) diameter pots with the axillary bud and leaf just above the potting soil level. Nurse grafting will be encouraged as the union is below the potting soil level. The potted grafts are placed into a shaded high humidity grafting case with the base temperature at about 21°C (70°F) for 2–3 weeks, after which they can start to be hardened-off. There is only a small volume of soil and the grafts therefore need to be carefully checked for water requirements. Also, fungal disease infection must be checked and the necessary action taken. After hardening-off, they are grown-on on the open greenhouse bench with the air temperature set at around 10°C (50°F). They may be pinched back when three pairs of leaves have formed to encourage basal breaks and a 45 cm (18″) tall split cane inserted to provide initial support by tying the new growth to it. The grafts are potted-on into either 15 cm (6″) diameter containers or into the traditional 10 cm wide × 15 cm deep (4 × 6″) "long tom" (British term used for this size pot) for sale in the late summer.

Grafting Procedure

Initial Rootstock Preparation

The prepared rootstocks are trimmed and cleaned up as necessary, ensuring that any debris is wiped away from around the hypocotyl or root piece.

Scion Preparation

(1) Cut the scion material into pieces 2.5 cm (1″) long first, each with one pair of leaves and one pair of developed buds. Ensure that the top cut is 6 mm (¼″) above the buds. The number of leaflets is reduced if necessary.

(2) Make a vertical cut down the center of the scion to produce two scions, each with a single bud and leaf.

Rootstock Preparation

Remove a thin sliver of tissue, 2 cm (¾″) long, from one side of the hypocotyl or root piece.

Matching-up

Carefully match the scion and rootstock so that the top of the scion is flush with the upper surface of the rootstock. The different length of the cuts on the scion and rootstock will leave a "tail" of exposed scion below the cut surface of the rootstock. This will encourage scion rooting.

Variations

There are variations of this graft. A veneer may be cut on the rootstock (as in basal whip grafting) so that no "tail" remains—this is sometimes used for grafting *Clematis armandii* cvs. (Evergreen Clematis). Alternatively, a small "church window" may be left above the top of the rootstock, or both a "church window" above and a "tail" below may be left.

Tying-in

Wind moist raffia or cotton twine in a spiral from the top to the base, leaving the axillary bud exposed.

Aftercare

The grafts are immediately potted-up, with the bud and leaf just above soil level, and placed in a grafting case at 21°C (70°F) (see p. 511). Precautions should be taken against the development and spread of fungal diseases (see miniature roses, p. 523).

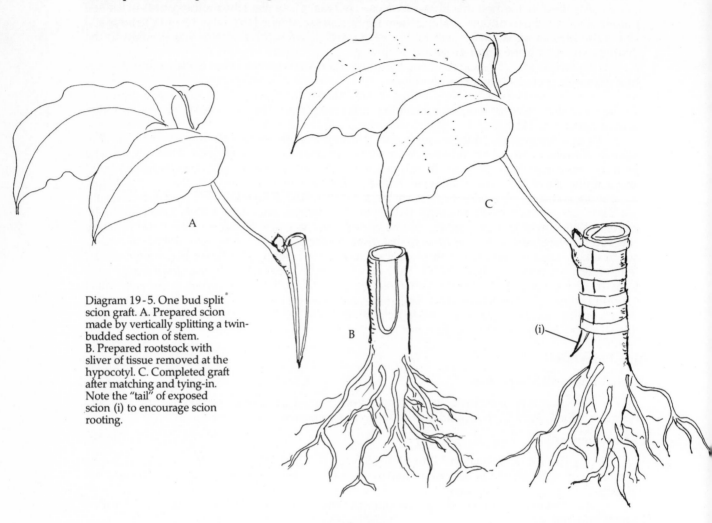

Diagram 19-5. One bud split scion graft. A. Prepared scion made by vertically splitting a twin-budded section of stem. B. Prepared rootstock with sliver of tissue removed at the hypocotyl. C. Completed graft after matching and tying-in. Note the "tail" of exposed scion (i) to encourage scion rooting.

RIND GRAFT

This graft has proved to be very valuable for a number of specialist miniature rose producers. The majority of miniature roses, particularly in North America, are now propagated by softwood cuttings, but rind grafting is still used economically by a few European producers. Micropropation will reduce further the need for grafting. Essentially, the technique depends on the use of a bare-root stock with a rind that will lift easily to accommodate a single-budded softwood scion. The plants are grown-on to produce a flowering pot plant for retail sales or bedded out in open ground for selling later that year.

The mother plants are prepared by potting-up pruned bare-root plants during October and November and then standing them down outside to obtain sufficient vernalization (cold period). The mother plants are brought into a warm greenhouse with an air temperature of 18–21°C (65–70°F) during early December to force the plants into growth. Thus, this is an example of softwood scion wood being used in grafting, as in *Clematis*. The amount of scion wood available can be increased by installing a high intensity light source to provide an 18-hour photoperiod.

Grafting, using 4–6 mm (1/6–1/4") caliper *Rosa canina* (Dog Rose), *R. multiflora* (Baby or Japanese Rose) or Laxa rootstocks may begin during late December and continue until early April. The soft growth has hardened sufficiently for removal and preparation when the flower buds are well formed. The scions are cut back to 2–3 axillary buds to ensure further breaks in growth. A further source of scion wood as the grafting season continues is from plants grafted earlier in the year. Cotton is ideal for tying-in these small grafts as it deteriorates, thus overcoming the necessity of removing the tie by hand.

Compared with many other plants, miniature roses seem to require higher base and air temperatures in the aftercare facility when softwood scion material is used for grafting. A layer of moistened peat, 23 cm (9″) deep, is placed on the bottom of the grafting case, and the grafts plunged into this up to the level of the hypocotyl or root collar. The base temperature is at 24–27°C (75–80°F) with a humid environment being maintained at the same time. Shading is vital to avoid excessive temperatures and damage to plant tissue. Callusing can be seen within 7–10 days, with hardening-off taking place over the next 3–4 weeks. The grafts can be either potted-up into 10 cm (4″) diameter pots or stood down in flats in a cold house until open-ground planting in April to May.

The soft growth of the scion mother plants and the high temperatures and humidity during the forcing stage and during aftercare mean that disease prevention is of paramount importance. Regular fungicidal sprays for mildew and Botrytis should be implemented. [Scion wood can also be immersed (wearing gloves) in a solution of fungicide after removal from the mother plants.] The completed grafts can be immersed in a fungicidal solution prior to being placed in the grafting case.

Dormant scion wood may be used for rind grafting miniature roses, but a continuous supply is not as readily available as is softwood. It does allow lower temperatures to be used for the aftercare. Whip grafting is sometimes used as an alternative to rind grafting. Both these techniques can be used for grafting of *Rosa* species and some of their hybrids ("botanical" roses).

Figure 19-8.
Miniature rose cultivar rind grafted onto *Rosa canina* (Dog Rose) seedling. Note the ordinary rubber band used for tying-in and the development of callus at the cut surface of the rootstock and at the base of the scion.

Grafting Procedure

Initial Rootstock Preparation

Use hand pruners to reduce the root system to 7.5–10 cm (3–4″) and to cut back the stem to retain 2.5 cm (1″) of hypocotyl.

Scion Preparation

(1) Remove the leaves, retaining a small length of petiole.
(2) Use a knife slanted at a 20–25° angle to cut a one-budded scion, 2–2.5 cm (¾–1″) long, beginning about 3 mm (⅛″) above the bud.

Rootstock Preparation

Make a vertical cut, 2 cm (¾″) long, on a clean area of hypocotyl. The knife blade may then be "rolled" to ease the rind away from the woody tissue.

Matching-up

Place the scion between the flaps of rind on the rootstock so that the bud is just below the apex of the hypocotyl. The exposed scion above the rootstock can be left to encourage callusing over the cut surface tissue of the hypocotyl.

Tying-up

Wind cotton twine twice around the top of the rootstock and then spiral it down the graft, finishing off with a half-hitch knot.

Aftercare

The grafts are packed into moist peat moss, 23–25 cm (9–10") deep, in deep flats or in a grafting case. The base temperature is set at 24–27°C (75–80°F).

POTTED ROOTSTOCK GRAFTING

Bench grafting onto pot-grown rootstocks is more widely used for woody ornamentals than bare-root rootstocks. To the outsider, there is perhaps an "air of mystique" about this method of propagation. Perseverance, both with the method of grafting and with the aftercare, will soon give the beginner an appreciation of the necessities for success. This is perhaps the best example of how the propagator has to understand plants, from the source and handling of scion wood through to the production of the liners following the grafting process. Some of the principles behind the method will be described, so that the bench grafter has a foundation upon which to build.

The three major advantages for using pot-grown rootstocks over bare-root stocks are as follows:—

(i) A greater range of plants may be grafted. This includes both conifers and broad-leaved trees having a heavy sap rise and therefore needing a greater degree of control, e.g., *Picea* (Spruce), *Cedrus* (Cedar), *Acer palmatum* (Japanese Maple) and *Betula* (Birch). In addition, many rarer trees can be propagated by this method when other techniques have not proved reliable, e.g., *Fagus sylvatica* 'Roseo-marginata' (European Beech cv.)

Figure 19-9. *Acer japonicum* 'Aureum' (Golden Full-moon Maple) is a tree that requires side grafting onto a pot-grown rootstock.

Figure 19-10. Propagation by bench grafting onto pot-grown rootstocks gives a nursery the opportunity to specialize in, and sell, important high-value crops. This is a quality crop of *Acer palmatum* cvs. (Japanese Maple) imported in from a specialist Japanese nursery. (George Kato, Kato's Nurseries, Aldergrove, B.C., Canada)

(ii) The fact that the rootstock is grown in a soil medium within the small volume of a pot means that it can be conditioned to some extent, both before and afer grafting. For example, drying off the soil medium to restrict the flow of sap at grafting time and during aftercare.

(iii) The rate of scion growth during the months following grafting and the establishment of the grafts in containers and open ground during the growing-on phase are both improved for many species.

As a general rule, a propagator who is experiencing problems with bare-root grafts during the aftercare and establishment periods should consider using pot-grown rootstocks instead.

Rootstocks

In addition to compatibility, the criteria for quality pot-grown rootstocks are as follows:—

(1) There should be a well-developed fibrous root system surrounding the ball of soil. Many conifer specialists will select a reliable seed source for their rootstocks, e.g., *Pinus* (Pine), to ensure good root development and straight stems on which to graft. A poor root system will result in variable success and low quality liners.

(2) The root system should not be subject to root rots. For example, *Platycladus (Thuja) orientalis* (Oriental Arborvitae) is used instead of *Chamaecyparis lawsoniana* (Lawson Cypress) as the rootstock for *C. nootkatensis* 'Pendula' (Weeping Yellow Cedar) in high rainfall areas such as the Pacific Northwest region of North America.

(3) The caliper size should be of a constant grade through the rootstocks—"pencil thickness" (ca. 6 mm/¼" caliper) being a guideline for many subjects. The stem should be straight and devoid of both multiple and side branches for ease of grafting. This means that the stocks must be thoroughly graded out, particularly seedlings, before potting-up.

(4) The rootstock should have the ability to "push" as much scion growth as possible during the months after the graft has successfully united. This is particularly important with some conifers (e.g., *Abies*, Fir, and *Picea*, Spruce) and deciduous trees (e.g., *Aesculus*, Buckeye or Horsechestnut, and *Quercus*, Oak) that have essentially one major flush of growth.

Seedling Rootstocks

Similar criteria apply here to the use of seedling rootstocks as explained under open-ground budding (p. 459) and bare-root grafting (p. 512). However, it is probable that some different seedling rootstocks not normally offered by the supplier will be required. There are two options in this case. Firstly, to encourage the supplier to grow the specific rootstocks required. Secondly, to purchase seed from a reputable seed house (p. 13) and produce the rootstocks on the nursery. *Hamamelis virginiana* (Common Witch Hazel) is a good example for this procedure.

As a general rule, seedling rootstocks require one complete growing season in the pot before use in dormant winter grafting. This timing is sometimes reduced in warmer climates—for example, *Acer palmatum* (Japanese Maple) seedlings can be potted in October and then stood down in a greenhouse for grafting in the following February. A sufficiently large root ball will not form unless the growing conditions are suitable. The time period to produce a seedling rootstock ready for grafting may be categorized as follows:—

(i) **Three year pot-grown rootstock**—Two seasons in an open-ground seed bed, with undercutting or transplanting after one season, then lifted and potted after the second season to complete the three-year cycle. For example, *Abies* (Fir), *Cedrus* (Cedar), *Picea* (Spruce) and *Pinus* (Pine).

(ii) **Two year pot-grown rootstock**—One season in the open-ground seed bed, lifted and potted to complete the two-year cycle. For example, *Acer palmatum* (Japanese Maple), *Alnus* (Alder), *Betula* (Birch), *Cornus florida* (Eastern Flowering Dogwood), *Liquidambar* (Sweet Gum) and *Quercus* (Oak).

(iii) **One year pot-grown rootstock**—One season in a liner pot from germination in spring and subsequently grown-on in a greenhouse/shade house (see p. 84). For example, *Betula pendula* (European White Birch) and *Alnus glutinosa* (Black or Common Alder).

Before potting up, the rootstocks must be graded or re-graded for stem caliper, root pruned, and side shoots removed from the main stem about 7.5–10 cm (3–4") above the root system. A useful short-term storage method if potting is delayed is to bundle the rootstocks and completely cover them with sawdust.

The choice of growing medium for the potted rootstock is important. Excessive drying out of the medium can cause problems during aftercare, destroying the newly developing roots, and re-wetting is difficult. I prefer a medium that is flexible in the time period for wetting and drying the rootball. This can be achieved by adding up to 30–35% good quality, partially sterilized (pasteurized) or fumigated loam to the selected nursery mix.

Loam-less potting mixes have also been used successfully for growing pot-grown rootstocks. However, they will dry out at a faster rate than loam-based mixes. The controlled-release fertilizer added to the mix should be one with an 18–24 month effect. The quantity of the controlled-release fertilizer can be reduced to lessen the risk of salt build-up stimulated by basal heat. The pH of a loam-less mix should be adjusted to 4.8–5.0 for calcifuge plants. Low pH peats and acid barks intended for general use may have to have the pH raised to 5.5 with magnesium (dolomitic) limestone.

Clay pots were traditionally used for growing the rootstocks, and are still occasionally used. The porosity of the clay meant that it was much easier to dry out the rootball prior to grafting. Rigid square or round plastic containers with a diameter of either 9 cm (3½") or 10 cm (4") are now usually standard. The square pot allows more pots to be accommodated in the grafting case if stood down vertically. The larger volume "long tom", 10 × 15 cm (4 × 6"), is excellent, despite using more potting soil. It allows a more substantial root system to develop on deeper rooted plants such as *Aesculus* (Buckeye, Horse-chestnut) and *Quercus* (Oak).

A successful technique used at Hillier Nurseries (Winchester) Ltd., Romsey, England, for rootstocks with large tap roots, such as *Juglans* (Walnut) and *Quercus* (Oak), is as follows. One-or two-year seedlings of a size suitable for grafting are lifted and the tap root is severed so that it will be 2.5 cm (1") less in length than the depth of the pot. They are then bedded in a peat moss and sand mix in a cold frame for one growing season so that the tap root develops numerous fibrous roots. The rootstocks are potted-up in the following winter, i.e., one year after the initial severing of the roots. The *Quercus* (Oak) is then grafted in the following September/October, while the *Juglans* (Walnut) is grafted early in the following year. A summary of the technique is tabulated below:—

Sever tap root	— February 1984
Bed in peat and sand	— One full growing season
Pot	— Winter 1984/85
Graft	— September/October 1985 (*Quercus*)
	January/February 1986 (*Juglans*)

The rootstocks are stood down in outdoor beds after potting, unless there is a problem with exposure or irrigation when the more controlled environment of a shade house with overhead irrigation is ideal. A covering of salt-free hemlock or fir sawdust, 6 mm (¼") deep, over the pots will reduce the need for irrigation, help to keep the rootball at a more constant temperature, and eliminate weeds. Shade structures are necessary for *Rhododendron*, *Hamamelis* (Witch Hazel), *Tsuga* (Hemlock) and *Fagus* (Beech). Pest and disease control is important, including inspection of the rootballs of conifers such as *Pinus* (Pine) and *Picea* (Spruce) to check for root aphids. These can be controlled by drenching the potting soil with diazinon. Red spider mites and spruce aphids can cause deterioration of the rootstocks, but a program using alternating organo-phosphorus insecticides will keep them in abeyance. Systematic fungicides, such as benomyl (Benlate®), will be needed to control foliar diseases such as mildew. A fungicidal drench, e.g., with thiophanate methyl + ethazol (Banrot®), will be helpful to prevent roots being infected with *Pythium* and *Fusarium* (Collar and Root Rots). Rootstocks infected with root rots should be discarded, as an unhealthy root system can significantly reduce the percentage take and subsequent scion growth.

Rootstocks from Cuttings

An alternative to seedling rootstocks is to use rootstocks raised from cuttings. Some nurseries have relied on this technique to provide *Rhododendron* 'Cunningham's White', *R.* 'Cunningham's Blush' and *R.* 'County of York' rootstocks for use with some of the more difficult-to-root hardy hybrids. Similarly, *Juniperus chinensis* 'Hetzii' (Hetz Blue Juniper) is popular in North America as a rootstock for some *J. scopulorum* cvs. (Rocky Mountain Juniper), e.g., 'Pathfinder'. I have noted *Cryptomeria japonica* 'Elegans' (Plume Cryptomeria) used as rootstock for such dwarf forms of the species as 'Bandai-Sugi', and *Taxus × media* 'Hicksii' (Hicks' Yew) for *T. baccata* 'Fastigiata Aurea' (Golden Irish Yew).

The circumstances in which to use rootstocks raised from cuttings include:—

(i) When clonal material is desired, e.g., *Rhododendron* 'Cunningham's White'.

(ii) To avoid bent stems at the point where the graft is to be placed. *Rhododendron ponticum* (Pontic Rhododendron) grown from seed has this disadvantage, as did *Ilex aquifolium* (English Holly) in the days when it was used for grafting some variegated forms of holly.

(iii) When a rootstock is desired in a short period of time. A pot-grown rootstock can be available within one year after rooting a cutting of sufficient size and stem caliper, e.g., *Cryptomeria japonica* 'Elegans' (Plume Cryptomeria).

The criteria for this technique to be economical are that sufficient cuttings are available, that they are graded to size and caliper before sticking, that they root easily within the available propagation facility, and that they subsequently develop a healthy root system.

Burlapped (Balled) or Bedded Rootstocks

This is essentially a compromise between the bare-root and the pot-grown rootstock. There are three methods to carry out this procedure and these are outlined below.

(1) Lay a damp thin-grade burlap (hessian) square on the bench and place on it a sufficient amount of moist peat moss for working into and around the root system (use the fingers for this). Place the rootstock on the peat moss and work it into the root system. The peat moss is compressed with the hand and then secured by tying-in the four corners of the burlap (hessian) square (using a similar tying technique to that used when burlapping open-ground conifers). After grafting, the burlap (hessian) square must be well covered by damp peat moss in the grafting case and not allowed to dry out. White root initials can be seen coming through the burlap (hessian) within 3–4 weeks. The burlap (hessian) is not removed but left to naturally deteriorate after potting or bedding out in the open ground. I have seen this technique used successfully for *Betula* (Birch) grafts when pot-grown rootstocks were not available. It is unlikely to be successful for coarse-rooted stocks and those that do not establish easily as it is necessary to have a reasonable fibrous root system before grafting. Do not use plastic or plastic-based materials as these will restrict the developing root system.

Figure 19-11.
Burlapped *Magnolia* sp. rootstocks have been used successfully for bench grafting some of the large-leaved *Magnolia* species and varieties, e.g., *M. ashei* (Ashe Magnolia).

(2) Transplanted rootstocks are allowed to grow *in-situ* for about two years in the open ground. They are lifted about two weeks prior to grafting, burlapped with a damp burlap (hessian) square and brought into the greenhouse at 10–15°C (50–59°F) to dry off the rootball. The care after grafting is similar to that described above.

In both the above methods it is important to examine a few rootballs at random before grafting. This is done by cutting longitudinally through the rootball and observing the root development. It can be done while lifting the rootstocks prior to burlapping, but is easier to see when the rootball is drier. I experienced a substantial loss of *Cedrus atlantica* 'Glauca' (Blue Atlas Cedar) grafts when using burlapped *C. deodara* (Himalayan Cedar) rootstocks. The needles became discolored and dropped within ten days of being placed in the plastic-covered grafting case. The problem was soon identified when the rootball was cut through—root development had only occurred in the upper 8 cm (3") of the ball. This was caused by the fact that the rootstocks had been initially transplanted into a compacted soil with a shallow "pan" that had restricted root development. The warm temperatures in the grafting case made conditions worse as they literally dried out the restricted root system. Normal watering application at the neck of the rootball was not sufficient to alleviate the problem. This is a good example of learning and adapting from one's own graft failures.

Rootstock stems for top-working are sometimes burlapped with peat moss being included around the roots before the material is secured. The practice is usually to lift appropriate stems from the open ground, grow-on in containers, and then graft at the appropriate time of year once they are established.

(3) A useful system for *Rhododendron* is to take root cuttings of *R.* 'Cunningham's White' or

R. ponticum (Pontic Rhododendron) in late summer to early fall and transplant them into a deep flat or bench with a depth of about 15 cm (6"). A suitable mix to use for transplanting the cuttings is a low-nitrate ericaceous potting mix in which there is greater emphasis on peat moss. Rootstocks with a well-developed root system are removed just prior to grafting, but are *not* burlapped. After side or whip grafting, the grafts are plunged into moist peat moss in the grafting case.

A similar principle has been used for grafting *Cedrus* (Cedar) and *Picea* (Spruce) except that a seedling is transplanted rather than a rooted cutting. Two-year seedlings are transplanted into a soil with a high percentage of peat moss, using 10 cm (4") square spacing, and grown on for one or two years to obtain a good rootball. When required for winter grafting, the rootstocks are carefully lifted (ensuring that the rootballs are kept intact), packed into wooden boxes and taken into the greenhouse. After grafting, they can be re-boxed and placed into the aftercare facility or, alternatively, bedded into peat moss placed on the floor of the grafting case.

Time of Year

There are essentially two periods during the year when grafting onto pot-grown rootstocks can be carried out. The first period is July to August, referred to as "Summer Grafting", and the second is December to February, referred to as "Winter Grafting". There is some flexibility in these time periods depending on geographical location and the species to be grafted.

Summer Grafting (July-August)

Many ornamental woody plants have completed their major growth phase by July, and there is a natural lowering of the sap rise from the roots into the stems. Thus, there is less risk of excessive sap rise immediately after grafting, which can result in loss of grafts—usually referred to as "flooding of the union". For this reason, plants such as *Acer palmatum* (Japanese Maple) are grafted by some propagators at this time of year. By December, when winter grafting begins, the rootstock has completed its natural growth cycle and is dormant. This means that growth is stimulated, with natural sap rise occurring, when it is brought into a warm greenhouse. In practice, this can be largely controlled by "conditioning" the rootstock beforehand. In summer grafting the sap rise is naturally on the "downward" flow, while winter grafting stimulates the "upward" flow. In most years, there has been sufficient time by July/August for the scion wood to have ripened so that it can be handled in the semi-ripewood condition.

George Chandler (formerly chief propagator at Stewarts Nurseries, Ferndown, Dorset, England) was a strong exponent of summer grafting for *Picea pungens* 'Koster' (Koster Blue Spruce), and I had the privilege of seeing some excellent grafts that he had done. *Quercus* (Oak) does not show a heavy rise of sap but Peter Dummer of Hillier Nurseries (Winchester) Ltd., England, has shown that September/October is reliable for the rarer species and cultivars. Some propagators prefer to graft *Hamamelis* (Witch Hazel) in August although it does not have a heavy sap rise.

Three further attractions of summer grafting, in addition to a natural lowering of the sap rise, are:—

(i) It relieves the pressure on labor and space caused by winter grafting.

(ii) It enables the propagator to utilize well-shaded cold frames in addition to the greenhouse for callusing the grafts. Conifer grafts can be both callused and over-wintered in cold frames, except in extremely cold areas.

(iii) The vascular tissue between the rootstock and scion unites prior to the onset of winter, thus encouraging a more even break of the scion in the following spring with the hope of obtaining increased growth.

To conclude, the decision to graft in the summer as an alternative or in addition to the winter period must be left to the individual. It is a subject that promotes discussion with varying opinions. In general, I feel that the best advice is to rely initially on winter grafting, using summer grafting as a back-up when necessary to fulfill the desired overall grafting totals for the nursery.

Winter Grafting (December-February)

This is the major period for bench grafting ornamentals with the scions either in the evergreen hardwood or deciduous dormant condition. One mistake that the novice can make is to try to extend the grafting season into March—by this time both the scion and rootstock have a greater natural ability for the sap to rise and for buds to swell and flush. In addition, the correct aftercare can become more difficult due to warmer temperatures and longer days.

Grafting Calendar

The grafting calendar needs to be planned in advance of the season. It will be determined largely by such factors as geographical location, past and projected nursery sales, availability of labor, scions and rootstocks, and available space.

An outline sequence used at Iseli Nurseries, Boring, Oregon, is to graft *Cedrus* (Cedar) in November (after Thanksgiving) through December; *Picea* (Spruce) from November through January; *Juniperus* (Juniper) in January and February; and *Pinus* (Pine) and *Larix* (Larch) in February.

Drying Off the Rootstocks

The process of drying off the rootstocks must begin about 2–3 weeks before grafting. This entails the reduction of moisture levels in the potting mix around the root system. There are two reasons for drying off. Firstly, it reduces the likelihood of "flooding of the union" through excess sap accumulating around the graft union. Secondly, the physiological activity of the rootstocks is initiated by bringing them into the warmer temperature used to dry out the rootball. It is necessary to promote this 2- to 3-week advancement of the rootstock development when grafting a completely dormant scion. Visual signs of development are new root growth beginning to develop around the perimeter of the rootball and, in some cases, the swelling of buds on the stems, for example in *Betula* (Birch).

The need to reduce the moisture level within the rootball is universally accepted by propagators, but there are sometimes conflicting views on the desirable degree of dryness to be attained. I have discussed this particular topic with some foremost propagators and these discussions, plus personal experiences, lead me to believe that a good guideline for winter grafting is to aim for about 50–60% moisture content of the potting mix—particularly for conifers. There are exceptions to this. For example, *Juglans* (Walnut) requires substantial drying off, while some propagators have found that *Betula* (Birch) should be considerably dried off, but not to the same high degree as with *Juglans* (Walnut). Conversely, damage to rootstocks of *Alnus* (Alder) has been found to occur if they are substantially dried off. The danger of excessive drying off is that the new white roots that have formed are killed off in the warm grafting case, and there will also be a greater need for early watering of the grafts before callusing develops—a practice to be avoided as far as possible. Placing the grafts in a closed case with a layer of moist peat moss at the base should lessen the need for additional watering. The overall objective should be to maintain a balance between allowing root and union development with a minimum of sap rise. This delicate balance is only achieved with experience.

There are two points of view regarding the drying off of rootstocks for summer grafting, particularly for *Acer palmatum* cvs. (Japanese Maple). Firstly, the rootstocks should be dried off until the young shoots show signs of wilting. Secondly, drying off is hardly necessary as the rootstock is in full leaf and is therefore physiologically active so that drying off can cause severe stress. In practice, both these methods have given good results. [A potting mix moisture content level of around 60% has been found to be a good compromise.]

Procedure

A few rootstocks are taken at random for inspection of the rootball. The three points to look for are:—

(i) That the rootball is well developed around the inside perimeter of the pot.

(ii) That it is free from root rots caused either by disease, especially *Verticillium* on *Acer* (Maple) and *Phytophthora* on conifers and rhododendrons, or by waterlogging. The rootstocks are under considerable stress during drying off, and experience has shown that *Fusarium* and *Pythium* infections can then affect the roots. *Picea* (Spruce) is particularly prone to this.

(iii) That the roots are free from pest infection, for example, root aphids. These rootstocks should be drenched with a malathion or diazinon solution for control. The rootstocks should also be free from Vine Weevil attack.

The rootstocks are brought into a greenhouse with the air temperature set at 10–12°C (50–54°F) about 2–3 weeks before grafting. Long stems of plants such as *Acer palmatum* (Japanese

Maple) should be cut back to 15–30 cm (6–12") for ease of handling. However, some propagators prefer to bring the pot-grown rootstocks into a cold greenhouse about 6–8 weeks prior to grafting.

The rootstocks (and rootballs) should be inspected daily. The drying out process should be slow—another reason for adding partially sterilized (pasteurized) loam to the potting mix because peat moss/sand mixes may dry out too quickly and are more difficult to re-wet. The degree of dryness can be assessed visually by the color of the rootball. It is helpful to have some control rootstocks outside to use for comparison until the procedure becomes "second nature". The rootstocks are ready for grafting when the rootball has approximately 50% moisture removed and about 1 cm (⅜") of white roots can be seen.

If the rootball is excessively wet, the following procedures may be implemented:—

(i) Bring the stocks into a cold frame, unheated greenhouse, shed or lean-to during October/November so that they are protected from the winter rains.

(ii) Remove the rootball from the pot, place on an open bench for 3–4 days and then replace in the pot.

(iii) Raise the air temperature by 5°C (9°F). Care needs to be taken in this case to ensure that the physiological activity does not become too advanced. This method is not ideal.

Scion Wood

Source, Mother Plants, Establishment and Maintenance

The principles for source, establishment and maintenance of mother plants to provide deciduous scion wood for grafting are discussed on p. 464. The improved performance obtained by establishing and manipulating hedges or individual specimens far outweighs the use of unpruned trees—particularly for *Acer* (Maple), *Alnus* (Alder), *Betula* (Birch), *Carpinus* (Hornbeam), *Fagus* (Beech), *Liriodendron* (Tulip Tree), *Quercus* (Oak) and *Ulmus* (Elm). Deciduous plants are pruned back hard during November to February. Evergreens are best pruned during late February to the end of March. Some specific examples are given below.

(i) Conifers—The establishment of mother plants to provide the correct numbers and type of scions is normally better in the long term than relying on production plants. However, some nurseries do prefer to take scions from production plants in the belief that they are the healthiest and most nutritionally robust, as well as being pest- and disease-free. Propagators of *Abies* (Fir), *Picea* (Spruce) and *Pinus* (Pine) would particularly benefit from the practice of establishing mother plants. *Abies* (Fir) and *Picea* (Spruce) should be encouraged to form more upright, vigorous terminal scions.

(ii) *Rhododendron*—As with cuttings, the vigorous pithy shoots that are often found on production plants should be avoided. It is often useful to site the mother plants in a shade house, mulching to keep the root systems cool and avoiding heavy applications of nitrogenous fertilizers. Heavy pruning should be avoided. Removal of the flower buds, and adventitious buds where desirable, before growth starts will increase breaks and growth. Scion material should be selected from the thinner well-ripened shoots.

Mother plants of some of the slower growing forms, which require greater extension growth, may be containerized and placed in an unheated, well-shaded greenhouse. I have seen this used successfully for some forms of *R. yakusimanum* (Yakusima Rhododendron) that require increased maiden growth. The plants may be moved to a shade structure after the growth flush has finished in order to ripen the wood.

(iii) *Hamamelis* (Witch Hazel)—A useful method, particularly in exposed areas, is to site mother plants in a structure clad with shade cloth fabric of woven polypropylene (as described on p. 252). The more controlled environment will aid in establishment of the plants and will increase the extension growth, and often the quality, of the scion wood. This technique can also be utilized for *Acer palmatum* (Japanese Maple) and other deciduous shrubs if necessary.

Selection of Scion Wood

Grafting onto pot-grown rootstocks is used for conifers and a wider range of trees and shrubs than bare-root grafting, and the selection of scion wood has to be more specific in a number of instances. Some examples are explained below.

Figure 19-12. A (left). A newly-established "orchard" of *Betula* (Birch), *Alnus* (Alder) and *Quercus* (Oak) species and cultivar mother trees to provide vigorous maiden growth scion wood for bench grafting. B (right). An eight-year-old established "orchard" of *Fagus* (Beech), *Sorbus* (Mountain Ash), *Gleditsia* (Honey Locust) and *Betula* (Birch) species and cultivars to provide scion wood. Note that annual pruning has retained the height of small trees to ease scion wood collection. (Hadlow College of Agriculture & Horticulture, Tonbridge, Kent, U.K.)

Figure 19-13. Well-established rows of *Abies* sp. (Fir), *Pinus* (Pine) and *Picea* (Spruce) to provide vigorous terminal scion wood for bench grafting. (Joh. Bruns Nursery, Oldenburg, West Germany)

Figure 19-14. A pruned hedge of *Picea pungens* 'Koster' (Koster Blue Spruce) provides scion wood and also crop shelter.

(i) *Picea pungens* cvs. (Colorado Spruce) —Select one-year-old vigorous terminal scions, 10–15 cm (4–6″) long. Each scion should have a dominant terminal bud and not less than three radial buds.

The importance of correct scion selection was brought home to me when I visited a nursery in Holland where one drift of *Picea pungens* 'Koster' (Koster Blue Spruce) had correctly selected scions while the other plants had received weak scion wood taken from axillary shoots towards the base and center of the mother plant. The four-year-old plants with the correct scion wood showed the dominant leader with symmetrical whorls of branches formed after each season's growth. Plants with the incorrect scions showed uneven growth, with side shoots competing for dominance and a lack of symmetrical whorls, and more attention to staking and pruning was required.

(ii) *Picea brewerana* (Brewer's Weeping Spruce) and *P. smithiana* (Himalayan Spruce) — Only the dominant terminal scion at the end of each branch should be selected. Scions from the weeping branches can be used but will promote poor growth with continuous staking and tying necessary for some years.

(iii) *Sequoia sempervirens* cvs. (Coast Redwood) —This plant is notorious for changes in growth after propagation due to topophysis. Scions should be selected from the more vertically growing shoots. The selection of horizontal shoots will promote subsequent lateral growth.

Figure 19-15.
Note the irregular growth pattern and lack of symmetrical whorls of side shoots resulting from incorrect selection of the scion.

(iv) *Sequoiadendron giganteum* **'Pendulum' (Weeping Giant Sequoia)** —Scions selected from open-ground mother plants in the fertile soils of the Pacific Northwest region of North America are often too large and insufficiently ripened for winter grafting. Smaller ripened scions are obtained by lifting the plants from the open ground and containerizing them into large boxes, so that watering and nutrition can be controlled and the root system restricted.

(v) Dwarf Conifers—A number of dwarf and slow-growing conifers need to be grafted. The size of scion wood needed means that it will be necessary to cut into two- to three-year-old wood. The resulting scion will have a dominant leader with a number of side shoots. Examples are *Picea pungens* 'Globosa' (Globe Colorado Blue Spruce), *Taxus baccata* 'Adpressa Aurea' (English Yew cv.) and *Cedrus libani* 'Green Prince' (Cedar-of-Lebanon cv.).

(vi) Deciduous Trees and Shrubs—In maritime climates, one-year-old wood can often be insufficiently ripe, especially for summer grafting. If this is the case, the scions should be prepared with a short length of two-year-old wood below the one-year-old wood. The actual carpentry is then carried out on the two-year-old wood. An additional advantage is that the physiological ages of the scion and rootstock are more closely matched. It is very important to check that all buds are healthy prior to grafting. Multi-stem scions are sometimes necessary for dwarf and slow-growing plant forms.

The majority of *Cornus florida* (Eastern Flowering Dogwood) selections that I have seen grafted have used one-year-old wood for the scions, but James Wells made an interesting observation in his book *Plant Propagation Practices*. The objective was to develop specimens with a well-branched head after 30–45 cm (12–18″) maiden stem growth. He described a practice used in New Jersey whereby they used 15 cm (6″) long scions of three- or even four-year-old wood with a minimum of two nodes. The subsequent growth was considerably stronger than when one-year-old terminal scions were used, as the latter have the tendency to produce side shoots during the maiden year at the expense of terminal growth.

Collection and Storage of Scion Wood

The principles for the collection and storage of scion wood are described in Chapters 17 and 18. Freshly cut scion wood should be used whenever feasible, so a general rule is to cut only sufficient for half-a-day's grafting. This is particularly important in summer grafting, when there is a much stronger possibility of the deterioration of scion wood. Short-term cold storage in a cool room is satisfactory if the scions are wrapped either in polyethylene containing a few water droplets or in moist sacking. Wrapping the scion wood in moist sacking and placing the parcel in a pile of moist sawdust is very satisfactory for a few days storage.

It may be necessary to collect scion wood of evergreens in November in cold exposed areas or in regions of high snowfall, and store until grafting in January to February. Thomsen Planteskole, Aalborg, Denmark, do this successfully for *Picea* (Spruce) by placing the scions in a polyethylene bag and cold storing at 4°C (39°F). There is some dehydration of the material, but the grafting success rate has been as good as for fresh collected scion wood.

Magnolia scions have been successfully cold stored for 3 months by covering them with dampened sphagnum moss and then placing in a polyethylene bag.

Tying-in and Waxing

The different types of tying materials are described in Chapter 4. Rubber strips or bands are the most widely used materials, but waxed cotton is preferred by some propagators. The ties are spiralled down the stem from the top and fixed with a half-hitch knot behind and just under the union. In side veneer grafting, the lip or veneer left at the base of the cut should not be covered with the tie as damage by "crushing" can occur at the critical site of the graft, with disastrous results. Also, there is a risk of bruising the tissue at the veneer. The ties should be tight, but excessive binding on scions with soft stems must be avoided. *Abies* (Fir) is an example of a conifer in which the union may fail if a constriction begins to form at the base of the scion.

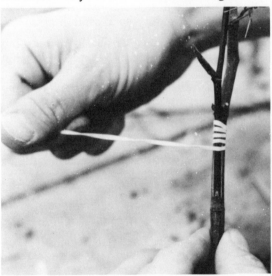

Figure 19-16. A rubber strip is used to tie-in a side veneer graft of *Fagus sylvatica* 'Riversii' (Rivers Purple Beech) on *F. sylvatica* (European Beech). Note that the tie has been slightly twisted as it is spiralled down the graft. This will ensure that the tie will lie flat around the scion and rootstock. (Note also that the matching-up is not perfect.)

Figure 19-17. Polyethylene tape used successfully for tying-in a *Pinus* (Pine) graft. Some propagators find that polyethylene is more difficult to handle for bench grafts but it does eliminate the need for waxing over.

The need to wax over the union is largely dependent on the aftercare procedure. As with bare-root grafting, it is not necessary to wax if the union is covered by peat moss. Also, waxing is often omitted when warm temperature and high humidity conditions are maintained in the grafting case because the possibility of tissue at the graft union becoming desiccated is minimal. For example, some nurseries that specialize in conifers prefer to enclose the grafts of *Juniperus* (Juniper) and *Chamaecyparis* (False Cypress) within a polyethylene tent for 3 weeks following grafting to create a warm, humid environment.

Waxing is advisable when humidity and air temperatures are low and movement of air is encouraged—for example, on the open bench or in a partial polyethylene tent. If in doubt, I would generally recommend waxing the union as there seems to be little evidence of it hindering a satisfactory union. Once again, the decision whether or not to wax depends on the propagator's own preferences and is based on experience, the plant material in question, aftercare facilities, and maintenance procedures. Hot waxes are popular for bench grafts, and cold latex waxes (Farwells Tree Doc®—Yellow and Green Cap) are reported to be very successful. Not waxing will significantly speed up the grafting operation.

The tip of the scion (where applicable) and union are both waxed. Sometimes both the scion and union of bench grafts of deciduous species are coated in wax.

Aftercare

It has already been emphasized that the aftercare is critical to the success or failure of the grafts. One foremost propagator believes that the success of bench grafting pot-grown rootstocks is 45% attributable to the quality and procedures used in preparing the rootstocks for grafting, 10% attributable to the actual carpentry carried out, and 45% attributable to the aftercare procedures. Practical experience is vital to fully understand and apply the aftercare procedures.

The important features relating to aftercare can be grouped and summarized as below.

(a) Facility

Pot bench grafts are normally callused in a grafting case facility (p. 160) constructed within the greenhouse. A cold frame (p. 106) can be successfully used in some cases—for example, for summer bench grafting of *Picea* (Spruce) and September/October grafting of *Quercus* (Oak). Propagators have made a number of modifications to the traditional grafting case by re-designing benches, using floor space, and utilizing polyethylene instead of glass. The polyethylene can be directly laid onto the grafts (contact polyethylene), supported by metal hoops, or hung down over the facility as a drape.

The photographs and text describe modifications in facility design and methods to stand-down the grafted rootstocks in the selected facility in order to promote a successful graft union.

(1) A layer of peat moss, 15–20 cm (6–8″) deep, is placed in the bed. It should be moist but not to the point of dripping when a handful is squeezed. The pots of grafts are placed in rows in the peat moss, angled at 45° and with the sides touching. The scion must be uppermost. The reason for the angling is so that any water droplets from condensation falling onto the grafts will accumulate on the underside of the scion rather than around the union, and it also allows more air to reach the scion. Other advantages suggested are firstly, that it could restrict the sap flow, and secondly, that it allows the glass or polyethylene cover of the grafting case to be placed closer to the peat moss and thus help to increase the humidity. This method is particularly popular in Holland. It can be especially helpful for some conifers, e.g., *Cedrus* (Cedar) and *Juniperus* (Juniper). When one row has been laid down, moss is loosely packed over the pots and the graft unions.

An alternative method is to reduce the layer of peat moss to 7.5–10 cm (3–4″) deep so that it covers only half to three-quarters of the depth of the pots.

Whichever method is used, the peat moss should not cover any foliage of ever-green material, particularly conifers.

(2) A layer of moistened peat moss is spread over the base of the grafting case to a depth of 1.3 cm (½″). The pots are stood down with the base just below the top surface of the peat moss.

The aim with the peat moss in both cases is to assist in providing more constant humidity and to slow down the drying out of the base of the rootball. The first method is normally used when placing unwaxed grafts in a grafting case with high humidity and air temperature. The second method is used where there is more movement of air, e.g., in a polyethylene tunnel or tent drape or on the open bench, and the grafts have been waxed.

I have seen one procedure where the peat moss was drenched with captan or benomyl before the pots were plunged or stood down. This was to help reduce the incidence of disease.

When all the pots are in place, supported polyethylene film, where applicable, is laid over the grafts and tucked in around the sides of the bench or bed. The height of the polyethylene above the grafts has ranged successfully from 10–45 cm (4–18″). The increased height makes ventilation easier. An ideal situation is to have the glass or polyethylene cover 10–15 cm (4–6″) above the grafts for the first 10 days, and then raise to 30–45 cm (12–18″).

One effective method to provide some environmental control during the first few days on an open bench that I have noted is to use a series of portable wooden frames clad with a lightweight, clear, rigid plastic. These frames can be moved to new batches of grafts as necessary.

Figure 19-18. A greenhouse installed with grafting cases. A primary advantage of benches is that the grafts normally can be more readily inspected to check that the correct aftercare procedures are being maintained. (Wells Nursery, Inc., Mount Vernon, WA, U.S.A.)

Figure 19-19. A wide-span greenhouse fitted with benches for grafting. Note the shade cloth fabric to provide shade as necessary, and the polyethylene cover to retain a humid environment around the grafts.

Figure 19-20. A polyethylene cover used directly over summer bench grafted *Acer palmatum* (Japanese Maple). (Peter Catt, Liss Forest Nursery, Liss, Hampshire, U.K.)

Figure 19-21. Individual glass jars inverted over *Camellia* grafts to create a closed environment. (Monrovia Nurseries, Azusa, CA, U.S.A.)

Figure 19-22. *Juniperus* (Juniper) grafts being packed at a 45° angle into moist peat moss in a grafting case. (Sheridan Nurseries, Oakville, ON, Canada)

Figure 19-23. *Pinus* (Pine) and *Picea* (Spruce) grafts packed into a simple grafting case consisting of wooden sides to which are attached wire hoops to support the polyethylene film. Note that the scion is uppermost when the grafts are angled.

A new development in grafting is the use of hot callusing pipes in which warm air is directed at the graft unions for 10–20 days to produce rapid callusing while the scion buds remain dormant. Previous hot callusing methods exposed the whole plant to warm temperatures, resulting in the beginning of growth by both the roots and buds. Experiments by H. B. Lagerstedt of the National Clonal Germplasm Repository, Corvallis, Oregon, have shown that the optimum temperature for *Corylus avellana* (European Filbert) and *Juglans nigra* (Black Walnut) is about 27°C (80°F). Further experiments have shown that the hot callusing pipe is of no great advantage for plants that normally callus readily over a wide range of temperatures, except that subsequent growth may be improved because they can be planted out earlier. However, the method is of great advantage for plants that do not normally callus readily—most species tested have callused within 21 days.

The hot callusing pipe system consists of a series of 6 m (20′) lengths of 3.8 or 5 cm (1½ or 2″) diameter polyvinyl pipes with perpendicular 1.3–1.5 cm (½–⅝″) wide slots made at 2.5 cm (1″) distances and extending for just less than half the diameter of the pipe. The pipes are insulated with a wrapping of 2.5 cm (1″) thick foam rubber slit at the points over the slots. The heat is provided by an electric heating cable or small hot water pipe running through the polyvinyl pipe and can be thermostatically controlled to maintain the desired temperature.

The rootstocks must be well-rooted and long scions are necessary to keep the buds as far as possible from the warm pipe. The graft union is completely sealed with overlapping strips of rubber or plastic grafting bands and is then placed in one of the slits in the foam rubber with the root system embedded in moist sawdust and the buds exposed to ambient air temperatures. The cut ends of *Corylus avellana* (European Filbert) are waxed to prevent drying.

Plants successfully callused with the hot callusing pipe include *Corylus avellana* (European Filbert), *Fagus* (Beech), *Juglans nigra* (Black Walnut), *J. regia* (English or Persian Walnut), *Cornus* (Dogwood), *Acer* (Maple), *Carya illinoinensis* (Pecan), *Sequoiadendron giganteum* 'Pendulum' (Weeping Giant Sequoia) and *Pseudotsuga menziesii* (Douglas Fir).

V. Holden, Holden Wholesale Nurseries, Inc., Silverton, Oregon, has modified the original design of H. B. Lagerstedt to give additional insulation properties. The pipes are laid 30 cm (12″) apart on the floor of an unheated greenhouse. Species successfully callused on this nursery include *Cercidiphyllum japonicum* (Katsura Tree), *Fagus sylvatica* (European Beech) and *Cedrus* (Cedar).

(b) Shading

The grafts will require shading in most locations. Little or no shading is required during December and January when external light conditions are poor, but it becomes more critical as the year proceeds. It is essential during summer grafting. The main function of shading is to reduce temperature build-up, which can be excessive under glass or polyethylene. Shading is most effective when it is outside and above the greenhouse. This will provide a greater cooling effect than if it is placed inside the greenhouse. It may still be necessary in some circumstances to have some shade cloth supported above the grafts inside the greenhouse as well as on the outside. A useful guideline used in Europe is to provide 80% shading for summer grafting and up to 50–70% shading, where applicable, for winter/spring grafting. [*NOTE:*—Some specialist nurseries in the western United States practice no shading for winter/spring grafting of some conifers, e.g., *Pinus* (Pine). However, it is essential to ensure that the rootstocks are not under stress or losses will occur.] The problems of excess light are when:—

- **(i)** The buds prematurely swell and new growth quickly flushes—particularly with *Acer* (Maple), *Tsuga* (Hemlock) and *Betula* (Birch)—due to a significant rise in air temperature.

    (ii) The air temperature rises and the humidity drops. This can scorch the foliage in severe cases, causing stress to the rootstocks. I learnt this from bitter experience with some *Pinus* (Pine) grafts just after they had been hardened-off during a prolonged dull and cloudy spell. One day of full sun on a public holiday resulted in brown and scorched scions and rootstocks. This was accentuated by the fact that the rootballs had been allowed to dry out.

As the light intensity increases, the glass of the greenhouse can be sprayed with an appropriate proprietary liquid shading preparation. Rolls of canes are used in some of the more traditional nurseries of Europe. The most convenient material is a woven polyethylene shade cloth which is suspended as a false ceiling and combined if necessary with a vertical curtain. A certain amount of shade can be provided by substituting "milky" polyethylene for clear. A false ceiling of woven polypropylene shade cloth is ideal for a large greenhouse, particularly if it is designed in sections so that areas can be pulled back when necessary.

Figure 19-24. Grafted *Pinus* (Pine) stood down onto a bench containing a layer of moist peat moss. Note that the greenhouse has been lined at the sides and over most of the roof with polyethylene to create a tent effect. This, plus the ability to roll the drapes up and down over the front of the bench, enables greater control of the environment around the grafts.

Figure 19-25. Two 6 m (20') lengths of polyvinyl chloride pipe used for hot callusing of *Corylus maxima* cvs. (Giant Filbert) grafts. Note that the root systems of the rootstocks are covered by moist sawdust, and that opaque polyethylene film covers the foam to keep it dry. (Reproduced by permission of Harry B. Lagerstedt, Clonal Germplasm Repository, Corvallis, OR, U.S.A.)

Figure 19-26. "Mock-up" to show the structure of the hot callus pipe without the outer foam insulation. Note the electric heating cables on each side of the narrow inner pipe, and the slit in the outer pipe where the graft is placed. (Reproduced by permission of Harry B. Lagerstedt, Clonal Germplasm Repository, Corvallis, OR, U.S.A.)

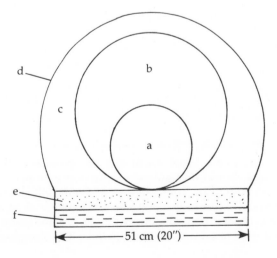

Diagram 19-6. Diagrammatic transervse section through a hot callus pipe. (Adapted from details viewed at Holden Wholesale Nurseries, Inc., Silverton, OR, U.S.A.)
Key
a—Inner 1.3 m (½") diameter plastic pipe to circulate hot water for basal heat.
b—Outer 5.0 cm (2") diameter plastic pipe with pre-cut slots to hold the grafts.
c—"Closed cell foam" covering outer pipe.
d—Polyethylene film to protect foam, secured onto wooden base.
e—Expanded polystyrene (Styrofoam®) for insulation.
f—2.5 cm (1") thick wooden base.

(c) Temperature and Humidity

Basal temperature regimes differ depending largely on location, experience and plant material. I have attempted to summarize the different systems and regimes used by various nursery operators to provide an initial guideline as shown below.

SYSTEM	BASAL TEMPERATURE	
	°C	°F
Open bench	16.5–18	62–65
Polyethylene tent or drape or Supported polyethylene ("low tunnel")	18–20	65–68
Grafting case with glass or Polyethylene 7.5 cm (3") above the grafts	20–21	68–70

Similarly, air temperature guidelines are as follows (it will be difficult to constantly maintain these levels in practice).

SYSTEM	AIR TEMPERATURE	
	°C	°F
Open bench	10–13.5	50–55
Polyethylene tent or drape or Supported polyethylene ("low tunnel")	15.5–18	60–65
Grafting case with glass or Polyethylene 7.5 cm (3") above grafts	21–24	70–75

The air temperature should be gradually reduced as the hardening-off process begins.

Some plants respond better to the higher temperatures and a humidity regime above 80%—for example, *Acer palmatum* cvs. (Japanese Maple). On the other hand, this can be detrimental with *Picea* (Spruce) because it encourages premature flushing of the scion buds before the union has adequately formed, resulting in loss of the grafts. Very high humidity levels can make the callus tissue that unites the scion and rootstock too soft, thus increasing the possibility of disease infection. Regular damping down of the pathways will help to keep up the humidity.

(d) Watering

Provided that the rootballs have the right moisture content at the time of grafting, it should not be necessary to give the first watering until callus tissue is seen to be developing between scion and rootstock. However, some propagators recommend that the grafts should not be watered until the buds on the scion begin to swell and extension growth is evident. The commencement of watering is also dependent on the medium, pot size and whether or not the pots have been plunged in peat moss. Grafts on an open bench have a tendency to dry out faster than those plunged in peat moss. Nevertheless, the rootballs should be randomly inspected to check their dryness. Evidence of the newly developing roots being lost means that earlier watering is necessary. The danger of overwatering during the initial 2–3 weeks is that it will encourage undesirable heavy sap rise. The amount of watering is increased as the grafts are hardened-off. For summer bench grafting, it is preferable to wait until there has been plentiful callus formation before watering.

Figure 19-27. The method and frequency of watering bench grafts is one of the most critical procedures during the aftercare period. A (left). Watering *Picea* (Spruce) grafts individually by hand. B (right). Misting conifer bench grafts on a floor-level bed after the growth has flushed. Note the even covering of water droplets being applied by the operator. (Terry Wiggin. Wells Nursery, Inc., Mount Vernon, WA, U.S.A.)

A simple way to apply water is with a hand-operated "watering gun" or a conventional watering rose that provides a close pattern of coarse water droplets. The water should be directed at the rootball.

Later, it is important to apply a fine spray of water over the grafts, particularly with evergreen shrubs and conifers and with deciduous material that has flushed. This is necessary under the following conditions:—

(i) When there is no polyethylene over the grafts during the night. The grafts should be sprayed lightly first thing in the morning.

(ii) When the grafts have been uncovered on dull days to encourage some air movement around them. A light spray should be given when the foliage has dried.

(iii) During the hardening-off process. The number of spray applications should be increased or decreased according to the weather and the stage of hardening-off.

The rootball experiences considerable hardship during the process of drying off, and with the subsequent restriction of water and high temperatures in the aftercare facility. It is vital that attention be directed to regular watering needs following hardening-off, so that good maiden scion growth will be achieved.

(e) Ventilation and Hardening-Off

Grafts in a grafting case with polyethylene placed just above them may require the polyethylene to be turned once or twice a week, shaking to remove excess condensation droplets before replacement. [Excess condensation on the underside of glass can be removed with a cloth.] Care should be taken not to inadvertently dislodge the scions during this process. If there is excessive humidity during dull weather, turn back the polyethylene for 1–2 hours and then replace. It may be necessary to remove the polyethylene for the night and replace early the following morning for evergreens, particularly conifers. It is important after ventilating to maintain the humidity and to replace water lost from the rootball by evaporation.

Tents, drapes, low polyethylene grafting tunnels and open benches encourage more air movement around the grafts, which I personally like to see. This is achieved after the first 10 days by lifting one side of the polyethylene on dull days for half-an-hour initially, gradually increasing the exposure time (to one hour, then two, and so on). An extractor fan can be fitted to the inside of one side of the greenhouse, thus encouraging the extraction of a slow movement of air from the opposite (inlet) end. This system has proved to be ideal for open bench aftercare.

The callus tissue hardens and becomes a darker color as hardening-off proceeds. The polyethylene can be removed after 4–6 weeks and replaced with shade cloth. The grafts are moved to a cold greenhouse or cold frame for final hardening-off.

A critical stage for the grafts is when the scion buds flush and growth reaches about 2.5–5 cm (1–2"), depending on the species. This is the testing stage on whether the scion and rootstock

Figure 19-28. Successful side veneer graft between *Fagus sylvatica* 'Tricolor' (Tricolor Beech) and *F. sylvatica* (European Beech). Note the evenness of the callusing along the cut surfaces; that the tying-in began well above the top of the cuts and finished well below the basal veneer; that the basal veneer was not covered by the rubber strip to allow callus development; and, that the rubber strip is just beginning to degrade.

Figure 19-29. Daily inspection of the grafts during the aftercare period is essential for success. (Neil Hall, Wells Nursery, Inc., Mount Vernon, WA, U.S.A.)

have united properly to form a joint vascular system. If the growth begins to wilt, the grafts are likely to be lost—I have noted that *Betula* (Birch) and *Picea* (Spruce) grafts are sometimes prone to this and can lead to considerable disappointment. Eriophid mites can result in poor growth of some broad-leaved trees such as *Fraxinus* (Ash).

The needles of conifers may drop during the aftercare period—*Cedrus* (Cedar) and, to a lesser extent, *Abies* (Fir) are prone to this. As long as the union has formed properly, the axillary buds will usually break to produce new shoots.

(f) Pest and Disease Control

The importance of controlling root aphids has already been discussed (p. 529). Red spider mites are particularly troublesome for conifers, especially *Picea* (Spruce), and control should be directed at the rootstocks and stock plants before material is grafted and brought into the greenhouse. Chemicals such as dicofol (Kelthane®), dienochlor (Pentac®) and cyhexatin (Plictran®) are recommended for control.

Brown Scale can be troublesome on broad-leaved evergreens. A dormant oil spray to the stock plants is recommended, while diazinon will kill the crawler stage.

Whitefly can be troublesome with *Hibiscus* (Rose-of-Sharon) grafts after they have broken into growth. This pest is usually introduced from infected plants in adjacent greenhouses. Regular applications of permethrin (Ambush®) will keep the problem in check.

Aphids can attack the new growth. Insecticidal soap can be sufficient when they first appear, otherwise dimethoate, malathion or diazinon should be considered.

Vine Weevil should be kept in check, particularly with *Rhododendron* and *Camellia*. Aldrin mixed in the potting mix is very effective if the law permits its use, otherwise treat with acephate (Orthene®).

Botrytis or Gray Mold (*Botrytis cinerea*) can be troublesome on grafts. The problem is enhanced in the warm humid conditions under polyethylene. *Cedrus* (Cedar) tend to drop their old needles in the spring and are particularly prone to *Botrytis* infection. *Betula* (Birch) is also prone to attack, with infection of both the soft growth of suckers from the rootstock and the new shoots from the scion. The shoots wilt, turn yellow to brown to black and subsequently infect the entire scion. Air movement should be encouraged and infected leaves and shoots, and complete grafts where necessary, removed. Physan® has been used successfully, firstly, to disinfect the knife blade, and secondly, the area of stem where the cuts are to be made. Fungicidal sprays or dusts containing captan or thiram applied at one or two weekly intervals will help to keep the disease in check. Chlorothalonil (Bravo®) is recommended as a fumigant for *Botrytis* control. Benomyl (Benlate®) and thiophanate methyl + ethazol (Banrot®) can be used as a drench for *Pythium* and *Fusarium* on the roots.

(g) Weed Control

Weeds such as *Cardamine hirsuta* (Hairy Bittercress or Popweed) is troublesome in the warm greenhouse. This weed germinates and the seed capsules mature and split within a few weeks, releasing seeds over the surfaces of other pots. Hand weeding is very time-consuming, plus there is a risk of disturbing the grafts. The problem can be largely eliminated by employing good cultural techniques such as using sterilized loam, clean pots, mulching the pots with sawdust or peat moss during the season prior to grafting, and removal of both weeds and the surface soil when the rootstocks are brought in for drying off. [Granular oxadiazon (Ronstar®) has proved to be an excellent herbicide for plants in containers.]

(h) Heading or Snagging Back

This process is necessary with side grafting to remove the sap drawer so that the scion and rootstock will grow as one. It is carried out in one, two or three stages, based largely on the plant material and the past experiences of the propagator.

Figure 19-30. Heading back conifer grafts moved to a double-span cold frame after removal from the grafting case. (Angers, France)

A sharp-pointed pair of hand pruners should be used for this operation. Particular care is required in the final removal of the sap drawer or small snag. Two slight variations of the technique for the final heading back are as follows:—

(i) The rubber grafting band is partially pushed down the stem and the union supported with the index finger. The snag is removed at a 30° angle, thus leaving exposed a part of the cut originally made on the scion and giving a "church window" effect. The exposed tissue is sometimes waxed over and eventually callus tissue should form from both the scion and rootstock to give greater strength to the graft. This method is slower than the second method.

(ii) Cut the snag at a 30° angle about 1.5 mm (1/16") above the graft union, supporting the scion during the process.

Sometimes it is advisable to leave cutting back the final snag until after potting or planting to reduce the risk of scion damage, e.g., *Acer palmatum* cvs. (Japanese Maple) and *Rhododendron*. The operator is then more likely to hold both the scion and rootstock rather than the scion only.

Side grafted *Alnus* (Alder), *Betula* (Birch), *Corylus* (Filbert), *Fagus* (Beech) and *Hamamelis* (Witch Hazel) usually can have the sap drawer removed in one step 8 weeks after grafting. *Rhododendron*, *Juniperus* (Juniper) and *Taxus* (Yew) are best handled in two stages, removing half the sap drawer after 4–6 weeks and the remaining snag 4–6 weeks later. *Acer* (Maple), *Abies* (Fir), *Cedrus* (Cedar), *Picea* (Spruce) and *Pinus* (Pine) are best done in three stages. In the first stage, half

Figure 19-31. Final heading back of *Betula pendula* 'Dalecarlica' (Cutleaf Weeping Birch) grafted on *B. pendula* (European White or Common Silver Birch). Note that the top of the rubber strip is rolled back; that the index finger is used to support the union; and, the position of the pruners while actually heading-back.

Figure 19-32. Some propagators like to wax over the cut surface after the final heading back.

the sap drawer is removed 6–8 weeks after grafting, followed by heading back to a 2.5 cm (1″) snag 6 weeks later. The timing of the third stage varies depending on whether the plants were winter or summer grafted. Winter grafted plants have the snag removed in the following July to August, summer grafted ones in early March before growth commences. This small snag acts as a final "safety valve" in case of a sudden sap rise.

An important point to remember, particularly with *Picea* (Spruce), is not to be too hasty in heading back. Experience has shown that heading back too soon will delay the development of new roots in the container. The young graft looks healthy but the scion makes little significant growth. In these circumstances, it is preferable to delay the final heading back until the August after winter grafting. Also, it seems advantageous to retain a small number of needles on this short snag if possible. [The motto with *Picea* (Spruce) grafts is that it is "better to head back later than early".] The recommendation for variegated pines is that they should be headed back over a two-year period.

(i) Caning and Tying-in

The union can be particularly brittle during the first season even when the graft has been successful—*Picea* (Spruce) and *Quercus* (Oak) being two examples of this. In this case, the tie should not be removed until the end of the growing season, unless a stem constriction is forming. This will provide some extra support.

Caning the young grafts with 45 cm (18″) canes is carried out for two reasons:—

(i) To give the graft union further support.

(ii) To support the subsequent scion growth in order to avoid bent stems.

The wood of some conifers, e.g., *Picea* (Spruce), can harden relatively quickly and it becomes more difficult to produce quality liners if staking and tying-in is not carried out before this occurs. *Alnus* (Alder) and *Betula* (Birch) are examples where growth is more vigorous over a longer period. In some cases, it will be necessary to reduce the length of the axillary (side) shoots to ensure a dominant leader.

Grafting Techniques

Bench grafting onto pot-grown rootstocks embraces virtually all the grafting and budding techniques previously described. However, it also utilizes a major group of grafts that have received little mention so far—the side grafts in which the scion is placed on the side of the rootstock. The cuts are made and matching done so that the scion arises at about a 30° angle from the vertical stem of the rootstock. Unlike the apical grafts, this leaves a portion of rootstock stem that is referred to as the "sap drawer".

It is generally considered that the purpose of the sap drawer is to regulate the flow of sap

Figure 19-33. Quality liners of a compact form of *Pinus densiflora* 'Umbraculifera' (Japanese Umbrella Pine or Tanyosho) following final heading back. (Wells Nursery, Inc., Mount Vernon, WA, U.S.A.)

Figure 19-34. A tie and cane being used to ensure that the terminal growth of a *Picea pungens* cv. (Colorado Spruce) is kept vertical. It also provides initial support to the graft union. Note the evenness of the whorl of side shoots resulting from correct scion collection.

Figure 19-35. Outdoor beds for conifer grafts after transferring from the greenhouses. (Wells Nursery, Inc., Mount Vernon, WA, U.S.A.)

Figure 19-36. A thorough understanding of scion/rootstock compatibility, and the correct procedures for rootstock preparation, carpentry and aftercare will achieve the desired result. David Roberts (left) and Peter Dummer (right) with one-year-old bench grafts of *Quercus* (Oak). Note the cold frames adjacent to the propagation greenhouse for hardening-off bench grafts and growing pot-grown rootstocks (Hillier Nurseries (Winchester) Ltd., Romsey, Hampshire, U.K.)

Figure 19-37. Quality open-ground conifers 4 years after bench grafting. Foreground—*Picea abies* 'Pendula' (Weeping Norway Spruce). Rear—*Cedrus atlantica* 'Glauca Pendula' (Weeping Blue Atlas Cedar). (Wells Nursery, Inc., Mount Vernon, WA, U.S.A.)

past the union. Very little sap from the rootstock actually enters the scion during the early stages of aftercare, so it is necessary to create a means by which the sap can pass by the union into the upper part of the stem. Otherwise the sap would accumulate and ooze out of the cut surfaces, resulting in the loss of the grafts by "flooding of the union". As the tissues of the scion and rootstock unite, an increasing quantity of sap is able to enter the scion. To compensate for this, the sap drawer is gradually reduced, normally in 2 or 3 stages, until it is finally removed. It has also been suggested that a sap drawer assists the callusing process in those woody plants that are slow to unite. This is one reason for using side grafting for such plants, whether or not they have a heavy sap rise. [One authority suggests that oozing of sap at the site of the graft is almost entirely dependent on the efficiency of drying out the rootball prior to grafting and the sap drawer has little to do with it.]

The different techniques for grafting onto pot-grown rootstocks may be grouped as follows:—

Side Grafts
       Side Veneer
       Side Wedge
       Side Inlay
Bud Grafts
       T- or Shield Bud
       Chip Bud
Apical Grafts
       Whip
       Whip and Tongue
       Basal Whip
       Wedge
       Rind
       Saddle
       Cleft or Inlay

The following grafting techniques are those prescribed for woody ornamentals. Bench grafting of some *Larix* (Larch), *Picea* (Spruce) and *Pinus* (Pine) is practiced in forestry to reproduce clonal material for planting as sources of superior seed. Details of the variations used may be obtained from the publication *Manual for Greenhouse Grafting of Conifers in the Maritimes* by R. D. Hallett, R. F. Smith and T. W. Burns (Maritimes Forest Research Centre, Fredericton, New Brunswick, Canada).

Side Grafting

There are several different variations for side grafting woody ornamentals on the bench.

SIDE VENEER GRAFT

This is the most widely used technique and is used for *Abies* (Fir), *Acer* (Maple), *Alnus* (Alder), *Betula* (Birch), *Picea* (Spruce), *Pinus* (Pine), etc. A small portion of wood is removed from the rootstock as low down as possible to reduce suckering, leaving a small veneer at the base of the cut. The scion is cut, matched and firmly tied into the rootstock.

Picea pungens 'Hoopsii' (Hoops Blue Spruce), a particularly attractive silver-blue foliaged cultivar of the Colorado Spruce, grafted onto *Picea abies* (Norway Spruce) is used to illustrate the technique, and to help consolidate some of the practices just described.

Grafting Procedure

Choice and Production of Rootstock

(1) Two-year transplanted or undercut open-ground rootstocks of *Picea abies* (Norway Spruce) are obtained and graded for caliper size. They are root pruned, the lower side shoots removed to clean up the area of the stem where the graft is to be made, and then potted up into 10 cm (4") diameter containers.

(2) The potted plants are stood down in rows in a bed either in the open or within a shade

structure. The surfaces of the pots are mulched with sawdust or peat moss. They are grown on for one growing season, with attention being paid to irrigation and to pest and disease control of the foliage and rootball.

(3) At the end of the growing season, a 3-year pot-grown rootstock will be available for winter grafting (caliper size of approximately pencil thickness, 6 mm/¼"). (The age of the rootstock will be less if used for summer grafting, but sufficient root development should have occurred.)

Time of Year

The most widely practiced time is winter grafting during December to February, although the alternative, summer grafting in July to August, is also used.

Drying off the Rootstocks

(1) Inspect the rootballs at random for moisture content, and pest and disease infection.

(2) Bring the rootstocks into a greenhouse about 2–3 weeks prior to grafting, and set the air temperature at 10–12°C (50–54°F.) This time period is adjusted according to the moisture content of the rootball and root activity.

(3) The rootstocks are ready for grafting when about 50–60% of the moisture is retained and a small amount of root growth can be seen around the perimeter of the rootballs.

Selection and Collection of Scion Wood

(1) Use pruners to collect terminal shoots from the mother plants. Each scion should be of the current season's growth, 10–15 cm (4–6") long, and have both a prominent terminal bud and not less than 3 adjacent radial buds.

(2) It may be necessary to cut into two-year-old wood if multi-branched scions are required. These may be larger and therefore the rootstocks should also be of a sufficiently larger caliper to allow matching.

(3) Place the scions in moist burlap (hessian) sacking or a polyethylene bag with a few drops of water, and keep cool until grafting—ideally the same day.

Initial Rootstock Preparation

(1) Use pruners to head back the stem of the rootstock to about 20 cm (8") to facilitate handling. It is important to retain sufficient foliage for the rootstock to grow satisfactorily.

(2) Clean up the base of the rootstock with a knife (not a grafting knife) to remove basal shoots. A dry rag is used to clean and remove loose debris from the grafting area on the stem.

Figure 19-38. Mother plants of *Picea pungens* 'Hoopsii' (Hoops Blue Spruce) to provide vigorous terminal scions for bench grafting. Note the distinct whorls of growth on the plants. (Boskoop, Holland)

Figure 19-39. Removing the basal needles from the base of the scion. Note that the tip of the scion is held towards the grafter.

Scion Preparation

(1) Remove the basal needles with the grafting knife for about 3–4 cm (1¼–1½″) up the stem. This is carried out by holding the tip of the scion towards you and revolving the scion in the hand while cutting off the needles. It is important that the stem tissue is not torn during this operation.

An alternative method is to rest the scion on a wooden block, with the tip of the scion towards you. The knife blade is directed away from you and the needles scraped off, with the scion being turned until all the needles are removed. If the needles tear the stem tissue, use the first method.

(2) Re-cut the base of the scion.

(3) Make a slightly sloping cut, 2.5–3 cm (1–1¼″) long, at the base of the scion. It is important that this cut is shallow and does not expose too much pith.

(4) Reverse the scion and make a sloping cut 3 mm (⅛″) long to meet up with the first cut.

Rootstock Preparation

(1) Hold the pot firmly with its base either on the bench or against your chest. The pot is tilted away from you, both for vision and for ease of making the cuts.

(2) Make a 4 mm (1/6″) long cut at a 30° angle at the base of the rootstock. Note that the final tying-in will be difficult if it is made too low.

(3) Make a straight or slightly angled cut, 2.5–4.0 cm (1–1½″) long, down towards the first cut. The tissue removed will expose the wood for matching with the scion.

(4) Clean the knife blade after each graft, or more often if necessary, by wiping on a pad or cloth soaked in white or methylated spirit.

Matching-up

Match the scion and rootstock so that both sides of the scion are flush with the sides of the cut on the rootstock.

If the scion is smaller in diameter than the rootstock, move it across so that they match on one side only.

Tying-in

Use a rubber grafting strip for tying-in. Make two turns at the top of the graft to secure it, then spiral down, leaving a short gap of 3 mm (⅛″) between each turn, and secure with a half-hitch knot below the graft. The base of the veneer should remain exposed.

It is helpful if the rubber strip is slightly twisted as it is spiralled down to encourage it to lie flat on the graft.

Waxing

If desired, hot or cold liquid wax is applied over and around the cut surfaces of the graft. (Refer to p. 533 for options on waxing.)

Figure 19-40.
Waxing over the cut surfaces and rubber strip, using a small paint brush.

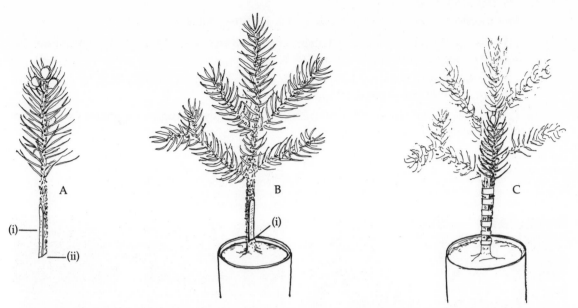

19-7. Diagrammatic representation of side veneer graft of *Picea pungens* cv. (Colorado Spruce). A. Prepared scion. (i)—slightly angled cut, 2.5–3 cm (1–1¼″) long; (ii)—reverse cut, 3 mm (⅛″) long. B. Prepared rootstock. (i)—4 mm (1/6″) cut at the base to form a veneer. C. Completed graft matched and tied-in.

Aftercare

Assuming the aftercare facility is a polyethylene tent, drape or tunnel, the grafts are either placed vertically on a layer of moistened peat moss, 1.3 cm (½″) thick, or plunged at a 45° angle in a 15–20 cm (6–8″) deep bed of peat moss, with the scion uppermost. The base temperature is maintained at 18–20°C (65–68°F), the air temperature at 15.5–18°C (60–65°F), and the humidity above 80%.

To encourage air movement, the grafts are ventilated on dull days and at night if necessary. The grafts are lightly sprayed with water during ventilation periods and subsequent hardening-off.

Unless plunged in peat moss, the rootballs in the pot must be regularly inspected for moisture content and root development. Watering is restricted until the buds on the stem swell and extension growth is evident. For summer grafting, wait until there has been copious callus formation. Heavy shading of the grafts is necessary during warm sunny weather. Hardening-off the grafts by gradually increasing the amount of ventilation begins after about 3–6 weeks and is completed by 8–12 weeks after grafting, by which time the polyethylene has been replaced with shade cloth. The grafts are regularly inspected for pest and disease infection—especially for red spider mites and spruce aphids.

Figure 19-41. The first stage of heading back is to reduce the stem of the rootstock (the sap drawer) by half about 6–8 weeks after grafting. A (right). Before heading back. B (far right). After heading back by half.

The rootstock (sap drawer) is headed back in three stages:—

(1) The sap drawer is reduced by half its length 6–8 weeks after grafting, by which time the wax covering the graft will begin to crack.

(2) The sap drawer is reduced to 2.5 cm (1″) above the union 6 weeks later, by which time the terminal bud has flushed into growth.

(3) The remaining snag is removed in the following July to August for winter grafting and in early March for summer grafting.

Figure 19-42. Young grafts bedded out in a cold frame for the summer after removal from the greenhouse. Note the snag retained after the second heading back—this will be removed in the following July/August.

Figure 19-43. A quality crop of *Picea pungens* 'Hoopsii' (Hoops Blue Spruce) 3 years after planting in the open ground. (Joh. Bruns Nursery, Oldenburg, West Germany)

Side Veneer Grafting of *Betula* (Birch)

The following diagram illustrates a completed side veneer graft for a deciduous broad-leaf tree. *Betula* (Birch) has been chosen as a typical example.

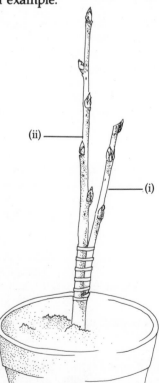

(ii)

(i)

Diagram 19-8. Completed side veneer graft of *Betula* (Birch) after matching and tying-in. (i)—scion; (ii)—rootstock.

<h2 align="center">SIDE WEDGE GRAFT</h2>

Method I

This technique differs from the side veneer graft in that no tissue is removed from the rootstock. Instead, a thin flap consisting of rind and a thin sliver of tissue remains attached to the base of the rootstock. Two slightly sloping cuts are made on the scion so that it can be matched and callused on two sides. These cuts should not taper to a point as the thin tissue is liable to be damaged and bent when placed in the rootstock, and it is also more prone to drying out.

Dexterity and knife control are necessary to form the flap. The stem of the rootstock is weakened if the flap is too thick, while the flap has little strength and is prone to damage when tying-in if it is too thin. The beginner is likely to cut completely through the flap if control of the knife is lost. The flap should *not* be used to hide poor carpentry on the scion!

The main reason for using the side wedge graft is because it provides additional cambial contact. This graft is preferable for species with thin flexible bark where all tissue elements can be retained in the flap. The flap must also be able to withstand bending. This graft is said to be useful for species with weak connecting tissues—for example, *Cedrus* (Cedar), some *Juniperus* (Juniper) and ericaceous plants. However, one reason given against its use on conifers is that cutting the scion on both sides results in a greater tendency to expose the pith which, in turn, encourages drying out of the scion. [If the bark slips when the second cut to form the wedge is made, then revert to the side veneer graft. Some propagators recommend that the outside cut on the scion should be only one-fifth the length of the inner cut.]

Figure 19-44. *Hamamelis mollis* 'Pallida' (Chinese Witch Hazel cv.) side wedge grafted onto *H. virginiana* (Common Witch Hazel). (This graft is sometimes referred to as a modified side veneer graft.) Note the callus development on both sides of the cut surface on the scion and the use of waxed cotton twine to tie-in.

Some propagators prefer to use the side wedge graft for deciduous trees and shrubs such as *Alnus* (Alder), *Betula* (Birch) and *Hamamelis* (Witch Hazel). There seems to be little or no experimental data to prove that this technique is better for these species than conventional side veneer grafting. Therefore, the choice of graft to use is usually left to the personal preference of the propagator.

Grafting Procedure

Example:	**Scion**	*Cedrus atlantica* 'Glauca' (Blue Atlas Cedar)
	Rootstock	*Cedrus deodara* (Himalayan Cedar)

As for side veneer grafting, except as indicated below.

Scion Preparation

(1) Cut the scion wood into individual lengths of about 12.5 cm (5″).
(2) Make two opposite slanting cuts, 2.5 cm (1″) long, but not tapered to a point.
(3) Make two 3 mm (⅛″) cuts at the base of the scion to give a smooth but firm base.

Rootstock Preparation

Form a thin flap 2.5 cm (1″) long, using the tip of the knife blade. Ensure that the flap is cut deep enough to include living tissue and not bark alone.

Matching-Up

Match the scion on two sides—one with the cut surface of the main stem of the rootstock, the other with the flap. Care should be taken not to push the flap sideways with the thumb as this can cause the rind and sliver of wood to separate. Revert to side veneer grafting if this is a continuing problem.

[A variation that is sometimes carried out is to reduce the length of the flap by two-thirds. The scion is prepared as for the conventional side veneer graft and the flap tied in behind it. This is useful if there is a tendency for the tie to bite into the base of the scion as the flap gives it some protection. I have seen this used successfully on *Abies* (Fir) and *Picea* (Spruce) as a modification to side veneer grafting.]

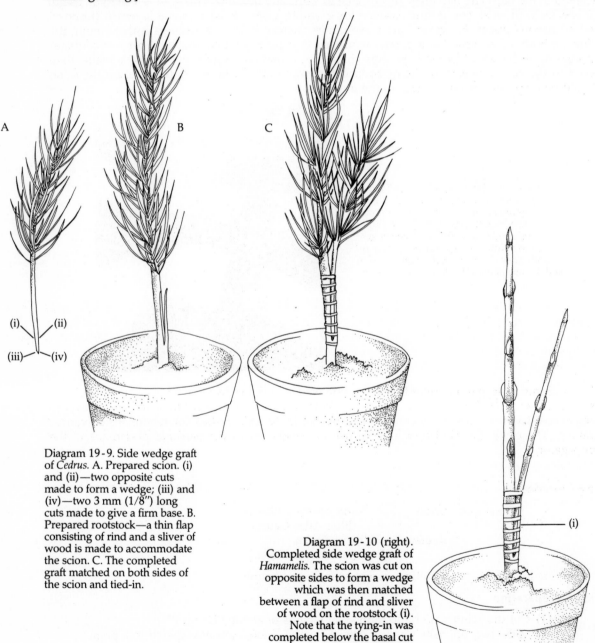

Diagram 19-9. Side wedge graft of *Cedrus*. A. Prepared scion. (i) and (ii)—two opposite cuts made to form a wedge; (iii) and (iv)—two 3 mm (1/8″) long cuts made to give a firm base. B. Prepared rootstock—a thin flap consisting of rind and a sliver of wood is made to accommodate the scion. C. The completed graft matched on both sides of the scion and tied-in.

Diagram 19-10 (right). Completed side wedge graft of *Hamamelis*. The scion was cut on opposite sides to form a wedge which was then matched between a flap of rind and sliver of wood on the rootstock (i). Note that the tying-in was completed below the basal cut on the rootstock.

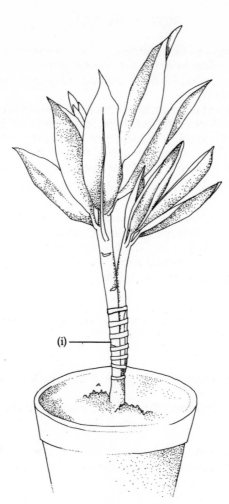

(i) —

Diagram 19-11. Completed side wedge graft of *Rhododendron.* The scion was cut on opposite sides to form a wedge which was then matched between a flap of rind and sliver of wood on the rootstock (i). Note that the tying-in was completed below the basal cut on the rootstock.

Method II

Some propagators use a modified version of the side wedge graft in which a single cut is made in the rootstock, ensuring that it does not enter into more than one-third of the caliper to avoid weakening the stock. (There is, therefore, not a thin flap formed as in Method I.) This graft is really only successful when the rootstocks are of larger caliper than the scions, and the wood of the scion is sufficiently firm not to be damaged while being placed into the rootstock.

Grafting Procedure

As for side veneer grafting except as below.

Scion Preparation

Make two slanting cuts, 2.5 cm (1″) long, on opposite sides of the scion and meeting at the base to form a firm wedge.

Rootstock Preparation

Make a single cut, 2.5 cm (1″) long, down into the rootstock.

Matching-Up

Slightly ease back the stem of the rootstock just above the top of the cut and match the scion to each side of the rootstock cut.

Aftercare

As for side veneer grafting.

SIDE INLAY GRAFT

This further modification to side grafting is more widely used in Europe than in North America. A flap is made but it differs from the side wedge graft in that one side remains attached to the rootstock. The scion is prepared as for the traditional inlay graft (see p. 558), and is then placed in behind the flap of the rootstock.

I have seen this graft used in cases where there was a thin scion and a considerably larger caliper rootstock as it helps to improve the matching. It is useful for *Chamaecyparis* (False Cypress), *Juniperus* (Juniper), *Taxus* (Yew) and the compact forms of *Picea* (Spruce) and *Abies* (Fir). It is a graft that requires considerable practice and skill to perfect the technique. It should not be attempted when the caliper of the rootstock is thin or where there is a risk of tearing the rind.

Grafting Procedure

| | Example: | Scion | *Chamaecyparis nootkatensis* 'Pendula' (Weeping Yellow Cedar) |
| | | Rootstock | *Platycladus (Thuja) orientalis* (Oriental Arborvitae) |

As for side veneer grafting except as below.

Scion Preparation

Make two adjacent sloping cuts, 2.5 cm (1″) long, so that they taper to a point. This gives a three-dimensional effect to the base of the cutting.

Rootstock Preparation

(1) Using the tip of the knife, take the blade 6 mm (¼″) horizontally and then downward to form a flap 2.5 cm (1″) long.

(2) Carefully ease the rind from the internal tissue with the knife blade.

Matching-Up

Hold the cut surfaces of the scion towards the rootstock and place it firmly beneath the rind so that both the cut surfaces are matched—one with the rind, the other with the stem of the rootstock.

Aftercare

As for side veneer grafting.

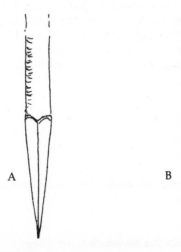
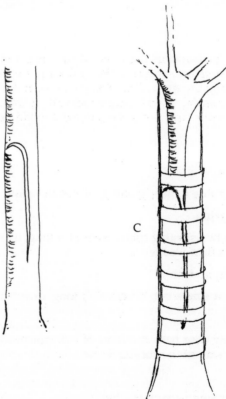

Diagram 19-12. Diagrammatic representation of a side inlay graft of *Chamaecyparis* (False Cypress). A. Prepared scion with two adjacent cuts tapering to a point. B. Prepared rootstock—a horizontal and a downward cut are made with the tip of the knife and the rind lifted. C. Matched and tied-in graft with the scion fitting snugly between the rind and the stem of the rootstock.

Budding (Bud Grafting)

This method utilizes a combination of the techniques used in both open-ground budding and bench grafting. In practice, it may be carried out either indoors like conventional bench grafting or *in-situ* on the container standing ground. The major techniques used are T-budding (p. 468), chip budding (p. 478) and stick budding (p. 487). The benefits that maybe gained by this method are summarized as follows:—

(i) Maximum use of scion wood is ensured as a single bud is matched with the rootstock. This can be particularly useful if scion wood is in short supply—for example, *Hamamelis* (Witch Hazel) and *Magnolia.*

Figure 19- 45.
Cercidiphyllum japonicum 'Pendulum' (Weeping Katsura Tree) chip budded onto a pot-grown rootstock of *C. japonicum* (Katsura Tree). Note the young terminal shoot arising from the bud chip.

(ii) The time of year for working the scion onto the rootstock is more flexible. Depending on the plant and method of bud grafting used, it can be carried out during January/February when the rootstock is prepared as the buds are swelling or during the spring and summer when it is in active growth.

(iii) The height of the maiden growth is sometimes increased over that of a side veneer graft carried out in January/February, e.g., *Magnolia*

Its limitations are that it is unlikely to be successful for conifers and some evergreen shrubs, while the range of deciduous shrubs and trees in which it is successfully used has so far been limited compared with standard procedures. Also, the scion has less initial food storage capacity than a conventional scion and this may be detrimental to both successful take and subsequent growth rate.

The systems used when budding onto a pot/container-grown rootstock are summarized in the following section. The procedures for T- and chip budding are described in Chapter 17.

Roses

It is a satisfactory method for propagating hybrid tea, floribunda and polyantha bush roses for retail selling in containers. One system widely practiced is to use second-grade or unsold first-grade bare-root bushes. They are pruned back hard to leave 2–4 buds above the original graft union and then grown-on in 21 cm (8″) diameter containers for sale the following summer.

An alternative method is to summer bud onto an established container-grown rootstock. A 5–8 mm (1/5–1/3″) caliper *Rosa canina* (Dog Rose) selection or seedling of the Laxa rootstock is potted into an 21 cm (8″) diameter container in late winter or early spring, and T-budded *in-situ* during the oncoming summer. The rootstock is headed back to just above the union the following

February, and multiple shoots from the bud (remember that there are a number of small axillary buds around the one dominant bud) will provide a saleable product for the next summer. The axillary buds can be encouraged to break by tipping the leader shoot when it is 10–12.5 cm (4–5") long. The disadvantage of this method is that it takes up container standing space for 1½ seasons, so it is very important that the final product be of high quality to command a good price. The economics of both systems need to be evaluated before beginning such an enterprise.

Initial experiments have recently been undertaken in Texas to reduce the production cycle for open-ground roses from the usual 20–24 month period by bench chip budding onto unrooted cuttings of *Rosa multiflora* 'Brooks 52' (Baby or Japanese Rose form) during December. Chip budding was carried out both by using a knife and the Liliput® budding tool (p. 201) and Parafilm® budding strips were effective for tying-in.

Trees

Ornamental trees can be produced in similar fashion to roses, with the rootstocks in 21 or 23 cm (8 or 9") diameter containers. They are T- or chip budded in the summer, headed back to the scion bud in February and sold from that summer into the next winter. If the bud fails, they can be whip and tongue grafted later. A maiden feathered tree makes an excellent product for garden center sales—for example, *Malus floribunda* (Japanese Flowering Crab Apple), *M. sargentii* (Sargent Crab Apple), *M. toringoides* (Cut-leaf Crab Apple), *Prunus serrulata* 'Amanogawa' (Amanogawa Cherry), *P.* 'Pandora', *P.* 'Accolade', *Acer platanoides* 'Drummondii' (Silver Variegated Norway Maple), *Sorbus aria* 'Lutescens' (White Beam cv.) and *S.* 'Joseph Rock'.

This system may be used as an adjunct to conventional open-ground grown stocks. Situations can arise such that the area available for lining out open-ground rootstocks may be limited one year, establishment of a particular rootstock could prove difficult, or particular care is necessary for a new potential saleable item. The maiden trees are removed from the container after the first growing season, root pruned and lined out in the nursery rows. As with roses, production costs will increase because of the costs of containers, potting mix and the extra handling.

A variation on the above system that I have seen used with *Sorbus* (Mountain Ash) is to bud the rootstocks in the summer and then to plant the rootstocks with dormant bud in open ground in the fall. Root pruning will encourage new roots to form after lining out and before the onset of winter. The rootstocks are headed back flush to the scion and bud in the following February, and then grown-on in the conventional manner. There was some doubt as to the quality of the subsequent maiden growth that was obtained.

Two items are worthy of mention in this section.

(i) *Liquidambar* (Sweet Gum)—I noted a most impressive crop of the clonal forms 'Burgundy', 'Festival' and 'Palo Alto' of *Liquidambar styraciflua* (American Sweet Gum or Liquidambar) at the Saratoga Horticultural Foundation in California. Advantage is taken of the favorable climate to which these selections respond, of the ability to extend the budding season with spring and summer budding, and of the flexibility gained by growing in containers.

The rootstocks, *Liquidambar styraciflua*, are direct sown in 9 cm (3½") containers at the turn of the year and subsequently potted into 15 cm (6") diameter containers. The rootstocks are budded from September to October when the caliper has reached "pencil thickness" (ca. 6 mm/¼"). Variable sowing dates and cultural procedures can enable budding to commence in April to take advantage of the Foundation's geographical location.

(ii) *Fraxinus* (Ash), *Sorbus* (Mountain Ash), and *Acer* (Maple)—The pot-grown rootstock—*Fraxinus excelsior* (European Ash), *Sorbus aucuparia* (European Mountain Ash) and *Acer platanoides* (Norway Maple)—are produced as for side grafting. During January-April, the rootstocks are chip budded low down onto the stem, tied-in with 1.3 cm (½") polyethylene tape, and the grafts stood down on an open bench in a greenhouse. A well-callused union will often develop within 21 days of budding if the greenhouse is heated to a minimum of 15.5°C (60°F). Shade must be provided, particularly when either the rootstock or the scion has flushed into growth. The tape is removed approximately 6 weeks later, the rootstocks headed back to just above the chip bud, and then grown-on.

It will be necessary to cold store dormant scion wood for budding in late February to April. This technique has also been successful on pot-grown rootstocks of *Gleditsia* (Honey Locust), *Malus, Prunus, Robinia* (Locust), *Tilia* (Linden), *Ulmus* (Elm) and *Zelkova*.

Hamamelis (Witch Hazel)

The culitvars of *Hamamelis mollis* (Chinese Witch Hazel) and *H. × intermedia* (Hybrid Witch Hazel) may be successfully chip budded onto pot- or container-grown rootstocks of *H. virginiana* (Common Witch Hazel) under the following conditions:—

(i) During January and February as an alternative to whip or side grafting.

(ii) During July and August onto a rootstock in its 21 cm (8″) diameter selling container. In this case, the rootstocks are headed back in the following March to the chip bud and then about 60–75 cm (2–2½′) of maiden growth can be achieved by the end of the growing season. It is important to support this growth by staking early in the season.

The chip buds, whether for winter or summer budding, should be taken from stock plants that have been pruned back to encourage vigorous, one-year-old vegtative growth, otherwise the buds are small and difficult to handle, leading to lower success rates.

Magnolia

A paper presented at the 1969 International Plant Propagators' Society (Great Britain and Ireland Region) Conference created considerable interest. It was based on David Knuckey's experience at the former nursery belonging to Treseders Nurseries (Truro) Ltd., Cornwall, with the T- and chip budding of *Magnolia* onto pot-grown seedling rootstocks. Budding began in August and continued into December, with best results being achieved during October-December when the scion wood was well-ripened. The greenhouse facility for the rootstocks contained a polyethylene tent in which a base temperature of 21–24°C (70–75°F) was maintained. Tungsten filament lights were installed to provide extended day length in the form of a 20-hour photo period with a two-second break every two minutes.

The graft was tied-in with waxed cotton and a grafting wax was used to cover the area. The retention of a small triangle of leaf lamina directly above the petiole was advantageous in the evergreen and some deciduous forms as it encouraged an early break of the axillary bud. Success rates of between 75–95% were ultimately achieved. The condition of the budwood was important in order to achieve the desired result.

Magnolia propagation is also a specialty of Charles E. Tubesing at the University of British Columbia Botanical Garden, Vancouver. Scions from around the world are being collected to provide material for the *Magnolia* collection in the Asian Garden component of this Botanical Garden. His method is less complex than the one just described. The Magnolias are chip budded from early February into the second week in April. However, he has also chip budded *Magnolia* onto rootstocks during August and September for forcing into growth the following March with equal success. The table outlines some of the scion/rootstock combinations used.

Figure 19-46.
Young terminal shoot arising from *Magnolia officinalis* var. *biloba* chip budded onto a pot-grown rootstock of *M. hypoleuca* (Japanese Whitebark Magnolia).

SCION	ROOTSTOCK
M. cylindrica	*M. kobus* (Kobus Magnolia)
M. officinalis var. *biloba*	*M. hypoleuca* (Japanese Whitebark Magnolia)
M. sprengeri var. *diva* 'Claret Cup' (Sprenger Magnolia cv.)	*M. dawsoniana* (Dawson Magnolia) *M. sprengeri* var. *diva* (Goddess Magnolia)
M. denudata (syn. *M. heptapeta*) (Yulan)	*M. kobus* (Kobus Magnolia) *M.* × *soulangiana* (Saucer Magnolia)
M. campbellii (Campbell Magnolia) *M. campbellii* spp. *mollicomata* (Downy Magnolia)	*M.* × *soulangiana** (Saucer Magnolia) *M. sprengeri* var. *diva* (Goddess Magnolia) *M. dawsoniana* (Dawson Magnolia)
M. dawsoniana (Dawson Magnolia)	*M. dawsoniana* (Dawson Magnolia) *M. sprengeri* var. *diva* (Goddess Magnolia)
M. sargentiana var. *robusta* (Robust Magnolia)	*M. acuminata** (Cucumber Tree) *M. dawsoniana* (Dawson Magnolia) *M. sprengeri* var. *diva* (Goddess Magnolia)

*Does not grow as rapidly as the scion, thus producing an unsightly although strong union.

The buds are tied in with 1.3 cm (½″) polyethylene tape and then stood down on an open bench in a greenhouse with the air temperature set at 18°C (65°F). The scions are well callused to the rootstocks in about 21 days, after which the tape is removed and the rootstock headed back to the scion chip.

The Saratoga Horticultural Foundation, San Martin, California, has perfected production systems for T-budding the evergreen *Magnolia grandiflora* (Southern Magnolia) cultivars, e.g., 'Russet' and 'Samuel Sommer', onto seedling rootstocks of *M. grandiflora*. One sequence used involves the moving of the rootstock from peat pots into 15 cm (6″) diameter containers during June and then placing these containers down within a lath structure. They are of sufficient caliper by the following April for T-budding to begin. Just prior to budding, the rootstock is reduced in height by one-third to one-half. The rubber budding strip is removed after about 4 weeks and is then later finally headed back. A maiden plant is ready for sale by the next fall. If fall budding, the final heading back of the rootstock is carried out during the following spring.

Among the factors that ensure a high percentage bud take are:—

(i) Ripeness of wood, size of bud, and the amount of pith around the small buds. Sufficiently ripened wood and the minimum amount of pith is ensured by cutting 0.6–1.0 m (2–3½′) long bud sticks, but using only the lower five buds.

(ii) It is beneficial to remove the wood from behind the bud. This also makes it easier for the budder to slip the shield between the two flaps of rind and obtain better matching—particularly when the bud is on the large side.

The semi-evergreen tree *Michelia doltsopa*, an asiatic member of the Magnoliaceae, may also be produced in a similar fashion by working onto *Magnolia grandiflora* seedling rootstocks.

Apical Grafting

The techniques of whip, whip and tongue, basal whip, wedge and rind grafts used for bare-root grafting are also used on pot-grown rootstocks (see pp. 514–526 for details). However, there are additional grafts that are mainly used for pot-grown rootstocks.

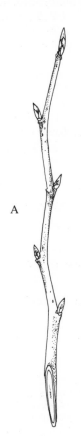

A

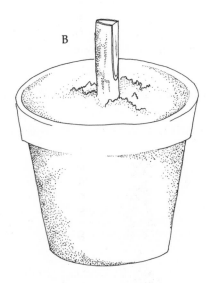

B

Diagram 19-13. Whip graft of *Fagus sylvatica* (European Beech). A. Prepared scion with a sloping cut. B. A shallow section of the rootstock is removed to match the scion. C. Completed graft matched and tied-in, leaving a small "church window" of exposed scion tissue (i). Note that *Fagus* (Beech) are more usually side veneer grafted.

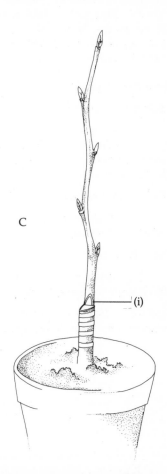

C

(i)

Figure 19-47. A young liner of *Gingko biloba* 'Variegata' (Variegated Maidenhair Tree) whip grafted onto *G. biloba*.

Figure 19-48. *Camellia* cv. propagated by wedge grafting.

SADDLE GRAFT

Saddle graft is a traditional bench graft that was used mainly for *Rhododendron,* although it has been largely superseded today by side grafting, whip grafting and cutting propagation. It has also been used for various *Aesculus* (Buckeye, Horse-chestnut) when grafted onto *A. hippocastanum* (Common Horse-chestnut).

This graft results in a very strong union, but is not easy to perfect and considerable practice is necessary. It is best used on large-diameter rootstocks, with the scion of similar diameter. Propagation of *Rhododendron* rootstocks from cuttings will help to ensure a straight stem on which to graft. It is advisable to remove the buds below and around the union to reduce subsequent suckering.

Grafting Procedure

Scion Preparation

(1) Use 10–12.5 cm (4–5″) long scions with a diameter similar to that of the rootstock.

(2) Use a knife to make two opposite slanting cuts, 2.5–3.0 cm (1–1¼″) long, down into the stem. If possible, the cuts are "rounded" at the point where they meet by widening the angle of the knife blade.

Rootstock Preparation

Make two opposite cuts, 2.5–3.0 cm (1–1¼″) long, rounding at the juncture to match the scion. (Adjustments to these cuts may be required during matching-up.)

Matching-up

Match the scion and rootstock on both sides of the cut surfaces, with the base of the scion flush with the base of the rootstock cut.

[*NOTE*—: Some propagators in North America make the cuts on the rootstock in the form of a wedge. The scion is then cut to match.]

Figure 19-49.
Matching-up a
Rhododendron saddle graft.
Note the shape of the cut
surface on the rootstock.

CLEFT OR INLAY GRAFT

The cleft or inlay graft may be used when the rootstock is of larger diameter than the scion (see also bare-root grafting, p. 520). *Campsis* (Trumpet Creeper), *Cytisus* (Broom), *Hibiscus* and *Wisteria* are among the genera in which it is practiced. Matching is ensured on both sides of the scion instead of the single side that results when it has to be moved over to the perimeter of a larger diameter rootstock in other methods. An inverted cleft or inlay graft is used if the scion is considerably larger in diameter than the rootstock.

This graft is also used in December and January for some of the slow growing and choicer *Daphne,* such as *D. aurantiaca* (Golden-flowered Daphne), *D. petraea* and *D. tangutica,* because of the thin stems of the scion and the larger diameter of the seedling *D. mezereum* (February Daphne) and *D. laureola* (Spurge Laurel) rootstocks. Daphnes can be unreliable in both rooting and establishment of cuttings. Grafting results in a saleable plant after one growing season compared with about three years for those raised from cuttings.

The graft requires considerable dexterity and skill to obtain two equal sloping cuts that widen in width as they lengthen. The cuts on the scion may have to be made slightly longer than those on the rootstock to ensure a small "church window" of exposed scion.

Grafting Procedure

Example: Scion   *Daphne petraea* 'Grandiflora'
Rootstock   *D. mezereum* (February Daphne)
—2-year seedling

Scion Preparation

(1) Cut terminal stems of one- or two-year-old wood into 6.5–7.5 cm (2½–3") lengths.
(2) Remove the leaves from the bottom 2.0–2.5 cm (¾–1") of the scion, using either a knife or the fingers.
(3) Make a sloping cut, 1.3–2.0 cm (½–¾") long, at the base of the scion.
(4) Make a second corresponding cut at a 45° angle to the first cut.

Rootstock Preparation

(1) Reduce the stem in height to about 4.0 cm (1½") above the pot surface.
(2) (a) Make two cuts starting at an identical point about 2.0–2.5 cm (¾–1") from the top of the rootstock. Each cut should go deeper into the stem tissue as it proceeds up the stem. Remove the tapered section of tissue formed by these cuts.

 (b) If the wood of the stem is relatively soft, an alternative method is to make a single vertical cut down the stem, again going deeper into the stem as one proceeds.

Matching-up

(a) Place the scion into the rootstock so that the outer uncut surface is flush with the perimeter of the rootstock and a 3 mm (⅛") "church window" of exposed tissue remains.

(b) If a vertical cut has been made on the rootstock, the scion is carefully pushed down into the rootstock as the blade is removed, so pushing out the two sides of the rootstock. The outer cut surface should be flush with the perimeter of the rootstock and a 3 mm (⅛") "church window" of exposed tissue should remain.

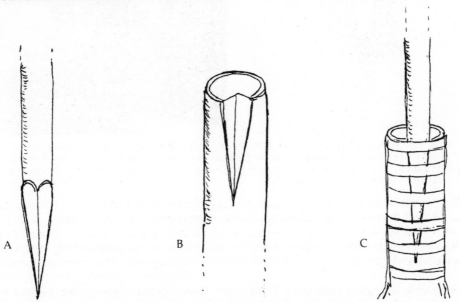

Diagram 19-14. Diagrammatic representation of a cleft or inlay graft. A. Prepared scion with two sloping cuts. B. Prepared rootstock with matching cuts slightly shorter than those on the scion so that a "church window" of exposed scion wood will be retained after matching-up. C. The completed graft after tying-in. (Note that this last diagram shows the reverse of the scion.)

UNROOTED CUTTING GRAFTS

The main difference between this method and the bench grafting techniques previously described is that the scion is grafted onto an unrooted rootstock. They are tied together and placed into a mist propagation unit with the objective of encouraging quick rooting of the rootstock and, at the same time, of creating conditions that will encourage cell differentiation to unite the scion and rootstock. It can also act as a nurse graft because roots may develop on the scion as well as on the rootstock during the aftercare process. This technique has been used successfully for *Rhododendron*, *Juniperus* (Juniper) and *Rosa* (Rose)—a main advantage being that the expense of providing an initial rooted rootstock is eliminated.

There are two differing ways in which this technique may be used. Firstly, it may be used as an alternative to pot-grown or bare-root rootstocks. Secondly, it may be used as an adjunct to cutting propagation, being used only for the plants that present problems when treated as conventional cuttings. Observations with *Rhododendron* show that it is important not to have excessive misting, to ensure that the medium covering the graft union in the flat is well aerated, and that a sufficient strength of hormone is applied to the unrooted cutting/rootstock to promote quick rooting.

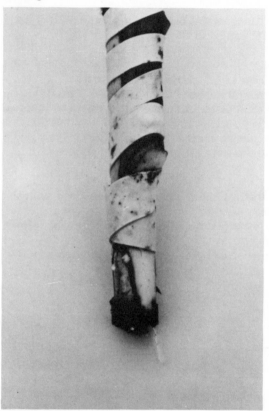 

Figure 19-50. A (left). An unrooted cutting graft. Note the beginning of root growth at the base of the cutting and the formation of callus just above the basal veneer on the rootstock. B (right). Successful unrooted cutting graft of *Rhododendron bureavii* on R. 'Cunningham's White' rootstock using the side veneer graft method. Note the well-developed root system in a peat moss/perlite mix.

The rootstock initially has no root system and therefore the efficiency of this system must be compared with conventional techniques before proceeding. The percentage grafting success rate should be evaluated first, and then the rate of establishment and of maiden growth to produce the liner also evaluated. Some who have tried this technique wrongly assess it only on percentage grafting success and ignore the rate of establishment and growth after removal from the mist unit.

Unrooted cuttings of *Picea abies* 'Nidiformis' (Nest Spruce) have given positive results as rootstocks for bench grafting *P. abies* 'Pyramidata' (Pyramidal Norway Spruce). Also, unrooted cuttings of *Juniperus horizontalis* (Creeping Juniper), *J. horizontalis* 'Plumosa' (Andorra Juniper) and *J. chinensis* 'Hetzii' (Hetz Blue Juniper) have been used successfully for selected cultivars of *J. scopulorum* (Rocky Mountain Juniper) and *J. virginiana* (Eastern Red Cedar)—the cuttings being 18–

20 cm (7–8") long. For *Rhododendron*, the rootstocks *R.* 'Cunningham's White', *R.* 'Cunningham's Blush' or *R.* 'County of York' (significantly less suckering) can be used.

Grafting Procedure

Example:	**Scion**	*Rhododendron yakusimanum* F.C.C. Form (Yakusima Rhododendron)
	Rootstock	*R.* 'Cunningham's White'
		R. 'County of York'

Method 1

(1) Take a one-year-old terminal shoot, 10–12.5 cm (4–5") long, remove the axillary buds and slice wound at the base by making two opposite cuts about 2.0 cm (¾") long. The axillary buds should be cut out to prevent suckering.

(2) Make a side veneer cut (see p. 546), 2.5 cm (1") long, just above the area where the slice wounds were made.

(3) Make a matching cut on a 7.5–10 cm (3–4") long scion, as for a side veneer graft.

(4) Match the graft and tie-in with a rubber strip, but do not wax over.

(5) Dip the base of the rootstock into 0.8% IBA in talc or a 2,500 ppm solution of IBA for 3–5 seconds.

(6) Place the completed graft in a medium of 2 parts peat moss to 1 part perlite, with the union just below the surface of the medium. The flat containing the rooting medium should have a depth of 10–12.5 cm (4–5").

(7) Place the flat in a mist propagation unit with a base temperature of 21°C (70°F).

(8) Remove the top of the rootstock above the union after the graft has united and there is sufficient root system on the rootstock to enable it to be successfully potted into a liner pot.

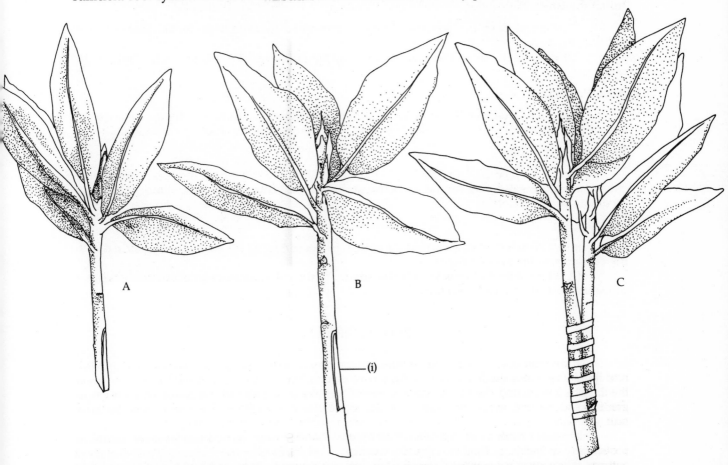

Diagram 19-15. Unrooted cutting graft of *Rhododendron*. A. Prepared scion. B. Prepared rootstock (unrooted cutting.) (i)—side veneer cut. C. Completed graft matched and tied-in. Note that the cuts are similar to those used for side veneer grafting.

Method 2

(1) Take a one-year-old terminal shoot, 10–12.5 cm (4–5″) long, and slice wound at the base by making two opposite cuts about 2.0 cm (¾″) long.

(2) Make an oblique cut, 2.0–2.5 cm (¾–1″) long, downward into the stem.

(3) Make a matching wedge (see p. 000) on the 7.5–10 cm (3–4″) long scion.

(4) Proceed as for Method I.

NURSE SEED GRAFTING

This occasionally used, specialized technique involves the use of a seedling that retains the cotyledons below soil level after germination. The shoot and root systems are removed and a dormant scion placed into the cotyledons. Nurse seed grafting is usually carried out in late February to early March. In practice, the range of plants where this technique has been success-fully used is limited to large seeded plants, such as *Aesculus* (Horse-chestnut), *Camellia*, *Castanea* (Chestnut) and *Quercus* (Oak). A union is quickly formed and root development encouraged on normally difficult-to-root plants because of the physiological make-up of a juvenile seedling during the early stages of development. Roots should normally form from the cut cotyledons, but some propagators have noticed that roots have developed from the actual scion wood.

More recently, Peter Dummer of Hillier Nurseries (Winchester) Ltd., England, has taken this technique a stage further by nurse grafting scions and seedling rootstocks of some different genera in the same natural order (family). The grafts are placed in a grafting case with the cotyledons 2.5–4.0 cm (1–1½″) beneath the surface of moistened peat moss. A quick union is encouraged by maintaining the base temperature at 21°C (70°F).

Grafting Procedure

Initial Rootstock Preparation

(1) Remove from the seed bed a newly germinated seedling with the first pair of leaves not fully expanded.

(2) Remove the shoot and roots by severing the petioles of the cotyledons just outside the seed coat.

Scion Preparation

Select a scion about 10 cm (4″) long and of relatively thin diameter (this depends on the size of the cotyledons). Make two sloping cuts about 2.0 cm (¾″) long to form a wedge.

Rootstock Preparation

Place the tip of the knife blade into the cotyledons between where the two petioles were cut and at right angles to the natural slit between the petioles. This should be of sufficient depth to accommodate the scion.

Matching-up

Insert the scion into the cotyledons so that the cut surface of the cotyledon is matched with the cambium of the scion wedge.

(A 0.4% solution of formalin may be applied to the cut surfaces of scion and rootstock as a preventative against fungal infection.)

TOP-WORKING

Top-working is a specialized method of grafting in which the scion, either as a stem with multiple buds or as a single bud, is normally worked onto the rootstock 0.3–1.8 m (1–6′) above soil level. With few exceptions, the timing and technique of grafting and budding are very similar to those already described for open-ground and bench grafting procedures. The differences are in the size and handling of the rootstocks and, very often, in the actual scion to be grafted.

Top-working is a very traditional technique that has been carried out for many decades, particularly in Belgium, England, France, Germany and Holland. I have been fascinated by the varying scion/rootstock combinations used in different nurseries in these countries. Many provide attractive forms of plants, while others are harsh and look somewhat hideous when planted out—although this is a personal opinion! The spectrum of woody ornamentals that can be top-worked is considerable, ranging from roses, ground covers, conifers, evergreen and deciduous shrubs to trees. In this section, the information is condensed on the scion/rootstock combinations, mainly based on personal observations and experience combined with other references. Six different top-working systems are later outlined.

The major reasons for top-working woody ornamentals are as follows:—

(i) It is a very effective way to produce unusual forms of plants. These vary from weeping (*Salix caprea* 'Pendula', Kilmarnock Willow) to globose (*Acer platanoides* 'Globosum', Globe Norway Maple) and fan-shaped (*Cotoneaster horizontalis*, Rock Cotoneaster or Rockspray) trees. Rhododendron enthusiasts occasionally top-work *Rhododendron* cultivars such as 'Elisabeth Hobbie' onto 91–102 cm (36–40") tall understocks of *R.* 'Anna Rose Whitney'. Iseli Nurseries Inc., Boring, Oregon, have produced a fascinating range of "artistic conifers" (e.g., to create a dramatic topiary effect) by inter-specific grafting of various weeping, horizontal and dwarf forms.

Figure 19-51. A specimen of *Salix caprea* 'Pendula' (Kilmarnock Willow) which is normally whip grafted onto *S. × smithiana* (or sometimes *S. daphnoides*, Violet or Daphne Willow).

Figure 19-52. *Prunus × cistena* (Purple-leaf Sand Cherry) makes an attractive novelty tree when top-worked on a stem of *P.* Myrobalan. Note the heavy winter pruning to encourage shoot development. (Angers, France)

Figure 19-53. *Hibiscus syriacus* 'Blue Bird' (Rose-of-Sharon cv.) top-worked onto stems of *H. syriacus*. (Angers, France)

It can also be extended into what is best described as "custom-built" trees. This can be the chip budding of 3 pairs of buds at 38–45 cm (15–18") intervals up the stem of the rootstock so that the growth can be immediately trained for espaliering (p. 570). A further example is top-working onto an inner-stem previously bottom-worked onto a rootstock. The virtues of the attractive shiny peeling bark of *Prunus serrula* (Birch-barl Cherry) may be used as an inter-stem for many of the hybrid Japanese cherries (see p. 446).

(ii) It provides specimen plants for both public and home landscaping, and also for use as avenue trees. The expansion of garden centers has provided the opportunity to sell excellent novelty plants, in the form of container-grown miniature to half-standard scion/rootstock combinations, at a premium price to the home gardener. However, some of the items offered are unlikely to provide a rapid throughput in sales, partly because of the individual customer's preferences for plant habit.

(iii) It provides the nursery operator with the opportunity to grow a plant to the point-of-sale in a shorter period of time. Top-working onto a 1.5–1.8 m (5–6') stem can often reduce the production period by 2–3 years.

Occasionally 0.6–1.0 m (2–3') tall specimens of *Chamaecyparis lawsoniana* (Lawson Cypress) or *Thuja occidentalis* (Eastern Arborvitae) may have the foliage reduced and then be grafted with numerous scions of *Chamaecyparis obtusa* 'Nana Gracilis' (Dwarf Hinoki Cypress). This slow-growing cultivar would normally take a number of years to reach such a height.

(iv) It can provide a method of producing a tree from forms that would otherwise require staking or develop into shrubs. Bottom-working of many weeping trees means that they have to develop a leader, which then needs staking and tying to ensure the stem is kept straight—for example, *Fraxinus excelsior* 'Pendula' (Weeping European Ash). Many slow-growing trees, such as the globose *Acer pseudoplatanus* 'Brilliantissimum' (Sycamore Maple cv.) would just develop into large shrubs if bottom-worked as they do not readily develop a leader. Thus, the only practical way of propagating these trees is by top-working.

(v) It is a useful method for inducing vigorous early growth in weak species that fail to perform when bottom-worked, e.g., *Quercus robur* 'Concordia' (Golden English Oak). It is also occasionally used when a quick bulk-up of further propagation material is required.

(vi) It is a procedure that has been used for decades in the top-working of conventional-habit Japanese Cherries, using cultivars of *Prunus serrulata* such as 'Kwanzan', 'Shirofugen' and 'Tai Haku' (Great White Cherry). Layers of *P. avium* Mazzard F12/1 are planted up, grown-on and then top-worked at about 1.8 m (6'). A straight stem is then ensured and the tree is saleable after 1 or 2 years of growth. It was also used in some areas where the soil in the open ground had become over-worked, thus lacking fertility and making it unsuitable to encourage sufficient growth in the early years after bottom-working so that the resulting trees were of poor quality, variable in height, and had a tendency to bent stems. This technique was used in the open-ground production of Japanese Cherries at some of the nurseries in the Bagshot/Chobham/Woking area in England where the greensand soils had been continually down-graded over the years by top soil being removed for burlapping plants as they were lifted, with little attention given to subsequent soil improvements and crop rotation. Top-working should not be used today as an excuse for poor cultural practices.

(vii) It provides the opportunity to change the cultivar or species of a tree, as is often done with fruit trees. Specimen plants of *Acer palmatum* (Japanese Maple) or some of its cultivars, for example, 'Atropurpureum' (Red Japanese Maple), may be worked with multiple scions (up to 20 per plant) of another cultivar when 1–2 m (3–6') tall to change the cultivar. Stick budding of Japanese Maples (see p. 487) lends itself very well to this technique. The procedure is useful if a particular *A. palmatum* cultivar has been over-produced for the market. The plants can be stick budded outdoors in late July/August or a greenhouse in September with a cultivar that is in more demand.

Open-ground trees that have been bottom-worked and allowed to grow-on for 1–2 years may be found to be surplus to requirements. An alternative to discarding is to top-work them. The weeping *Cotoneaster* × *watereri* 'Pendulus' (a.k.a. 'Hybridus Pendulus') can be worked on stems of other members of the Watereri group, e.g., 'St. Monica' and 'Cornubia', while the weeping *Laburnum anagyroides* 'Pendulum' (Weeping Golden-chain Tree) can be worked on stems of *L.* × *watereri* 'Vossii'. (Voss' Long-cluster Golden-chain Tree) previously bottom-worked onto *L. anagyroides* (Golden-chain Tree). The more upright *Cytisus battandieri* (Atlas or Moroccan Broom) can also be worked on stems of *Laburnum* × *watereri* 'Vossii'. This raises production costs, but the increase can be offset by choosing a scion to re-work that can be sold at a premium price.

[(vii) It has been recorded that some dwarf plants that do not set seed will produce viable seed after top-working. This has been known to occur on dwarf forms of *Pinus strobus* (Eastern White Pine) and *Tsuga canadensis* (Canadian Hemlock), particularly those arising from Witch's-brooms.]

Top-working has its limitations, among which are:—

(i) The increased cost of the rootstocks because they have to be taller and also generally larger in caliper than for conventional grafting. It may take up to 4–5 years to produce rootstocks of a sufficient size for top-working, versus 1–3 years for conventional ones.

(ii) The larger size means that more handling is needed for bench grafting, with increased height and weight provisions, and that more room will be occupied in the aftercare facility. The facility may have to be extended in height, width and length, particularly when grafting plants such as *Aesculus* × *carnea* 'Briotii' (Ruby Horse-chestnut) onto 1.5–1.8 m (5–6') stems of *A. hippocastanum* (Common Horse-chestnut).

(iii) The graft union can be unsightly, although it is largely hidden by the foliage of weeping deciduous forms during the summer months. Trees such as *Prunus* (Cherry) and *Ulmus* (Elm) are particularly notorious for this. It gives an unsightly and artificial appearance to the tree, particularly when the graft is at eye level. For this reason, I do not like to see top-working of the non-weeping *Prunus*, but would rather see a stem run up and trained to form a head from a bottom-worked rootstock.

Figure 19-54.
Some species propagated by top-working can produce a very unsightly union at eye level as the tree matures. This *Prunus serrulata* cv. (Japanese Flowering Cherry) was probably top-worked onto a *P. avium* Mazzard F12/1 rootstock.

OPEN-GROUND TOP-WORKING

Open-ground top-working is used essentially for ornamental trees and roses. The main points to consider when contemplating top-working are as follows:—

(i) The rootstock stem must be straight. It is vital that they are of top quality, whether bought in or grown on the nursery. Common faults in low-grade stems are bent stems or "kinks". A "kink" in the lower part of the stem is prevalent in the *Rosa rugosa* (Rugosa Rose) rootstocks used to produce tree (standard) roses by top-working. This is normally due to the selected leader bud breaking away at a wide angle after the rootstock is headed back in the rootstock production area. The formation of flowering buds during the growth phase is also known to induce "kinks" in the stem.

(ii) The rootstock has sufficient caliper at the point at which the scion is to be placed. The stems should have sufficient strength not to bend as the scion develops and increases in weight, thus causing the tree to be top-heavy. Therefore, stem caliper of the rootstock needs to be "balanced" with the expected growth rate and habit of the scion.

(iii) It is important to pay attention to the method of stem support (where applicable) and the protection of the scion. The scion is considerably more exposed than on bottom-worked rootstocks and is therefore more prone to both physical damage and desiccation. Excessive wind can break the scion away from the rootstock right at the union.

The actual techniques for grafting and budding are similar to those described for bottom-working open-ground trees. The differences are that multi-stemmed and longer scions (sometimes two scions) may be used for grafting, while three scion buds are used in budding instead of one. Chip budding (see p. 478) is particularly useful for top-working in the summer because of its tendency to produce a stronger and better united union by the time the new growth emerges the following spring when compared with T-budding in some climates.

(a) Weeping Trees

A very popular tree for top-working is the double pink-flowered *Prunus serrulata* 'Kiku-shidare-zakura' (Double Weeping Flowering Cherry), sometimes referred to as 'Cheal's Weeping Cherry'. It is top-worked at a height of between 1.5–1.8 m (5–6'), generally with scions similar to those described for whip and tongue grafting on bottom-worked trees. One variation that I have noted is to use a scion up to 25–30 cm (10–12") long in order to produce a larger head to the tree. A thin cane is placed adjacent to both scion and rootstock after grafting and firmly tied-in, thus providing the scion with support in wind. A polyethylene bag or a layer of polyethylene film (preferably milky (opaque) film) is then tied in below the union so that it completely covers the scion to help reduce wind desiccation. The bag or film is slit when the buds have flushed and growth is about 1.3 cm (½") long, and is removed entirely a few days later.

Another variation noted in Angers, France, is to use large multi-stemmed scions with about four lateral shoots coming off the leader shoots. These were effectively used for grafting *Fraxinus excelsior* 'Pendula' (Weeping European Ash) onto *F. excelsior* (European Ash).

A technique used in Belgium for *Robinia* (Locust) is to graft two scions opposite each other. This method provides quality trees of either *Robinia pseudoacacia* 'Umbraculifera' (Mop-head Acacia) or the deep rose-pink flowered *R. hispida* (Rose Acacia) when top-worked on *R. peudoacacia* (Black Locust or False Acacia).

The best method for summer budding is to chip or T-bud 3 scion buds in a spiral at the desired height to help to ensure a balanced head. If one bud fails, the remaining two can be pruned back early in the year to promote breaking of the axillary buds and thus still produce a satisfactory tree. If only one bud remains, it is preferable to graft over in the following February to March. Alternatively, two buds may be sited opposite each other, but this has the disadvantage that grafting over has to be done if one bud fails. Other ornamental trees which are top-worked by budding include *Prunus subhirtella* 'Pendula Plena Rosea' (Double Weeping Rosebud Cherry), *Acer platanoides* 'Globosum' (Globe Norway Maple) and *Ulmus glabra* 'Camperdownii' (Camperdown Elm).

Figure 19-55. Top-worked rootstock stems of *Fraxinus excelsior* (European Ash). Note the use of small polyethylene bags tied-in below the union to reduce scion desiccation.

Figure 19-56. One of a pair of buds of *Fraxinus excelsior* 'Pendula' (Weeping European Ash) top-worked by T-budding onto stems of *F. excelsior* (European Ash). The photograph shows the shoot development commencing after the rootstock was headed back to the pair of buds in March after T-budding the previous year.

(b) Standard (Tree) Roses

This traditional crop provides one of the best examples of top-working. They are top-worked as miniature standards with a minimum clear stem of 30 cm (1'), half-standards with 75 cm (2½'), standards with 1.0 m (3½'), and as weeping standards with 1.4 m (4¾') of clear stem.

Cultivars such as *Rosa* 'Little Buckaroo' and *R.* 'Cinderella' are used for miniature standards, while a whole range of hybrid tea and floribunda roses, including *R.* 'Fragrant Cloud' and 'Pascali', are budded for the half-standards and standards. *Rosa* 'Dorothy Perkins' is a popular choice for weeping standards. Effective standards can be produced by budding some of the species roses, such as *R. moyesii* (Moyes Rose) and *R. hugonis* (Father Hugo's Rose or Golden Rose-of-China), and the hybrids *R.* 'Max Graf' and 'Highdownensis'. These can be worked onto stems of *R. rugosa* (Rugosa Rose), *R.* 'Hollandica' (a.k.a. 'Scherpe Boskoop'), the *R. canina* (Dog Rose) cultivars 'Dessiatoff', 'Inermis' and 'Pfänder', or on thornless *R. multiflora* (Baby or Japanese Rose).

With the exception of miniature standards, the rootstock stems are planted 38 cm (15″) apart with 1.0 m (3′) pathways. Alternative methods of supporting the stems before budding include:—

(i) Stake and tie after planting to ensure that the stems do not fall into the rows.

(ii) Tie-in the heads of the stems in groups of 3 or 4 to prevent them from bending into the rows. This is particularly useful for twin-row planting systems and if the budder prefers a "free" standing stem for budding. Staking and tying-in is carried out after budding. [Note:—Some budders like to have a "free" stem in which to place the bud as against budding a stem that is rigid and tied into a wire.]

The buds are best placed in a spiral, leaving a short length of rootstock about 15 cm (6″) long above the top bud. This snag can be used to tie into the wire to support the plant. If the support wire is below the scion buds, this snag is removed during the following February to early March. Alternatively, two buds may be sited opposite each other. Another method used is to allow some of the lateral shoots to develop at the top of the rootstock stem and then place a single bud into each of these shoots. This latter method is useful for some of the weeping roses to give a wider head to the plant. Chip budding is particularly useful for standard rose production when the rind does not lift satisfactorily for T-budding.

Figure 19-57. T-budding standard (tree) roses onto stems of *R. rugosa* (Rugosa Rose). Note that the budder holds the stem at waist level to improve handling and visibility. (Hillier Nurseries (Winchester) Ltd., Romsey, Hampshire, U.K.)

Figure 19-58. The result of T-budding standard (tree) roses. Three buds have been placed in a spiral around the stem and tied-in with degradable rubber ties.

Figure 19-59. The season after T-budding standard (tree) roses. New growth has commenced from each of the buds. The terminal shoot is normally pruned back when it reaches 10–15 cm (4–6″) in length to encourage side shoot development.

(c) Conifers

Open-ground top-working of conifers is little practiced, although it has been used in dryer and warmer climates for winter side grafting of *Larix decidua* 'Pendula' (Weeping European Larch) onto *L. kaempferi* (Japanese Larch) and side grafting of *Pinus mugo* (Mugo Pine) as a miniature or full standard.

BENCH TOP-WORKING

This embraces a much wider range of plants by utilizing more scion/rootstock combinations, particularly in conifers, trees and evergreen shrubs. The principles and techniques are essentially similar to those previously described under bench grafting.

When any form of top-working is carried out in an enclosed environment it is important to remember that the scions are a good deal higher above the ground then in conventional grafting and therefore, once again, shading is vital to prevent scorch to the new scion growth. The following examples illustrate top-working using bench grafting.

(i) *Acer pseudoplatanus* 'Brilliantissimum' (Sycamore Maple cv.)—This slow-growing tree makes a strong impact with its pink foliage in the spring, and is an ideal subject for top-working. *Acer pseudoplatanus* (Sycamore Maple) trees are selected for top-working as half- or three-quarter standards during the late fall or winter, lifted, root pruned, and shoot pruned to leave a clean stem. They may either be containerized and stood down in a shade house or heeled into sawdust or peat moss. Rootstocks in containers are brought into a frost-free greenhouse 2–3 weeks prior to the grafting time in February. Heeled-in rootstocks are burlapped, with additional peat moss/loam medium being placed around the roots just prior to burlapping to prevent them from drying out. An alternative method is to line out the heeled-in rootstocks directly into the border soil of a structure clad with glass or polyethylene.

Figure 19-60. A (left). *Acer pseudoplatanus* 'Brilliantissimum' (Sycamore Maple cv.) top-worked onto stems of *A. pseudoplatanus* (Sycamore Maple) and bedded out in a polyethylene greenhouse after grafting. B (right). A whip grafted multiple-budded scion of *A. pseudoplatanus* 'Brilliantissimum'.

Two multi-stemmed scions are side veneer grafted at the desired height, the union waxed and the air temperature kept frost-free. The temperature can be raised to around 15.5°C (60°F) if desired. Alternatively, a single multi-stemmed scion may be whip grafted. A saleable tree can be produced by the following fall if these trees are kept under glass or polyethylene for growing-on during the season after budding.

(ii) *Acer platanoides* **'Globosum' (Globe Norway Maple),** *Aesculus* × *carnea* **'Briotii' (Ruby Horse-chestnut),** *Fagus sylvatica* **'Pendula' (Weeping Beech) and** *Fraxinus excelsior* **'Pendula' (Weeping European Ash)**—These are large trees that can be top-worked in January to February. They are burlapped with a peat moss and loam medium around the root system and brought into a greenhouse maintained at 12–15°C (54–59°F) about 2 weeks before grafting. Two side veneer grafts, using conventional scions, are placed at the desired height. The grafted trees are then placed side by side in a large polyethylene tent constructed within the greenhouse so that high humidity and air temperature of 21°C (70°F) can be maintained around them. The trees can be planted up in the open ground after hardening-off. An alternative to burlapping is to side graft bare-root rootstocks, which are then placed into a deep bed of moist peat moss. However, there is a greater risk that the newly developed roots will dry out following planting in the open ground.

(iii) Miniature Standard Conifers—A specialist crop is the top-working of certain conifers such as *Picea pungens* 'Globosa' (Globe Colorado Blue Spruce), *Pinus mugo* 'Prostrata Wells' (Wells' Prostrate Mugo Pine), *P. sylvestris* 'Glauca Nana' (Dwarf Blue Scots Pine) and *P. densiflora* 'Umbraculifera' (Japanese Umbrella Pine or Tanyosho). The rootstock needs to be of sufficient length so that a conventional side graft can be placed at least 30 cm (12") above the surface of the medium. This means that it is necessary to either pot-up increased caliper seedling rootstocks or to grow the rootstock for two years in a larger pot instead of one year.

Figure 19-61. A. (left). Top-worked compact form of *Pinus densiflora* 'Umbraculifera' (Japanese Umbrella Pine or Tanyosho) side veneer grafted onto stems of *P. sylvestris* (Scots Pine). B. (right). Top-worked specimen plant of *P. sylvestris* 'Glauca Nana' (Dwarf Blue Scots Pine) ready for sale some years after grafting.

Juniperus squamata 'Blue Star', the attractive silver-blue foliaged form of the Single-seed or Scaly-leaved Nepal Juniper, can be top-worked during January and February onto rootstocks of unsold *J. scopulorum* 'Skyrocket' (a.k.a. *J. virginiana* 'Skyrocket') (Skyrocket Juniper) or *Thuja occidentalis* 'Pyramidalis' (Pyramidal Arborvitae) for sale as a novelty plant. The rootstocks should be cleaned up at the time of grafting by removing all side branches to about 7.5 cm (3″) above the point at which the scion is to be grafted. Two to three scions can then be side grafted in a spiral.

Figure 19-62. Open-ground plants of *Juniperus scopulorum* 'Skyrocket' (*J. virginiana* 'Skyrocket') (Skyrocket Juniper) containerized in the fall for top-working in the following February and over-wintered in a polyethylene greenhouse. Note the method of stacking the containers to utilize space more efficiently, and that the stems have been partially cleaned up by removing the majority of side shoots. (Joerg Leiss, Sheridan Nurseries, Oakville, ON, Canada)

Figure 19-63. Top-worked specimen of *Juniperus squamata* 'Blue Star' (Single-seed or Scaly-leaved Nepal Juniper cv.).

(iv) Espaliered Trees—An interesting technique pioneered recently in western Canada by Geoffrey Schwyn of Westham Island Nursery, British Columbia, is the container production of espalier fruit trees. First-grade layers of *Malus* M.26 are purchased and potted-up into 27 cm (10½″) diameter containers. During July, 2 or 3 pairs of opposite buds are chip budded at 38 cm (15″) intervals up the stem—each pair of buds being a different cultivar of similar vigor. Tying-in is made easier by placing a short strip of sticky tape across the front of the bud shield and adjoining rootstock after the chip bud has been matched. This prevents the buds falling out and allows the operator to efficiently tie-in the pair of buds with one strip of polyethylene tape.

A prefabricated trellis is fitted at the back of the rootstock and held rigid by the fact that the basal posts are designed to slip flush against the inner surface of the container. The rootstock is tied directly onto a stake adjacent to the center of the trellis to ensure that the stem is kept straight.

The buds break in the next spring and the new growth is tied to and trained along and up the trellis. The final "custom" product is sold to garden centers in the following fall. This system could be used for selling espaliered ornamental *Malus* and *Pyrus* (Pear).

Figure 19-64. Nursery rows of container-grown M.26 rootstocks chip budded in the previous summer. Note the evenness of height following heading back to the upper pair of buds in late February. (Westham Island Nursery, Delta, B.C., Canada)

Figure 19-65. A close-up of the bud chip on M.26 rootstock. Note the position of the pruners in relation to the bud chip when heading back, and the sticky tape remaining from the previous summer when it was used to prevent dislodgement of the bud chip while tying-in. (Westham Island Nursery, Delta, B.C., Canada)

Figure 19-66. The shoots from two pairs of buds of *Pyrus* (Pear) being espaliered in early August onto a single wooden trellis slotted into the container. (Geoff Schwyn, Westham Island Nursery, Delta, B.C., Canada)

(v) *Malus* **and** *Prunus*—A specialist crop grown by R. Sorenson of Homestead Nurseries, Clayburn, B.C., was instigated by demands from local retail sales outlets and is the production of container-grown half- and full-standard ornamental *Prunus* and *Malus*. The aim is to provide a tree during the early part of the year that can be easily handled by both the garden center operator and the customer. The majority of the scions used are species and cultivars suitable for small and medium-sized subdivision gardens.

First grade layers of *Prunus avium* Mazzard F12/1 and *Malus* M.M.106 are purchased and heeled-in outdoors, with the roots well covered by sawdust. The scions are whip grafted as half- or full-standards during January onto these rootstocks, tied-in with rubber grafting strips, and waxed so that both scion and union are covered. The grafts are tied into bundles of 10–15 and moved to a well-aerated, unheated, polyethylene structure

Figure 19-67. A (left). Top-worked *Prunus avium* Mazzard F12/1 stems bundled and labelled ready for callusing in the greenhouse. Note that the root systems are covered by a mixture of moist sawdust and peat moss. B (right). Top-worked container-grown ornamental *Prunus* whip grafted the previous January and intended for garden center sales. (Rick Sorenson, Homestead Nurseries, Clayburn, B.C., Canada)

with the root systems well covered by sawdust. Shading is provided as necessary. Callusing between scion and rootstock is seen after 3 weeks, and the grafts can be potted into 27 cm (10½″) diameter containers 4–5 weeks after grafting, just prior to the swelling of the buds. These are placed under polyethylene for 6 weeks, then moved outdoors and grown-on for a full season before selling the following year. Pruning of the side shoots is carried out up to three times during the growing season to build up the head of the tree.

Ornamental *Malus* and *Prunus* used for this system at Homestead Nurseries are *Malus* 'Profusion', *M. sargentii* (Sargent Crab Apple), *M. floribunda* (Japanese Flowering Crab Apple), *M.* 'Red Jade' (Red Jade Crab Apple), *Prunus* 'Accolade', *P.* 'Pink Perfection', *P. serrulata* 'Shirotae' (Mount Fuji Cherry), and *P. subhirtella* 'Autumnalis' (Autumn Flowering Higan Cherry).

(vi) *Acer palmatum* **cvs. (Japanese Maple)** —A unique method of top-working constitutes an integral part of the production system of Tsai-Ying Cheng, founder of T.C. Plants Inc., Hillsboro, Oregon. She produces custom-made, container-grown *Acer palmatum* cultivars in a variety of shapes by inter-lacing and wiring the stems. Some 3–10 seedlings of *A. palmatum* have their main stems inter-laced and are then potted and allowed to establish. Following establishment, each stem is side grafted at the required height. Scions used include many of the cut-leaved cultivars such as *A. palmatum* 'Burgundy Lace', 'Dissectum Filigree' and 'Dissectum Garnet'.

As a result of her previous micropropagation experiences, Tsai-Ying Cheng has evolved a side grafting method for both top-working and conventional production of *A. palmatum* cvs. virtually all the year round. This success has been mainly achieved by the method of grafting, soaking the scion in a medium containing auxins and cytokinins, and using a degradable adhesive plastic tie.

A specialty of Iseli Nurseries Inc., Boring, Oregon, is to stick bud (p. 487) multi-scions onto 1–2 m (3–6′) tall, container-grown plants of *A. palmatum*. It is important to retain sufficient new growth from the top of the rootstocks in the following spring as this draws sap up the stem and thus prevents root die-back while also providing some shade. The new growth arising from between the buds and at the base of the rootstock is removed.

Figure 19-68. A (left). A specimen plant produced by inter-lacing 8 stems and then top-working each of the stems with a dissected cultivar of *Acer palmatum* (Japanese Maple). B (right). A recently top-worked plant of a dissected cultivar of *A. palmatum* produced by inter-lacing and wiring the stems. This will eventually be sold as a fan-shaped specimen plant. (T. C. Plants, Hillsboro, OR, U.S.A.)

(vii) *Euonymus fortunei* **cvs. (Winter Creeper Euonymus)** —A number of the popular *Euonymus* ground cover cultivars, e.g., *E. fortunei* 'Emerald 'n Gold' and 'Gaiety', sell as novelty products when grafted onto stems of *E. europaea* (European Spindle Tree). Two side veneer grafts per stem are made in late January/February. and then the container-grown plants are sold after 1 or 2 years of growth.

APPENDIX 19-1

A Selected List of Scion/Rootstock Combinations for Ornamental Trees and Shrubs Propagated by Bench Grafting

NOTE:—The grafting times in this list have been taken as an optimum range for both North America and Europe. The geographical location of a nursery may mean that grafting is carried out before (or after) the times listed here.

SCION	ROOTSTOCK	TIME OF YEAR	BARE-ROOT (B.R.) OR POT-GROWN (P.G.)	TYPE OF GRAFT	COMMENTS
Acer campestre cvs. (Hedge Maple) [e.g., 'Schwerinii']	*A. campestre* (Hedge Maple)	Aug or Jan–Feb	P.G.	Side	Sometimes bare-root grafted in Aug–Sept and potted-up when union unites.
A. cappadocicum cvs. (Coliseum Maple) [e.g., 'Aureum', Yellow Coliseum Maple]	*A. cappadocicum* (Coliseum Maple)	Aug or Jan–Feb	P.G.	Side	Sometimes top-worked. (Effectively propagated by layering.)
A. davidii cvs. (David Maple) [e.g., 'Ernest Wilson']	*A. davidii* (David Maple) or related species in "Snake-bark" gp of Maples	Aug or Jan–Feb	P.G.	Side	
A. griseum (Paperbark Maple)	*A. nikoense* (Nikko Maple)	Aug. or Jan–Feb	P.G.	Side	Good seed sources of *A. nikoense* often very difficult to locate. Softwood cutting propagation has been successful.
A. heldreichii (Balkan Maple)	*A. pseudoplatanus* (Sycamore Maple)	Jan–Mar	B.R. P.G.	Side	
A. japonicum cvs. (Full-moon Maple) [e.g., 'Aureum', Golden Full-moon Maple]	*A. palmatum* (Japanese Maple)	July–Aug or Jan–Mar	P.G.	Side	
A. palmatum cvs. (Japanese Maple) [e.g., 'Dissectum Nigrum']	*A. palmatum* (Japanese Maple)	July–Aug or Jan–Mar	P.G.	Side	Also open-ground budded in Aug on *A. palmatum*.
A. platanoides cvs. (Norway Maple) [e.g., 'Crimson King', Crimson King Maple]	*A. platanoides* (Norway Maple)	Aug or Jan–Feb	P.G.	Side or Whip	More commonly open-ground budded. *A.* × *dieckii* (Dieck's Maple) successfully bench grafted onto *A. platanoides*.
A. pseudoplatanus cvs. (Sycamore Maple) [e.g., 'Worleei', Golden Sycamore]	*A. pseudoplatanus* (Sycamore Maple)	Aug or Jan–Feb	P.G.	Side or Whip	More commonly open-ground budded.

SCION	ROOTSTOCK	TIME OF ·YEAR	BARE-ROOT (B.R.) OR POT-GROWN (P.G.)	TYPE OF GRAFT	COMMENTS
A. rubrum cvs. (Red Maple) [e.g., 'Red Sunset']	*A. rubrum* (Red Maple)	Aug or Jan–Feb	P.G.	Side or Whip	More commonly open-ground budded. Softwood cutting propagation becoming more popular in N. America mainly due to incompatibility of some of the newer cvs. with *A. rubrum* seedling rootstocks when open-ground budded.
A. saccharum cvs. (Sugar Maple) [e.g., 'Temple's Upright']	*A. saccharum* (Sugar Maple)	Aug or Jan–Feb	P.G.	Side	
A. trautvetteri	*A. pseudoplatanus* (Sycamore Maple)	Jan–Mar	B.R. P.G.	Side	*Note:*—A "rule of thumb" sometimes used for compatibility of *Acer* is that species with a "milky" sap are not compatible with species with a "non-milky" sap and vise-versa.
A. velutinum (Persian Maple)	*A. pseudoplatanus* (Sycamore Maple)	Jan–Mar	B.R. P.G.	Side	
Aesculus × *carnea* (Red Horse-chestnut) [e.g., 'Briotii', Ruby Horse-chestnut]	*A. hippocastanum* (Common Horse-chestnut *A.* × *carnea* (Red Horse-chestnut)	Jan–Feb	P.G. B.R.	Whip, Basal Whip or Chip Bud	It is preferable to select the type species (e.g., *A.* × *carnea* or *A. indica*) as rootstock as *A. hippocastanum* can result in stem over-growth at the union.
A. hippocastanum (Common Horse-chestnut) [e.g., 'Baumanii', Double-flowered Horse-chestnut)	*A. hippocastanum* (Common Horse-chestnut)	Jan–Feb	P.G. B.R.	Whip, Basal Whip or Chip Bud	Commonly open-ground budded.
A. indica 'Sydney Pearce' (Indian Horse-chestnut cv.)	*A. hippocastanum* (Common Horse-chestnut) *A. indica* (Indian Horse-chestnut)	Jan–Feb	P.G. B.R.	Whip, Basal Whip or Chip Bud	Use at least 2-yr-old seedlings if budding onto the rootstock— gives improved take.
Alnus × *cordinca*	*A. cordata* (Italian Alder)	Jan–Feb	P.G.	Side	
A. glutinosa cvs. (Black or Common Alder) [e.g., 'Imperialis']	*A. glutinosa* (Black or Common Alder)	Jan–Feb	P.G.	Side	
A. incana cvs. (White Alder) [e.g., 'Aurea', Yellowleaf White Alder]	*A. incana* (White Alder)	Jan–Feb	P.G.	Side	Softwood cutting propagation is very effective and becoming more widely used.
Amelanchier lamarckii 'Ballerina'	*A. canadensis* (Shadblow Serviceberry)	Jan–Feb	P.G.	Whip, Side	*Sorbus intermedia* (Swedish White Beam) and *Cotoneaster bullatus* (Hollyberry

SCION	ROOTSTOCK	TIME OF YEAR	BARE-ROOT (B.R.) OR POT-GROWN (P.G.)	TYPE OF GRAFT	COMMENTS
A. lamarckii 'Rubescens'	*A. canadensis* (Shadblow Serviceberry)	Jan–Feb	P.G.	Whip, Side	Cotoneaster) also suggested as rootstocks.
Aralia chinensis cvs. (Chinese Aralia) [e.g., 'Aureovariegata']	*A. chinensis* (Chinese Aralia)	July or Jan–Feb	P.G. or balled & burlapped	Side or Chip Bud	
Arbutus × *andrachnoides*	*A. unedo* (Strawberry Tree)	Aug or Jan–Feb	P.G.	Side	*A.* × *andrachnoides* can be propagated by cuttings.
Berberis linearifolia cvs. [e.g., 'Orange King']	*B. thunbergii* (Japanese Barberry)	Jan–Feb	B.R. P.G.	Whip	*B. thunbergii* 'Atropurpurea' (Red Barberry) seedlings are sometimes preferred as root-stocks as subse-quent sucker growth is more distinctive.
B. × *lologensis* cvs. [e.g., 'Apricot Queen']	*B. thunbergii* (Japanese Barberry)	Jan–Feb	B.R. P.G.	Whip	
Betula pendula cvs. (European White or Common Silver Birch) [e.g., 'Tristis']	*B. pendula* (European White or Common Silver Birch) *B. pubescens* (Downy Birch)	Jan–Feb	P.G.	Side	*B. pubescens* best used for wet soils. Cutting propagation is effective for many cvs.
Betula spp. [e.g., *B. ermanii*]	*B. pendula* (European White or Common Silver Birch) *B. pubescens* (Downy Birch)	Jan–Feb	P.G.	Side	Some spp. and cvs. successfully open-ground budded.
Camellia reticulata cvs. (Net-veined Camellia) [e.g., 'Captain Rawes']	*C. japonica* (Common or Japanese Camellia)	Jan–Feb	P.G.	Side or Whip	A California practice is to graft some Camellia hybrids, e.g., 'Flower Girl' (*C. reticulata* × *C. sasanqua*), on *C. japonica* or *C. sasanqua* (Sun or Sasanqua Camellia). Also in California, scion is wedge grafted onto other cvs., e.g., *C.* 'Betty Sheffield Supreme', to initially build-up stock.
Carpinus betulus cvs. (European Hornbeam) [e.g., 'Fastigiata']	*C. betulus* (European Hornbeam)	Sept or Jan–Feb	P.G.	Side Whip or Basal Whip	Sometimes grafted bare-root in Sept. and potted-up when graft union has taken.
Castanea sativa cvs. (Spanish Chestnut) [e.g., 'Aureomarginata']	*C. sativa* (Spanish Chestnut)	Jan–Feb	P.G. B.R.	Whip	
Cercis canadensis cvs. (Eastern Redbud) [e.g., 'Forest Pansy']	*C. canadensis* (Eastern Redbud) *C. siliquastrum* (Judas Tree)	Jan–Feb	P.G.	Stick-budding, Side	Stick-budding used successfully in California.

SCION	ROOTSTOCK	TIME OF YEAR	BARE-ROOT (B.R.) OR POT-GROWN (P.G.)	TYPE OF GRAFT	COMMENTS
C. siliquastrum cvs. (Judas Tree) [e.g., 'Bodnant']	*C. siliquastrum* (Judas Tree)	Jan–Feb	P.G.	Stick-budding Side	
Cornus controversa 'Variegata' (Giant Dogwood cv.)	*C. controversa* (Giant Dogwood) *C. alternifolia* (Pagoda Dogwood)	Jan–Feb	P.G.	Side	Rooted cuttings of *C. alba* 'Elegantissima' (Silver-leaf Dogwood) have been used as a rootstock but subsequent growth is slow.
C. 'Eddies White Wonder'	*C. florida* (Eastern Flowering Dogwood) *C. nuttallii* (Western Flowering Dogwood)	Jan–Feb	P.G.	Side	*C. florida* is preferred due to transplanting losses when using *C. nuttallii* rootstocks. Tests in British Columbia indicate that *C. kousa* (Kousa Dogwood) may be a satisfactory rootstock.
C. florida cvs. (Eastern Flowering Dogwood) [e.g., 'Apple Blossom']	*C. florida* (Eastern Flowering Dogwood)	Jan–Feb	P.G.	Side	
C. kousa var. *chinensis* (Chinese Kousa Dogwood)	*C. florida* (Eastern Flowering Dogwood)	Jan–Feb	P.G.	Side	
C. nuttallii cvs. (Western Flowering Dogwood) [e.g., 'Ascona']	*C. florida* (Eastern Flowering Dogwood) *C. nuttallii* (Western Flowering Dogwood)	Jan–Feb	P.G.	Side	See under *C.* 'Eddies White Wonder'.
Corylus avellana cvs. (European Filbert or Hazelnut) [e.g., 'Contorta', Harry Lauder's Walking Stick]	*C. avellana* (European Filbert or Hazelnut) *C. maxima* (Giant Filbert)	Jan–Feb	P.G. B.R.	Whip	*C. colurna* (Turkish Filbert) has been used successfully in Holland. Easier to distinguish sucker growth.
Cytisus battandieri (Atlas or Moroccan Broom)	*Laburnum anagyroides* (Common Laburnum)	Jan–Feb	P.G.	Whip	May be raised from seed.
Daphne cneorum cvs. (Garland Flower) [e.g., 'Variegata']	*D. mezereum* (February Daphne) *D. laureola* (Spurge Laurel)	Jan–Mar	P.G.	Inlay, Whip or Side	In Holland, growth better on *D. mezereum*. Root sections or seedlings used.
D. petraea cvs. [e.g., 'Grandiflora']	*D. mezereum* (February Daphne) *D. laureola* (Spurge Laurel)	Jan–Mar	P.G.	Inlay, Whip or Side	
Daphne spp. [e.g., *D. aurantiaca*, Golden-flowered Daphne; *D. tangutica*]	*D. mezereum* (February Daphne) *D. laureola* (Spurge Laurel)	Jan–Mar	P.G.	Inlay, Whip or Side	Grafting is effective for many of the slow-growing species.
Elaeagnus macrophylla	*E. pungens* (Silverberry, Thorny Elaeagnus)	Aug–Sept	P.G.	Side	
E. pungens 'Maculata' (Golden Elaeagnus)	*E. umbellata*	Sept	P.G.	Side	Today, normally propagated by semi-ripe wood cuttings due to problems of suckering with rootstock.

SCION	ROOTSTOCK	TIME OF YEAR	BARE-ROOT (B.R.) OR POT-GROWN (P.G.)	TYPE OF GRAFT	COMMENTS
Fagus sylvatica cvs. (European Beech) [e.g., 'Tricolor', Tricolor Beech]	*F. sylvatica* (European Beech)	Jan–Feb	P.G.	Side	Whip grafting has also been successful.
Fraxinus americana 'American Purple' (White Ash cv.)	*F. excelsior* (European Ash) *F. pennsylvanica* var. *lanceolata* (Green Ash)	Jan–Feb	P.G.	Whip	Most *Fraxinus* are open-ground budded. Overgrowths at the graft union are likely to occur when the smaller species of *Fraxinus* are worked onto vigorous rootstocks.
F. bungeana (Bunge Ash)	*F. ornus* (Flowering or Manna Ash)	Jan–Feb	P.G.	Whip	
F. floribunda (Himalayan Manna Ash)	*F. ornus* (Flowering or Manna Ash)	Jan–Feb	P.G.	Whip	
F. mariesii (Maries Ash)	*F. ornus* (Flowering or Manna Ash)	Jan–Feb	P.G.	Whip	
F. pennsylvanica cvs. (Red Ash) [e.g., 'Summit']	*F. pennsylvanica* var. *lanceolata* (Green Ash)	Jan–Feb	P.G.	Whip	In England, *F. pennsylvanica* var. *lanceolata* rootstocks are generally recommended for *F. pennsylvanica* var. *lanceolata* cvs.
Gleditsia triacanthos var. *inermis* cvs. (Thornless Honey Locust) [e.g., 'Sunburst', Sunburst Honey Locust]	*G. triacanthos* var. *inermis* (Thornless Honey Locust)	Jan–Feb	P.G.	Whip	Often open-ground budded. Thornless rootstock selections make handling easier.
Halesia spp. & cvs. (Silver-bell) [e.g., *H. monticola* 'Rosea', Mountain Silver-bell cv.; *H. diptera* var. *magniflora* Two-winged Silver-bell var.]	*H. carolina* (Carolina Silver bell) or *H. monticola* (Mountain Silver-bell)	Jan–Feb	P.G.	Whip	
Hamamelis × *intermedia* cvs. (Hybrid Witch Hazel) [e.g., 'Ruby Glow']	*H. virginiana* (Common Witch Hazel) *H. japonica* (Japanese Witch Hazel) *H. vernalis* (Spring or Ozark Witch Hazel)	Aug or Jan–Feb	P.G.	Side or Whip	The less hardy evergreen *Distylium racemosum* (Isu Tree) has been used but slower scion growth results. Many cvs. successfully open-ground budded in Aug. *H. vernalis* rootstock makes it easy to distinguish suckers from scion growth.
H. japonica cvs. (Japanese Witch Hazel) [e.g., 'Sulphurea']	*H. virginiana* (Common Witch Hazel) *H. japonica* (Japanese Witch Hazel) *H. vernalis* (Spring or Ozark Witch Hazel)	Aug or Jan–Feb	P.G.	Side or Whip	

SCION	ROOTSTOCK	TIME OF YEAR	BARE-ROOT (B.R.) OR POT-GROWN (P.G.)	TYPE OF GRAFT	COMMENTS
H. mollis cvs. (Chinese Witch Hazel) [e.g., 'Pallida']	*H. virginiana* (Common Witch Hazel) *H. japonica* (Japanese Witch Hazel) *H. vernalis* (Spring or Ozark Witch Hazel)	Aug or Jan–Feb	P.G.	Side or Whip	
Hibiscus syriacus cvs. (Rose-of-Sharon) [e.g., 'Woodbridge']	*H. syriacus* (Rose-of-Sharon)	Jan–Feb	B.R.	Wedge, Inlay or Whip	Successfully root from hardwood cuttings but subsequent growth is considerably slower.
Juglans regia cvs. (English or Persian Walnut) [e.g., 'Franquette']	*J. regia* (English or Persian Walnut)	Jan–Feb	P.G.	Whip	
Kalmia latifolia cvs. (Mountain Laurel) [e.g., 'Ostbo Red']	*K. latifolia* (Mountain Laurel)	Jan–Feb	P.G.	Side	Micropropagation and conventional cuttings have largely replaced grafting.
Ligustrum lucidum cvs. (Glossy Privet) [e.g., 'Tricolor']	*L. ovalifolium* (California Privet)	Jan–Feb	P.G. B.R.	Whip, Side	The more hardy *L. vulgare* (Common Privet) also used for *Ligustrum* (Privet) in general.
Liquidambar styraciflua cvs. (American Sweet Gum) [e.g., 'Golden Treasure']	*L. styraciflua* (American Sweet Gum)	Jan–Feb	P.G.	Whip	Many cvs. successfully root from softwood cuttings.
Liriodendron chinense (Chinese Tulip Tree)	*L. tulipifera* (Tulip Tree)	Jan–Feb	P.G.	Whip	
L. tulipifera cvs. (Tulip Tree) [e.g., 'Aureomarginata']	*L. tulipifera* (Tulip Tree)	Jan–Feb	P.G.	Whip	
Magnolia campbellii cvs. (Campbell Magnolia) [e.g., 'Darjeeling'] *M. dawsoniana* cvs. (Dawson Magnolia) [e.g., 'Chyverton'] *M. sargentiana* var. *robusta* (Robust Magnolia) *M. sprengeri* cvs. (Sprenger Magnolia) [e.g., Diva', Goddess Magnolia]	*M. campbellii* (Campbell Magnolia) *M. sprengeri* (Sprenger Magnolia) *M. dawsoniana* (Dawson Magnolia)	Jan–Feb	P.G.	Whip, Side or Chip Bud	Although scions compatible with *M. kobus* (Kobus Magnolia) and *M. × soulangeana* (Saucer Magnolia), the more vigorous scion growth encourages an overgrowth of the scion giving an unsightly union.
M. grandiflora cvs. (Southern Magnolia) [e.g., 'Little Gem']	*M. grandiflora* (Southern Magnolia)	Jan–Feb	P.G.	Side, Chip Bud or T-Bud	Successfully T-budded during the summer.
Other *Magnolia* spp. & cvs. [e.g., *M. cylindrica; M. denudata,* Yulan; *M. salicifolia*]	*M. kobus* (Kobus Magnolia) *M. × soulangeana* (Saucer Magnolia)	Jan–Feb	P.G.	Whip, Side or Chip Bud	Best grafted on type species or closely related species. However, most *M. stellata* (Star Magnolia) and *M. × soulangeana* (Saucer Magnolia) forms are propagated by softwood cuttings.

SCION	ROOTSTOCK	TIME OF YEAR	BARE-ROOT (B.R.) OR POT-GROWN (P.G.)	TYPE OF GRAFT	COMMENTS
Mahonia trifoliolata var. *glauca*	*Berberis thunbergii* (Japanese Barberry)	Jan–Feb	P.G.	Whip	
Michelia doltsopa	*Magnolia grandiflora* (Southern Magnolia)	Jan–Feb	P.G.	Side, Chip Bud or T-Bud	Can be propagated by semi-ripewood cuttings.
Photinia × fraseri 'Indian Princess' (Fraser's Photinia cv.)	*Chaenomeles japonica* (Japanese Flowering Quince)	Jan–Feb	P.G.	Whip	Place graft union deep in container when liners are potted-up to encourage scion rooting.
Populus tremula 'Erecta' (Upright Trembling Aspen)	*P.* Brooks No. 6	Jan–Feb	Unrooted hardwood cuttings	Whip	
Prunus mume cvs. (Japanese Flowering Apricot) [e.g., 'Beni-shi-don']	*P. cerasifera* (Myrobalan Plum) St. Julien A *P. persica* (Peach)	Jan	P.G.	Whip	
Pyrus salicifolia 'Pendula' (Weeping Willow-leaved Pear)	*P. communis* (Common Pear)	Jan–Feb	P.G. B.R.	Whip	Pears usually summer budded in the open ground or onto container-grown rootstocks. Interstock of *P. communis* 'Beaurré Hardy' used to overcome incompatibility problems with Quince rootstock.
Quercus spp. & cvs.					It is important to select the rootstocks from within the appropriate group for long-lasting unions.
e.g., *Q. coccinea* 'Splendens' (Scarlet Oak cv.)	*Q. palustris* (Pin Oak) *Q. rubra* (Red Oak)	Sept–Oct or Jan–Feb	P.G.	Side or Whip	
Q. frainetto (Hungarian Oak)	*Q. robur* (English Oak)	Sept–Oct or Jan–Feb	P.G.	Side or Whip	
Q. × hispanica	*Q. ilex* (Holly Oak)	Sept–Oct	P.G.	Side	
Q. macranthera	*Q. robur* (English Oak)	Sept–Oct or Jan–Feb	P.G.	Side or Whip	
Q. petraea 'Purpurea' (Durmast or Sessile Oak cv.)	*Q. robur* (English Oak)	Sept–Oct or Jan–Feb	P.G.	Side or Whip	
Q. robur 'Fastigiata' (Pyramidal English Oak)	*Q. robur* (English Oak)	Sept–Oct or Jan–Feb	P.G.	Side or Whip	
Q. rubra 'Aurea' (Red Oak cv.)	*Q. rubra* (Red Oak)	Sept–Oct or Jan–Feb	P.G.	Side or Whip	Experience in Holland has shown that *Q. rubra* cvs. give unpredictable results.

SCION	ROOTSTOCK	TIME OF YEAR	BARE-ROOT (B.R.) OR POT-GROWN (P.G.)	TYPE OF GRAFT	COMMENTS
Rhododendron spp. & cvs.	*R. ponticum* (Pontic Rhododendron) *R.* 'Cunningham's White'	Jan–Mar	P.G. or burlapped	Side	Important to select rootstocks within same series as scion. Cutting grafts of more difficult-to-root rhododendrons, using easy-to-root rootstocks (e.g., *R.* 'Catawbiense Boursault' or 'Cataw'biense Grandiflorum'), have been successfully carried out in Oct. *R.* × *loderi* is a hybrid between *R. fortunei* and *R. griffithianum* and it has been suggested that seedlings or cuttings of one of the parents may act as suitable rootstocks for this form.
R. macabeanum	*R. grande* (Silvery Rhododendron)	Jan–Mar	P.G. or burlapped	Side	Saddle graft sometimes used.
R. sinogrande	*R. grande* (Silvery Rhododendron)	Jan–Mar	P.G. or burlapped	Side	Saddle graft sometimes used.
R. yakusimanum (Yakusima Rhododendron)	*R.* 'County of York' *R. ponticum* (Pontic Rhododendron) *R.* 'Cunningham's White'	Jan–Mar	P.G. or burlapped	Side	*R. yakusimanum* cvs. graft well in Aug–Sept. *R. ponticum* prone to excess suckering.
Rosa 'Mermaid'	*R. canina* (Dog Rose)	Jan–Feb	P.G.	Whip or Rind	
Salix spp. & cvs.					Great majority of *Salix* spp. root successfully from softwood and deciduous hardwood cuttings. See top-working for weeping cvs.
e.g., *S. magnifica*	*S.* × *smithiana* *S. daphnoides* (Violet or Daphne Willow)	Jan–Feb	P.G.	Whip	
Sorbus megalocarpa	*S. meliosmifolia* *S. alnifolia* (Dense-head Mountain Ash)	Jan–Feb	P.G.	Whip	
Syringa vulgaris cvs. (Common or French Lilac) [e.g., 'Katherine Havemeyer']	*S. vulgaris* (Common or French Lilac) *S. tomentella* (Felty Lilac) *S. josikaea* (Hungarian Lilac)	Jan–Feb	P.G. or B.R.	Whip	*S. josikaea* and *S. reflexa* have very distinctive leaves thus making easy-to-recognize suckers in gardens. *S. tomentella* results in

SCION	ROOTSTOCK	TIME OF YEAR	BARE-ROOT (B.R.) OR POT-GROWN (P.G.)	TYPE OF GRAFT	COMMENTS
	S. reflexa				fewer suckers. *Ligustrum ovalifolium* (California Privet) used as a nurse graft. Softwood cutting propagation, open-ground budding and layering also used.
Viburnum carlesii (Korean Spice Viburnum)	*V. lantana* (Wayfaring Tree) *V. opulus* (European Cranberry Bush)	Jan–Feb	P.G.	Whip	Softwood cutting propagation more popular. Suckering a problem with *V. lantana* rootstocks. *V. opulus* produces more easily identifiable suckers.

APPENDIX 19-2

A Selected List of Scion/Rootstock Combinations for Ornamental Conifers Propagated by Bench Grafting

NOTE:—The grafting times in this list have been taken as an optimum range for both North America and Europe. The geographical location of a nursery may mean that grafting is carried out before (or after) the times listed here.

SCION	ROOTSTOCK	TIME OF YEAR	BARE-ROOT (B.R.) OR POT-GROWN (P.G.)	TYPE OF GRAFT	COMMENTS
Abies spp. & cvs. (Fir)	Type species or *A. alba* (Silver Fir) *A. nordmanniana* (Nordmann Fir)	Dec–Feb	P.G.	Side	*Abies cephalonica* (Greek Fir) or *A. pinsapo* (Spanish Fir) have been suggested as suitable rootstocks, growing better in the U.K. on a range of soils.
Calocedrus decurrens cvs. (Incense Cedar) [e.g., 'Aureovariegata']	*C. decurrens* (Incense Cedar)	Aug–Sept	P.G.	Side	
Cedrus atlantica cvs. (Atlas Mountain Cedar) [e.g., 'Glauca', Blue Atlas Cedar]	*C. deodara* (Himalayan Cedar)	late July–Aug or Jan–Feb	P.G.	Side	
C. deodara cvs. (Himalayan Cedar) [e.g., 'Aurea', Golden Himalayan Cedar]	*C. deodara* (Himalayan Cedar)	late July–Aug or Jan–Feb	P.G.	Side	
C. libani cvs. (Cedar-of-Lebanon) [e.g., 'Sargentii', Sargent's Cedar-of-Lebanon]	*C. deodara* (Himalayan Cedar)	late July–Aug or Jan–Feb	P.G.	Side	

SCION	ROOTSTOCK	TIME OF YEAR	BARE-ROOT (B.R.) OR POT-GROWN (P.G.)	TYPE OF GRAFT	COMMENTS
Chamaecyparis lawsoniana cvs. (Lawson Cypress) [e.g., 'Triomf van Boskoop']	*C. lawsoniana* (Lawson Cypress)	Aug–Sept	P.G.	Side	Very few cvs. now grafted. Most readily propagate success-fully from cuttings.
C. obtusa cvs. (Hinoki, Hinoki Cypress) [e.g., 'Nana Gracilis', Dwarf Hinoki Cypress]	*C. lawsoniana* (Lawson Cypress) *C. pisifera* 'Plumosa' (Plume Cypress) *Thuja occidentalis* (Eastern Arborvitae)	Jan–Feb	P.G.	Side	*C. pisifera* 'Plumosa' is more resistant to Phytophthora. Grafting of dwarf *Chamaecyparis* can lead to undesirable vigor compared to cutting propagation. *C. pisifera* controls growth better than *C. lawsoniana*.
C. nootkatensis cvs. (Yellow or Alaska Cedar) [e.g., 'Pendula', Weeping Yellow Cedar]	*Platycladus (Thuja) orientalis* (Oriental Arborvitae)	Aug or Jan–Feb	P.G.	Side	Does not grow well on *C. lawsoniana* rootstocks.
Cryptomeria japonica cvs. (Japanese Cedar) [e.g., 'Lobbii', Lobb Cryptomeria]	*C. japonica* seedlings or rooted cuttings (Japanese Cedar)	Jan–Feb	P.G.	Side	
Cupressus glabra 'Pyramidalis' (Smooth-barked Arizona Cypress cv.)	*C. macrocarpa* (Monterey Cypress)	Jan–Feb or Aug–Sept	P.G.	Side	*C. sempervirens* (Italian Cypress) is a recommended root-stock in Holland.
C. macrocarpa cvs. (Monterey Cypress) [e.g., 'Lutea', Golden Monterey Cypress]	*C. macrocarpa* (Monterey Cypress)	Jan–Feb or Aug–Sept	P.G.	Side	
C. sempervirens 'Stricta' (Columnar Italian Cypress)	*C. macrocarpa* (Monterey Cypress) *C. sempervirens* (Italian Cypress)	Jan–Feb or Aug–Sept	P.G.	Side	
Gingko biloba cvs. (Maidenhair Tree) [e.g., 'Fastigiata']	*G. biloba* (Maidenhair Tree)	Jan–Feb	P.G.	Whip	
Juniperus scopulorum cvs. (Rocky Mountain Juniper) [e.g., 'Wichita Blue']	*J. virginiana* (Eastern Red Cedar) *J. chinensis* 'Hetzii' rooted cuttings (Hetz Blue Juniper)	Jan–Feb	P.G.	Side	Most cvs. propa-gated by cuttings.
Larix decidua cvs. (European Larch) [e.g., 'Fastigiata']	*L. decidua* (European Larch) *L. kaempferi* (Japanese Larch)	Jan–Feb	P.G.	Side	
Picea abies cvs. (Norway Spruce) [e.g., 'Inversa']	*P. abies* (Norway Spruce)	late July–Aug or Dec–Feb	P.G.	Side	Many of the dwarf *P. abies* cvs. root successfully from cuttings.
P. breweriana (Brewer's Weeping Spruce)	*P. abies* (Norway Spruce)	late July–Aug or Dec–Feb	P.G.	Side	*NOTE:*—Generally, preference for summer grafting *Picea* in Holland, for winter grafting in N. America.
P. omorika cvs. (Serbian Spruce) [e.g., 'Pendula']	*P. abies* (Norway Spruce)	late July–Aug or Dec–Feb	P.G.	Side	
P. orientalis cvs. (Oriental Spruce) [e.g., 'Aurea']	*P. abies* (Norway Spruce)	late July–Aug or Dec–Feb	P.G.	Side	

SCION	ROOTSTOCK	TIME OF YEAR	BARE-ROOT (B.R.) OR POT-GROWN (P.G.)	TYPE OF GRAFT	COMMENTS
P. pungens cvs. (Colorado Blue Spruce) [e.g., 'Hoopsii, Hoops Blue Spruce]	*P. abies* (Norway Spruce)	late July– Aug or Dec–Feb	P.G.	Side	
Pinus spp.					Normally graft 2-needled pines on 2-needle rootstock and similarly "3 on 3" and "5 on 5".
e.g., *P. densiflora* cvs. (Japanese Red Pine) [e.g., 'Umbraculifera', Japanese Umbrella Pine, Tanyosho]	*P. sylvestris* (Scots Pine)	Nov–Jan	P.G.	Side	Some propagators have found *P. contorta* (Shore or Lodgepole Pine) to be compatible with 2-, 3- and 5-needled pines.
P. mugo cvs. (Mugo Pine) [e.g., 'Mops']	*P. sylvestris* (Scots Pine)	Nov–Jan	P.G.	Side	*P. mugo* rootstocks will keep plants of *P. mugo* cvs. more compact subsequently.
P. parviflora cvs. (Japanese White Pine) [e.g., 'Tempelhof']	*P. strobus* (Eastern White Pine)	Nov–Jan	P.G.	Side	
P. pumila cvs. (Dwarf Stone or Siberian Pine) [e.g., 'Compacta']	*P. strobus* (Eastern White Pine)	Nov–Jan	P.G.	Side	
P. strobus cvs. (Eastern White Pine) [e.g., 'Nana']	*P. strobus* (Eastern White Pine)	Nov–Jan	P.G.	Side	
P. sylvestris cvs. (Scots Pine) [e.g., 'Aurea']	*P. sylvestris* (Scots Pine)	Nov–Jan	P.G.	Side	
Platycladus (Thuja) orientalis cvs. (Oriental Arborvitae) [e.g., 'Conspicuus']	*P. orientalis* (Oriental Arborvitae)	Aug–Sept	P.G.	Side	Many *P. orientalis* cvs. root successfully from cuttings.
Pseudotsuga menziesii 'Fletcheri' (Douglas Fir cv.)	*P. menziesii* (Douglas Fir)	Dec–Feb	P.G.	Side	Foresters formulating seed orchards have experienced incompatibility when seedling rootstocks have been used for some clones.
Sequoia sempervirens cvs. (Coast Redwood) [e.g., 'Adpressa']	*S. sempervirens* (Coast Redwood)	Aug–Sept or Jan–Mar	P.G.	Side or Whip	A number of Californian clones root effectively from cuttings, e.g., 'Aptos Blue'. *Sequoiadendron giganteum* (Giant Sequoia) stated to be an appropriate rootstock and is hardier.
Sequoiadendron giganteum (Giant Sequoia) [e.g., 'Pendulum', Weeping Giant Sequoia]	*S. giganteum* (Giant Sequoia)	Aug–Sept or Jan–Feb	P.G.	Side or Whip	*Sequoia sempervirens* can be used but only in warmer climates due to hardiness.

SCION	ROOTSTOCK	TIME OF YEAR	BARE-ROOT (B.R.) OR POT-GROWN (P.G.)	TYPE OF GRAFT	COMMENTS
Taxodium distichum var. *nutans* (Pond Cypress) (a.k.a. *T. ascendens* 'Nutans')	*T. distichum* (Common Bald Cypress)	Jan–Feb	P.G.	Whip	
Taxus baccata cvs. (English Yew) [e.g., 'Adpressa Aurea']	*T. baccata* (English Yew)	Jan–Feb	P.G.	Side or Whip	Many *T. baccata* cvs. root successfully from cuttings.
Tsuga canadensis cvs. (Canadian Hemlock) [e.g., 'Pendula', Canadian or Sargent Weeping Hemlock]	*T. canadensis* (Canadian Hemlock)	Jan–Feb	P.G.	Side	Propagators have successfully used *T. canadensis* rootstocks for *T. heterophylla* clones and vice versa.
T. heterophylla cvs. (Western Hemlock) [e.g., 'Greenmantle;']	*T. heterophylla* (Western Hemlock)	Jan–Feb	P.G.	Side	

APPENDIX 19-3

A Selected List of Scion/Rootstock Combinations for Ornamental Deciduous and Evergreen Broad-leaved Trees, Conifers and Shrubs Successfully Propagated by Top-working

NOTE:—The grafting times in this list have been taken as an optimum range for both North America and Europe. The geographical location of a nursery may mean that grafting is carried out before (or after) the times listed here.

SCION	ROOTSTOCK	TIME OF YEAR	BARE-ROOT (B.R.) OR POT-GROWN (P.G.)	TYPE OF GRAFT	COMMENTS
Acer palmatum 'Burgundy Lace' *A. palmatum* 'Dissectum' cvs. (Japanese Maple cvs.)	*A. palmatum* (Japanese Maple)	July–Aug or Jan–Feb	P.G.	Side	Usually top-worked at a height of 20–60 cm (8–24"). Some *A. palmatum* cvs. used to frame-work established plants using stick-budding. Use of a high humidity tent in California in February results in a very quick union.
A. platanoides 'Globosum' (Globe Norway Maple)	*A. platanoides* (Norway Maple)	Jan–Feb	P.G. or root-balled	Side	Can be budded onto stems of *A. platanoides* 'Emerald Queen'. Use of an interstock can result in more upright growth of 'Globosum'.

SCION	ROOTSTOCK	TIME OF YEAR	BARE-ROOT (B.R.) OR POT-GROWN (P.G.)	TYPE OF GRAFT	COMMENTS
A. pseudoplatanus 'Brilliantissimum' *A. pseudoplatanus* 'Prinz Handjery' (Sycamore Maple cvs.)	*A. pseudoplatanus* (Sycamore Maple)	Jan–Feb	P.G. or root-balled	Side or Whip	Interstock of *A. pseudoplatanus* cvs. sometimes used.
Aesculus × *carnea* 'Briotii' (Ruby Horse-chestnut)	*A. hippocastanum* (Common Horse-chestnut)	Jan–Feb	P.G. or root-balled	Side or Whip	More commonly open-ground low-worked by budding.
A. pavia 'Koehnei' (Red Buckeye cv.)	*A. hippocastanum* (Common Horse-chestnut) *A. pavia* (Red Buckeye)	Jan–Feb	P.G. or root-balled	Side or Whip	*A. hippocastanum* is likely to result in stem overgrowth at union. Preferable to use type species, e.g., *A. pavia.*
Betula nana (Dwarf Birch)	*B. pendula* (European White or Common Silver Birch)	Jan–Feb	P.G.	Side	Also open-ground budded in Aug. Many propagators prefer to low-work the grafts to prevent a swollen union at eye level.
B. pendula 'Youngii' (Young's Weeping Birch)	*B. pendula* (European White or Common Silver Birch)	Jan–Feb	P.G.	Side	
B. pendula 'Trost's Dwarf'	*B. pendula* (European White or Common Silver Birch)	Jan–Feb	P.G.	Side	'Trost's Dwarf' makes an effective patio tree.
Caragana arborescens 'Pendula' (Weeping Siberian Pea Shrub)	*C. arborescens* (Siberian Pea Shrub)	Jan–Feb	P.G.	Whip	
C. arborescens 'Walker' (Walker Siberian Pea Shrub)	*C. arborescens* (Siberian Pea Shrub)	Jan–Feb	P.G.	Whip	
C. frutex 'Globosa' (Russian Pea Shrub cv.)	*C. arborescens* (Siberian Pea Shrub)	Jan–Feb	P.G.	Whip	
Catalpa bignonioides 'Aurea' (Golden Indian Bean)	*C. bignonioides* (Indian Bean) *C. speciosa* (Western Catalpa)	Jan–Feb	Balled & burlapped	Whip	Both cvs. usually low-worked to prevent swollen graft at eye level.
C. bignonioides 'Nana' (Umbrella Catalpa)	*C. bignonioides* (Indian Bean) *C. speciosa* (Western Catalpa)	Jan–Feb	Balled & burlapped	Whip	
Cedrus atlantica 'Glauca Pendula' (Weeping Blue Atlas Cedar)	*C. deodara* (Himalayan Cedar)	late July–Aug or Jan–Feb	P.G.	Side	Some propagators prefer to low-work to avoid swollen union at eye level.
Chamaecyparis obtusa 'Nana Gracilis' (Dwarf Hinoki Cypress)	*C. lawsoniana* (Lawson Cypress) *C. pisifera* (Sawara Cypress)	Jan–Feb	P.G.	Side	Multiple scions—frame-working. *C. lawsoniana* should not be used in areas subject to Root Rot (*Phytophthora cinnamomi*).
Corylus avellana 'Contorta' (Harry Lauder's Walking Stick)	*C. colurna* (Turkish Filbert)	Jan–Mar	B.R.	Whip	
C. avellana 'Pendula' (Weeping European Filbert or Hazelnut)	*C. colurna* (Turkish Filbert)	Jan–Mar	B.R.	Whip	
C. maxima 'Purpurea' (Purple Giant Filbert)	*C. colurna* (Turkish Filbert)	Jan–Mar	B.R.	Whip	

SCION	ROOTSTOCK	TIME OF YEAR	BARE-ROOT (B.R.) OR POT-GROWN (P.G.)	TYPE OF GRAFT	COMMENTS
Cotoneaster adpressus var. *praecox* (Early Cotoneaster)	*C. bullatus* (Hollyberry Cotoneaster) *C. frigidus* (Himalayan Cotoneaster) *C.* × *watereri* cvs. (Waterer Cotoneaster)	Jan–Feb	P.G.	Whip	*C. frigidus* often preferred as it has stronger stem. Also open-grounded grafted and budded.
C. horizontalis (Rock Cotoneaster, Rockspray)	*C. bullatus* (Hollyberry Cotoneaster) *C. frigidus* (Himalayan Cotoneaster) *C.* × *watereri* cvs. (Waterer Cotoneaster)	Jan–Feb	P.G.	Whip	Monrovia Nursery (California) speciality is to graft at 75 cm (30″) for sale as "Patio-trees". Cvs. used include *C. congestus*, *C.* 'Coral Beauty', *C. salicifolia* 'Repens' and 'Emerald Carpet', and *C. apiculatus*.
C. 'Hybridus Pendulus' (a.k.a. *C.* × *watereri* 'Pendulus')	*C. bullatus* (Hollyberry Cotoneaster) *C. frigidus* (Himalayan Cotoneaster) *C.* × *watereri* cvs. (Waterer Cotoneaster)	Jan–Feb	P.G.	Whip	
Crataegus laevigata 'Gireoudii' (English Hawthorn cv.)	*C. laevigata* 'Coccinea Flore Pleno' (Paul's Scarlet Hawthorn)	Jan–Mar	B.R.	Whip	Double-working— the already-budded rootstock should provide a good straight stem.
C. monogyna 'Flexuosa' (Common Hawthorn cv.)	*C. laevigata* 'Coccinea Flore Pleno' (Paul's Scarlet Hawthorn)	Jan–Mar	B.R.	Whip	
Cytisus battandieri (Atlas or Moroccan Broom)	*Laburnum anagyroides* (Common Laburnum)	Jan–Feb	P.G.	Inlay or Whip	
C. scoparius cvs. (Scotch Broom)	*Laburnum anagyroides* (Common Laburnum)	Jan–Feb	P.G.	Inlay or Whip	
Elaeagnus pungens 'Maculata' (Golden Elaeagnus)	*E. umbellata*	Jan–Mar	P.G.	Side	Sometimes potted-up following bare-root grafting.
Euonymus fortunei 'Emerald n' Gold' (Winter Creeper Euonymus cv.)	*E. europaeus* (European Spindle Tree)	Jan–Feb	P.G.	Side	Other evergreen *Euonymus* sometimes top-worked are the *E. fortunei* cvs. 'Emerald Gaiety' and 'Sheridan Gold'.
Fagus sylvatica 'Purpurea Pendula' (Weeping Copper Beech)	*F. sylvatica* (European Beech)	Jan–Feb	P.G.	Side	Often low-worked to avoid swollen union at eye level.
Fraxinus excelsior 'Pendula' (Weeping European Ash)	*F. excelsior* (European Ash)	Jan–Feb	P.G.	Whip	Effectively open-ground budded or grafted.
Hedera helix 'Pixie' *H. helix* 'Silverdust' (English Ivy cvs.)	× *Fatshedera lizei* (Botanical-wonder)	Aug Oct–Nov	P.G.	Side	Two scions used to fill out head of plant. Specialist Californian product for patios.

SCION	ROOTSTOCK	TIME OF YEAR	BARE-ROOT (B.R.) OR POT-GROWN (P.G.)	TYPE OF GRAFT	COMMENTS
Hibiscus syriacus 'Hamabo' (Rose-of-Sharon cv.)	*H. syriacus* (Rose-of-Sharon)	Jan–Feb	P.G.	Whip, Wedge	*H. syriacus* cvs. are sometimes top-worked to produce a novelty tree.
Juniperus horizontalis 'Blue Chip' (Creeping Juniper cv.)	*J. virginiana* 'Skyrocket' (Skyrocket Juniper)	Jan–Feb	P.G.	Side	Top-worked at 75 cm (30") by Monrovia Nurseries (California) for sale as "Patio-trees".
J. horizontalis 'Emerald Spreader'	*J. virginiana* 'Skyrocket' (Skyrocket Juniper)	Jan–Feb	P.G.	Side	
J. horizontalis 'Wiltonii' (Wilton Carpet or Blue Rug Juniper)	*J. virginiana* 'Skyrocket' (Skyrocket Juniper)	Jan–Feb	P.G.	Side	
J. procumbens 'Nana' (Dwarf Japgarden Juniper)	*J. virginiana* 'Skyrocket' (Skyrocket Juniper)	Jan–Feb	P.G.	Side	
J. sabina 'Buffalo' *J. sabina* 'Calgary Carpet' (Savin Juniper cvs.)	*J. virginiana* 'Skyrocket' (Skyrocket Juniper)	Jan–Feb	P.G.	Side	
J. scopulorum 'Tolleson's Blue Weeping' (Rocky Mountain Juniper cv.)	*J. virginiana* 'Skyrocket' (Skyrocket Juniper)	Jan–Feb	P.G.	Side	
J. squamata 'Blue Star' (Single-seed or Scaly-leaved Nepal Juniper cv.)	*J. virginiana* 'Skyrocket' (Skyrocket Juniper)	Jan–Feb	P.G.	Side	*Thuja occidentalis* 'Pyramidalis' (Pyramidal Arbor-vitae) successfully used for 'Blue Star'.
Laburnum alpinum 'Pendulum' (Weeping Golden-chain or Scotch Laburnum)	*L.* × *watereri* 'Vossii' (Voss' Long-cluster Golden-chain Tree)	Jan–Mar	B.R.	Whip	Potted after grafting.
Larix decidua 'Pendula' (Weeping European Larch)	*L. decidua* (European Larch) *L. kaempferi* (Japanese Larch)	Jan–Feb	P.G.	Side	
L. kaempferi 'Pendula' (Japanese Larch cv.)	*L. decidua* (European Larch) *L. kaempferi* (Japanese Larch)	Jan–Feb	P.G.	Side	
Malus prunifolia 'Pendula' (Weeping Plum-leaved Apple)	M.M. 106 *M.* 'Bittenfelder'	Jan–Mar	P.G. or B.R.	Whip, Whip & Tongue	More commonly open-ground budded or grafted.
M. 'Royal Beauty'	*M. sylvestris*	Jan–Mar	P.G. or B.R.	Whip, Whip & Tongue	
Morus alba 'Chaparral' *M. alba* 'Pendula' (Weeping Mulberry) *M. alba* 'Venosa' (White Mulberry cvs.)	*M. alba* var. *tatarica* (Russian Mulberry)	Jan–Mar	B.R.	Side	
M. bombycis 'Issai'	*M. alba* var. *tartarica* (Russian Mulberry)	Jan–Mar	B.R.	Side	
M. latifolia 'Spirata'	*M. alba* var. *tartarica* (Russian Mulberry)	Jan–Mar	B.R.	Side	

SCION	ROOTSTOCK	TIME OF YEAR	BARE-ROOT (B.R.) OR POT-GROWN (P.G.)	TYPE OF GRAFT	COMMENTS
Picea abies 'Inversa' (Norway Spruce cv.)	*P. abies* (Norway Spruce)	late July–Aug or Dec–Feb	P.G.	Side	Produced as miniature standards—45–60 cm (18–24").
P. pungens 'Globosa' (Globe Colorado Blue Spruce)	*P. abies* (Norway Spruce)	late July–Aug or Dec–Feb	P.G.	Side	
Pinus mugo 'Prostrata Wells' (Wells' Prostrate Mugo Pine)	*P. sylvestris* (Scots Pine)	Nov–Jan	P.G.	Side	
P. strobus 'Nana' (Dwarf White Pine)	*P. strobus* (Eastern White Pine)	Nov–Jan	P.G.	Side	
P. sylvestris 'Glauca Nana' (Dwarf Blue Scots Pine)	*P. sylvestris* (Scots Pine)	Nov–Jan	P.G.	Side	Normally produced as miniature standards—45–60 cm (19–24").
Piptanthus nepalensis (Evergreen Laburnum) (a.k.a. *P. laburnifolius*)	*Laburnum anagyroides* (Common Laburnum)	Jan–Mar	B.R.	Whip	Also open-ground budded or grafted.
Prunus × *cistena* (Purple-leaf Sand Cherry)	*P. cerasifera* (Myrobalan Plum) Myrobalan B. *P. mahaleb* (Mahaleb Cherry)	Jan–Feb	P.G. B.R.	Whip	Also open-ground budded or grafted. Unsightly union at eye level due to stem overgrowth may develop when top-working many *Prunus,* particularly with *P. avium* and *P. avium* Mazzard F12/1 rootstocks.
P. fruticosa 'Globosa' (European Dwarf or Ground Cherry cv.)	*P. avium* (Mazzard, Gean Cherry)	Jan–Mar	B.R.	Whip	
P. 'Okame'	*P.* Mazzard F12/1	Jan–Feb	P.G. B.R.	Whip	Occasionally top-worked.
P. serrulata 'Shirofugen'	*P. avium* (Mazzard, Gean Cherry) *P.* Mazzard F12/1	Jan–Mar	B.R.	Whip	*P. serrula* (Birch-bark Cherry) used sometimes as an inter-stem budded onto *P. avium.*
P. subhirtella 'Pendula Plena Rosea' (Double Weeping Rosebud Cherry)	*P. avium* (Mazzard, Gean Cherry)	Jan–Mar	B.R.	Whip	Occasionally top-worked.
P. triloba 'Multiplex' (Flowering Almond cv.)	Myrobalan B. *P. cerasifera* (Myrobalan Plum) St. Julien A Brompton	Jan–Feb	B.R.	Whip	Inter-stock of Brompton has been used in Holland when incompatibility problems arise with other rootstocks.
Rhododendron 'Elisabeth Hobbie'	*R.* 'Anna Rose Whitney'	Jan–Mar	P.G. or root-balled	Side	
Robinia hispida var. *macrophylla* (Smooth Rose Acacia)	*R. pseudocacia* (Black Locust)	Jan–Feb	P.G.	Whip, Whip & Tongue	Also open-ground budded and grafted.
R. pseudocacia 'Umbraculifera' (Mop-head Acacia)	*R. pseudocacia* (Black Locust)	Jan–Feb	P.G.	Whip, Whip & Tongue	

SCION	ROOTSTOCK	TIME OF YEAR	BARE-ROOT (B.R.) OR POT-GROWN (P.G.)	TYPE OF GRAFT	COMMENTS
Rosa 'Dorothy Perkins'	*R. canina* 'Pfander' (Dog Rose cv.)	Jan–Feb	P.G. or B.R.	Whip, Rind	Normally open-ground budded.
R. 'Little Buckaroo'	*R. multiflora* (Baby or Japanese Rose) *R. canina* 'Inermis' (Dog rose cv.)	Jan–Feb	P.G. or B.R.	Whip, Rind	
R. moyesii (Moyes' Rose)	*R. canina* 'Pfander' (Dog Rose cv.)	Jan–Feb	P.G. or B.R.	Whip, Rind	Occasionally produced as a novelty tree (standard) rose.
Salix caprea 'Pendula' (Kilmarnock Willow)	*S.* × *smithiana*	Jan–Mar	B.R.	Whip	Can also be grafted onto unrooted cuttings of *S.* × *smithiana* rootstock. Sometimes grafted and sold as *S. caprea* 'Kilmarnock' (male form) or *S. caprea* 'Weeping Sally' (female form).
S. hastata 'Wehrhahnii' (Halberd-leaved Willow cv.)	*S.* × *smithiana*	Jan–Mar	B.R.	Whip	Some nurseries open-ground bud and then spring graft if bud fails.
S. helvetica	*S.* × *smithiana*	Jan–Mar	B.R.	Whip	
S. purpurea 'Pendula' (Weeping Purple Willow)	*S.* × *smithiana*	Jan–Mar	B.R.	Whip	
Sophora japonica 'Pendula' (Weeping Japanese Pagoda Tree)	*S. japonica* (Japanese Pagoda Tree)	Jan–Feb	P.G.	Side	
Ulmus × *elegantissima* 'Jacqueline Hillier'	*U. glabra* (Scotch or Wych Elm)	Jan–Feb	P.G.	Whip, Whip & Tongue	
U. glabra 'Camperdownii' (Camperdown Elm)	*U. glabra* (Scotch or Wych Elm)	Jan–Feb	P.G.	Whip, Whip & Tongue	Effectively open-ground budded or grafted
U. glabra 'Crispa' (Fern-leaf Elm)	*U. glabra* (Scotch or Wych Elm)	Jan–Feb	P.G.	Whip, Whip & Tongue	
U. glabra 'Nana' (Scotch Elm cv.)	*U. glabra* (Scotch or Wych Elm)	Jan–Feb	P.G.	Whip, Whip & Tongue	
U. parvifolia 'Geisha' (Chinese Elm cv.)	*U. glabra* (Scotch or Wych Elm)	Jan–Feb	P.G.	Whip, Whip & Tongue	
Wisteria venusta (Silky Wisteria)	*W. sinensis* (Chinese Wisteria)	Jan–Feb	P.G.	Side	In southern California material propagated by soft-wood cuttings has longer growing season compared to grafted plants.

REFERENCES AND SUGGESTED SOURCES FOR FURTHER READING

Adcock, G. 1969. Propagation of Picea breweriana. *Gardeners Chronicle & New Horticulturist,* February 7, 1969, pp. 29–30.

Allen, T. 1971. Propagation of *Clematis. Comb. Proc. Inter. Pl. Prop. Soc.* **21**: 245–246.

Buckley, A. R. 1957. The grafting of *Juniperus virginiana* varieties on unrooted cuttings. *Proc. Pl. Prop. Soc.* **7**: 81–83.

Burton, J. H. 1952. The grafting of some Maples. *Proc. Pl. Prop. Soc.* **2**: 71–73.

Carville, L. L. 1970. Environmental control for grafting. *Comb. Proc. Inter. Pl. Prop. Soc.* **20**: 232–238.

Curtis, W. J. 1962. The grafting of Koster Spruce *Cedrus atlantica* Glauca, Copper Beech, Pink and Variegated Dogwoods. *Comb. Proc. Pl. Prop. Soc.* **12**: 249–253.

Davies, F. T., Jr. & Y.-S. Fann. 1983. New propagation practices show promise for field-grown roses. *Amer. Nurseryman* **157**(3): 73–77 (February 1, 1983).

Dummer, P. C. R. 1968. Birch grafting. *Comb. Proc. Inter. Pl. Prop. Soc.* **18**: 69–72.

———. 1970. Propagation of Daphnes. *Gardeners Chronicle,* June 5, 1970, pp. 21–23.

———. no date. The propagation of Acers. Unpublished mss., Hillier Nurseries (Winchester) Ltd., England.

Foster, S. M. 1980. Grafting Apples. *Comb. Proc. Inter. Pl. Prop. Soc.* **30**: 321–323.

Gaggini, J. B. 1971. A time measurement study: bench grafting of woody plants under glass. *Comb. Proc. Inter. Pl. Prop. Soc.* **21**: 275–292.

Hallett, R. D., R. F. Smith & T.W. Burns. 1981. *Manual for Greenhouse Grafting of Conifers in the Maritimes.* Inform. Rep.,M-X-117, Maritimes Forest Research Centre, Canadian Forestry Service, Fredericton, N.B.

Howard, B. H. 1976. Chip-budding potted stocks under glass. *Comb. Proc. Inter. Pl. Prop. Soc.* **26**: 155–157.

Humphrey, B. 1978. Propagation by grafting under glass at Hilliers Nursery. *Comb. Proc. Inter. Pl. Prop. Soc.* **28**: 482–490.

Itaya, G. 1981. Producing budded *Magnolia grandiflora* cultivars. *Comb. Proc. Inter. Pl. Prop. Soc.* **31**: 616–619.

Jaynes, R. A. & G. A. Messner. 1967. Four years of nut grafting Chestnut. *Comb. Proc. Inter. Pl. Prop. Soc.* **17**: 305–311.

Knuckey, D. 1969. Bud-grafting Magnolias. *Comb. Proc. Inter. Pl. Prop. Soc.* **19**: 221–222.

Lagerstedt, H. B. 1981. A device for hot callusing graft unions of fruit and nut trees. *Comb. Proc. Inter. Pl. Prop. Soc.* **31**: 151–159.

———. 1981. The hot callusing pipe, a grafting aid. *Ann. Rpt. Northern Nut Growers Ass'n* **72**: 27–33.

———. 1984. Hot callusing pipe speeds up grafting. *Amer. Nurseryman* **160**(8): 113–117 (October 15, 1984).

Lane, C. 1976. Production of Norway Maple cultivars by bench grafting. *Comb. Proc. Inter. Pl. Prop. Soc.* **26**: 150–153.

Leiss, J. 1967. Grafting, outdoors, deciduous and broadleaf. *Comb. Proc. Inter. Pl. Prop. Soc.* **17**: 303–305.

Macdonald, A. B. 1979. Discussion Group Report. Propagation of *Picea. Comb. Proc. Inter. Pl. Prop. Soc.* **29**: 260–265.

———. 1982. Propagating success. *GC & HTJ* **191**(20): 25–26 (May 14, 1982).

———. & C. G. Lane. 1978. Bench grafting techniques. *GC & HTJ* **184**(8): 33–34 (August 25, 1978).

———. 1978. Bench grafting of ornamental trees. *GC & HTJ* **184**(10): 27–29 (September 8, 1978).

———. 1978. Bench grafting of ornamental trees. *GC & HTJ* **184**(12): 35, 37, 39 (September 22, 1978).

———. 1980. A graft in time. *GC & HTJ* **188**(21): 31, 33, 34 (November 21, 1980).

———. 1980. Veneer of skill. *GC & HTJ* **188**(23): 24, 25, 27 (December 5, 1980).

McDaniel, J. C. 1958. Procedures to increase take in budding and top-grafting. *Proc. Pl. Prop. Soc.* **8**: 159–162.

Mezitt, R. W. 1973. Grafting to obtain unusual shapes and forms. *Comb. Proc. Inter. Pl. Prop. Soc.* **23**: 335–338.

Ryan, G. F. 1970. Selection and time of collection of material for stocks and scions. *Comb. Proc. Inter. Pl. Prop. Soc.* **20**: 225–231.

Savella, L. 1971. Top grafting of Japanese Maples and Dogwoods. *Comb. Proc. Inter. Pl. Prop. Soc.* **21**: 395–397.

Sheat, W. G. 1948. *Propagation of Trees, Shrubs and Conifers.* Macmillan & Co. Ltd., London, U.K.

Stoner, H. E. 1974. Grafting from scion to plant. *Comb. Proc. Inter. Pl. Prop. Soc.* **24**: 401–405.

Strametz, J. R. 1983. Hot-callus grafting of filbert trees. *Comb. Proc. Inter. Pl. Prop. Soc.* **33**: 52–54.

Thomsen, A. 1978. Propagation of conifers by cutting and grafting. *Comb. Proc. Inter. Pl. Prop. Soc.* **28**: 215–220.

Tubesing, C. E. 1983. Chip budding magnolias: Part I. *Magnolia* **19**(1): 17–19.

_____ . 1983. Chip budding magnolias: Part II. *Magnolia* **19**(2): 6–14.

Vertrees. J. D. 1978. *Japanese Maples.* Timber Press, Portland, Oregon.

Wickens, D. J. 1977. Bench root grafting of Wisteria. *Comb. Proc. Inter. Pl. Prop. Soc.* **27**: 55.

Wolff, R. P. 1973. Successes and failures in grafting Japanese Maples. *Comb. Proc. Inter. Pl. Prop. Soc.* **23**: 339–345.

SECTION G

SECTION G

Chapter 20

MICROPROPAGATION

Micropropagation is a specialized method of propagation in which very small pieces of plant tissue are regenerated in an artificial medium under sterile conditions. It embraces the regeneration from shoot and root tips, callus tissue, leaves, seed embryos, anthers, and even single cells. The shoot tip is the most commonly cultured woody plant part and its culture and regeneration is therefore the main subject of this chapter.

The first experiments on micropropagation of plant material under sterile conditions were carried out at the turn of this century. Many of them were unsuccessful because there were few refinements in laboratory procedures, so contamination of the cultures was inadequately controlled. Considerable advances were made after 1939 when research workers in the United States and France successfully established plant callus tissue. This foundation work by researchers such as P. R. White was the stimulus that encouraged others to exploit the field of micropropagation.

The benefits of plant tissue culture became more generally known in the horticultural world with its use as a technique to assist in making virus-free plants in the various virus-testing programs throughout the world. This was quickly followed by its use in the multiple cloning of orchids. Commercial advances were seen in greenhouse crops such as carnations, chrysanthemums and ferns, followed by some hardy herbaceous perennials. During the last decade, much research emphasis has been placed on the micropropagation of woody plants.

Pioneer workers in micropropagation were F. Skoog and T. Murashige, with the latter continuing the work at the University of California at Riverside. The research enthralled and encouraged other workers, and T. Murashige is now considered a world authority on procedures and on the components of sterile media for a wide range of horticultural crops. His paper *Plant Propagation through Tissue Cultures* is probably one of the most cited references for micropropagation.

The exciting discovery by G. Morel in France during the 1950s that one shoot tip of the orchid *Cymbidium* could proliferate into a multitude of plants was a major break-through that resulted in large quantities of many orchid species becoming commercially available at greatly reduced prices. During the last decade, Twyford Plant Laboratories, Glastonbury, England, has become a leader in Europe in developing micropropagation technology and in using it for a considerable range of greenhouse crops. The export of the resulting small plants to several European countries accounts for around 80% of their total sales.

The leaders in the micropropagation of ornamental woody plants are undoubtedly located in the Pacific Northwest of North America. One person who has been largely responsible for this growth is W. C. Anderson of the Northwestern Washington Research and Extension Center at Mount Vernon, WA. His research work on the micropropagation of fruit trees and ornamentals such as *Rhododendron* laid a foundation upon which others are building.

Two nurserymen in the Pacific Northwest, Bruce Briggs of Briggs Nursery in Olympia, WA, and Les Clay of Les Clay & Son Ltd. in Langley, B.C., have been particularly active and successful in using and adapting this specialized technique for major horticultural crops—particularly *Rhododendron* and *Kalmia* (American or Mountain Laurel).

A company named Microplant Nurseries, Inc., Gervais, Oregon, was founded in 1980 to specialize mainly in the micropropagation of ornamental shade trees and fruit tree rootstocks. The ornamental shade trees successfully cultured include *Betula* (Birch), *Acer platanoides* cvs. (Norway Maple), *A. rubrum* cvs. (Red Maple), ornamental *Malus* (Crab) and *Prunus cerasifera* cvs. (Myrobalan

Plum). This is a very positive move to encourage nurseries to grow ornamental trees on their own roots so eliminating the need for budding and grafting (and consequent failures).

Major advantages gained from using micropropagated *Acer rubrum* cvs. (e.g., *A. rubrum* 'Autumn Flame', 'October Glory' and 'Red Sunset') liners for open-ground planting in Oregon are:—

(a) Micropropagated liners have a more balanced shoot:root ratio compared to liners propagated from softwood cuttings. Micropropagated liners can be planted the same year they are cultured. [Liners from softwood cuttings are over-wintered in cold storage and then planted in the spring of the following year—experience has shown that the less developed root systems of these liners results in over-wintering and establishment losses.]

(b) The stem internodes are considerably closer to each other when compared to pot-grown liners propagated from softwood cuttings. This means that the heavy pruning of the main stems of the liners that is done after the first year's growth following planting can be made closer to the ground (at a more constant height). This results in a straighter tree and a more uniform crop.

We are now seeing micropropagation having a major impact in the development of woody ornamentals, particularly rhododendrons, daphnes, roses, kalmias, some maple species, and apple and cherry rootstocks onto which fruiting and ornamental cultivars are budded. *Betula* (Birch), *Amelanchier alnifolia* cvs. (Common or Western Saskatoon) and *Syringa vulgaris* cvs. (Common or French Lilac) have all been commercially micropropagated. Micropropagation in France and Britain has made a considerable impact in the bulking-up of miniature roses. Bush roses have been commercially produced through micropropagation, providing an alternative technique to the traditional open-ground budding. Micropropagation has resulted in well-graded crops of container-grown roses.

Figure 20-1.
The number of basal lateral breaks is increased in micropropagation of roses. The liner on the left was raised by micropropagation while the liner on the right was raised from a conventional softwood cutting. (Efford Experimental Horticulture Station, Lymington, Hampshire, U.K.)

The micropropagated product may be sold from the nursery as:—

1. Multiple shoots (Stage 2), with the customer preparing their own "micro-cuttings".

2. *In vitro* rooted plantlets.

3. Liners ready for potting or open-ground planting.

4. Developed container and open-ground plants.

There is a considerable amount of published information available on micropropagation in publications of professional organizations such as the *Combined Proceedings* of the International Plant Propagators' Society, and *HortScience,* the journal of the American Society for Horticultural Science. A useful reference book for nursery operators contemplating a micropropagation laboratory is *Plants from Test Tubes. An Introduction to Micropropagation* by Lydiane Kyte (Timber Press, Portland, OR). A number of the relevant publications for woody ornamentals are listed at the end of this chapter.

Rather than merely summarizing published information, this chapter is aimed at describing the procedures used in the "working laboratories" on production nurseries, particularly those in the Pacific Northwest of North America.

ROLE OF MICROPROPAGATION

Advantages of Micropropagation

Micropropagation has many applications for ornamental woody plants. These are summarized below.

(1) As a means to remove viruses from plants. As previously discussed in Chapter 16, the removal of the meristem from a heat-treated plant and its subsequent culture under sterile conditions has formed the basis of all virus-free programs for *Prunus* and *Malus,* such as the E.M.L.A. Scheme in Britain, the I.N.R.A. Scheme in France and the British Columbia Landscape Plant Improvement Association (B.C.L.P.I.A.), Canada.

The elimination of viruses by micropropagation can be used as a means to improve clones of plants in clonal improvement programs for ornamental woody plants.

(2) As a very effective and rapid method to multiply clonal material. The ability to keep the material within its "juvenile-like" phase and the selection of the correct media are the critical elements in realizing this objective. It is particularly useful for increasing material in the following situations:—

(a) For rapid bulking-up of plants.

(b) For a selected seedling or mutation in a plant breeding program to permit an earlier release date, e.g., *Rhododendron.*

(c) For plants that are normally difficult to root, e.g., *Kalmia latifolia* cvs. (Mountain Laurel) and *Lapageria rosea* (Chilean Bellflower).

Figure 20-2. The micropropagation of *Kalmia latifolia* cvs. (Mountain Laurel) has overcome the difficulties of conventional cutting propagation, resulting in the availability of considerable numbers of many of the new cultivars.

(d) For rare plants and species in conservation programs; e.g., the research program at the Royal Botanic Gardens, Kew, England.

The speed with which woody plant material can be increased in a commercial laboratory is indicated in the table.

Potential Average Multiplication Rate for Deciduous Azalea— assuming the cultivar is capable of producing 10 shoots every two months.	
Second month	1 shoot in 1 test-tube → 10 shoots
Fourth month	10 shoot apices in 10 test-tubes → 100 shoots
Sixth month	100 shoot apices in 100 test-tubes → 1000 shoots

Apple rootstocks provide another example of the speed with which plants can be multiplied. Microplant Nurseries, Inc. began with 500 shoot apices of the rootstock E.M.L.A. Malling Merton (M.M.) 111 in April 1984 and had some 50,000 plants rooted in the laboratory and ready for acclimatization in the nearby greenhouse by mid-January 1985. The developed liners were ready for open-ground planting by April 1985—one year after culturing of the original 500 shoot apices. Unlimited labor and materials, if available, could have provided 1 million rooted plants by the summer of 1985.

(3) As a means of propagating all year rather than being confined to the seasonal variations common to conventional techniques. This objective is achieved by the ability to keep propagation material under cold storage for extended periods. Such storage is valuable not only for storing the initial clonal material in a "clone bank" but also to regulate the plants in keeping with supply and demand for the final product.

(4) As a particularly convenient way to export plants to other parts of the world. They may be exported as a mass of proliferated shoots that the buyer can then re-multiply and propagate or as small rooted shoots. Costs are reduced because of the small size and weight of the package in relation to the number of plants. Certain plant quarantine restrictions are also overcome because the material has been grown on a soilless sterile medium.

Figure 20-3. Micropropagated material is a particularly convenient method of exporting plant material, largely because of its small size, light weight, and the sterile growing medium. Note the sack and release tube above the box for dispensing Styrofoam® chips to aid packaging. (Briggs Nursery, Olympia, WA, U.S.A.)

Moisture levels are critical when shipping cultured material, therefore attention to retaining high humidity levels is as important as insulating the packages to reduce temperature variation.

(5) As a means of radically reducing both the number of stock plants and the size of stock plant beds because the mother stock remains *in vitro* at the laboratory.

(6) As a means of significantly reducing the actual size of the propagation area. A most extreme comparison is stooling or mound layering where a considerable amount of outside land is utilized. Micropropagation offers the opportunity to bring "the stool bed into the test-tube"—a technique that is being successfully utilized to supply mother plants for stool beds as part of the overall production programs by Oregon Rootstock Inc., Woodburn, OR. These mother plants are virus-, *Phytophthora*- and nematode-free.

(7) As a means of providing a higher-quality saleable product—for example, liners of *Acer rubrum* (Red Maple), *Amelanchier alnifolia* (Common or Western Saskatoon) and *Rhododendron*. The sterile conditions mean that the material is free from pests and diseases—a problem associated with conventional propagation methods.

One aspect of the higher quality that has impressed me, particularly with *Rhododendron* liners, is the increased number and even development of the axillary shoots breaking at the base of the plant. This ensures an excellent framework for growing-on to larger sizes in containers or the open ground.

(8) As a means of exploiting the technology in other methods of conventional propagation. For example, the cut surfaces of scions of *Acer palmatum* cvs. (Japanese Maple) have been immersed in a micropropagation medium just prior to matching-up during grafting to success-

Figure 20-4. E.M.L.A. Malling Merton apple rootstocks liners initially propagated by micropropagation for subsequent planting in the open ground as mother plants for stool beds. (Gayle Suttle, Microplant Nursery, Inc., Gervais, OR, U.S.A.)

Figure 20-5. Micropropagation can significantly increase the number of basal lateral breaks on many rhododendrons, as can be seen in this photograph of *R.* 'Vulcan'. (Briggs Nursery, Olympia, WA, U.S.A.)

fully promote cell differentiation and improve callusing.

(9) As a specialized method of raising plants from seed. Complete plants can be propagated from the immature cotyledons. Embryo culture can be utilized for rare and/or small quantities of seed to speed up a breeding program, or in cases where breaking seed dormancy presents considerable problems.

Limitations of Micropropagation

Micropropagation has its limitations and should not be regarded as the answer to all propagation problems. Some of the limitations are summarized below.

(1) The initial capital investment in laboratory and equipment can be high. The financial commitment necessary has been quoted in the range of $15,000 to $250,000 (U.S.), depending on the size of the laboratory and the refinement of procedures desired. However, some nursery operators have been successful with a relatively low-cost investment.

(2) Additional salary costs. Micropropagation requires a skilled, usually specially trained laboratory manager and skilled, disciplined support staff.

(3) It is not yet commercially successful with a variety of species, including most conifers, *Acer palmatum* (Japanese Maple), *Cornus florida* (Eastern Flowering Dogwood) and *Stewartia*. It is one thing to culture a plant experimentally and another to develop procedures that will provide sufficient plant material to make it economically viable. The correct nutrient medium and the levels of growth regulators to establish, regenerate and multiply the plant material, and the ability to develop the required growth and rootability have not been discovered for a number of species, so conventional propagation techniques are still better suited for successful commercial production of a number of woody ornamentals.

(4) There are problems with some species associated with the formation of roots and successful establishment of the shoots in conventional production areas after removal from the test-tube or jar. Essentially, one is taking a young growing shoot from a sterile, controlled environment and placing it into another environment over which the grower has far less control.

The major problems have been with obtaining a sufficient root system, controlling disease infection, and obtaining the correct air and water ratios in the rooting and growing-on media. However, many of these problems have been resolved, not so much by research workers, but from the experience and knowledge of the nursery operator able to adapt and combine traditional growing methods with modern laboratory technology.

(5) Possible over-production of plant material. Any operation turning to micropropagation must assess the market situation very thoroughly and carefully. Over-supply in the industry is often endemic using conventional methods. It can be greatly aggravated by the rapid production associated with micropropagation.

Conclusions

Micropropagation should be seen as a technology to be used in conjunction with conventional propagation techniques. There seems little value in using it for the wide range of deciduous shrubs, such as *Spiraea* (Spirea), *Philadelphus* (Mock-orange), *Potentilla* (Cinquefoil) and *Kolkwitzia* (Beautybush), that root so readily from softwood cuttings in low-cost facilities; or for *Berberis* (Barberry), *Cotoneaster* and *Ligustrum* (Privet) species used for hedging plants; or until successful commercial micropropagating procedures are developed for *Fagus sylvatica* cvs. (European Beech) and *Picea pungens* cvs. (Colorado Spruce) currently propagated successfully by bench grafting. Micropropagation should be regarded as a "tool" to refine the production of some high value crops, and to produce healthier plant material. Micropropagation is a "tool" for the propagator to use intelligently.

PERSONNEL

Labor costs are typically in the range of 75–85% of the total micropropagation production costs. Therefore, the personnel must be carefully selected.

The ultimate success of a micropropagation facility depends on the selection and hiring of an effective laboratory manager. The first requirement for a laboratory manager is an analytical mind, with a thorough education in plant science and/or pathology. The second requirement is a reasonable horticultural background. Understanding the fundamental concepts—in this case woody plants and taxonomy—makes it easier to conceive the necessary changes in procedure or medium required when the laboratory is confronted with an additional or new genus or species to culture and then establish in the growing-on houses. The third requirement is an ability to communicate well at all levels in the nursery, whether with management or with employees, and, at the same time, be capable of supervising and training a small team of technicians. The specialized nature of the work must not allow the laboratory manager and his team to become isolated in their own restricted environment. They must be aware of how their work fits into the overall production of the nursery. Finally, the laboratory manager must have the disposition to pay attention to detail in formulating procedures, media preparation, accurate record keeping and, not least, the power of close observation so that necessary adjustments are made as the result of both successes and failures.

Conversely, the reason for installing a micropropagation laboratory and the benefits to the overall well-being of the company should be carefully explained to all levels of the regular production staff. It is easy for the established staff to feel resentful and suspicious if this is not done. They may become critical of the venture—and this may be difficult to overcome. The overall aim must be to ensure that the staff is kept informed at all stages of the development plans.

The alternative to hiring a laboratory manager from outside is to select someone from the existing propagation staff. It is of no use to expect such a person to manage the laboratory effectively in a matter of weeks. The individual selected must be enrolled in micropropagation courses and, ideally, required to work for a period in an established, respected laboratory elsewhere.

A small team of technicians may be required if the laboratory is of sufficient size. A person with little or no previous laboratory experience will often perform well, and could be recruited from the present staff. It is important to explain to candidates at the interview that a lot of the work will be detailed and routine, but must be carried out with considerable dexterity and speed. Previous experience in either plant science or medical laboratories is an excellent prerequisite, but not necessarily essential. It is very important that these new technicians receive a thorough training so that they develop a basic understanding of the plant physiology underlying micropropagation, the importance of sterile procedures, and develop efficient routine work habits.

Work in the laboratory is often carried out in a confined area with a continual background hum from the motors of the laminar flow cabinet(s) used for the initial culturing and when transferring material. The tedium of such conditions can be relieved if the management develops a flexible definition of the technicians' job description(s)—for example, working at the laminar flow cabinet during the morning and making up culture media in the "kitchen" in the afternoon.

LABORATORY FACILITIES

There are essentially three choices when siting the laboratory facility on the nursery:—

(1) Within an existing building.

(2) An extension to an existing building—for example, to the existing office area.

(3) Construction of a completely new facility.

The final decision will depend largely on the capital available and on how the facility fits in with the everyday operations of the nursery. Some nurseries begin by using the first alternative until sufficient capital is accumulated to invest in a completely new facility. However, it is important to allow sufficient space in the second and third alternatives for future expansion, as it is easy to outgrow the original site. The laboratory should be sited within easy access to related areas in the nursery—in particular to the propagation house where the shoots will be removed from the test tube, rooted and plantlets grown.

The laboratory can be sited within a greenhouse complex. This is not ideal as there is a greater risk of transferring fungal infection from the production areas to the laboratory. Difficulties in controlling the air temperature are also likely to occur.

It is not intended to provide building specifications for the facility, but four general points should be noted:—

(1) Every effort must be made to prevent any contamination of plant material within the laboratory. Close attention should be paid to installing doorways, clean-up areas, rooms for staff to change from outdoor to laboratory clothing, and good work flow patterns to prevent the introduction of contaminants into the sterile area.

(2) There should be sufficient lighting and ventilation for both laboratory personnel and plant material.

(3) A claustrophobic atmosphere should be avoided by installing windows with an outside view.

(4) There should be adequate passage-ways between rooms to allow the movement of trolleys and carts, and adequate cupboards and shelves for the storage of glassware, chemicals, etc.

The laboratory will need sufficient electricity (including enough outlets) to run the equipment, and, ideally, a standby generator for the culture room in case of an electrical failure. The temperature-controlled rooms should be supplied with safety cut-out switches to prevent over-heating which can quickly kill cultures. Warning systems should be installed in all essential circuits to attract attention in case of failure. Alarm bells can be connected to such a system to warn of critical failures.

The laboratory usually consists of five main rooms, which should lead naturally one into the other, following the sequence of activities. They are:—

(1) The Media Preparation Room or "Kitchen"—This room contains the autoclave, balances, chemical storage cupboards, hand tools, pH meter and dishwasher, and is where the media are formulated, equipment sterilized and chemicals stored.

(2) The Transfer Room—This room contains the laminar flow cabinet(s) through which there is a continuous stream of sterile air. The culturing and transferring of plant material is carried out in this room.

(3) The Culture or Growing Room—This room provides a well-illuminated and temperature-controlled environment for the maintenance of the developing plant material, both after initial establishment and subsequent transfers.

(4) The Cold Storage Facility—This facility is optional. It is used for holding plant material in tubes or flasks for future use.

(5) The Washroom—This room is essential for staff to clean-up and change into laboratory clothing to help to maintain the sterile environment required in a micropropagation facility.

Typical approximate sizes of the Media Preparation, Transfer and Culture rooms in a laboratory capable of an output up to 5,000 *Rhododendron* shoots per week for rooting are indicated below. Note that this output will vary according to the plant material used, due to inherent differences in maturation times and the number of shoots produced per tube.

Media Preparation Room	— 21 m² (225 sq. ft.)
Transfer Room	— 9 m² (100 sq. ft.)
Culture Room	— 27 m² (288 sq. ft.)
	(this provides approximately 24 shelves for the cultures)

EQUIPMENT FOR A MICROPROPAGATION LABORATORY

It is essential to buy quality equipment from the beginning. The cost will vary according to the size of the laboratory, but a number of simplified items are available that will produce a very satisfactory end result. For example, a kitchen pressure cooker can be used instead of an autoclave to sterilize media and equipment in the smaller laboratory.

It is imperative to adhere to strict standards of tidiness and cleanliness to prevent contamination of the cultures. Facilities are necessary for efficient cleaning of equipment, and all the floors should be tiled so that they can be easily maintained—never use carpets. A good fluorescent light source, an extractor fan for ventilation, and adequate garbage disposal facilities are important.

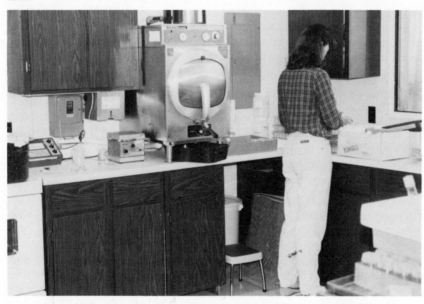

Figure 20-6.
A clean and tidy media preparation room. The equipment shown includes the autoclave (center), pH meter (at left hand side of bench) and storage cupboards. (Briggs Nursery, Olympia, WA, U.S.A.)

The following list of comments will provide a guideline to the essential items required for the Media Preparation, Transfer and Culture rooms.

Media Preparation Room

Equipment

Refrigerator—For storage of media, stock solutions and chemicals that may degrade in sunlight and/or warm temperatures. A freezer section is useful for storing stock solutions of growth regulators for long periods.

Metallic Sink—One or two metallic sinks are needed for washing equipment.

Dishwasher—A restaurant- or industrial-grade dishwasher is particularly useful for cleaning the large quantities of glassware used in the laboratory.

Range—This can be a conventional kitchen range. The materials used to make the gelatin or agar for the media must be heated to incorporate the nutrients and hormones for micropropagation. A range is more convenient and safer than a small hotplate standing on a counter.

Autoclave or Pressure Cooker—Necessary for sterilizing glassware, equipment and media. It should be capable of reaching temperatures up to 120°C (250°F) at a pressure of 345 kPa (15 lb/sq.in.).

pH Meter—Correct pH levels of the media are vital for success, therefore an accurate automatic pH meter is essential.

Balance—An accurate balance capable of measuring to three decimal places is required.

Stirrers—Electrically-powered, motorized or magnetic stirrers are used to mix the agar/nutrient media. Both powered and magnetic units have controls to allow different speeds of mixing.

Automatic Pipet Dispenser—This is particularly useful for dispensing accurate quantities of medium to a large number of test tubes. It saves a considerable amount of time compared to manual techniques. There are many different types of dispensers and ways to dispense—some are mechanical and others are manually operated. For example, a wheel, valve or selector collar on the pipet is set to measure the amount of solution to be released. Some types can automatically reproduce 20–30 samples per minute.

The dispensing of small quantities of media into test tubes is more easily done with a manually-operated buret (burette). Media are normally poured by hand into dishes, jars and boxes.

Storage Cupboard for Chemicals—Either a wooden or metal cupboard is used to store bulk chemicals used in the media. Chemicals must be handled in a systematic way. Each chemical must be clearly labelled and dated immediately on arrival in the laboratory. Buffer solutions should be stored in labelled color-coded bottles. It is useful to divide the cupboard into two compartments, one for the organic chemicals and the other for inorganic chemicals. The chemicals should be stored in alphabetical order within the respective compartments. A separate compartment at floor level will be needed to store chemicals purchased in large quantities, for example, sodium hypochlorite which is used as a disinfectant. Dark bottles will be needed to store chemicals such as indole-3-acetic acid (IAA) and iron solutions that break down in light.

Distilled or Deionized Water—Tap water contains many impurities and so is unsuitable and unreliable for micropropagation purposes. Therefore, a source of purified water is required to wash materials and equipment before sterilizing in the autoclave, and for making solutions. Larger laboratories usually find that it is more economical to rent or buy distillation equipment to provide a regular supply *in situ*. Distilled or deionized water for scientific use can be purchased in large carboys, but it must be obtained from a reliable source.

Pots, Pans and Waterbath—These are used to make the media. They should be made of glass or stainless steel in 6, 9, and 13 litre sizes (approximately 6.5, 9.5 and 14 quarts). Note that the pots and pans should fit into the autoclave.

Glassware and Plastic Containers—Test tubes are required for the media and cultures and may be purchased in one of two types. Borosilicate-glass disposable culture tubes come without caps, which must be purchased separately. It is important that the caps fit tightly to the tubes, e.g., with molded pressure fins, and that they are made of non-toxic, autoclavable, unbreakable polypropylene. Pre-sterilized culture tubes are more expensive, but are supplied with caps.

Mason or Kilner Jars are used for culturing, although a cheaper alternative is to use clear square polypropylene boxes with tight-fitting lids. Glass baby food jars fitted with autoclaved caps are particularly useful. Polypropylene plastic jars are good, and will not crack. Although more costly initially, plastic containers are normally best. Buy only jars made of plastic materials that can be autoclaved (e.g., polypropylene and polycarbonates)—some plastics, especially polyethylene, will warp or melt under high temperatures. There are a number of different types of plastic containers available that are specifically designed for micropropagation.

Other necessary items include the usual components of a working laboratory, such as flasks, beakers, graduated cylinders (100–1000 ml), graduated pipets, glass rods to use as stirrers, petri dishes, etc.

Racks—Two types of racks are required for the test tubes. The first is a rack that will hold up to 80 test tubes vertically while the medium is being sterilized in the autoclave. These racks must have an epoxy coating to prevent deterioration while in the autoclave.

The second type of rack is referred to as a tissue culture rack and normally holds 10 test tubes. These racks are designed to hold the test tubes at a 45° angle so that the nutrient medium will set at the desired slope and are used to hold test tubes containing the growing plantlets in the culture (growing) rooms. Alternatively, some types of manufactured unit containers (Chapter 5) for greenhouse seedling production and rooting cuttings can be used. The test tubes are placed into the cavities of the container.

Dissecting and Transfer Hand Tools—These include scalpels and forceps, which must be made of high-quality stainless steel to avoid risk of corrosion. Scalpels are used to excise shoots and to cut portions of differentiated material after the initial culture has multiplied. Forceps are used to transfer material from one culture to another, and also to remove the shoots from the culture container when they are finally severed for rooting in a mist propagation or fogging facility. Several sizes should be available for each technician, with fine to medium points and differing lengths for efficient use with the different culture containers and material being propagated.

Clothing and Safety Procedures

Laboratory coats are not essential but do give a professional appearance and help to prevent staining or damaging personal clothing. Shoes specifically to wear only in the laboratory are essential, not only to prevent contamination of the cultures but also as a protection against chemical spillage or injury. Never allow anyone to work in sandals or with bare feet. Rubber gloves are necessary when working with the sterilant sodium hypochlorite or other caustic compounds.

Fire extinguishers suitable for chemical and electrical fires must be available either inside or just adjacent to the laboratory. Check with the local fire officials for suitable extinguishers. A set of safety regulations should be formulated, ensuring that they are fully understood by staff, and permanently posted in the laboratory. Review and update these regulations regularly. [A useful guideline to safety procedures in the laboratory is *Laboratory Health and Safety Procedures*, published by the Workers' Compensation Board of British Columbia, Canada.]

Transfer Room

Equipment

Laminar Flow Cabinet with an HEPA (High Efficiency Particulate Air) Filter—This is the main piece of equipment in the transfer room. It is the unit within which the excision and transfer of material is carried out under sterile conditions. Each cabinet is fitted with fluorescent lights and filters that are 99.97% effective against dust particles down to 0.3 microns in size. The optimum size of a cabinet is about 115 cm (45") high and 90 cm (36") wide, with a working surface about 60 cm (24") deep. The noise level should be below 65 decibels. The cabinet should be placed in an area which is free from sudden drafts so that its action is not adversely affected.

The cabinet works on the principle of sterile air flowing across the working surface from the back to the front. The back of the cabinet consists of an HEPA filter made of submicron glass fiber paper. Outside air enters the top of the cabinet through a replaceable filter to remove large particles, passes into a sealed compartment and is then blown through the HEPA filter to remove small particles down to 0.3 microns. This sterile air is released into the working area and causes the air already present to move forward at a uniform rate towards the operator. This rate should be 24–30 m (80–100') per minute to ensure that particles do not settle on the working surface. The flow rate of the sterile air should be checked at least once a year to ensure that the machine is working properly. A thin piece of paper can be held in the cabinet to check that there is an air flow before commencing work—its movement confirms that sterile air is passing over the working area. Alternatively, the air flow can be detected with the flame of a bunsen or alcohol burner—the flame will bend away from the cabinet.

The majority of laboratories buy manufactured units, but simple home-made cabinets have been very successful and will lower the initial capital outlay. Specifications for building your own cabinet can be found in *Getting Started in Tissue Culture—Equipment and Costs* by L. P. Stoltz (*Comb. Proc. Inter. Pl. Prop. Soc.*, Vol. **29**, p. 376).

The equipment needed on the working surface in the cabinet is largely determined by

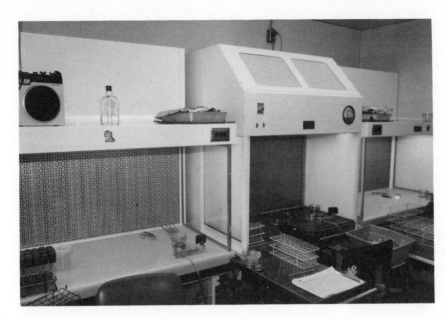

Figure 20-7.
The principle equipment in the transfer room is the laminar flow cabinet. Note the large filter towards the rear of the cabinet to ensure that sterile air flows towards the operator. Other equipment visible includes an alcohol lamp, test tube racks, petri dishes, and a clipboard for daily record keeping.

the method used to sterilize the instruments (forceps, scalpels, etc.). The methods used for sterilization include:—

(i) **Flame and Alcohol Dip**—The flame is provided by an alcohol lamp or bunsen burner (the Touch-O-Matic® bunsen burner is particularly satisfactory for flaming). The instruments are dipped into alcohol (ethanol 95%) and the excess burnt off in the flame before use.

Sterile petri dishes, previously sterilized by autoclaving, are used as the surface on which to cut the plant material. Alternatively, a glass plate sterilized by flaming the alcohol-covered surface may be used.

There has been some concern over safety using flame and alcohol techniques, but commonsense laboratory procedures reduce the danger to a minimum.

(ii) **Sodium Hypochlorite (Bleach)**—This method requires compartmented dishes or pans into which the petri dishes for cutting the material can be placed. The three-compartment dishes have proved to be satisfactory with one compartment containing 0.5% sodium hypochlorite, the second 0.05% sodium hypochlorite, and the third being used for waste plant material (see p. 619 for the work pattern when using bleach).

Sodium hypochlorite has been losing favor in micropropagation facilities, mainly because employees have found the substance irritating to the nose, and there has been some corrosive action on some tools plus damage to plant tissue of some species—even with the very weak concentration of 0.05%.

(iii) **Bacti-Cinerator®**—This is an electrically-powered device that has a heated ceramic core. The tips of the instruments are sterilized by placing them in the core for 5–7 seconds. The core temperature reaches 872°C (1600°F) which is sufficient to kill fungi and bacteria. The instruments are very hot after removal and it is therefore necessary for staff to have several sets of instruments to allow sufficient cooling-down time before use. Ancillary equipment for this method is a holder into which the forceps and scalpels are inserted to cool after removal from the Bacti-Cinerator®. The Bacti-Cinerator® has been gaining popularity and is a quick and efficient sterilization method.

[Ultra-violet light is sometimes used for long-term sterilization, with the instruments being placed under the light for 30 minutes before use. It is not recommended for short-term sterilization as an alternative to flame and alcohol dip, sodium hypochlorite or the Bacti-Cinerator®. Ultra-violet light is harmful to skin and eyes and therefore UV sterilization should be done when the cabinet is not in use.]

Irrespective of the sterilization method used, a hand magnifier and binocular microscope (20–30× power) are needed in the cabinet for use when excising shoots. Alternatively, a magnifying glass fixed to a head band can be used—the magnifier is brought down over one eye when needed. The magnifier, whichever model is chosen, should have a 7.5 cm (3") focal length with a magnification of ×3 to ×5.

Culture or Growing Room

This is normally the largest room of a micropropagation facility. The current recommended optimum temperature is 22–24°C (71–75°F), therefore this room should have its own ventilation and thermostatically-controlled heating systems for effective temperature control. Too high a temperature is said to be a cause of vitrification (water-soaking) of plant tissue. The air intake unit should be filtered to remove dust. Virtual elimination of all dust particles in the air can be achieved by fitting the room with its own HEPA filtration unit (0.5 μm filter) to filter the air—but this will substantially increase the overall capital costs. However, home-made systems can be made to reduce investment costs, but should be tested regularly to ensure that they meet the standard requirements of dust removed from the air.

The light source should be fluorescent tubes, but the ballasts should be removed and located just outside the culture room to reduce the problem of heat build-up. Ensure that the ballasts and lights are carefully labelled during installation so that repairs can be made easily. Note that fluorescent lights with separated ballasts are more expensive. The tubes should be dusted regularly to remove any dust particles accumulating on the upper surface of the tube. Dust decreases both the longevity of the tube and the amount of light that reaches the shelves.

Clean floors are essential—they should be tiled and regularly cleaned with a damp mop. Avoid sweeping with a brush as this stirs up dust.

The test tubes containing plant material are stored on shelves. Each shelf unit can consist of angle-iron supports carrying four shelves about 50 cm (20") apart. Sufficient space is required between the shelves to allow efficient air circulation. Heat build-up underneath the cultures is a problem when a solid surface is used for the shelves. Spacers, 2.5 × 2.5 cm (1 × 1") in size, are placed on each shelf to form a base on to which the trays are placed to provide better air circulation. Alternatively, heavy wire screening can be used for the shelves instead of a solid surface. Fluorescent light tubes are attached to the underside of each shelf to provide sufficient light for the cultures on the shelf below. The amount of light required by the cultures will determine the number of fixtures installed on each shelf.

There are two ways to retain the test tubes. The first is to use square-compartmented polystyrene trays such as those used as unit containers to root cuttings individually in conventional propagation. The second method is to use custom-built trays, 60 × 60 cm (24 × 24") square, that hold 5 rows of test tubes lying at approximately 45° angles. Each tray will conveniently hold 100 culture tubes. Jars can be conveniently held in plastic or wire flats and then placed on the shelves.

Additional equipment includes time-clocks to control the day length and a second thermostat fitted to an alarm system to warn if the temperature rises or falls excessively. This thermostat should be set to operate when the temperature varies by 2.5–3.0°C (4–5°F) from that desired. It should turn off the heating cycle and also activate a warning light and an alarm bell outside the room.

[Figures quoted on culture densities for *Kalmia latifolia* (Mountain Laurel), assuming about 15 shoots (propagules) from each culture over a period of eight weeks, are that each 0.1 m² (1 square foot) of shelf space allows the production of around 2250 shoots per annum.]

DOCUMENTATION

It is imperative that all operations in a micropropagation laboratory be documented in an orderly and thorough way. Mistakes can be more easily detected and rectified if there is documentation for each step in a procedure. Documentation will show, for instance, which member of staff carried out the various procedures for a particular culture so that work habits can be corrected if contamination has occurred. Alternatively, the problem may be due to a wrong growth regulator combination, which can be discovered by checking the records kept during the media preparation stage.

The following three sets of recording sheets are used successfully at Briggs Nursery, Olympia, Washington, and will provide a useful basis on which to develop forms for use in other micropropagation programs. See Tables 20-1 to 20-3 for the exact layout and use of the sheets.

> A—Media Preparation Sheet
> B—Production Sheet
> C—Plant Transfer Sheet

Figure 20-8. The culture room must provide easy access to the shelves, be well illuminated, and have an accurate, temperature-controlled environment. (Reproduced by courtesy of Microplant Nurseries, Inc., Gervais, OR, U.S.A.)

Figure 20-9. A code system using a series of different colored test tube caps is a convenient method to quickly locate tubes containing different media. Note the installation of fluorescent light tubes above each shelf, and the test tubes held at approximately 45° angles in trays. (Les Clay & Son Ltd., Langley, B.C., Canada)

Figure 20-10. A plastic rack containing cultures of rhododendrons. Note that each test tube is individually labelled.

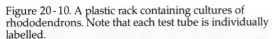

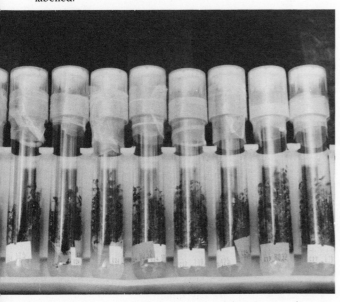

Figure 20-11. Kilner jars laid on their sides on shelves in the culture room.

TABLE 20-1. Example of Media Preparation Sheet

SOL'N NAME: **RHO II**   LOT # **ex. 128**   DATE MADE **3-21-84**

PREPARED BY **SMc**   VOLUME **10 ℓ**

DISPENSED INTO CONTAINER **test tubes**   pH **4.5**

COMPONENT	MFG. & LOT #	WEIGHT OR VOLUME DESIRED 1 ℓ	ACTUAL 10 ℓ	COMMENTS
A	90*	20 mℓ	200 mℓ	✓　　　a
B	85	20 mℓ	200 mℓ	✓
C	50	10 mℓ	100 mℓ	✓
Fe EDTA	70	10 mℓ	100 mℓ	✓
myo-inositol	12C-1085**	0.1 g	1.0 g	✓
2 iP	6F-825	5 mg	50 mg	✓
IAA	9B-1650	1 mg	10 mg	✓
pH	-	4.5	4.5	✓
Sucrose	-	20 g	200 g	✓
Agar	21C-420	4 g	40 g	✓

* Batch #

** Chemical manufacturer's lot #

a—check each component as you proceed in case you are distracted.

Source: Briggs Nursery, Olympia, WA, U.S.A.

TABLE 20-2. Example of Production Sheet

VARIETY: *Rhod.* 'Boule de Neige' 0101[a]
SOURCE: Briggs Nursery[b]
GOALS: (production #s needed to produce)

DATE	INIT.	# IN	# OUT CULTURE	# HOURS	MEDIA BATCH #	SHELF LOCATION	NOTES
6-7-84	SME	120 (2T) *	510 (2T) **	2.25 hrs.	# 128	A-1 A-2	shoots very healthy

* 120 test tube in St. 2   a—computer number of material   Source: Briggs Nursery, Olympia, WA, U.S.A.
** 510 test tube in St. 2   b—source of material

TABLE 20-3. Example of Plant Transfer Sheet

| | FROM | | | TO | | | | | | |
PLANT NAME	NUMBER	CODE	AMOUNT	NUMBER	CODE	AMOUNT	BIN	DATE	DEAD	OTHER
Rhod. 'Boule de Neige'	0101	2T	120	0101	2T	510	A-1 A-2	6-7-84	10 (2T) mold	Plants healthy

a—transfer report; b—transfer report; c—loss adjustment part   Source: Briggs Nursery, Olympia, WA, U.S.A.

A coding system is necessary when labelling the culture tubes or bottles. The code should consist of a reference number or letter for the plant name, the date of initial culture or subsequent transfer, and the initial(s) of the staff member responsible. A color-coded system to assist in making the cultures more identifiable may be superimposed onto this. Two examples are as follows:—

(1) A series of colored labels with a different color being used for each month of the year.

(2) A series of colored test tube caps that directly identify the medium being used. For example, a cap color code system used for media at Les Clay & Son Ltd., Langley, British Columbia, is as follows:—

Blue	—Extra low concentration of cytokinin and auxin
White, Red, Yellow, Green	—Low concentration of cytokinin and auxin, but double the strength of the blue caps
Black	—High hormone and high cytokinin—double the strength of the white, red, yellow and green caps
Turquoise, Brown	—Experimental media
Purple	—Woody plant media, specifically used for *Kalmia*
Pink	—No hormone
Olive-green, Clear	—Conifer species

Finally, an accession book should be kept in which is recorded the date of purchase (where applicable) and the clonal and seed source of all plant material used in the micropropagation program.

STAGES OF MICROPROPAGATION

The process of micropropagation can be essentially divided into four stages:—

Stage 1   —The cleaning and establishment of the plant material in aseptic culture (Initiation and Establishment).

Stage 2   —The promotion of active regeneration so that multiple shoots develop (Multiplication).

Stage 3   —The encouraging of root initiation and development at the base of the shoot (*In-vitro* Rooting).

Stage 4   —The transplanting, potting and establishment of the rooted shoots in a greenhouse (Acclimatization).

NOTE:—Stage 3 is sometimes omitted and rooting then occurs in Stage 4.

INITIAL PREPARATION OF PLANT MATERIAL FOR CULTURE

Research has stressed the formulation of appropriate media to use for ornamental woody plants but, until more recently, no recommended procedures for the initial preparation of the plant material that the newcomer could follow were formulated. However, the preparation phase of micropropagation is vital, as the tissues cannot be used if the shoot is not properly surface-sterilized. Success involves not only efficient procedures in the laboratory, but also good husbandry of the mother plants in the nursery. Guidelines can be formulated from the following comments, in which rhododendrons are used as the example.

Mother Plants

The greenhouse is the best site for growing the mother plants. They can be either container-grown or dug from the open ground and then bedded out in a border or containerized.

Because one shoot can be the clonal source of many thousands of plants over a short period of time, it is absolutely vital that both the source and clone are correctly identified. A mistake at this stage can lead to both financial loss and embarrassment. Where possible, the mother plants should be virus-tested. I feel strongly that the nursery operator undertaking micropropagation has a great deal of responsibility to the whole trade when selecting the initial mother material.

One concern that has worried nursery operators purchasing micropropagated material is that some genetic change may occur as a result of the propagation system used. Variegations sometimes occur in the early stages with the *Rhododendron* cultivars 'Vulcan', 'Madame Masson' and 'Virgo', but the liners largely grow out of it. Each nursery operator undertaking tissue culture must retain a mature specimen of each clone so that the subsequent clonal material can be checked against the original plant over the years for habit, flower color, etc. Comparison will show if any permanent genetical variations have occurred.

A well-managed husbandry program for the mother plants should be initiated—paying particular attention to pest and disease control. Leaf axils can harbor contaminants, therefore overhead watering should be avoided wherever possible. A polyethylene bag can be placed over some shoots if overhead contamination is likely to be a problem. This technique is particularly useful when collecting shoots from outdoor mother plants as they are more likely to collect debris around the leaf buds and axils, thus making cleaning more difficult.

Removal of Shoots

Shoots, 2–6 cm (¾–2½″) long, are removed when they are in the softwood phase of growth. This is best carried out in the early morning when the mother plants are under less stress. The air temperature within the greenhouse can be raised to force the mother plants into growth if shoots are required earlier than usual. Rhododendrons such as *R.* 'Egret' and *R.* 'Wigeon' (two excellent introductions by the Scottish nurseryman and plant collector, Peter Cox) respond readily to this forcing, with shoots being ready for removal during February. The shoots are removed with a knife, a label made, and shoots and label placed in a labelled polyethylene bag containing a few drops of water. The bag is taken to the laboratory where the shoots are placed in a tray of sterile water, together with the label made when they were collected.

CLEANING OF SURFACE TISSUE

The aim of this procedure is to surface-sterilize the plant material so that it is free from micro-organisms. The shoots (explants) used for culturing are not normally more than 6 cm (2½″) long. The leaves are carefully removed with a scalpel, leaving a leafless stem to be cultured because this:—

(i) Encourages the axillary buds to break so that there will be shoot tips for subsequent proliferation.

(ii) Reduces the amount of surface area that can harbor contaminants.

Figure 20-12.
The preparation of a *Rhododendron* shoot for surface sterilization. The removal of the leaves encourages the axillary buds to break and reduces the surface area that can harbor contaminants.

The most widely used and reliable chemical compound for surface-sterilizing plant tissue and equipment during all stages of micropropagation is bleach (sodium hypochlorite). Calcium hypochlorite is also used, but the sodium hypochlorite is easier to prepare as a solution. Sodium hypochlorite is better known as domestic laundry bleach and is sold under various trade names. Commercially available bleaches contain 5–5.25% sodium hypochlorite, and standard micropropagation practice is to use a 1 in 10 dilution (0.5% sodium hypochlorite) of the commercial product for routine surface sterilization. There are occasions, e.g., with more delicate tissues, when a 1 in 100 dilution (0.05% sodium hypochlorite) may be required.

The pH of the solution may be altered if desired. For example, a solution with a low pH (i.e., more acidic) is less effective in combating fungi than an alkaline solution but more effective in combating bacteria.

The shoot is placed into a Kilner-type jar containing a small amount of water and a few drops of soap solution. The jar is vigorously hand-shaken for two to three minutes to remove surface debris. The shoot is then transferred to another jar containing a surface sterilant (e.g., a 0.5% solution of sodium hypochlorite) and hand-shaken for fifteen to twenty minutes. Mechanical shaking using magnetic stirrers or orbital shakers has been used, with mixed success. The rather tedious hand shaking seems to be most efficient as the shoot moves around in a very haphazard way, rather than in a continuous flow pattern. Some researchers have found ultrasonic cleaners successful, but there is the risk of both cell and cell wall breakdown and subsequent necrosis.

Figure 20-13. The leafless *Rhododendron* shoot after being shaken vigorously in a soap solution in a Kilner jar to remove surface debris.

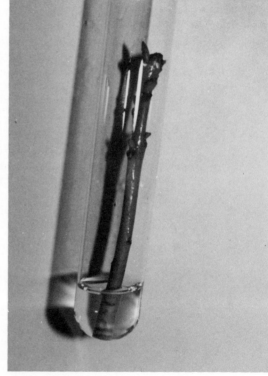

Figure 20-14. The surface-sterilized *Rhododendron* shoot in a test tube containing a liquid medium to encourage shoot tip development.

Alternative surface sterilants have been investigated by Steven McCulloch of Briggs Nurseries, with varying degrees of success. These include several alcohols at strengths ranging from 70–90%. They were found to be effective in combating only a relatively narrow range of micro-organisms. However, alcohols are useful for removing surface waxes from the stems in order to make other surface sterilants more efficient. Dyes such as methylene blue have surface-sterilant properties, but are not effective against many micro-organisms. Mercury-based compounds have been found to be effective against bacteria but inactive against fungal spores. The preservatives used in food preparations, such as propionic and benzoic acids, were found to be harmful to subsequent shoot growth. Tincture of iodine and potassium permanganate solutions may be useful alternatives to the standard bleach.

THE MEDIA

As with conventional propagation, the excised shoots need a medium in which to grow. The medium used in micropropagation must be sterile and contain all necessary components for plant growth and development. An omission or an incorrect ratio of compounds will result in failure of tissues to differentiate successfully. The purest chemicals are required—use analytical-grade chemicals whenever possible.

A considerable amount of methodical research has been devoted to the correct formulation of media for specific plants—especially trees. For example, Microplant Nurseries Inc. have approximately 10 modifications of media for *Malus* (Apple) culture alone. This research, in turn, has resulted in a range of recommended media named after the research worker(s) who developed them—for example, Murashige and Skoog, Knop's Solution, White's Medium and Knudson C. These media were particularly effective for callus culture, embryos, root cultures, and shoot tip and orchid seed respectively.

As the technology of micropropagation progressed there was a proportionate increase in the range of plants successfully cultured. In a number of instances, slight modifications of a basic research medium led to successful use with commercial greenhouse crops such as ferns, orchids, *Saintpaulia* (African Violet) and *Gloxinia*. W. C. Anderson of the Northwestern Washington Research and Extension Center, Mount Vernon, WA, carried out a considerable amount of research during the 1970s on the correct media for rhododendrons. His modification of the Murashige and Skoog formula resulted in the Anderson Media for the culture of rhododendrons.

Constituents of the Media

The constituents of the media may be conveniently grouped as follows.

(1) Inorganic Salts

These are the major, minor and trace elements necessary for plant growth. Listed below are the elements and some of the compounds that may be purchased to obtain them.

ELEMENT	COMPOUND	FORMULA
Nitrogen (N)	Potassium Nitrate Sodium Nitrate Ammonium Nitrate Ammonium Sulfate Calcium Nitrate, Tetrahydrate	KNO_3 $NaNO_3$ NH_4NO_3 $(NH_4)_2SO_4$ $Ca(NO_3)_2.4H_2O$
Phosphorus (P)	Sodium Dihydrogen Phosphate Potassium Dihydrogen Phosphate	$NaH_2PO_4.4H_2O$ KH_2PO_4
Potassium (K)	Potassium Chloride Potassium Sulfate Potassium Nitrate Potassium Dihydrogen Phosphate Potassium Hydroxide	KCl K_2SO_4 KNO_3 KH_2PO_4 KOH
Magnesium (Mg)	Magnesium Sulfate (Epsom Salts)	$MgSO_4.7H_2O$
Calcium (Ca)	Calcium Chloride, Dihydrate Calcium Nitrate, Tetrahydrate	$CaCl_2.2H_2O$ $Ca(NO_3)_2.4H_2O$

ELEMENT	COMPOUND	FORMULA
Iron (Fe)	Ferrous Sulfate complexed with ethylene diamine tetraacetic acid	$FeSO_4.EDTA$
	Ferrous Chloride	$FeCl_2$
	Ferric Citrate	$FeC_6H_5O_7.5H_2O$
Boron (B)	Boric Acid	H_3BO_3
Iodine (I)	Potassium Iodide[1]	KI
Zinc (Zn)	Zinc Sulfate, Heptahydrate	$ZnSO_4.7H_2O$
Copper (Cu)	Cupric (Copper) Sulfate	$CuSO_4.5H_2O$
Manganese (Mn)	Manganese Sulfate	$MnSO_4.H_2O$

[1]·Potassium iodide (KI) is toxic at high levels. Use only in small amounts to provide trace Iodine. It is not used in many media.

Other compounds used may include the following:—

Cobalt Chloride	$CoCl_2$
Cobalt Chloride, Hexahydrate	$CoCl_2.6H_2O$
Ferrous Sulfate, Heptahydrate	$FeSO_4.7H_2O$
Manganese Sulfate, Tetrahydrate	$MnSO_4.4H_2O$
Disodium EDTA (Disodium ethylene diamine tetraacetate)	$Na_2.EDTA$
Sodium Phosphate (dibasic)	Na_2HPO_4
Sodium Molybdate, Dihydrate	$Na_2MoO_4.2H_2O$
Sodium Sulfate	Na_2SO_4

(2) Organic Compounds

The major groups of organic compounds used in cultures are described below.

(a) Sucrose and Glucose—Sucrose is normally used as the major source of carbon (carbohydrate) which is required for the development of plant tissues and organs.

(b) Vitamins—These are necessary for normal plant growth, especially of the actively growing tissues. Several vitamins act as enzyme co-factors; that is, a substance that must be present in order for the enzyme to be active. Plants normally make the vitamins themselves, but excised shoots in tissue culture may produce an insufficient amount. Therefore, substances (known as pre-cursors) must be added to the medium to provide a source from which the plant tissue can manufacture the necessary vitamins.

Thiamine hydrochloride (Vitamin B_1), pyridoxine hydrochloride (Vitamin B_6) and nicotinic acid (Niacin) are the commonly added vitamins. These can be stored as stock solutions for up to one month in a refrigerator to prevent breakdown. There have been some reports of adverse effects when other vitamin sources are used with thiamine hydrochloride.

(c) Amino Acids and Amides—These compounds assist in the differentiation of tissue and are used in the synthesis of protein.

Compounds used include aspartic acid, glutamic acid, glycine and tyrosine. The L-isomer of these compounds should be used as the D-isomer does not occur naturally and is biologically ineffective. Care should be taken when adding more than one amino acid or amide as certain combinations have a negative effect when mixed together.

(d) *myo*-Inositol—*myo*-Inositol is a cyclic alcohol that promotes growth of some cultures. It is apparently a pre-cursor of membrane and cell wall constituents. Growth is usually improved with the addition of this compound to the medium.

(e) **Phloroglucinol**—This is a compound derived from phlorizin (or phloridzin). Research at East Malling Research Station, England, showed that phloroglucinol encouraged an increase in shoot development and rooting of *Malus* shoots. The reasons for its effectiveness are not clearly understood, and it should be considered only as a special additive in certain cases when all else has failed. Commercial micropropagation laboratories have had mixed results when using phloroglucinol.

(f) **Growth Regulators**—These essential constituents of the media are the auxins, cytokinins and gibberellins. The auxins are necessary for the promotion of root growth and cell elongation. They are normally provided in the form of either indole-3-acetic acid (IAA) or indolebutyric acid (IBA)—the latter is more stable. Naphthaleneacetic acid (NAA) is also used and, to a much lesser extent, (2,4-dichlorophenoxy) acetic acid (2,4-D). The level of auxin can affect the rate of root formation. For example, high levels of IBA and NAA are known to cause fused and thickened roots of the Cherry rootstock *Prunus* Mazzard F12/1, thus making subsequent establishment difficult.

Cytokinins are necessary for the initiation of shoot buds and leafy tissue and are supplied in the form of kinetin, zeatin, benzyladenine or N_6(2-Iso-pentyl)-adenine (2iP). The ratios of the auxin and cytokinin are critical*—for example, high levels of IAA will inhibit the action of the cytokinin. To avoid this, IAA may not be included in the first medium, the tissue being transferred to a medium containing IAA after sufficient shoot differentiation has occurred. *Betula pendula* (Common Silver Birch) shows the effect of cytokinin well—small pieces of callus will readily form buds when cytokinin is included in the medium. Cytokinins are also used to promote the formation of buds on immature cotyledons of seed embryos (e.g., *Pinus sylvestris,* Scots Pine). These will subsequently grow into shoots.

Gibberellins, of which gibberellic acid (GA_3) is the best known, cause elongation of stem internodal tissue and also act with the auxins to promote root growth when the culture is kept in the dark. In practice, the gibberellins are not widely used but they do offer a way to extend shoot growth when desired. This, for instance, would allow the shoots to be more easily cut into sections for rooting in the mist unit. There is some speculation that gibberellins inhibit root development in some species.

(g) **Natural Organic Complexes**—There are a wide range of natural organic complexes that have been considered necessary for successful propagation. However, T. Murashige points out that variability can occur in complexes obtained from different sources and also that variations can occur from one batch of cultures to the next in the laboratory. He recommends that they should be used only when conventional media have failed. Examples of natural organic complexes are banana puree, coconut milk and yeast extract.

(3) Support Material

The final constituent of the medium is a solidifying material to support the plant tissues. Agar, made from a seaweed extract, is most commonly used for this support material. The support material may be either solid or semi-solid, although solutions containing no agar are used in some circumstances.

Semi-solid and solid gels are most widely used in plant micropropagation laboratories and provide support as against submersion in a liquid for the differentiating tissue. Note that the agar may vary in composition and quality due to inherent differences of source and manufacturing processes. Commercial experience has shown that these differences (e.g., source and batch lot) may have significantly varying results. It is advisable to test several brands of agar when beginning micropropagation of a species, choose the best brand, and buy a large batch of it at one time.

The gel is made in the laboratory by adding the purchased purified agar powder to hot water. Deionized water, preferably glass-distilled, should be used, not tap water. The agar powder is stirred with the hot water to provide a concentration of between 0.5–1.0% for semi-solid media. A concentration of agar higher than 1% will produce a gel that is too hard, restricting the growth of most species. The required chemicals are added and the solution is permitted to cool.

---

*NOTE: One of the "classic" papers on micropropagation was published in 1957 by Skoog and Miller (*Symp. Soc. Exp. Biol.* **11**: 118–130). The authors found that shoot, root or callus formation could be predicted by the interaction of auxin and cytokinin in tobacco cells. For example, a high cytokinin and low auxin concentration promoted shoot formation whereas a lower cytokinin and higher auxin concentration encouraged root formation. An intermediate level of these growth regulators initiated callus formation.

More recently, a compound called Gelrite® has been introduced as an alternative to agar. It is cheaper and gives a much clearer gel on solidifying. Early tests with this compound were not successful. However, refinements by the manufacturer have resulted in greater success when used at a concentration of around 0.2%, although there have been some difficulties because it can set too quickly.

Liquid media contain all the chemicals needed by the tissue but not agar. Liquids make it easier for re-culturing but they provide less support to the cultures, particularly during handling. Only distilled or deionized water should be used and aeration should be provided (as in hydroponics) for the developing tissues. Some other means of additional support for the plant tissue or agitation of the liquid may need to be employed. Agitation must be weak to prevent cells breaking off from the developing tissue. Support in liquid media is provided in three ways, depending on the plant being cultured.

(a) A filter paper bridge is used to support the shoot tip. The paper acts as a wick from the liquid medium, so making it available to the cultured tissue.

(b) Rotating the flask containing the tissue at 1 rpm. This technique is successfully used in the micropropagation of orchids.

(c) Vigorously agitating the flasks in a shaker unit at 400 rpm. This technique is more commonly used with cell suspension cultures than with shoot tip cultures.

pH of the Medium

The pH level of the medium is important, with the optimum normally ranging between 4.5–5.7. A pH meter to measure the pH is essential, as well as stock solutions of the necessary buffers, acids and bases. Sulfuric acid and potassium hydroxide are preferred to adjust the pH. Sodium hydroxide should be avoided as plant tissues are sensitive to sodium. Hydrochloric acid should not be used because of the sensitivity of plants to chlorine.

Formulation of the Media and Autoclaving

Many problems in micropropagation are caused by mistakes during media preparation. Care must be taken to ensure that all amounts are measured exactly and that all constituents are added to the medium. Most media should be used within 14 days of formulation and autoclaving.

Each chemical substance used in formulating the medium must be accurately weighed or measured out by pipet. Distilled/deionized water is added to make up the mixture to the desired volume. Ensure that the medium is thoroughly mixed before proceeding. Dispense the medium into sterile test tubes, flasks, jars or "boxes" (between 13–15 ml of the medium is usually dispensed into a 50 ml (22 × 175 mm) test tube). Immediately cap, label and then autoclave for 15–20

Figure 20-15.
Placing racks of capped test tubes containing prepared medium into the autoclave for sterilization. (Briggs Nursery, Olympia, WA, U.S.A.)

minutes. It is important that the medium is not kept in the autoclave longer than the recommended time as prolonged heat causes the medium (particularly the sugar and sucrose) to degrade. The medium is sometimes autoclaved in bulk and then dispensed under sterile conditions into sterile test tubes. A convenient method for labelling the containers is to use a label dispenser similar to those used in supermarkets for pricing foods (e.g., Sato Corporation KSA 4078). The label should show the date and type of material and, where relevant, the computer number of the batch of plant material to be cultured. A convenient method of easier identification is to use a different colored label for each month of the year, or a cap color coding system (see p.610).

Prepared media can be purchased in packages (similar to powdered soup) directly from the supplier if the nursery operation is reluctant to formulate their own media. These pre-mixed media are dissolved in distilled water, made up to the desired concentration and then thoroughly mixed. Initially, there was concern with the use of these pre-packed media because culture results varied from one batch to the next. Pre-mixed media are now improved in quality and offer a convenient method for the beginner.

Tabulated below are five media that have been used successfully for a number of woody plants.

(1) Greshoff and Doy Medium (Modified)

Has been used on *Betula* (Birch), some conifers (e.g., *Thuja,* Arborvitae), *Rosa* and *Quercus* (Oak).

COMPONENT	FINAL CONC. OF MEDIUM (mg/l)	COMPONENT	FINAL CONC. IN MEDIUM (mg/l)
$(NH_4)_2SO_4$	200	$ZnSO_4.7H_2O$	3
KNO_3	1000	$CuSO_4.5H_2O$	0.25
$CaCl_2.2H_2O$	150	Thiamine HCl	1.0
KCl	300	Nicotinic acid	0.1
H_3BO_3	3	Pyridoxine HCl	0.1
KH_2PO_4	90	Glycine	2.0
Na_2HPO_4	30		
KI	0.75	$FeSO_4.7H_2O$	27.8
		$Na_2.EDTA$	37.3
$CoCl_2.6H_2O$	0.25	*myo*-Inositol	100
$Na_2MoO_4.2H_2O$	0.25	Sucrose	20 g/l
$MgSO_4.7H_2O$	250	Agar	6 g/l
$MnSO_4.H_2O$	10		

(2) Murashige and Skoog (1962) Medium (MS) (Modified)

This medium has been successfully used on a large range of herbaceous perennials, and also for some specific woody ornamentals—notably *Malus* and *Prunus*.

COMPONENT	FINAL CONC. IN MEDIUM (mg/l)	COMPONENT	FINAL CONC. IN MEDIUM (mg/l)
NH_4NO_3	1650	$Na_2.EDTA$	37.35
KNO_3	1900	$FeSO_4.7H_2O$	27.85
H_3BO_3	6.2	Thiamine.HCl	0.4
KH_2PO_4	170	Nicotinic acid	0.5
KI	0.83	Pyridoxine.HCl	0.5
$Na_2MoO_4.2H_2O$	2.5	Glycine	2.0
$CoCl_2.6H_2O$	0.025	*myo*-Inositol	100
$CaCl_2.2H_2O$	440	Indolebutyric acid	0.1
$MgSO_4.7H_2O$	370	B.A.P. (benzyl-aminopurine)	0.5–1.0
$MnSO_4.4H_2O$	22.3	Sucrose	30 g/l
$ZnSO_4.7H_2O$	8.6	Agar	5–10 g/l
$CuSO_4.5H_2O$	0.025		

(3) Anderson Media—Rhododendron Multiplication and Rooting Media

These media were developed by W. C. Anderson at Northwestern Washington Research and Extension Center, Mount Vernon, WA. The rooting medium will induce rooting formation while the multiplication medium will induce bud initiation.

Medium 1—Rhododendron Multiplication Medium

COMPONENT	CONCENTRATION (mg/l)	COMPONENT	CONCENTRATION (mg l)
NH_4NO_3	400	$NaH_2PO_4.H_2O$	380
KNO_3	480	*myo*-Inositol	100
$MgSO_4.7H_2O$	370	Adenine Sulfate $2H_2O$	80
$FeSO_4.7H_2O$	55.7	Thiamine	0.4
$Na_2.EDTA$	74.5	Hydrochloride	
$CaCl_2.2H_2O$	440	Indoleacetic Acid	1.0
$MnSO_4.H_2O$	16.9	N^6 (2-Isopentenyl)-	5.0
$ZnSO_4.7H_2O$	8.6	Adenine	
H_3BO_3	6.2	Sucrose	30 g/l
KI	0.83	pH	4.5
$CoCl_2.6H_2O$	0.025	Agar: either	
$CuSO_4.5H_2O$	0.025	Gibco-phytagar	8.0 g/l
$Na_2MoO_4.2H_2O$	0.25	or Gelrite®	1.75 g/l

Medium 2—Rhododendron Rooting Medium

This has one-quarter the strength of the inorganic salts in the multiplication medium.

COMPONENT	CONCENTRATION (mg/l)	COMPONENT	CONCENTRATION (mg/l)
NH_4NO_3	100	$NaH_2MoO_4.2H_2O$	0.063
KNO_3	120	$NaH_2PO_4.H_2O$	95
$MgSO_4.7H_2O$	92.5	*myo*-Inositol	25
$FeSO_4.7H_2O$	13.9	Activated Charcoal	600
$Na_2.EDTA$	18.6	Indolebutyric Acid	5.0
$CaCl_2.2H_2O$	110	Sucrose	30 g/l
$MnSO_4.H_2O$	4.2	pH	4.5
$ZnSO_4.7H_2O$	2.2	Agar (Gibco—	5.5 g/l
H_3BO_3	1.6	Commercial Grade	
$CoCl_2.6H_2O$	0.006	Phytagar)	
$CuSO_4.5H_2O$	0.006		

(4) McCown and Lloyd—Woody Plant Medium

This medium was developed by B. H. McCown and G. Lloyd at the University of Wisconsin, Madison, and has been successful for shoot-tip and callus cultures of *Betula* (Birch), *Kalmia* (American Laurel), *Rhododendron* and other woody ornamentals.

COMPONENT	CONCENTRATION (mg/l)	COMPONENT	CONCENTRATION (mg/l)
NH_4NO_3	400	$CuSO_4.5H_2O$	0.25
$Ca(NO_3)_2.4H_2O$	556	$FeSO_4.7H_2O$	27.8
K_2SO_4	990	$Na_2.EDTA$	37.3
$CaCl_2.2H_2O$	96	Thiamine HCl	1.0
KH_2PO_4	170	Nicotinic acid	0.5
H_3BO_3	6.2	Pyridoxine HCl	0.5
$Na_2MoO_4.2H_2O$	0.25	Glycine	2.0
$MgSO_4.7H_2O$	370	*myo*-Inositol	100
$MnSO_4.H_2O$	22.3	Sucrose	20 g/l
$ZnSO_4.7H_2O$	8.6	Agar	6 g/l

Further details of some of these media, for example, the Anderson Media, may be found in some commercial literature such as that from Gibco Laboratories (Grand Island Biological Company, P.O. Box 200, Chagrin Falls, Ohio 44022). Media modifications that can be made for the various stages of the culture process are also found in this literature. Nursery operators intending to install a micropropagation laboratory are well advised to carefully study the references listed at the end of this chapter.

Figure 20-16.
A crew of operators carrying out the transfer procedures at the laminar flow cabinets. (Reproduced by courtesy of Microplant Nurseries, Inc., Gervais, OR, U.S.A.)

TRANSFER OF TISSUE

The clean explants (p. 611) are placed in an initiation medium and allowed to differentiate and multiply in number. The material is then re-cut, divided and transferred into test-tubes or jars containing a medium in which to increase numbers.

The transfer of material for multiplication and rooting is carried out within the laminar flow cabinet in the transfer room. It is vital that all the work is carried out under the sterile air stream in the cabinet. One way to assist this is to paint a red line just inside the entrance of the cabinet. This provides a visual warning to the operator that the plant material must remain inside the line.

It is important that strict sterile techniques be maintained to prevent subsequent contamination. The supervisor must thoroughly train, and regularly check, staff working at the laminar flow cabinets to ensure maximum speed without contamination. Two ideas to instill into the staff are that the cabinet surfaces are *always* "contaminated" and that each movement in the transferring process has the objective of preventing possible infection.

All instruments must be sterilized prior to the transfer of material—if in doubt, always re-sterilize. Ethanol (95% strength) may be used as the sterilant with the excess being burnt off in a flame before use. Alternatively, bleach may be used with the instruments being dipped first into a 1:10 (0.5% sodium hypochlorite) solution and then into a 1:100 (0.05% sodium hypochlorite) solution. A methodical work pattern must be established so that the instruments are automatically sterilized every time they are used.

A procedure for transfer of material from one tube to another tube or to the larger culture jar that I have seen used successfully by a commercial micropropagation laboratory is summarized below. Sodium hypochlorite was used to sterilize the instruments.

(1) Gloves are worn, with the cuff turned up so that the sodium hypochlorite does not run down the arm.

(2) The cap of the test tube containing the culture is removed.

(3) Forceps are used to remove the plant tissue from the test tube and place it onto moistened paper towel in a petri dish.

Figure 20-17. Sterilizing the opening of the test tube and tip of the forceps with a flame from an alcohol lamp. (Monrovia Nursery, Azusa, CA, U.S.A.)

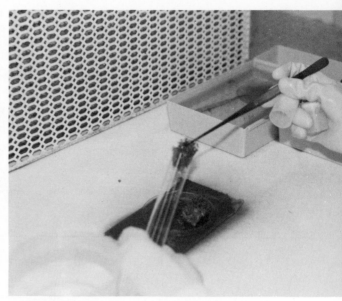

Figure 20-18. Using forceps to remove proliferated *Rhododendron* shoots from a test tube. Note that the test tube cap is retained in the right hand to speed up the operation.

Figure 20-19. Using forceps and scalpel to divide and cut proliferated shoots into smaller pieces for transfer. Note that there is moistened filter paper underneath the petri dish to prevent it from slipping on the working surface of the cabinet.

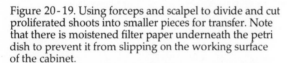

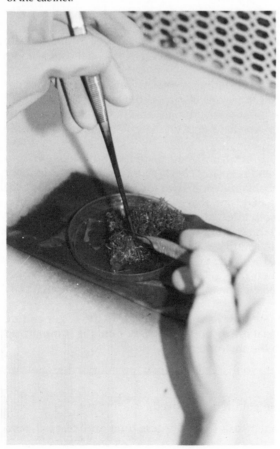

Figure 20-20. Transferring divided stem tissue into a small jar for re-culturing. Note that the cuff of the rubber glove is turned over to prevent sodium hypochlorite running down the arm of the operator.

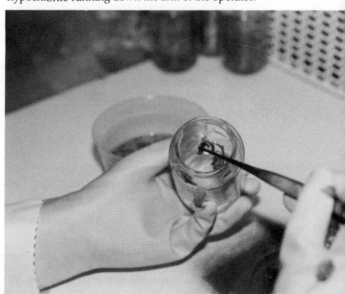

[Petri dishes are used to hold the tissue, with a paper towel square soaked in 1:100 bleach solution being placed (with forceps) in each dish. A similarly moistened piece of paper towel can be placed underneath the dish to prevent it moving around on the working surface.]

(4) A scalpel is used to cut the stems as quickly as possible into 1.3–2.0 cm (½–¾″) lengths.

(5) Forceps are used to divide the severed stems and then to place one or more stem sections onto the new gel medium, either in a test tube or other container.

This procedure is repeated, ensuring that all hand tools are re-sterilized after each usage, until there is sufficient quantity of material to move into the culture room.

[*NOTE:*—Some laboratories have found that sodium hypochlorite has damaged plant tissue and inhibited rooting with some species. An alternative procedure is to cut the tissue on dry sterile paper towels and regularly wipe down the bench with a disinfectant, e.g., Omega®. Forceps and scalpels are sterilized in ethanol and/or a flame before each container is opened.]

CULTURE ROOM CARE

The function and general layout of the culture room has been described earlier (see p. 606). It is important to maintain a steady temperature of around 24°C (75°F). The air volume inside a test tube expands and contracts as the temperature varies. There is a strong possibility that non-sterile air will be pulled into the test tube, thus contaminating the culture, if the temperature falls to 16.5–18°C (62–65°F). Cotton placed inside the test tube cap before the cap is put on can act as a filter to potential contaminants. Some laboratories do not use cotton when using custom-made micropropagation test tubes (e.g., Belco Kaputs®) as the caps fit very tightly.

A minimum 14–16 hour light period per day should be maintained. The intensity of light may depend on the plant being cultured—for example, 2000 Lux (200 ft. candles) for *Rhododendron*, *Kalmia* (American Laurel) and *Arctostaphylos* (Manzanita), but up to 5000 Lux (500 ft. candles) for *Acer* (Maple), *Clematis*, *Prunus* (Cherry) and *Malus* (Apple). The overhead lights encourage the shoots to grow upward. Inadequate light leads to disorganized development that results in bent stems and poor multiplication. A light meter should be used to check the light intensity.

Daily checks must be made to identify contaminated cultures. Fungi grow very fast on the medium but tend to be restricted to the top surface of the culture media. Bacteria (e.g., *Bacillus subtilis*), which also multiply rapidly in the medium, cloud or discolor the culture and can be seen scattered within it, instead of restricted to the surface. Any infected tubes or jars are autoclaved and immediately discarded. Slight contaminations have been overcome by surface sterilizing the plant tissue a second time.

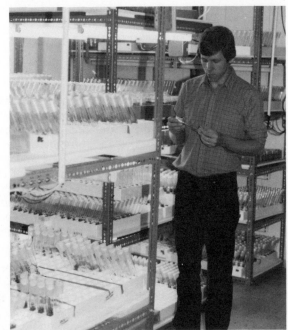

Figure 20-21. The cultures must be checked daily for any signs of contamination. Note the use of expanded polystyrene (Styrofoam®) trays with cavities to support the test tubes. (Briggs Nursery, Olympia, WA, U.S.A.)

Sometimes the plant tissue takes on a "water-soaked" appearance, normally referred to as vitrification. The exact cause of vitrification has created considerable discussion; there are currently at least three people doing full-time research at universities to discover the causes and effects. This type of effect can be avoided by using a stiffer agar mix or by changing agar brands. One laboratory has found that the addition of 10 mg cysteine hydrochloride to the medium will help to overcome vitrification.

The plant material is normally kept in the culture room for 1–2½ months. They are ready for either re-culturing (normally every 3–4 weeks) or for rooting in a mist propagation or fogging facility when the multiple shoots are about 5.0–7.5 cm (2–3″) high.

Figure 20-22. A healthy culture of *Rhododendron* shoots in the culture room about 6 weeks after a successful transfer.

One problem likely to occur is that the shoots are too soft and short to be easily handled. One method that has been found successful for *Rhododendron* is to place the cultures under low light intensity in a designated area in the laboratory for about two weeks prior to rooting in the mist propagation unit. This elongates the stems, making them easier to handle. The reduction of light has sometimes had the additional benefit of promoting rooting in those species or cultivars that are difficult to root. Some success has been achieved by using a low concentration of gibberellic acid in the medium (note that autoclaving can reduce the concentration by half).

COLD STORAGE OF PLANT TISSUE

The benefits provided by using domestic refrigerators for the cold storage of plant tissue include the following.

(i) To store or "bank" clonal stock material for future use. This provides a ready source for bulking-up plant material if and when the demand arises. Also, the amount of space required is minimal compared to traditional stock plants. A successful method of storage at Microplant Nurseries, Inc., Oregon, is to place the tissue in plastic petri-dishes which are then sealed with water-proof tape and placed in a refrigerator at 2°C (35.6°F) without artificial light. It is often possible to store cultures for 18–24 months without subculturing, depending on species or cultivar. However, for long-term stock maintenance purposes, the dishes are removed from the refrigerator once a year and placed into light to allow differentiation. A shoot tip is then removed, returned to a fresh petri-plate and stored for a further year. A culture line may be maintained indefinitely in this way.

(ii) To aid production scheduling. A laboratory can bulk-up large quantities of material year round and allow greenhouse growers to pot at their convenience. Research carried out at Microplant Nurseries, Inc., has demonstrated the considerable benefits that may be gained from storing large quantities of micropropagated tree species. The material is stored in darkness at 2°C (35.6°F), either as "clumps" ready to be cut into individual shoots (micro-cuttings) or as *in vitro* rooted plantlets. This procedure allows for a large quantity of plant material to be subsequently handled in the customer's greenhouse during spring when day length and temperatures are adequate to promote rapid shoot and root growth. It illustrates the point that a micropropagation laboratory must meet the demand of a typical production pattern in the average nursery if the laboratory is to be successful. Cold storage provides the flexibility to meet this objective.

(iii) To restrict the development of cultures temporarily. This is of use when there is short-term over-production, low demand, current establishment and growing-on areas cannot take further material, or in winter.

(iv) To provide a pre-chilling treatment. This results in dramatically superior greenhouse growth and uniformity for some deciduous tree species when compared with non-chilled material. Research carried out at Microplant Nurseries, Inc. and at A. McGill & Son, Fairview, Oregon, clearly showed that improved growth of several crab apple varieties and pear rootstocks resulted from a minimum of 6 weeks chilling.

ROOTING, ESTABLISHMENT AND LINER PRODUCTION

It is vital to develop and follow the correct procedure for the establishment of cultured plant material. Ideally, successful establishment must be in the 90–95% range—success rates below 70% are unlikely to warrant the investment of capital and labor for the laboratory.

Understandably, research on micropropagation has so far been much more oriented to mastering the correct procedures in the laboratory, rather than concentrating on the establishment of the plant material under nursery conditions. Therefore, it has been left largely to the nursery operators themselves to pioneer the correct procedures for establishing woody ornamental material. More recently, the perseverance and willingness of nursery operators to adapt or change procedures has led to the perfecting of methods to establish such crops as *Acer rubrum* (Red Maple), *Betula* (Birch), *Rhododendron* and *Kalmia*. It has been suggested that a grower experienced in propagating *Rhododendron* from seed should be able to adapt quickly to techniques of successfully rooting and establishing micropropagated material. The system that is now widely used for woody ornamentals on commercial nurseries is to sever and root small individual stems (micro-cuttings), rather than to allow the roots to develop during the culturing phase.

The six factors that will largely determine the success of establishment of micropropagated material are outlined below. In practice, they are inter-related.

(1) Personnel

The nursery staff caring for the plant material must fully understand the needs for successful establishment, must be observant, and must carry out their work in a conscientious manner.

(2) Humidity

Water stress due to rapid loss of water is one of the major reasons for failure when the plant material is moved to a new environment. This has been found to be more of a problem with woody material than with herbaceous perennials.

Research at Oregon State University, Corvallis, has shown that micropropagated material lost considerably more water during the establishment phase than plant material propagated using conventional techniques. Microscopic examination showed that the stomata of micropropagated material were continually open for 2–3 days after removal from the laboratory while those of material raised under conventional techniques opened and closed. There is also very little leaf cuticle. Water is lost through open stomata, therefore it could be concluded that this is the major factor for the increased water stress in micropropagated material. The initial desired level of the surrounding humidity should be 90–95%. This level can be best achieved artificially either by regular applications of fine water particles from a mist propagation unit or by installing a fogger. Some research has been done on ways to promote earlier development of the opening and closing of stomata in micropropagated plant cultures. These methods include placing the material under pre-determined periods of darkness, foliar feeding, and placing in a high humidity environment for two weeks while being established.

(3) Temperature

The optimum air temperature to encourage rapid plant development in the establishment phase is considered to be between 18–21°C (67–70°F). The required high level of humidity can mean that disease infection of the plant tissues is encouraged if the air temperature is reduced to below 18°C (65°F).

(4) Fungal Infection

Damping-off diseases and secondary infection by *Botrytis cinerea* (Gray Mold) have caused serious losses of both rooted and unrooted material. Strict hygiene, maintaining the correct environment of both the air and rooting/growing media, and a regular fungicide program will go a long way towards solving this problem.

(5) Aeration of Rooting/Growing-On Media

Experience has shown that many failures during the establishment phase are due to insufficient aeration of the media used for the rooting, hardening-off and initial growing-on phases. The aim should be to maintain an air to water ratio of about 30%. Perlite or crushed pumice (volcanic rock) are two particularly useful medium constituents to increase the aeration capacity.

(6) Light Intensity

The use of high-intensity sodium vapor and metal halide lamps to increase light intensity and day length has been found to be helpful during the rooting of the severed micropropagated shoots. These should have a rating of 2000–5000 Lux (200–500 ft. candles) and be set for a 16-hour photoperiod. It is particularly important that increased light be given during the winter as the shoots have come from a well-illuminated laboratory.

Nursery Procedures

There are two systems which are used for the rooting of the individual shoots:—

1. Transferring the shoots to a different medium and allowing rooting to occur in the laboratory (Stage 3). The end product from the laboratory is a rooted plantlet. Changes in the media are necessary to promote root initiation and development to occur. The salt concentration is usually reduced, the cytokinin eliminated, modifications made to the hormone concentration, and activated charcoal is sometimes added.

2. Taking the cultures from the laboratory, severing the stems and rooting individual shoots (micro-cuttings) (Stage 2) in a greenhouse propagation facility. The end product from the laboratory is a micro-cutting. This method is currently more commonly used in commercial laboratories for woody ornamental plants, thus it forms the basis of the following information.

[Some laboratories may offer their customers the choice of micro-cuttings or rooted plantlets when purchasing plant material—for example, Microplant Nurseries, Inc.]

This section, discussing the principles for successful establishment of tissue cultured material in greenhouses, describes the procedures used successfully at three nurseries.

Figure 20-23. A petri dish containing rooted plantlets of *Malus* (Apple) growing in an agar-based medium. (Reproduced by courtesy of Microplant Nurseries, Inc., Gervais, OR, U.S.A.)

Figure 20-24. A rooted plantlet of *Acer rubrum* 'Red Sunset' (Red Maple cv.) 2 weeks after the shoot was stuck into the agar rooting medium. (Microplant Nurseries, Inc., Gervais, OR, U.S.A.)

(i) A. McGill & Son, Fairview, Oregon
Rooting

A procedure for successfully establishing young plantlets of *Acer platanoides* (Norway Maple), *A. rubrum* (Red Maple), *Betula* (Birch), ornamental *Malus* (Crab Apple) and ornamental *Prunus cerasifera* (Myrobalan Plum) has been developed by A. Chianello at this nursery. The plantlets are shipped to the nursery in petri dishes or small tubs, with each petri dish containing approximately 25 plantlets growing in an agar medium. The plantlets are cold stored at 1–3°C (34–38°F) if transplanting does not proceed immediately following arrival.

Employees wash their hands in a Physan® solution before handling the plantlets. Any tools used for transplanting are also immersed in this sanitation solution. The operator holds the leaves with the fingers as close to the crown of the plantlet as possible to ensure that it is removed from the agar with roots intact.

The 3 cm (1¼″) square pots are filled with a growing medium containing equal parts of very fine bark and Lite-Grow® (a peat moss and vermiculite mix). This medium is drenched with a fungicide/fertilizer solution (1 part to 100 parts of water) delivered through a precision injector during preparation. The stock solution is formulated by mixing 600 g of benomyl (Benlate®) and 600 g of calcium nitrate in 5 l of water (1 lb of each in 1 U.S. gal). Eighty of these square pots are placed in a flat for ease of handling.

Excessively long roots are trimmed at transplanting time, a small cavity is made in the medium with a pointed stick and the root system is evenly distributed in this cavity. All the root system must be covered by the growing medium, taking care not to let any of the medium remain on the leaves.

Following transplanting, the plantlets are settled in with a fine spray of water containing the fungicide/fertilizer mix used during medium preparation. The flats are placed in a plastic tent where a mist unit is installed and the plants are provided with a minimum basal heat of 15.5–18°C (60–65°F). The flats are removed from the tent after 3–5 days and placed down onto the greenhouse bench. A liquid feeding program is implemented to provide 250–300 ppm N, 50–100 ppm P and 150–175 ppm K.

Hardening-off and Liner Production

The plantlets are grown-on in the greenhouse to produce a 22.5–30 cm (9–12″) tall liner suitable for mechanically planting in open ground. One to two weeks prior to planting, the liners are placed in a shade house to harden-off. The liners are irrigated immediately after planting.

The liners may also be allowed to become dormant in the flats, kept in refrigerated cold storage at 2–4°C (36–39°F) over the winter, and then planted in the open ground as dormant liners in the spring.

Micro-cuttings

Micro-cuttings are established using the same techniques described above, except that they are placed in polyethylene mist tunnels until the roots have developed.

Figure 20-25. A greenhouse containing healthy liners of *Acer platanoides* cvs. (Norway Maple), *A. rubrum* cvs. (Red Maple), *Betula* (Birch) and *Prunus cerasifera* cvs. (Myrobalan Plum). These liners were all grown from rooted plantlets shipped from the micropropagation laboratory. (A. McGill & Son, Fairview, OR, U.S.A.)

Figure 20-26. Young liners of *Acer rubrum* 'Red Sunset' (Red Maple cv.) almost ready for open-ground machine planting. (A. McGill & Son, Fairview, OR, U.S.A.)

(ii) Briggs Nursery, Inc., Olympia, Washington

Rooting

The test tubes or jars are taken from the laboratory to the greenhouse used for rooting the propagules when they contain an adequate number (approximately 15–30 per test tube) of shoots approximately 5.0–7.5 cm (2–3″) long. The propagation staff in the greenhouse are seated at surface-clean benches. They first remove the test tube caps, then remove the contents of the tube with forceps. The shoots must be washed to remove the old medium and sugar, otherwise mold will grow on it and may kill the cuttings before they root. The shoots are then severed into 2.5 cm (1″) lengths with a scalpel, the pieces teased apart, and stuck singly into a rooting medium of 1 part perlite, 1 part peat moss and 1 part Douglas Fir (*Pseudotsuga*) bark. The medium is supplemented with a small amount of calcium carbonate and Micromax®. Small containers, 10 × 10 × 7.5 cm (4 × 4 × 3″), that will hold 16–25 shoots are used. Sixteen of these containers will fit into a flat 60 × 60 × 7.5 cm (24 × 24 × 3″).

This procedure must be carried out precisely and quickly. The risk of desiccation is reduced by having a hand-operated spray bottle available to regularly mist the severed shoots. Rooting hormone has been unnecessary for most rhododendrons and kalmias grown.

The flats are placed in a mist propagation unit fitted with nozzles that will produce very fine water droplets. A time clock is set to give a burst of water spray every fifteen minutes for the first 3–5 days, after which it is reduced to about once per hour. The frequency of misting is partly determined by the time of year. However, Briggs Nursery has recently installed a Mee Industries fogging system (high pressure fog) and this has been found to be even more suitable than mist after the first 7–10 days. The base temperature is maintained at 24°C (75°F), while the air temperature is set at 21°C (70°F). Metal halide lights above the flats maintain an output of 5000 Lux (500 ft. candles) at night or during periods of low light intensity during the day. A photoperiod of 12 hours is generally used. During the winter, the cuttings are rooted inside polyethylene tents with only limited misting.

Hardening-off

The cuttings are sufficiently well-rooted to be removed from the propagation bench approximately 4–6 weeks after sticking. The flats are taken to a separate greenhouse where the air temperature is maintained between 18–21°C (65–70°F). The plants are watered precisely up to three times a day for the first few days (depending on the weather), and watering is then gradually reduced to an average of once per day. It is advisable to keep the rooting medium slightly on the dry side to increase aeration, which, in turn, increases the number and length of roots.

Liner Production

The cuttings are hardened-off for 2–3 months after which they are sufficiently rooted for potting-up into 6 cm (2¼″) square containers for liner production. The rooted cuttings are removed from the 10 cm (4″) rooting containers and graded into 3–5 grades to reduce variation within the subsequent liner crop.

The potting mix is:—
  50% Sawdust—salt-free Douglas Fir (*Pseudotsuga*)
  20% Sphagnum Peat Moss
  20% Perlite
  10% Bark
To each 1 m³ (1 cu. yd.) of mix is then added:—
  Osmocote® (18–6–12)—3.3 kg (5.5 lb)
    (8–9 month release)
  Dolomite—2.4 kg (4 lb)
  Micromax—222.5 g (6 oz)
  Iron sequestrene—222.5 g (6 oz)

After potting, the potential liners are placed pot-rim to pot-rim in carrying flats which are then placed on the floor of the greenhouse.

A weekly spray of fungicides is applied during the rooting and early phases of liner production, alternating the active ingredient with each application. Problems have been experienced with benomyl (Benlate®) in that it both dwarfed and scorched *Rhododendron* and *Kalmia*. A fungicidal spray using a combination of captan and benomyl (Benlate®) is now used in rotation with daconil at 2-week intervals. Metalaxyl (Subdue®) is applied at 12-week intervals because of its effectiveness against *Phytophthora cinnamomi* (Root Rot). It is applied at the rate of 37.5–75 g in 500 l

Figure 20-27. A proliferation of *Rhododendron* shoots that are long enough to be removed from the jar and severed with forceps and/or scalpel.

Figure 20-28. An operator works at a bench to stick 16–25 sections of single shoots into a 10 × 10 × 7.5 cm (4 × 4 × 3″) plastic container. (Briggs Nursery, Olympia, WA, U.S.A.)

Figure 20-29. Close-up of the sticking procedure. Note the clear plastic container with loosely packed severed shoots, and the way in which the sticking container is tilted towards the operator. (Briggs Nursery, Olympia, WA, U.S.A.)

Figure 20-30. Regular hand misting during the sticking operation is important as the shoots are very sensitive to moisture loss. The completed flats are moved to a mist or fogging propagation facility. (Briggs Nursery, Olympia, WA, U.S.A.)

of water (1–2 oz. per 100 U.S. gallons). Red spider mites are sometimes a major pest problem, but are effectively controlled by using alternate sprays of cyhexatin (Plictran®), fluvalinate (Mavrik®) and permethrin (Pounce®).

The liners develop into an excellent graded product either for sale to another nursery or for growing-on in containers or in the open ground. Two major features of the liners obtained are firstly, the evenness of grade and secondly, the ability of the young plants to produce a high proportion of side shoots, thus providing a strong foundation for a larger-sized quality plant. Some cultivars of *Rhododendron,* e.g., *R* 'Vulcan', do occasionally produce variegated leaves or shoots. However, this has not been found to be a problem as the liners eventually grow out of it and it has not, so far, reappeared during later stages of plant development.

Figure 20-31. A container of rooted *Rhododendron* shoots 10 weeks from sticking. (Briggs Nursery, Olympia, WA, U.S.A.)

Figure 20-32. The rooted cuttings are removed from the containers, carefully separated and graded. (Briggs Nursery, Olympia, WA, U.S.A.)

Figure 20-33. Note the extensive root system on the small cutting removed from the container. (Briggs Nursery, Olympia, WA, U.S.A.)

Figure 20-34. The flats of graded cuttings are transferred to a crew working at a mobile potting bench where the cuttings are potted into netted pots. (Briggs Nursery, Olympia, WA, U.S.A.)

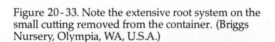

Figure 20-35. The rooted cutting is held gently in one hand and the index finger of the other hand is used to make a depression in the growing medium. It is important to cover all the root system with the growing medium. (Briggs Nursery, Olympia, WA, U.S.A.)

Figure 20-36. Flats holding the containers of newly potted plants move along under a very fine mist to keep the tissues turgid. (Briggs Nursery, Olympia, WA, U.S.A.)

Figure 20-37. The flats are stood down at floor level in the greenhouse for growing-on. Note that timbers are placed under the flats to create air circulation under the containers and that there is access to all four sides of each block of trays. (Briggs Nursery, Olympia, WA, U.S.A.)

Figure 20-38. A healthy, well-branched liner of *Rhododendron* 12–14 weeks after potting. (Briggs Nursery, Olympia, WA, U.S.A.)

Figure 20-39. Liners of *Rhododendron* 'Vulcan' bedded out into a growing medium retained in a wooden pallet. (Briggs Nursery, Olympia, WA, U.S.A.)

(iii) Les Clay & Son Ltd., Langley, British Columbia

Rooting

The shoots are removed from the test tubes and severed when there are sufficient numbers about 1.3–5.0 cm (½–2″) long, using a procedure similar to that described for Briggs Nursery. The work of the propagation staff is arranged so that one person does not spend more than half-a-day sticking cuttings. This is to prevent development of the boredom that can be associated with the precise work required.

The cuttings are stuck in flats measuring approximately 30 × 50 cm (12 × 20″) square, which conveniently hold 260 cuttings per flat. The rooting medium used is made up of 2 parts peat moss to 1 part perlite. *Kalmia* and some *Rhododendron* (e.g., *R.* 'Cynthia' and *R.* 'Pink Pearl') have produced a better root system when the ratio of peat moss to perlite is increased to 3:1. No rooting hormone is applied to cuttings of *Rhododendron* and *Kalmia*. The completed flats are hand misted and then placed on a bench measuring 2.75 × 18 m (9 × 60′) with overhead mist lines. Greater control of the environment, particularly humidity and temperature, is achieved by enclosing the bench and mist lines with polyethylene to make a large tent-like structure. High-intensity sodium vapor lamps, which provide 1000 Lux illumination (100 ft. candles) at the bench level, are sited above the tent to provide lighting for 16 hours per day and during periods of low light intensity.

Figure 20-40. A tent propagation facility for rooting the cuttings. Note the sectioned drapes to facilitate daily inspection of the cuttings. (Les Clay & Son Ltd., Langley, B.C., Canada)

Figure 20-41. Flats of *Rhododendron* and *Kalmia* cuttings inside the polyethylene tent fitted with a mist line. High-intensity sodium vapor lamps are installed above the tent to provide up to 16 hours of daylight during periods of low light intensity. (Les Clay & Son Ltd., Langley, B.C., Canada)

The base temperature is set to maintain a level of 21–24°C (70–75°F) while the air temperature is retained at a minimum of 10°C (50°F) at night and 21–24°C (70–75°F) during the day. Cooling pads have been installed and found to be very effective in reducing the air temperature during hot weather. Mist application is controlled by a time clock set to work during daylight hours, while a humidifier is turned on in the evenings or at night to keep up the humidity levels. *Rhododendron* shoots begin to root within 10–25 days but remain within the polyethylene tent for around 6 weeks. *Kalmia* is slower to root and requires 8 weeks before hardening-off.

Once the cuttings begin to root, a liquid fertilizer (10-52-10) is applied weekly at a dilution of 1 part in 1000 parts of water. A layer of coarse sand is placed over the surface of the rooting medium once the cuttings have rooted to help to control mosses and liverworts. If mosses and liverworts are a continuing problem, it is wise to experiment with chemical controls applied at low concentrations at regular intervals beginning soon after sticking. These chemical controls include dodine acetate (Cyprex®), maneb (Dithane M-22®), a mixture of Physan® and a micro-copper compound such as Microcop®, and dichlorophen (Algofen®). The objective is to prevent the mosses and liverworts from forming instead of controlling them after they have developed. These chemicals must be tested first to see whether they cause leaf scorch or inhibit rooting before they are universally used on the nursery.

Hardening-Off

The well-rooted cuttings are given a minimum two-week hardening-off period on an open bench adjacent to the polyethylene tent. Mist lines above the flats are manually operated as required.

Liner Production

The aim is to produce a plant of maximum quality and size in the minimum size of container. Therefore, a square container with dimensions of 6 cm (2¼") was chosen. The liners are kept under overhead mist for the first month after potting-up and then moved out to the growing-on houses.

Botrytis cinerea (Gray Mold) is the major disease problem during the rooting, hardening-off and liner production phases. It is prevented by regular applications of benomyl (Benlate®), fenaminosulf (Dexon®) or captan at half the recommended rate. Full strength applications are used if an outbreak of *Botrytis cinerea* occurs. Lindane (25% wettable powder) is applied at 1.5 g per 1 l (0.2 oz in 1 U.S. gal) for fungus gnats and springtails. Acephate (Orthene®) applied at 3 ml per 1 l (0.2 fl. oz. in ½ U.S. gal) is used, if necessary, for vine weevil control. The liners should be ready for sale about four months after potting-up.

Figure 20-42. Inspecting young *Rhododendron* and *Kalmia* liners and plants propagated the previous year. (Les Clay & Son Ltd., Langley, B.C., Canada)

CONCLUSIONS

This chapter has been designed to give the reader a practical introduction to micropropagation using a relatively narrow range of woody ornamentals as examples. Micropropagation is a highly specialized propagation method and therefore a greater depth of knowledge, both in technique and the range of plants successfully cultured, should be obtained by consulting the references listed below for further reading. A visit to a working micropropagation laboratory and to a nursery successfully establishing micropropagated material is strongly recommended.

Figure 20-43. Shoots of *Nandina domestica* cvs. (Heavenly or Sacred Bamboo) being rooted in containers individually covered with polyethylene. (Monrovia Nursery, Azusa, CA, U.S.A.)

Figure 20-44. A container of rooted *Nandina domestica* 'Nana Harbour Dwarf' (Heavenly or Sacred Bamboo cv.) cuttings ready to be divided for potting as liners. (Monrovia Nursery, Azusa, CA, U.S.A.)

REFERENCES AND SUGGESTED SOURCES FOR FURTHER READING

Anderson, W. C. 1978. Rooting of tissue cultured rhododendrons. *Comb. Proc. Inter. Pl. Prop. Soc.* **28:** 135–139.

Cameron, A. 1982. A cultured advance. *GC & HTJ* **191**(12): 12–13, 15 (March 19, 1982).

Chée, R. 1984. How to produce millions of shoot tips in a year. *Amer. Nurseryman* **159**(10): 55–56, 58, 60–61 (May 15, 1984).

Cheng, T.-Y. 1978. Propagating woody plants through tissue culture. *Amer. Nurseryman* **147**(10): 7–8, 94–102 (May 15, 1978).

————. 1978. Clonal propagation of woody plant species through tissue culture techniques. *Comb. Proc. Inter. Pl. Prop. Soc.* **28:** 139–155.

Cross, D. 1982. Multiplying miniatures. *GC & HTJ* **192**(1): 18–20 (July 2, 1982).

de Fossard, R. A. 1976. *Tissue Culture for Plant Propagation.* Univ. of New England Printery, Armidale, N.S.W., Australia.

Dunstan, D. I. 1981. Transplantation and post-transplantation of micropropagated tree-fruit rootstocks. *Comb. Proc. Inter. Pl. Prop. Soc.* **31:** 39–45.

Gamborg, O. L. & L. R. Wetter, Editors. 1975. *Plant Tissue Culture and Methods.* NRC Prairie Regional Laboratory, Saskatoon, Sask.

George, E. F. & R. D. Sherington, 1984. *Plant Propagation by Tissue Culture.* Exergenics Ltd., Eversley, Hants, U.K.

Hartmann, H. T. & D. E. Kester. 1975. 3rd ed. *Plant Propagation: Principles & Practices.* Prentice-Hall, Inc., Englewood Cliffs, N.J. pp. 509–532.

————. 1983. 4th ed. *Plant Propagation: Principles & Practices.* Prentice-Hall, Inc., Englewood Cliffs, N.J.

Jones, O. P. 1976. Effect of phloridzin and phloroglucinol on apple shoots. *Nature* **262:** 392–393, 724.

————. 1976. Propagation of deciduous trees by cuttings, Part 2. Propagation *in vitro. ARC Research Review* **2:** 74–75.

Kyte, L. 1983. *Plants from Test Tubes. An Introduction to Micropropagation.* Timber Press, Portland, Oregon.

———— & B. Briggs. 1979. A simplified entry into tissue culture production of rhododendrons. *Comb. Proc. Inter. Pl. Prop. Soc.* **29:** 90–95.

Latham, G. 1978. Woody plant tissue techniques. *GC & HTJ* **183**(24): 34–37 (June 16, 1978).

Lazarte, J. E. 1981. Woody tissue culture research. *Comb. Proc. Inter. Pl. Prop. Soc.* **31:** 649–655.

Lineberger, R. D. 1981. Tissue culture approaches commercial production. *Amer. Nurseryman* **154**(8): 14–15, 69–70 (October 15, 1981).

Lloyd, G. & B. H. McCown. 1980. Commercially-feasible micropropagation of Mountain Laurel, *Kalmia latifolia,* by use of shoot-tip culture. *Comb. Proc. Inter. Pl. Prop. Soc.* **30:** 421–427.

Marchant, B. 1982. Acclimatizing plants produced by tissue culture. *Amer. Nurseryman* **156**(6): 31–33 (September 15, 1982).

Marston, M. E. 1973. Applications of tissue culture to plant propagation. *Nurseryman & Garden Centre,* February 1, 1973, pp. 161–162.

————. 1973. Applications of tissue culture to plant propagation—2. *Nurseryman & Garden Centre,* February 8, 1973, p. 211.

McCulloch, S. M. & B. A. Briggs. 1982. Preparation of plants for micropropagation. *Comb. Proc. Inter. Pl. Prop. Soc.* **32:** 297–306.

Murashige, T. 1974. Plant propagation through tissue cultures. *Ann. Rev. Plant Physiol.* **25:** 135–166.

Skoog, F. & C. O. Miller. 1957. Chemical regulation of growth and organ formation in plant tissues cultured in vitro. *Symp. Soc. Exp. Biol.* **11:** 118–130.

Smith, W. A. 1981. The aftermath of the test tube in tissue culture. *Comb. Proc. Inter. Pl. Prop. Soc.* **31:** 47–49.

Stokes, M. J. 1974. Plant propagation by means of aseptic techniques. *Comb. Proc. Inter. Pl. Prop. Soc.* **24:** 196–206.

————. 1980. Current aspects of commercial micropropagation. *Comb. Proc. Inter. Pl. Prop. Soc.* **30:** 255–268.

Stoltz, L. P. 1979. Getting started in tissue culture—equipment and costs. *Comb. Proc. Inter. Pl. Prop. Soc.* **29:** 375–382.

Thorpe, T. E., Editor. 1982. *Plant Tissue Culture, Methods and Applications in Agriculture.* Academic Press, London and New York.

Wong, S. 1981. Direct rooting of tissue-cultured rhododendrons into an artificial soil mix. *Comb. Proc. Inter. Pl. Prop. Soc.* **31**: 36–39.

Workers' Compensation Board, B.C. no date. *Laboratory Health and Safety Procedures.* Workers' Compensation Board, Richmond, B.C.

Wright, N. 1983. Ideal subjects. Containerised roses by micropropagation. *GC & HTJ* **194**(6): 14–15 (August 5, 1983).

Zinmerman, R. H. 1981. Tissue culture for the practical plant propagator—state of the art. *Comb. Proc. Inter. Pl. Prop. Soc.* **31**: 559–562.

Figure IPPS-1.
Members of the Great
Britain and Ireland
Region of IPPS
examining nursery
production methods
during a study tour in
West Germany.

Figure IPPS-2.
Members of the Western
Region (U.S.A.) of IPPS
sharing information on
micropopagation with
Bruce Briggs of Briggs
Nursery, Olympia, WA,
U.S.A.

INTERNATIONAL PLANT PROPAGATORS' SOCIETY (IPPS)

The reader of this book may well find that his or her interest in propagation can be encouraged by belonging to the International Plant Propagators' Society.

The success of the International Plant Propagators' Society, founded in 1951, is due to the enthusiasm and participation of its members, who are willing "to seek and to share" their propagation knowledge.

This Society brings together nursery propagators, students, researchers, extension advisors and college instructors. Such a group of people provides a fascinating forum for exchanging ideas, learning new techniques, expanding plant knowledge and meeting fellow professional propagators.

The Society is truly international with Regions in western, eastern and southern North America, Great Britain and Ireland, Australia and New Zealand. This provides an opportunity to exchange knowledge with overseas members.

The benefits of membership include:

1. The opportunity to attend the annual meetings of any of the other Regions.

2. Nursery and botanical garden visits to learn about the practical aspects of propagation, nursery production and plant materials.

3. A bound copy of the COMBINED ANNUAL PROCEEDINGS, containing the conference papers of *all* Regions of the Society—over 600 pages in each volume.

4. The quarterly newsletter, THE PLANT PROPAGATOR, containing papers on propagation, news items and book reviews.

5. Helping to provide educational opportunities for young people interested in plant propagation as a career.

More information about the Society can be obtained by contacting the International Secretary/Treasurer, John A. Wott, Center for Urban Horticulture, Seattle, WA 98195, U.S.A.

INDICES

INDEX TO COMMON NAMES

Aaron's-beard: *Hypericum calycinum*
Abelia, White: *Abelia × grandiflora*
Acacia: *Acacia*
  False: *Robinia pseudoacacia*
  Mop-head: *R. pseudoacacia* 'Umbraculifera'
  Rose: *R. hispida*
  Smooth Rose: *R. hispida* var. *macrophylla*
Actinidia: *Actinidia*
  Bower: *A. arguta*
  Kolomikta: *A. kolomikta*
Albizzia: *Albizia*
Alder: *Alnus*
  American Green: *A. viridis* subsp. *fruticosa*
  Black: *A. glutinosa*
  Common: *A. glutinosa*
  Italian: *A. cordata*
  Red: *A. rubra*
  White: *A. incana*
  Yellowleaf White: *A. incana* 'Aurea'
Almond: *Prunus dulcis*
  Chinese Flowering: *P. glandulosa* 'Sinensis'
  Double: *P. dulcis* 'Roseoplena'
  Double Pink Flowering: *P. glandulosa* 'Sinensis'
  Dwarf Flowering: *P. glandulosa*
  Dwarf Russian: *P. tenella*
  Flowering: *P. triloba*
  White Dwarf Flowering: *P. glandulosa* 'Alboplena'
Anemone: *Carpenteria*
  Bush: *C. californica*
  Tree: *C. californica*
Apple: *Malus*
  Weeping Plum-leaved: *M. prunifolia* 'Pendula'
Apricot: *Prunus armeniaca*
  Japanese Flowering: *P. mume*
Aralia: *Aralia*
  Chinese: *A. chinensis*
  Variegated Chinese: *A. chinensis* 'Variegata'

Arborvitae: *Thuja*
  Eastern: *T. occidentalis*
  Goldspure: *Platycladus orientalis* 'Conspicuus'
  Oriental: *Platycladus orientalis*
  Pyramidal: *T. occidentalis* 'Pyramidalis'
Arbutus, Trailing: *Epigaea repens*
Arrowwood: *Viburnum dentatum*
Ash: *Fraxinus*
  Bunge: *F. bungeana*
  Claret: *F. oxycarpa* 'Raywood'
  European: *F. excelsior*
  Fallgold Black: *F. nigra* 'Fallgold'
  Flatspine Prickly: *Zanthoxylum simulans*
  Flowering: *F. ornus*
  Golden: *F. excelsior* 'Jaspidea'
  Green: *F. pennsylvanica* var. *lanceolata*
  Himalayan Manna: *F. floribunda*
  Manna: *F. ornus*
  Maries: *F. mariesii*
  Moraine: *F.* 'Moraine'
  Narrow-leaved: *F. angustifolia*
  Patmore: *F. pennsylvanica* var. *lanceolata* 'Patmore'
  Pointed-fruit: *F. oxycarpa*
  Prickly: *Zanthoxylum*
  Raywood: *F. oxycarpa* 'Raywood'
  Weeping European: *F. excelsior* 'Pendula'
  White: *F. americana*
Aspen: *Populus*
  European: *P. tremula*
  Quaking: *P. tremuloides*
  Upright Trembling: *P. tremula* 'Erecta'
Aucuba, Japanese: *Aucuba japonica*
Azalea: *Rhododendron*
  Chinese: *R. molle*
  Pontic: *R. luteum*
Azara, Variegated Boxleaf: *Azara microphylla* 'Variegata'

Bamboo, Heavenly: *Nandina domestica*

  Sacred: *Nandina domestica*
Barberry: *Berberis*
  Chrome-flower: *B. polyantha*
  Darwin: *B. darwinii*
  Dwarf Magellan: *B. buxifolia* 'Nana'
  Japanese: *B. thunbergii*
  Red: *B. thunbergii* 'Atropurpurea'
  Red-leaf Japanese: *B. thunbergii* 'Atropurpurea'
  Rosemary: *B. × stenophylla*
  Warty: *B. verruculosa*
  Wilson: *B. wilsoniae*
  Wintergreen: *B. julianae*
Basswood: *Tilia americana*
Bayberry: *Myrica pensylvanica*
Beautyberry: *Callicarpa*
Beautybush: *Kolkwitzia amabilis*
Beech: *Fagus*
  Bronze: *F. sylvatica* 'Atropunicea'
  European: *F. sylvatica*
  Purple: *F. sylvatica* 'Atropunicea'
  Rivers Purple: *F. sylvatica* 'Riversii'
  Roblé: *Nothofagus obliqua*
  Southern: *Nothofagus*
  Tricolor: *F. sylvatica* 'Tricolor'
  Weeping: *F. sylvatica* 'Pendula'
  Weeping Copper: *F. sylvatica* 'Purpurea Pendula'
Bellflower, Chilean: *Lapageria rosea*
Birch: *Betula*
  Common Silver: *B. pendula*
  Cutleaf Weeping: *B. pendula* 'Dalecarlica'
  Downy: *B. Lubescens*
  Dwarf: *B. nana*
  European White: *B. pendula*
  Glandular: *B. glandulosa*
  Himalayan: *B. utilis*
  Young's Weeping: *B. pendula* 'Youngii'
Bitter Tree, Korean: *Picrasma quassioides*
Bittersweet: *Celastrus*

Daphne: *Daphne*
  Balkan: *D. blagayana*
  February: *D. mezereum*
  Golden-flowered: *D. aurantiaca*
  Lilac: *D. genkwa*
  Pink Winter: *D. odora* 'Aureo-
    marginata'
  Red Winter: *D. odora* 'Rubra'
  Somerset: *D.* × *burkwoodii*
    'Somerset'
  Variegated Somerset: *D.* × *burk-
    woodii* 'Somerset Variegata'
  Winter: *D. odora*
  White Winter: *D. odora* 'Alba'
Deutzia: *Deutzia*
  Double Rose: *D. scabra* 'Plena'
  Fuzzy: *D. scabra*
  Slender: *D. gracilis*
Dogwood: *Cornus*
  Blood-twig: *C. sanguinea*
  Chinese Kousa: *C. kousa* var.
    chinensis
  Eastern Flowering: *C. florida*
  Giant: *C. controversa*
  Kousa: *C. kousa*
  Pagoda: *C. alternifolia*
  Red-bark: *C. alba*
  Red Flowering: *C. florida*
    'Cherokee Chief'
  Red-osier: *C. stolonifera*
  Siberian: *C. alba* 'Sibirica'
  Silver-leaf: *C. alba*
    'Elegantissima'
  Tatarian: *C. alba*
  Western Flowering: *C. nuttallii*
  Westonbirt: *C. alba* 'Westonbirt'
  Yellow-edge: *C. alba* 'Spaethii'
  Yellow-twig: *C. stolonifera*
    'Flaviramea'
Dove Tree: *Davidia involucrata*

Eglantine: *Rosa rubiginosa*
Elaeagnus: *Elaeagnus*
  Golden: *E. pungens* 'Maculata'
  Thorny: *E. pungens*
Elder: *Sambucus*
  American: *S. canadensis*
  Box: *Acer negundo*
  European: *S. nigra*
  Golden American: *S. canadensis*
    'Aurea'
Elm: *Ulmus*
  Camoerdown: *U. glabra*
    'Camperdownii'
  Chinese: *U. parvifolia*
  Dutch: *U.* × *hollandica*; *U.* ×
    hollandica 'Major'
  English: *U. procera*
  Evergreen: *U. parvifolia*
  Fern-leaf: *U. glabra* 'Crispa'
  Jacan Japanese: *U. japonica*
    'Jacan'
  Japanese: *U. japonica*
  Sapporo Autumn Gold: *U.*
    'Sapporo Autumn Gold'
  Scotch: *U. glabra*

  Siberian: *U. pumila*
  Wych: *U. glabra*
Empress Tree: *Paulownia tomentosa*
Enkianthus, Red-veined: *Enkianthus
    campanulatus*
Eucryphia: *Eucryphia glutinosa*
Euonymus, Winter Creeper:
    Euonymus fortunei

Fern, Littleleaf Common Sweet:
    Comptonia peregrina var.
    asplenifolia
Filbert: *Corylus*
  European: *C. avellana*
  Giant: *C. maxima*
  Golden European: *C. avellana*
    'Aurea'
  Purple Giant: *C. maxima*
    'Purpurea'
  Turkish: *C. colurna*
  Weeping European: *C. avellana*
    'Pendula'
  Yellow European: *C. avellana*
    'Aurea'
Fir: *Abies*
  Alpine: *A. lasiocarpa*
  Corkbark: *A. lasiocarpa* var.
    arizonica
  Douglas: *Pseudotsuga menziesii*
  Dwarf Corkbark: *A. lasiocarpa*
    'Compacta'
  Grand: *A. grandis*
  Greek: *A. cephalonica*
  Noble: *A. procera*
  Nordmann: *A. nordmanniana*
  Silver: *A. alba*
  Spanish: *A. pinsapo*
  White: *A. concolor*
Fire Tree, Chilean: *Embothrium
    coccineum*
Flannelbush: *Fremontodendron cali-
    fornicum*
Fleece Flower: *Polygonum*
  Bukhara: *P. baldschuanicum*
Fleece Vine, Chinese: *Polygonum
    aubertii*
Forsythia: *Forsythia*
  Border: *F.* × *intermedia*
  Lynwood: *F.* × *intermedia* 'Lyn-
    wood'
Fothergilla: *Fothergilla*
  Alabama: *F. monticola*
  Large: *F. major*
Fremontia, California:
    Fremontodendron californicum
Fringe Tree: *Chionanthus*
  Chinese: *C. retusus*
  White: *C. virginicus*

Garland Flower: *Daphne cneorum*
Glory-bower: *Clerodendrum*
  Harlequin: *C. trichotomum*
Glory Vine, Crimson: *Vitis
    coignetiae*
Golden-chain Tree: *Laburnum
    anagyroides*

  Voss' Long-cluster: *L.* × *watereri*
    'Vossii'
  Weeping: *L.* × *anagyroides*
    'Pendulum'
Golden Rain Tree: *Koelreuteria
    paniculata*
Gooseberry, Chinese: *Actinidia
    chinensis*
Gorse: *Ulex europaeus*
Grape: *Vitis*
  Wine: *V. vinifera*
Greenbrier: *Smilax*
Gum: *Eucalyptus; Liquidambar*
  Black: *Nyssa sylvatica*
  Cider: *E. gunnii*
  American Sweet: *L. styraciflua*
  Formosan Sweet: *L. formosana*
  Sweet: *Liquidambar*

Handkerchief Tree: *Davidia
    involucrata*
Hawthorn: *Crataegus*
  Common: *C. monogyna*
  English: *C. laevigata*
  Paul's Scarlet: *C. laevigata*
    'Coccinea Flore Pleno'
  Plum-leaf: *C.* × *prunifolia*
  Scarlet: *C. pedicellata*
  Single Pink English: *C. laevigata*
    'Rosea'
  Single-seed: *C. monogyna*
  Toba: *C.* × *mordenensis* 'Toba'
Hazel: *Corylopsis; Hamamelis*
  Buttercup Winter: *C. pauciflora*
  Chinese Witch: *H. mollis*
  Common Witch: *H. virginiana*
  Contorted: *Corylus avellana*
    'Contorta'
  Hybrid Witch: *H.* × *intermedia*
  Japanese Witch: *H. japonica*
  Ozark Witch: *H. vernalis*
  Spring Witch: *H. vernalis*
  Willmott Winter: *C. willmottiae*
  Winter: *Corylopsis*
  Witch: *Hamamelis*
Hazelnut: see under European
    Filbert
Heath: *Erica*
Heather: *Calluna; Erica*
  Bell: *E. cinerea*
  Scotch: *C. vulgaris*
  Spring: *E. carnea*
Hemlock: *Tsuga*
  Canadian: *T. canadensis*
  Canadian Weeping: *T. canaden-
    sis* 'Pendula'
  Mountain: *T. mertensiana*
  Sargent Weeping: *T. canadensis*
    'Pendula'
  Western: *T. heterophylla*
Hinoki: *Chamaecyparis obtusa*
  Dwarf: *C. obtusa* 'Nana Gracilis'
Holly: *Ilex*
  Altaclara: *I.* × *altaclerensis*
  Broad-leaved Silver: *I.
    aquifolium* 'Marginata'

Double-file: *V. plicatum* f. *tomentosum*
Fragrant: *V. farreri*
Korean Spice: *V. carlesii*
Violet, African: *Saintpaulia*
Virginia Creeper: *Parthenocissus quinquefolia*

Walking-stick, Harry Lauder's: *Corylus avellana* 'Contorta'
Walnut: *Juglans*
Black: *J. nigra*
California Black: *J. hindsii*
Cut-leaved: *J. regia* 'Laciniata'
English: *J. regia*
Persian: *J. regia*
Wayfaring Tree: *Viburnum lantana*
Weigela, Old-fashioned: *W. florida*
White Beam: *Sorbus aria*
Swedish: *S. intermedia*
Willow: *Salix*
Bay: *S. pentandra*
Corkscrew: *S. matsudana* 'Tortuosa'
Daphne: *S. daphnoides*

Dragon-claw: *S. matsudana* 'Tortuosa'
French Pussy: *S. caprea*
Goat: *S. caprea*
Halberd-leaved: *S. hastata*
Kilmarnock: *S. caprea* 'Pendula'
Laurel: *S. pentandra*
Salamon Weeping: *S.* × *sepulcralis*
Violet: *S. daphnoides*
Weeping Golden: *S. alba* var. *vitellina* 'Pendula'
Weeping Purple: *S. purpurea* 'Pendula'
White: *S. alba*
Wingnut, Caucasian: *Pterocarya fraxinifolia*
Winter Hazel: see under Hazel
Wintergreen, Creeping: *Gaultheria procumbens*
Wintersweet: *Chimonanthus praecox*
Wisteria: *Wisteria*
Chinese: *W. sinensis*
Japanese: *W. floribunda*
Silky: *W. venusta*

Witch Hazel: see under Hazel
Wolfwillow: *Elaeagnus commutata*
Woodbine: *Lonicera periclymenum; Parthenocissus*
Dutch: *L. periclymenum* var. *belgica*

Yaupon: *Ilex vomitoria*
Yellow Horn: *Xanthoceras sorbifolium*
Yellowwood, Chinese: *Cladrastis sinensis*
Yew: *Taxus*
English: *T. baccata*
Evergold English: *T. baccata* 'Semperaurea'
Golden Irish: *T. baccata* 'Fastigiata Aurea'
Hicks': *T.* × *media* 'Hicksii'
Yulan: *Magnolia denudata* (syn. *M. heptapeta*)

Zelkova, Japanese: *Zelkova serrata*

INDEX TO SCIENTIFIC NAMES

Please note: boldface page number indicates a photograph(s); italicized page number denotes a drawing(s).

V. lantana 17, 42, 65, **447**, 581
V. opulus 17, 23, **23,** 25, 46, 65,
  68, 581
V. plicatum 'Summer Snowflake'
  228, **230**
  f. *tomentosum* 438
V. × *rhytidophylloides*
  'Alleghany' **235**
V. tinus **278**
Vinca 316, 386
V. minor 'Variegata' 220
Vitis 23, 196, 199, 200, 201, 202,
  241, 289, 294, 318, 319, **373,**
  430, 431, 439
V. coignetiae 308
V. vinifera 308

Weigela 231, 298, 308, 310, 317, 327,
  388
W. florida 313
  'Foliis Purpureis' **292**
  'Minuet' see *W.* 'Minuet'
  'Rumba' see *W.* 'Rumba'
  'Variegata' **171**
W. 'Minuet' 232
W. 'Rumba' **230,** 232
W. 'Samba' 232
W. 'Tango' 232
Wisteria 263, 318, 430, *431,* 446,
  510, 511, 513, 517, 518, 558
W. floribunda 439
  'Macrobotrys' 518
W. sinensis 65, 221, 439, 446, 518,
  589

W. venusta 589

Xanthoceras sorbifolium 401

Yucca 60

Zanthoxylum ailanthoides **392**
  Z. piperitum 401
  Z. simulans 398
Zelkova 554
  Z. serrata 4, 495
    'Village Green' 495

GENERAL SUBJECT INDEX

Please note: boldface page number indicates a photograph(s); italicized page number denotes a drawing(s).

VERMONT STATE COLLEGES

0 0003 0890392 1

DATE D

SEP 09 2016

SEP 09 2016

Hartness Library
Vermont Technical College
One Main St.
Randolph Center, VT 05061

DISCARD